Reference and Subscription Books Reviews

1976–1977

Reprinted from *Booklist*

Volume 73

September 1, 1976–July 15, 1977

Prepared by the
American Library Association
Reference and Subscription Books Review
Committee
Edited by Helen K. Wright

AMERICAN LIBRARY ASSOCIATION

Chicago 1978

Copyright © 1976, 1977 by the
American Library Association

Permission to quote any review in full
 or in part must be obtained from the
 Office of Rights and Permissions of the
 American Library Association.
Permission to quote a review in full
 will be granted only to the publisher
 of the work reviewed.

Library of Congress Catalog Card
 Number 73-159565

International Standard Book Number
 0-8389-3207-X

Printed in the United States
 of America

Contents

The table of contents contains an alphabetical list of titles of works which is divided into two sections: (1) reviews and (2) notes and comments. An author index follows the text.

Preface, vii
Reference and Subscription Books
 Review Committee, ix
Guest Reviewers, xi

REVIEWS

Acronyms, initialisms, & abbreviations dictionary, 1
Airplanes and balloons, 50
The ALA yearbook, 2
American art directory, 1976 3
American dance band discography, 1917-1942, 4
The American film institute catalog of motion pictures, 5
Animals that burrow, 50
Animals with shells, 50
Argentina, 88
Ballet and dance, 50
The baseball encyclopedia, 6
A bibliography of English history to 1485, 9
Biographical dictionaries master index, 10
Birds and migration, 50
The book collector's handbook of values, 1976-1977, 11
Book review digest: author/title index, 1905-1974, 11
The book trade of the world, v.II, 12
Brazil, 88
Bridges and tunnels, 50
The British comic catalogue: 1874-1974, 13
Building, 50
Butterflies and moths, 50
Canada, 88
Childhood in poetry, 14
Children's book review index, 14
Children's literature review, 14
Clocks & watches, 15
Cloth and weaving, 50
The complete color encyclopedia of antiques, 15
A comprehensive bibliography for the study of American minorities, 38
Concise color encyclopedia of science, 17
A concise encyclopedia of antiques, 18
Cowboys, 50
Deserts, 50
Dictionary of American history, 19
A dictionary of Japanese artists, 20
Directory of research grants 1976-77, 21
The documentary history of the first federal elections, 1788-1790, v.I, 22
The dog family, 50

Electricity, 50
Encyclopedia of American agricultural history, 23
Encyclopedia of American history, 24
The encyclopedia of minerals and gemstones, 25
Encyclopedia of mystery and detection, 26
An encyclopedia of small antiques, 27
The encyclopedia of sports, 28
Encyclopedia of the musical theatre, 28
Encyclopedia of the Third Reich, 29
Energy atlas, 30
England, 88
Environmental legislation, 31
Ethnic information sources of the United States, 31
Famous actors and actresses on the American stage, 32
Farms and farmers, 50
Fire, 50
Fishing, 50
Food and drink, 50
The foundation center source book, 1975/1976, 33
The fresh & salt water fishes of the world, 34
Fuel and energy, 50
Gateways to readable books, 35
Gemstones of North America, 35
Geography and cartography, a reference handbook, 36
Germany, 88
Gypsies and nomads, 50
A handbook of American minorities, 38
Handy key to your "National Geographics", 39
Health and disease, 50
Horses and ponies, 50
Illustrated dictionary of place names, United States and Canada, 40
Illustrated encyclopaedia of the classical world, 40
Index to handicrafts, model making, and workshop projects, 41
Insects that feed on trees and shrubs, 42
The international authors and writers who's who, 43

International bibliography of the book trade and librarianship, 45
The international who's who, 45
Ireland, 88
Israel, 88
The jungle, 50
Lakes and dams, 50
A library of literary criticism: modern Latin American literature, 46
Light and color, 50
The living word vocabulary, 47
Longman illustrated companion to world history, 48
Macdonald first library, 50
Major libraries of the world, 53
Make it: an index to projects and materials, 53
Modern science dictionary, 54
Monkeys and apes, 50
Mountains, 50
The movies, 50
The national directory for the performing arts and civic centers, 55
The national directory for the performing arts/educational, 55
The Netherlands, 88
The new Columbia encyclopedia, 56
The new illustrated encyclopedia of world history, 57
The new Oxford atlas, 58
New York art yearbook, 1975-1976, 59
The ocean world of Jacques Cousteau, 59
The official encyclopedia of baseball, 6
Official rules of sports and games, 1976-77, 61
Outdoor recreation, 62
The Oxford companion to German literature, 63
Paper and printing, 50
Parliaments of the world, 64
Pears cyclopaedia, 1976-1977, 65
Personal name index to 'the New York times index' 1851-1974, 66
Peterson's annual guides to undergraduate and graduate study, 66
Photography, 50
Pirates and buccaneers, 50
The planet we live on, 67
Political science bibliographies, 69
Pollution, 50
A popular guide to government publications, 70
Ports and harbors, 50
The Princeton encyclopedia of classical sites, 71
Rivers and river life, 50
Roads and highways, 50
Rocks and mining, 50
Science fiction book review index, 1923-1973, 72
Signals and messages, 50
Sir Banister Fletcher's a history of architecture, 72
Size, 50
Skyscrapers, 50
Snakes and lizards, 50
Soviet Asia, 73
Spiders, 50
Sports, 62
The sports encyclopedia: baseball, 6
The story of cars, 50
Subject guide to children's books in print, 74
A survey of musical instruments, 75
Television, 50
The theater, 50
Time and clocks, 50
Towns and cities, 50
Trains and railroads, 50
Treasures of Italy, 76
Trees & shrubs, 76
Trees and wood, 50
United States local histories in the Library of Congress, 77
The universe, 50
Vanishing animals, 50
Violets of the United States, 78
Water resources of the world, 79
The way to play, 80
Weather, 50
Webster's collegiate thesaurus, 80
Webster's new students dictionary, 81
Webster's sports dictionary, 82
Who was when?, 83
Who was who in American history—arts and letters, 84
Who's who among black Americans, 85
Who's who in American art, 1976, 3
The world book dictionary, 86
The world chronology series, 88
World directory of environmental organizations, 90
The world guide to antiquities, 91
World guide to universities, 92
The world of learning, 1976-1977, 92

NOTES AND COMMENTS

Along the northern border, 116
America: history and life, 93
American and British genealogy and heraldry, 94
American architects from the Civil War to the First World War, 94
American book prices current, 1975 95
The American clock, 95
American drama criticism supplement II, 95
American literary scholarship: an annual, 1973, 96
American literary scholarship: an annual, 1974, 96
American music 1698-1800, 96
American picturebooks from Noah's ark to the beast within, 96

American-Southern African relations, 97
American women and the labor movement, 1825-1974, 97
Anniversaries and holidays, 97
Annual bibliography of British and Irish history, 98
Annual index to popular music record reviews 1974, 98
Antebellum black newspapers, 98
Artillery of the world, 98
Asimov's biographical encyclopedia of science and technology, 99
Bibliography of American ethnology, 99
A biographical dictionary of film, 100
Biographical dictionary of the federal judiciary, 100
The birds of California, 101
Birdwatcher's guide to wildlife sanctuaries, 101
The black American reference book, 101
Black American writers past and present, 102
Black Americans in aviation, 102
Black separatism, 102
Bombers in service, 103
Books for cooks, 103
Books for inner development, 103
Bowker serials bibliography supplement 1976, 104
The Bradford book of collector's plates 1976, 104
British music yearbook, 104
Business information sources, 104
Canadian book review annual, 1975, 105
Canadian books for children, 105
Canadian essay and literature index, 106
Catalogue of the world's most popular coins, 106
The Catholic encyclopedia, 106
Chambers biographical dictionary, 107
Chambers dictionary of science and technology, 107
Checklist of the world's birds, 108
Children's authors and illustrators, 108
Children's books in the Rare Book Division of the Library of Congress, 108
Choice: a classified cumulation, 109
Choosing the right dog, 110
Choral music in print, 110
The classic motorcycles, 110
Cloak and dagger bibliography, 110
Collectors' guide to nineteenth-century photographs, 111
Colombo's Canadian references, 111
The color treasury of gemstones, 111
Comparative guide to American colleges, 112
Comparative guide to two-year colleges and career programs, 112
The complete book of United States coin collecting, 112
The complete guide to salt and fresh water fishing equipment, 113
Concise encyclopedia of Jewish music, 113
The concise heritage dictionary, 113
Congressional quarterly's guide to Congress, 113
Conservation directory, 1976, 114
Consumer complaint guide 1977, 114
Consumer protection guide 1977, 114
Consumer sourcebook, 114
A consumer's arsenal, 115
Contemporary novelists, 115

Cookery Americana, 116
Cooking for entertaining, 118
Cooking in old Creole days, 116
The cooks' catalogue, 119
Cool, chill, and freeze, 116
Corporate profiles for executives and investors, 1976-77, 119
Country experts in the federal government, 119
The country life collector's pocket book, 120
Current journals in the sciences, 120
Diary for the business traveler, 1977, 120
Dictionary of British antique glass, 120
A dictionary of British surnames, 121
Dictionary of business finance and investment, 121
The dictionary of butterflies and moths in color, 121
Dictionary of geological terms, 122
A dictionary of gestures, 122
Dictionary of Ming biography, 1368-1644, 122
A dictionary of philosophy, 122
A dictionary of the old West, 1850-1900, 123
Dictionary of tools used in the woodworking and allied trades, c1700-1970, 124
Directions for cookery in its various branches, 116
Directory of corporate affiliations, 1976, 125
Directory of franchising organizations 1976, 125
Directory of library reprographic services, 125
Directory of newspaper libraries in the U.S. and Canada, 126
Directory of registered lobbyists and lobbyist legislation, 126
Directory of special programs for minority group members, 126
The economics of minorities, 127
Educators guide to free guidance materials, 127
Educators guide to free health, physical education and recreation materials, 127
Educators guide to free science materials, 127
80 years of bestsellers, 1895-1975, 127
The encyclopedia of Africa, 128
The encyclopedia of air warfare, 128
Encyclopedia of American steam traction engines, 129
The encyclopedia of comic book heroes, 129
Encyclopedia of German-American genealogical research, 129
Encyclopedia of hand-weaving, 130
Encyclopedia of information systems and services, 130
Energy fact book 1976, 131
English language cookbooks, 1600-1973, 131
Enjoy Europe by car, 131
The equal rights amendment, 132
Executive and management development for business and government, 132
The family guide to Cape Cod, 132
Federal government: Congress, 133
A field guide to Pacific states wildflowers, 133
A field guide to the butterflies of the West Indies, 133
A field guide to the mammals, 133
A field guide to the nests, eggs, and nestlings of British and European birds, 134
50 major film-makers, 134
Fifty years of prairie cooking, 116
Fighters in service, 103

Fischler's hockey encyclopedia, 135
5,000 questions answered about maintaining, repairing, and improving your home, 136
A folk music sourcebook, 136
Foreign affairs bibliography, 136
The foundation grants index, 1974   136
From radical left to extreme right, 137
Getting skilled, 137
Glass, 138
A glossary of Faulkner's South, 138
Government publications, 138
The great world encyclopedia, 138
Grosset & Dunlap's all-sports world record book, 140
Group work in the helping professions, 140
Guide to basic information sources in English literature, 141
Guide to Cretan antiquities, 141
A guide to critical reviews: part II, 141
Guide to drug information, 141
Guide to reference books for school media centers, 142
Guide to special issues and indexes of periodicals, 142
A guide to the birds of Panama, 142
The Hamlyn junior encyclopedia of nature, 143
The Hamlyn junior science encyclopedia, 144
The Hamlyn younger children's encyclopedia, 144
A handbook for travellers in India, Pakistan, Nepal, Bangladesh and Sri Lanka (Ceylon), 145
A handbook of African names, 145
A handbook of American literature, 145
Handbook of practical cookery, 116
Harper dictionary of contemporary usage, 146
Helicopter directory, 146
Helicopters of the world, 98
High living, 116
Historical and cultural dictionary of Thailand, 146
Historical and cultural dictionary of Vietnam, 146
Historical dictionary of Honduras, 147
A history and bibliography of American magazines, 1810–1820, 147
Home cookery, 116
How to locate reviews of plays and films, 148
The illustrated encyclopedia of rock, 168
The improved housewife, 116
Incredible, 148
Index to black poetry, 148
Index to book reviews in historical periodicals 1973, 148
Index to book reviews in historical periodicals, 1974, 148
Index to inspiration, 149
Index to literary biography, 149
Industry analysts in the federal government, 119
Information sources in power engineering, 149
Interlibrary Users Association journal holdings in the Washington-Baltimore area, 1977, 150
The international antiques yearbook, 1976, 150
International bibliography of Jewish affairs, 1966–1967, 151
The international butterfly book, 151
International congress calendar, 1976, 151
International film guide 1976, 152
International guide to library, archival, and information science associations, 152
Jane's dictionary of military terms, 152
Jane's dictionary of naval terms, 152
The Kansas home cook-book, 116
Keywords, 153
Kings, rulers and statesmen, 153
Large type books in print, 1976, 154
Larousse dictionary of wines of the world, 154
A library of literary criticism: modern American literature, 154
Literary research guide, 154
Livres canadiens pour enfants, 105
The London stage, 1890–1899, 155
Manuscripts guide to collections at the University of Illinois at Urbana-Champaign, 155
Maps to anywhere, 156
Mathematics dictionary, 156
Mexico especially for women, 157
Midwestern home cookery, 116
Military aircraft of the world, 157
Military vehicles of the world, 98
Missiles of the world, 98
Modern collector's dolls, 157
Motion picture market place 1976–1977, 157
Motion picture performers, 158
Mrs. Porter's new southern cookery book, 116
Music titles in translation, 158
The national directory of grants and aid to individuals in the arts, international, 158
Naval, marine and air force uniforms of World War 2, 159
The Negro almanac, 159
The new guide to study abroad, 160
News dictionary 1975, 160
NIH factbook, 160
Official Eastern North America map and chart index catalog, 161
Official Western North America map and chart index catalog, 161
Oil terms, 161
Old and middle English poetry to 1500, 162
Olympic sports official album, 172
One hundred recipes for the chafing dish, 116
1,000 great lives, 162
Organ music in print, 162
The Oxford children's dictionary in colour, 163
Pan Am's USA guide, 163
Performing arts research, 163
Pictorial souvenirs & commemoratives of North America, 163
The picture reference file, 164
Plants that *really* bloom indoors, 164
The pocket book of furniture, 164
Policies of publishers, 165
Political handbook of the world, 1976, 165
Popular song index, 165
Quotations in history, 166
Railways of the modern age since 1963, 166
Reference materials on Mexican Americans, 167
Research in progress in English and history in Britain, Ireland, Canada, Australia, and New Zealand, 167
Reverse acronyms, initialisms, & abbreviations dictionary, 167
Rock 100, 168
RSPB guide to British birds, 168

Screen world, 1976, V.27,   168
Sea fiction guide,   169
A short guide to the study of Ethiopia,   169
Significant American artists and architects,   169
Significant American authors, poets, and playwrights,   169
Significant American blacks,   169
Significant American colonial leaders,   170
Significant American government leaders,   170
Significant American historians and educators,   170
Significant American Indians,   170
Significant American inventors,   170
Significant American military leaders,   170
Significant American musicians, composers, and singers,   170
Significant American presidents of the United States,   170
Significant American scientists,   170
Significant American social reformers and humanitarians,   170
Significant American sport champions,   170
Significant American women,   170
Significant Americans,   169
Six little cooks,   116
Sociology of America,   171
Sources of information in water resources,   171
Southwestern cookery,   116
Sports olympiques album officiel,   172
Stamp collectors' handbook,   172
State constitutional conventions: 1959–1975,   173
The statesman's year-book world gazetteer,   173
Sub-aqua illustrated dictionary,   173
Subject guide to humor,   174
A supplement to the Oxford English dictionary,   174
Tanks and other armoured fighting vehicles 1942–1945,   103

Travel market yearbook, 1975/1976,   175
Treasures of Britain and treasures of Ireland,   175
The treasury of houseplants,   176
TV season 74–75,   176
TV season 75–76,   176
Ukrainians in North America,   176
U.S. government scientific & technical periodicals,   177
The vice-presidents and cabinet members,   177
Washington information directory, 1976–77,   177
Water publications of state agencies,   178
Webster's secretarial handbook,   178
The weekend education source book,   178
Which wine,   179
Who's who in golf,   179
Who's who in Greek and Roman mythology,   179
Who's who in labor,   180
Who's who in public relations (international),   180
Who's who in the United Nations and related agencies,   180
Who's who in twentieth century literature,   181
A Winterthur guide to American Chippendale furniture,   181
A Winterthur guide to American needlework,   182
A Winterthur guide to Chinese export porcelain,   182
Women in public office,   182
The word book,   183
The world atlas of food,   183
The world encyclopedia of comics,   183
World of fashion,   184
World uniforms and battles, 1815–50,   184
Writings on American history: a subject bibliography of articles, 1973/74,   184
The year book of world affairs, 1976,   185

Author Index,   186

Preface

Reference and Subscription Books Reviews is published by ALA on the first and fifteenth of every month except August as a separate publication within *Booklist* magazine. This is the eleventh cumulation of *Reference and Subscription Books Reviews* and third in the new series of annual compilations. The 101 reviews and 249 notes and comments originally appearing in *Booklist* between September 1, 1976 and July 15, 1977 are reprinted in this volume. Evaluations of 41 biographical or bio-bibliographical reference sources; 102 guides, factbooks, and manuals; 5 general English language and 32 subject encyclopedias; 37 special and general dictionaries, thesauri, or other kinds of wordbooks; 21 indexes; 8 atlases and gazetteers; 46 bibliographies; 29 directories; 13 almanacs, annuals, and yearbooks; and a wide range of other reference works are included. In comparison to the previous year there was almost a tenfold increase in the number of directories examined and more than twice as many guides, special subject treatments, wordbooks, and dictionaries have been handled in reviews or notes.

In the present cumulation of titles, the reader will note that some are of especial interest to black Americans. These include two biographical dictionaries, an almanac, index, and several useful bibliographies. The Bicentennial was graced by reference works created to celebrate the occasion, though not as many as had been anticipated. Standing out in this group because of its exemplary conception, scholarship, and design was the *Atlas of Early American History* (Princeton University Press). Baseball, insects, birds, fish, and mammals were also well represented by encyclopedias, handbooks, and field guides. Finally, the public's preoccupation with World War II was sustained by a spate of publications dealing with Nazi Germany and the military hardware, uniforms, and other paraphernalia of the period.

The Reference and Subscription Books Review Committee considers two types of publications: reference books likely to be of general interest (defining *reference book* as a publication designed by arrangement and treatment to be consulted for specific facts rather than to be read consecutively); and other books, if sold by subscription. Titles are brought to the Committee's attention by announcements in trade and professional publications, referral from other ALA review media, correspondence from publishers, and recommendations from Committee members. The Chairperson selects titles in conformity to guidelines stipulated and periodically revised by the Committee. Priorities governing acceptance of titles entail consideration of factors such as significance, potential sales impact upon the library and home markets, anticipated intensity of *Booklist* subscribers' interest, and to a certain extent price. Among standard reference works, general encyclopedias are primary candidates for review. Those published in new editions are evaluated every five years. Also reviewed at five-year intervals are annuals, yearbooks, and almanacs. Other general reference books such as unabridged dictionaries, biographical directories, atlases and gazetteers, general bibliographies, statistical compendiums, and indexes to periodical literature are next in priority order. Recently Committee coverage was widened to include medical and law reference books addressed to the lay reader. Still excluded from consideration are very technical, narrowly specialized, and foreign language works.

The fifty members of the Committee are appointed by the ALA Executive Board to serve for one- or two-year terms not to exceed six consecutive years. The members include a cross section of accomplished professional librarians: subject and reference specialists, library school faculty, administrators, and young adult and children's librarians. More than twenty former members with exemplary experience as reviewers and special subject skills also contribute to the Committee's production.

Upon acceptance of a title for review, one member is assigned primary responsibility for preparation of a draft review. The completed draft is circulated to the entire Committee for commentary on content, structure, and style. Referring to guidelines set forth in the Committee *Manual*, members note any errors, omissions, awkward or opaque language, or inattention to standard procedure. Clear characterization of the work under review—its organization and scope; publication history and editorial credentials; designation of the appropriate user; evaluation of accuracy, currency, and objectivity; comments on the adequacy of bibliographies, indexes, and cross-references; appraisal of the format—these are among the elements examined and remarked upon in every review. Above all, there is an attempt to combine clear description and analysis, comparison with similar titles, and astute judgment in an integrated and thoroughly substantiated statement that is fair to the author, publisher, and probable purchaser. Every review, before publication, is criticized and revised until divergent opinions on form and content have been resolved. It has in effect been endorsed (or signed) by the entire Committee before it appears in print. In these days of increased accountability and declining budgets, expenditures for reference books must be more critically examined than ever before. Therefore, timely appearance of reviews is essential. Recognizing this pressing need, the Committee will strive to increase the tempo and volume of coverage without diminishing the rigor of its judgment.

Reviews and notes in this volume are in two alphabetical sequences by title. Appended to each reprint is a citation of the issue and page of *Booklist* in which it originally appeared.

In closing, it must be evident that creation of the reviews in this publication has been a cooperative endeavor, the product of skilled, persistent and dedicated Committee members. For the Chairperson, it is both pleasurable and instructive to be associated with such individuals, persons whose only remuneration is well-deserved praise. Helen K. Wright, Committee editor and secretary, is also to be commended for her proficiency, tact, and unceasing efforts as coordinator and advocate of the Committee and its handiwork.

RICHARD SWEENEY HALSEY
Chairperson
ALA Reference and Subscription
Books Review Committee, 1975–

Reference and Subscription Books Review Committee 1976–1977

RICHARD SWEENEY HALSEY, Associate Professor, School of Library Science, State University of New York, Albany, New York (Chairperson, 1976-1977)

JOYCE L. BARNUM, Reference Division, University of Washington Libraries, Seattle, Washington

MALCOLM E. BLOWERS, Associate Professor and Head Librarian, Findlay College, Shafer Library, Findlay, Ohio

ONVA K. BOSHEARS, JR., Dean, School of Library Service, University of Southern Mississippi, Hattiesburg, Mississippi

ROBERT N. BROADUS, Professor, School of Library Science, University of North Carolina, Chapel Hill, North Carolina

LORENE BYRON BROWN, Assistant Professor, School of Library Science, Atlanta University, Atlanta, Georgia

DOROTHEA L. COACHMAN, Media Specialist, Hanover Park High School, East Hanover, New Jersey

CARL T. COX, Professor, Graduate School of Information Science, University of Tennessee, Knoxville, Tennessee, (deceased)

WINIFRED F. DEAN, Reference Bibliographer, Cleveland State University Libraries, Cleveland, Ohio

ROBERT H. DUMAS, City Librarian, Decatur Public Library, Decatur, Illinois

JULIA EMMONS, Assistant Professor, Division of Librarianship, Emory University, Atlanta, Georgia

ANITA W. FARBER, University of Texas at Austin, General Libraries, Austin, Texas

DOROTHY FIELD, Reference Librarian, Science and Technology Department, Indianapolis Public Library, Indianapolis, Indiana

JAMES K. FOYLE, Assistant Dean, University of Denver, Graduate School of Librarianship, Denver, Colorado

LOUVAN B. GEARIN, Librarian, Steger Junior High School Library, Webster Grove, Missouri

SUZANNE K. GRAY, Coordinator of Science, Boston Public Library, Boston, Massachusetts

LAUREL GROTZINGER, Professor, School of Librarianship, Western Michigan University, Kalamazoo, Michigan

NANCY E. GWINN, Information and Publications Officer, Council on Library Resources, Washington, D. C.

BRUCE C. HIGH, Librarian, The Baylor School, Chattanooga, Tennessee

PATRICIA M. HOGAN, Information Librarian, North Suburban Library System, Wheeling, Illinois

D. RONALD JOHNSON, Acquisitions Librarian, William Randall Library, University of North Carolina, Wilmington, North Carolina

JOHN C. LARSEN, Assistant Professor, School of Library Service, Columbia University, New York, New York

CHARLES LOWRY, Social Science Reference Bibliographer, University of North Carolina, Charlotte, North Carolina

RUTH N. LYNN, Children's Librarian, Skokie Public Library, Skokie, Illinois

JOSEPHINE MCSWEENEY, Professor, Pratt Institute Library, Pratt Institute, Brooklyn, New York

JEAN A. MAJOR, Graduate Library School, University Library, Indiana University, Bloomington, Indiana

R. KAY MALONEY, Graduate School of Library Service, Rutgers University, New Brunswick, New Jersey

ARTHUR S. MEYERS, Branches Manager, St. Louis Public Library, St. Louis, Missouri

MARION L. MULLEN, Head, Reference Department, Bird Library, Syracuse University, Syracuse, New York

MARGUERITE M. MURRAY, formerly Coordinator Children's Services, Montgomery County Department of Public Libraries, Rockville, Maryland

DIANE ORTIZ, Graduate Assistant, Department of Political Science, University of Nevada, Las Vegas, Nevada

CHARLES PATTERSON, Associate Professor, School of Library Science, Louisiana, State University, Baton Rouge, Louisiana

WILLIAM T. PETERS, Director, Grosse Pointe Public Library, Grosse Pointe, Michigan

ROBERT M. PIERSON, Associate Director of Libraries, University of Maryland, College Park, Maryland

CLAIRE PYLE, Head, Branch Services, Carnegie Library, Pittsburgh, Pennsylvania

THOMAS A. RAINES, Head, Literature Department, Memphis Public Library, Memphis, Tennessee

LOIS L. REILLY, Performing Arts Librarian, Oakland University Library, Rochester, Michigan

MARIAN E. RICHESON, Director, Public Legal Education, Information and Training, Legal Services Commission, Vancouver, British Columbia

BETTY B. ROSENBERG, Senior Lecturer, Graduate School of Library Science, University of California, Los Angeles, California

LELIA B. SAUNDERS, Assistant Director, Arlington County Department of Libraries, Arlington, Virginia

BRUCE SCHMIDT, Director, Southfield Public Library, Southfield, Michigan

ALAN EDWARD SCHORR, Government Publications and Map Librarian, University of Alaska, Fairbanks, Alaska

SHIRLEY SHISLER, Head, Reference Department, Des Moines Public Library, Des Moines, Iowa

JOHN STALKER, Trevor Arnett Library, Atlanta University, Atlanta, Georgia

MARGARET F. STIEG, School of Library Service, Columbia University, New York, New York

CAROL B. TANZER, Materials Coordinator, Oklahoma County Libraries, Oklahoma City, Oklahoma

MILDRED VANNORSDALL, Professional Library, Chicago Public Library, Chicago, Illinois

MARVIN D. WILLIAMS, JR., Senior Librarian, Head of Cataloging, State Library Division, Tennessee State Library and Archives, Nashville, Tennessee

KEN AKIRA YAMASHITA, Administrative Assistant to the Director, Chicago Public Library, Chicago, Illinois

Guest Reviewers

HELEN L. BENNETT, Reference Libraries, University of Missouri, Kansas City, Missouri

LESLIE BJORNCRANTZ, Curriculum and Reference Librarian, Northwestern University Library, Evanston, Illinois

BERNICE BRUNER, Chief, Division of Work with Schools and Children, Evansville Public Library, Evansville, Indiana

ELEANOR BUIST, 90 LaSalle Street, New York, New York

RAY CARPENTER, Associate Professor, University of North Carolina, School of Library Science, Chapel Hill, North Carolina

FRANCES NEEL CHENEY, formerly Associate Director of Peabody Library School, Nashville, Tennessee

DONALD G. DAVIS, JR., Assistant Professor, Graduate School of Library Science, University of Texas, Austin, Texas

JACK W. DICKEY, Physics Library, University of Iowa, Iowa City, Iowa

HELGA H. EASON, Head, Community Relations, Miami-Dade Public Library System, Miami, Florida

JOHN J. FARLEY, Dean, School of Library Science, State University of New York, Albany, New York

NORMAN FINKLER, Director, Montgomery County Department of Public Libraries, Rockville, Maryland

JACK FORMAN, Eastern Massachusetts Regional Library System, Boston Public Library, Boston, Massachusetts

MARGARET H. GRAZIER, Professor, Division of Library Science, Wayne State University, Detroit, Michigan

ROGER C. GREER, Professor, School of Information Studies, Syracuse University, Syracuse, New York

RUTH M. HADLOW, Coordinator, Work with Children, Cleveland Public Library, Cleveland, Ohio

FRANCES H. HALL, Law Library, Southern Methodist University, Dallas, Texas

HENRY C. HASTING, Head, Reference Department, Gary Public Library, Gary, Indiana

LUCILLE HATCH, Professor, Graduate School of Librarianship, University of Denver, Denver, Colorado

NORMAN HORROCKS, Director, School of Library Service, Dalhousie University, Halifax, Nova Scotia

CHARLOTTE LEONARD, Coordinator, Children's Services, Dayton Public Library, Dayton, Ohio

ALBERT P. MARSHALL, Dean of Academic Services, Eastern Michigan University, Ypsilanti, Michigan

RACHEL S. MARTIN, Reference and Serials Librarian, Furman University Library, Greenville, South Carolina

HUGH PRITCHARD, Reference Librarian, University of New Hampshire, Durham, New Hampshire

GARY R. PURCELL, Director, Graduate School of Library and Information Science, University of Tennessee, Knoxville, Tennessee

JAMES H. RICHARDS, JR., Library Gettysburg College, Gettysburg, Pennsylvania

MARJORIE L. ROGERS, 3064 Taylor Avenue, Cincinnati, Ohio

STEWART P. SCHNEIDER, South County Trail, West Kingston, Rhode Island

VIRGINIA C. SCHWARTZ, Milwaukee Public Library, Milwaukee, Wisconsin

CAROL E. SELBY, Head, Humanities Division, Eastern Michigan University Library, Ypsilanti, Michigan

MARGARET R. SHEVIAK, Associate Professor, Graduate Library School, Indiana University, Bloomington, Indiana

ELIZABETH SILVESTER, Head, Reference Department, McLennan Library, McGill University, Montreal, Quebec

MARGARET SMART, Documents Librarian, Colorado School of Mines, Golden, Colorado

MARY E. STILLMAN, Professor, Albright College, Reading, Pennsylvania

RUTH WALLING, Associate University Librarian, Emory University, Atlanta, Georgia

WILEY J. WILLIAMS, Professor, Peabody Library School, Nashville, Tennessee

RAYMUND F. WOOD, Associate Professor, Graduate School of Library Science, University of California, Los Angeles, California

Reference and Subscription Books Reviews

Acronyms, initialisms, & abbreviations dictionary: a guide to alphabetic designations, contractions, acronyms, initialisms, abbreviations, and similar condensed appellations. Covering aerospace, associations, biochemistry, business and trade, domestic and international affairs, education, electronics, genetics, government, labor, medicine, military, pharmacy, physiology, politics, religion, science, societies, sports, technical drawings and specifications, transportation, and other fields. v. 1. Edited by Ellen T. Crowley; assistant editors: Christopher Crocker, Donna Wood; contributing editor: Harry Schecter; editorial consultant, Miriam M. Steinert. 5th ed. Detroit, Gale Research Co., 1976. 757p. 29cm. cloth $38.50.

The fourth edition of the *Acronyms, Initialisms, & Abbreviations Dictionary,* published in 1973 and hereafter referred to as *AIAD,* was briefly noted in the June 1, 1974, issue of *Reference and Subscription Books Reviews.* This is the first formal review of this work by the Committee.

Ellen T. Crowley has been chief editor of *AIAD* during the 16 years of its existence. She acknowledges the contribution of terms and editorial advice from various individuals and organizations, including Eric Partridge, IBM's Data Processing Division, the U.S. Air Force's Translations and Abbreviations Section, and the National Library of Medicine.

Our society's increased dependence on acronyms, initialisms, and abbreviations is attested to by the statistics of this title's growth. Its first edition, appearing in 1960, contained only 12,000 entries; the fifth edition lists 130,000. The Preface notes that although the use of the three forms of contraction may be traced back to ancient times, its golden age arrived with the creation of New Deal agencies and the onset of World War II. In the 1970s, the presence of these ugly linguistic devices became ubiquitous. In addition to the forms of contraction identified in its title, the *AIAD* includes "many alphabetic symbols in which the letters do not always correspond to the words which they represent."

Inclusions are limited to U.S. contractions with the exception of a few foreign terms with internationally known meanings. These terms are translated for the reader. The subject range is vast, encompassing data processing and food, religion and slang. According to the editor, new, updated, and important but formerly overlooked terms appear in this latest version of *AIAD,* while "obsolete entries have not been deleted, but merely noted or cross-referenced."

Editorial policies are described in the introductory matter. All items are included that may be even loosely defined as being acronyms, initials, or abbreviations. Unpronounceable acronyms, initials not beginning with the first letter of the first word, and alphabetic symbols such as chemical elements are included. All entries are in capitals with periods omitted; when a word within the term is in capitals, such words are AIAs themselves and have separate references. However, when common usage indicates, capitals and lower case are combined, e.g., CofC, PhD. Arrangement is alphabetical by acronym/initial/abbreviation, and spacing or lower case letters do not affect this arrangement. Various meanings for the same entry appear in alphabetical sequence, and entries of identical letter combinations with differing intervening characters follow an arbitrary order, e.g., BS; B-S; B/S; B&S, BofS; B2S. A final point of policy defines the acronym itself as the basic reference: if it is found in a different form in several sources, it is used in all forms without comment.

Because the quality of inclusions and variety of fields represented in the *AIAD* are both so extensive, its users could falsely conclude that its coverage is exhaustive. A listing of fields and types of acronyms/initialisms/abbreviations not included would preclude this possibility and reduce potential reader frustration and disappointment.

Also, the title page notes the existence of "Other volumes: volume 2—*New Acronyms, Initialisms, and Abbreviations* (an annual supplement to volume 1); volume 3—*Reverse Acronyms, Initialisms, and Abbreviations Dictionary,*" while the cover of the *AIAD* does not bear markings identifying it as volume 1.

If the legitimacy of single-letter abbreviations cannot be questioned, their utility for reference work can. Many of these entries appear in *AIAD* with several, e.g., *C* and *M*, absorbing more than two columns of space. A few of the initialisms, (e.g., *A* used as a contraction of "about," "act," "adult," "American," "annual," "April," or "at") can be located in other sources, while some of the other abbreviations seem superfluous, e.g., *A* for "American League" (baseball) when there is also an entry under *AL,* and *B* for "black-and-white" (television program or movie) when there is already an entry under *B & W.* It is unlikely that librarians would consult *AIAD* to confirm the meanings of familiar abbreviations (e.g., the alphabetic symbols for chemical elements, *R* for "Restricted" or "Republican") because these latter examples are explained in most unabridged or desk dictionaries. Much more valuable to the user are the inclusions of single-letter terms that bear no apparent relation to the uncurtailed original expressions, e.g., *A* used for "Hail" (meteorological symbol), "High Medium" (Moody's bond rating), or "mass number" (symbol).

AIAD's initialisms and abbreviations are taken from a miscellany of sources, and the fact of their use is considered sufficient grounds to justify inclusion. However, this admits many seemingly idiosyncratic entries, e.g., in a full column of *AD*'s are found the terms "A Drink," "Advice," "Alternate Days," and "Archduke," the latter three possibly intelligible within circumscribed contexts, the first suggesting only Alice in Wonderland.

The shorthand type of abbreviation is a very common entry which has little value for the general public if its use is confined to "house" practice or internal communications. The Committee suspects that few readers would ever look up *ACT* for the terms "active," "activity,"* "actual,"* "actuate"*; *ACTG,* "acting," "actuating"*; *ACTL,* "actual"*; *ACTN,* "action"; *ACTR,* "actuator"*; *ACTV,* "activate,"* "activity"*; *ACTVT,* "activate"*; ACTVTR, "activator"*; ACTY, "activity."* The asterisked terms indicate that there are two or more abbreviations for the term. The entries for ACT take one-half column; those for ACTA through ACTY, a full column; therefore, the search for an item may well be impeded by the extraneous entries.

The parenthetical addition of category or identifier is exceedingly useful, so useful that it should be used more frequently, particularly for the acronyms. When there are multiple terms for the same acronym, searchers may find a choice confusing if several are in the same or similar fields. For example, under SMART, there are ten entries, four of which have categories (two are data processing abbreviations, one is an Air Force term, and one stands for a simulation game); under MARC, there are ten entries and only four have categories (LC; Air Force; program using regional councils of government to serve as clearinghouses for federal grants; New York).

The Committee did not submit the AIAD to a formal accuracy test, but one error was noted in passing: BOLD—Bibliographic On-Line Library Display (Data Processing)—should not include the word "library." Further probing revealed incomplete representation of terms in the field of librarianship. Of 49 appearing in the July 1976 Library Journal, only 39 were found in AIAD. Omitted were AFRAM, BiN, CARDSET, DIALOG, LIBS100, METRO, MUSCLE, NYSILL, RENCON, YA. This suggests a catch-as-catch can editorial attitude because ORBIT, BALLOTS, OCLC are included, while METRO and YA, of venerable age, are overlooked.

FYI (For Your Information) is in, but JIC (Just in Case) is out. NARC (Narcotics) is cited as an FBI term, while the television designation (narcotics officer) is omitted.

Contractions of vulgarisms are laundered and parenthetically noted as (Bowdlerized versions). BS becomes "Bullsling(er)," while FU, FUBAR, FUBB and SNAFU substitute "foul" for the standard four-letter word. SOB is left intact.

Despite the preceding criticisms, its large quantity of conveniently organized entries makes the Acronyms, Initialisms, & Abbreviations Dictionary a valuable reference source. The dictionary is sturdily bound to withstand heavy use and lies flat when open. The typography is small but legible, and the text is presented in double columns with wide margins to maximize readability. This work is recommended for large libraries. Libraries with little budgetary leeway should consider the AIAD's publication pattern—annual supplements and a new edition every two or three years—as a critical factor when considering whether convenience of ownership is worth the dollar investment. Small libraries may find Ralph De Sola's Abbreviations Dictionary: Abbreviations, Acronyms, Anonyms, Contractions, Initials and Nicknames, Short Forms and Slang Short Cuts, Signs and Symbols, new international 4th ed; American Elsevier Pub. Co., 1974, $24.50 (Reference and Subscription Books Reviews Sept. 1, 1975) a satisfactory and less expensive substitute.

(Feb. 15, 1977, p.918)

423.5 Acronyms || Abbreviations [OCLC] 76-10036

Airplanes and balloons.
†629.13 Airplanes—Juvenile literature || Balloons—Juvenile literature [OCLC] 75-19991

See page 50

The ALA yearbook:
a review of library events 1975. Editor in chief, Robert Wedgeworth. Chicago, American Library Association, [1976]. 494p. illus. 29cm. cloth $25.

The ALA Yearbook proposes "to provide an authoritative and readable source of information about activities, events, and organizations that reflect the diverse interests of the American Library Association for the year ending on December 31, 1975." It reaches, as the subtitle indicates, considerably beyond these limits and covers trends in librarianship as a whole. While emphasis is on current information, this first yearbook and centennial publication covers more retrospective material than its title suggests.

The ALA Yearbook is divided into three major parts. The first contains three long feature articles: ALA at 100 by Edward G. Holley, Independent Learning and the Future Role of Public Libraries by Samuel B. Gould, and Micrographics: An Eventful Forty Years—What Next? by Allen Veaner. The next part is a review of the library year, comprised of 143 short articles arranged alphabetically and ranging between one-half page to more than nine pages in length. Academic Libraries, Biographies, Buildings, Intellectual Freedom, Public Libraries, and School Libraries and Media Centers receive the most extensive treatment. Articles are discursive, but some statistics and tables are included. Forty-four biographies of outstanding persons who have contributed to librarianship are found under the heading Biographies. Although most of the biographees are librarians, a goodly portion come from other walks of life, e.g., Congressman Carl Perkins; bookseller and Lincoln scholar, Ralph G. Newman; founder of Reading Is Fundamental, Margaret C. McNamara; illustrator and author, Gerald McDermott; scholar and University of Chicago professor of history, John Hope Franklin. Fourteen deceased persons are in an Obituaries article.

The third section is made up of a series of 53 reports, one from each of the 50 states and reports from the District of Columbia, Britain, and Canada. Several appendixes conclude the yearbook: Organizations and Associations, Prizes and Awards, and Notable Books.

The ALA Yearbook is published by the American Library Association and edited by its executive director, Robert Wedgeworth. Its board of 16 advisers includes some of the most distinguished persons in American librarianship. Two hundred and eleven well-qualified contributors wrote the articles. For example, Russell Bidlack, former chairman of the ALA Committee on Accreditation, authored the Accreditation article. Ann Morgan Campbell, executive secretary of the Society of American Archivists, produced the article on Archives; Jack Dalton, chairperson of the ad hoc committee which prepared the Statement on Professional Ethics approved in 1975, contributed the capsule summary on ALA's formulation of an official code of ethics; Richard Darling, president of the Freedom to Read Foundation, prepared the material on the foundation; Carol Ishimoto, head of the cataloging and processing department at the Harvard College Library, contributed Cataloging and Classification; Carol Starr, coordinator of young adult services at the Alameda County Library System and editor of the Young Adult Alternative Newsletter, described young adult library services; and Elbert Watson, director of the Huntsville Public Library and a recent past president of the Alabama Library Association, was responsible for the state report on Alabama.

Although the yearbook is to be commended for matching appropriate topics and experts, the result is an uneven product. Lack of uniformity and symmetry is, in fact, one of the chief defects of the ALA Yearbook. Little direction seems to have been given to the contributors, and while some authors cover topics thoroughly, others unduly stress local situations and interests or provide shallow summaries. This inconsistency is most apparent in the state reports. The Virginia report covers changing demography, the economy, professional activities, proposed VLA reorganization, meetings and workshops, buildings, appointments, and retirements. The Vermont report, on the facing page, covers interdependence, building and remodeling, workshops, VLA activities, and deaths; while Utah offers "Polyadies and Quiddities," genealogical treasure house, Whitmore Library, LDS church library, multi-state center library, Utah's regional library, Utah State Library Commission, bookmobile program, UNET, CLR/NEH grant, and "Of Rascals and Bandits." Since ALA Yearbook is the only source of information on the state associations, this important section would be more useful if it had been organized to allow for comparison of factors common to all states. Imbalance is also evident in the article on *Principal Libraries of the World* in which the scope of a "special collection" appears to vary widely. Surely Columbia University Library with only three special collections cited is underrepresented vis-à-vis Cornell, a slightly smaller library, with its listing of thirty-eight. Surprisingly, Boston and Philadelphia public libraries, and Princeton, Newberry, and Cambridge University are not in this elect group.

Apparently editorial policy permitted considerable latitude in style and in the expression of personal views. For example, the Utah state report is individualistic in tone and content. Also, not all would agree with the *Young Adult Literature* correspondent's contention that 1975 will be remembered for the publication of *The Doonesbury Chronicles* by Gary Trudeau that "gladdened every heart" or with the opinion, expressed in the lead article, that David Clift and Carl Milam remained too long as executive secretaries of the association.

The lack of uniformity can also be seen in the topics chosen for treatment. Italian-Americans receive special treatment in *Italian-Americans and Libraries,* while there are no comparable articles on numerous other Americans. Similarly, the British Library, the Bibliothèque Nationale, the State V. I. Lenin Library, and the new Iranian Library, the Pahlavi National Library (a library which as yet exists only on paper), are the only national libraries treated. The Committee hopes that future plans, undisclosed in the Introduction, will redress this type of inequity.

Since most of the articles are discursive and impressionistic, a favorable reaction will in many cases depend on the extent to which the reader agrees with the perceptions of the writer. A few simple errors such as misspellings of names and the incorrect captioning of a photograph of Low Library at Columbia University were noted. This library ceased to function in that capacity some 40 years ago. In general the articles maintain an admirably high level of accuracy despite such minor and annoying flaws.

There is a roster of contributors showing their affiliations and articles in the yearbook at the beginning of the volume, and the yearbook concludes with an Index to titles of articles, persons, places, subjects, and many of the illustrations. The Committee noted no errors in the Index.

Regrettably, there are few cross-references in the body of the text; they seem to be provided mainly from places where there is no information to the place where pertinent material is located. The article on *Automation* would have been enhanced by references to *Networks* and *Machine-Readable Data Bases.*

The yearbook is printed on thick, nonglare paper, but some of the pictures and heavy type have bled. Exceptionally wide outer margins in the *Review of the Library Year* section, with its abundance of pictures and tables, produce a very tasteful effect. The binding is sturdy.

The volume is lavishly illustrated with black-and-white photographs and some cartoons. While the illustrations generally explicate the text with which they are associated, not all of them are of the highest quality. In the article *Principal Libraries of the World,* the picture of the main reading room at the Harvard University library is so light that the viewer has to be familiar with the room to appreciate fully its proportions. On the other hand, the patrons in the New York Public Library reading room are shown sitting in stygian darkness. Other illustrations fail to enhance the content of the related articles. For example, a picture of a CRT terminal and microfiche reader, part of the New York Times data bank at the Dallas Public Library, is adjacent to articles on *Research* and the ALA *Resources and Technical Services Division,* but neither of these writeups mentions the Dallas Public Library acquisition. Also, the photograph of a group of mostly male individuals sporting unreadable name tags walking across the White House drive adds little insight to the *Washington Report* article, and the two—the only two—pictures of the Huntsville-sponsored event "Reflections of Yesterday" seem a trifle excessive in the Alabama report.

Although this first edition is not without flaws, it is a well designed and attractively printed new annual. It offers a readable overview of institutions, issues, and organizations, and the synopses of state activities are a promising effort to scan yearly library activities at this level. There are, of course, the *Bowker Annual of Library and Trade Book Information* and the many directories of libraries and librarians which preempt much of the scope of such a work. The yearbook sensibly does not try to absorb the functions of these publications. For example, it does not give as many or such comprehensive statistics as the *Bowker Annual,* although it does give some statistics not cited in the *Bowker Annual,* e.g., bibliography and index compilation. The *ALA Yearbook* has chosen instead to augment existing sources and provide a less formalized, more personal interpretation of ongoing activity in the library profession. It is, therefore, recommended to individuals and libraries with a need for comprehensive information on American librarianship.

(Apr. 1, 1977, p.1191)

†020.62274 American Library Association—Directories || Libraries—U.S.—Directories

American art directory, 1976.
Edited by Jaques Cattell Pr. 46th ed. New York, R. R. Bowker Co., 1976. xiv, 536p. 29cm. cloth $37.50.
†705 Art—Periodicals || Art—U.S. || Art—Canada || Artists—Directories   99-1016

Who's who in American art, 1976.
Edited by Jaques Cattell Pr. 12th ed. New York, R. R. Bowker Co., 1976. xiv, 756p. 29cm. cloth $37.
†705 Artists, American [OCLC]   36-27014

Earlier editions of *Who's Who in American Art* (*WWAA*) and the *American Art Directory* (*AAD*) have been reviewed in *Reference and Subscription Books Reviews* (May 1, 1974, p.959, and May 15, 1974, p.1014, respectively). These long-established directories are triennial works which complement each other. According to the Preface of *WWAA,* beginning with the current editions, both volumes will appear biennially. The *WWAA* provides information on persons active in the art world and the *AAD* deals primarily with art organizations. Together they form a major source of directory information in the field of art. In general, they are limited to U.S. and Canadian data, although there are some additional inclusions. Both titles have been prepared with the cooperation of the American Federation of Arts, which has been involved with the two works and their predecessor, the *American Art Annual,* since 1913. Data for both works were obtained from questionnaires completed by the person or organization concerned. If there was no response, there is no representation, although the Preface to *Who's Who in American Art* suggests that "in some instances" biographical entries may contain information from other sources.

WWAA lists in a single alphabet approximately 8,500 entries for artists, art historians, art administrators, dealers, librarians, and collectors living in or native to the U.S. and Canada. Although the Preface claims that coverage includes Mexico as well, the Geographical Index indicates only 87 persons with Mexican residence. Twenty-four artists living outside North America are also included.

Each biographical entry includes date and place of birth, education, career history, exhibition and publication information, prizes and awards, and current mailing address. An extensive key to abbreviations is provided for the many standard abbreviations used in the biographical entries. A new feature in this edition is the identification, following each personal name entry, of the biographee's field of activity (sculptor, collector, cartoonist, critic, etc.).

Following the 626-page biographical section are a Geographic Index and a Professional Classification Index. The Geographic Index arranges the personal names alphabetically under country. For U.S. and Canadian residents, there is a further breakdown by state or province and city.

The Professional Classification Index uses the self-assigned occupational classifications supplied by the biographees. More than half of the subjects have listed themselves in two occupational categories. A check of the 18 names identified in the Index as art librarians reveals that three of the biographees are not so identified at the head of their respective entries, although they have had some library experience earlier in their careers. In their entries, one is classified as "film maker," another as "archivist," and the third as both "art administrator" and "photographer."

Users of the Professional Classification Index may be annoyed by the inconsistent use of the word "art" as a prefix. Why "art book dealer," "art consultant," and "art librarian," on the one hand, but simply "collector," "critic," "curator," and "publisher" on the other?

As in previous editions, a Necrology concludes the work. Persons who have died since publication of the preceding edition are identified by occupational category, and birth and death years are included.

This edition of WWAA is sturdily bound and lies flat when opened. In an apparent attempt to cut costs, the typeface has been reduced in size from previous editions. Although the text of individual entries is crowded and difficult to read, the pages are easier to scan because each entry is a clean block of type with sufficient space to separate it from its neighbors. Margins are somewhat narrow, but this is not a serious fault because a new edition will probably be published before rebinding should be required.

The *American Art Directory* provides information for U.S. and Canadian art organizations and related topics (museums, schools, state arts councils, state departments of education and public school art supervisors, magazines and newspapers, scholarships, exhibitions, and booking agencies for traveling exhibitions) in several alphabetically arranged lists. An Index of institutions and broad categories of exhibitions (African art, bronzes, textiles, etc.) concludes the work. Beginning with this edition, the *AAD* contains the directory of competitive national, regional, and statewide exhibitions which previously appeared in *WWAA*. This information fits more logically with *AAD* data.

Information was obtained by questionnaire, and the editors state that no effort was made to check information "beyond that which was given on the questionnaires," disclaiming liability for inaccuracies or omissions. However, not all obvious candidates for inclusion are found. ARLIS/NA, an organization of U.S. and Canadian art librarians which has been in existence since 1973, is not entered.

The *AAD* lists art organizations alphabetically with address, principal officers, establishment date, purpose, membership dues, activities, and publications. Museums are arranged geographically by state or Canadian province. A 41-page section of major museums abroad includes entries from five Iron Curtain countries, although there are none from the USSR.

Art schools are also arranged by state or province with a brief section listing selected art schools abroad. Entries for each school include name of director, faculty size, establishment date, entrance requirements, degrees offered, current enrollment, fees, and major fields of study. This section is very misleading for students. It is only eight pages long and lists only 96 schools. The Committee wonders how the schools were selected. Of the 96 schools, 48 have asterisks indicating that they did not respond to the questionnaire. Among these, the Committee queries the currentness of the information on the one Burmese school listed and why the State Art Institute of the Estonian Soviet Republic is the only art school entered from Russia.

Art magazines are cited alphabetically, with frequency, editor, address, and subscription price given. Newspapers are those regularly carrying art notes; the art editors are identified. Arrangement of this list is geographical. Magazine representation is international, but the newspapers are exclusively North American.

Scholarships and fellowships are arranged alphabetically by sponsoring organization. Stipends and eligibility requirements are given. Only two of the 373 organizations listed as offering scholarships are located outside the U.S. and Canada. This section should be used with caution, because the selection is both incomplete and idiosyncratic.

The listing of open exhibitions is arranged by state and includes eligibility requirements. The agencies which supply traveling exhibitions are arranged alphabetically, and entries include the types of exhibitions available and rental and transportation fees.

The comprehensive Index which concludes the *AAD* contains a number of inaccurate or misleading name or subject entries. For example, the Index includes entries for individual collections, but not every collection mentioned in the entries is represented in the Index. (When the searcher turns to the indicated page, the collection may be difficult to locate in the closely spaced entry.) Preceding the Index is a disclaimer that certain information may be lacking because of inadequate responses to the questionnaires, but this does not seem to be an adequate explanation for the inconsistencies and errors. Names appearing in the Index do not agree with the actual *AAD* entry. Page numbers are inaccurate. Subject entries in the Index show no great care in their choice.

The *AAD* has the same sturdy binding as *WWAA*, and it lies flat when opened. The typeface used is larger than that in *WWAA*, but lengthy entries are not always easy to read. Indentation is used to mark the start of new paragraphs, but sometimes there is no leading between sections, and the result is an unbroken forbidding column extending from the top to the bottom of the page. Right-hand margins are not justified as they are in *WWAA*. Page scanning is easy as each institution is entered in capital letters and set off from adjacent entries.

Who's Who in American Art and the *American Art Directory* are recommended for public and academic libraries. For art librarians, these new editions are indispensable.

(Mar. 1, 1977, p.1033)

American dance band discography, 1917–1942.
By Brian Rust. 2v. New Rochelle, N.Y., Arlington House, 1975. 2066p. 24cm. cloth $30; to schools and libraries, 25 percent discount.

Brian Rust, the author of this new two-volume set, is certainly one of the most authoritative and productive writers on jazz discography. He is an Englishman who from 1945–60 worked in the BBC Gramophone Library "spending his days finding the right records for programmes, and doubtless his nights in memorizing and criticizing their contents" (*Gramophone*, June 1971, p.112). Since 1960 he has free-lanced, writing and reviewing for *Gramophone*, and has produced probably the most complete discography of jazz and popular music for the years 1897 to 1942 in two complementary sets of volumes. The earlier set is entitled *Jazz Records, 1897–1942* (Storyville Publications, 1970). The second set is the one presently under review, although an effort will be made to evaluate the first set as well.

In his Introduction Rust "seeks to list all known recorded works of dance bands, famous and obscure, remembered or forgotten." As the title shows, the bands are limited to American groups, with 1942 chosen as the cutoff year, because with the entry of the U.S. into World War II, recording came to a halt. The author feels that dance band recording never regained momentum after the war, that the music itself changed as, earlier, the advent of jazz had changed all that went before it, and that this period (1917–42) encompasses the best years of American dance music. This publication is concerned with this type of music, as distinct from jazz with its improvisational quality. For coverage of 78rpm recordings of jazz, one must refer to Rust's earlier publication, *Jazz Records, 1897–1942*.

The publisher's claim that 2,373 bands are included in the *American Dance Band Discography* seems accurate, as there are 288 entries in the *A*'s and *B*'s alone. There are some omissions, however. No Negro dance bands are included, as Rust has done a thorough study of these in *Jazz Records*. Glenn Miller is left out, because his discography is covered in John Flowers' *Moonlight Serenade* (Arlington, 1972), and Benny Goodman is missing, because he is covered in *BG on the Records* by D. R. Connor and W. H. Hicks (Arlington, 1969). Although these two books are in print, librarians who prefer all-inclusive reference works may be disappointed by these omissions.

The records (all 78rpm discs) are arranged chronologically by date of original "take" under the name of the band leader or the band. Personnel and soloists are included and updated for each entry so that the reader can trace the history of each recording group's development. Entries include the original American, subsequent American and Canadian, and all known British manufacturer numbers for each recording. Matrix numbers, arrangers, and soloists are also cited for many titles. Some of the information is in code which is explained at the front of volume 1. Entries include pseudonyms used by bands recording for various labels; hence one learns that "The Old Virginians" on the Aco label were really "The Ambassadors," and that "The Maryland Dance Orchestra" was in fact many orchestras, including Ben Bernie's group and the "Bar Harbor Society Orchestra." Entries are arranged by name of orchestra if it is not a personal name, or by last name of conductor, even though entries begin with first names. Thus, although Ted Fiorito is listed in this way, material is located in the *F*'s under Fiorito. There are very few cross-references, and band leaders' names are preferred entries, so that Isham Jones' Rainbo Orchestra is entered only under *Jones*. At the end of volume 2, there is an Index to all musicians named, including those of band members and soloists.

The work is in two sturdy volumes of over 1,000 pages each with continuous pagination, in small but clear printout type, with the entries centered and capitalized. It is bound in linenlike brown buckram and seems capable of withstanding average usage.

Jazz Records, 1897–1942 is also a two-volume set, similar in organization and format but slightly smaller. There is some overlapping of scope in the two sets, but the contents are different. Some dance bands recorded a very few times in the jazz idiom, and these have been included in *Jazz Records*. Most of the output of these bands remains in *American Dance Band*, however. Thus, Eddie Duchin's band takes up nine pages in *American Dance Band* but has only one entry in *Jazz Records*. There are many bands which are represented in only one of the two sets. Wingy Manone, Duke Ellington, Louis Armstrong, and Count Basie appear exclusively in *Jazz Records*. Horace Heidt, Ted Fiorito, Sammy Kaye, and Wayne King appear only in *American Dance Band*.

Another difference lies in the record companies analyzed. The *American Dance Band* indexes only the products of American and a few British companies, 121 in all. *Jazz Records* includes British and continental companies as well as American, 180 in all. In addition, *Jazz Records* indexes the recordings of many soloists. One can find discographies for Mildred Bailey, Bessie Smith, Bing Crosby, Ethel Waters, Mary Lou Williams, and the Andrews Sisters, among many others. The *American Dance Band* does not have separate entries for soloists.

Comparison should be made with Roger Kinkle's *Complete Encyclopedia of Popular Music and Jazz 1900–1950* (Arlington, 1974) reviewed in *Reference and Subscription Books Reviews*,

July 15, 1975, p.1200. In this set, only the first three of the four volumes contain recordings. Volume 1 is a chronological list of popular music by type with a selective discography not comparable with the comprehensive listing prepared by Rust. In 1923, for instance, *Kinkle* lists only three recording numbers for Vincent Lopez as compared to 55 in *American Dance Band*. Volumes 2 and 3 of *Kinkle* are biographical dictionaries which include jazz and popular musicians, radio, stage, movie personalities, conductors, and show people. As the *American Dance Band* does not include entries for soloists, *Kinkle* may fill a gap. Although *Jazz Records* does not include biographies, the discographies for performers are much more complete, e.g., for Mildred Bailey, *Kinkle* lists only 36 recordings while *Jazz Records* contains a six-page discography. For soloists involved less in jazz than in popular or show music, neither *American Dance Band* nor *Jazz Records* contributes much. For Helen Morgan, *Jazz Records* and *American Dance Band* each represent her with only one recording, whereas *Kinkle* lists 17 records and 2 which were made later than 1942. However, Rust does justice to the missing show people in a third publication, *The Complete Entertainment Discography from the Mid 1890's to 1942* (New Rochelle, N.Y.: Arlington, 1973), prepared in collaboration with coauthor Allen G. Debus.

Libraries having active music collections and a public interested in popular music will want both *American Dance Band Discography* and *Jazz Records*, and perhaps the *Complete Entertainment Discography*. The three titles provide a fairly complete inventory of popular recordings created prior to 1942. University, special, and large public libraries; popular culture enthusiasts; and collectors of popular music recordings may want all three works. The *American Dance Band Discography* is recommended as a worthy addition to the field of popular music discography. *(Sept. 15, 1976, p.199)*

016.7899'12 Music, Popular (Songs, etc.)—U.S.—Discography || Dance—Orchestra music—Discography [CIP] 75-33689

The American film institute catalog of motion pictures: feature films 1961–1970 and indexes. Richard P. Krafsur, executive editor. 2v. New York, R. R. Bowker Co., 1976. 29cm. buckram $90. plus shipping and handling.

The American Film Institute, founded in 1967 by the National Endowment for the Arts and the Ford Foundation, was launched with stated goals which include the preservation of archives and the execution of a publication program. The two-volume catalog under review, labeled F6, covers feature films produced during the 1960s. So far, the only other cumulation to be published is F2 which was confined to feature films created in the U.S. during the 1920s decade. The long-term objective of the American Film Institute is publication of nineteen titles consisting of three separate series plus a historical volume entitled *Film Beginnings, 1893–1910*. F1-F6, S1-S6, and N-1-N6 are to cover features, short, and newsreel films respectively. The six decades 1910 through 1969 will be encompassed.

F2, published in 1971, was limited to feature films produced in the U.S. By the sixties, filmmaking had assumed an international character so that coverage in the two-volume catalog under review has been expanded to include all qualifying films regardless of country of origin. To be eligible, a film must have been commercially exhibited, have a minimum running time of 45 minutes, and have been available with an English-language soundtrack or subtitles.

The 1961–70 catalog, F6, includes two separate volumes. The first volume is an alphabetical listing of each film by title, with copious cross-references leading from working titles, original titles, or alternate titles to the main entry. The second volume contains indexes. Information about each of the 5,775 films, to the extent available, is arranged in the following order: title, country of origin, reissue, entry number, producer, sponsor, distributor, date of release, sound/silent, color, gauge, length, production credits, cast, genre, source, synopsis, subject, and notes. Acquisitions staff and film librarians will welcome, in particular, the identification of distributors.

For example, one may confirm that the film "Camelot" was released in October 1967, premiered in New York on October 21, was created in technicolor, and runs 179 minutes. Persons involved in the production are identified in addition to members of the cast; a synopsis of the plot and the titles of the songs appear; and subjects under which the film may be classified—nobility, knighthood, jousting, illegitimacy, trials, age of chivalry, and others—are enumerated. Finally, a note states that scenes were filmed in Spain.

The Index volume of 976 pages contains a Credit Index, a Literary and Dramatic Source Index, a Subject Index, and a National Production Index. The Credit Index, comprising three-quarters of the book, lists "all personal, group, institutional, and corporate names credited in the *Catalog* with any aspect of film production and distribution or with the performance of film roles." Under each name is a roster of films, arranged by year of release in the U.S. An entry number refers to the appropriate page in the first volume. No errors in indexing were detected. The Literary and Dramatic Source Index is an alphabetical listing of the authors of plays, operas, ballets, short stories, screenplays, and novels, identifying the exact titles of works from which films have been derived. The Subject Index enumerates, under each subject heading, film titles in which the subject figures importantly. The range of subject headings is rich in its diversity (e.g., *police, pianists, Jesus, San Francisco—Haight-Ashbury, helicopters, motherhood, winter, white house, Ku Klux Klan, dogs,* and *United States—history—war of 1898*). Finally, the National Production Index lists films according to national origin with the exception of films produced solely by United States production companies.

The volumes are sturdily bound in red cloth with silver lettering and an embossed design on the front covers. The pages in the alphabetical catalog volume contain double columns with film titles in boldface type; the index volume has four columns per page. Legibility in both formats is satisfactory.

A selective and fairly current Bibliography of 100 items—books, periodicals, annuals and serials, and national production catalogs—implies that much scholarly effort stands behind this endeavor. Fully one-third of the titles are in foreign languages, e.g., Swedish, Polish, Czechoslovakian, Yugoslavian, French, and so on. Even in its initial state, covering just two decades of feature films, this series assembles a vast amount of information not available in any other place.

It appears certain that the *American Film Institute Catalog* will become a major reference work on American movies. It is recommended to large public and academic libraries. Special film libraries will find it invaluable. *(Feb. 15, 1977, p.920)*
011   Moving-pictures—Catalogs   [CIP]   79-128587

Animals that burrow.
†591.5264   Burrowing animals—Juvenile literature || Animals, Habitation of—Juvenile literature   [OCLC]   75-20511
See page 50

Animals with shells.
†594   Shellfish—Juvenile literature   [OCLC]   75-20513
See page 50

Argentina:
a chronology and fact book, 1516–1973. Compiled and edited by Russell H. Fitzgibbon. Dobbs Ferry, N.Y., Oceana Publications, 1974. 148p. 24cm. cloth $7.50.
982   Argentine Republic—History—Sources || Argentine Republic—History—Chronology   [CIP]   73-20375
See page 88

Ballet and dance.
†793.3   Ballet—Juvenile literature || Dancing—Juvenile literature   [OCLC]   75-20501
See page 50

The baseball encyclopedia:
the complete and official record of major league baseball. [Edited by Fred Honig. 3d ed.]. New York, Macmillan, 1976. 2,142p. 25cm. cloth $25.
796.357'021   Baseball—Statistics   [OCLC]   73-21291

The official encyclopedia of baseball.
[By] Hy Turkin and S. C. Thompson. 8th rev. ed., [1976]. New York, Barnes, [c1976]. 715p. 25cm. cloth $14.95 (This ed. now o.p.)
†796.357'021   Baseball—Statistics

The sports encyclopedia: baseball.
[By] David S. Neft, Roland T. Johnson, Richard M. Cohen, and [Jordan A. Deutsch]. New York, Grosset, [c1976]. 494p. 29cm. cloth $17.95; paper $9.95.
†796.357'64   Baseball—Statistics   [OCLC]   73-15137

The Baseball Encyclopedia, The Official Encyclopedia of Baseball, and the *Baseball* volume of *The Sports Encyclopedia* are three compilations of baseball statistics currently being published with frequent new and revised editions appearing since 1970. In this omnibus review, the Committee will examine these works separately and then compare them in terms of major emphases and unique features.

The third edition of *The Baseball Encyclopedia* was edited by Fred Honig with the assistance of a large editorial staff. Joseph L. Reichler served as editorial consultant. Reichler has written numerous books on baseball, including *Baseball's Great Moments.* For *The Baseball Encyclopedia,* his position as special assistant to the baseball commissioner enabled him to provide additional information and raw material for use by the Macmillan editorial staff.

The Baseball Encyclopedia is a voluminous collection of data including analysis of demographic, biographic, and career statistics for major league players, managers, and teams from 1876 through 1975, with a supplementary section on the National Association, 1871–75, even though it was not considered a major league because of its loose organization and sporadic scheduling from 1871 through 1875. Compilation of this information required extensive original research and the conversion of earlier data for fielding and batting averages and measures of pitching effectiveness into their modern equivalents. Hits, stolen bases, errors, earned run averages, and assists were defined in a variety of ways in the late 1800s and early 1900s. Using the records of Lee Allen, historian of the Baseball Hall of Fame, and John Tattersall, who for 40 years collected statistics on early games, plus local newspapers and archives, the editorial staff compiled and organized millions of data elements. In order to assure reasonable accuracy and consistency, the editors formed a Special Baseball Records Committee to draw up a code of rules recording past play of the game, particularly during the period before 1920. This committee's 17 guidelines are presented in an Appendix.

Part one—a brief history of the development of professional baseball, focusing primarily on interleague conflicts and challenges in baseball's early years and on player-owner conflicts in recent decades—introduces this work. Part two, "Special Achievements, Records, and Awards," provides rosters of Cy Young Award winners, those named Rookie of the Year, Baseball Hall of Fame members, no-hit games, and unusual team and individual records presented in chronological sequence. Part three lists complete lifetime team rosters for each of the major league teams including references to name and location changes; thus, the entry for the Atlanta Braves roster refers the user to the Boston Braves. Both players and managers, even those who appeared in only one game and may not have had an official time at bat, are listed along with years of service.

Part four lists individual single season and lifetime batting, pitching, and fielding records from 1876 through 1975. For 1870 through 1919, data that is estimated is italicized. Depending on the category, the top 15 or 20 single season performers are noted. For example, Babe Ruth, Lou Gehrig, and Ted Williams account for 13 of the top 20 slugging averages, while Nolan Ryan and Sandy Koufax hold 6 of the 15 season strikeout records. Career records provide much longer listings; 139 lifetime batting averages of .300 or better, 167 players who scored 1,000 or more runs, and 70 pitchers who won 200 or more games are indicative of this coverage.

In part five every major league team roster is listed for each year from 1876 and arranged in order of its final standing. Won-lost record, manager, basic player roster with detailed individual batting, fielding, and pitching statistics are provided. Team entries are followed by a summary of individual batting and pitching leaders for the league. Since only regular players are included in these team rosters, they are by no means complete listings of team members. Comprehensive player listings are provided in another section.

Part six lists the teams and players and provides available statistics on individual and team performance for the National Association, baseball's first professional league. Since many of these players later joined major league teams, this is a useful supplement to later career statistics. Managers, especially for the early years of baseball, are often hard to identify; however, part seven, the "Manager Register," attempts to list every manager and his managerial record by year and by team for each year since 1876. Some managers lasted only one or two games, but they are dutifully identified and their won-lost records presented. Part eight, the "Player Register," requires more than 800 pages of text. Every man who could be identified as having appeared in a major league game from 1876 through 1975 is listed, except players who were primarily pitchers. Each player is listed under his playing name; there are only a few *see* references from real names. Since most players are known almost exclusively by their playing names, these cross-references appear to be useful but not indispensable. Information for each player includes birth date, birthplace, death date if deceased, name variations and nicknames, height, weight, year-by-year performance statistics in regular season games, cumulated career statistics, and world series performance. Joe Cobb, who appeared in one game for Detroit in 1918 as a pinch-hitter, receives the same detail as the venerable Ty Cobb with his 24-year career and more than 11,000 times at bat. Obviously Ty Cobb's entry is 24 times as long because it provides full information for each year of his involvement with the sport. In addition, achievements are noted for such players as Ty Cobb who ranks high among lifetime leaders in performance. Cobb's entry ranks him first in career hits, runs, stolen bases, and batting average and second, third, and fourth in some other categories. Within this same section, only pitchers who played in other positions or appeared as pinch hitters in at least 25 games are covered.

Part nine details major league career statistics for pitchers active since 1876, including those whose careers consisted of pitching to but one batter. Won-lost record, earned run average, strike-outs, hits yielded, relief pitching record, and similar data are presented for each year with identification of team or teams played for; cumulated career figures are calculated and separate coverage of league playoff or world series data is provided. Vital statistics are provided along with nicknames and name changes. As in the "Player Register," few *see* references are provided from legal names or other playing names.

Part ten covers "World Series and Championship Playoff Series" beginning with the 1903 series. Each game and its highlights are succinctly presented, followed by team and individual batting and pitching statistics for the series. A separate section identifies world series lifetime batting and pitching leaders based on a minimum of 50 times at bat for the former category and 25 innings pitched for the latter. All-star games receive brief coverage in part eleven. The outcome and highlights of each game, pitchers, and home run hitters are provided. However, all-star team rosters of players and managers are not provided; nor are they identified elsewhere in the volume.

Three brief appendixes complete *The Baseball Encyclopedia*. Appendix A lists the official records, archival collections, trade (e.g., *The Sporting News*), and city newspapers used in data collection and research for this volume. Appendix B records the decisions of the special committee on record-keeping procedures. Appendix C chronicles major changes which have occurred in playing and scoring rules in the last 100 years. An awareness of major rule changes can be a critical factor in interpreting baseball history.

The following look-up pattern clarifies how *The Baseball Encyclopedia* functions as a reference tool. To find material on Terry Moore, St. Louis Cardinal outfielder 1935–42 and 1946–48, one must consult the "Player Register" for yearly and aggregate statistics, the "Manager Register" to cover his 1954 stint as manager of the Philadelphia Phillies, the "Pitcher Register" for his one pitching assignment in 1939, and the yearly team entries for his usual position (centerfield in 1942) and his fielding average as well as the team's final standing. The "World Series" section for the 1942 and 1946 years gives Moore's batting record for the series games, and he, of course, appears in the "Team Roster" for St. Louis as a player and for Philadelphia as a manager. The "Player Register" is the logical place to initiate the search since this entry will identify his team, positions played including any appearance as a pitcher, reference to any managerial appointment, identification of brothers, father, or sons who also performed as professional ball players or managers, and other information which leads the user to other entries or sections.

The Sports Encyclopedia: Baseball is one of a Grosset & Dunlap series of reference books dealing with major sports. Volumes on professional football and professional basketball have already been published. David Neft and Roland Johnson also compiled *The All Sports World Record Book,* and Jordan Deutsch has to his credit *The Scrapbook History of Baseball.* While the authors do not discuss their research process, they do cite many persons who assisted them, including Joseph Reichler, consultant for *The Baseball Encyclopedia,* and Pete Palmer, reviser of *The Official Encyclopedia of Baseball.*

The Sports Encyclopedia: Baseball is a detailed statistical handbook divided into several chronological segments which the authors consider significant. A series of essays describing the highlights of each year since 1900 supplements the statistical data. It appears that Jordan Deutsch wrote ten baseball poems which precede the main text, but no other specific authors are identified.

An introductory essay covering the period 1876–1900 explains the reasons for using 1876 as the beginning date for major league baseball and identifies some of the problems in record keeping for the early years. Nine balls for a walk, underhand pitching, and a 45-foot pitching distance are a few of the earlier specifications of the game that make comparisons between nineteenth- and twentieth-century baseball players inconclusive. Outstanding batters and pitchers of the 1876–1900 period are identified, followed by team standings and basic statistics for the top batters and pitchers for each year. Boldface type identifies the highest individual or team achievement for each year (most hits, most innings pitched, most games won). The stars of this early era, who finished their careers by 1900, are listed along with their vital statistics and lifetime batting/pitching records.

The next section covers 1901–1919 in much the same manner but in greater depth. Highlights and the world series of each year occupy a half page, followed by the team-by-team rosters of players and their seasonal achievements. Positions played, age, games played, times at bat, runs, hits, stolen bases, batting average, and many other statistics are provided for each man who appeared in the lineup, even for a single time at bat. Pitchers are described in terms of won-lost records, games, saves, innings, hits, strikeouts, and similar elements of the pitching game. World series box scores and player performance figures complete the annual coverage. Cumulated listings of batters and pitchers for the period 1901–1919 provide total performance information for players who completed their careers during this time.

This pattern is repeated for the periods 1920–1945, 1946–1960, and 1961–1975. Variations from the earlier coverage are the enlargement of team rosters, lists of team players who missed full seasons because of World War II military service, and the addition of league playoffs in 1969.

A comparatively small section (25 pages) entitled "Leaders and Features" covers such diverse topics as yearly pennant winners, batting crown winners, and pitching leaders in a series of tables; single season leaders in various batting categories, such as number of hits, doubles, home runs, are given in rank order by player followed by similar listings for pitchers. In these listings, players' names sometimes recur. Ty Cobb's name appears eleven times among the seasonal batting averages of .375 or better; Cy Young is listed three times among single season pitching winners. Lifetime or career leaders in the same categories, team leaders, world series leaders, no-hit games since 1901, awards, Hall of Fame membership, a special look at designated hitters, and a comparison of "Black, Latin, and White" ballplayers complete the coverage. Most of these features cover only one or two pages of text. There are no illustrations or indexes, although the main body of the volume is in chronological order and alphabetical by player in the roster sections.

The Official Encyclopedia of Baseball was first published in 1951 and is going into its ninth revised edition. After the deaths of Hy Turkin and S. C. Thompson, subsequent editions were prepared by Roger Treat, then by Mrs. Peter Rowe Treat, and currently by Pete Palmer, who has also served as the editor of *The All-Time Rosters of Major League Baseball Clubs,* another of S. C. Thompson's baseball reference works. Hy Turkin, a sportswriter for the New York *Daily News,* built upon the baseball files of S. C. Thompson, augmenting this data with information from local newspapers and health department files of cities around the country and by visits to cemeteries and various other sources of data. The evolution of baseball from ancient bat-and-ball religious rites, the early American variations and modifications of the British game of rounders, and the post-Civil War development of national interest in intersectional competition are briefly treated in the opening chapter of *The Official Encyclopedia of Baseball.* Chapter II deals with the history of professional major league baseball, beginning with the establishment of the National Association of Professional Base-Ball Players in 1871.

The history of the National League, beginning in 1876, and the American League, from its founding in 1901, are treated separately with many succinct references to influential owners, managers, and players, along with brief treatments of major financial crises and gambling corruption during the early years. Also mentioned are the several leagues formed to challenge the established major league control of the professional sport. Brief sections of Chapter II discuss the American Association and Union Association of the 1880s, the Players League of 1890, and the Federal League of 1913. This historical treatment is followed by year-by-year final club standings, including won-lost records and managers' names, an alphabetical listing of every city with a major league team or teams, physical design of all current major league stadia (in a series of black-and-white illustrations), and annual league and team single game attendance records. In addition to the stadium illustrations, these first two chapters include black-and-white pictures of baseball action and portraits and photographs of several major personages associated with the development of the sport. While few in number, the illustrations are generally clear and well-chosen.

Chapter III, the "All-Time Register of Players and Managers," seeks to identify and provide career information about every person who has appeared in a major league game since the beginning of the 1871 season. The editors' claim that more than 10,000 players' names are represented seems justified. Depending on availability of information, each player and manager is included in a single alphabet, with nickname, birthplace and date, and playing record by club and by season, with yearly and lifetime batting average (except for pitchers), games played, and whether the player batted and threw left or right handed. Batting information is not provided for pitchers; instead the number of games pitched and the won-lost record is provided by year with a career cumulation as the final entry. Cross-references from legal names to playing names are provided in many instances, although the legal or family names of many famous ballplayers are not included under player entries or as cross-references.

Chapter IV discusses each world series and provides the box score summary for each game including pitchers and attendance for most games. Attendance, gate receipts, players' shares, and series winners are presented in a single table, and a summary of team participation indicates the number of series and number of series games won and lost. An "All Time Register of World Series Players" provides name, year, team, position, number of games, and batting average or pitching record by year and cumulatively.

Chapter V lists top performers in a wide variety of categories, such as number of games, number of hits, pitching victories, batting average, slugging percentage, consecutive batting and fielding streaks, and many other categories of statistical information.

Chapter VI identifies the player in each league with the highest batting average, most hits, most singles, doubles, triples, home runs, runs batted in, stolen bases, pitchers' won-lost records, earned run average, and number of players struck out. Lifetime club leaders in batting and pitching and winners of awards (e.g., the Most Valuable Player Award) complete this chapter.

In chapter VII many unusual feats of the past 100 years are noted. Vander Meer's double no-hitter, Di Maggio's 56-game hitting streak, and Ruth's 60 home runs are highlighted.

Chapter VIII provides the history and roster of the National Baseball Hall of Fame, a list of pitchers of nine inning no-hit games, and all-star game box scores since 1933.

Chapters IX through XIII present a brief history of umpiring, an all-time roster of umpires, baseball administration and league regulations, along with brief discussions of such diverse topics as writers, fans, spring training, nicknames, black players, ballads, and playing tips. The final chapter deals with the evolution of playing rules and the current official rules of play. A brief glossary and scoring guide conclude the volume. There is no index to any section, but the players' register is in alphabetical sequence.

Since all three of these titles devote the overwhelming preponderance of their space to individual player performance, the amount and quality of coverage of pitchers, managers, and other players seems critical. *The Official Encyclopedia of Baseball* identifies the largest number of players and managers, especially because of its inclusion of the 1871–76 period, and a few individuals from the 1900s also appear only in this volume. However, this work also provides the least detail in its entries. *The Baseball Encyclopedia* ranks only slightly behind *The Official Encyclopedia of Baseball* in number of names and gives much more data on each player. *The Sports Encyclopedia: Baseball* lists only a few professional baseball players who finished their careers before 1900. Players active in 1901 or later are covered with essentially the same degree of specificity as that provided by *The Baseball Encyclopedia.* To collect yearly statistics for a player, the user must examine annual team rosters in *The Sports Encyclopedia: Baseball,* while detailed annual tables are provided under the player's name in *The Baseball Encyclopedia.* Many conflicting entries were located, especially the birth dates of early players. The birth dates reported in *The Official Encyclopedia of Baseball* were frequently in disagreement by one or more years with the other two sources, yet this source discusses the editors' practice of securing death certificates which "invariably revealed the man to be one to four years older than his 'baseball age.' " In one sample, demographic information was in conflict more than 50 percent of the time. *The Baseball Encyclopedia* provided the most detailed information on playing names, nicknames, and players who were related to each other and is most likely to provide place of death. *The Official Encyclopedia of Baseball* added some death dates not included in the other sources. Conflicting data on batting averages, won-lost records, and similar standard elements are common for the pre-1901 era, the period of constantly changing rules. Record keeping became increasingly standardized during the early decades of the twentieth century. Only a few small data conflicts were located for players who began their careers during or after the 1920s.

The Baseball Encyclopedia adds several extra dimensions to its player coverage. Boldface type shows league-leading performances by individual players; and all-time rankings are given at the bottom of appropriate columns.

Annual team data ranks next in importance. For this coverage *The Sports Encyclopedia: Baseball* lists teams by manager and order of finish and provides a complete roster of all team members during the season with cumulative season performance statistics. *The Baseball Encyclopedia* offers a similar type of coverage but lists only the major team members, the regulars, rather than the total roster. It includes unique information on put-outs, assists, errors, and fielding averages and additionally summarizes league batting, base running, and pitching leaders, along with team batting, fielding, and pitching records. *The Official Encyclopedia of Baseball* provides only final team standings and managers' names.

Managerial information is provided in maximum detail in *The Baseball Encyclopedia* but only sketchily in the other two encyclopedias. This title lists both player and nonplayer managers, with vital statistics, team managed, won-lost record, final standing, and career record.

Each encyclopedia offers a few unique features. *The Official Encyclopedia of Baseball* devotes the most space to history and essays on topics such as baseball writers and umpires; *The Sports Encyclopedia: Baseball* divides its retrospective coverage into several chronological periods and discusses the impact of the 1973 "designated hitter" ruling; and *The Baseball Encyclopedia* provides a brief history of the sport, discussion of the establishment of special awards, rules changes, and lifetime team rosters. In all three titles, the statistics on players, pitchers, managers, and teams form the major portion of coverage, and each title offers something of consequence. *The Baseball Encyclopedia* is most exhaustive in detail and is characterized by high quality printing with excellent boldface type and an attractive format. *The Sports Encyclopedia: Baseball* is printed on high quality opaque paper, provides detailed statistics since 1900 in very compact legible print, and is superior in year-by-year team detail. *The Official Encyclopedia of Baseball* presents the largest number of player names by a small margin over *The Baseball Encyclopedia*, is most heavily cross-referenced, and brings to light early players' birth dates which are inconsistent with dates cited in other standard sources. Regrettably *The Official Encyclopedia of Baseball* also provides the most skeletal statistics on players and teams and is not characterized by high quality printing. Several different typefaces are mixed together in the "World Series Player Roster" with light and dark print on the same page. While all three titles are sturdily bound, their narrow inner margins make rebinding impractical.

The Baseball Encyclopedia, The Sports Encyclopedia: Baseball, and *The Official Encyclopedia of Baseball* provide extensive coverage of baseball statistics through 1975. All three volumes are recommended for purchase by public, academic, and secondary school libraries. Large libraries will probably wish to acquire all three titles; smaller libraries should select the encyclopedia with the content of most interest to their clienteles. *(June 1, 1977, p.1517)*

A bibliography of English history to 1485:
based on the sources and literature of English history from the earliest times to about 1485. By Charles Gross. Edited by Edgar B. Graves. [2d ed.] London, Oxford Univ. Pr. [1975]. xxiv, 1103p. 24cm. cloth, $40.

This work is an extensively revised and greatly expanded edition of Charles Gross' *The Sources and Literature of English History from Earliest Times to About 1485* (2d ed., Longmans, 1915). Authorities generally agree that Gross' *Sources . . .* is the best bibliography of English history from its prehistoric and Celtic beginnings to 1485, the date coinciding with commencement of coverage in the next title in this Oxford University Press series, *Tudor Period, 1485–1603.* It is valuable for both its selection of material and for its annotations.

In 1935 the Royal Historical Society invited the Mediaeval Academy of America to collaborate in the preparation of a revision of Gross' *Sources. . . .* Although learned societies and universities supported this early effort toward revision, the Second World War interrupted the project. Revived in 1949, the project moved slowly but steadily until 1956 when a Ford Foundation Grant enabled the American Historical Association in cooperation with the British Academy, the Mediaeval Society of America, and the Royal Historical Society to revise and complete a planned series of British Bibliographies. The societies cooperating in the venture appointed the Anglo-American Committee for British Bibliographies to select editors for specific volumes and to give general supervision to the project. The titles in the series, in addition to *Bibliography of English History to 1485,* are *Tudor Period, 1485–1603,* 2d ed. (1959) edited by Conyers Read, the *Stuart Period, 1603–1714,* 2d ed. (1970) edited by Godfrey Davies and revised by Mary Freer Keeler, and *The Zenith of Empire, 1851–1914,* forthcoming, edited by H. J. Hanham.

Edgar B. Graves, Professor Emeritus of History, Hamilton College, Clinton, New York, was selected as editor in chief for the revision of Gross' *Sources. . . .* Eminently qualified through education, experience, and research, he worked with an advisory committee of British and American scholars.

Professor Graves states: "The general principles on which this bibliography has been fashioned are broadly those set forth by Charles Gross." Graves rather closely conforms to the pattern described by Gross, who in his Preface stated that the bibliography . . . should give some account of the contents and a brief estimate of the value of the books named . . . does not profess to be exhaustive; it comprises only select lists of books; worthless and obsolete treatises are omitted. . . . Greater fullness has been sought in the sections concerning the original sources; and it is hoped that no printed source of prime importance has been overlooked.

Graves, in his Introduction to *A Bibliography of English History to 1485,* says of the revision: "Like previous editions, it includes for the pre-Norman period some fundamental studies on Welsh and Irish history; but it comprises for the period from 1066 to 1485 only those studies about non-English areas which relate directly to England. . . . The extension of knowledge; particularly in the fields of economic and cultural history, has necessitated some rearranging for the pre-Norman period and considerable reorganization for the subsequent period."

The bibliography is divided into five parts and subdivided into 23 chapters. The five parts are: (1) General Works and Auxiliary Sciences, (2) Archives, Source Collections, and Modern Narratives, (3) From Prehistory to Anglo-Saxon Conquests, (4) The Anglo-Saxon Period, and (5) From Normans to Tudors. Each chapter is divided into appropriate sections as necessitated by the subject or period. To illustrate: chapter XI, Anglo-Saxons and Celts: Sources, is divided into the five subdivisions: (1) Chronicles and Annals, (2) Administrative Sources, (3) Church Sources, (4) Literature and Learning, and (5) Non-Literary Sources. An eleven-page Table of Contents clearly outlines this arrangement of subjects and facilitates effective access to pertinent groupings of items in the bibliography.

The bibliography has retained virtually all the entries of Gross's *Sources* . . . which were appropriate for the first two parts, but greatly expands the number of entries which fall into the chronologically arranged three final parts. The total number of entries has increased from 3,234 to 7,221 numbered citations with fully 70 percent of the bibliography comprising the three final parts.

Each part of the bibliography is preceded by a brief note explaining the value of some of the more important entries in the group. Sometimes the scope and organization of cited sources are also described. Most entries are annotated. Unannotated entries are self-explanatory such as number 7034 "PEARSALL (DEREK) John Lydgate. Lond. and Charlottesville (Virginia) 1970 (a biography)." Brief comments accompany other entries such as number 7038 "BENNETT (JACK A. N.), ed. Essays on Malory. Lond. 1963. Seven essays by seven scholars." Many entries contain a listing of the contents as illustrated by entry 5582 "LE NEVE (JOHN). Fasti ecclesiae anglicanae, 1300–1541. Institute Hist. Research, London, 1962–7." Listed are the titles and authors of the eleven chapters and the twelfth chapter which serves as the introduction, errata, and index. The majority of the entries have descriptive or critical annotations which provide information on the background and/or value of the work.

The total number of entries in *A Bibliography of English History to 1485* is difficult to determine for two reasons: (1) some titles have multiple entry numbers, and (2) many unnumbered citations are included in the annotations. For example, THE HONOR AND FOREST OF PICKERING, edited by Robert Turton, appears as four separate entry numbers (3203, 3630, 3884, and 3890) and REGISTRUM VULGARITER NUNCUPATUM, *The Record of Caernarvon,* edited by Henry Ellis, Record Comm. 1838 is entered twice (numbers 4943A and 6828). Annotations vary to meet the requirements of the section under which the book is entered. However, the annotation for entry number 4188 includes citations of eight *see also* references which are unnumbered in the *Bibliography* . . . ; entry number 4943 has one unnumbered citation in the annotation. Probably the total of 7,221 entries cited above is a conservative figure.

Graves has made excellent use of cross-references. He frequently refers to related entries by number, thus expanding the user's knowledge of materials.

A Bibliography of English History to 1485 has been fully indexed by author and subjects not represented in the Contents section.

The book is printed on nonglare paper with main entries in large uppercase type. Annotations are in smaller but very legible type. The type shows through the page slightly, but this is not distracting. The binding and sewing are sturdy enough to withstand wear, and the margins are wide enough to permit rebinding.

A Bibliography of English History to 1485 has no equal. The careful and scholarly attention given the selection and annotation of entries, and the well-designed organizational pattern qualify it as the definitive work in its field. It is recommended for libraries which serve research needs in English history.
(Nov. 1, 1976, p.416)

016.942 Gt. Brit.—History—To 1485 [OCLC]

Biographical dictionaries master index:

a guide to more than 725,000 listings in over fifty current who's whos and other works of collective biography. 3v. Editors: Dennis La Beau and Gary C. Tarbert. 1st ed., 1975–1976. Detroit, Gale Research Co., 1975. 29cm. buckram $65.

This alphabetical listing of about three quarters of a million names culled from 53 current English-language biographical directories is a welcome application of computer technology. Publication dates of the works begin in 1940 (the date of the first volume of *Current Biography*), and go up to 1975. Most were published in the 1970s. By itself the four word main title connotes a vast undertaking inclusive of the major historical and national retrospective compilations such as the *Dictionary of American Biography* and *Chambers's Biographical Dictionary*. The new master index, however, is limited primarily to North America, but there is some international coverage.

About one third of the directories indexed are well-known tools, not limited to a particular occupation. They include *Biography News, Canadian Biography, International Who's Who, Who's Who,* and the Marquis series of national and regional directories. The other two thirds are specialized directories for authors, scientists, scholars and educators, government officials, sports notables, politicians, communications personnel, artists and architects, musicians, actors, and actresses. Although no directories for lawyers or physicians are included, many of the prominent members of these professions are represented in the who's who volumes.

Each entry consists of the biographee's name and birth date as given in the indexed publication and a code designating the source from which the entry word was taken. The "Key to Title Codes for Use in Locating Sources" is printed on the endpapers on the front and back cover of each volume. The full bibliographic description showing which edition or year of a given title is indexed appears only with the introductory pages of the first volume. Because of the continual replacement of older editions of biographical directories in most libraries, this information is essential for users and should have been displayed prominently in each of the three volumes.

By listing names exactly as they are found, the *Biographical Dictionaries Master Index* repeats any discrepancies among the sources. As stated in the Introduction, the user must be aware of the need to look in the *Biographical Dictionaries Master Index* itself under any variations which may affect alphabetizing, particularly for names with suffixes and prefixes and for Spanish and non-Roman alphabet names. For example, there are entries for Bonvoison, Baron Pierre de and De Bonvoison, Baron Pierre de; Sir Alec, Alec F., Sir Alexander Frederick, and Alexander Frederick Douglas-Home; and Patty Duke is listed with two birthdates, 1946 and 1947. Beatrice Lillie is listed from nine different directories with three different birth dates, and from two more as Lady Peel and Lady Beatrice Peel. The repetition of names and their variants as they appeared in the original publications consumes space and creates pitfalls for the unwary user. Conversion to single uniform entries of names in future editions would be a major improvement. The only cross-references in the *Biographical Dictionaries Master Index* are those already given in the indexed directories.

A promised feature for planned biennial revisions is the inclusion of references "to the latest available sketch for each individual, whether this be an updated sketch in a revised edition of the source work or a sketch from a former edition for a person who is no longer listed." If the editors are able to accomplish this in addition to adding the names from new titles, the result should be increasingly useful in eliminating the problem of locating "dropped" biographees and relevant years and editions.

Other than the Marquis Company's *Index to All Books, 1975 –* , which lists names in 11 of their publications (9 of which are indexed in the *Biographical Dictionaries Master Index*), there is no comprehensive index of current biography comparable to the *Master Index.* Omitted from the *Master Index* and included in *Index to All Books* are *Who Was Who in America* v.5 and *Who's Who in Religion* (1st ed. 1975). Other recently published titles not picked up by the *Master Index* include *American Men and Women of Science: Agricultural, Animal and Veterinary Science* (1974) and *Who's Who in the United Nations and Related Agencies* (1975).

The first edition of the *Biographical Dictionaries Master Index* is a highly useful key to the contents of a large and representative cross section of current biographical directories primarily, but not exclusively, of living persons in the U.S. and Canada. It is recommended for public and academic libraries.

(Jan. 1, 1977, p.682)
920'.073   U.S.—Biography—Indexes || Canada—Biography—Indexes   [CIP]   75-19059

Birds and migration.
†598.2   Birds—Juvenile literature || Birds—Migration—Juvenile literature   [OCLC]
75-19979
See page 50

The book collector's handbook of values 1976–1977.
By Van Allen Bradley. rev., enl. 2d. ed. New York, G. P. Putnam's Sons, c1975. xxi, 566p. illus. 24cm. cloth $20.

Van Allen Bradley, compiler of *The Book Collector's Handbook of Values,* was the author for many years of the syndicated column about rare books and their prices, "Gold in Your Attic," which appeared in the *Chicago Daily News* and other newspapers in the U.S. and Canada. The response to his column prompted the author to write a book under the same title (New York: Fleet, 1958), which was followed in 1961 by a sequel entitled *More Gold in Your Attic.* A revised edition of Bradley's first book appeared in 1968 under the title *The New Gold in Your Attic.*

In contrast to the compiler's previous works, which were intended primarily for the general public, *The Book Collector's Handbook of Values,* the first edition of which was published in 19:2, aims to be of value to book collectors, librarians, scholars, and booksellers as well. The compiler also expresses the hope that the book will be used by "readers who are interested in scarce and rare books as items to buy and treasure rather than to sell."

While the author's previous titles were confined solely to American books and pamphlets, the *Handbook* covers both English and American works. The minimal detail provided in the earlier volumes has been expanded to include a wider range of relevant bibliographical description.

The scope of the *Handbook* is limited, however, to works of the nineteenth and twentieth centuries. Books by literary authors predominate. A further limitation is the exclusion, with some exceptions, of items with a retail value of less than $25 in the current market. Entries are restricted, for the most part, to books in fine condition and in their original bindings. Only a few of the unique items (signed copies or copies containing writing by the author, presentation copies, etc.) are priced because their value is generally atypical.

The 16,000 titles in the *Handbook,* 1,000 of which are new to the present edition, are listed alphabetically by author. Entry is made under authors' names as they appear on the title pages. Consequently, many works are entered under authors' pseudonyms. Cross-references are provided from the authors' real names.

Auctorial entry is used only when the authorship is direct and stated on the title page. Editors and compilers are not given main entries, and books published anonymously are not entered under their known authors. For example, T. S. Eliot's anonymous *Ezra Pound and His Metric Poetry* is listed by title. The first entry under Eliot's name is a cross-reference directing the user to this and two other works by Eliot, as well as to three other author entries for works with which he provided a preface, acted as translator, or had a similar connection. Unfortunately, this method of cross-referencing is not explained in the Introduction and, as the cross-references are typographically identical to the entries, they could easily be overlooked by any user unfamiliar with the system.

In addition to authors and titles, entries cover those "bibliographical points" which the compiler considers most useful in identifying first editions, first issues, first states, etc. These usually include a description of the binding, a note on the illustrations, and the place and date of publication. Many entries include valuable notes by the compiler on the items listed. One can learn, for example, that Allen Ginsberg's *Howl* was first circulated in mimeographed form and that copies of the mimeographed edition are worth three or four times as much as copies of the first printed version.

Entries conclude with up-to-date (as of mid-1975) price information based on the catalogs of leading antiquarian booksellers in England and America and on book auction records of the major galleries. Auction prices are identified with a capital "A" and the year of record. A representative price spread is provided for most entries as the prices of rare books are subject to considerable variation depending on condition and geographical location.

The compiler's Introduction (reprinted from the first edition) provides concise information on such matters as identifying first editions, the nature of the rare book trade, and the difference between auction and catalog prices. In the Preface to the Second Edition, Bradley comments on major trends since 1972, particularly the sharp increase in prices for literary first editions, Americana, and art and color plate books, as well as the increasing difficulty in locating perfect copies.

The volume is attractively printed, providing considerably more space between entries than is often found in listings of this type. It is illustrated with a number of small (approximately one and three-fourths by three inches) reproductions of first-edition title pages of famous works. The black cloth binding appears to be sufficiently sturdy.

Because of its limited scope, the *Book Collector's Handbook of Values* will not satisfy the requirements of most serious book collectors. For the beginner, however, and for the collector interested primarily in nineteenth- and twentieth-century English and American books, the *Handbook* provides much valuable information in convenient form. Libraries which have found the first edition useful will want to obtain the second edition for its up-to-date price information. Other libraries not requiring the more extensive listings provided by such works as *American Book Prices Current* and *The Bookman's Price Index* may wish to consider purchasing the *Handbook.*   *(Jan. 15, 1977, p.74)*
016.09   Bibliography—Rare books || Books—Prices || Book collecting || Book prices   [OCLC]
75-13906

Book review digest: author/title index, 1905–1974.
Edited by Leslie Dunmore-Leiber. 1st ed. New York, H. W. Wilson Co., 1976. 4v. buckram $245, U.S. and Canada; $270, other countries.

In 1905, the H. W. Wilson Company, then of Minneapolis, began publication of a work entitled *The Cumulative Book Review Digest: Evaluation of Literature* with the intention "to make the descriptive notes so comprehensive, and the digests so full and accurate, that librarians who do not have access to the review themselves, will be able to arrive at substantially correct appreciations of the value of the books reviewed." The

Wilson Company has continued this endeavor over the past 70 years, and *Book Review Digest* is now one of the standard selection tools used in most libraries.

At intervals during its 70-odd years of existence *Book Review Digest* issued bound-in cumulative author and title indexes. These, when they appeared, have saved users time by eliminating the need to search more than one alphabet when trying to track down review excerpts. The Wilson Company has now cumulated all name and title entries from the beginning of the *Book Review Digest* through 1974 and issued a four-volume index. The *Book Review Digest: Author/Title Index, 1905–1974* indexes reviews of over 300,000 books of adult and juvenile fiction and nonfiction.

The editor, Leslie Dunmore-Leiber, was assisted in this venture by two assistants, Jason B. Honig and Barbara Schreiber.

Each of the four volumes in the set includes three introductory sections: a prefatory note, some directions for use with sample entries, and an alphabetical list of periodicals from which reviews were cited and excerpted for the period 1905 through 1974 along with the years during which they were used in *Book Review Digest*. This list includes cross-references from variant as well as earlier and latest titles.

The index itself is arranged in a single alphabet with titles and personal and corporate names interfiled. Personal name entries include not only principal authors, but also compilers, editors, joint authors, translators, illustrators, and pseudonymous or variant names. *See* and *see also* cross-references are provided to accommodate the differing spellings, filing rules, and principal listings used by *Book Review Digest* during its publishing history. For example, Bernice Richmond and Bernice (Nelke) Robinson are confirmed as being different names for the same person. Edward Carrick is identified as the pseudonym for E. A. Craig; Russia. State Planning Commission is also listed as Union of Soviet Socialist Republics. State Planning Commission; and Ibáñez, Vicente Blasco is provided with references to and from another form of his name, Blasco Ibáñez, Vicente.

Under each author's name titles are listed alphabetically, with those attributed to individuals listed before any titles for which the author was collaboratively responsible, (e.g., Reddick, Lawrence Dunbar. *Crusader Without Violence.* 1950. Jt. author, *Worth Fighting For. See* McCarthy, A. 1965).

Book Review Digest volumes in which digests of reviews appeared are indicated opposite each title and also reference is made after listings of collaborators and the various forms of authors' names represented in *Book Review Digest*. This greatly reduces the time spent checking back and forth within the four volumes of the index, because the entry found by a user generally sends him directly to the appropriate volumes of *Book Review Digest*.

A potentially useful feature of the index is the listing of separate monographs within series under the title of the series. For example, under *Survey of International Affairs, 1939–1946*, volumes 2, 3, 4, 5, and 10 with their titles are listed with the years of their occurrence in *Book Review Digest* between 1953 and 1959. Unfortunately, this feature is not as helpful as might be hoped. Only series initially entered in *BRD* under the series name are listed in the work under review. Therefore, for such well-known series as The Reference shelf, the Headline series, and Twayne's English authors series [United States, etc.], there is no representation of separate titles under series headings.

The Committee found no incorrect references within the index itself or from the index to the particular *Book Review Digest* volumes.

The set is sturdily bound in maroon buckram; and the print, two columns to a page, is small but clear. The paper is of good quality. Titles are indented under authors, and italics are used for *see* and *see also* references. These volumes will withstand normal library use, but if rebinding should become necessary, margins would be adequate.

The prime value of a set such as this resides in its usefulness as a contents key. It also has value in that it reconciles past inconsistencies in the spelling and filing of names which have appeared in the *Book Review Digest*. Additionally, it brings together entries for works reviewed in different years. *Book Review Digest: Author/Title Index, 1905–1974* is a handy, useful, and accurate index to a standard library tool. It is recommended for all academic and large public libraries.

(Jan. 1, 1977, p.683)

028.1   Book review digest—Indexes || Books—Reviews—Periodicals—Indexes   [CIP]
75-43680

The book trade of the world. v. II:

The Americas, Australia, New Zealand. Edited by Sigfred Taubert. Wiesbaden/Gütersloh/London/New York, Verlag für Buchmarkt-Forschung, André Deutsch, Bowker, [1976]. 377p. maps. 23cm. plastic-covered case binding $36 plus shipping and handling.

The Book Trade of the World, volume II, *The Americas, Australia, New Zealand (BTW II)* is part of an intended three-volume set designed to provide basic information about the world's book trade. The first volume, which was published in 1972, was confined to Europe with only peripheral attention given to international aspects of the trade. The present volume deals with North and South America, Australia, and New Zealand; a third volume will cover Africa and Asia. While only the second volume is under review here, it and the first volume have identical formats, and the Committee presumes that the third volume will follow the same plan. The editor indicates that a fourth volume containing an overall index is a possibility; this certainly would be welcome as there are no indexes in the individual volumes.

The editor of this and the previous volume is Sigfred Taubert, whose career in the book trade began in Germany in 1932. He is now director of the Frankfurt Book Fair. Taubert states in the Foreword that the work is intended to assist booksellers in various parts of the world in saving time and energy in their dealings with one another by providing information required in the international book trade in comprehensible form.

In most cases the editor's approach to gathering the necessary information has been to contact appropriately credentialed experts and ask them to prepare entries for their countries. For example, the person chosen to prepare the entry for the U.S. is Daniel Melcher, whose career in the book trade is long and illustrious. National coverages are assigned space based on the number of book titles produced annually. Taubert states that only in "unavoidable cases" has he asked authors for editorial changes and never in situations involving politics or ideologies. The latter proviso is especially evident in the section devoted to Cuba, which exudes pride of accomplishments achieved under the Castro regime and contains revolutionary rhetoric.

Information has been arranged alphabetically by country. Under each country the information about the book trade is distributed under a maximum of 35 headings. Information about the book trade of the U.S. requires all 35 headings; for Surinam only 7 of the headings are necessary. A listing of the various headings indicates the range of information provided. Each country's entry begins with an outline map showing its principal cities. Section 1, "General Information," contains general statistics, mostly of the standard sort, but also including the percentage of illiterates and the consumption of newsprint, as well as general printing paper, per inhabitant. Section 2, "Past and Present," is a brief (usually a page or less) history of the country's book trade. The sections that follow are (3) "Retail Prices"; (4) "Organization"; (5) "Trade Press"; (6) "Book-Trade Literature"; (7) "Sources of Information, Address Services"; (8) "International Membership"; (9) "Market Research"; (10) "Books and Young People"; (11) "Training"; (12) "Taxes"; (13) "Clearing Houses"; (14) "Copyright"; (15) "National Bibliography, National Library"; (16) "Book Production"; (17) "Translations"; (18) "Book Clubs"; (19) "Paperbacks"; (20) "Book Design"; (21) "Publishing"; (22) "Literary Agents"; (23) "Wholesale Trade"; (24) "Retail Trade"; (25) "Mail-Order Bookselling"; (26) "Antiquarian Book Trade, Auctions"; (27) "Book Imports"; (28) "Book Exports"; (29) "Book Fairs"; (30) "Public Relations"; (31) "Bibliophily"; (32) "Literary Prizes"; (33) "The Reviewing of Books"; (34) "Graphic Arts"; (35) "Miscellaneous."

Four modes of discourse are used: narrative description, addresses, bibliographies, and statistical charts. These appear in varying ratios, depending upon the topic being treated. Despite the diverse sources of the narratives, style and content are remarkably consistent. Less uniformity is shown in the information presented in statistical charts. The nature, format, and extent of statistical data vary widely from country to country, and one should not expect to make absolutely reliable comparisons using this work.

Perhaps the two most important reference elements are the addresses and bibliographies. The *International Literary Market Place* (*ILMP*) also includes the former information but in considerably more detail. One learns in *BTW II*, under "Mexico" (item 18), for example, that book clubs are not very important. They are dismissed in three lines; and yet *ILMP* lists the addresses of two. Again, in *BTW II* under "Australia" (item 22), the address of the "only resident literary agent" appears; *ILMP* lists seven with Australian addresses. It is clear that in such matters *BTW II* is not intended to be exhaustive. One should also emphasize the fact that *BTW II* omits the names and addresses of individual publishers, bookstores, and the like; only their trade associations are so represented. The bibliographies appear to provide a useful guide to further reading. According to the editor's Foreword, there has been no attempt to make them comprehensive. A large proportion of the works cited are in Spanish.

Both volumes which have appeared so far are bound in an attractively designed brown plastic material. The typography is clear; however, the outline maps are so stripped of detail that they are only marginally useful. The printing reflects a high standard of craftsmanship. The book uses an arrow, meaning "see," a symbol commonly used in German reference works, but, as this is not explained in the work, it may cause some momentary confusion for the reader unfamiliar with it.

The Book Trade of the World, volume II, is a compilation of a large amount of material not readily available elsewhere. This is especially true of information about the Latin American book trade. The entries are intended to be descriptive, not exhaustive, and may need to be supplemented on occasion by other sources. In addition, since the second volume occasionally makes reference to information in the first, especially on the subject of copyright, both volumes should be obtained. The second volume of *The Book Trade of the World* is recommended for college and university libraries and for public libraries maintaining comprehensive reference collections.

(July 15, 1977, p.1744)

†380.145070   Booksellers and bookselling   72-142165

Brazil:
a chronology and fact book, 1488–1973. Compiled and edited by Russell H. Fitzgibbon. Dobbs Ferry, N.Y., Oceana Publications, 1974. 150p. 24cm. cloth $7.50.

981   Brazil—History—Sources || Brazil—History—Chronology   [CIP]   73-17058

See page 88

Bridges and tunnels.
†690.598   Bridges—Juvenile literature || Tunnels—Juvenile literature   [OCLC]   75-19988

See page 50

The British comic catalogue: 1874–1974.
[By] Denis Gifford. Westport, Conn., Greenwood Pr., 1975. xiv, 210p. 29cm. linson 2 $30.

The author claims that this is the "world's first attempt at a catalogue of comics. It aims to list the title of every comic published in Great Britain, from the first one in 1874 to the most recent in 1974: some 1,900 titles in a century of comics." Denis Gifford has collected comics for more than 40 years, and he has written a number of books on film, cartoons, comics, and other aspects of popular culture, including the two-volume *British Film Catalogue 1895–1970* (New York: McGraw-Hill, 1974), *Chaplin* (New York: Doubleday, 1973), and *Karloff* (Phila.: Curtis, 1973). According to a Greenwood press release, "he drew some of the most memorable characters in British comics."

In the Introduction, the author surveys the development of comics, pointing out the genre was originally intended for adults and was created in England 25 years before it appeared in America. This preliminary historical account deals with the comic strip, color comics, comic supplement, special give away, American, wartime, library, international, underground, reprint, and amateur comic. Unfortunately, a precise definition of the term "comic" is not offered.

The present catalog begins with the first regularly published separate comic paper which was tabloid size with funny drawings on the front, back, and center, and which was published every Monday. It includes not only comics printed, published, or created (written or drawn) in Great Britain, but also reprints of U.S. and foreign materials. It lists those apparently all-British comics drawn or printed elsewhere in Europe. Amateur comics that have been published or sold at conventions or in specialized shops have also been included.

A section describing how to use the catalog follows the Introduction. Abbreviations are also explained at this point. The catalog proper is arranged alphabetically by title, in double columns. Comics of the same title are arranged chronologically with cross-references from alternative titles. Incomplete or uncertain data are so indicated. Coverage under each title includes as much of the following information as is available or applicable: date, number of issues, publisher, distributor, price, number of pages, color and printing, page size, British Museum holdings, description, premiums offered, editor, companion comics, incorporations, artists, reprints, and contents. A majority of the entries examined by the Committee contained most of these information elements.

Cross-references in the catalog are accurate, and no blind entries were noted in the Index to Artists. However, minor alphabetical misarrangements were found in the catalog entries.

Following the 191-page catalog, there is a 17-page Index to Artists, again arranged alphabetically in two columns, with the works of each person also arranged alphabetically.

The British Comic Catalogue does not profess to be a comprehensive source and its author invites corrections of errors and suggestions for inclusion in a second edition. The present book stands well as a pioneering effort, an easy-to-use product of a lay practitioner's scholarship and enthusiastic involvement. The binding will probably tolerate the limited use to which the catalog will be exposed. Recommended as an effective reference tool but only for libraries that specialize in popular culture or anticipate a demand by collectors of British comics.

(Jan. 1, 1977, p.683)

016.7415   Comic books, strips, etc.—Gt. Brit.—Bibliography   [OCLC]   75-35486

Building.
†690   Architecture—Juvenile literature   [OCLC]   75-20508

See page 50

Butterflies and moths.
†595   Butterflies—Juvenile literature || Moths—Juvenile literature   [OCLC]   75-20509

See page 50

Canada:
a chronology and fact book, 875–1973. Compiled and edited by Brian H. W. Hill. Dobbs Ferry, N.Y., Oceana Publications, 1974. 153p. 24cm. cloth $7.50.
971   Canada—History—Chronology || Canada—History—Sources   [CIP]   73-7929

See page 88

Childhood in poetry:
a catalogue, with biographical and critical annotation of the books of English and American poets comprising the Shaw childhood in poetry collection, library of the Florida State University, with lists of the poems that relate to childhood, notes, and index. 2d Supplement, 2v. By John MacKay Shaw. Detroit, Gale Research Co., [1976]. illus. 29cm. cloth $87.50 for 2v. set; v.II, Indexes, available separately $45.

The first five volumes of John Mackay Shaw's catalog, *Childhood in Poetry*, covered 100,000 poems appearing in 10,000 books and were published in 1968. A supplement followed in 1972. Volume I of the second supplement (1976) continues the catalog by describing those books added to the collection since 1972, and volume II "cumulates, extends and replaces" all previous indexes found in the main catalog and first supplement.

The Shaw Collection, which is housed in the Library at the Florida State University, is made up of books, including many first editions, which Shaw collected and donated to the university. Shaw is a well-known private collector, enthusiast, and connoisseur of children's poetry. His highly personal but knowledgeable taste comes through as one browses through the catalog. Shaw's collection includes poetry written for, about, and by children and poetry which is adopted by children and used by them, such as poems traditionally recited in school. Other miscellaneous materials, not necessarily about childhood, can also be found in the catalog. Random examples include such titles as *Book Collecting: A Beginner's Guide* by Seumas Stewart, *Literary Associations of the English Lakes* by Hardwick Drummond Rawnsley, and *From Primer to Pleasure in Reading* by Mary F. Thwaite. According to the publisher, the entire catalog provides bibliographic information for more than 200,000 poems and 21,000 volumes. An incidental extra dividend provided by the catalog is its analysis of a great deal of literature buried in nineteenth-century periodicals.

The catalogs are arranged alphabetically by author. Bibliographic information is given, as well as a summary of the contents, often some description of the format, such as "blue pictorial boards, red cloth spine," and the entry is usually followed by typical passages quoted from the volume, such as "Room at the Top" from F. Raymond Coulson's *A Jester's Jingles:*

> When I was an urchin (in knickers) / And revelled in cake with my tea, / Kind pedagogues, parents and vicars / Bestowed much advice upon me. / And one glowing precept they never / Lost any occasion to drop, / To stimulate youthful endeavor / "There's plenty of room at the top."

There are numerous *see* references from author or illustrator to other volumes. A few typical pages or illustrations from particular books are reproduced in black and white.

Volume II of the second supplement is the index volume to the entire catalog. It may be purchased separately. The Index consists of three sections, Keyword Poem-Title List, Short Title List and Key, and Book Title Index. The short titles are listed under authors' names. The lists from the base set, first and second supplements, are filed separately, since the numbering systems do not appear to be compatible. The Book Title Index is an index to the entire set, arranged alphabetically by title.

Childhood in Poetry has been compiled with great care given to textual detail. The large volumes are attractive, easy to read, and absorbing to browse through. The Shaw Collection would be of value to researchers primarily. Few public or school libraries would need so specialized a tool as the catalog, but collections/libraries supporting the study of children or scholarly investigation of adult attitudes toward children and concepts of childhood will find the catalog useful: some other libraries will require only the Index volume, which provides full entries for titles in the Shaw Collection. The latter volume, if used in combination with the Index to *Children's Poetry* and *Granger's Index to Poetry,* should provide enough access to keywords and titles to satisfy most patrons using large library systems or special collections.   *(Feb. 1, 1977, p.853)*
†808.819′52   Children's poetry—Bibliography || Children—Poetry—Bibliography   67-28092

Children's book review index.
v. 1, 1975 cumulation. Gary C. Tarbert, ed.; Sharon K. Hall, assistant ed. Detroit, Gale Research Co., 1976. 254p. 22cm. cloth $18.

In 1975 the editorial team which is responsible for Gale's *Book Review Index* (*BRI*), reviewed by the Reference and Subscription Books Review Committee Nov. 15, 1965, began to produce the *Children's Book Review Index* (*CBRI*), which cites all reviews of children's books listed in *BRI*. The Index is issued three times a year with an annual cumulation published early in the next year.

CBRI cites reviews appearing in periodicals devoted specifically to children's literature, e.g., *Bulletin of the Center for Children's Books, Horn Book,* and *Junior Bookshelf.* It also cites children's book reviews in general educational and literary journals, such as *Childhood Education, Instructor,* and *Saturday Review,* and in periodicals devoted to specialized fields of interest, e.g., *Art Journal, Natural History,* and *Social Studies.* Also represented are reviews from newspapers such as the *Christian Science Monitor* and *New York Times.* Altogether, more than 250 periodicals and newspapers are covered.

A publisher's note indicates that the volume cites all reviews of children's books from kindergarten through grade 5 or through age 10. However, examination of the titles included confirms that the span is wider, running from preschool up to the eighth grade.

The format and accuracy of *Children's Book Review Index* are the same high quality as that of *Book Review Index.* Arranged alphabetically by author, each entry gives the author's name, book title, reviewing publication abbreviation, reviewing publication volume number, date of issue, and page number.

CBRI lacks sufficient cross-references, e.g., Collodi, Carlo. See Lorenzini, Carlo; Seuss, Dr., Pseud. See Geisel, Theodor Seuss. One serious lack in the present cumulation is that Mollie Hunter's books are listed under McIlwraith, Maureen Mollie Hunter McVeigh, with no reference to or from Hunter, Mollie. A title index would also add greatly to use of the book for reference purposes.

Following a brief Introduction, the periodicals cited are listed in an alphabetic sequence according to the abbreviations used to identify them in review citations.

The volume is bound in sturdy cloth, with the title, editor, and year plainly indicated on the cover and spine. The paper is of good quality, and the typeface is clear and very readable.

Children's Book Review Index is a convenient and reasonably priced reference tool for children's and elementary school librarians and others interested in children's literature who do not have easy access to *Book Review Index.* It is recommended.
(Feb. 1, 1977, p.853)
015   Books—Reviews || Children's literature—Book reviews   [OCLC]   75-27408

Children's literature review:
excerpts from reviews, criticism, and commentary on books for children and young people. Ann Block and Carolyn Riley, editors. v.1. Detroit, Gale Research Co., 1976. iv, 201p. 29cm. cloth $25.

Patterned after *Contemporary Literary Criticism, Children's Lit-*

erature Review is projected to be a "multi-volume work of indefinite but considerable size." This review will consider the potential of the set based upon examination of volume 1. Summative judgment will be withheld until the set is completed or until such time as a number of volumes are available for comparison.

Contemporary Authors and *Something About the Author,* both bio-bibliographical reference sets, have already been issued by the publisher and are intended to be used with this new "digest of comment." *Children's Literature Review* will consist of excerpted reviews of children's literature, each semiannual volume to cover works by approximately 40 authors. The editors expect that at least 45 books and about 35 periodicals will be represented in each volume. The list of projected authors is incomplete, and suggestions are invited. The authors included are largely contemporary, but writers of an earlier period are included if the criticism of their work "is directed to a contemporary audience." For instance, volume 1 contains a section on Louisa May Alcott in which reviews published in recent years reevaluate the impact of her books. Laura Ingalls Wilder will be covered in future volumes.

For each of the authors included, there are several pages of excerpted criticism and citations. The section for Betsy Byars, as an example, contains 30 excerpted criticisms as well as citations for further research. Typically, each section gives birthdate, a very short identifying note about the author, in some cases excerpts of general criticism, and then excerpts and citations of critical reviews arranged under separate titles by the author. There are three indexes which will cumulate in each volume: an author index, an index to critics, and an index to works used in the text.

The editors have included a variety of reviews from many sources. The excerpts are generally interesting and reflect different points of view.

In the case of controversial books, such as *The Slave Dancer* by Paula Fox, excerpts are representative of various opinions, and the Eleanor Cameron/Roald Dahl confrontation over the alleged exploitation of the Oompa-Loompas in *Charlie and the Chocolate Factory* is also fairly documented.

Since the set is designed to be used in conjunction with *Contemporary Authors* and *Something About the Author,* cross-references to these volumes are made and bio-bibliographic data are omitted. For instance, although the publication dates are given for various titles listed under an author's name, no other bibliographic information is included. This sometimes leads to obscurity, as in the case of *Scoppettone, Sandra,* who is listed in the Author Index as joint author with Louise Fitzhugh, but who is nowhere mentioned in the text. The lack of bibliographic specifics for books may pose an inconvenience for some users. Full bibliographic information is given, however, for all excerpted criticism and for citations.

Volume 1 of *Children's Literature Review* represents only a minute proportion of contemporary children's literature so that it would be premature to assess the usefulness of this new tool. If subsequent volumes proceed according to plan, children's librarians, media specialists, and students can anticipate wider coverage in this source than in *Book Review Digest.*

(Mar. 1, 1977, p.1034)

028.5   Children's literature—History and criticism—Periodicals || Children's literature—Book reviews—Periodicals   [OCLC]   75-34953

Clocks & watches.

[By] Alan Smith; drawings by Peter Fitzjohn. London, The Connoisseur, [1975]. 222p. illus. 23cm. (The Connoisseur illustrated guides) paper over boards $14.95.

The Connoisseur Illustrated Guides are designed to help interested students and collectors "overcome the basic problems of identifying an object, placing it in the context of its period and style and forming a reasonable judgement of its comparative quality." With this new Connoisseur guide, Alan Smith, senior lecturer in the Department of Art History, University of Manchester, has written a book surveying clocks and watches produced within the last 500 years. Particular emphasis is placed on English horology, but some space is devoted to the timepieces of other European countries, America, and Japan.

Basically, the text is chronologically arranged in chapters which cover the period from approximately 1550 to the present. Two chapters serve as a brief introduction to the subject; the first discusses measurement of time by sundials and nocturnal, water, glass, and sand clocks, while the second attempts to provide insight into some of the major principles of clock and watchmaking as well as to create appreciation of the craftsman and his tools.

Throughout *Clocks & Watches,* the text is placed on the bottom half of the page, and illustrations of the clocks discussed appear at the top of the page. The illustrations consist of more than 400 line drawings, each of which is designed to help the reader recognize general features or details explained in the text. In addition, 26 selected representative pieces are pictured on eight color plates. Together, illustration and text provide the beginning student or collector with an introduction to the evolving materials, design, and technique associated with English horology.

A List of Plates is provided at the front of the book, and a Select Bibliography follows the last chapter. The Bibliography is in six categories: general reading, specialized works, precision clocks and electrical time-keeping, mechanical information and manufacturing methods, American clocks and watchmaking, and journals; it appears to be current, with many 1960 through 1973 imprints.

The Index is in one alphabet and includes all individual and corporate names of clock and watchmakers listed in the text as well as all major terms relating to the subject. However, some terms italicized in the text which relate directly to clocks and watches are not indexed. These appear to be mainly words or phrases dealing with the design or ornamentation of clock or watch faces, cases, and mechanisms. A check of Index references revealed no inaccuracies.

Found throughout the text are cross-references to other relevant articles, plates, or items in the Bibliography. Cross-references are accurate and, together with the Index, provide effective access to the book's contents.

Clocks & Watches is printed on heavy nonglare paper. Clear and easy to read, the text is arranged in two columns per page. The line drawings by Peter Fitzjohn are clear, and the color fidelity of the plates is excellent. The sewn binding is sturdy and should withstand normal library use.

Clock & Watches is an attractive book offering guidance to interested students and collectors. Since, however, it is devoted to collecting and does not provide comprehensive information, only fine arts libraries or public and academic libraries serving clock buffs may want to acquire this book. Recommended.

(Mar. 1, 1977, p.1036)

681'.11   Clocks and watches—Collectors and collecting   [OCLC]   75-322706

Cloth and weaving.

†677.02   Textile industry—Juvenile literature   [OCLC]   75-20504

See page 50

The complete color encyclopedia of antiques.

Compiled by the Connoisseur. Edited by L. G. G. Ramsey. rev. and expanded ed. New York, Hawthorn Books, [c1975]. 704p. illus. (part col.) 29cm. cloth $37.50.

The first edition of this work was published in 1962 as *The Complete Encyclopedia of Antiques* and was reviewed in *Booklist and Subscription Books Bulletin* for February 1, 1963. It consisted of material adapted from the five volumes of *The*

Concise Encyclopedia of Antiques (New York: Hawthorn, 1955–61) and the two volumes of *The Concise Encyclopedia of American Antiques* (New York: Hawthorn, 1958). In adapting and rearranging the material for the 1975 encyclopedia, the editor reduced to 1,472 pages the 3,248 pages of the seven volumes on which it was based.

The description of this new 1975 version of the encyclopedia as an "expanded edition" must be understood in terms of its scope rather than its length, as the total number of pages has been further trimmed to 704. This has been accomplished by replacing the 512 full-page plates in the earlier edition with illustrations placed on the text pages, by increasing the size of the volume from 26 to 29 centimeters, and by the use of smaller type. There has been no reduction in the text of the encyclopedia, although several sections (viz., the sections on *Books and Bookbinding, Painting, Sculpture and Carving,* and the material on drawing from the section on *Prints and Drawings*) in the earlier edition have been dropped.

New to this edition are sections covering *The Aesthetic Movement; The Arts and Crafts Movement; Art Nouveau; Art Deco; Antiquities;* and *Ethnographica,* areas which have become important to collectors since the publication of the first edition of the encyclopedia. New material on Oriental antiques has been added to several sections (e.g., the *Furniture* section now includes five and one-half pages on Chinese and Japanese furniture).

The work retains its original subject organization in 17 sections arranged in alphabetical order. Each section begins with a short general introduction followed by treatment from the relevant national standpoint and, when appropriate, discussion of special aspects. Each section ends with a glossary.

The longest sections are those covering *Furniture* (117p.), *Pottery and Porcelain* (115p.), *Silver* (77p.), *Prints* (65p.), and *Glass* (56p.). The sections on the movements of the late nineteenth and early twentieth centuries (*The Aesthetic Movement,* etc.), *Barometers, Clocks and Watches, Metalwork,* and *Needlework and Embroidery* have between 20 and 50 pages devoted to them, while *Antiquities, Arms and Armour, Carpets and Rugs, Coins and Medals, Ethnographica, Jewelry, Mirrors,* and *Scientific Instruments* are covered in fewer than 20 pages each.

L. G. G. Ramsey, editor of the British periodical *The Connoisseur* from 1951 to 1973, served as editor of both editions of the encyclopedia. The 99 contributors listed in the first edition are listed again on page 7 of the new edition. In view of the deletion from the new edition of the sections previously noted, the Committee wonders whether all the contributors whose names are listed actually contributed to the encyclopedia. As in the first edition, authors of sections are not identified. The Committee's review of the 1962 edition noted that "Most of them are British, members of museum staffs and frequent contributors to the *Connoisseur.*"

Authors of the new material in the present edition are listed following the original list of contributors noted above. While the sections which each of these four added contributors wrote are indicated, no further information is provided.

In his Preface to the new edition, Bevis Hillier, the present editor of *The Connoisseur,* points out that the original edition attempted to provide only a broad introduction to complex subjects, reserving complete information for topics of more limited scope. An attempt was also made to achieve a balance "between academic scrupulousness and popularizing attractiveness of presentation." Adherence to these criteria cannot, however, account for the unevenness of treatment among some of the topics included in the encyclopedia.

The Committee's review of the first edition noted that "The discussion of British silver consists entirely of advice to the collector, with no historical information or names of silversmiths." Coverage of this topic has not been expanded in the new edition. The treatment of Italian silver, on the other hand, consists of a brief historical introduction followed by a list of 53 "Notable Italian Silversmiths" with concise information on their work. Although the section on American clocks covers their development through 1850, the discussion of British clocks does not get much beyond the middle of the eighteenth century. Such imbalance is not surprising because of the encyclopedia's origins as a compilation of magazine articles.

Sections new to this edition (e.g., *Arts and Crafts Movement, Esthetic Movement, Art Nouveau, Art Deco, Antiquities, Ethnographica*) have been added to provide coverage of areas of growing interest to collectors, but no effort seems to have been made to update text carried over from the previous edition. The section on American glass, for example, does not go beyond the middle of the nineteenth century, whereas items from the latter half of the century as well as the early decades of the present century are much in demand by collectors today (e.g., carnival and depression glass). Many of today's collectors would challenge the statement in the section on American clocks characterizing the years after 1850 as a "period of mass production of inexpensive clocks" which "yielded very few items which may now be considered desirable from the collector's standpoint." Comparison of the text and glossaries in several corresponding sections of the original and new editions reveals no substantive changes. Only a few corrections, such as the elimination of the blind cross-reference from *reverse* to *obverse* in the glossary on *Arms and Armour* and the rectification of an error in alphabetization at the beginning of the glossary on *Glass,* were noted.

Perhaps the most striking aspect of the new edition is the inclusion of 500 new color photographs, the presence of which is announced by the addition of the word "Color" to the original title of the work. An equal number of black-and-white photographs and 300 line drawings are also included. The introduction of judiciously selected colorplates and improved placement and distribution of illustrations more than compensate for the reduction in the total number of graphics. While glossy stock has not been used, excellent reproduction has been achieved in most cases.

An unannotated Bibliography of approximately 775 items follows the final section. Arrangement of the Bibliography repeats that of the sections and subdivisions of the encyclopedia. A substantial number of books from the 1960s and early 1970s have been added. There are about 775 items in all—200 more than in the first edition.

The 15-page Index which concludes the volume covers both the text and glossary portions of the encyclopedia in some detail. All entries in the glossaries are not indexed however, and the criteria for selecting the entries which are indexed are not stated. Some very brief entries are indexed (e.g., "Egyptian black," p.492), while more detailed entries (e.g., "Iron-red," p.496) are sometimes not represented. Names are included in the Index, but name entries for artists and craftsmen no longer include the parenthetical references to the fields in which they worked. A helpful feature is the inclusion of references to information contained in illustration captions. The illustrations themselves, however, are not indexed.

References are provided from the text sections to relevant entries in the glossaries. The glossaries include *see* references directing the user from entries not used to those where information on the topic may be found. A few references also direct the user to other entries under which additional information is provided.

The volume is serviceably bound in dark red cloth. While the layout is pleasing, inner margins are too narrow to permit rebinding. The smaller typeface in the new edition tends to make extended reading in the work somewhat less inviting than it was previously.

Libraries whose patrons have an interest in antiques need at least one comprehensive encyclopedia of the field. Many such works are available today, most of them somewhat less expensive than *The Complete Color Encyclopedia of Antiques*. Its comparatively high price, inconsistent revision, unevenness in coverage, and British emphasis raise questions as to whether this would be a satisfactory acquisition for most libraries in the U.S. Recommended only for libraries which desire comprehensive representation in this field and to antique dealers and enthusiasts. *(Apr. 1, 1977, p.1192)*

†745.103   Collectors and collecting—Dictionaries || Art—Collectors and collecting || Furniture—Collectors and collecting   74-7888

A comprehensive bibliography for the study of American minorities.
[Comp. by] Wayne Charles Miller. 2v. New York, New York Univ., 1976. xix, 1380p. 29cm. $95.

016.30145'0973   Minorities—U.S.—Bibliography   [OCLC]   74-21636

See page 38

Concise color encyclopedia of science.
Compiled [By] Robin Kerrod. Michael W. Dempsey, editor in chief. New York, Crowell, 1975 [c1973] 256p. illus. (part col.) 31cm. pyroxylin-coated cover $9.95.

Concise Encyclopedia of Science was first published in 1973 in Great Britain by Purnell and Sons, Ltd. It carried the cover title *Purnell's Concise Encyclopedia of Science.* Robin Kerrod, the editor, is a British author who has written a number of short books for young people on science subjects (cars, satellites, rocks and minerals). Eric Davis, who is listed in the book as Senior Lecturer at Polytechnic of South Bank was the science and technology consultant. David George is cited as schools advisor and Angela Sheehan as executive editor.

Although there is no prefatory explanation of this encyclopedia's purpose, the dust jacket states that it was planned as a source of information for the whole family and aims to describe comprehensibly and illustrate "every imaginable scientific topic." "Written as an introductory overview, this simple but never simplistic volume explores in an orderly and easy-to-use format every aspect of the physical sciences. In language that young people can easily grasp, the text includes in-depth explorations of both the theoretical and the applied aspects of chemistry, physics, technology, physics and astronautics. From electronics and computers to submarines and navigation, from mining and metals to skyscrapers and the stars, from soaps to satellites, automobiles to aircraft, every theory and process is clearly explained."

Despite the title, which implies coverage of both life and physical sciences, only the latter and their technological applications are represented in this encyclopedia. Although there is a Table of Contents, the book lacks introductory matter which might explain the arrangement of subjects.

Each entry covers a two- to three-page section. In a number of cases, several successive entries are subdivisions of major subject areas. The first six sections, for instance, all deal with some aspect of space science (*Rockets into Space, Satellites into Orbit, Space Probes, Man in Space, Steps into Space, Destination Moon*). These are followed, without any transition, by *Atoms and Elements, Radioactivity,* etc. From *Atomic Energy* the book proceeds to *Common Plastics,* from *Plastics Technology* to the *Electromagnetic Spectrum,* and from *Photography* to *Railways and Locomotives.*

At no time is there any indication in the design or typography of the Table of Contents or in the body of the encyclopedia itself when there is such a major change of topic. Other groups of sections deal with civil engineering and construction, various aspects of the chemical industry, astronomy, textiles, the automobile, aircraft, and farming and foods.

Many major sections are followed by two- to three-page spreads citing important examples and giving short descriptive paragraphs for each (important minerals, metals and their uses, pioneering days of rail, common plastics, pioneers of the textile industry, etc.).

There are many illustrations throughout; either two or three small ones on a page or one illustration covering about a quarter to a third of the page, is used. Every page contains at least one illustration, either diagram or photograph. Throughout the book, two pages of exclusively color illustrations are followed by two pages of black and whites in a continuing alternating pattern. While many of the diagrams are of good quality, the main function of many of the large photographs seems to be to fill space. Captions are in smaller type, not always clearly set off from the text. Although a list of acknowledgments at the back of the encyclopedia credits "all the people and organizations who have provided photographs and assisted in the preparation of illustrations," source of individual illustrations are not identified.

The editors characterize this work as being "simple but never simplistic," and most technical terms are explained immediately after their initial appearance in italics. However, there are some terms used without any attempt at definition.

The heavy industrial and technological emphasis is pervasive. At the end of the section on soaps and detergents there is a brief statement that "the increasing use of detergents at first created pollution problems at sewage farms. Processes were upset and excessive frothing occurred in the water." In the section on paints, lead paint is described as "one of the older types of paint still successfully used." It is disappointing to find so little attention paid to environmental problems caused by some of these industrial activities. In the section on natural plastics, Kerrod states that "our own bodies are made up of complicated molecules based on linked carbon atoms. And so are those of other living things, including plants. It is not surprising that we can obtain or make plastic substances from plants. The best example of this is the latex we tap from the rubber tree and make into rubber.... Other natural plastics include rosin and shellac...." The paragraph concludes with a discussion of celluloid and cellulose acetate, "both made from cellulose." Nowhere is an attempt made to explain cellulose, or other carbohydrates. In fact, the only reference to carbohydrates and proteins in the Index is to p.238 where, under the heading *staple foods,* there is a discussion of the ingredients of bread. No other explanations appear.

Another example from the sequence on plastics is in the two-page spread featuring some common plastics and their properties. There are separate entries for the generic name acrylics as well as one for Perspex, the trade name by which methacrylate resins are known in Great Britain and for Lucite, the name for many methacrylate products in the U.S. The last sentence in the Lucite paragraph is misleading. The Lucite trademark does apply to both the methyl methacrylate monomer and to the plastics made from it, but it is incorrect to describe the properties of the polymer and then say "its proper name is methyl methacrylate monomer."

The section on atomic energy contains another example of careless editing. The text describes nuclear fission and the chain reaction. On the same page, there is a black-and-white photograph of "the gigantic fireball after the explosion of a hydrogen bomb." Near the end of this caption it is pointed out that the hydrogen bomb itself is the result of nuclear fusion, but that a small fission bomb is used as a triggering device. A picture of the well-known mushroom cloud of an exploding fission bomb would have been a more appropriate illustration on that page. Such a picture is shown on the following page, on a smaller scale.

Although there are descriptions of rather complicated machines and processes, nowhere are the basic concepts of physics upon which they are predicated fully explained.

Since the encyclopedia contains no post-1973 information, it is not surprising that discussion of alternate forms of energy (solar, wind and geothermal) which have received so much attention since the 1973 energy crisis is omitted. Similarly, one should not expect to find, in the large amount of space devoted to space science, in-depth information about Skylab and Viking. However, the complete lack of laser coverage is surprising because this technology has existed since 1960.

In general, young people and their parents looking for "simple but not simplistic" explanations of scientific and technological topics can find these more adequately represented in general encyclopedias such as the *World Book Encyclopedia* or *Collier's Encyclopedia*. These sources are, however, much more expensive. A less costly alternative is *Compton's Illustrated Science Dictionary* (Encyclopaedia Britannica, Inc., 1971) which contains a short paragraph for each term and a diagram to illustrate it and includes coverage of all the biological sciences but does not include industrial information.

Following the main text, and preceding the Index, there are two special two-page sections (inventors and inventions, weights and measures) and a single page devoted to Nobel Prizes. After a brief paragraph extolling the phrase "necessity is the mother of invention" and praising the genius of Thomas Edison, there follows a table of inventions and inventors from Gutenberg's invention of movable type in 1450 to Bacon's invention of the fuel cell in 1959. Most of the second page is taken up by a biography of Edison.

The section on weights and measures starts with a statement regretting the imminent demise of the English system of measures as a result of the movement towards complete metrication. It lists metric units, English or Imperial units (with U.S. equivalents where necessary), conversions between the two systems as well as the International System (SI) of Units. These are followed by melting and boiling points of all the elements, as well as their coefficients of expansion. While these are concepts which should be explained, the complete tables are unnecessary in a nontechnical work for young people. Nobel prizewinners for physics and chemistry are listed giving the year of the award and the name and nationality of the recipient from 1901 to 1972, but not listing topics.

The Index is accurate and comprehensive. The only cross-references used are *see* references, often given from a scientific term to the common English term. The encyclopedia includes no bibliographies after topics, or even a general list of suggested readings for anyone wishing to acquire additional information on a topic.

The entire volume is printed on good opaque paper and is sturdily bound. The typography is clear, and although the typesize used for captions is rather small, it is not difficult to read. Rebinding may be a problem, because the margins are narrow and many illustrations extend to the edge of the page.

The *Concise Color Encyclopedia of Science* may have some value for young people and their families as a book for browsing which covers a variety of technological subjects. Because of its uneven coverage, its arbitrary sequencing, its use of language not easily understood by the non-scientist, and its poor choice of illustrations as well as its lack of usefulness as a reference tool, it is not recommended. *(Dec. 15, 1976, p.626)*

†600 Technology || Science [OCLC]   73-13688

A concise encyclopedia of antiques.

[By] Geoffrey Wills. New York, Van Nostrand, 1976. 304p. 23cm. illus. (part col.) paper composition $15; to schools and libraries, 10 percent reference discount.

This work might be more accurately titled "A Concise Encyclopedia of ENGLISH Antiques" since it is devoted to "articles made and used in the past, principally in England, but including those from foreign lands that influenced London and provincial craftsmen." While the chronological scope of the volume extends from approximately 1500 to 1890, coverage of American antiques is limited to the colonial period.

Geoffrey Wills is a native of Great Britain who has had 24 books on all phases of antiques (glass, chandeliers, ivory, copper, brass, pottery, and porcelain) published in his homeland. In 1976 he had six books in print in the U.S. in addition to the *Concise Encyclopedia.* Potter, Hawthorn, Herman, St. Martin's, Weatherhill, and Arco have handled his books in the U.S. He has also contributed numerous articles to such British specialist journals as *The Connoisseur, Country Life,* and *Apollo.*

The encyclopedia is organized into two main parts. Part I (p.9–90), "Decorative Styles," provides a "brief survey of the evolution of public taste in architecture and the broad area of the arts and decoration, with biographical notes on significant architects, painters, and sculptors in each period." There are approximately 100 such notes covering figures from the fifteenth to the late nineteenth centuries. The survey is divided into nine chronological periods beginning with the Tudor Period (1500–1600) and concluding with the Later Victorian Period (1860–90). Each section begins with a one- to two-page review of the principal trends and developments of the period, followed by entries for the leading architects, painters, and sculptors of the time.

Part II, which includes more than 1,000 entries, consists of 5 sections, each devoted to a major category of antiques: "Furniture" (50 pages), "Pottery and Porcelain" (57 pages), "Glass" (56 pages), "Silver" (29 pages), and "Copper, Bronze, Pewter and other Metals" (29 pages). The sections are subdivided into topics appropriate to the subject of the section. The section on "Furniture," for example, includes the subdivisions "Woods," "Ornament and Style" and "Articles of Furniture." Entries are arranged alphabetically within the subdivisions. Thus, the entries under "Woods" begin with *Alder* and *Amboyna* and conclude with *Yew* and *Zebra,* while those under "Ornament and Style" begin with *Acanthus* and conclude with *Vitruvian Scroll.* While most of the entries are brief (averaging two or three sentences in length), longer entries provide adequate coverage of major topics in each section.

The volume concludes with a 16-page Index to text and illustrations which facilitates reference use. A random check disclosed that the Index is accurate. *See* references in the text and the Index direct the user from entry terms not used to those under which information on the topic is covered. There are no bibliographic references or lists of books for further reading.

Black-and-white illustrations, ranging in size from a column in width and an inch in height to a full page, appear on almost every other page of the encyclopedia. Eight full-page color photographs showing interiors representative of various periods and styles are distributed throughout the first half of the volume. The illustrations are of good quality.

The volume is bound in brownish gold paper board and will not be able to withstand extensive use. Large, clear type and spacious layout contribute to easy readability. Inner margins are wide enough to permit rebinding.

Although the title of the book seems to promise more than the work delivers, the *Concise Encyclopedia of Antiques* contains much useful information effectively organized and attractively presented. Recommended for libraries and individuals requiring a compact volume on English antiques. *(June 1, 1977, p.1520)*

745.1'03 Antiques—England—Dictionaries || Antiques—U.S.—Dictionaries [CIP]   75-22082

Cowboys.

†636.01 Cowboys—Juvenile literature [OCLC]   75-19975

See page 50

Deserts.

†574.526'5 Deserts—Juvenile literature [OCLC]   75-19970

See page 50

Dictionary of American history.
[Managing ed., Louise Bilebof Ketz.] 2d. rev. ed. 7v. plus index [not published as of May 1977]. New York, Scribner, [c1976, 1961, 1940]. 29cm. pyroxylin coated Tyvek $340; to schools and libraries $280.

The first edition of the *Dictionary of American History* was published in 1940 in five volumes. At that time, *Subscription Books Bulletin* recommended it for "high school, public and college libraries." The dictionary soon became a standard ready-reference tool for all aspects of American history because its expertly written articles provided easy access to reliable, basic information on a very wide range of topics. The first edition enjoyed the reputation of being an essential reference work. In 1961 a supplement to update and expand the dictionary's coverage was published. In 1970 "it was decided ... to publish a complete revision, in the light of historiographical changes over the past thirty years, rather than publish a second supplementary volume." It was also decided that the new edition should be issued as part of the commemoration of the American Bicentennial; it was therefore published on July 4, 1976.

The Committee has deliberately delayed the present review, waiting for the set's Index, which, though scheduled for December 1976 publication, had not appeared as of June 1977. Without the Index, rapid and complete access to the set's mass of resources is denied.

According to the managing editor, the six-member editorial board examined each entry in the 1940 edition and in the 1961 supplement to determine whether it was to be reedited, updated, rewritten, or deleted. The board also decided to expand coverage by adding articles on American history which deserved inclusion but which had been ignored, had occurred since 1940, or had been overlooked in the 1961 supplement. The board also decided to expand general coverage of the arts and sciences. Black Americans and American Indians were justly identified as subjects needing more and totally revised representation. The result of these decisions is this seven-volume set containing more than 6,000 articles written by approximately 1,400 different authors. The articles are generally very concise, averaging about 175 to 200 words, but some are short (e.g., 25 words on "Buffalo Chips") and some long (e.g., 18 pages on "Labor"). As the title suggests, articles are arranged in alphabetical order. In the first edition, the arrangement was word-by-word; in the current edition, a letter-by-letter scheme is used. The title of each article appears in boldface capitals. Each article is signed by the author(s), and most contain short bibliographies. Almost all of the articles are the work of single authors, but a few are signed by two. Entries in the bibliographies are arranged alphabetically by author's name and contain only author and title information without any type of publication data or page citation. If a journal article is cited, the volume number of the journal is included but not the page number of the article. In fact, page citations which appeared in the first edition have been deleted from the revised edition.

As in the first edition, the articles cover events, concepts, or things; since the dictionary is meant to be used in conjunction with the publisher's *Dictionary of American Biography*, there are no biographical articles. There are no graphics except for a map showing the location of American Indian tribes. As in the first edition, there are texts of the Declaration of Independence and the Constitution. In the 1940 edition, however, the text of the Constitution was made much more useful by the inclusion of numerous marginal cross-references to articles which explained the various articles of the document or provided historical insight. Unfortunately, these have been dropped from the revised edition.

There have been major changes in the new edition. The editorial board has achieved its goal of expanding the coverage of arts and sciences. Where the first edition and supplement were silent on *Physics; Physics, High Energy; Physics, Nuclear; Genetics; Genetics, Applied; Semiconductors; Masers and Lasers; Computers;* and *DNA*—there are now informative articles by experts. There are also new or much expanded articles on *Music, Folk Art, Theater, Dance,* and *Painting.* This is by no means a complete listing, but it gives some idea of the augmented coverage.

In addition, the editors attempted to correct the "obviously inadequate and often biased" first edition coverage of the American Indian. All of the earlier first edition articles have either been completely rewritten or extensively revised. The editors state that they have added 25 additional articles on this subject. The bibliographies have also been completely reworked and updated. Whereas F. W. Hodge's *Handbook of American Indians* (1907–10) was the only source cited in the majority of articles in the 1940 edition, now additional and more up-to-date titles appear. Robert F. Spencer of the University of Minnesota and Kenneth M. Stewart of the University of Arizona assumed the responsibility for revising this coverage, and they have contributed more than 130 articles on all aspects of the history of the American Indian.

Another area in which the editors rightly sought revision and expansion was that of Afro-American history. This task was undertaken by Henry N. Drewry of Princeton University, who "commissioned some forty new articles and supervised the complete revision of approximately sixty additional entries from the original *Dictionary* and supplement." Drewry also wrote the entirely revised article *Afro-Americans* as well as 22 other articles on various aspects of black history. The articles on *Slavery; Suffrage, Afro-American;* and *Education, Afro-American;* for example, have been rewritten and contain revised, updated bibliographies. There are new articles on *Civil Rights Movement; Literature, Afro-American; Black Infantry in the West;* and *Black Panthers,* to name only a few. An indication of the change in tone in the coverage of this area of American history is that the brief article *Race Problem* in the first edition has been replaced with a rather long one entitled *Race Relations.*

Other articles which the editors thought in need of extensive revision were those dealing with American religious history, various churches, and denominations. Glenn T. Miller, St. Mary's University (Maryland), apparently has been responsible for this area and has contributed 33 articles on American religious history. This is not to say that all the articles on the American religious experience have been rewritten or even revised; 24 articles from the first edition by William W. Sweet have been largely unchanged.

In addition, there are new articles on *Anthropology* and *Ethnology, Political Science, Demography,* and *Psychology;* but the other social and behavioral sciences still are not represented.

Needless to say, the editors have introduced recent happenings. There are entries on *Watergate, Nixon, Resignation of, Students for a Democratic Society, Moon Landing,* and *Vietnam War,* to list only a few. In addition, 1970 census figures are cited in the articles on individual states and major cities. Information in the dictionary is reasonably current, with the latest date observed being April 30, 1975, in the Vietnam War article. Late 1974 seems to be the most common cutoff date.

Few articles from the 1940 edition have been deleted. However, there have been some rearrangements and changes of entry, e.g., the article *Indian Dances* in the first edition reappears under the heading *Dances, American Indian* in this edition. There are now articles on broad subjects which contain information formerly found in shorter, more specific articles. These specific headings no longer appear as titles for articles but do appear as *see* references to one or more of the newer large articles. Due to this rearrangement, some of the old headings have been dropped altogether. Another form of change of entry has been to group all formerly separate articles on one subject, e.g., the Civil War, which appeared as separate articles in the first edition, under one heading, e.g., *Civil War*. These smaller articles have been changed very little and are still the work of individual authors. The bibliographies, however, have been interfiled, with one bibliography appearing at the end of the large covering article.

The managing editor's claim that significant portions of the dictionary have been either expanded and/or revised is clearly justified; other assertions, however, need to be examined. The Foreword states that the total number of entries is 7,200, but the Committee estimates the number to be 6,045. The publisher also claims that 1,200 (19 percent) of the total number of articles "have been completely rewritten," that 4,500 (73 percent) "have been reedited, rechecked, and updated," and that 500 (8 percent) are new to this revision. These figures are consistent with Committee findings. By the term "rewritten," the editors mean that while the entry appears in either the first edition or the supplement, the article was replaced by another, written by a new author. The terms "reedited, rechecked, and updated," however, are not so easy to define, given the reality of what was accomplished in the revision process. It was assumed that the editorial staff examined each entry, double-checked the facts, and changed statements when necessary; this was done in some cases. But the editorial staff went further and found it necessary, for some reason, to readjust almost every article that was not rewritten. Most of these editorial changes are cosmetic. In some articles punctuation has been slightly modified, commas substituted for hyphens, for example. Most of these minor alterations reflect the stylistic taste of the editors because some of the authors have been dead for many years. In addition, there are examples of genuine clarification and improvement through "reediting." One beneficial editorial change is the inclusion of the full names of people mentioned in the articles. In the first edition only surnames appear. This can often lead to confusion when trying to find additional information.

Another major editorial modification, begun in the supplement volume and continued in the revision, has made the dictionary a far less useful reference tool. This is the elimination of "q.v."'s to direct the reader to related discussions found elsewhere in the dictionary. In the revision there is no way of knowing if an aspect of a topic has been covered by its own article. The publishers claim that "1,000 cross-references have been added" to the revision, but these appear to be *see* references, printed in boldface identical to article headings, and not true *see also* references. An example is the heading *American Literature*, which directs the user to *Literature*. There are few true cross-references so that the user is severely handicapped. For example, *Afro-American Culture* and *Afro-Americans* briefly treat topics which are more fully explored in *Colleges, Afro-American; Education, Afro-American; Literature, Afro-American;* and *Music, Afro-American;* and yet there are no cross-references to these articles. Such references are needed all the more because all articles about blacks are not listed under a uniform heading, such as "Afro-American...." There are numerous other instances of this failure. (The current absence of an index only exacerbates the problem.)

The Committee's review of the first edition concluded that the "bibliographies are not a strong feature of the set. Many are excellent but there is an unevenness in the number of references and in their value." The same can be said of the current edition. It can be assumed that the new entries have up-to-date bibliographies. Also, those bibliographies for rewritten articles can be assumed to have been checked carefully by their new authors. It is the vast majority of bibliographies (73 percent), however, which remain disappointing. In a random sample of articles, fully 45 percent of the sample bibliographies have not been revised. Another 9 percent have had one or more titles deleted, with the remaining ones carried over from the first edition. A further 5 percent of the earlier bibliographies have been deleted altogether. Only 8 percent of those bibliographies not revised by new authors have undergone any type of change. This means that about 54 percent of the bibliographies are at least 40 years old. Admittedly there have been no new editions of some of those titles, and others may be the only ones available for a particular topic. However, it seems unlikely that Dudley G. Wooten's *Comprehensive History of Texas,* published in 1898, is still the best source for "Terry's Texas Rangers" or that Henry Adams' *History of the United States,* first published in 1909–11 and last revised in 1931, is the best work on *Standing Order*. And George Otto Trevelyan's *George III and Charles Fox* (1912–14) surely must have been superseded as the best possible source of further information on *Peace Resolutions of the British Parliament*. Assessment of the continuing appropriateness of such titles must be made by persons steeped in the disciplines, but doubts remain. There has been some attempt to delete titles which the previous reviewer found to be either "sectional, out of print or fairly rare," but little or nothing has been added to take their place. And how many more of those 40-year-old titles are now themselves out of print?

The dictionary's format is successful. Its text is printed in double columns on opaque paper, and it has generally adequate margins. The type is larger in this edition than in the first, and the lines have been better spaced, making the revision much easier to use and to read. Each volume averages about 475 pages. The set is well bound in blue plastic.

Because of its updated and expanded coverage of all aspects of American history and because of its value as a ready-reference tool, this 1976 revision of *Dictionary of American History* is recommended for school, public, and academic libraries.

(July 15, 1977, p.1745)

†973.03   U.S.—History—Dictionaries   76-6735

A dictionary of Japanese artists:

painting, sculpture, ceramics, prints, lacquer. By Laurance D. Roberts. Tokyo, New York, Weatherhill; distributed by Lippincott, 1976. 299p. 27cm. cloth $22.50.

Any librarian who has to deal with the identities of past and present Japanese artists will find this new publication a helpful breakthrough. The author, a specialist in Oriental art, graduated from Princeton in 1929. He worked first at the Philadelphia Museum of Art and later at the Brooklyn Museum, of which he was director until 1946. From 1946 to 1960, he was director of the American Academy in Rome. Subsequently he helped organize and later headed the New York State Council for the Arts. Princeton University awarded him an honorary degree in 1960.

Japanese artists are difficult to identify because of their penchant for choosing to be known by many names other than their own. This is true particularly for early artists, as Japanese commoners were not allowed to adopt family names until after 1890. Accordingly, artists often chose names of adopted families or of great teachers and schools (if they were outstanding students). They could also choose pseudonyms (called *azana* or "art names"). Sometimes they used elaborate puns on their own names (called *go*) and they often used different names for different types of work or as their mood dictated. All this provided endless possibilities, and Shigemasa, for instance, has signed himself 19 different ways—so far as we know—he *may* have used names as yet undiscovered. The confirmation of these numerous identities has severely taxed many an art historian's scholarship and tenacity; so Dr. Roberts must be commended for his resolute effort to bring order out of chaos.

Each entry is under what is presumably the best-known name (*azana*): Harunobu, for instance. This is followed by the family name (N: Suzuki, in Harunobu's case); by the familiar or nickname (FN Jikei); and the various *go* (Choeiken or Shikojin for Harunobu). The Japanese characters for all names are cited at the conclusion of each listing. At the end of the volume, there is a 30-page Index of Alternate Names, which refers to main entries, and also an Index of Japanese characters based on the order of radicals used in A. N. Nelson's *Modern Readers' Japanese English Character Dictionary* (Tuttle, 1966).

The biographical content of the entries is usually brief. Media in which artists worked, birth and death dates, family background if known, teachers, schools and stylistic characteristics, and, in most instances, one- or two-line critical summaries are included. There are also a list of museum collections owning the artists' works and brief bibliographies, both cited in abbreviated form. An explanatory code is provided in Appendix I for the collections and in the Bibliography list at the back of the volume. The appendixes also include a list of art organizations and institutions with which artists were often connected, a list of art periods for Japan, Korea, and China, and a list of pre-Meiji Japanese provinces with their present names and prefectures. There is also a glossary of Japanese terms employed in the entries. Especially important is the Index of Alternate Names, as there are no cross-references in the text.

The *Dictionary* goes as far back as the eighth century for such semi-legendary artists as Enkin, who is known only by inscriptions on some masks in the Shoso-In collection. The most recent entrants are "artists who were born before 1900, or, if born later, who died before 1972." As the title suggests, important crafts as well as painting and sculpture are included. Because some of the artists are "shadow figures" who are sometimes no more than names in the literary records of temples or signatures on a few works of art, and because information may be drawn from sources which do not use Japanese characters (thus making distinctions between artists with similar names difficult), the author warns that "inaccuracies may have crept into these references." He also says that "there is no pretense on the part of the author that either the list of artists or any single entry is complete."

Bearing in mind that Western knowledge of Japanese artists is less complete than that of occidental artists and that new personalities are continuously emerging or sometimes merging with those already known, the effort at clarification or at least tabulation represented by Dr. Roberts' *Dictionary* is valuable, even allowing for possible faults and inaccuracies. There are very few entries for Japanese artists in Thieme and Becker's *Allgemeines Lexikon der bildenden Kunstler,* Vollmer's *Allgemeines Lexikon der bildenden Kunstler des XX Jahrhunderts,* and the Bénézit *Dictionnaire des Peintures, Sculpteurs, Dessinateurs et Graveurs.* A check of the *A*s and *B*s showed eleven duplicate entries in *Thieme-Becker,* eight in *Vollmer,* and fourteen in *Bénézit,* but the last dictionary only identifies the artist and dates his activities. *Thieme-Becker* includes all of the various names, the characters for each name, and a few cross-references from subsidiary names to main entries. *Vollmer* gives alternate names but does not include the Japanese characters. *Bénézit* rarely includes alternate names or characters.

The *Dictionary of Japanese Artists* is of a comfortable size to handle, flexibly bound in blue buckram, though with margins rather narrow for rebinding. There are two columns per page, printed in small but clear type, with entries in bold type and key words at the top of each column. There are no illustrations.

A Dictionary of Japanese Artists would be useful in any library having among its patrons students, collectors, or amateurs interested in East Asian art. Recommended. *(Apr. 1, 1977, p.1194)*

†709.52   Art, Japanese—Dictionaries || Artists, Japanese—Dictionaries   76-885

Directory of research grants 1976–77.
Compiler, William K. Wilson; Editor, Betty L. Wilson. 2d. ed. Phoenix, AZ 85018, 3930 E. Camelback Rd., Oryx Pr., [c1976]. xvii, 235p. 29cm. buckram $34.75.

Directory of Research Grants 1976–77 is the second edition of a reference title which provides information on sources of research-grant support. William and Betty Wilson again have produced a valuable resource tool for researchers and research administrators, faculty, and students who are seeking funding of research proposals.

William Wilson, coordinator of sponsored research at the State University of New York, Fredonia, has utilized for the work the Grant Information System data base, which covers federal and state programs, foundation programs, and programs sponsored by other commercial and noncommercial organizations. Although some programs sponsored in countries other than the U.S. are included, this listing is not worldwide in scope.

The directory includes preliminary material: Contents; Preface—describing purpose, scope, and entries; "The Many Faces of a Grantsperson," a two-page essay on the various roles persons seeking grants must play; "Grant Proposal Preparation," excellent guidance for the proposal writer; "Bibliography"; "Subject Heading Equivalency List," a display of two-letter codes for the subject areas in which the grants are categorized; "Grant Programs," the main listing of 1,545 programs. There are three appendixes: Grant Names—October 1976; Sponsoring Organizations—October 1976; Sponsoring Organizations, By Type—October 1976.

The Preface of the 1976–77 edition has been altered slightly from that in the first edition to reflect the change in arrangement of the new edition; "The Many Faces of a Grantsperson" is new to this volume; "Grant Proposal Preparation" is identical in both editions.

Both the Bibliography and the "Subject Heading Equivalency List" reflect updating of material. The second edition has ten additional titles, for a total of 23 citations listed in its selected bibliography of the best books available on the subject; one title has a 1976 publication date; fourteen are undated. Two new subject areas—*Energy* and *Geriatrics*—bring the total number of subject areas covered to 34.

The entry for each grant program usually gives the following information: the name of the grant; an annotation describing the subject area and emphasis of the program; amount of grant; date application is due; and name and address of sponsor to contact. Entries are numbered consecutively, and appendixes of grant names and sponsoring organizations refer to the appropriate entry number.

The arrangement of the main listing, "Grant Programs," represents a major departure from the 1975–76 edition and a gain in convenience for the user. Whereas the first edition was arranged alphabetically by a two-letter subject code (*AC* Archaeology, *AE* Adult Education, *AG* Agriculture), the second edition is arranged alphabetically by the subject itself (*Accident Prevention, Adult Education, Agriculture, Archaeology*). Within subject areas, the 1975 volume was subarranged by a classification code number comprising subject code letter, date deadline for application, further requirements, and sequence number. For example, the number DE .04.02.R.004 indicated the grant was in the field of dentistry, the application was due by April 2, receipt of the application satisfied the deadline requirement, and that this was the fourth grant program listed in the subject area within the stipulated application deadline. The 1976–77 directory has dropped this classification scheme and subarranges entries within subject areas alphabetically by grant name.

A second major format modification is in the presentation of data on programs suitable for inclusion in more than one subject area. In the first edition, entries were repeated. In the second, the entry is under one subject area with cross-referencing from the others. This creates, in effect, a sizable reduction in number of entries in the 1976–1977 volume. Whereas the first edition included about 2,900 entries, only about 1,330 different grant-support programs were represented. Actual separate entries in the 1976–77 directory number 1,545, an increase of approximately 200 programs.

Comparison of the two editions reveals that the annual updating of the directory is justified due to fast-moving changes in the funding field. For example, of the entries under *Drug Abuse,* seven are the same in both editions; eight new entries appear in the 1976–77 edition; ten entries have been deleted, twelve cross-references have been added, and three 1975 entries have been converted to cross-references. The editor also indicates that quarterly revisions of the names and codes of all the grant programs currently in the Grant Information System will be distributed to subscribers to that system.

The directory is sturdily and attractively bound and lies flat when opened. The inner margins are too narrow to permit rebinding, but this is not a detrimental factor because the useful lifespan of the work is short. The white opaque paper, clear print, and generous spacing of entries make the pages easy to read. Grant-program names and cross-references are in darker type; subject areas are in both dark type and boldface. Running heads, giving subject areas and inclusive entry numbers, are provided at the top of each page.

The need for accurate, up-to-date information on availability of, and application for, grants is well met by the *Directory of Research Grants.* The simplified arrangement of the 1976–77 edition and the appendixes provides efficient subject, title, and organizational access to a wealth of material. Institutions serving researchers and scholars, including those which have the 1975 edition, will want to have the 1976–77 *Directory.* Recommended. *(June 15, 1977, p.1592)*

001.44   Scholarships—U.S.—Directories || Research grants—U.S.—Directories   [OCLC]
76-47074

The documentary history of the first federal elections, 1788–1790. v.l.

Edited by Merrill Jensen and Robert A. Becker. [Madison, Wis.], Univ. of Wisconsin, [1976]. xxxi, 896p. maps. 24cm. cloth $30.

In 1952, the National Historical Publications Commission, in association with the National Archives, began collecting copies of all contemporary documents relating to the ratification of the Constitution, the first federal elections, the first federal Congress, and the ratification of the Bill of Rights. The primary purpose was to assemble material for *The Documentary History of the Ratification of the Constitution,* the first two volumes of which were published in 1976. However, in 1966 two additional editorial projects were established: the Documentary History of the First Federal Elections at the University of Wisconsin and the Documentary History of the First Federal Congress at George Washington University. The volume under review is the first of a three-volume set resulting from the work at the University of Wisconsin; the second and third volumes are "now in preparation."

Merrill Jensen, editor of both titles, is Vilas research professor of history at the University of Wisconsin–Madison and is well known for such works on the Revolutionary period as *The Articles of Confederation: An Interpretation of the Social-Constitutional History of the American Revolution, 1774–1781* (Madison, Wisconsin, University of Wisconsin Press, 1940) and *The New Nation: A History of the United States during the Confederation, 1781–1789* (New York, Knopf, 1950). He is a strong proponent of the view that adoption of the Constitution represented a victory for conservatives, who desired a strong central government. Among the works which Jensen has edited is a volume of the English Historical Documents series, *American Colonial Documents to 1776* (London, Eyre and Spottiswoode, 1955). Robert A. Becker holds a doctorate in history from the University of Wisconsin and is assistant professor of history at Louisiana State University.

The three volumes of *The Documentary History of the First Federal Elections, 1788–1790* are intended to provide a selection of excerpts from official documents, letters and diaries, contemporary newspapers, and other sources dealing with the election of the members of the first federal Congress and the first presidential electors in each of the 13 states arranged "in a chronological order determined by the dates of elections to the United States House of Representatives." This order of arrangement was chosen because "the great legislative innovation of the Constitution was the creation of a House of Representatives to be elected by the voters of the states." The third volume is to include a chapter on the election of the president and vice-president.

Volume I opens with a General Introduction which points out the significance of the elections in 1788, 1789, and 1790 and explains the content and arrangement of the work. Acknowledgments describe in some detail the origin of the three related editorial programs, the methods used in their implementation, and the sources of their funding. "Editorial Policies and Procedures" outlines the decisions made on such matters as literal reproduction of official documents, excerpts and elisions, use of brackets, identification of individuals, and so on. Other aids provided for the user are "Short Title List of Sources Cited" containing 33 items; "List of Symbols for Manuscript Depositories"; a brief essay and full-page table on "Population and Representation, 1787, 1792"; "Chronology of the Elections with Names of Men Elected"; "Presidential Electors and Their Votes"; and "Calendar for the Years, 1788–1790."

A very brief chapter made up of an introduction and two documents deals with "The Constitution, the Confederation Congress, and Federal Elections." The second chapter, "The Confederation Congress and the First Federal Election Ordinance of 13 September 1788," includes an introduction, a note on bibliographical sources, a note on procedure followed in the Confederation Congress, a list of members attending the Congress in 1788 with exact dates of attendance, a Confederation Congress chronology from June 21, 1788, when New Hampshire ratified the Constitution, to September 13, 1788, when the Election Ordinance was adopted, and more than 100 pages of documents arranged in chronological order. Each document has a boldface heading supplied by the editors and appropriate notes about sources, identification of persons, such as writers and recipients of letters, and related materials.

The remaining four chapters in this first volume deal with the elections in South Carolina, Pennsylvania, Massachusetts, and New Hampshire in that order. Each follows the same pattern: a full-page map of the state showing either election districts or counties as they were in 1788–89, an introduction from two-and-a-half to five-and-a-half pages long, a note on sources, a chronology of election-related events in the state, documents giving a detailed picture of official actions, the election campaigns, the election results with accompanying comment, and, finally, biographical sketches of all candidates for United States representative, United States senator, and presidential elector in the state.

The maps of the states come as a pleasant surprise to the reader because there is no list of them at the front of the volume; nor are there references to them in the Index. Sources are cited for the maps of South Carolina and Pennsylvania but not for those of Massachusetts and New Hampshire.

Each "Note on Sources" is a brief bibliographical essay discussing such matters as the form and location of the legislative records of the state; important letters and diaries; newspapers published in the state during the election period and their relative value for research; and notable printed sources, both contemporary and recent.

The biographical sketches of each candidate give years of birth and death when known, place of birth, and information about education, career, and political activities and note briefly the course of the subject's life after the election. Information about a good many politically active men not included in either the *Dictionary of American Biography* or the *Biographical Directory of the American Congress* can be found here. The editors also claim greater precision and accuracy for their biographical sketches. The 33-page Index has been carefully planned to make the mass of material contained in the volume available to users. There are index entries for names of persons, names of places, subjects, and types or forms of material. For each person indexed, a full name and the state of residence are shown followed by a reference, marked *id.,* to the location of a biographical sketch or a note, if one exists; appropriate subheadings follow and then come listings of letter(s) from and to the subject and diaries. Those who wrote letters and other documents or received letters concerning the elections, serious candidates for office during the elections, and those who played important roles in legislatures are indexed; but many other names mentioned in roll-call votes or elsewhere are not. There are entries for each of the 13 states and Kentucky with very detailed entries for the 4 states on which this volume concentrates. It should be noted that many town and county names appear under these state names as subheadings, but there are *see* references only from *Lancaster* and *Philadelphia*. There are also entries for the names of all places considered for the location of the federal capital.

The Index contains entries for some topics "as issues" (e.g., *religion, as an issue*) and some for definitions of terms (e.g., *federal year*). Under the heading, *candidates, biographical sketches of,* the names are arranged first by state and then by office. Headings such as *chronologies, newspaper comments on,* and *roll calls* provide useful lists to facilitate searching. There are, however, no entries for the titles of newspapers, books, or pamphlets quoted.

In addition to the *see* and *see also* references in the Index, there are cross-references in some of the editorial notes.

The Index is printed two columns to the page without running heads, but the main entries are in small capitals and subheadings are indented even when arranged in paragraph form. The introductory paragraphs at the beginning of the Index assist the user in understanding its arrangement. There is no statement about the possibility of a cumulated index for the three volumes of the set.

The first volume of *The Documentary History of the First Federal Elections, 1788–1790,* is printed on nonglare opaque paper and is bound in blue cloth stamped in gold. The print is small but clear, and the page layout is attractive. There are running heads indicating chapter, month, and year, a special convenience in the long sections of documents. The margins are somewhat narrow, especially the inner ones, so that rebinding will be difficult. The review copy tended not to lie flat when opened.

No other work attempts to provide so much source material on this important aspect of the early history of the United States. Other collections of documents are more generalized or have selected another facet of the general topic for emphasis; for example, *The History of American Presidential Elections, 1789–1968* by Arthur M. Schlesinger, Jr. (New York, Chelsea House Publishers in association with McGraw-Hill, 1971–   ) devotes only about 30 pages of its 4 volumes to documents relating to the presidential election in 1789. Jensen and Becker have brought together documentary material from sources such as the state legislative journals which are not easily available and are difficult to search; they have also provided helpful explanatory sections, notes, and finding devices.

In keeping with the policy of the Reference and Subscription Books Committee, recommendation will be deferred until publication of the 3-volume set has been completed. However, large public and academic libraries as well as historical libraries will wish to give this title their careful consideration.

(June 1, 1977, p.1521)

329'.023   Elections—U.S.—History—Sources || U.S.—Politics and government—1789-1797—Sources   [CIP]   74-5903

The dog family.
†636.7   Dogs—Juvenile literture   [OCLC]   75-19999
See page 50

Electricity.
†537   Electricity—Juvenile literature   [OCLC]   75-19995
See page 50

Encyclopedia of American agricultural history.
By Edward L. Schapsmeier and Frederick H. Schapsmeier. Westport, Conn., Greenwood Pr., 1975. 467p. 24cm. cloth $25.

The *Encyclopedia of American Agricultural History* is an alphabetical compilation of short articles concerned with the history of agriculture in the U.S. Topical coverage ranges from agricultural agencies to pests to legislation and spans a time period from colonial America to the early 1970s.

The present volume is the first edition of the encyclopedia. The writers are history professors who have coauthored other books on American agricultural history, including one survey, *Abundant Harvests: The Story of American Agriculture*.

The *Encyclopedia of American Agricultural History* was intended to be as "comprehensive as possible." Among the estimated 2,500 entries, one finds many concerning federal legislation, such as the Forest Pest Control Act of 1947 and the Sugar Act of 1764. Institutions and organizations such as the National Cowboy Hall of Fame and Friends of the Earth are included. The volume identifies agricultural publications, e.g., *The Quarter Horse Journal* and *Agri Finance*. One of the strengths of the *Encyclopedia of American Agricultural History* for reference use is the number and variety of biographical entries. Government officials and other political figures, agricultural educators, historians and researchers, artists, writers, inventors—and a host of other individuals, both historical and current figures, who are identified with American agriculture—are represented. Included among the bits of curious biographical information are articles about "the father of the state fair" (Elkanah Watson), the principal developer of *Prairie Farmer* (John S. Wright), and "the red fox of Kinderhook" (Martin Van Buren). Terms such as *Dust Bowl, making hay, pellagra, rural reapportionment, turnpikes,* and *lightning rod* are also defined. Articles concerning nineteenth and twentieth century events predominate; material from earlier times represents less than 10 percent of the entries. The variety and range of subject material bear out the stated purpose of the book which is to "provide a reference tool for the novice as well as the scholar, the browser seeking nostalgia and the student checking a precise fact."

Although representation of biographical figures is gratifyingly expansive, some readers may be disappointed by the omission of W. Atlee Burpee, Squanto, and the recently ascendant Jimmy Carter. The choice of strictly agricultural topics is not carefully calibrated. Included are *individualism, operant conditioning, outhouse,* and *meteorology*—such general terms that their presence seems superfluous. On the other hand, one finds nothing on anthrax, the Japanese beetle, or Venezuelan equine encephalitis, Jersey Giants (the breed of chicken) or Jersey cows, American class chickens, contour plowing, sorghum, or peanuts.

The encyclopedia entries generally vary in length from three to ten lines to one column. Entries seldom use more than one page of text, and no illustrations are provided. Within entries, however, the information offered is significantly extended by liberal cross-references. Thus, a reader has available as much detail as he or she needs by pursuing the cross-references selectively or comprehensively. The language itself is clear and the tone impartial and serious, though not always scholarly; interpretation is sometimes offered, but not bias.

The arrangement of the *Encyclopedia of American Agricultural History* is alphabetical, word by word. Fifty-five special topical indexes draw together all pertinent references to such subjects as *abolitionists, crops and commodities, equipment and implements, ideologies and beliefs, pioneer and rural life, rural revolts,* and *tariffs and trade.* The number of terms listed under each topical index ranges from fewer than 10 to more than 200; many indexes have around 50 terms brought together under a topical heading.

Most encyclopedia entries have several *q.v.* references within the body of the entry, and additional cross-references are available as separate entries. Many entries have at least one bibliographic citation for further reading. Unfortunately, no index or listing appears in the volume to draw together these references. The physical format is satisfactory.

There is no really comparable work. Some of the same information exists in general reference books on American history, such as the *Oxford Companion to American History.* However, coverage in the *Encyclopedia of American Agricultural History* is more detailed, more specific, and more inclusive. Many of the biographees are treated in several major biographical tools, but the *Encyclopedia of American Agricultural History* concentrates them within a single source.

The Schapsmeier book is an exceedingly useful subject reference tool because of its inclusive coverage of American agricultural history and because it provides easy access to the material. Further, this representation of agriculture is notably better than that offered by any general reference in U.S. history. The *Encyclopedia of American Agricultural History* is recommended for use in public, secondary school, and academic libraries.

(Jan. 15, 1977, p.742)

630'.973   Agriculture—U.S.—History—Dictionaries || Agriculture—Dictionaries   [CIP]
74-34563

Encyclopedia of American history.
Edited by Richard B. Morris; associate editor, Jeffrey B. Morris. bicentennial ed. New York, Harper & Row, Publishers, [c1976]. xiv, 1245p. maps. 25cm. cloth $25.

The 1976 or Bicentennial edition of this useful one-volume handbook on the American past has been thoroughly revised. The *Encyclopedia of American History* first appeared in 1953 and was favorably reviewed in *Subscription Books Bulletin* October 1953. The first revision, published in 1961, was also recommended by the Reference and Subscription Books Review Committee June 15, 1962. The third and fourth editions, appearing in 1965 and 1970 respectively, were not reviewed by the Committee.

Richard B. Morris, professor emeritus of history, Columbia University, and the author of numerous historical works, has been the editor of the encyclopedia from its beginning. His son, Jeffrey B. Morris, special assistant to the executive vice-president for academic affairs, Columbia, is now listed as associate editor, and the distinguished historian, Henry Steele Commager, continues to serve as chief consulting editor. One or more consulting editors are identified for each of ten subject areas in the present edition. Of these 17 individuals, 9 are professors and one is a university librarian; the others are associated with such institutions as the Henry E. Huntington Library, the Solomon R. Guggenheim Museum, and the Smithsonian Institution. All appear to be suitably qualified in their fields, and some are very well known. Consulting editors for the fields of medicine and public health and of music have been added in this edition. The Foreword to the Bicentennial edition cites three other persons for specific kinds of assistance.

The arrangement of the encyclopedia is the same as in previous editions. "Basic Chronology," the first and largest section, contains primarily political and military facts arranged in chronological order from prehistoric times to January 1, 1974, and in some cases to April 1975. The second section, "Topical Chronology," provides information on seven broad subject areas divided into subsections and then arranged chronologically from whatever period seems appropriate to the subject up to 1973 or 1974. Between these two chronological sections are found a list of the presidents and their cabinets, a table showing party strength in Congress from 1789-91 to 1975-77, a list of the justices of the Supreme Court, and the texts of the Declaration of Independence and the Constitution. In former editions, cabinet members were arranged by the office held; in this edition, they appear under each president with the years of their appointments identified.

The third major section of the encyclopedia, "Five Hundred Notable Americans," contains biographical sketches arranged in alphabetical order. According to the Foreword, those included were chosen by "an extensive poll among historians and specialists in a variety of fields." Finally, there is a 53-page Index.

The volume has increased in size from 850 pages in 1970 to 1,245 pages in the current edition, and every subdivision in each section has been enlarged. In some cases information left unchanged in the previous revisions has now been brought up to 1973 or 1974. The special supplementary section, which contained new material in the 1970 edition, has been eliminated. Headnotes intended "to organize and assimilate the discrete facts that follow and to furnish some sense of pattern and significance" have been added for each subsection. In the "Topical Chronology" *Mass Media* is a new section; *Dance* and *Music* are added subsections under *Thought and Culture* as is *Medicine and Public Health* under *Science, Invention, and Technology.* The number of biographical sketches has been increased from 400 to 500.

Entries before 1763 in the "Basic Chronology" vary, sometimes covering a period of years and in other cases only a single year, month, or day. For example, one finds: "1642–52. Berkeley's First Administration," "1539. De Soto in Florida;" and "1763, 10 Feb. Treaty of Paris." After 1763, each year is listed separately with articles both on events occurring on specific dates and articles on larger subjects arranged under it. There are discussions of each presidential campaign; descriptions of important legislative acts, treaties, and reports; and brief articles on topics such as *Decline of Dollar Diplomacy* (p.386), *Indochina* (p.462–63), *Deterioration of U.S. Relations with Cuba* (p.489–90), and *Presidential Impoundments* (p.539). The tone is generally objective.

The "Topical Chronology" now contains the following sections: *The Expansion of the Nation; Population, Immigration, and Ethnic Stocks; Leading Supreme Court Decisions; The American Economy; Science, Invention, and Technology; Thought and Culture* (the largest single section); and *Mass Media.* The Supreme Court decisions are in chronological order with both the popular name and legal citation given, although occasionally a number of related cases are grouped together (i.e., "1937. New Deal Cases"). The other six sections are divided into two to eight subsections with material arranged chronologically under each. Again, in order to give a coherent account of changes and trends, a broad heading with related dates is used in many cases and specific events are subsumed under it. For example, under the heading "1780–94. Scientific Societies," four societies and one museum are named, dates of founding are given, and some brief additional information is supplied.

The biographical sketches average 46 lines or about a column. They give day, month, and year of birth and death where known, the city and country of birth and death, a characterization of the person's field(s) of prominence, selected information about education and positions held, and a description of his or her most important accomplishments. Where appropriate, titles of selected works (books, musical compositions, paintings, ballets) are given. Of the 500 biographees, 47 are living persons, and 26 of these are new in this edition. Twenty-five women are listed; the six added to this edition are all established names:

Mary Cassatt, Martha Graham, Anna Mary Robertson Moses, Louise Nevelson, Frances Perkins, and Margaret H. Sanger. There are eleven blacks, six premiering in this edition. They are Benjamin Banneker, Edward Kennedy Ellington, Ralph Ellison, Marcus Garvey, Thurgood Marshall, and Asa Philip Randolph. Similarly, all have earned a permanent place in the annals of American civilization. No athletes and few performing artists have been included. The sketches are only sufficient to give the reader an understanding of the person's importance in American history; they are too superficial to stand as independent biographical summaries.

The 1976 edition of the encyclopedia contains 42 maps and charts in contrast to 37 in the 1970 edition. There are 16 full-page maps. The maps are clear and uncluttered and are usually located close to related text. Five of the maps are credited to Rand McNally, but no sources are given for the others. They enhance the text but cannot serve as a substitute for an historical atlas.

The volume contains many useful lists and tables, nearly all with their sources stated. Unless limited to a historical period, they are usually brought up to 1972 or 1973. All are printed in very clear, readable type. Included are such interesting items as a diagram showing the way in which townships and sections were laid out under the public land survey system, a map showing the Triangular Trade Routes of colonial times, and a graph showing ownership of electrical appliances in 1972 when the energy crisis gave such information new meaning.

The Foreword notes the use of *Historical Statistics of the United States: Colonial Times to 1957* (1960) and related supplementary materials in compiling the encyclopedia, but no other reference sources which might be helpful to the reader are cited nor are any reading lists included.

The encyclopedia contains a variety of finding aids. There is a detailed Table of Contents and a list of maps and charts. In the first two sections, page references within the text direct the reader to related material elsewhere in the volume. The Index, printed three columns to the page, refers to all three sections and to the maps. The detail in which the latter have been indexed seems to vary. There is no mention of a map under *railroads*, but there is under *canals*. Nicknames, quotations, slogans, and titles are indexed. The Index includes some *see* and *see also* references. In using the Index while examining the volume, it proved to be accurate, but it was often time-consuming to locate an indexed item because of the need to read an entire page to find it. Reference to columns or quarters of a page would eliminate this problem. Although the number of pages devoted to the Index has been increased, some entries are in very small type, indicating an effort to minimize expansion of this part of the volume.

Material added to the 1976 revision reflects current concerns. There are subsections dealing with the Vietnam War and Watergate. A subsection, *Black Americans Since the Civil War*, has been added in the "Topical Chronology;" a reference from *Negroes* to *Blacks* appears in the Index; and more information about black history and the contributions of blacks to American culture can be found throughout. There are eleven subdivisions under *Women* in the Index instead of five, and the following new headings appear: *Abortion Laws, Birth rate, Divorces, Equal Rights Amendment, Family Planning Services and Population Research Act, Married Women's Property Act, New York, Pill (birth control),* and *Voting rights—of women. Chavez, Cesar; Cubans in U.S.; Mexican Americans;* and *Puerto Ricans in U.S.* appear in the Index. Still excluded are Chicano and Latino.

The *Encyclopedia of American History* is intended both for reference use and for reading "as a narrative," but the flow of its prose is often interrupted by dates in parentheses, page references to additional information, abbreviations, and telegraphic language. Some subsections, such as *Newspapers* and *Periodicals,* turn into lists or catalogs. Material on a subject is inevitably scattered as a result of having three sections, each approaching American history in a different way. To get a complete and balanced account of a particular event or subject, one must often read about it in several places. Occasionally, short items are given under a date with insufficient explanation of their significance. Nevertheless, many sections are genuinely readable so that the browser is well rewarded and usually gains more than mere odd facts, "firsts," and other tidbits. The Foreword, in fact, contains a thoughtful warning about "firsts" in history.

The bicentennial edition of the encyclopedia is bound in brown cloth with gold lettering on the spine. The creamy paper is opaque and without glare. The volume lies flat when opened and seems likely to withstand considerable handling. As in earlier editions, the narrow inner margins would cause trouble if rebinding became necessary. Otherwise the layout of the pages is good. Topics and years (in the "Basic Chronology") are used as running heads. The changes made in this edition in the way indentions and various type sizes are used to facilitate location of information on a page are helpful. The typefaces used, including the smallest in some tables, are clear and readable.

Three works with which the encyclopedia may be compared are the *Concise Dictionary of American History,* the *Oxford Companion to American History,* and *Encyclopedia of American Facts and Dates.* All are one-volume works attempting to cover the full range of American history. The first two are arranged alphabetically rather than chronologically; neither has maps or other illustrations. The *Concise Dictionary* does not include biographical sketches as such, but many persons may be identified by using its detailed Index. Unfortunately, neither the *Concise Dictionary of American History* nor the *Oxford Companion to American History* has been revised or updated since their first publication in 1962 and 1966 respectively.

The *Encyclopedia of American Facts and Dates,* first appearing in 1956, is arranged chronologically in tabular style under four fields of interest. It aims to cover the "most interesting events from America's past," but it omits "obvious" dates in order to give more emphasis to cultural and popular material. It is a frankly popular work based on secondary sources but with an excellent detailed index. A sixth edition was published in 1972.

The Bicentennial edition of the *Encyclopedia of American History* is a major revision of a useful and reliable work, distinguished because of its authority, comprehensiveness, and effective arrangement. Owners of earlier editions will wish to consider its purchase. Recommended for public, school, and college libraries and for home use. *(Apr. 15, 1977, p.1290)*

†973'.03   U.S.—History—Chronology || U.S.—History—Dictionaries   [CIP]   74-15839

The encyclopedia of minerals and gemstones.
Edited by Michael O'Donoghue. New York, Putnam, [c1976]. 304p. col. illus. diagrs. 30cm. cloth $22.50.

This encyclopedia is printed in Italy and copyrighted by Orbis Publishing Ltd. of London and Istituto Geografico de Agostini of Novara. The editor, Michael O'Donoghue, and contributors are British. O'Donoghue also edits *Gemmological Newsletter* and *Synthetic Crystals Newsletter* and is a member of the Council of the Gemmological Association of Great Britain.

The first half of the volume introduces minerals and the gems fashioned from them so that the amateur who wishes to may become a knowledgeable collector, gemmologist, or lapidary, or may merely take pleasure in minerals and the beauty of gemstones. An Introduction places gemmology in historical context; the remainder of the first half of the book consists of seven chapters on minerals, collecting, and gemmology. The titles and contributors of the introductory chapters are "The Chemistry of Minerals" (14 pages) by Dr. Robert Thompson, research petrologist in the Department of Geology at Imperial College, London; "The Crystalline State" (18 pages) by Dr. John

Bradley, senior lecturer in physics at the Middlesex Hospital, London; "Geology for the Collector" (29 pages) by Dr. Alan Woolley of the Department of Mineralogy at the British Museum (Natural History); "Minerals Valuable to Man" (12 pages) by Robert Symes of the Department of Mineralogy at the British Museum (Natural History); "The Fashioning of Stones" (45 pages) by Colin Winter, a practicing lapidary and Fellow of the Gemmological Association of Great Britain; "Identifying Minerals" (8 pages) and "Conserving and Displaying Minerals" (10 pages) by O'Donoghue.

All chapters are clearly written in language comprehensible to the general reader. Scientific terms are italicized and defined within the text, which is often further amplified by charts and diagrams. Color illustrations appear on almost every page.

The second half of the volume, entitled "The Mineral Kingdom," is a systematic presentation of "the essential information on over one thousand minerals. These are nearly half of all those known to science, and include all those that the vast majority of mineralogists will ever be able to examine, whether they be enthusiastic collectors or professionals." Except for some digressions to identify important relationships among minerals, the sequence of entries follows the "order of the Chemical Index of Minerals (CIM) published by the British Museum (Natural History) in London. The first section of CIM consists of the elements and their alloys; further minerals are entered according to traditional subdivisions into oxides, sulphates, silicates, phosphates and so forth. They are further grouped by their metals, according to their atomic weight."

Further access to the entries is through the Index, by name, or through the appended Identification Tables, which characterize minerals by crystal form and habit, luster and color, cleavage and parting, fluorescence in ultraviolet light, phosphorescence following illumination with ultraviolet light, thermoluminescence, hardness according to Mohs' scale, streak, refractive index and birefringence, and specific gravity. The entries average from two to ten per three-column page and vary in number depending on the size and number of color photographs and diagrams on the page. There are about three color photographs to a page; many of these are half-page, and five are full-page. The information in each entry is given in standard order: "name of mineral; chemical composition; general properties; mode of occurrence; localities in which it is found; mode of treatment; fashioning details."

There are more than 500 color photographs and more than 150 diagrams. Both color and clarity are excellent.

There is a one-page, two-column "Glossary," the scope of which is greatly augmented by citations in the Index to definitions in the texts of the introductory chapters. There is also a half-page of "Conversion Tables" for linear, square, and volume measures and weight. "Important Addresses" lists 30 associations and museums of gemmological and mineralogical interest in Australia, Canada, Czechoslovakia, France, Iran, Switzerland, United Kingdom, U.S., USSR, and West Germany. There is a two-page, double-column, briefly annotated bibliography in five divisions: chemistry, crystallography, geochemistry, and physics; geology and mineralogy; periodicals and serials; gemmology; and gem-cutting.

The six-and-one-half-page Index, four columns per page, includes minerals, subjects, and names in the introductory chapters. It also includes cross-references. Bold designates the minerals listed in "The Mineral Kingdom," and italics designate illustration captions. The type is large and clear, and there is ample white space between the columns.

The book is printed on opaque heavy stock, with very readable type; the two-column layout of the seven chapters constituting the first half is attractive. The smaller type used in the three-column "The Mineral Kingdom" is clear and legible. There is some bleeding of illustrations into the inner margin. The cover is made of heavy cloth, and the sewn binding is strong.

Comparison may be made with two books reviewed in *Reference and Subscription Books Reviews* Feb. 1, 1976. *Encyclopedia of Minerals* by W. L. Roberts (New York: Van Nostrand, 1974) is a catalog of 2,200 minerals presented with detailed scientific data and small but utilitarian identification photographs in color. Its sober format is not meant to appeal to the amateur or general reader, for whom "The Mineral Kingdom" section of *O'Donoghue* is more congenial; nor does *Roberts* have the introductory material. This material may be found in a more comprehensive presentation in *The Collector's Guide to Rocks and Minerals* by J. R. Tindall and Roger Thornhill (New York: Van Nostrand, 1975) reviewed with *Roberts*. *O'Donoghue* presents the material in both *Roberts* and *Tindall and Thornhill* in a form suitable for the beginning enthusiast.

The Encyclopedia of Minerals and Gemstones is recommended for school and public libraries seeking informative and inviting introductory material for amateurs, hobbyists, and rock hounds. The introductory chapters are excellent for the young and for general readers, and the superb illustrations and diagrams are valuable in their own right. This book would be appropriate for purchase by individuals. The usefulness of "The Mineral Kingdom" section for museum, college, and university libraries would need to be evaluated in the context of holdings of comparable manuals. ***(May 15, 1977, p.1443)***

553   Mineralogy || Mineralogy—Collectors and collecting || Gem cutting   [OCLC] 76-1419

Encyclopedia of mystery and detection.

Editors-in-chief, Chris Steinbrunner and Otto Penzler; senior eds., Marvin Lachman and Charles Shibuk. New York, McGraw-Hill Book Co., [1976]. xii, 436p. illus. 25cm. kivar $19.95; to schools and libraries, 20 percent discount.

Mystery and dectective fiction have always been popular but only recently have they received serious attention as a literary genre. The editors of the *Encyclopedia of Mystery and Detection* believe the genre to be "the most important literary development of the twentieth century." Accordingly, they have brought together a wide range of factual material, dealing primarily with authors of mystery and detective fiction but also covering both detectives and criminals in books, as well as films, plays, television and radio programs, and comic strips. Eleven entries cover broader categories, such as *Scientific Detectives; Pulp Magazines; Locked-Room Mysteries; "Had-I-But-Known" School;* and *Collecting Detective Fiction.* Although most of the information concerns British and American authors and their works, other authors, primarily European, can also be found. Examples are Georges Simenon, Robert van Gulik, and the Swedish team of Maj Sjöwall and Per Wahlöö. The material ranges from historical to modern, from Edgar Allan Poe to Ross McDonald, from Boston Blackie to Rabbi David Small.

Editors-in-chief Chris Steinbrunner and Otto Penzler are briefly identified along with the other contributors in a list following the title page. Steinbrunner has worked as a television writer and producer and is currently regional vice-president of the Mystery Writers of America and editor of its journal. Penzler is editor of the *Ellery Queen Newsletter,* owner of a large collection of memorabilia and detective fiction (first editions), and founder of The Mysterious Press, a publishing house specializing in mystery fiction.

Marvin Lachman and Charles Shibuk are listed as senior editors. Lachman is a "regular contributor to *The Armchair Detective* and other scholarly journals devoted to the genre," and Shibuk is the author of "The Paperback Revolution" column in the same magazine and vice-president of the Theodore Huff Memorial Film Society. The eight contributing editors are identified variously as editor of *The Rohmer Review,* editor of *The Armchair Detective,* author of *Cheap Thrills* (a history of pulp fiction), member of The Baker Street Irregulars, authority on radio detectives, and reference librarian and authority on the detective story in the dime novel. They all share an enthusiasm for and have written about the subject covered by the encyclopedia.

According to the Introduction, the encyclopedia "is designed for the use of scholars and librarians who may have noticed the paucity of reference material about the subject, as well as for the mystery reader and filmgoer who may want to know more about his favorite writers, directors, books, films, detectives, and so on." The 600 entries are unsigned but presumably were written by the various editors. In gathering information, they examined standard reference works dealing with general literature as well as biographies, bibliographies, and critical works about individual authors. In addition, they consulted a number of specialized works. These are listed in a Selective Bibliography preceding the entries and provide a fairly complete representation of standard sources appearing to date.

The editors have attempted to insure the accuracy of the information presented. "Almost every living writer included in the *Encyclopedia* has read his or her own entry and made corrections and emendations where necessary. In the case of major deceased writers, the entries have been seen by experts, biographers, friends, or close relatives." The editors also claim to have consulted "many of the world's leading authorities and scholars" in compiling the entries; some, e.g., Jacques Barzun and Nigel Morland (a writer and editor in the field of criminology) are listed without identification in the acknowledgments. Comparison of biographical entries with those in standard biographical sources showed that the encyclopedia's versions agreed except for a few discrepancies in dates of birth, death, and publication.

The articles are written in a lively, readable style. They vary in length according to the prominence of the author or popularity of the character, for example, from a few lines for author Francis Durbridge to six pages for Sherlock Holmes. In general, the editors have attempted to include fuller information for some lesser known writers, while restricting information about such prominent authors as Theodore Dreiser or Balzac to material relating to their mystery fiction. No claim is made for comprehensiveness, and indeed, comparison with Barzun and Taylor's *A Catalogue of Crime* (New York: Harper & Row, 1971) shows that many minor figures have been omitted. Biographies of authors range from historical figures to current persons and include both an account of their lives and, in many instances, critiques of their works. Checklists of book titles follow the articles about major characters. The titles are arranged chronologically according to first publication, and alternative English and American titles are provided. Where a writer is represented with one article and his series detective with another, books about the detective are listed under the detective's name. For example, John D. MacDonald, creator of Travis McGee, is also well known for books featuring other characters. These are discussed under the entry for MacDonald, while a checklist of novels featuring McGee appears under the entry for the character; cross-references tie the entries together. Where appropriate, the checklists are followed by discussions of films, radio series, television series, and plays that have derived from the writings. Many of these provide synopses, information about source of plots and characters, dates, production companies, directors, and leading players. Other than the general list appearing in the front of the book, bibliographical sources for articles are not cited. The encyclopedia therefore complements rather than supplants such bibliographical works as the Barzun work mentioned above or Hagen's *Who Done It?* (New York: Bowker, 1969).

Cross-references are plentiful, both within the text, designated by small capital letters, and as *see* entries for pseudonyms, joint authors, etc. An alphabetical arrangement is used throughout. There is no index, although a title index would have been useful, there being few title entries.

One of the most attractive aspects of the volume, in addition to its readability, is its layout, utilizing more than 300 illustrations. They include both historical and current motion picture stills, early dust jackets, book illustrations, and portraits of authors. The reproduction of illustrations is excellent, and they are well placed, generally within the confines of the relevant article. The arrangement of the material is in two columns, with boldface capitals and white space distinguishing the entries. Running heads help one locate material. Margins are wide enough to permit rebinding, and the volume lies flat when opened. The print is clear, and the paper is of medium weight and opaque.

The Encyclopedia of Mystery and Detection is a browser's delight. While differing in its content from the usual academic reference volume, its information is generally accurate. With its popular, lively style, it will appeal primarily to fans of the genre, who will find, in one volume, "biographies" of favorite characters, photographs of actors who portrayed them, checklists of titles in which they appear, plot synopses, and brief critical estimates—along with "something about the author." Most public libraries will find the encyclopedia a useful addition for lending as well as reference. It is recommended to homes and libraries as a supplement to the more authoritative bibliographies and criticisms of this literary genre.

(Feb. 15, 1977, p.921)

808.8'016   Detective and mystery stories—Dictionaries || Detective and mystery plays—Dictionaries || Detective and mystery films—Dictionaries   [CIP]   75-31645

An encyclopedia of small antiques.

[By] James Mackay. New York, Harper, [c1975]. 320p. illus. (part col.) 25cm. cloth $22.50.

James Mackay served as an assistant keeper of the British Museum from 1961 until 1972. Since 1961 he has written numerous books on antiques and collecting stamps and coins. His previous works include *Airmails 1870–1970* (Batsford), *Antiques of the Future* (Studio Vista), *Greek and Roman Coins* (Barker), and *Value in Coins and Medals* (Johnson).

An Encyclopedia of Small Antiques was published simultaneously by Harper in the U.S. and by Fitzhenry & Whiteside in Canada. It is a first edition intended particularly for the collector who, because of financial and/or space limitations, is obliged to confine his collecting to objects of modest dimensions. This means that large articles, including furniture, have been omitted. While attempting to provide adequate coverage of most aspects of small antiques, the encyclopedia concentrates on "areas and periods which offer the greatest opportunity to the collector, particularly the applied arts of western Europe and North America over the past three centuries."

The encyclopedia contains about 400 entries in alphabetical order. They average several paragraphs. While the majority of entries is devoted to specific objects (e.g., clocks, figures, mugs, paperweights), a number of somewhat longer articles covers generic subjects (e.g., antiquities, miniatures, railway relics) and the major media (bronze, brass, glass). *See also* references direct the user to related information in other articles.

There are, however, no *see* references directing the user from entry terms not used to those which are. Thus one must discover by searching that earthenware is discussed under *Pottery* and that barometers are treated under *Scientific instruments*. The lack of an index also impedes the location of specific points of information covered in the longer articles.

Many of the objects treated in the entries are illustrated in the more than 350 black-and-white photographs and 32 full-page colorplates. The quality of the black-and-white photographs ranges from fair to very good, while that of the colorplates is superior.

A Bibliography of approximately 450 items, limited to English-language monographs, follows the text and includes works published as recently as 1975. The Bibliography is arranged under 13 broad categories (e.g., glass, metalwork, silver, textiles). Entries include only author, title, and publication date; they are not annotated.

The volume is sturdily bound in dark blue cloth and employs a somewhat small but clear typeface. The inner margins are extremely narrow, and since those on the right-hand pages contain picture captions, rebinding would not be feasible. While the layout is attractive, the colorplates are sometimes separated from the related text by several intervening pages. Paperweights, for example, are discussed on pages 185–187 while the related colorplate appears on page 196.

Most comprehensive encyclopedias of antiques provide basic coverage of the types of items included in *An Encyclopedia of Small Antiques*. Because this volume focuses more closely on a wide range of small antiques, it can be recommended for libraries and individuals requiring such specialized treatment.

(June 1, 1977, p.1522)

†745.1'03 Art objects—Collectors and collecting ‖ Antiques—Dictionaries   75-4145

The encyclopedia of sports.

[By] Frank G. Menke; revisions by Suzanne Treat. 5th rev. ed. South Brunswick and New York, A. S. Barnes and Co; London, Thomas Yoseloff Ltd., [c1975]. 1125p. illus. 25cm. cloth $25.

The first edition of *The Encyclopedia of Sports* was published in 1939. Beginning with the third edition, Roger L. Treat edited the work. Now that Menke and Treat are both deceased, the current fifth edition is edited by Treat's daughter-in-law, Suzanne Treat. The Reference and Subscription Books Review Committee reviewed and recommended the encyclopedia in the April 1946 and July 1954 issues of *Subscription Books Bulletin*. In design the latest revised edition of *The Encyclopedia of Sports* is essentially unchanged from the 1953 edition. Major athletic and competitive events are covered historically, records and champions of the sport are listed, and basic rules of competition are provided. Baseball, wrestling, angling, yachting, automobile racing, checkers, dog shows, and water skiing are among the diversity of sports covered. The 71 articles are arranged alphabetically, and there is an 11-page Index. There are several related articles treating amateur athletes, associations, Olympic and Pan-American games, and a new article which includes less generally popular sports such as boccie, codeball, skate sailing; a list of sport museums and halls of fame; metric equivalents of yards, feet, and inches; and the Associated Press Mid-Century poll of greatest athletes and outstanding events.

The Index provides selective references to major sports figures; it does not include every all-star team member, record holder, and title holder. Approximately two-thirds of the Index is devoted to listing the 71 major articles with extensive alphabetical entries for information contained in that article. For example, *baseball* has a column and a half devoted to such topics as *all-star games, home run hitters,* and *World Series*. The remaining Index entries refer to many of the sports figures and associations discussed in the historical and descriptive section of each article. No blind references were located, although a few textual and Index misspellings occur, and many persons given prominent coverage in the text are not cited in the Index.

Several diagrams of playing courts, gymnastic equipment, and harness horse racing equipment supplement the text. The humorous cartoons which were interspersed throughout earlier editions have been deleted.

A comparison of the fourth and fifth editions revealed very little change, except for the updating of records through 1972 and description of major rule changes, association changes, and highlights. The fourth edition contained many new introductory paragraphs to articles followed by much the same text as in earlier editions. The fifth edition follows the fourth edition very closely, but there are major revisions of several articles, such as those on *Billiards, Bowling,* and *Dog Racing*. *Automobile Racing* adds drag racing and expands the treatment of sports cars.

However, automobile speed racing records are for piston-driven vehicles only. No jet or turbine-powered vehicles are mentioned. "Roller Derby" (third edition) and "Women in Sports" (fourth edition) are among the articles deleted from this edition. Women's competition and records are included in appropriate articles, e.g., *Swimming, Field Hockey, Bowling,* and *Tennis*.

Overall, only a small percentage of the text is changed from the fourth edition. Despite the addition of 25 more pages in the fifth edition (1,100 pages to 1,125 pages), this does not represent a gain in information value for the user because of an increase in type size. Some articles have been shortened by deleting the 300 games in bowling and nationally ranked duckpin bowlers; the *Miscellaneous* article has been shortened by 12 pages, and minor American and international soccer league winners are no longer listed.

The print in the fifth edition is larger and more readable than that of the fourth edition, and the volume lies reasonably flat when opened. Some articles need revision. It is difficult to believe that Professor Harvey Lehman's 1938 research on prime athletic condition and peak performance ages as reported in the first edition is as valid in 1976 as it was over a quarter of a century ago. The *Gymnastics* article cites the Swiss Turn Verein as the team to beat for the A.A.U. championship. Neither the Swiss Turn Verein nor the Swiss Gymnastic Society has won the team championship since 1947. Obviously, the "Famous Gymnasts and Teams" section of the *Gymnastics* article has not been adequately updated.

With many articles, a by-line "Courtesy of ..." appears immediately following the main heading. One may assume that in most instances, the cited authority reviewed and approved the article. However, this is not stated in the Foreword and in at least one case, the connection between the article and the cited authority appears to be no more than *pro forma* in nature. An illustration of this is the *Canoeing* article. The texts of the fourth and fifth editions covering the history of canoeing are identical; yet the fourth edition credits Frank Havens of the Washington Canoe Club, and the fifth edition credits William A. Smoke of the National Paddling Committee. Clarification of by-lined individuals' involvements either as reviewers, revisers, authors, or authenticators would add considerably to the credibility of articles.

The Encyclopedia of Sports contains a wealth of information about champions, trophies, and records and the history of major sports not located in general encyclopedias. For major topics such as baseball, football, hockey, and the Olympics, much greater detail and currency is available in other sources, such as *The Sporting News National Football Guide, Official National Basketball Association Guide,* and the *Pro and Amateur Hockey Guide,* but this book should remain a standard for most libraries. Although the quality of coverage could be improved through a more thorough revision of existing articles and some expansion of Index entries (primarily of major trophies, awards, associations, and key sports figures), the basic coverage and structure remain sound. Bibliographic references to sources of additional information are not included.

The inner margins of the fifth edition of *The Encyclopedia of Sports* are too narrow for good rebinding results, but the volume is sturdy enough to withstand extensive use. Recommended for those libraries which lack this work or whose fourth edition needs replacement. *(Sept. 1, 1976, p.50)*

†796'.03 Sports [OCLC]

Encyclopedia of the musical theatre.

[By] Stanley Green. New York, Dodd, c1976. vi, 488p. 24cm. cloth $17.50.

Encyclopedia of the Musical Theatre is a ready-reference book covering the most prominent people, productions, and songs of the musical theater in New York (including off-Broadway) and

London from the late 19th century to 1975. Musical theater is defined as "productions generally called musical comedy, musical play, musical farce, musical spectacle, just plain musical, revue, operetta, and, if offered for a regular commercial run, opera." Minstrel shows, one-man shows, vaudeville and like forms of entertainment are not included.

Arranged in one alphabet are names of people (actors, actresses, composers, lyricists, librettists, directors, choreographers, producers) along with song and show titles; song titles are enclosed in quotation marks to distinguish them from show titles. Entries run from one or two sentences to several columns.

Entries for persons include the real name if different from the professional name (e.g., "Arden, Eve [née Eunice Quedens]"), a year-by-year listing of all musical stage productions with which the person was associated in New York or London, including, in the case of an actor/actress, the parts played.

Entries for plays give, in this order, composer and/or lyricist, play or book on which the musical is based if any, songs, place of first production (city, theater, date), number of performances, credits (producer, costumer, choreographer), and cast (performers and role played). The sequence is repeated for the second opening if applicable. This information is followed by a summary of the plot, cast replacements in the case of a long-run production, touring company cast, and film version information.

In song entries one finds the names of composer and lyricist, name of character and performer in the role who sang the song in the production, and the circumstances in which it was sung, e.g., "'Bye, Bye, Baby.' Music by Jule Styne, lyric by Leo Robin. Jaunty farewell—with a reminder to be faithful—sung by Jack McCauley to Carol Channing (as Lorelei Lee) as the lady is about to embark on a transatlantic voyage in *Gentlemen Prefer Blondes* (N.Y. 1949). . . . "

To have included a full entry for every musical ever produced, let alone every song and show with which each major actor/actress was associated, would have created a volume of unwieldy size. Thus, Stanley Green has had to be selective. While the dust jacket and the Preface state that the most "significant" or "prominent" productions and people are included, no criteria for judging significance or prominence have been indicated. One finds 15 productions listed under *Astaire, Fred*, but there are entries in the encyclopedia for only *Funny Face, Lady Be Good, Band Wagon*, and *Gay Divorce*. Paralleling this, songs in the entry for the show *Where's Charley* total nine; of these, five have entries of their own. Conversely, there is an entry "*Autumn in New York*" (song) from *Thumbs Up!* but no entry for the show; and for "*Ol' Man River*" there is the note that it was written for Paul Robeson but "introduced in *Show Boat . . .* by Jules Bledsoe . . ."; there is no entry for Bledsoe, Jules. But one should not cavil at this as the book contains pertinent information on more than 200 musicals, more than 1,000 songs, and about 600 brief biographies.

Stanley Green, the compiler, is a musical theater dèvotèe as well as author of several books on the subject: *Starring Fred Astaire, The World of Musical Comedy, The Rodgers & Hammerstein Story, Ring Bells and Sing Songs*. He acknowledges the help in this compilation of several "bibliothecal specialists" of the Theatre Collection, New York Public Library at Lincoln Center, and the Walter Hampden Memorial Library at The Players, New York.

There are references to books for further reading at the end of some of the entries, as well as a bibliography of "Librettos & Lyrics," "Reference," and "Song Collections" at the end of the book. Also included is a discography, a list of awards and prizes, and a table of long runs—runs over 1,000 performances in New York or London.

The book is sturdily bound in gray buckram and opens easily. The two-column pages are not crowded, and various typefaces are utilized so that the different kinds of information are readily located within entries. Inner margins, while not generous, should be adequate if rebinding is needed.

Altogether, *Encyclopedia of the Musical Theatre* is a fascinating fund of factual information which should delight any librarian who has ever been asked, "Was there a character named Marcus, or something like that, in 'The Music Man'?" Recommended for academic, public, and school libraries.

(July 15, 1977, p.1747)

782.8'1 Musical revue, comedy, etc.—Dictionaries || Theater—New York (City) || Theater—London [CIP] 76-21069

Encyclopedia of the Third Reich.

By Louis L. Snyder. New York, McGraw-Hill Book Co., 1976. [xx] 410p. illus. 24cm. permacote $24.95; to schools and libraries, 20 percent discount.

In the work under review, historian Louis L. Snyder has provided a tool that he hopes, ". . . presented without praise or polemic, will give users the essential facts of the Third Reich." One recalls Santayana's quotation, "Those who do not remember the past are condemned to relive it," which William L. Shirer used as an epigraph in his *The Rise and Fall of the Third Reich*.

During his student days in Germany, 1928–31, Snyder witnessed the demise of the Weimar Republic and rise of National Socialism. His first book, *Hitlerism: The Iron Fist in Germany*, was published in 1932. Since then, he has taught in universities and has written a number of important works on nationalism, World War II, and aspects of German history.

The present book aims to cover the period of German history from the rise of National Socialism to the fall of the Third Reich. Also included are selected entries relating to the Weimar and the Bonn Republics whenever the persons and events were "closely associated with Hitler and the Nazi regime." Although the author doesn't specifically say so in the Preface, this book is an attempt to provide a comprehensive, inclusive work on all aspects of the period. "The names of the biographees selected are those that would be recognized by most historians of the Third Reich as of some significance. The amount of space devoted to each entry was judged by its relative importance to historians of the era." While much of the source material for the encyclopedia came from the author's own collection gathered over nearly a half century, he expresses special appreciation to the Wiener Library of London, an institution strong in documentation of every phase of Nazi history and of political development during the totalitarian era in Europe.

Following the Preface is an 18-page "Calendar of Significant Dates in the History of the Third Reich," arranged by year and then by day, beginning with Hitler's birth (April 20, 1889) and ending with the execution of war criminals at Nuremberg (October 16, 1946). With only a few exceptions, the dates are consistent with those in William L. Langer's *An Encyclopedia of World History*, a standard source for dates of historical events.

The main body of the book comprises nearly 2,000 entries, alphabetically arranged, on people, events, ideas, social life, military organizations, politics, and aspects of the war. The articles are in two columns, with running heads at the top of each page and bold capitals for each entry. Birth and death dates are given in parentheses following personal names. Place-names and other terms are usually entered under the German word or well-known phrase, with the English translation or original term in parentheses. *See* references lead the reader from forms not used, for example, from Terezin to *Theresienstadt;* from Storm Detachment, Storm Troopers, and Sturmabteilung to *SA;* "Today Germany! Tomorrow the World!" to "*Heute Deutschland! Morgen Die Welt!*"; and from White Rose to *Weisse Rose*. Many q.v. references in the articles lead the user further. For example, in *Reischstag Fire,* additional articles are indicated on the men accused of the fire, Nazi leaders involved with the trial, and subsequent events. Following many articles are sources for further information.

A sampling of articles by the Committee verified the accuracy and thoroughness of the work under review. Refugees and resisters, military formations and leaders, concentration camp operations, home front activities, minutes of conferences and documents, words of songs, quotations, statements of policy and philosophy, code names for military actions, and many other facets of the period are defined and described. There are only rare instances of repetition, such as in the overlapping information in the *Blood Purge* and *Ernst Roehm* (SA leader) entries. Generally each article stands independent of the others. The author succeeds in his goal of describing the many inhumanities of the time "without polemic." Good balance and restraint are shown in the article on Hitler with its discussion of three levels of value judgments on his life and career. The writing style throughout is clear.

Numerous black-and-white illustrations—photographs (with sources), drawings, maps, cartoons, organization charts, stamps—add to the book's reference value. Portraits of leaders of the anti-Nazi Resistance are a special strength. However, no photograph of Roehm was found, and the painting of Nietzsche is not a good likeness, but these are exceptions.

Another valuable reference aid is the extensive two-part Bibliography at the end: approximately 800 books on the Third Reich and 200 periodical articles. Both sections are arranged by author and include titles in English and German. The lists include items published in the 1970s as well as earlier, standard works.

Encyclopedia of the Third Reich is the culmination of a noted historian's 45-year study of the subject and fills a reference need. No other dictionary or encyclopedia in English is solely devoted to the Third Reich. The work is balanced, comprehensive, and easy to use. The book is sturdily bound. Recommended for homes and high school, public, and college and university libraries. *(Feb. 15, 1977, p.922)*

943.086'03 Germany—History—1933-1945—Dictionaries || National socialism—Dictionaries [CIP]   75-25740

Energy atlas:

a who's who resource to information. Washington, D.C., Fraser/Ruder & Finn, 1976. various paging. 28cm. paper $25 or $35 for Energy Atlas and Capital Contacts in Consumerism.

Energy Atlas is a directory of about 50 federal energy-related departments and agencies, 100 Congressional committees and organizations, some 50 private and public state and local assistance organizations, and the executive and legislative energy agencies of each of the 50 states. The Introduction refers to "150 non-governmental groups"; apparently the assistance organizations and the state agencies are intended to be the 150. The Committee's examination of the book reveals that most of the agencies categorized as "State and Local Assistance Organizations" are clearly not "non-governmental." The volume concludes with a Publications section, three Appendixes, a Glossary, and an Index.

Fraser/Ruder & Finn are communications counselors who have been in business since 1975. Their headquarters office is in New York; other American offices are in Chicago, Dallas, Houston, Los Angeles, San Francisco, and Toronto. They also operate in six cities throughout the world.

No cutoff date is specified for *Energy Atlas*. On the one hand, Earl Butz's resignation on October 4, 1976, is taken into account because John Knebel is listed as Acting Secretary. On the other, the 1973 (rather than 1976) edition of *Encyclopedia of Associations* (Gale Research Co.) is cited, and the list of GPO bookstores does not include Houston, the newest (1976) and largest of the 24 stores. Nor are plans for updating the atlas stated. Council of State Governments, National Governors Conference, Rural Electrification Administration of the U.S. Department of Agriculture, and state associations of REA electric borrowers are examples of agencies covered.

The work is divided into nine separately paged sections: (A) Executive Office of the President; (B) Executive Departments; (C) Independent Agencies and Commissions; (D) Congress; (E) State and Local Assistance Organizations; (F) States; (G) Publications; (H) Appendixes and Glossary; and (I) Index.

In each of the first six sections—more than four-fifths of the volume—similar information is provided for each entry: agency name, mail address, telephone number, statement of agency jurisdiction in energy matters, key energy-related personnel (names, titles, telephone numbers). "What's What" would have been more appropriate than the "Who's Who" in the subtitle, which misleadingly implies that the work is predominantly biographical in nature.

The seventh section, Publications, consists of five parts covering periodicals, guidebooks and directories, professional and trade journals, digests and abstracts, and selected government publications. There seems to be no logical reason for the peculiar and arbitrary separation of "periodicals" and "professional and trade journals." In all but the last-named category, each entry includes address, price, frequency, and a descriptive contents note. For government publications, the title, order number, year (1970–75 only), and price are identified. The editors do not explain why a portion of the guidebooks and directories and all of the government publications have numbered entries.

In the eighth section, the three Appendixes are text statements on the federal programs dealing with energy management, solar heating and cooling, and wind energy. The Glossary, following the Appendixes, briefly defines 200 terms such as *beneficiation, degree day,* and *trommel screen* but fails to indicate any authority for the definitions.

The Index (ninth section) is in six alphabets, contains only 137 page references, and provides access to just the entries for federal and congressional offices. Arranged under six "where to find out about" captions, it is in the following sequence: (1) availability or management of energy resources, (2) energy efficiency, (3) financial assistance, (4) health regulations, (5) allocation of energy resources, (6) alternative energy sources. Similar coverage for nonfederal organizations is not provided. There are no index references to individual names; nor is there one alphabet of all the agency names and/or of all the publications cited.

Examination of entries revealed a few errors in titles, alphabetization, and spelling. *Federal Energy Guidelines* (p.G-6) is in fact the subtitle of three of the volumes of Commerce Clearing House's *Energy Management*. The titles *Energy Dialog* and *Energy Digest* precede *Energy Daily* (p.G-4). The professional journals of the Institute of Electrical and Electronics Engineers are entered before *Industrial Heating* and *Industry Week* (p.G-20 and 21). In the States section, Alaska precedes Alabama and Texas precedes Tennessee. Joe Evans (p.D-4) should be Evins.

Running heads and an orderly layout make it easy to find information on the page. The book has non-glare paper and lies flat when opened.

To summarize, the uneven currency, the absence of a comprehensive index, and the failure to identify sources consulted and plans for updating make *Energy Atlas* of limited value to library users requiring recent and accurate information. Not recommended. *(July 1, 1977, p.1666)*

333.8 Power resources—U.S.—Directories || Energy policy—U.S. || Power resources—Bibliography [OCLC]   76-46681

England:

a chronology and fact book, 1485–1973. Compiled and edited by Robert I. Vexler. Dobbs Ferry, N.Y., Oceana Publications, 1974. 186p. 24cm. cloth $7.50.

942 Gr. Brit.—History—Chronology || Gr. Brit.—History—Sources [CIP]   73-17067

See page 88

Environmental legislation:
a sourcebook. Edited by Mary Robinson Sive. New York, Praeger (Praeger Special studies in U.S. economic, social, and political issues), [1976]. xxiv, 516p. 24cm cloth $35.

Environmental Legislation, a Sourcebook provides a sampling of federal and state laws, executive orders, state constitutional provisions, and federal regulations concerning the environment. Its purpose is to introduce citizens interested in public affairs to the scope of environmental problems addressed by legislation and the solutions thereby attempted. It also intends to provide reference material for students in environmental law courses at undergraduate and continuing education institutions. Only laws in force in 1975 are included. Most of these were enacted within the past ten years, and the editor considered historical significance in making her selection. Only legislation with fairly stringent requirements and sanctions, intended to regulate and not merely to promote study, is included. No attempt is made to assess the success of environmental legislation.

Mary Robinson Sive, the editor, admits her "pro-environment" bias. She is an information specialist and a former librarian who served as director of the Education and Library Department of the Environment Information Center in New York City.

The volume begins with a nine-page Foreword, *The Frontiers of the National Environmental Policy Act,* by Irving Like, a New York lawyer experienced in environmental litigation and legislative drafting. Like explains how the act and other environmental legislation have given citizens the right to use litigation to participate in government and corporate decision-making. He contends that decisions governing the production and consumption of goods and services harbor the roots of pollution problems.

The Foreword is followed by a half-page of Acknowledgements, a table of contents which includes chapter subdivisions, a one-page list of Abbreviations, a short Glossary of legal terms, and a ten-page Introduction delineating the scope and purpose of the volume.

The body of the book is divided into 14 chapters, each of which is devoted to a particular environmental topic such as air, historic preservation, land use, noise, solid waste, toxic and hazardous substances, and water. Each chapter begins with an introduction explaining the problems involved and the policies employed as remedies, followed by the texts of legislation.

The complete text of the laws is not given. Since the *Sourcebook* is not intended for lawyers or legal researchers, the editor determined that excerpting was an appropriate way to emphasize the most significant provisions as well as save space. She has, however, attempted to include declarations of policy, major substantive provisions, language held particularly significant by courts and commentators, and significant definitions.

There are four Appendixes. Appendix A, "Organizations, Government Agencies, Public Interest Law Firms," cites a few useful guides such as the *Washington Information Directory, Environment U.S.A.,* and *Conservation Directory* and lists addresses of ten agencies providing legal assistance for environmental protectionists. Appendix B is a three-page explanation, "How to Find the Law." Appendix C, "Statutes, Enactments, and Areas of Concern," serves as an index to the volume, with titles of the excerpted federal and state legislation listed by jurisdiction. A three-page list, "Areas of Concern," comprises a subject index. Appendix D, "Supplementary Readings," is a 22-page collection of bibliographies entitled "Monographs," "Environmental Law Texts and Treatises," "Reference Books and Annuals," "Compilations of Laws," "Bibliographies," "Periodicals," and "Articles on Administrative Decision Making." These bibliographies list recent publications; some entries are briefly annotated.

Binding and format are satisfactory; right margins are uneven because the book has been reproduced from typewritten copy. However, the print is very legible.

The *Sourcebook* provides broad coverage on the subject of environmental legislation including laws from more than 40 states. The chapter introductions are lucid and provide orientations to the subjects. The inclusion of the more significant portions of statutes instead of the complete text is satisfactory for the audience for which the book is intended. The excerpts are identified by legal citations that facilitate access to the complete texts if needed. The table of abbreviations, glossary, bibliographies, and explanation of how to find laws will aid those unfamiliar with legal literature. The Index provided in Appendix C is somewhat brief but satisfactory.

The *Sourcebook* does not purport to state the law on any of the subjects encompassed. However, it does provide an introduction to environmental legislation for students and others interested in environmental problems. Libraries which subscribe to *Environment Reporter* (Washington, D.C., Bureau of National Affairs, Inc., 1970–) or *Environmental Law Reporter* (Washington, D.C., Environmental Law Institute, 1971–), both of which contain complete texts of federal and state legislation and regulations, may not need this volume. However, there may be people whose needs will be better filled by this edited and excerpted collection. For libraries serving such patrons, *Environmental Legislation: a Sourcebook* is recommended. *(July 15, 1977, p.1747)*

344'.73 Environmental law—U.S. [CIP]   75-61

Ethnic information sources of the United States:
a guide to organizations, agencies, foundations, institutions, media, commercial and trade bodies, government programs, research institutes, libraries and museums, religious organizations, banking firms, festivals and fairs, travel and tourist offices, airlines and ship lines, bookdealers and publishers' representatives, and books, pamphlets and audiovisuals, on specific ethnic groups. Managing ed., Paul Wasserman; associate ed., Jean Morgan. Detroit, Gale Research Co., 1976. xviii, 751p. 28cm. cloth $45.

The contents of this book are described by its subtitle. In the growing library of publications supporting ethnic studies in the U.S., this guide will provide much useful information not readily available elsewhere. It is "addressed to individuals who come to the United States from foreign countries or regions as visitors or permanent residents," persons related in some way to ethnic groups or who plan to go to a foreign region, students, educators, information workers, and those engaged in commerce with specific ethnic groups. Excluded are blacks, American Indians, and Eskimos because of these groups' extensive representation in other sources. Inexplicably the Vietnamese are also excluded.

Designed to bring together many types of information, the volume treats 90 identifiable ethnic groups (Afghans to Yugoslavs), including two religious groups (Buddhists and Moslems) and a number of ethnic groups that no longer constitute independent nations, e.g., Latvians, Armenians, Basques, and Welsh. The arrangement is alphabetical, with a table of contents as well as a Guide to Ethnic Arrangement which has adequate *see* and *see also* references. Under each ethnic group heading there are 26 major headings, included whenever material was found for the categories. The subtitle lists many of these headings; others, lumped under more general terms in it, are fraternal, professional, public affairs, cultural and educational, and charitable organizations, foundations, UN missions, information offices, embassies and consulates, newspapers and newsletters, magazines, radio programs, and films.

Information was compiled through questionnaires, correspondence, library research, ethnic publications, and interviews with experts and individuals in travel and tourist offices and especially embassies. The data provided are clear, up to date, and accurate. Access to the data is provided by the table of contents, the guide, and two indexes. The Organizations Index lists all those cited whether by full name or by acronym. The Publications Index includes the many newspapers, magazines, and books by title only.

Ethnic Information Sources of the United States is very easy to use, is sturdily bound in light gray cloth, and is printed in the familiar two-column format used in other Gale encyclopedias on good quality white paper. Comparison with the *Encyclopedia of Associations* (Detroit: Gale Research, 1956–   ) and the *Encyclopedic Directory of Ethnic Organizations* (Littleton, Colo.: Libraries Unlimited, 1975) reveals that while both of these are essentially directories, *Ethnic Information Sources of the United States* is much more. The addresses of embassies, UN missions, consulates, information offices, museums, tourist agencies, and banks; lists of radio programs, festivals and fairs, books, pamphlets, and audiovisual material are all useful features not included in the other two titles. The book lists comprise a wide selection, with a good representation of current publications as recent as 1975 but ranging back to 1876 where appropriate.

On the other hand it must be said that as a directory *Ethnic Information Sources* falls considerably short of the *Encyclopedic Directory of Ethnic Organizations* and virtually duplicates the ethnic organizations given in the *Encyclopedia of Associations*. It would have been helpful if the broadcast bands of radio stations carrying ethnic programs had been given, as well as the sources of films cited. The Publications Index could have been broadened to include films, but an even more useful aid would have been a geographical index.

Despite these shortcomings the volume accomplishes a useful purpose. It should be noted that coverage of banks, festivals and fairs, and numerous trade associations offers information helpful to those considering commercial ventures with an ethnic orientation. Because of the presence of this and other categories of data not found in existing directories, *Ethnic Information Sources of the United States* may be recommended as complementary to the other directories cited for any library supporting the growing field of ethnic research. *(Apr. 1, 1977, p.1194)*

301.45'1071073 Minorities—U.S.—Societies, etc.—Directories || Minorities—U.S.—Information services [CIP] 76-4642

Famous actors and actresses on the American stage: documents of American theater history. [By] William C. Young. 2v. New York & London, Bowker, 1975. 26cm. cloth $55.

Famous Actors and Actresses on the American Stage is a significant and scholarly assemblage of contemporary writings on the performances and personalities of representative stage artists appearing in America from the mid-eighteenth century to the present.

William Curtis Young is well qualified to author this book. He has been professor of English and humanities at various U.S. and foreign colleges and universities, recipient of Ford Foundation and American Library Association grants, associate editor of *Theatre Documentation,* contributing editor of *Educational Theatre Journal,* and visiting lecturer in English at the University of Kansas. He is author of *Famous American Playhouses* (Chicago: ALA, 1973) in this same series of Documents of American Theatre History and of other works in the field of drama.

The quoted writings or "documents" were selected from a wide variety of sources including newspaper and journal reviews and articles, histories of the American theater, and biographies. A valuable feature is the inclusion of material from autobiographies and interviews providing insight into performers' concepts of acting and their interpretation of particular roles.

Names are arranged alphabetically in two volumes and numbered from 1 (Edwin Adams) to 218 (Blanche Yurka). Quoted selections from reviews, articles, diaries, and biographical writings follow brief vitae and career synopses. Running page heads facilitate use.

The number of documents by or about the actors varies from one to eight. The documents may be short paragraphs or run several pages in length. Typically three or four of these selections, with footnotes indicating their sources, are provided for each entrant. Citations follow each selection. Acting teams such as Weber and Fields, Lunt and Fontanne, and the Marx Brothers are treated as single units rather than divided into separate entries.

Brief paragraphs by Young provide an introductory background and running commentary on each selection, contributing to a sense of continuity.

Although this work is not a biographical directory, a minimum amount of personal information about each subject is noted, such as birth date, place of birth, death date, husband or wife, circumstances of American debut, and famous roles. Anecdotal material and theatrical history are only tangentially touched upon.

An intriguing illustration precedes the coverage of each stage personality. These include reproductions of photographs, paintings, engravings, woodcuts, prints, and other media and most frequently show the actor in a particular role. Also noted are year of the performance and source of the picture. A list of these illustrations, arranged alphabetically by actor, appears in the front of each volume. If the actor is portrayed playing a part, the part and/or play are also indicated. However, page references are not given.

-The Index to the set at the end of volume 2, consisting of 61 double-columned pages, is extensive and detailed. References are to the numbered sections and subparagraphs rather than to page numbers, making it difficult to locate some of the citations, especially those for main numbers instead of specific subparagraphs with texts encompassing several pages.

Actors' names, authors (when verified), critics, theaters and theatrical companies, directors, designers, producers, titles of plays, and characters (followed in parentheses by the play in which they appear) are all indexed. Cross-references are given from the briefer appellations of characters to the full name, such as "Judge (*Winterset*) see Gaunt, Judge."

Some inaccuracies and inconsistencies were noted. For instance, there are cross-references from Laurette Cooney to Laurette Taylor and from Fannie Borach to Fanny Brice, but not from Willis Claude Dunkenfield to W. C. Fields nor from Mary Moss to Laura Keene. Some index reference citations cannot be found or are incorrect.

Identification of 255 actors out of the thousands who appeared over two centuries obviously required the exercise of highly selective judgment and was conditioned as well by the availability of suitable materials. The author has given (1) "Preference . . . to performers of the eighteenth and nineteenth centuries, since such material is much more difficult for the modern reader to obtain than on twentieth century actors. (2) actors and actresses . . . who tower over all their peers and are accepted as the greatest performers of their time by a majority of the public and critics. (3) actors and actresses (who) could never be considered giants of the stage, but have created some great roles and served the theater nobly and well for many years. . . . (4) The twentieth century actors and actresses posed the greatest problems, for it is very difficult for a contemporary to assess whether or not a performer's work is of lasting value." Some musical comedy stars are included. Young makes it clear that for these as well as for representatives of legitimate theater, prototypes of various acting movements or dramaturgical innovation were chosen. "Omissions in no way signify that a performer is not or was not great or significant on the American stage, but merely that space has limited the scope of the work."

Examination of the contents of *Famous Actors* reveals that the compiler has indeed abided by his own objectives and limitations. It is also evident that a substantial percentage of the generally recognized all-time "greats" are included.

An Index by Decades lists actors and actresses alphabetically under ten-year periods from 1750 to 1970 according to their active life on the American stage. The largest concentration of actors represented in this index occurs in the 1920s.

The past and present popularity of Shakespeare's works is shown by the fact that the greatest number of Index entries appear under his name, as well as under his plays such as *Macbeth, Julius Caesar,* and *Othello.* Second to Shakespeare in quantity of citations is Sheridan because of the many entries for *The School for Scandal* and *The Rivals.* Edwin Booth is the actor with the most references closely followed by Edmund Kean and Edwin Forrest, while Sarah Bernhardt is the leader among the actresses.

The most frequently quoted drama critics are Brooks Atkinson and John Mason Brown.

A good selection of variety and musical comedy luminaries such as W. C. Fields, Bert Williams, Will Rogers, Ethel Merman, Alfred Drake, Fanny Brice, Julie Andrews, Carol Channing, and Al Jolson gives deserved recognition to these forms of stage entertainment.

A selective bibliography lists newspapers, journals, and magazines, ten general histories of the theater, and more than 350 recommended books on actors and acting, including numerous imprint dates from the latter half of the nineteenth century.

Comparable in intent to *Famous Actors* in a related area of the performing arts is *American Film Directors* (compiled and edited by Stanley Hochman, New York: Ungar, 1974) which also consists of quoted commentary, in this case on the techniques of film directors. The material in both books can be utilized in the study of changing philosophies and methods of artistic criticism.

Format, paper, and typography of these volumes are particularly attractive and the binding is sturdy.

Actors and Actresses on the American Stage presents a fascinating panorama of acting and actors in the American theater from its earliest beginnings. This is a collection to arrest the imagination because of the insights revealed in writings of contemporaneous critics as well as in autobiographical accounts, interviews, and other sources. These attractively produced volumes should become a standard reference source of original commentaries for students of acting and the theater and are recommended for drama collections in university, college, and larger public libraries. *(May 15, 1977, p.1444)*

792'.028 Actors—U.S. [CIP]   75-8741

Farms and farmers.
†630 Agriculture—Juvenile literature [OCLC]   75-19981
See page 50

Fire.
†530.43 Fire—Juvenile literature [OCLC]   75-19967
See page 50

Fishing.
†688.79 Fishing—Juvenile literature [OCLC]   75-20520
See page 50

Food and drink.
†641.3 Food—Juvenile literature [OCLC]   75-20503
See page 50

The foundation center source book, 1975/1976: documentation on large grant making foundations; entity description; policies, programs, application procedures; grants. Edited by Terry-Diane Beck and Alexis Teitz Gersumky. 2v. New York, The Foundation Center, distributed by Columbia University Pr., 1975 and 1976. 29cm. buckram, $65. a v. (limited discount available).

The Foundation Center is an independent educational institution chartered by the Board of Regents of the University of the State of New York. It gathers and disseminates information on philanthropic foundations through its library services, publications, and research. The Foundation Center's Library contains an extensive collection of books, documents, and reports on the foundation field and current files on the activities and program interests of more than 26,000 foundations. Well-known as the publisher of *The Foundation Directory* (see *Reference and Subscription Books Reviews,* November 15, 1975) and *Foundation News,* the Center has now begun a new series, the two-volume *Foundation Center Source Book,* 1975/1976.

The Source Book is edited by Terry-Diane Beck and Alexis Teitz Gersumky who were assistant editor and editorial associate, respectively of the fifth edition of *The Foundation Directory.*

The purpose of *The Source Book* is "to relate the needs of fund seekers to the activities of foundations and to assist foundations in making their programs known to a wider public."

The 1975 *Foundation Directory* lists 2,533 foundations which have assets of at least $1,000,000 or make minimal annual grants of at least $500,000. In selecting foundations for inclusion in *The Source Book,* only those with assets of at least $7,000,000 were considered. From this upper level group of 580 foundations, 227 with national or significant regional program interests were chosen. Local foundations with primary interests within a state, community foundations, and operating foundations primarily concerned with managing their own programs were excluded. Also excluded were foundations whose response to requests for information was too limited to enable the editors to determine qualifications or to compile a complete entry. Some were omitted in order to maintain editorial and production schedules and may be included in later editions, although a definite publication plan for the series has not been announced. Omitted foundations are listed in volume 2 with an explanation for their exclusion. The two books do not form a unified set. One hundred foundations, arranged alphabetically (Amoco through Whitehead), appear in volume 1 while an entirely different alphabet of 127 presumably later respondents (Alcoa through Xerox) is represented in volume 2. There are no cross-references between volumes to assist the user. Information is provided for each foundation under three headings: Entity Data; Policies, Programs, Application Procedures (when this information was made available to the Foundation Center); and Grants. The data are usually for the calendar or fiscal year ending in 1974. The Entity Data section is about the same as that which appears in *The Foundation Directory* but revised and updated. It consists of the address; place and date of establishment; names of donors; purpose and activities; financial data including amount of assets (market or ledger value), gifts received, expenditures, and grants (low and high); and names of officers and trustees, along with the employer identification number. A photographic reproduction of the cover of the foundation's latest annual report and an abstract of its contents are sometimes included.

The Policies, Programs, Application Procedures section is made up of photoreproduced statements provided by the foundations or from information contained in foundation annual reports. This section is missing for some foundations listed in volume 1 and for most of those listed in volume 2.

The Grants section contains lists of grants photoreproduced from annual reports or from reports filed with the Internal Revenue Service.

Both volumes of *The Source Book* contain the same one-page introduction and brief description of the Foundation Center with a list of its national and regional reference collections. Each volume has a table of contents listing the foundations included. Neither volume has an index. However, the Index of Fields of Interest; the Index of Foundations by State and City; and the Index of Donors, Trustees, and Administrators in *The Foundation Directory* can be used to some advantage with this set.

The Source Book binding matches that of *The Foundation Directory.* Although these volumes are somewhat heavier, they appear sturdy enough to withstand heavy use. The size and style of print, while readable, varies throughout since the set is made up largely of photoreproduced pages from a variety of documents.

The Source Book provides a broad range of examples of the contributions of foundations to American society. Fund seekers should find the information concerning application procedures useful. The lists of grants may enable fund seekers to determine whether their proposals fall within the scope of a particular foundation's program, assuming of course that the program has not changed since the year reported. Much of this information, however, is available elsewhere. Annual reports are usually available from foundations on request. They may be purchased on film from the Foundation Center or consulted at the Center's regional libraries. The information in the Entity Data section duplicates that provided by *The Foundation Directory,* most of which is derived from 1972 or 1973 data while the *Foundation Grants Index,* which is published as part of the bimonthly *Foundation News,* lists foundation grants of $5,000 or more. The advantage of the *Source Book* is that it brings all of this information together within a single work.

Another source of grant information is the *Taft Information System Foundation Reporter* (Washington: Taft Products, 1976, $275 a year including the monthly *News Monitor of Philanthropy,* and *Hotline*). This, the latest volume in the series, lists 391 major foundations selected on the basis of the amount of assets, quantity of grants, geographical focus and location, and fields of interest. It does not, however, list all of the foundations included in *The Source Book.* The *Taft Reporter* provides about the same information as that included in the Entity Data section of *The Source Book,* although the latter is sometimes more up to date. In addition, the *Taft Reporter* provides brief biographical information about foundation administrators and board members, the names of persons to contact when submitting requests, and information about the history and operation of the foundations. It also has separate indexes to fields, foundation names, foundations by state, geographic grant distribution, individuals, and types of grants. The *Taft Reporter* has a grants section for each foundation which lists examples of funding programs by areas of interest which sometimes number as many as 50, but are not intended to be exhaustive in their representation of potential foundation involvements. About two full pages with single-spaced type are devoted to each foundation. In *The Source Book* the number of pages for each foundation varies from about 4 or 5 to over 70, depending on the number of grants listed. The pages are sometimes only half full, however, and the type is often double spaced. The grants section is not usually arranged by areas of interest.

The Source Book provides basic information about a number of the largest foundations with national or regional interests, including some information concerning application procedures and a complete list of grants for the most recent year for which data were available to the Foundation Center. This latter information has not previously been available so conveniently. It is, however, an expensive set and already dated. But it is less expensive and sometimes more up to date than the *Taft Reporter* which includes information on 164 more foundations, although not as complete a listing of grants. For these reasons *The Foundation Directory Source Book* is recommended for libraries which would normally expect to provide grant information to patrons. *(Nov. 1, 1976, p.416)*

361.7'6 Endowments—U.S. [OCLC]

The fresh & salt water fishes of the world.
By Edward C. Migdalski and George S. Fichter; illustrations by Norman Weaver. New York, Knopf, 1976. 316p. illus. 30cm. cloth $25.

More than 1,000 species of fish, representing all of the 43 orders and the 212 most commonly known families, are described in this book intended for "popular consumption." Migdalski, an ichthyologist with Yale University's Bingham Oceanographic Laboratory and Peabody Museum of Natural History, is an author of several books for anglers. Fichter, former instructor in biology and conservation at Miami University of Ohio, has written and edited many nature books and guides. Drawing on many published sources as well as on their own observations, they have produced a very readable text.

The material is arranged by order and family, giving family characteristics, habits, and habitat, with added information of interest to sport fishermen and fish enthusiasts. For example, under *Jacks and Pompanos* the authors state: "Of all the jacks—and to many people, of all the fishes in the sea—the Florida pompano, *Trachinotus carolinus,* is by far the most delicately flavored. It is netted commercially, bred in ponds, and sold for high prices in markets and restaurants. It is also caught on hook and line with small artificials (bucktails or jigs) or with sand fleas, clams, or similar natural baits. On light tackle, the pompano makes an exciting catch; some weigh 3 pounds or even as much as 5 or 7 pounds, but most weigh a pound or less."

Pertinent information on tank fishes is included for fish enthusiasts, including some warnings, as "piranhas are voracious predators, dangerous even to humans. They are not proper fishes for home aquariums, as they will bite anything that moves and have no respect for the hand that feeds them." More suitable are the upside-down catfishes that swim on their back when mature. "All members of this genus are hardy and live peaceably with other fishes in an aquarium."

In addition to the more scientific information, a historical frame of reference often is provided. For example, the reader learns of the carp's importation in the 1880s, when bands played and parades celebrated its arrival in the United States. "But enthusiasm soon soured. Carps made themselves so much at home that they began to crowd out the native species."

However, much of the commentary deals with the habits and habitats of fishes with the minimum of technical terminology, since the volume is not addressed to the research ichthyologist. The text is further enlivened by 500 handsome full-color illustrations and 186 drawings, which accompany the descriptions, each giving the common and scientific names and sizes in feet and centimeters. The illustrator, Norman Weaver, is considered one of the world's outstanding painter-illustrators in the field of natural history.

An introductory section covers the world of fishes: technicalities, fishes from past to present, the fish's body and its functions, and commercial and sport fishes. Appended are a brief bibliography of 30 titles, all in English and chiefly recent, and salt water records of fishes caught by rod and reel. An accurate and attractively designed Index gives common names in roman type, scientific names in italics, and indicates pages on which illustrations occur with boldface numerals.

The format is excellent—heavy paper, large type, good color in illustrations, and stout binding.

The volume may be compared with an earlier title, *Living Fishes of the World,* by Earl S. Herald (New York, Doubleday, 1961. 303p.). Also systematically arranged and with a semiscientific and popular approach, it was prepared by the curator of San Francisco's Steinhart Aquarium. Illustrated with more than 300 photographs, half in full color, and by more than 60 photographs, it contains a Glossary, Bibliography, and Index. *The Fresh & Salt Water Fishes of the World* has the advantage because of its inclusion of recent findings as well as superior illustrations by Norman Weaver.

The experience and prestige of the authors, the broad appeal

of *The Fresh & Salt Water Fishes of the World* and its well-organized text, the readable style, and the beautiful illustrations recommend this guide for both homes and libraries.
(July 15, 1977, p.1748)

597 Fishes [CIP] 76-13704

Fuel and energy.
†621.3 Fuel—Juvenile literature || Power resources—Juvenile literature [OCLC] 75-20512
See page 50

Gateways to readable books:
an annotated graded list of books in many fields for adolescents who are reluctant to read or find reading difficult. By Dorothy E. Withrow, Helen B. Carey, Bertha M. Hirzel. 5th ed. New York, H. W. Wilson Co., 1975. 23cm. 299p. cloth $12.
This edition of *Gateways to Readable Books* includes over 1,100 books covering a wide range of adolescent interests.

Dorothy E. Withrow is the only one of the authors who wrote previous editions. However, Ruth Strang, originator and coauthor of each of the first four editions, and Ethlyne Phelps, one of the authors of the third and fourth editions, were consulted in the preparation of the present edition. New authors Dorothy E. Withrow and Helen B. Carey were formerly reading clinic supervisors for the Philadelphia public schools; Bertha M. Hirzel is reading consultant, North Penn School district secondary schools, Landsdale, Pennsylvania.

An Introduction, worth reading on its own, includes a brief history of publication, an analysis of updating, a survey of illiteracy in the U.S. and the efforts made to combat it. Discussions of what makes a book easy to read and the values of wide reading, suggestions for use of the bibliography with individuals and with groups, procedures used in building this bibliography, "Lists of Recommended Books for Retarded Readers," and general sources of information on books are also included.

According to the Introduction, the breakdown of kinds of items included is as follows: 962 trade books (78 retained from the previous edition); 40 reading texts (12 retained); 126 books in series (49 retained); 41 magazines and newspapers (34 retained—including only 1 children's newspaper, *My Weekly Reader*); and 9 simplified dictionaries (8 retained). This indicates that 85 percent of the material is new in the present edition.

Twenty-eight subject categories are used, including Adventure, Aeronautics and Outer Space, Animal Life and Adventure, Biography, Careers, Community Problems, Family Life and Problems, Folk Tales and Myths, Girls' Stories, Health and Safety, and History and Geography. Some of these categories are broken down into smaller units, e.g., Adventure: Historical, Personal, Stories; Community Problems: Regional, Rural, Suburban, Urban. In comparing the subject categories with those in the 1966 edition, the following substitutions and additions were noted: Aeronautics (formerly under Aviation); Outer Space (new entry with Aeronautics); Community Problems (formerly under Family and Community Life); Family Life and Problems (now a separate entry); War Stories; Minorities; Nationwide Problems (all new entries); Mystery and Suspense (replaces former heading Mystery Stories); Science (secondary headings changed—Anthropology and Archaeology replaces Prehistoric World, and Ecology and Pollution, Electronics and Computers, Nature, Oceanography have been added).

In checking titles under broad subject categories, it is evident that the authors have covered current and traditional interests of adolescents such as archaeology, auto racing, bikes, boxing, civil rights, crime, delinquency, detective stories, drugs, macrame, marriage, motorcycles, the occult, pollution, race relations, and war.

Following the general listings of titles within subject categories are annotated Reading Texts and Workbooks, Books in Series, Magazines and Newspapers, and Simplified Dictionaries.

Bibliographic information on each title is complete, with paperback editions noted. Prices are not included because of their rapidity of change.

The titles in the bibliography were selected with "the idea that a book should be highly interesting to adolescents, should keep them reading through the sheer pull of its intrinsic interest, and should give them the feeling that reading is rewarding." Only books below the tenth-grade level of difficulty were included. In the Introduction the authors discuss standards they employed for judging content, style, and physical make-up of titles.

The annotations are brief but offer enough information to indicate the nature of the books and to identify themes that should appeal to the reluctant reader. While these are designed for the teacher or librarian, they can also stimulate the student.

Generally the procedures used in building this bibliography were: examination of bibliographies compiled for reluctant and retarded readers of adolescent age, observation of reluctant and retarded readers in clinics and classrooms, in-depth reading of new materials for this age level, and reexamination of titles in the last edition.

The authors state that estimates of reading difficulty are based on averages of formulas and on expert opinion. The estimated grade level is indicated after each title. The majority of books included are of fifth- and sixth-grade level of difficulty. The authors point out that the single indication of grade difficulty "should be considered as a central tendency having a possible range of difficulty above and below the level indicated." The authors stress the need to use this list with flexibility. Suggestions are offered, but "the teacher must find out what his own pupils *can read, are reading,* and *should read.*"

Near the end of the volume is a Directory of Publishers and Distributors. Following this are Author, Title, and Reading Difficulty Indexes.

The volume is sturdily bound in buff cloth. The pages lie flat when the book is opened. The print is clear, and the arrangement is easy to follow.

Like its predecessors, this edition of *Gateways to Readable Books* should prove very useful to teachers and librarians in selecting materials for reluctant readers, grades 7 to 12. It is recommended. *(Oct. 1, 1976, p.274)*

028.52 Slow learning children, Books for [CIP] 75-12933

Gemstones of North America.
By John Sinkankas. New York, Van Nostrand Reinhold, [c1959, 1976]. 2v. illus. (part col.) chart. diagrs. 24cm. cloth v.I $27.50; v.II $30; to schools and libraries, 20 percent discount.

Volume I of *Gemstones of North America* was published in 1959 without volume designation; volume II is very similar in format and its title page reads "In Two Volumes."

John Sinkankas is a member of the American Gem Society and a Fellow of the Mineralogical Society of America. He has written books and articles on mineralogy and gemmology, including *Gem Cutting: a Lapidary's Manual* (2d ed., 1962) and *Prospecting for Gemstones and Minerals* (New York: Van Nostrand Reinhold, 1970).

The author intends to provide geological and mineralogical information along with a history of mining for collectors, gemmologists, geologists and mineralogists, miners, and students. While volume I provides the basic scientific description of each stone, both volumes are largely devoted to detailed description of localities, deposits, and mining activities in various regions and states arranged under each gemstone. The quality of the gemstones is discussed and price data are provided. There are often photographs of the region.

Chapter I, volume I, "The Properties of Gemstones," is a 24-page definition with six diagrams describing the qualities of organic gemstones, rocks, minerals, and crystals, the geometry of crystals, crystal growth, cleavage, specific gravity, the effect of light upon gems, dispersion, color in gems, and special optical effects. The other chapter headings in both volumes (v.I, chapters 2–7; v.II, chapters 1–6) are identical: "Principal Gemstones," "Important Gemstones," "Quartz Family Gemstones," "Rare and Unusual Gemstones," "Massive and Decorative Gemstones," and "Organic Gemstones." The content, however, is not duplicated: the second volume consists "almost entirely of new material," providing information on re-exploited older deposits discussed in volume I and on gemstone sources discovered since 1959 as well as data from recent mineralogical analyses.

The gemstones discussed in volume I appear in the second volume only if new information is available. New gemstones have been added: prosopite under "Important Gemstones;" anatase, tugtupite, hemimorphite, and legandite under "Rare and Unusual Gemstones"; but while 23 of the 49 gemstones in volume I are not listed, basalt breccia, hypersthene gabbro, hematite, serandite, nepheline syenite, rodingite, copper in basalt, dolomite, mariposite, meerschaum, and bauxite are listed under "Massive and Decorative Gemstones." Thirteen of the thirty-four gemstones listed in volume I are omitted in volume II. Pearls and shell under "Organic Gemstones" becomes saltwater pearls and shell and freshwater pearls and shell, and ivory is added.

The sections on turquoise exemplify the differences and relationships between the two volumes. Volume I (p.207–28) describes the gem and its uses in comparison with other gemstones, gives a brief history, notes its chemical properties and natural formations (with photograph), its crystal structure, and provides advice on lapidary care. Under "Localities" there is a description of mines or workings in eight states, Baja California, Sonora, and Zacatecas in Mexico. In volume II (p.119–43) there is a section on the "unprecedented demand for turquois in the last decade," a table of "Turquois Retail Prices, Rough, Summer 1974," giving locations, mines, and other details. There is a page and a half of "Mineralogical Notes" augmenting the information in volume one. A table of "Property Comparisons: Turquois —Variscite" is provided as the demand for turquoise has stimulated the mining of variscite, which may be used as a substitute in jewelry. The description of localities and mines in volume I covers 15 pages, 20 pages in volume II.

Both volumes are extensively illustrated with photographs, diagrams, and maps: 178 (eight in color) in volume one; 126 (16 in color) in volume two. There are also many unnumbered tables. Three appendixes appear only in volume I: an 18-page "Glossary," including precise definitions, without amplification, of scientific terms (e.g., *anhydrous*—lacking water of crystalization) and many words from the Spanish used in mining areas (e.g., *agua, arroyo, hacienda, loma, mesa*); a "Tabular Review of Gemstone Deposits," which describes the rock classes and types of gemstones found in each; and "Notes on Collections and Collecting," a brief introductory statement.

In each volume is a "Geographical and Locality Index" to the volume. Greenland, Canada, U.S. (including Alaska), Mexico, Central America, and the West Indies are covered. Specific locations and associated gemstones are listed under each region along with text page references. Each volume has its own General Index (not cumulated in volume II). In volume I there are some *see* and *see also* references; in both volumes there are plentiful bibliographical citations within the entries. Indexes to both volumes must be used for complete analysis.

The 207-item Bibliography in volume I is superseded by a 2,661-item Bibliography in volume II. Both monographs and journal articles (mainly in English with a few in German and Spanish) are cited. The bibliography is arranged alphabetically by author, with a Geographic and Gemstone Index divided thus: General and Regional Works; Guidebooks, Topographical Mineralogies, Catalogs; Historical locations (further subdivided by region, state, province, etc.); Individual Gemstones (further subdivided by stone and with cross-references provided). The Bibliography indexing is not repeated in the general Index.

Preceding the Bibliography is a 13-page critical bibliographical essay, "A Brief History of North American Gemological Literature," which describes the earliest accounts of gemstones, the first catalogs of minerals and mining localities, and the growth of the literature, including journals and regional guides.

Both volumes are sturdily bound, open readily to lie flat, have ample margins, and have clear, large type. The work is not intended as a substitute for collector's guides which provide more detailed information. A comparison with the fifth revised edition of *Gem Hunter's Guide* (New York: Crowell, 1975) and J. E. Ransem's *Gems and Minerals of America* (New York: Harper, 1974), both reviewed in *Reference and Subscription Books Reviews* Feb. 1, 1976, shows their quite different approach.

Gemstones of North America is recommended for libraries having mineralogy and geology collections and also to those serving prospectors or rock hounds. It is a scholarly and thorough introduction to the nature of gemstone deposits in North America. *(May 15, 1977, p.1446)*

553'.8 Precious stones—North America [CIP]   59-13853

Geography and cartography, a reference handbook.
[By] C. B. Muriel Lock. 3d ed. rev. and enl. London, Clive Bingley; Hamden, Conn., Linnet Books, [c1976]. 762p. 22cm. cloth $32.50.

Geography and Cartography, a Reference Handbook is a combined and revised edition of two earlier works written by Clara Beatrice Muriel Lock—*Geography and Cartography: A Reference Handbook* (1st ed. London: Clive Bingley; Hamden, Conn.: Linnet Books, 1968; 2d ed. 1972) and *Modern Maps and Atlases* (London: Clive Bingley; Hamden, Conn.: Archon Books, 1969). In addition to these titles, Dr. Lock is the author of *Reference Materials for Young People* (Hamden, Conn.: Archon Books, 1967; 2d ed. 1970), a Fellow of the Royal Geographical Society, cofounder of *Library Science Abstracts,* and former lecturer in bibliography and general librarianship at the Birmingham School of Librarianship.

In the Foreword, Lock states: "This handbook had its origin in the belief that a quick reference book covering some of the main focal points of geographical study would be useful to both geographers and librarians. It has not been the intention to maintain a balanced coverage either regionally or thematically ... but to draw attention to the outstanding scholars ... and to some of the organizations and sources of the greatest continuing significance."

This volume is a minor revision of the second edition of *Geography and Cartography* and includes excerpts from *Modern Maps and Atlases.* Its 1,393 numbered entries are arranged in alphabetical order, primarily by title for monographs, atlases, serials, and projects or by names of individuals or institutions. Entries range from a few lines to many pages and treat a wide range of geographical/cartographical material, such as significant books, atlases, maps or periodicals; eminent geographers/cartographers (deceased); trade, industrial, and professional organizations; and the history of cartography and exploration. The book does not include geographical/cartographical terms which can be found in appropriate dictionaries. The entries have primarily descriptive, nonanalytical annotations.

Geography and Cartography is the only reference handbook for the disciplines of cartography and geography and is useful for locating information on institutions, publications, projects, and, especially, deceased geographers/cartographers. As stated in the Foreword to the first edition, the scope and coverage are by no means comprehensive or balanced, and there is an acknowledged emphasis on the United Kingdom. Many entries include a Bibliography of works related to the subject of the entry or works written by the biographee. There are both *see* references and cross-references (q.v.) to other subjects which are entries. There is an accurate and detailed subject, author, and title index. The alphabetical arrangement precludes the necessity for a table of contents. The type is clear; margins are adequate for rebinding, and the volume lies flat when open. The volume is sturdily bound and should hold up well under normal reference use.

This handbook is easy to use and makes available in a single volume a variety of information regarding geography and cartography. The material covers the period from the fifth century B.C. to the early 1970s, though emphasis is placed on the nineteenth and twentieth centuries. Approximately 50 percent of the entries relate specifically to the United Kingdom or Commonwealth nations with the remainder covering all regions of the world, though Europe and North America alone account for another 30 percent of the coverage. There are entries for R. A. Skelton, the eminent cartographer; *Bibliographie geographique internationale; American Geographical Society; Istituto Geografico de Agostini; International Map of the World* series; Wright and Platt, *Aids to Geographical Resarch; Directorate of Overseas Surveys;* the geographer Ellen Churchill Semple; Chauncy Harris, *International List of Geographical Serials;* and the *International Geophysical Year.* The entries, especially those for individuals, older atlases/monographs, and general entries which require little revision to maintain accuracy, are satisfactory. Unfortunately, some entries have not been revised, and many are for topics which some would not consider of the "greatest continuing significance."

The 1972 edition of *Geography and Cartography* contained 1,283 entries. The new edition includes 1,393 entries, an increase of 9 percent. Approximately 35 percent of the entries from the 1972 edition remain unchanged in the 1976 edition; 50 percent underwent minor (usually stylistic) changes; 5 percent were deleted; and only 10 percent were extensively revised, and for some of these, the revision consisted of merely increasing the size of the Bibliography (and not substantially altering the text). Consequently, 12 percent of the entries are new to this edition.

A List of eight Extended Entries precedes the body of the book: Atlases; Audiovisual Aids; Bibliographies, National; Classification; Education in Geography and Cartography; Globes; Map Librarianship; and Maps. Coverage of these subjects varies in length from three to twenty-nine pages. The entry for *Map Librarianship* is chapter five of the author's *Modern Maps and Atlases* with the addition of some cross-references and an expanded Bibliography. The Classification entry is also taken from *Modern Maps and Atlases.* Interestingly, the list does not contain "Cartography," a 39-page entry excerpted from *Modern Maps and Atlases;* nor does it include the entry "Ordnance Survey." Another lengthy entry, *Bibliographies, National,* is badly outdated (see below), and it is difficult to believe it was specially written for this volume.

There are basically two problems with *Geography and Cartography:* balance and currency. Even though Lock states that it was not her intent to provide balanced coverage, the lack of balance and the related question of what is included and what is omitted are important considerations. There are many entries which probably do not belong in a handbook on geography and cartography. For example, *Lancashire Textile Industry* (book); *Far East Trade and Development* (periodical); *Soil Biology and Biochemistry* (periodical); *Annotated Bibliography of Afghanistan; International Wool Secretariat; Preliminary Bibliography of the Natural History of Iran; Colombo Plan; Der Welt des Islams* (periodical); *Institution of the Rubber Industry; Dictionary of Rubber Technology;* and *Encyclopedia of Latin American History.* Other entries, such as regional and national bibliographies and encyclopedias, are only remotely related to geography and cartography. Perhaps, instead of including titles such as the *Encyclopedia of Latin American History,* it would have been more pertinent to have entries for serials such as the *Revista geografica* or the *Boletin* of the Sociedad Mexicana de Geografia y Estadistica. Likewise, instead of having an entry for a general list such as *Theses on Asia,* why not include Sukhawal, *Bibliography of Theses and Dissertations in Geography on South Asia* (Council of Planning Librarians, 1973)? A number of Festschriften are included, but the only major index to the contents of geographical Festschriften Schwickerath and Schmidt's *Inhaltverzeichnis der Festschriften zur Ehrung und Wurdigung deutscher österreichischer und schweizer Geographen sowie der Festschriften zu Jubilaen geographischer Gesellschaften Deutschlands, Österreichs und der Schweiz* is omitted.

There are no entries for the following significant topics or titles: Winch, *International Maps and Atlases in Print; Index to Maps in Books and Periodicals; Geographical Bibliography for American College Libraries;* Alexander, *Guide to Atlases; Lexikon geographischer Bildbände;* Army Map Service; Defense Mapping Agency; LC's *Bibliography of Cartography;* Schmidt and Streuman, *Verzeichnis der geographischen Zeitschriften, periodischen Veröffentlichungen und Schriftenreihen Deutschlands;* Eckert, *Die Kartenwissenschaft: Forschung und Grundlagen zu einer Kartographie als Wissenschaft;* and the Herman Dunlop Smith Center for the History of Cartography. Moreover, there is an entry for the Oxford University Exploration Club but not for the Explorers Club of New York. There is an entry for the *Atlas over Sverige* but not for the *Atlas over Danmark.* The *Gazetteer of the Persian Gulf, Oman and Central Asia* is included but not the *Gazetteer of Canada* series. Similarly, the *Pergamon General Historical Atlas* is listed but not Shepherd's *Historical Atlas.* Though Debenham's *Discovery and Exploration* is listed, more recent general atlas-histories of exploration are not. There are no entries for Powell, King, Hayden, or Wheeler, outstanding American explorers of the nineteenth century.

With respect to currency, most of the entries have remained relatively unchanged since the publication of Lock's two earlier works. *Geography and Cartography* contains numerous entries which are outdated. For example, there is an entry for the *U.S. Coast and Geodetic Survey* (which was abolished in 1970) but no entry for its successor, the National Oceanic and Atmospheric Administration, which includes the National Ocean Survey, an important source of nautical and aeronautical charts. For the U.S. Geological Survey, Lock lists the *Monograph* series of the U.S. Geographical Survey as still being active; the last *Monograph* was number 55 published in 1929. Lock also includes an entry for the *Polar Bibliography,* citing it as an ongoing series despite the fact that the last issue appeared in 1959. No mention is made of two more detailed and comprehensive bibliographic series issued by the U.S. government relating to the literature of the arctic regions. These are only a few illustrations of the inadequate revision.

The following are further examples of entries which contain outdated information: *Geo Abstracts; Handbook of Latin American Studies; Antarctic Bibliography; Arctic Bibliography; Bibliography of Agriculture; Bibliotheca Cartographica; National Atlas of Canada; Goode's World Atlas;* and the *Times Atlas of the World.* The lengthy essay on *Map Librarianship* omits the important 1973 issue of the *Drexel Library Quarterly,* Roman Drazniowsky's *Map Librarianship* (Metuchen, N.J.: Scarecrow, 1974), and the most complete bibliography on the subject. It also fails to note the Western Association of Map Libraries and its valuable *Information Bulletin.*

The lengthy entry, *Bibliographies, National,* is arranged by regions and then by individual nations. An examination of the short section for the U.S. clearly demonstrates the lack of currency. The last *National Union Catalog* cited is the 1958–62 cumulation. There is no mention of the 1963–67 and 1968–72 cumulations, nor the *Pre-1956 Imprints* series. There is a reference to *United States Research Reports;* this title changed in 1965 and again in 1971. Lock does not trace *Dissertation Abstracts* past 1969 when its title changed to *Dissertation Abstracts International.* Lock describes as still extant a series being issued by the General Land Office. The latter agency was abolished in 1946. There is no mention of numerous geographical/cartographical publications from the Library of Congress, National Archives, or other government agencies. An examination of the sections for the United Kingdom, Ghana, and Sri Lanka (identified by Lock as Ceylon) revealed many major omissions. For example, the British Museum's *General Catalogue of Printed Books;* the 1962 supplement to Pitcher, *Bibliography of Ghana;* and the *Statement of Books Printed in Ceylon* (1885–1939) are omitted.

Although *Geography and Cartography* is the only handbook of its kind, its haphazard policy of inclusion and outdatedness make it a flawed reference tool. Libraries owning the 1972 edition need not purchase this new edition. Recommended only for libraries with extensive geographical and cartographical collections. *(Mar. 15, 1977, p.1116)*

910'.3   Geography—Dictionaries || Cartography   [CIP]   76-8273

Germany:
a chronology and fact book, 1415–1972. Compiled and edited by Robert Vexler. Dobbs Ferry, N.Y., Oceana Publications, 1973. 184p. 24cm. cloth $7.50.
943   Germany—History—Chronology || Germany—History—Sources || Germany—History—Bibliography   [CIP]   73-7792

See page 88

Gypsies and nomads.
†301.451'042   Nomads—Juvenile literature || Gypsies—Juvenile literature   [OCLC]   75-20500

See page 50

A handbook of American minorities.
[Comp. by] Wayne Charles Miller. New York, New York Univ., 1976. xi, 225p. 29cm. $15.
016.30145'0973   Minorities—U.S.—Bibliography   [OCLC]   74-21636

A comprehensive bibliography for the study of American minorities.
[Comp. by] Wayne Charles Miller. 2v. New York, New York Univ., 1976. xix, 1380p. 29cm. $95.
016.30145'0973   Minorities—U.S.—Bibliography   [OCLC]   74-21636

A Handbook of American Minorities consists of 39 essays "designed to provide basic historical overviews of many American minorities and to provide bibliographical introductions to some of the most useful sources for the study of them." It is intended as a guide for the beginning student, and it also affords a comparative approach for the person possessing "some expertise in one minority." No claim is made that the work is exhaustive. For further bibliographic materials, the student is advised to consult *A Comprehensive Bibliography for the Study of American Minorities,* the other work reviewed here.

Wayne Charles Miller received a doctorate in English from New York University in 1968. Since 1970 he has been professor of English at the University of Cincinnati. Literature of the minorities is his chief field of research. Several fellowships and research grants enabled him to pursue this study over a five-year period. Included among his published works is *A Gathering of Ghetto Writers,* an anthology which opens with a long critical analysis of minority authors' accomplishments.

In the handbook Miller was assisted by ten contributors, six of whom are credited with seven specific essays. None of these persons could be located in standard biographical sources. One cannot be precise concerning their qualifications. Credit is also given to graduate students at the University of Cincinnati for their work on this project. Since the introductory material is meager and the essays are not signed, and because no notes support the text, the absence of scholarly credentials is regrettable. The Committee assumes that responsibility for the accuracy of the text and the validity of value judgments rests with Wayne Miller.

The material is organized by geographic area of origin. The first two groups are Afro-Americans and Arab-Americans. Twelve groups of Western European origin include French, German, Spanish, Irish, Italian, Jewish, Greek, and the various Scandinavian emigrants. Sixteen other groups represent Eastern Europe including the Balkans; some of these are of Slavic, Polish, Czech, Slovak, Yugoslav, Slovenian, and Croatian extraction. Representing Asia are Chinese, Japanese, and Filipino-Americans; from the West Indies the Puerto Rican and Cuban Americans, but nothing concerning other West Indian people such as Jamaicans, Haitians, Barbadians, and Virgin Islanders. Finally, there are the American Indians and the Mexican Americans. No definition of the term "minority" is given. It is not clear why the German, Italian, and Irish are included, while the Welsh, Dutch, and Scots are not.

The essays vary in length. A long article covers the black-American experience. Opening with a fairly extensive historical narrative that begins with the earliest explorers and concludes with the followers of Martin Luther King Jr. and Jesse Jackson, the account concludes with the following subdivisions: Bibliographies; Encyclopedias, Handbooks and Guides to Collections; Journals and Periodicals; Biographies and Autobiographies; History and Sociology; Folklore; Music; Slave Narratives; Poetry; Fiction; and Drama. Within each of these sections, the reference material is woven into well-written, informative paragraphs. The bibliographic essay dealing with the black American is the only one that is subdivided in this detail.

For certain minorities, material is limited to a few references. For example, the account of the Albanian-American experience contains only two short paragraphs with three sources cited. The essay concludes thus: "The Albanian-American experience is one that invites serious study." Similar recommendations accompany the Slovenian, the Croatian, the Serbian, and the Latvian articles, which are also brief. Most of the essays fall somewhere between these two extremes, perhaps six to eight pages of text containing 75 to 100 sources.

The handbook is of very broad scope. There are references to historical, statistical, and fictional works. Periodicals and newspapers are cited, as are music, art, and drama sources. Although the Preface does not incorporate a statement about foreign-language sources, an examination of the book indicates that only English-language items are represented. Many references are to recent material: about half of the sources have been published within the last 15 years. Often the works are evaluated.

The handbook is easy to read; it is written in a fresh and thought-provoking style.

The book is bound in blue cloth with gold lettering on the spine. The two-column page, printed on quality stock, is fairly legible. Since the volume is relatively slim with its 225 sewn pages, it is not likely that rebinding would be required.

A Comprehensive Bibliography for the Study of American Minorities is the parent work from which the *Handbook of American Minorities* was derived. Each historical-bibliographical essay appears verbatim in the two works. However, added to each essay are a great many enumerative lists of bibliographic references, many of them annotated. The essays average between 30 and 40 pages in length. The bibliography contains 29,300 entries, and the claim that "it does represent the most comprehensive bibliographical coverage of American minorities extant, and includes references to more specialized bibliographies for every minority group and for every discipline in which they are available" appears to be reasonable. Selection has been made with the aim of facilitating research students. Monographs and other full-length studies are listed for those minority groups about which much has been written; if little has been written, articles and pamphlets have been cited.

The bibliography devotes 20 percent of its space to black-American materials. Extensive coverage, about 10 percent, is also given to American Indians. American Jews and Mexican-Americans follow in order of emphasis. Slightly less attention is given the Irish, Italian, and Spanish-American. The remaining 31 groups receive minimal representation because source material in the English language is limited.

Materials are classified thus: Bibliographies, Guides to Collections, Periodicals, History, Sociology, Politics, Education, Religion, Biography and Autobiography, Language, Literary History and Criticism, Fiction and Dialect Writings, Poetry and Drama, Music, and the Plastic Arts. Entries are arranged alphabetically by author in each classification. Author, title, place, publisher, date, and frequently a brief annotation are given. Price is not listed. Annotations are descriptive and specific for fiction, as illustrated by these novels of French-Americans:

Allen, Hervey. *Anthony Adverse.* New York; Farrar & Rhinehart, 1933. Tale of fortunes and gambling, set in New Orleans Creole Society.

Kerouac, Jack. *Doctor Sax.* New York, Grove, 1959. An account of a French-American adolescence by the high priest of the "Beat Generation."

Sixteen pages of general bibliography follow the specific bibliographies. Fourteen pages of citations appear under the general heading Multi-Group Studies, and two pages are captioned Selective List of General Sources. Since the entire work is bibliographic, these listings are of only slight interest.

There are two indexes, an Author Index and a Title Index. Both are thorough; each runs about 200 pages and includes roughly 20,000 listings. The Committee found no errors in indexing.

A Comprehensive Bibliography for the Study of American Minorities promises to be very valuable to students, scholars, writers, and researchers for some time. No other currently available work covers exactly the same material. In view of the modest price of the *Handbook,* it is likely that college libraries and medium-sized public libraries will want to acquire it. The *Comprehensive Bibliography* two-volume work, however, may be a justifiable purchase only for large public libraries and university libraries. Both works are recommended.

(July 1, 1977, p.1667)

Handy key to your "National Geographics": subject and picture locater, 1915–December 1975. Charles S. Underhill, compiler. 12th ed., Charles S. Underhill, Box 127, East Aurora, New York, 1976. 59p. 9cm. paperbound $3.50; two or more copies $3 each.

This paperbound booklet is a key, rather than an index, to all the issues of the *National Geographic* published from 1915 to December 1975. Charles S. Underhill, its compiler, states that it is "cumulated and issued every two years in a complete revision to enable librarians, teachers, and others to locate in a single alphabetical listing all the incomparable educational and pictorial wealth in the 'National Geographic Magazine.'"

As should be expected for a geographical magazine, a majority of the broad subject entries are countries (42 percent), islands (10 percent), and geographic regions (4 percent). The second most numerous type of entry is the general topic (33 percent), such as agriculture, architecture, arts and crafts, history, science. The remaining entries are for individual and tribe names (8 percent) and miscellaneous topics (3 percent).

See references are abundant, constituting about 30 percent of the total entries.

There are separate entries for Walter Disney, Frances Drake, Elsie May Bell Grosvenor and Gilbert Hovey Grosvenor, Elizabeth II, and six U.S. presidents. Other U.S. presidents and Elizabeth I are listed under *U.S. History* and *England—History.* Some cities are listed alphabetically under the heading *Cities,* while others are represented under headings for countries. This arrangement is arbitrary and inconvenient. For example, U.S., English, French, and many European or African cities appear under *Cities,* while Chinese, Russian, and German cities are referred to under headings for these three countries. Islands are assigned individual headings, except for Indonesia, the Pacific Islands, and West Indies.

Location of specific information listed only under a broad heading is made accessible by alphabetic subdivisions. For example, *Agriculture* has four major subdivisions: crops, methods, livestock, and historical. *Crops* is further subdivided by the names of individual crops arranged alphabetically. This approach is not as convenient as the straightforward listing of specific subjects as main entries. Nevertheless, the *Key* is not difficult to master if the user first reads the Foreword and Explanation. Further, the broad subject headings often bring the constituent elements of a large subject together for easy consideration.

Headings may include one listing (*Abraham; Germany, East*) or hundreds of listings (*Fish, Crustacea and Other Marine Life; Industry; Physical Geography*). The arrangement of citations under headings and subheadings may be geographical (*Indians, No. American*), chronological (*U.S. History*), or typological (*Aviation, Birds*). Under *Aviation,* one finds separate subdivisions for *Heavier than Air, Gliders, Lighter than Air;* and under *Birds,* there are groupings under *Tropical, Temperate, Water Birds, Birds of Prey,* and so on. Therefore, related subjects are usually found in close proximity.

"Under each heading priority is given to the most general and of these to the best illustrated and most recent. Following the general articles are those on more limited areas or aspects of the entry topic, qualified by a word or two." For each entry, the month and year (e.g., S60) are given. Titles, authors, and paging are omitted, but usually an explanatory phrase is given. For example, the first entry under Japan is "Mr74 modern, industrialized, overcrowded city life." If there are noteworthy features, such as maps, paintings, drawings, or foldouts, these are indicated by "map," "pn," "drg," "fdt map and pics." Feature articles are marked "f" or "feat." A key to these abbreviations is given on page [2].

The two-column format facilitates quick scanning. Main entries and *see* references are in boldface capital letters. Entries referred to in the *see* and *see also* references and major subdivision headings are in lightface capital letters and are relatively easy to locate. Citations are separated by semicolons, with the month and year, which always precede any descriptive material, serving as dividers.

While a random check of issues of the magazine indicated that a few articles are not listed under logical headings, *The Handy Key to Your "National Geographics"* lives up to its name. The main disadvantage of the *Key* is its idiosyncratic indexing. This fault is more than counterbalanced by its arrangement of articles in descending order of importance and its indication of articles' special features such as foldouts, use of high-speed photography, inclusion of paintings, maps, and drawings. Libraries subscribing to the *National Geographic* will find this a useful acquisition. Recommended. *(Mar. 1, 1977, p.1036)*

910.5 Pictures—Indexes [CIP] 56-1375

Health and disease.
†613 Hygiene—Juvenile literature ‖ Medicine—Juvenile literature [OCLC] 75-20516
See page 50

Horses and ponies.
†636.1 Horses—Juvenile literature [OCLC] 75-19990
See page 50

Illustrated dictionary of place names, United States and Canada.
Edited by Kelsie B. Harder. New York, Van Nostrand Reinhold Co., [1976]. xiv, 631p. illus. 23cm. cloth $18.95.

Kelsie B. Harder, editor of the *Illustrated Dictionary of Place Names, United States and Canada,* chairs the English department of the State University of New York at Potsdam, and is also executive secretary of the American Name Society and former editor of its journal *Names.* The publisher notes that he was "instrumental in initiating the Place-Name Survey of the U.S. and helped establish five regional institutes to promulgate the study of names in the U.S. and Canada."

The dictionary lists over 15,000 U.S. and Canadian places: villages, towns, cities, counties, states, and provinces, also parks, historic sites, and major land and coastal features—bays, capes, gulfs, islands, lakes, rivers, forests, mountains, and valleys. For Canada only major places and features are listed.

Entries are alphabetical, letter by letter. There are *see also* references, both in specific instances and under headings such as *Cape* and *East.*

Main entries are for place-names with explanations given for their origins. Immediately following these are the places bearing the same name. For example, *Fayette* is explained as "American shortened version of the name (sometimes spelled La Fayette) of the Marquis de Lafayette." Under this are eleven Fayette counties, five Fayette cities, and six Fayettevilles. The county seat is given for each county; for each city, the county in which it is located is given and if it is the county seat, this fact is mentioned. Another example is *Cleveland* which has five main entries, for five different persons named Cleveland, and lists a total of thirteen different geographic entities. Other names derive from Indian names or descriptors, resemblances, fruits, trees, and animals found at the spot.

Main entries are easily identified by heavy black uppercase letters well separated from the preceding text. Additional entries are in italics under the main description, and any further commentary is indented. There are two columns to a page, and the type is clear and very easy to read on creamy-colored paper. The volume lies flat when opened and seems quite sturdy. However, inner margins are very narrow and rebinding would be a problem should it become necessary.

Approximately a third of the pages contain handsome black-and-white illustrations representing a variety of media culled from several different sources. The majority are from the New York Public Library. They range in size from less than a quarter of a page to a full page; most are either quarter or half page. Almost all are on the same page or adjacent pages to the names being illustrated.

The illustrations range from portraits of persons to photographs of a 1932 automobile assembly line for Detroit, the Indianapolis "500" Race, two Liberty Loan posters of World War I vintage near the entry for Liberty, a steamboat in a Cajun bayou for Louisiana, a photograph of an iron mine in the Mesabi Range, and a lithograph drawing of Oklahoma City ten months after its first home was built.

While the illustrations do not aid in the definition of the names and are not vital to the dictionary, they provide visual stimulation, and in many cases bring out unusual attributes of places.

Harder includes Acknowledgements, a four-and-one-half page Introduction which deals with the nature of naming and describes the dictionary as being "intended for the generalist and for those who wish a ready reference to a place and a name, especially as to its location and origin." A one-page Style Note describes the entries, and a four-and-one-half page Bibliography completes the volume.

There are several books comparable to the one under review. Alfred H. Holt's *American Place Names* (Crowell, 1938, reprinted by Gale, 1969) bears a similar title, but *Holt* is concerned with pronunciation only, not with definitions.

Most like the Harder dictionary is George R. Stewart's *American Place Names* (Oxford, 1970). In his Acknowledgements Harder says that Stewart's earlier *Names on the Land* (Houghton-Mifflin, rev. and enl., 1958) provided his first inspiration to study names, and that "Professor Stewart's pervasive influence can be seen throughout this dictionary as it can be seen throughout any modern dictionary of place names."

Stewart's book is limited to the continental U.S. while *Harder* includes also both Hawaii and Canada. *Stewart* has about 12,000 entries; *Harder* has 15,000. Each dictionary contains many names not found in the other. In most cases where the same names are found, definitions agree although their lengths vary. *Harder* tends to be more informal and chatty.

Only one outright error was identified—Harder states that *Lake Erie* is the "largest of the Great Lakes." He later corrects himself by referring to *Lake Superior* as the "largest and farthest north of the Great Lakes." This is a minor failing when considered in the context of the volume's many riches.

The *Illustrated Dictionary of Place Names, United States and Canada* is recommended as an additional source for the derivation of place-names for all types of libraries and also for home use where its illustrations will provide moments of pleasant browsing. *(Dec. 15, 1976, p.627)*

917.3'003   Names, Geographical—U.S. || U.S.—History, Local   [CIP]   75-26907

Illustrated encyclopaedia of the classical world.
[By] Michael Avi Yonah and Israel Shatzman. New York, Harper & Row, [c1975 by The Jerusalem Publishing House Ltd.]. 509p. illus. (part col.) 25cm. cloth $20.

In recent times there have been many English-language dictionaries of classical antiquities, most of which stem from the two-volume work of Sir William Smith, which first appeared in 1842. The Smith volumes have served as a model for such fine works as *Harper's Dictionary of Classical Literature and Antiquities* (1896) and the more recent (1949) *Oxford Classical Dictionary,* each of which has appeared in more than one edition.

The present work, which contains approximately 2,300 articles, follows the usual pattern of these alphabetical dictionaries, and includes place-names, proper names (up to about the end of the fourth century of our era), mythological names, and some social, historical, or literary terms, such as education, proletarii, logographers, epic poetry, sculpture, and villa. These subject terms are, however, in the minority; about 90 percent of the entries are proper names.

Entries vary from a few pages (*Festival, Rome, Sculpture*) to a few lines (*Abacus, Meddix, Syrinx*). The average is about 15 lines. Within the text all Latin or Greek words are printed in italics; Greek words, such as *kourotrophos,* are in the Roman alphabet. As a space-saving device the subject of an article is referred to in that article only by the initial letter. Thus Eurydice is referred to in the article itself as E., and elegiac poetry is referred to as EP. However, this is not carried to extremes. In the article on *Coinage, Greek,* the words coinage and coins are spelled out in full. British spelling (colour, plough, civilisation) has been used in the volume, but its incidence, because of the nature of the subject matter, is rather rare. Asterisks are employed to call attention to information about a person, place, or thing described elsewhere in the volume. Contrary to usual practice, the asterisks precede rather than follow the referenced words, e.g., "Allyates, King of Lydia . . . was succeeded by his son, *Croesus." These cross-references are quite numerous, two or three of them in even the briefest article, so that the reader is seldom if ever left to guess about some unfamiliar name or topic.

More than half of the articles, especially the shorter ones, lack bibliographies. The rest have only one or two, seldom more, titles of books appended to them. The complete titles are cited in a three-page List of Abbreviations in the front of the book, which forms a kind of single-alphabet bibliography. At the conclusion of the book, just before the Index, all items are consolidated in a three-page Select Bibliography, divided by topics—History, Literature, Philosophy, etc. Many of the works cited at the ends of articles and in the bibliographies have small superscript numbers, ranging from 2 to 7 appearing above the last word of the title. These enigmatic numbers are not explained in the Foreword or text. Place and publisher are not provided for any of the listed works.

None of the articles in the text is signed; nor is there any list of contributors. The late Michael Avi Yonah was an archaeologist who taught at the Hebrew University, Jerusalem, and Israel Shatzman also teaches at the Hebrew University. Both have written extensively on historical and archaeological subjects.

The text is attractive and legible; double-columned, using a serif type, with only eight lines to the inch for ease of reading. No errors of spelling were detected, but a paragraph with one or more missing lines of text was noted. As in the *Oxford Classical Dictionary*, there is an Index of cognate or equivalent names, terms, and subjects not used as entries, with helpful references to headings employed in the work; e.g., Antaeus—Heracles, Hellanodikai—Olypian Games, Satyricon—Petronius. In addition to the illustrations accompanying the text, the work has five pages of maps of the classical world and fifteen chronological tables (12 showing regional successions and years and 3 listing foundation dates of Greek and Roman colonies).

Some of the editorial decisions seem arbitrary. The prefatory "Notes on the Use of the Encyclopaedia" states that persons are listed by their more familiar names (e.g., Cicero rather than Tullius). But the name "Tully" was in common use in the eighteenth and nineteenth centuries, and the complete absence of any cross-reference anywhere in the book from Tully to Cicero is not helpful to someone who does not already have this knowledge. The famous Roman historian Dio Cassius is referred to as Cassius Dio, but there is no entry for him under Cassius, or any cross-reference. He is listed only under *Dio*. In what might originally have been only a typographical error, the Marcomanni are called "The People of the Marshes," instead of "The People of the March or Borderland."

Commentary on the rampant licentiousness of the classical world is muted. There is no article on prostitution, or any reference to it in places where it might be mentioned, such as under *Temple;* nor in the article on *Pompeii* is there any hint of the pornographic murals. Under the heading *Hetairoi* there is discussion only of the male "companions," soldiers who formed part of the royal bodyguard. There is no mention whatever of female hetairai, and there is no mention of Phryne, the most famous of these hetairai and the presumed model for Praxiteles' Aphrodite of Cnidus. Nor for that matter is there mention of that other "companion," Thais, who sat beside Alexander, in Dryden's poem, and "fired another Troy."

There are approximately 300 mostly black-and-white illustrations scattered throughout the book, many of them full page. The 33 colorplates are arranged in groups of two or four at a time, printed on both sides of the page and, though they give the appearance of having been tipped in, they are part of the continuous pagination and are firmly sewn into the spine. They are mostly photographs of paintings, murals, statues, and an occasional outdoor scene and are therefore similar to the black-and-white illustrations which likewise reproduce vases, mosaics, statues, temples, villas, and other aspects of classical life and art. The quality of reproduction is uniformly good, the colorplates are printed on a semigloss surface which is easy to use or to study.

The placement of black-and-white pictures is generally in close proximity to pertinent articles, but most of the colorplates are not as conveniently located. For example, the articles on *Armies, Greek* and *Armies, Roman* are interrupted by a page of colorplates showing paintings found at the Cnossos excavations of bullfighters and other persons. However, there is no article for Cnossos. Only if the reader refers to Cnossos in the Index will she or he find cross-references to Crete, Minoans, etc. Such circuitous routing should not be required in a reference tool. Conversely, there are no references in the text to related colorplates. For example, in the article on *Brygus* (an Athenian potter), on p.101, there is no mention of a full-page color illustration of his work on p.34.

Comparison of this new work with existing dictionaries or one-volume encyclopedias of the classical world is instructive. Similar to the work under review are several in-print titles, including the current reprint of the 1897 edition of *Harper's Dictionary of Classical Literature and Antiquities,* priced at $27.50, the second edition (1970) of the *Oxford Classical Dictionary* ($30), and the *Classics Illustrated Dictionary* (1974), also published by Oxford University Press, at $8.50.

Of these three, the first contains about five times as many illustrations, but they are smaller and in black and white only. *Harper's* has several other points to commend it. It gives the Greek form of all Greek words and names; it is more inclusive with more than 10,000 entries; its articles are longer and more erudite.

The second edition of the *Oxford Classical Dictionary* (1970), was favorably reviewed by the Reference and Subscription Books Review Committee on October 1, 1971. The *Oxford* lacks illustrations, but the scholarship of its approximately 300 contributors, and the extensive bibliographies at the end of almost all articles make it a favored one-volume reference work in its field. All entries are signed, and it is two-and-a-half times as large a work as the book under review, making it a good value by comparison, since it costs only one-and-a-half times as much.

Finally there is the small-sized (200 pages) *Classics Illustrated Dictionary*, a translation of the Dutch *Klassiek Vademecum,* published in 1974 by Oxford University Press, and priced at $8.50. The book is very well illustrated, in black and white only, having about one illustration per page, some of them being full page. The text is of course shorter than any of the other books being mentioned, with articles ranging from one line to about 30 lines, about an average of 8 lines.

In passing it should not be forgotten that very many of the entries in any of these classical dictionaries, and certainly all of the important ones, will be found in most adult-level, general encyclopedias.

Illustrated Encyclopaedia of the Classical World does combine some of the best features of several existing works of the same type. Its black-and-white illustrations are pertinent and useful; its colorplates, while they add to the art value of the work, fail to realize their potential reference value because of their inadequate coordination with the text. Finally, the previously noted editorial shortcomings diminish the usefulness of the *Illustrated Encyclopeadia*. Unless one puts a high premium on the colored plates, this source is not as satisfactory as the more authoritative *Oxford Classical Dictionary*. Alternatively, if one seeks only a brief, quick-reference type of answer, with an illustration in many cases, the smaller *Classics Illustrated Dictionary* would seem to be a better value.

Libraries already owning *Harper's* or the *Oxford Classical Dictionary,* as well as general adult-level encyclopedias, probably do not need this new work. The *Illustrated Encyclopaedia of the Classical World* is recommended only for libraries with a sufficient demand for information on this topic to justify addition of a supplementary resource to their shelves.

(Nov. 15, 1976, p.493)

†930.09 Classical dictionaries [OCLC]   73-14245

Index to handicrafts, model making, and workshop projects.
Compiled by Pearl Turner. 5th supplement, 1968–1973.

Westwood, Mass., F. W. Faxon Co., Inc., [1975]. 629p. 21cm. cloth, $18.

This fifth supplement to *Index to Handicrafts, Model Making, and Workshop Projects* extends the coverage of material on crafts and amateur workshop projects through 1973. Supplements, all published by F. W. Faxon Company, have appeared at approximately five-year intervals. Represented in the *Index* are books, parts of books, and periodical articles.

Eleanor C. Lovell and Ruth M. Hall compiled the original *Index* and the first two supplements. Harriet P. Turner and Amy Winslow collaborated on the third supplement covering the years 1950–1961, and E. Winifred Alt compiled the fourth supplement spanning 1962–1967. Pearl Turner, the present compiler, has recently retired as curriculum librarian at California State Polytechnic College, San Luis Obispo, and is now devoting her full attention to index construction.

As in previous volumes, an extensive Bibliography of items analyzed in the Index is included at the beginning of the volume. The Bibliography of approximately 1,000 titles published between 1968 and 1973 is arranged alphabetically by author and includes author's full name, title, publisher, and date. In this supplement grade levels of juvenile books are given for the first time, and "BIP" after an entry indicates the book is listed in the 1973 edition of *Books in Print.*

Following the Bibliography is a list of 14 periodicals also indexed in this supplement. Pearl Turner continues the policy of not including any periodical indexed in *Readers' Guide to Periodical Literature.* Five periodicals are newly represented in the supplement: *Arts and Activities, Family Circle, Family Handyman, Popular Crafts,* and *School Shop.* Still omitted are *Creative Crafts, Pack of Fun, Decorating Craft Ideas,* and *Popular Handicrafts and Hobbies,* magazines which are easily obtained at the newsstands and which contain an abundance of items not indexed elsewhere.

The index proper comprises 570 pages and is 121 pages larger than the fourth supplement of 1969.

Titles of sources are listed under alphabetically arranged subject headings. There are headings for projects, e.g., decoys, plant boxes, greeting cards; raw materials used in crafts, e.g., plaster of paris, egg boxes, postage stamps; techniques, e.g., marbling, grinding and polishing, découpage, scrimshaw; and repair of equipment and maintenance, e.g., washing machines, oscillators, milling tools, lathes, dampness in buildings, gutters (roof), and kitchens-remodeling.

An improvement over the earlier edition is the use of heavy black type to indicate the author of the book or periodical title being indexed. This makes it much easier to spot the source within each entry to which one must refer in the Bibliography for complete descriptive data. Authors and titles are not shortened, and only a few of the periodicals are abbreviated; so it is not necessary to turn very often to the Bibliography for clarification. Numerous cross-references are used, and the subject headings are the same as those used in earlier supplements or taken from the *Readers' Guide.* The high level of accuracy in the previous editions is maintained.

It is not feasible to compare subject coverage between supplements because of fluctuations in the volume of available publications in different categories during this century. The increased number of entries confirms publishers' responses to the rising interest in handicrafts. The multiple-page listings under such headings as *collage, macrame, jewelry, modeling,* and *string work* reflect recent trends. Included in this supplement are repair books and operating instructions for many types of tools and equipment like those found in industrial arts text books. Books of needlework and basic instruction in art have been excluded, but explanations of special techniques such as etching, batik, woodworking, and découpage are included. These inclusions make Turner's index more comprehensive than the Shield's *Make It* (reviewed below) which stresses projects and media rather than techniques or equipment care and repair.

The last 20 pages of the volume now include a list of all titles cited in the original *Index to Handicrafts* and the first four supplements which were in print as of 1973. Grade levels, if given in *Books in Print,* have been added in parentheses. New editions or revisions are noted as are any changes in the names of publishers. Only American and British titles are included.

Although the book is bulky, the margins are wide, and pages lie flat. Employment of contrasting type and complete author and title citations instead of abbreviations make the supplement a handy reference guide. Even so, the addition of running heads at the top of each page could further improve convenience of use. The tan buckram binding and gold lettering match the two previous supplements.

A comparison of all the books whose authors begin with *A, G, M,* and *S* which were analyzed in either *Shields* or *Turner* resulted in these findings: 21 percent of the titles were in both books; 67 percent of the *Turner* titles were not in *Shields;* and 34 percent of the *Shields* titles were not in *Turner.* Both indexes do not include titles published after 1973.

While there is some duplication, each index serves a different purpose and supplements the other. Libraries having to answer many reference questions on handicrafts, materials, and associated equipment will welcome the fifth supplement to the Faxon series, *Index to Handicrafts, Model Making, and Workshop Projects.* Recommended. *(Oct. 15, 1976, p.340)*

†016.7455   Handicraft—Bibliography || Manual training—Bibliography || Mechanical models—Bibliography || Ship models—Bibliography || Indexes   [OCLC]

Insects that feed on trees and shrubs:

an illustrated practical guide. [By] Warren T. Johnson and Howard H. Lyon, with the collaboration of C. S. Koehler, N. E. Johnson, [and] J. A. Weidhaas. Ithaca, N.Y. and London, Comstock Publishing Associates, a division of Cornell Univ. Pr. [c1976]. 464p. illus. diags. 31cm. cloth $35.

Insects That Feed on Trees and Shrubs is a reference manual covering essential information about insects, mites, and other animals associated with ornamental woody plants. In the past, efforts to investigate and control plant pests have been primarily directed to those that infest food and fiber crops, but as cities and suburbs grow, greater value is being placed on parks and greenbelts for aesthetic, ecological, and other reasons. This book, according to C. S. Koehler, who wrote its Preface, is an "attempt to add one brick to the foundation" of "urban entomology."

The book is directed to the needs of agricultural advisers, teachers, students, nurserymen, gardeners, and others who are responsible for maintaining trees and shrubs. The writers have assumed a general knowledge of ornamental plants and their common names. Their approach to entomology is pragmatic; they seek to provide assistance in the identification of insects and other animals that are or can be injurious. Over 700 of the approximately 2,500 species of insects and mites said to be destructive of ornamental plants in the U.S. are discussed, listed, or illustrated in this book.

Warren T. Johnson is a professor of entomology at Cornell University and a specialist in the biology and control of insects and diseases of ornamental woody plants. Howard Lyon is a photographer in the Department of Plant Pathology at Cornell. The Committee surmises that Johnson had primary responsibility for the text and that Lyon was responsible for the illustrations, all of which are in color. In addition the three collaborators listed on the title page have good credentials: C. S. Koehler is extension entomologist at the University of California (Berkeley) and a specialist in forest protection, bark beetles, cone insects, and adelgids; J. A. Weidhaas is entomology extension specialist at Virginia Polytechnic Institute and State University and specializes in ornamental and beneficial insects, coccinclids, and mites. N. E. Johnson is manager, Southern Forestry Research, and manager, Tropical Forestry Research at Weyerhauser Company. The particular contributions of the collaborators are not indicated.

The work is divided into two principal sections: "Insects That Feed on Conifers" and "Insects That Feed on Broad-leaved Evergreens and Deciduous Plants." Both sections have the same format: the left-hand page of each double-page spread is devoted to text and captions for the full-color composite photographic plates on the right-hand page. There is no discernible basic principle of organization within each section. Some entries represent families of insects, such as the bagworm; others deal with individual species such as the Eastern tent caterpillar; some groupings include taxonomically distinct but superficially similar species such as mealy bugs and the woolly pine scale, or other entries group together several species which share the same or similar host plants such as the cypress bark and cedar bark beetle. The Committee cites this apparent lack of formal organization not as a criticism, but merely as a note that since practical considerations have resulted in groupings that do not permit taxonomic or alphabetical organization, greater reliance must be placed upon other avenues of access. Two keys to the text and illustrations are provided: a "Reader's Aid to Identification of Insects" and an Index. The "Reader's Aid . . ." is a simple one-page summary of headings with references to related plates in the guide. Under two main categories of insects, those that feed on conifers and those that feed on broad-leaved evergreens and deciduous plants, there are references to plates showing foliage eaters, borers, sucking insects, thrips, gallmakers, mites, and miscellaneous pests other than insects such as birds, mammals, slugs, and snails.

As indicated above, the right-hand pages of the book proper are devoted to photographic plates. These 212 colorplates, containing three to eight pictures to a page, commonly exhibit such features as the manifestation of injury (sometimes with a second, close-up photo to provide detail), the pest on the host plant, cocoon or pupa of the pest, split or debarked tree revealing the ravages of the predator, insect eggs in their natural setting, scars at point of entry, and the like. If necessary, attention is called to details by arrows or encirclement of the feature in the illustration. If size has not been indicated in the text or caption and is not evident from the background, a scale line is marked alongside the pest and the size indicated in millimeters. Captions on the opposing page describe the feature being exhibited and when necessary indicate the pest and the plant usually by scientific name. Most of the captions are sufficiently specific. The plates offer exceptionally clear and realistic representations of the various pests.

In addition to the photographic plates, there is also illustrative matter incorporated into the text pages: tables showing seasonal histories of pests, labeled and unlabeled drawings of insects, black-and-white photographs of diseased or injured plants, maps showing life cycles of insects, etc. This latter material is infrequently and inconsistently presented and its inclusion is apparently determined on a case-by-case basis.

The articles on the left-hand page range in length from about one-third to nearly a full page. Information includes names of host plants; diagnostic data such as symptoms, size, appearance of the pest, and how and where it feeds; geography of infestation; life history of the pest; modes of control.

An important and intentional omission is advisory information on pesticides. Chemical pest controls are excluded because of rapid changes in technology and the importance of local conditions and experience in determining proper applications. The authors have instead provided an appended section, "Sources of Information on Pest Control," which refers readers to county extension agencies, land grant institutions and state experiment stations in the U.S., and provincial or regional agencies charged with pest control in Canada. On the other hand, information on insect parasites which are the natural enemies of pests and on bacteriological and fungal applications useful in control of injurious insects and not readily available elsewhere is included.

At the end of each article there are numerical references to items in an appended "Selected References," which lists in a numerical sequence 322 publications—books, journal articles, and leaflets issued by federal and state agencies and by museums of natural history in the U.S. and Canada. Within the articles, references are made to related matter in other articles or to plates other than those on opposing pages. The system of internal referencing is generally adequate and accurate.

A brief Glossary of about 80 terms, and two Indexes conclude the guide. An Index of Insects, Mites, and Other Animals lists plant predators by both common and scientific (Latinate) names. While there are a few omitted references for scientific names, the Index to pests generally provides satisfactory access to the contents of the work. An Index to Insects by Host Plant lists plants, generally by common name, followed by names of pests which infect or injure them. Both indexes provide cross-references from common names not used to those employed in the guide, *see-also* references to related entries, and boldface page references to biological and distribution information. The indexes are spread four columns to the page with the pest index occupying nearly four pages and the index by host plant occupying seven pages. The "Reader's Aid to Identification of Insects," referred to above, provides a partial index to the plates.

Insects That Feed on Trees and Shrubs is an attractively designed and well-made volume. The text is printed two columns to the page on coated stock of suitable opacity and lies flat when opened. Gutter margins will permit rebinding if it should be necessary.

Insects That Feed on Trees and Shrubs is a distinctive reference work generally different in scope and presentation from other manuals on plant pests. Its purpose is well-defined, and a high standard is maintained in text and illustration. While not without fault, the indexes provide adequate access to the book. *Insects That Feed on Trees and Shrubs* is recommended for those responsible for maintaining ornamental woody plants and for libraries serving such persons. *(Dec. 1, 1976, p.559)*

595.7   Plant parasites ‖ Insect–Plant relationships ‖ Insects—Food ‖ Plant diseases   [OCLC] 75-12255

The international authors and writers who's who.
Ernest Kay, editor. 7th ed., 1976. Cambridge, Melrose Pr. Ltd., 1976; distributed in U.S. by Rowman & Littlefield. xiv, 676p. 25cm. pyroxylin-impregnated cloth, $37.50.

In recent years, the International Biographical Centre at Cambridge, and its publishing arm, Melrose Press Ltd., have produced numerous contributions to the biographical reference literature. An omnibus review of such tools, published in *Reference and Subscription Books Reviews* (5/1/74), cited their *Dictionary of International Biography, Dictionary of Scandinavian Biography, International Who's Who in Poetry,* and *The World Who's Who of Women.* The book reviewed here is an international biographical directory of contemporary writers which includes novelists, poets, dramatists, editors, critics, journalists, educational authors, and script writers for radio and television. It excludes authors of "the one-off book, pamphleteers and highly technical or specialized writers." (Foreword)

The editorial director, Ernest Kay, also manages the biographical center and press. He has authored several monographs, edited numerous directories, and contributed to newspapers and magazines throughout the world. His awards include the Gold Medal of the United Poets-Laureate International and a 1973 nomination for a Nobel Prize as well as honorary degrees in literature, philosophy, and journalism.

The International Authors and Writers Who's Who has an apparent contradiction in publishing data, this volume being at the same time a seventh edition and an entirely new work. The editors explain in their Foreword that the International Biographical Centre acquired the publishing rights to the *Authors and Writers Who's Who* which had been produced in its first six editions (1934–1971) by Burke's Peerage Ltd. At the time of obtaining the publication rights, Melrose Press Ltd. was already involved in developing its own biographical directory. In fact, as noted in the Foreword to this volume, three different titles were involved: (1) *County Authors Today* which was intended to cover Scotland, Wales, and England; (2) *American Authors Today* planned to be in 50 volumes; and (3) *The World Who's Who of Authors*. *County Authors Today* was discontinued after completion of 9 volumes because of rising costs and changes in county structure, and *American Authors Today* turned out to be too complex a project. Therefore, in 1973 the International Biographical Centre began production of a volume originally entitled *The World Who's Who of Authors,* and in 1974 sent out its first questionnaires to individuals who would have been included in *American Authors Today* and *County Authors Today*. In addition, "many authors' organizations, particularly in the United States, cooperated closely and supplied us with the names of their members. Authors' agents and book publishers of many nations were also helpful." (Foreword) It was at this point that the Centre acquired the Burke's Peerage title, combined its coverage with their own, and emerged with *The International Authors and Writers Who's Who* in a seventh edition. This title is to be used for all future editions.

The International Authors and Writers Who's Who uses the same format and organization as other biographical reference tools published by the Centre. The basic information is supplied by authors through questionnaires, edited by the publisher, and verified by the included biographees. The A–Z arrangement is supplemented, in this volume, by (1) a Table of Abbreviations; (2) a brief addendum which, inexplicably, includes 31 individuals whose last names range from Aleckovic to Dupray; (3) a list of pen names of the individuals included in the biographical section with cross-references to the names under which their entries appear; and (4) a list of literary agents, arranged by country, with the majority falling under the United Kingdom and the U.S. The explanatory note included with the section on pen names indicates that some authors chose to be listed under their pen names, and when this occurred their names were omitted from the pseudonym appendix. No additional cross-references are included in the body of the work so that quick access to these authors will depend on the user's knowledge of pseudonyms and the authors' preferred listings.

Each entry is set apart from others by spacing, indention, and a capitalized surname. The entry name is followed by pen name, if used, birth date and place, a designation of position or occupation (e.g., writer, university professor of mental health, industrialist, poet, travel writer, clerk in Holy Orders), education (including institution and degree), selected monograph titles (usually with date of publication), other kinds of contributions as an author (e.g., "Contr. to num. Hungarian pubs." or "Contr. to elec. & sci. jrnls."), memberships, honors, and present address. The editors have imposed a space allocation for each entry regardless of number of publications, awards, or special contributions. Entries may be as short as 5 to 6 lines (approximately 50 words) but never exceed 15 or 16 lines (approximately 150 words). This creates some misleading impressions about the productivity or significance of an author. For instance, Isaac Asimov, who has well over 150 titles to his credit, receives no more space than many less prolific and less versatile authors. This editorial guideline was particularly noticeable when comparing *The International Authors and Writers Who's Who* to its major predecessor, the *Authors and Writers Who's Who*, 6th ed., published by Burke's Peerage Ltd. in 1971. Robert Gayre of Gayre and Nigg, Baron of Lochoreshyre, world-renowned ethnologist, is described with some 500 words and 50 lines in the 6th edition, while he has 15 lines in *The International Authors and Writers Who's Who*. On the other hand, *The International Authors and Writers Who's Who* does include over 10,000 entries which, while emphasizing United Kingdom authors, now gives comparable coverage to U.S. writers, and includes numerous literary figures from other parts of the world. This would not have been possible if some editorial limits had not been imposed. In addition, each biographee is, in submitting data, able to highlight titles and career elements which are, presumably, significant to him or her. It should also be noted that the cited publications often include items published in 1974, which indicates that the editors updated their biographical records.

Any publication which is based upon the willingness of respondents to return questionnaires will, of course, miss some names. Furthermore, the concept of international coverage is normally limited by political or communicational barriers which may restrict responses or limit recommendations. However, an examination of the list of literary agents included at the end of the volume as well as a sampling of entries indicates that the editors have succeeded in providing a basic directory of writers of the Western world. The Far East, especially China, and some African and South American nations have no or very limited representation. On the other hand, the strong coverage of the U.K. and the U.S. is such that a number of authors from these areas, especially academicians who are not usually found in more popular listings, may be located in this volume. A comparison of a sample of biographees from *The International Authors and Writers Who's Who* and the multivolumed *Contemporary Authors* revealed that the latter title provided information on two-thirds of the individuals sampled in *The International Authors and Writers Who's Who*. Of the remaining one-third, many are either in academic institutions or involved in the less formal aspects of writing such as the production of television scripts or textbooks, and are, therefore, harder to identify. Although *Contemporary Authors* provides more data about the background and interests of individuals, *The International Authors and Writers Who's Who* cites publications and current addresses. At the same time, the user must be reminded that the editor identifies few specific criteria relative to final selection of biographees, i.e., as noted earlier, pamphleteers and highly technical or specialized authors are not included.

The International Biographical Centre does not tie inclusion of an individual to purchase of the volume; it is not specifically a vanity press. However, it is also not clear whether or not any preliminary selection or later weeding occurs after a name is submitted as a candidate, and the Centre does offer a variety of purchase plans for individuals who have submitted biographies.

The International Authors and Writers Who's Who is sturdily bound and printed on opaque paper. Spacing and design are uncluttered and attractive. However, the two-columned pages are narrow with minimal margins, and include an average of 15 entries per page printed in relatively small typeface which creates eyestrain if scanned for a prolonged period of time. The thin pages tend to stick together, and users need to be careful that they do not miss or confuse any entry since there are no running heads to guide in movement from page to page.

Biographical tools constitute an important and popular segment of most library collections. In particular, knowledge of current literary figures is in common demand. Despite the obvious impossibility of providing complete coverage, *The International Authors and Writers Who's Who* is a careful revision *and expansion* of a well-received earlier title; it offers a large amount of reasonably accurate data not readily accessible to users. It is, therefore, recommended as a supplementary source for larger reference collections in public and academic libraries. For smaller collections without multivolumed sets, it might well serve as a basic source on authors and writers. *(Nov. 1, 1976, p.417)*

†928.025 Authors—Directories

International bibliography of the book trade and librarianship.
[Edited by Helga Lengenfelder and Gitta Hausen.] 11th ed., 1973–1975. New York and London, Bowker, München, Verlag Dokumentation, 1976. 704p. 22cm. cloth $49.50 plus shipping and handling.

The eleventh edition of the *International Bibliography of the Book Trade and Librarianship* is a translation of *Fachliteratur zum Buch- und Bibliothekswesen* which is volume 2 of the *Handbuch der Internationalen Dokumentation und Information* series. Helga Lengenfelder and Gitta Hausen also edited the tenth edition which covered the 1969 to 1973 period. They were assisted by Ingelore Schmid-Dankwart and Annemarie Wegner.

The bibliography includes over 9,000 monographs, most of them published from 1973 to 1975, although "supplementary material from the period 1969 to 1973 has been added." The editors state that "all publications were considered that pertain internationally to the history of books and the book trade, to topical questions of bookselling and publishing (including historically orientated works in this field), and to library and archive science." In marginally related fields such as modern printing technology, documentation and information science, only directly relevant and introductory works are included.

The material is arranged by place of publication; countries are listed alphabetically by German name within main geographical categories of Europe, Africa, the Americas, Asia, and Oceania. This practice leads to such results as Sharon E. Chapple's *Canadian Experience with MARC* (1974) being listed in the section on the Netherlands because it was published by IFLA in the Hague. Stanley Morison's *German Incunabula in the British Museum* (1975) is located under "U.S." because it was published by Hacker Art Books in New York. Each country's publications, depending on the volume of reported items, are then organized into six major categories in a classified arrangement devised by the Staatsbibliothek Bremen. The categories are: Script and Bibliology; Book Trade and Publishing; Printing and Bookbinding; Library Science; Documentation and Information; and Archives. Library Science, the largest category, has 14 subdivisions, several of which are even further divided. The book has three indexes, an Author/Editor/Compiler Index, a Subject Index (in English), and a Directory of publishers with addresses.

For each entry, author, title, subtitle, a German or English translation for titles in lesser-known languages, frequency of publication for periodicals, details concerning edition, year or volume number, place of publication, publisher, year of publication, number of pages, illustrations, details of series, ISBN or ISSN, kind of binding, price, and further details (of multivolume works) are given whenever available. The information was compiled from national and subject bibliographies, as well as publishers' catalogs and brochures.

The bibliography is in a modern type printed on opaque paper, but the ink on the reverse side shows through slightly. There are very narrow inner margins that inhibit the book from lying flat and will make rebinding difficult.

The *International Bibliography of the Book Trade and Librarianship* is unique because no other single bibliography covers the book trade and library science materials as exhaustively. Recommended for all libraries which need comprehensiveness in these areas. *(July 1, 1977, p.1668)*

†016.025   Book industries and trade—Bibliography || Library science—Bibliography   73-700

The international who's who.
40th ed., 1976–77. London, Europa Publications, Ltd., [1976]; dist. in the U.S. by Gale. 1908p. 26cm. cloth $70.

This is the fortieth annual edition of a work which began publication in 1935. *International Who's Who* was first reviewed by the Reference and Subscription Books Review Committee in *Subscription Books Bulletin,* October 1937, and most recently in *Reference and Subscription Books Reviews,* May 1, 1974.

International Who's Who, 1976–77 is a current biographical source which covers prominent individuals from all over the world in many professions. A sampling of ten pages uncovered persons of 23 different nationalities and in fields as diverse as politics, music, medicine, diplomacy, engineering, business, religion, astrophysics, law, education, biology, literature, geology, the armed forces, art, and journalism.

The team of editors responsible for the directory's compilation is not identified. Information is received by questionnaire directly from the biographees, and each edition is updated to incorporate most recently submitted data. A comparison of the 1976–77 volume with the previous year's edition revealed new names or new information in at least one entry, and frequently in many, on about 90 percent of the pages examined. Of course, not all persons return or update their listings each time, but errors found were few and minor and involved recent changes in political fortune and the like.

A complete entry can include all of the following components: name, degrees, profession, birth date and place, parents' names, name(s) of spouse and date(s) of marriage, number of children, education, list of past and present employment, honors and awards, memberships, publications, leisure interests, address, and telephone (frequently both home and business).

New biographees are added each year as persons rise into prominence; 500 names have been added this year. Other names are dropped because of death, retirement, or loss of eminence or newsworthiness. For persons whose deaths have come to the attention of the editors since the previous edition, names and dates of death are noted in a two-page, double-columned Obituary List. If the death occurred after the date page copy was set, the entry is starred. Persons who have recently retired and whose biographies have not otherwise changed, have their entries reduced to reference to the previous edition. Some names are dropped without explanation and without reference to the biography in previous editions. It is therefore necessary to check previous editions for names not found in the current volume.

In addition to the Obituary List, helpful aids include a seven-page listing of the abbreviations used in the entries and a five-page inventory of Reigning Royal Families in 25 countries including Belgium, Bhutan, Denmark, Liechtenstein, Thailand, Tonga, the United Arab Emirates, and United Kingdom.

The format is similar to that of Marquis and other Europa *Who's Who* volumes. Entries are two columns to a page; names are in boldface and stand out well. Arrangement is alphabetical, and running heads facilitate locating information. The print is small but clear, and the paper is good. The binding is sturdy and should withstand long wear; the margins are ample so that rebinding would be no problem. Despite the directory's considerable bulk, its pages lie flat to accommodate convenient use.

Information on many of the *International Who's Who* entrants is available in other biographical directories. A sampling of names showed most of the British and a sprinkling of Soviet, U.S., and Spanish names are also in *Who's Who, 1976–77;* the French names largely duplicate those in *Who's Who in France, 1975–76,* and eminent Americans are mostly covered in *Who's Who in America, 1976–77.* Middle- and Far-Eastern notable personalities can be found (usually with the same wording) in the "Who's Who" sections of *Far East and Australasia, 1975–76, Middle East and North Africa, 1975–76.* However, it would require many of these other sources, kept up to date with latest editions, to provide an equivalent breadth of coverage.

Because it consolidates in one volume vitae on many prominent persons from many different countries, *The International Who's Who, 1976–77* is recommended for all libraries whose patrons need such information. Small libraries may find it more

feasible to acquire this single title instead of a variety of separate biographical directories to cover important foreign nationals.
(June 15, 1977, p.1593)

920.1   Biography—Dictionaries   [OCLC]   35-10257

Ireland:
a chronology and fact book, 6000BC–1972. Compiled and edited by William D. Griffin. Dobbs Ferry, N.Y., Oceana Publications, 1973. 154p. 24cm. cloth $7.50.

941.5   Ireland—History—Sources || Ireland—History—Chronology   [CIP]   73-12694
See page 88

Israel:
a chronology and fact book, 2500BC–1972. Compiled and edited by Barnet Litvinoff. Dobbs Ferry, N.Y., Oceana Publications, 1974. 136p. 24cm. cloth $7.50.

956.94   Palestine—History—Chronology || Israel—History—Chronology || Zionism—History—Sources   [CIP]   73-12571
See page 88

The jungle.
†574.526'4   Jungle ecology—Juvenile literature   [OCLC]   75-19998
See page 50

Lakes and dams.
†627.8   Lakes—Juvenile literature || Dams—Juvenile literature   [OCLC]   75-20507
See page 50

A library of literary criticism:
modern Latin American literature. Compiled and edited by David William Foster and Virginia Ramos Foster. 2v. New York, Frederick Ungar Publishing Co., 1975. v.I, 539p.; v.II, 508p. 24cm. cloth $38. 20 percent discount to schools; 15 percent discount to libraries.

The first such cumulation of its kind, *Modern Latin American Literature* is intended as a reference tool for students, scholars, librarians, and researchers interested in the criticism of the writings of twentieth-century Latin American authors and poets.

The compilers are David William Foster, professor of Romance languages, Arizona State University, and Virginia Foster, professor of Spanish, Phoenix College. This husband and wife team "have written numerous articles and reviews for all the major periodicals devoted to Hispanic studies and comparative literature." Jointly, they have written a *Manual of Hispanic Bibliography* (1970), *A Research Guide to Argentine Literature* (1970), and *Luis de Gongora* (1973). In addition, David has published several volumes of criticism on Hispanic poetry and prose. Following the format of other sets in Ungar's "Library of Literary Criticism," *Modern Latin American Literature* presents "twentieth century Latin American writers through the eyes of leading critics in their own countries and abroad, with particular stress on their reception in the United States."

Approximately half of the critical excerpts are translations from the Spanish and Portuguese. Some of these originate in the writer's native country, others elsewhere in Latin America and in Spain and Portugal. Still others are taken from American journals written either wholly or partly in Spanish or Portuguese, such as *Hispania, Revista ibero-americana,* and *Luso-Brazilian Review;* many of the contributors to these journals are American professors writing in Spanish or Portuguese.

The other half of the excerpts come mainly from English-language sources. Most of these were selected judiciously from a wide variety of American publications; British critics, too, are well represented. There is also a sampling taken from French, German, Italian, and Swedish sources.

The master list of Periodicals Used cites 143 well-known journals. The compilers' selection of the best journals concerned with Latin American literary criticism is both comprehensive and well balanced though some Latin American countries are not represented by indigenous journals.

Approximately half of the journals (74) are published in the U.S. and range from the *New York Times Book Review* and *Atlantic Monthly* to the lesser-known *Bulletin of the Rocky Mountain Modern Language Association* (Boulder, Colo.) and *Northwest Review* (Eugene, Oreg.) Other countries represented are England (14), Argentina (13), Mexico (8), France (8), Brazil (5), Portugal (4), Colombia (3), Cuba, Peru and Puerto Rico (2 each), and Chile, East Germany, Ecuador, Paraguay, Spain, Sweden, Uruguay, and Venezuela (1 each). Not represented by journals, though writers therefrom are included in *MLAL,* are Bolivia, Dominican Republic, Guatemala and Nicaragua. In addition, numerous excerpts have been gleaned from books of literary criticism.

The editors have chosen 137 writers for inclusion in *MLAL.* To qualify for representation in this work authors had to fall into one of the following six categories: (1) living writers and those who died after 1900 whose major work or influence belongs to the twentieth century; (2) essayists who have an important place in literature; (3) writers important in the formation and development of a Latin American literary tradition; (4) authors who have attracted sufficient serious critical commentary to allow for a representative selection (this necessarily excludes many promising younger writers); authors whose works have been reviewed in journals available in the U.S.; and (6) writers who continue to hold a place in or have begun to become part of the programs of American universities, or who have attracted serious attention in the nonacademic American press.

The Committee's examination of 40 anthologies and books of literary criticism of Latin American writers verifies that most of those selected for inclusion in *MLAL* are well known and generally recognized as significant by critics. All except 21 were mentioned by at least one critic; 72 were cited at least three times.

It is noteworthy that 8 of the 21 not mentioned in the 40 anthologies checked are Brazilian writers. This is not surprising, because according to the *MLAL* editors, "Brazilian periodicals are simply impossible to obtain here, even through loan services." This inaccessibility could account for the relative sparseness of Brazilian representation in books of commentary on Latin American writers. Eight other writers also neglected by critics are from countries which had no more than two journals listed in the sources used for *MLAL.* Again, one may infer that journals from these countries may be difficult to obtain in the U.S.

For each of the 21 writers not represented in the group of authorities checked by the Committee, the editors have excerpted four to eight commentaries which vouch for these writers' eligibility for inclusion.

While the selection of writers can be justified, some of the exclusions seem illogical. It is difficult to see why Guillermo Valencia (Colombia) discussed by 6 of the 40 anthologies examined by the Committee was left out. Robert Roland Anderson's *Spanish American Modernism: A Selected Bibliography* (Tucson, Ariz.: Univ. of Arizona Pr., 1970) lists 119 citations for Valencia; so he qualifies under the guidelines of "sufficient critical commentary" and his dates are 1873–1943, but he is, nevertheless, denied representation. Other omissions include Luis Carlos Lopez (Colombia, 1883–1950), mentioned by five critics, Pedro Prado (Chile, 1886–1952) whom John E. Englekirk in *An Outline of History of Spanish American Literature* calls "the intellectual and esthetic leader of his generation in Chile," and Ricardo Palma (Peru, 1833–1919) who Englekirk states was "Peru's greatest literary personality." Also omitted are Ernesto Cardenal (Nicaragua, 1925–   ) and Violeta Parra, famous poet and folklorist from Chile, both of whom are among the most read poets of Latin America in American universities.

Included in the volume are 28 writers from Brazil and Argentina respectively. Representation of other countries is as follows: Mexico—24, Uruguay—11, Chile—8, Peru—7, Cuba—6, Colombia—5, Ecuador and Venezuela—4, Puerto Rico and Guatemala—3, Bolivia and Paraguay—2, and Dominican Republic and Nicaragua—1. Conformance to the criterion of the need for "sufficient serious (and worthwhile) critical commentary to allow for a representative selection" eliminated such writers as Rufino Blanco-Fombona and Miguel Otera Silva (Venezuela), Pablo Antonio Cuadro and Ernesto Mejia Sanchez (Nicaragua), Alfonso Hernández-Catá and Fina García Marruz (Cuba), and Eloy Farina Nunez and Herit Campos (Paraguay). The Committee notes the exclusion of a few influential writers such as Manuel Gutiérrez Najera (Mexico) who "exerted great influence on modernist prose," and José Asuncion Silva (Colombia), who John E. Englekirk feels might have become Spanish America's greatest poet had he not committed suicide at age 32, because they died in the mid-1890s. Adherence to a self-imposed injunction that limits inclusions to living writers of the twentieth century has kept out some authors who achieved posthumous renown.

The subjects are listed alphabetically. For each writer, birth and death dates and country are given. These personal facts are followed by four to eight excerpts from journals or books with complete bibliographical data. The excerpts range in length from a short paragraph to a page and a half with the majority running slightly less than a page. Each selection provides an interpretation and/or criticism of the writer's works which complements the other excerpts so that the reader receives a balanced impression of each writer's themes, literary devices, and caliber.

The compilers note that "Many of the selections included here have been translated into English for the first time—not only from Spanish and Portuguese but from other languages as well.... Hispanic prose style continues to be markedly hypotactic with clauses within clauses within clauses. The critic's tone is often less neutral or objective than is usual in English-language criticism, and there is greater reliance on personal or subjective criteria. Moreover, Hispanic criticism often seems to rival the text it is discussing in its use of difficult syntax or in its display of lexical variety. When translated into English, such writing yields an impressionism or theatricality American critics generally deplore. We have aimed to present such Latin American criticism in more concrete, less rhetorical English. In a few instances, however, we have selected examples of the criticism we consider to be objectionable in approach because it is indicative either of the type of analysis a particular writer has attracted or of a trend of impressionistic criticism that continues to be published, despite the efforts of those Latin American critics who insist on rigorously defined premises and methods."

The selection of reviews, especially those by such outstanding American scholars as Fred P. Ellison, Raymond S. Sayers, Jack E. Tomlins, and Seymour Menton, is excellent, and the translations are accurate and concise. Harold Conti deserves a better presentation, but the works of the major writers, such as Jorge Luis Borges, Alejo Carpentier, Julio Cortázar, José Lezama Lima, Eduardo Mallea, Pablo Neruda, Octavio Paz, João Guimaraes Rosa, Juan Rulfo, Ernesto Sabato, César Vallejo and Mario Vargas Llosa, are well described and thoughtfully interpreted.

"For the sake of uniformity and clarity, one literal translation has been used consistently for each title mentioned in the critical passages...." The editors "have also imposed a uniformity on Brazilian orthography, still not completely standardized."

Because the books are a compilation of literary criticism and not a critical evaluation, no comparative qualitative appraisal of the writers cited is attempted. Not even in the Introduction is there any summation of the work of the 137 writers included in the two volumes of *MLAL* or any indication of their contributions, individually or collectively, to the body of world literature.

Most users would have found such a judgmental framework invaluable, particularly since it seems rather difficult to obtain much information on Latin American writers in the average U.S. library.

The set offers several excellent features which provide easy access to the contents. In the front of both volumes can be found complete lists of authors arranged alphabetically and by country. All periodicals used for citations are also listed.

In the back of each volume is an alphabetically arranged list of Works Mentioned in the critical selections. For each work, the title (in English and Spanish) and date of publication are given. Omitted are place of publication and publisher. Also lacking is the name of the translator for the English version.

Volume II also provides Copyright Acknowledgments for the excerpts used, a thorough Cross-Reference Index to Authors included in this Index and an "Index to Critics."

The books are sturdily bound in buckram, and they lie fairly flat when open. The nonglare paper is of good quality, and the typeface is distinct and easy to read.

Each author section follows the same pattern. The author's name and dates, which serve as the heading, are printed in heavy boldface. Below, in a lighter type, is listed the author's country. The critical excerpts follow without introduction or indention. Only the paragraphs within each excerpt are indented. The citation (author, journal, volume, date, pages) completes the excerpt. No attempt is made to begin each author section at the top of a page. However, easy access is provided by the bold headings.

Despite exclusions of a number of influential authors who died before 1900 and several important new authors who could not be represented by "sufficient serious critical commentary," *A Library of Literary Criticism: Modern Latin American Literature* is a much-needed reference tool which provides information not easily located in other sources. It is recommended for public, college, and university libraries. *(Oct. 1, 1976, p.275)*
860'.9 Latin American literature—20th century—Book reviews [CIP]   72-81713

Light and color.
†535.6 Light—Juvenile literature ǁ Color—Juvenile literature [OCLC]   75-19978

See **page 50**

The living word vocabulary
the words we know: a national vocabulary inventory. By Edgar Dale and Joseph O'Rourke. [Chicago, Field Enterprises, c1976; dist. by Dome, Inc., 1169 Logan Ave., Elgin, IL 60120.] [iv] 868 [i.e., 869p]. 29cm. buckram $49.95. vinyl loose-leaf $39.95.

Choice of words should be determined not only by the ideas one wishes to communicate but by the words one's audience may be expected to understand. Hitherto, claim the authors of *The Living Word Vocabulary,* writers wanting to assess the appropriateness of their diction to their readers' levels of comprehension "have had to depend upon personal judgment and non-semantic frequency studies...."

TLWV is a list of more than 43,000 items (words used in particular senses) indicating at what grade level what percentage of persons tested comprehended each item, e.g., that at level 4, 93 percent identified the *ABC's* as "the alphabet" but that at level 16 only 40 percent identified *absinthe* as "a strong alcoholic beverage." The assumption is that in writing for third and fourth graders one may use *ABC's* with abandon but that in writing for college seniors one may risk *absinthe* only if one provides a definition or loads one's context with clues. The potential usefulness of such data is obvious. Perhaps less obvious is that such data may be expected to change: it may surprise some readers to be told that more readers at level 6 understand *drag* as "a dull affair" than readers at level 8 understand *drag* as "to search river bottoms."

Findings exhibited in *The Living Word Vocabulary* are based on the results of three-choice word tests administered to an undisclosed number of subjects. According to the authors, testing began in 1954 and is still in progress. School and college students at grade levels 4, 6, 8, 10, 12, 13, and 16 have been participating in this project administered by Ohio State University. The results are used by the editors of *The World Book Encyclopedia*. "Final scores" between 67 and 84 percent are desirable, explain the authors. "A word of a certain grade level," they note, "may be used without definition in an article for use by readers one grade below that level." The authors also point out that a "word with a score of 50 percent or less is generally a *hard word* and should be reconsidered before using [i.e., being used] in written material."

The 43,000-plus items are in one alphabetical sequence beginning thus:

GRADE	SCORE	WORD—WORD MEANING
04	79%	a—one, any
08	72%	A—musical note
16	37%	aardvark—animal
12	65%	ab—away, off, from
12	51%	A.B.—bachelor of arts

and ending thus:

12	81%	zygote—a fertilized egg
12	52%	zymurgy—the study of fermentation

The implication is that *A* may be safely used for eighth graders, as may *zygote* for twelfth graders; but college seniors cannot be expected to grasp *aardvark* "right off." *A.B.* is interesting in that only 51 percent of twelfth graders understand it (i.e., it is, for them, on the borderline of hardness), whereas, we learn elsewhere in the volume, *bachelor* in the same sense of "first college degree" is understood by 85 percent of eighth graders.

Missing in all this are complete data. The pages contain excessive amounts of white space, and the font is pica. With a smaller font, all seven scores—those achieved at grade levels 4, 6, 8, 10, 12, 13, and 16 (and testing dates)—could surely have been shown. Then, in addition to knowing that 72 percent of eighth graders recognized *A* as "musical note," we would know what percentage of students at each grade level recognized it and when they did so (1954). It is not clear why Dale and O'Rourke give but one score for each item and how they select which score to give. A low score at the highest level, e.g., 38 percent at level 16 understanding *baleful* as "evil," *probably* means that at lower levels even lower scores would be achieved; but can one be sure? A satisfactory score at a high level does not tell one at what lower level an item passed from hard to comprehensible: thus 68 percent at level 12 understand *badger* in the sense of "to annoy"; but what of level 10? And what of low scores at upper-middle levels? Only 24 percent at level 12 recognize *bairn* as "a child": what of levels 13 and 16? Does *bairn* at *any* point become comprehensible? Is it possible that more readers at level 4 understand *bairn* than at level 12? It is to be hoped that the next spin-off from the testing program will summarize results for all grade levels so that the whole continuum of readability may be inferred. Moreover, although data strike one as being recent, one cannot be sure. The editors observe: "A significant number of items in this volume were updated within the current year." Even if for *significant* one substitutes 10 percent, 40 percent, 60 percent, or whatever, the currency of data on any particular item still remains unrevealed.

The volume, bound in workaday buckram, is cumbersome but is solidly constructed, and it lies flat when open. The quality of reproduction of typescript varies, but no instances of illegibility were noted. The work is available in a three-ring notebook edition, the purpose of which is not stated.

Joseph O'Rourke is a research associate at Ohio State University; Edgar Dale, long associated with Ohio State, is one of the most distinguished, even venerated figures in educational research.

The Living Word Vocabulary goes far toward meeting a real and felt need; therefore the Committee recommends it to libraries serving writers and teachers, noting, however, that it must be used with caution. The Committee would welcome a second edition featuring more nearly complete displays of findings as well as indications of the timeliness of the scores reported.

(June 1, 1977, p.1523)

†428.04 Vocabulary English language—Word frequency || Word recognition 76-19222

Longman illustrated companion to world history.
Edited by Grant Uden. 2v. London and New York, Longman Group Ltd. (in association with Kestrel Books), [1976]. 1040p. illus., 24cm. permacote $35.

This product of seven years' work attempts to approach world history from an impartial point of view, "to stand outside Britain altogether . . . , even though this would involve the omission, or at least playing down, of many familiar names, events and places." The "Companion is not intended to be primarily a work of quick reference . . . . Rather, it is hoped that it will be congenial to browse in, sometimes for instructional purposes, sometimes simply because it is interesting to do so . . . [and] that the reader will find much that is outside the range of mere academic convention."

Editor Grant Uden brings to the *Longman Illustrated Companion to World History* experience in writing works on topics as diverse as the Napoleonic era, naval history, chivalry, British biography and printing, lifeboats, and book collecting. He has also edited the *Dictionary of Chivalry* (New York: Crowell, 1975). Robert J. Hoare, Book Lists Compiler for the *Companion*, has produced more than a dozen children's titles, including readers and a number of multivolume sets on subjects varying from the American West and chivalry to air and sea travel. Jane Dorner, in charge of picture research; Anthony Colber, the work's illustrator, and John Flower, the cartographer for volume I, all have ample credentials. The 51 contributors "come not only from school and university; but also from the world of commerce, the law, colonial service, agriculture, libraries, museums and technical organisations." Less than a third could be identified in standard biographical sources.

The two volumes, *A-K* and *L-Z*, include more than 2,000 articles, varying from a short paragraph to four pages. The entries are arranged in two columns and are set off from one another by solid horizontal lines. Within articles, dates are enclosed in parentheses, and metric equivalents appear in brackets after English measurements.

Access is provided by cross-references and an Index to the entire work at the end of volume II. The Index to personal and place-names, topics, and historical events is followed parenthetically by the date where necessary. Illustrations are also indexed. Main entries are indicated by boldfaced numbers, secondary entries by arabic numbers in plain type, and line and halftone illustrations by italicized numbers. Maps and colorplates are noted with reference to pagination or plate number, but not volume. There are also *see* references from unused to used headings in the Index. In general the Index is very reliable and assists in best utilization of the work, but occasionally, personal and place-names which are not main entries have been overlooked. For instance, of some 24 names appearing in the article *Russian Authors, Painters and Composers*, three—Chagall, Glinka, and Borodin—are missing from the Index. The Great Wall appears under the entry for China but not as a separate entry.

The internal cross-references are somewhat less effective. They take several forms appearing within and at the end of articles: "(*see* separate entry)," "*See* Colour section*,*" "*See also*" references to main entries, "*See*" for maps, "*See also*

PLACE NAMES." While adequate, this internal reference system should not be used without the Index. *See* references to color-plates do not include plate numbers which must be obtained from the Index. In addition, it is not always immediately apparent what one should look for in the Index when an article is followed by *see* references; often it is the main entry but sometimes not. Some highly relevant main entries have no *see* reference. For example, in the article on Islam, no cross-reference is provided to the entry *Koran.*

While uniformly good, the writing style varies from that in articles written at a quite elementary level to those of considerable complexity and sophistication. As might be expected, British oriented historical terminology and spellings are used, e.g., "American Civil War" or "Bloodless Revolution," "omnibus" and "jewellry" are used. This may present some minor difficulties.

The volumes are sturdily bound and, when opened, lie flat. The print is easily readable. The paper is opaque and has a mat surface. However, the gutter binding is narrow and will present problems if rebinding is necessary.

In spite of the editors' intention, the two volumes have a substantial Europocentric, if not British, bias. For instance, *Black Death* is principally a discussion of the effects of that disease in Britain. In the entry for the fifteenth century and others beginning with the twelfth century, the European emphasis is pervasive. *Gardens* is a discussion of the classical origins and later development of European, especially British, gardens sans any reference to oriental examples and *Housing* is similarly biased. *Plough* discusses British innovations to the exclusion of major U.S. achievements, and John Maynard Keynes receives prime billing in the *Economics* entry. European and British topics are accorded the lion's share of space. For example, the discussion of *Hampton Court* is as lengthy as the article on the *Pyramids* and four times as long as the *Taj Mahal. Hadrian's Wall* has a separate entry but the Great Wall of China does not. *Christianity* is given about twice as much attention as *Islam,* three times as much as *Buddhism,* and five times as much as *Hinduism. Bill of Rights* is defined as the 1689 "Act giving statutory force to the terms on which William III and Mary II were accepted on the throne of England." Excluded entirely is any reference to the first ten amendments to the Constitution of the U.S., the American Bill of Rights.

Of the sampled entries, 20 percent are biographical. Five of 13 are British, 4 European, and 1 American. A further indication of relative emphasis is the inclusion of main entries for even minor European royal houses from the Middle Ages onward, while only the Han and Ming dynasties of China and none of the Caliphates or various Mongol lines receive main entries.

The sparsity of factual data in some of the articles weakens an otherwise satisfactory text. For instance, the only cited activities of Francis I of France are his invasions of Italy and defeat and capture at Pavia. While somewhat more substantial, the sketch of Bismarck is still a superficial account of the "Iron Chancellor's" career, especially since no bibliography is appended. To flesh out biographical information, it is necessary to use the Index. The style and content of the *Economics* article are oversimplified. It omits important developments in "post-industrial" societies and fails to come to grips with the rather important differences between the "free market" economies of the West and the "command economies" of the Communist bloc and some developing nations. *Silver* fails to mention the sources of the massive increase of bullion after the discovery of America or its effects on prices in Europe. The descriptions of small, usually third world, countries as a rule omit most modern political and economic developments, and generally cultural background is given no attention. Inclusion of anecdotal incidents in British history, such as Catherine Howard's haunting of Hampton Court, reduce space available for firmer and more consequential matters.

In addition to events and persons considered historical, the editors have included a large number of miscellaneous topics. Approximately 37 percent of the entries fall into this group, which includes articles on such diverse topics as the astrolabe, dance, marionettes, silver, radio, playing cards, and transport. The principle for selection of these miscellaneous topics is never elucidated. The editors have chosen entries which are rather encyclopedic in scope and seem to reflect technological, cultural, social, institutional, and topical issues of broad historical significance. This is also the case with selection of many biographical entries, which, in addition to political and military leaders, include educators, inventors, scientists, explorers, artists, technicians, philosophers, political economists, professionals, agriculturists, religious leaders, individuals who have had an impact on economic and social movements, and legendary historical figures.

"The suggestions for further reading are intended mainly for young people, though readable adult books are not excluded." Half of the articles have no bibliographical references, but the proportion is a bit higher for items devoted to British historical topics. Rarely is more than one citation given, but most are representative works dating from the second half of the sixties. Many of the works cited will be available in American libraries, but on the whole the number of bibliographic citations is not an inducement to use the text.

There are 210 color illustrations grouped in two sections, one in the middle of each volume. The overwhelming majority are reproductions of paintings or photographs of architecture; all are clearly captioned. Fidelity and detail are excellent. These embellish more than they explicate the text. By contrast, the black-and-white text illustrations—maps, reproductions of paintings, line drawings, photographs of buildings, individuals, landscapes, and the like—do contribute to comprehension of the written material. These black-and-whites are evenly distributed among the various kinds of articles. Fully a third of the biographical and two-thirds of the geographical articles are illustrated with portraits or maps. There are two world maps in the endpapers: "Discovery of the World" (journeys of Norsemen to that of Charles Wilkes) and the "Modern World." In all, there are more than a thousand illustrations.

A few minor criticisms of these illustrations can be made. The black-and-whites are not always captioned, and although they generally fall within the lines setting off the article to which they pertain, this relationship is not always obvious. The Committee wishes that Longman and other reference books publishers would begin to include the approximate age of individuals in portraits. Where size is not immediately evident, a scale for illustrations would enhance the text. In addition, illustrations of technical subjects, such as the astrolabe, should label parts referred to in the text. Finally, in a few of the illustrations, reduction in size—most are a third to a half of the single column—makes the details difficult to distinguish. Acknowledgments for all copyrighted illustrations and plates are given following the Index in volume II.

Though "not intended to be primarily a work for quick reference," the reference value of the *Companion* may be compared to that of similar tools. There is currently no work which combines all its features—events, persons, places, topical entries, illustrations, and bibliographies. William L. Langer, *The New Illustrated Encyclopedia of World History* (New York: Abrams, 1975, $65), a two-volume expansion of his *An Encyclopedia of World History* (Boston: Houghton Mifflin, 1972, $17.50), has 2,000 illustrations. It covers in a chronological arrangement with much more detail the historical and many of the topical and biographical items in the *Companion.* Likewise, *Webster's Biographical Dictionary* (Springfield, Mass.: Merriam-Webster, 1974, $15) is richer in biographical detail and provides fuller cross-referencing. Neither *Langer* nor *Webster's Biographical Dictionary* includes bibliographies. The kinds of illustrations in the *Companion,* while attractive and appropriate, are available in numerous standard reference sources, notably general and subject encyclopedias.

The editor's claim that the "*Companion* breaks new ground in the field of history reference books" is marginally justifiable. Libraries will want to consider whether the work adds to the effectiveness of their reference services. "The *Companion* has been prepared with eleven- to fifteen-year-olds in mind," but for that audience it is recommended as a supplementary reference only in school and public libraries which already have strong holdings of reference works presenting American overviews of world history. *(Feb. 15, 1977, p.922)*
903 History—Dictionaries [CIP] 75-35742

Macdonald first library.
Editorial consultant, Sylvia Van Sickle. 50v. London, Macdonald Educational Ltd. [dist. in the U.S. by Purnell Reference Books, a division of Macdonald Raintree, Inc., 205 W. Highland Ave., Milwaukee, WI 53203, 1975]. each v. 38p. illus. (part col.) 19cm. tyvek $199.50 plus shipping and handling, $3.99 ea.; to schools and libraries, $149.50 plus shipping and handling, $2.99 ea.; minimum order $75; paper $.69 ea.

- **Airplanes and balloons.**
†629.13 Airplanes—Juvenile literature || Balloons—Juvenile literature [OCLC] 75-19991
- **Animals that burrow.**
†591.52б4 Burrowing animals—Juvenile literature || Animals, Habitation of—Juvenile literature [OCLC] 75-20511
- **Animals with shells.**
†594 Shellfish—Juvenile literature [OCLC] 75-20513
- **Ballet and dance.**
†793.3 Ballet—Juvenile literature || Dancing—Juvenile literature [OCLC] 75-20501
- **Birds and migration.**
†598.2 Birds—Juvenile literature || Birds—Migration—Juvenile literature [OCLC] 75-19979
- **Bridges and tunnels.**
†690.598 Bridges—Juvenile literature || Tunnels—Juvenile literature [OCLC] 75-19988
- **Building.**
†690 Architecture—Juvenile literature [OCLC] 75-20508
- **Butterflies and moths.**
†595 Butterflies—Juvenile literature || Moths—Juvenile literature [OCLC] 75-20509
- **Cloth and weaving.**
†677.02 Textile industry—Juvenile literature [OCLC] 75-20504
- **Cowboys.**
†636.01 Cowboys—Juvenile literature [OCLC] 75-19975
- **Deserts.**
†574.526′5 Deserts—Juvenile literature [OCLC] 75-19970
- **The dog family.**
†636.7 Dogs—Juvenile literture [OCLC] 75-19999
- **Electricity.**
†537 Electricity—Juvenile literature [OCLC] 75-19995
- **Farms and farmers.**
†630 Agriculture—Juvenile literature [OCLC] 75-19981
- **Fire.**
†530.43 Fire—Juvenile literature [OCLC] 75-19967
- **Fishing.**
†688.79 Fishing—Juvenile literature [OCLC] 75-20520
- **Food and drink.**
†641.3 Food—Juvenile literature [OCLC] 75-20503
- **Fuel and energy.**
†621.3 Fuel—Juvenile literature || Power resources—Juvenile literature [OCLC] 75-20512
- **Gypsies and nomads.**
†301.451′042 Nomads—Juvenile literature || Gypsies—Juvenile literature [OCLC] 75-20500
- **Health and disease.**
†613 Hygiene—Juvenile literature || Medicine—Juvenile literature [OCLC] 75-20516
- **Horses and ponies.**
†636.1 Horses—Juvenile literature [OCLC] 75-19990
- **The jungle.**
†574.526′4 Jungle ecology—Juvenile literature [OCLC] 75-19998
- **Lakes and dams.**
†627.8 Lakes—Juvenile literature || Dams—Juvenile literature [OCLC] 75-20507
- **Light and color.**
†535.6 Light—Juvenile literature || Color—Juvenile literature [OCLC] 75-19978
- **Monkeys and apes.**
†599.8 Primates—Juvenile literature [OCLC] 75-19972
- **Mountains.**
†551.43 Mountains—Juvenile literature [OCLC] 75-19994
- **The movies.**
†791.43 Moving pictures—Juvenile literature [OCLC] 75-20518
- **Paper and printing.**
†681.767′6 Printing—Juvenile literature || Paper—Juvenile literature [OCLC] 75-20502
- **Photography.**
†771 Photography—Juvenile literature [OCLC] 75-19997
- **Pirates and buccaneers.**
†364.135 Pirates—Juvenile literature || Buccaneers—Juvenile literature [OCLC] 75-19965
- **Pollution.**
†614.7 Pollution—Juvenile literature [OCLC] 75-20517
- **Ports and harbors.**
†338.476′272 Harbors—Juvenile literature [OCLC] 75-19987
- **Rivers and river life.**
†574.526′32 Rivers—Juvenile literature || Stream ecology—Juvenile literature [OCLC] 75-19983
- **Roads and highways.**
†625.7 Roads—Juvenile literature [OCLC] 75-19986
- **Rocks and mining.**
†622.3 Rocks—Juvenile literature || Mines and mineral resources—Juvenile literature [OCLC] 75-19982
- **Signals and messages.**
†001.51 Communication—Juvenile literature || Signs and symbols—Juvenile literature [OCLC] 75-20519
- **Size.**
†620.004′4 Weights and measures—Juvenile literature [OCLC] 75-19966
- **Skyscrapers.**
†690.523 Skyscrapers—Juvenile literature [OCLC] 75-19971
- **Snakes and lizards.**
†598.1 Snakes—Juvenile literature || Lizards—Juvenile literature [OCLC] 75-19985
- **Spiders.**
†595.4 Spiders—Juvenile literature [OCLC] 75-19964
- **The story of cars.**
†629.222 Automobiles—Juvenile literature [OCLC] 75-19993
- **Television.**
†791.45 Television—Juvenile literature [OCLC] 75-19996
- **The theater.**
†792 Theater—Juvenile literature [OCLC] 75-20515
- **Time and clocks.**
†529.78 Time—Juvenile literature || Clocks and watches—Juvenile literature [OCLC] 75-19977
- **Towns and cities.**
†301.36 Cities and towns—Juvenile literature [OCLC] 75-19989
- **Trains and railroads.**
†625.27 Railroads—Juvenile literature || Railroads—Trains—Juvenile literature [OCLC] 75-19973
- **Trees and wood.**
†674 Lumbering—Juvenile literature || Trees—Juvenile literature [OCLC] 75-19974
- **The universe.**
†523.1 Astronomy—Juvenile literature [OCLC] 75-19980
- **Vanishing animals.**
†591.52 Rare animals—Juvenile literature || Extinct animals—Juvenile literature [OCLC] 75-20510
- **Weather.**
†551.6 Weather—Juvenile literature || Meteorology—Juvenile literature [OCLC] 75-19969

According to the publisher's promotional material, *Macdonald First Library* was originally published in Great Britain in 70 volumes to give "young children who are learning to read . . . a simple but comprehensive introduction to many aspects of everyday life. Each book studies a particular theme and the topics cover such subject areas as history, sciences, social studies, and the arts." In 1975, 50 volumes of the series were updated and Americanized for sale in the U.S. Actually, of the 50 volumes, only 5 deal with the arts, and 7 can be considered to relate to social studies, while the other 38 cover science and technology. Furthermore, using the Fry graph for estimating readability, the Committee has determined that only 27 of the 50 volumes are at a reading level within the first to third grade range. The other 23 vary in reading level from fourth to tenth grade.

According to Purnell, "this colorful series has since appeared in fifteen languages and has sold four million copies." The American Teacher Advisory Panel responsible for the books under review consists of Valerie Jameson, the Creative Teaching Workshop in New York City; Patricia Sherman and Marsha Carlin, the Children's Center in Tenafly, New Jersey; and Angie Finn, from Community School #30 in New York City. Sylvia Van Sickle, editorial consultant, is a New York free-lance editor who has worked for McGraw-Hill, Xerox Learning Systems, American Book Company, and Appleton. The series now lacks an Index, but the publishers inform that on September 1, 1977, a fifty-first volume index priced at $4.95 to libraries will be published. "The new volume will be titled (2000+) 'Two Thousand Plus' and will provide in 96 pages of easy-to-read type, a carefully graded dictionary definition and a volume/page number cross reference to over (2000) two thousand terms used in 'First Library.' In addition there will be a section on how to use 'First Library' and a straightforward introduction to the concept and use of reference books. Because First Library volumes are not numbered, numbered press-on labels which will enable the teacher or librarian to establish a true reference set...." Contributions are unsigned.

No criteria are offered for determining subjects covered or the amount of space devoted to each. Volumes on the arts are *Ballet and Dance, The Theater, The Movies, Photography,* and *Building* (about architecture, not construction); in the social sciences *Size, Towns and Cities, Ports and Harbors, Signals and Messages, Gypsies and Nomads, Pirates and Buccaneers,* and *Cowboys.* Volumes dealing with science and technology are *Time and Clocks, The Universe, Light and Color, Fire, Electricity, Rocks and Mining, Weather, Mountains, Deserts, Rivers and River Life, Lakes and Dams, The Jungle, Trees and Wood, Spiders, Butterflies and Moths, Animals With Shells, Animals That Burrow, Birds and Migration, Snakes and Lizards, Monkeys and Apes, Vanishing Animals, Health and Disease, Bridges and Tunnels, Trains and Railroads, Roads and Highways, Airplanes and Balloons, The Story of Cars, Television, Pollution, Farms and Farmers, Horses and Ponies, The Dog Family, Food and Drink, Fishing, Fuel and Energy, Paper and Printing, Cloth and Weaving,* and *Skyscrapers* (about construction, not architecture). Historical information has been incorporated into many of the volumes.

Examination of the individual texts brings to light a number of passages which are both interesting and easy to understand. Such passages include tips for taking good pictures (*Photography*), the steps taken in laying a highway (*Roads and Highways*), the operation of sea locks (*Ports and Harbors*), carbon dating (*Time and Clocks*), and printing methods (*Paper and Printing*).

However, confusing, incomplete, or oversimplified statements are often made. In *Birds,* flight is explained thus: "The air below the wing is thicker than the air above the wing. The thick air below the wing pushes the bird up. This is how birds fly in the air. Wings move quickly through the air. This is what makes the air below the wing thick. If the wing moved slowly, the air below the wing would not be thick. The bird would fall." A more accurate explanation is that when a bird's wings swing up, air passes through the feathers, but that when they swing down, the air is not allowed to pass through, thus pushing the bird up. In addition, when a bird flaps its wings the air moves more quickly over the curved top of the wings than it does over the bottom. This makes the air pressure below the wings greater than the air pressure above, holding the bird up.

Thunder is described as "the noise caused by lightning as it travels to the ground." In reality, lightning does not always travel to the ground; it can also pass between clouds. The sound of thunder is actually caused by the violent expansion of air heated by lightning.

Occasionally, theories are stated as fact. *Fire* describes how man began to use fire: "Long, long ago men lived without fire.... Sometimes fires were started by lightning.... Then one day a brave man took a burning branch from a tree struck by lightning. He used the branch to make his own fire.... Soon men learned how to make fire." The lack of a prefacing phrase such as "Some scientists now believe that...." is misleading and furthers the erroneous idea that most children would rather read facts in story form.

Incomplete information is a fairly frequent problem. In *The Universe,* the earth's revolution around the sun and its effect on seasonal changes are described. However, the earth's rotation on its axis, causing day and night, is not mentioned. The book simply states that "The sun shines up in the sky in the daytime. The stars shine at night."

Sometimes, information seems misplaced. "Eclipses" have been included in *Fire,* but not in *The Universe.* The volume called *Signals and Messages,* which could have been titled "Communication," includes information on mime and dancing, also covered in the volumes on *The Theater* and *Ballet and Dance,* but fails to mention the telephone, telegraph, or codes.

Occasionally facts are omitted, which could cause confusion. Discussion of the tallest buildings in the world in *Skyscrapers* mentions the Empire State Building and the World Trade Center in New York City but omits mention of the Sears Tower in Chicago, completed in time for the 1975 revision date of this set. In another example, *Birds* states that "toucans live in American jungles" but fails to specify Central and South America.

From time to time, terms are used which are either not immediately explained or not explained at all. Shakespeare is mentioned in *The Theater,* but his identity and importance are not described, even though many young American children may not be familiar with him. The five positions of *Ballet* are described five pages before their illustration appears. The egg-laying platypus is compared to a reptile in *Animals That Burrow,* but "reptile" is not defined.

In spite of revision for the U.S., some undefined British idioms are used (e.g., "cat's-eyes" for road reflectors, "Plow" for the constellation commonly called the Big Dipper in the U.S., "balaclava" for a type of woolen pullover head and neck covering, and "pony travel" for horseback riding). A number of animal names which are probably not familiar to American children are used in passing (e.g., kestrel, linnet, wombat, petrel, tuatara, and puffin). Since their habitats are far removed from England, these animals may not be familiar to British children either. Most regrettable of all, there are no references to most of the animals' homelands. In addition, a British point of view has not been entirely revised in an illustration entitled "school children," showing uniformed girl pupils leaving a private school, a drawing showing cars driving on the left-hand side of the road, and the description of asteroid Ceres as being "only as big as Britain."

The writing style in many of the volumes of the *Macdonald First Library* tends to be choppy, repetitive, and dull. Few transitions are made between topics within a volume, and one third of the books end without summarizing statements. Examination of the books does not bear out the publisher's statement that the books were written with "a straightforward, controlled text," for "young children who are learning to read."

Only one book, *Size,* was found to be at a first- to second-grade level. Four of the books, *Light and Color, Rivers and River Life, Snakes and Lizards,* and *Towns and Cities* have a second-grade reading level. Four fall between the second and third grades in reading level: *Ports and Harbors, Spiders, Birds,* and *Roads and Highways.* Seventeen of the books are written at a third-grade level: *Time and Clocks, Rocks and Mining, Mountains, Deserts, Lakes and Dams, The Jungle, Animals With Shells, Monkeys and Apes, Vanishing Animals, Horses and Ponies, The Dog Family, Trains and Railroads, The Story of Cars, Farms and Farmers, Cloth and Weaving, Pirates and Buccaneers,* and *Cowboys.* Three books fall between the third and fourth grades: *Airplanes and Balloons, Trees and Wood,* and *The Movies.* The seven books written at a fourth-grade level are: *Weather, Animals That Burrow, Fuel and Energy, Bridges and Tunnels, Fishing, Building,* and *Ballet and Dance.* Three have a reading level between the fourth and fifth grades: *Butterflies and Moths, Skyscrapers,* and *The Theater.*

The Committee could not determine an average reading level for eight of the volumes, because they proved to have uneven readability. Vocabulary and sentence length in *The Universe* ranges from the first to the seventh grade, and both *Fire* and *Food and Drink* vary between the second and fifth grades in reading level. *Photography* ranges from the third to the sixth grade, *Gypsies and Nomads* and *Paper and Printing* from the third to the seventh grade, *Signals and Messages* from the fourth to the seventh grade, and *Health and Disease* from the fourth to the tenth grade. Valid reading levels for *Electricity* and for *Television* were not attainable because of limitations in use of the Fry Readability Graph.

There are no tables of contents in the *Macdonald First Library.* The publisher claims that a "two-page index completes each volume." Actually, each book ends with a one-page Index averaging between 20 and 40 entries. No cross-references are supplied in either the texts or the indexes, and there is no comprehensive index of all volumes. A check of a sample of entries in 25 volumes revealed an error rate of 10 percent. Indexing is so selective that it limits the usefulness of the volumes.

Even though pronunciation guides would have been helpful, they are not included. Children may have difficulty pronouncing such terms as "douroucouli," "macaques," "cirrocumulus," "cumulonimbus," "corroboree," "didjeridoo," "chamois," and "guanaco."

The illustrations in the *Macdonald First Library* consist of some maps, charts, and diagrams and color drawings of average quality. Many of them are incompletely identified. Although some drawings are well labeled, those of "Mont St. Michel," "an Inca Town," and "monorail" are simply described as such without any further elaboration being provided in their captions or the surrounding text. Others, like the two portraits of Marcel Marceau, are not identified at all. *Mountains* contains a drawing of 22 well-known peaks without any height or locational data. There is no explanatory material to let a child know that this is an arbitrary representation to demonstrate comparative heights and bears no resemblance to these mountains' actual geographical dispersion.

Some maps are poorly labeled and may therefore confuse the reader. On the map of "The world's biggest ports," the names of some towns are misplaced and other names are hard to distinguish because they bleed into the center seam. An untitled map of world jungles shows them as tiny brown spots on solid green continents. A reversal of colors would be helpful, as would identification of the 13 unlabeled jungles. In contrast, a map of world deserts is appropriately colored and correctly labeled.

At times, the illustrations themselves are incomplete. A drawing of the phases of the moon as seen from Earth mislabels the new moon as "full moon" and omits the sun's role. The discussion of the 12 signs of the zodiac is accompanied by an illustration of but 10 signs.

Other drawings do not fulfil their purposes. The reader of *Birds* is instructed to look at six pictures of a bird in flight and to "see how the outside part of the wing moves. The inside part hardly moves at all." This phenomenon is not easily observable in the illustrations. In a drawing of "Some trees compared in size," actual comparison is made impossible because the 11 trees are not arranged side by side and their relative proportions are incorrectly depicted.

Virtually the same illustration is used in two of the books. In *Deserts,* the man shown crossing the mountains with his yaks is called a "Tibetan," while in "Mountains," the same man in a differently colored jacket is called a "Mongol." Mongols, incidentally, are variably described in *Deserts, Mountains,* and *Gypsies and Nomads* as "nomads who travel in the Gobi," live in Tibet, and live in Mongolia without any indication of where these places are located.

Women are underrepresented in the illustrations of the *Macdonald First Library.* Although they make up 51 percent of the world's population, only 26 percent of the human beings illustrated for which a sex could be identified are women. Furthermore, the majority of these females are shown in conventional feminine activities such as playing with dolls, cooking, cleaning, shopping, typing, caring for children, and harvesting crops. There are a few exceptions, including three doctors, two pirates, two factory workers, a film editor, and an animator. While both male and female dancers are shown, only one female symphony-orchestra musician, a harpist, is depicted. All of the directors, camera operators, carpenters, electricians, musicians, and stunt people shown in *The Movies* are men.

Minority representation has been attempted in the *Macdonald First Library,* but most illustrations of nonwhites are found in scenes of Asia or Africa. However, textual coverage seems to be impartial. One passage in *Cowboys* is a good example: "Cattle trails often led through 'Indian country.' Native Americans didn't want cowboys and big herds of cattle moving through the land where they lived and hunted. Texas cattle trails passed through land near the Comanches. These Native Americans fought bravely and fiercely to defend their living and hunting grounds."

Examination of the physical format of the volumes shows the type to be large, legible, and well spaced, although not always evenly inked. For the most part, each sentence begins a new line. A few cases of skewed lines and words printed too closely together were noted, as well as occasional errors in grammar and punctuation. The library binding is sturdy, and the covers are washable. Paper is of adequate quality. Inner margins are narrow, and illustrations often bleed into the seams. The books do not lie flat when opened.

Interest levels, as suggested by the publisher, encompass the second grade through high school, but the books' small size and larger-than-average print might seem babyish to children above the fourth grade. The publisher's suggestion that these books be used as high interest low reading level materials does not seem justified, since many of the books, such as *Television, Paper and Printing, Electricity, The Universe,* and *Photography,* which might interest children of the fourth grade and up, have congenial-looking formats but demand sixth- and seventh-grade reading abilities.

Examination of the list of topics covered in the *Macdonald First Library* reveals that some subjects of special current interest, such as *Vanishing Animals, Pollution,* and *Fuel and Energy* have been included as well as those of enduring interest to children in the early elementary grades; *Spiders, Snakes and Lizards, Trains and Railroads, the Story of Cars, Airplanes and Balloons, Pirates and Buccaneers,* and *The Movies.* However, a number of both school-related and popular topics have been overlooked, even in the heavily emphasized areas of science and technology. Such topics include prehistoric animals, insects, amphibians, rodents, sharks, the human body, rockets and space travel, trucks, fire engines, monsters, codes, magic, the circus, cartoons, and sports.

In summary, the *Macdonald First Library* has the following drawbacks: unbalanced coverage, oversimplification, unclear and incomplete information, choppy and repetitive writing with an excessive number of Briticisms, a condescending tone, wide variation in reading level, inadequate indexing, no pronunciation guides, poorly labeled illustrations, and stereotyped representation of women and men. Although particular volumes may have some value as supplementary material for classrooms or the circulating sections of school or public-library children's collections, the *Macdonald First Library* cannot be recommended for purchase as a reference set.

(June 15, 1977, p.1593)

Major libraries of the world:

a selective guide. [By] Colin Steele. London and New York, Bowker, [c1976]. 479p. 24cm. $18.50 plus shipping and handling.

In his Preface, Colin Steele describes *Major Libraries of the World* as a "practical guide to 300 Major Libraries of the World." While "major library" is not defined, the book presumably covers national libraries, institutions with significant holdings, and select special libraries, such as Library and Archive Collections of the Institute for Sex Research at Indiana University, Bloomington. There are also a number of libraries important for their rare materials, such as the Biblioteca Ambrosiana in Milan. The results of the extremely small selection are that very few libraries can be listed for any city. For example, Washington, D.C., is covered by only the Folger Shakespeare Library and Library of Congress and Chicago by Chicago Public, John Crerar, Newberry, and University of Chicago libraries. St. Louis rates no listing at all. The author makes the point, in explaining his selection, that a few libraries are not included because they did not respond to letters or because they asked to be omitted.

The compiler, Colin Steele, assistant librarian at the Bodleian Library, Oxford, is the author of several books and articles on history, bibliography, and librarianship. He was awarded a British Academy American Fellowship in 1974; he took this at the Newberry Library. He has traveled widely, especially in the Americas.

The 300 libraries are arranged alphabetically by country, then by city, then individually. Representation by country is U.S.—40, Great Britain—23, East and West Germany—23, Italy and France—16 each. Twenty-five nations, including Algeria, Chile, Ethiopia, Finland, Ghana, Uganda, Vatican City, Malta, Jamaica, the Panama Canal Zone, Indonesia, and Iraq, have only one. There is no index.

Judging by the kind and amount of information given, the book is intended for the traveling scholar, although its purpose is nowhere stated. For each library, address and telephone number, history, special collections and treasures, exhibition areas, hours, public transport, parking, admission regulations, information facilities, services, catalogs, classification used, copying and photographic services, and friends-of-the-library group are given. This information was compiled by questionnaire and appears to be reasonably current. Holdings for New York Public Library are cited for 1973; for Cracow University, end of 1973; and for Tokyo National Diet Library, March 1975.

Also included are a number of very small black-and-white photographs of libraries and illustrations to please the bibliophile, such as a page from the first Croatian printed book and one from the Glagolitic Missal (1483) held by the National and University Library in Zagreb. Placed in the very wide outer margins of the directory, these photographs generally lack crispness of definition and are too diminutive to show detail. They neither enhance the book aesthetically; nor do they add information.

The book is printed on opaque, nonglare paper in a distinctive modern sans-serif type, which is very legible. There are very wide outer margins to accommodate the illustrations, but as these are at most one to a page, there is a great deal of wasted space. The binding is of mediocre quality black cloth.

Major Libraries of the World is, in spite of such shortcomings as a lack of clearly defined purpose, a very useful directory. There is no comparable one-volume source; others, like the *International Library Directory,* give only addresses, even though their coverage is more omnivorous. The amount of information *Major Libraries of the World* provides on individual libraries is available only in each country's library directory, and there are many nations which have not developed such a reference tool. Furthermore, Steele's selection reflects a secure knowledge of the field, as he has included key libraries one would expect to find in such a directory, e.g., the Leningrad Library of the Academy of the Sciences of the USSR and the Universtätsbibliothek in Heidelberg. Recommended for large public and research libraries. *(July 15, 1977, p.1749)*

†027.0025 Libraries—Directories

Make it: an index to projects and materials.

[Compiled by] Joyce F. Shields. Metuchen, N.J., Scarecrow Pr., 1975. 22cm. cloth, 485p. $15.

In her introduction called "The Whyfor and Howsomever," Joyce Shields reveals that her experience working with the reference service of the Oak Park, Illinois public library made her aware of the need for a new index covering the many titles being published to serve the expanding craft industry. Joyce Shields is currently Collection Development Consultant, Niagara Falls Public Library and Nioga Library System in Western New York state.

Make It is an index to 475 books on projects and materials involving needlework, weaving, plastics, ceramics, electronics, leather, metal, wood, and natural materials. It also covers a generous number of titles pertaining to the renovative arts, i.e., junkcrafting. Not included are works which are limited to the creation of one product in one medium, such as a book on making crepe paper flowers. Also omitted are books on cooking, general sewing, repair work, and experiments.

A list of the 467 books analyzed in the index follows after the introduction. These titles published between 1968 and 1974 are arranged alphabetically by author giving the author's full name, title, publisher, and date. In a column to the left of this information is part of the author's name which is the code referred to in Part I of the index. Almost always this is the complete last name and whenever more than one title is given, the name is followed by (1), (2), (3), etc. If the title is produced by a journal, a shortened form of the journal's name, and the periodical's name is used as author, i.e., *Better Homes* for *Better Homes and Gardens* is used. For monographs of indeterminate authorship, complete titles are cited. All of the sources are in English, and almost all are published in the U.S. Although juvenile books are included along with those for the skilled artisan, no grade or age level is indicated. There are no references to magazine articles or pamphlets.

Part I, Index to Projects pages 29–366 is an alphabetical listing of the subject headings with references indented beneath. Chapter titles, code name of the book, and paging are given. If the title is not self-explanatory, further information is included in parentheses, e.g., under MIRRORS, A bower of flowers (felt). This latter feature is especially helpful, because it eliminates the need to scan all likely references in order to locate one utilizing a specific material or technique. Another helpful feature is the breakdown of projects into specific headings. For instance 22 references are grouped under the general heading BELTS. Then the subject is analyzed further under BELTS-BEADED; CROCHETED; EMBROIDERED; FELT; KNITTED; LEATHER; MACRAME; METAL; NEEDLEPOINT; PAPER; PLASTIC; SEASHELLS;

WOOD; WOVEN; with a total of 91 additional references to all these different kinds of belts. In contrast, the Turner *Index to Handicrafts* (see review above) has two headings *Belts* and *Belts, Leather* with a total of 65 references. Eleven references to leather belts are placed under the general heading *Belts* instead of under the specific heading *Belts, Leather,* so the user of the index must depend entirely upon the title for guidance. In addition, the Shields' book has numerous cross-references to bring specific projects to the attention of the reader quickly.

Part II, *Index to Material* (pages 367–477), is an alphabetical listing of all types of raw materials with references listed below of projects utilizing these materials. Egg cartons, plastic lemons, dry cleaning bags, pine cones, clothes dryer lint, clay, copper, toothpicks, spider webs, pill bottles—all are among the raw materials listed. This feature, unique to *Make It,* will be especially appreciated by the Scout leaders, activity directors, craft teachers, conservationists, and others who have an abundance of some of these common objects and materials and wonder how to make the best use of them.

Running heads at the top of each right hand page aid the user in locating desired information. However persons not familiar with the two-part arrangement could confuse the project and materials indexes because of their similarity in format. Guide words at the top of the page or, better yet, use of differently colored paper for the two sections could have minimized this possibility.

The volume is bound in serviceable brown cloth with chalk white lettering, and it lies flat when opened. Its layout is attractive and functional. However, the subject headings are this book's most striking feature. The subject headings are those used in the dictionary catalogs of the Library of Congress and *Readers' Guide,* but original headings have also been devised that are in the crafts vernacular. It is gratifying to be able to locate references under terms familiar to craftsworkers such as *whimmy diddles, theorem painting, kafir pianos, luminaria, syminographs, pine cone turkeys, God's Eye*—headings not found in the Turner index, although references to these same projects can with patience be found under its very general headings.

An examination of several of the books indexed revealed that projects are selectively represented. Apparently unless specific how-to-do-it instructions are included in a text, it does not qualify for inclusion even though there may be self-explanatory illustrations. This observation applies to both the Shields and Turner books.

The two indexes complement each other, and even if the complete set of Faxon's *Index to Handicrafts* is available, *Make It,* because of its congenial subject headings and additional representation of titles, is useful and recommended. Public libraries and organizations serving hobbyists, the disabled, or the elderly, parents, and the conservation minded will all find this is a very useful reference. *(Oct. 15, 1976, p.342)*

016.7455   Handicraft—Indexes   [CIP]   74-17114

Modern science dictionary.
[By] Adelaide Hechlinger. 2d enl. ed. Palisades, N.J., Franklin, 1975. 848p. illus. 21cm. cloth on boards $20.

The first edition of the *Modern Science Dictionary* was reviewed by the Reference and Subscription Books Review Committee in the July 15, 1960, issue of *Booklist and Subscription Books Bulletin.* At that time the Committee stated that "although it contains useful material, the omission of syllabication and pronunciation, the poor organization of related terms, the unsatisfactory definitions, and the ineffective illustrations make it an insufficient guide for high school students and lay persons." The review concluded by not recommending the dictionary for libraries or homes.

The second enlarged edition is identical to the first edition. The only change is the addition of a 43-page section containing the "phonetic spelling of hard-to-pronounce words" and an "addenda section" of 49 pages where words not included in the first edition are defined in a separate alphabet.

Adelaide Hechtlinger, the compiler, teaches at the Bronx High School of Science. She is the author of several high school biology books. Dr. Morris Meister, who wrote the preface to the first edition, founded the Bronx High School of Science. In the endorsement which he wrote for the second edition, he is listed as president of Bronx Community College, although he apparently retired ten years ago. He is also a former president of the National Science Teachers Association.

The dictionary contains some 16,000 entries including about 1,000 in the addenda section. Arrangement throughout is word by word. Definitions, usually no more than single 15-word sentences, are in 2 columns per page. Compound words are usually listed in direct order (*indirect lighting, indirect stain,* etc.). There are, however, some inverted entries (*illumination, direct; illumination, indirect*). Since there is no system of cross-references, there is no way to connect the entry for *illumination, indirect* with that for *indirect lighting.*

The result of the enlargement and revision of *Modern Science Dictionary* is that one must check the main alphabet, the addenda, and the phonetic listing to find both definition and pronunciation. Pronunciations are provided for just under 500 entries, a small fraction of the 16,000 terms in the dictionary. Etymologies are not given, and there are no cross-references.

The dictionary has been compiled for use by high school students. It purports to cover vocabulary used in all branches of high school science as well as the terminology descriptive of "the most important technical accomplishments of our nuclear age" and to be "suitable for both the student and the average adult." While the selection of terms for inclusion in any dictionary may be subjective, the quality of selection for this work is open to some criticism.

There is an entry for *E.E.G. = electroencephalogram* but not for "E.K.G." There is, however, an entry for *electrocardiogram (ekg).* Three definitions are given for "plate," but the earth sciences definition (as in plate tectonics) is omitted. There is no entry for Richter scale (measure of earthquake severity), but there are definitions for *Indian summer* and *broadcasting.* There is a definition for *astrodynamics* but not for "astronaut" or "cosmonaut." The definitions themselves are simplistic, (e.g., "fluoridation—adding one part per million of fluorine to drinking water to lessen decay"; "north pole—the north end of the axis of the earth").

The dictionary includes some biographical resumés; these are one-sentence summaries, without dates, describing scientists' nationalities, fields, and most important contributions. Criteria for selection are not clear. Many Nobel Prize winners are listed, although not all are so identified. "Curie, Marie and Pierre" are listed, as is "Curie, Eve." Irene Curie is excluded, but there is an entry for "Joliot, Irene Curie and Frédéric." Marconi is described only as inventor of telegraphy; his Nobel Prize is not mentioned. In some cases the scientists' contributions (e.g., "van der Waals equation" and "Lorentz electromotive force") are given entries while their biographical sketches are omitted.

The second edition contains the same illustrations as the first. Randomly scattered throughout the book are nine pages, each of which contains nine small, numbered line drawings. Below the drawings is a one-word key to each picture without any indication of scale. These drawings are of such poor quality as to be of little use in clarifying a definition. The definitions do not include references to the drawings.

There is a need for an inexpensive dictionary of scientific terms suitable for high school use. Both the *McGraw-Hill Dictionary of Scientific and Technical Terms* (New York: McGraw-Hill, 1974) and the *Chambers's Dictionary of Science and Technology* (New York: Barnes and Noble, 1972) are much more expensive, and their definitions, though exellent, include many terms which laymen and high school students would not need. The *Dictionary of Science Terms,* edited by G. E. Speck and Bernard Jaffe (New York: Hawthorn, 1965), has fewer and longer definitions. *The Penguin Dictionary of Science* (New York: Schocken, 1971), somewhat British in its orientation, would include most terms needed. It must also be pointed out that many of the terms in *Modern Science Dictionary* are also defined in *Webster's Third New International Dictionary* and the *Random House Dictionary of the English Language. Compton's Illustrated Science Dictionary* (Chicago: Encyclopaedia Britannica Educational Corp., 1971) is planned for the same audience as *Modern Science Dictionary. Compton's* includes about 5,000 terms compared to the nearly 16,000 in *Modern Science Dictionary.* Almost all terms in *Compton's* were found in *Modern Science Dictionary. Compton's* includes the pronunciation and definitions, as well as an example of usage for each entry. Numerous helpful illustrations, always on the same page as the definition, further enhance its effectiveness.

Modern Science Dictionary is well printed on good opaque paper with adequate margins. The binding is sturdy so that the volume should stand up under reasonable use.

With the exception of the new separate section of "phonetic spelling of hard to pronounce words," the features that the Committee found unsatisfactory in the first edition of *Modern Science Dictionary* are still present. The added inconvenience of having to check three separate alphabets to find a definition and pronunciation for a word, the ineffective illustrations, the lack of etymologies and cross-references, the unevenness of the definitions make this an inadequate guide for high school students and the general public. It is not recommended for homes or libraries. *(Mar. 15, 1977, p.1119)*

503 Science—Dictionaries || Reference books, Medical   [OCLC]   75-319165

Monkeys and apes.
†599.8   Primates—Juvenile literature   [OCLC]   75-19972

See page 50

Mountains.
†551.43   Mountains—Juvenile literature   [OCLC]   75-19994

See page 50

The movies.
†791.43   Moving pictures—Juvenile literature   [OCLC]   75-20518

See page 50

The national directory for the performing arts and civic centers.
Editors: Beatrice Handel, Janet Spencer, and Nolanda Turner. 2d ed. Dallas, Handel; dist. by Baker & Taylor, [1975]. 972p. 28cm. cloth $35.

†790.025   Performing arts—Directories || Theater—Directories || Concerts—Directories || Art centers—U.S.—Directories

The national directory for the performing arts/educational.
Editors: Bea Handel, Nolanda Turner, and Janet Spencer. Dallas, Handel, 1975. 28cm. cloth $40; the set $70.

†790.07025   Performing arts—Study and teaching—Directories || Theater—Study and teaching—Directories || Music—Instruction and study—Directories || Universities and colleges—U.S.—Directories

The 1975 edition of *The National Directory for the Performing Arts and Civic Centers* is much larger (972p.) than the 1974 edition (604p.) and now has a companion volume, *The National Directory for the Performing Arts/Educational.* The 1974 one-volume edition was reviewed in *Reference and Subscription Books Reviews* Feb. 15, 1974. In the 1975 edition, there is a newly-added list of 99 contributors. These are mainly arts councils and commissions of various states, libraries, chambers of commerce, and individuals whose credentials and affiliations are not identified.

Representation of states varies considerably. New York and California each are credited with six consultants. For Colorado there is only one; for Michigan, three; for Iowa and Illinois, two each; and for Oklahoma, surprisingly, there are seven. This unevenness in depth of reporting seems to be paralleled by variability in fullness of listings. *The National Directory, Civic Centers* (hereinafter referred to as *NDCC*) was compared with the *Annual Directory* issue of *Musical America,* which is titled *1975 Directory of Performing Arts,* and with the 1972 edition of the *Musician's Guide* (New York: Music Information Service, 1972). Sections that all three publications had in common were those which enumerate orchestras and opera companies. A check of the entries for Michigan and California revealed considerable discrepancies. For Michigan, the *NDCC* lists 13 symphonies; the *Musician's Guide,* 30; and *Musical America,* 29. For California, *NDCC* lists 116 orchestras; *Musician's Guide,* 100; and *Musical America,* 70. A count of opera groups for California showed 43 listed in the *NDCC,* 59 in the *Musician's Guide,* and 16 in *Musical America.* For Michigan, *NDCC* lists 6; *Musician's Guide,* 13; and *Musical America,* only 3.

Although the editors of *NDCC* state in their Introduction, "College and university activities which are open to community participation are included," many groups of this kind have been omitted. It is surprising to find no mention of the University of Michigan Choral Union or the University of Michigan Gilbert and Sullivan Society which include both local citizens and students in their performances. Small city orchestras which are a combination of townspeople and students are also inconsistently represented. Other missing well-known organizations are Flint Symphony Orchestra, Detroit Symphony Youth Orchestra, The Kenneth Jewell Chorale, The Cranbrook Festival, Detroit Institute of Arts Concert Series, Meadowbrook Summer Festival, and the Willoway Theater. This suggests that the list of contributors should be broadened to include associations, local groups such as the Detroit Adventure, museums with regular performing arts programs, music divisions of some of the large public libraries, and perhaps also more chambers of commerce from smaller cities. A similar increase in the number of informants for other states would also be beneficial.

Its shortcomings aside, one must admire the ambitiousness of the *NDCC* project. The cities and towns of this country harbor a multitude of active theater groups which border on the professional and give satisfaction to participants and spectators alike. Compilation of a comprehensive and error-free inventory of these groups and their activities would constitute an extraordinary accomplishment. Needless to say, minor errors were noted in *NDCC* including incorrect addresses and telephone numbers, misspellings, and faulty alphabetization. No major mistakes were noted.

Substantial revision is evident in the 1975 edition. Under the arrangement by states, some entries have been dropped and some added. Alabama has 11 newly-added towns. Phoenix has 10 new entries where it had only 3 in the 1974 edition. Anchorage has 8 entries, double its previous total. A list of Broadway producers active in 1973 and 1974 has been appended to the volume, and the New York City performance facility list is much improved. Altogether 55 facilities have been added. The categories within the entries are still "Facilities," "Dance," "Instrumental Music," "Vocal Music," "Performing Arts Series," and "Theatre," and the kinds of data remain mostly unchanged, but more information has been added for many listings. "Instrumental Music" still consists largely of orchestras with inadequate inclusion of chamber groups. Again, as with theater companies, the abundance and transient nature of semiprofessional chamber ensembles may make it impractical to cover them adequately in this kind of publication.

The new volume has at least enlarged its representation of the more stable kinds of performing organizations. The second part of the set, *The National Directory for the Performing Arts/ Educational,* consists of a listing of colleges and universities in the United States which offer courses and degrees in "dance, instrumental music, vocal music, theatre, film arts, television and visual arts, and others, which may include clown and mime, martial arts, radio, etc." Entries are arranged by state and then by school, giving the address, type of support (private, state, etc.), and classification by number of years offered including fifth-year graduate courses. The names of deans or divisions of the schools supervising the activities are included. The rest of each entry is divided into "Arts Areas"; "Performing Series," which includes concerts, touring companies, and lectures sponsored by the school; "Facilities," listing auditoriums, concert hall, theaters, etc. This section may repeat information which is in the *NDCC* but in less detail. Finally, academic programs are listed with the names of department heads, size of faculty, and number of students enrolled, degrees available, financial assistance, performing groups, workshops, and festivals.

In short, there is a good summary of what students in the performing arts can find on approximately 1,600 U.S. campuses. Errors noted in this volume were again mostly editorial; repeated entries, misspellings, this sort of thing. Comparison with the section of *College Blue Book* entitled "Degrees Offered by College and Subject" (New York: Macmillan, 1975) revealed nearly identical representations of college programs. The *Blue Book,* of course, included more colleges, but most of those with performing arts courses of various kinds are to be found in the educational volume of *The National Directory.*

Both volumes in *The National Directory for Performing Arts* have a number of indexes. The *NDCC* has an Index by categories and also an Alphabetical Index. The educational volume also has a categorical Index, an Index by State and City, and an Alphabetical Index. The format and red-and-blue binding of the 1974 edition have been retained. The page layouts are uncrowded, and a variety of typography makes them easy to read.

These two volumes of the *National Directory of Performing Arts* effectively gather material which could otherwise be found only in many sources. In spite of the fact that there are certain neglected items, these directories still constitute the best single source that deals with performing arts organizations and education in this country. The Committee hopes that the editors will persist in their efforts to upgrade and improve this reference tool. Medium-sized and larger public libraries and special libraries will certainly want both directories. High school libraries may wish to acquire only the educational volume. Recommended.

(July 1, 1977, p.1668)

The Netherlands:
a chronology and fact book, 57BC–1971. Compiled and edited by Pamela and J. W. Smit. Dobbs Ferry, N.Y., Oceana Publications, 1973. 152p. 24cm. cloth $7.50.
949.2   Netherlands—History—Chronology || Belgium—History—Chronology   [CIP]
73-5599
See page 88

The new Columbia encyclopedia.
Edited by William H. Harris and Judith S. Levey, 4th ed. New York, Columbia Univ. Pr., 1975; distributed by Lippincott. 31cm. illus. maps. xiii, 3052p. standard ed. $79.50; deluxe ed. $135.

Since its first appearance in 1935, *Columbia Encyclopedia* has been a standard one-volume desk reference encyclopedia providing information on a wide range of subjects in concise format and in non-technical language for the average adult. The Reference and Subscription Books Review Committee reviewed the second edition of *Columbia* in July 1951 and the third edition May 15, 1964. The fourth edition, published on its fortieth anniversary and retitled *The New Columbia Encyclopedia* continues that tradition. Distribution of subject matter appears to be slightly changed from the previous edition's distribution of 40 percent biographical entries, 40 percent geographical, and 20 percent subject entries. The new edition has about 46 percent biographical matter; geographical entries comprise 30 percent, and miscellaneous subjects are covered in about 24 percent of the articles. The encyclopedia continues to provide basic information on a wide range of subjects and presentations are generally neither complicated, overly involved, nor very long. Richard M. Nixon receives one-and-a-half columns; *Chemistry* fills two columns; *Physics* is almost four columns long; the American Revolution is treated in less than four columns, and *Anthropology, Sociology,* and *Political Science* are cursorily covered in little more than half a column each.

The chief editors of this edition, William H. Harris, Columbia University Press's chief reference book editor, and Judith S. Levey, were assisted by some 170 editorial personnel. The introductory pages also include a roster of 92 academic consultants, 68 percent of them with Columbia University, and 29 percent from other educational institutions such as Yale University, University of California at Berkeley, Julliard, University of Leicester, New York Botanical Gardens, and the Smithsonian Institution. Since two or more persons were involved in the preparation of each entry, they are unsigned. The editors accept ultimate responsibility for the content.

Some of the features of this new edition include greater coverage of non-Western countries and people; more advanced and detailed coverage of science entries; more charts and tables of data, such as lists of Shakespeare's plays, rulers of the more important countries, and constellations. Further, in the new edition, metric equivalents have been added in parentheses after English standard units of measurement.

The articles are arranged alphabetically, with each article heading appearing in boldface type. Smaller boldface type is used to indicate subdivisions of the main topic. For instance, the *Strauss Family* article contains subdivisions for Johann (the elder), Johann (the younger), Josef, and Eduard. Space is saved through reliance on cross-references, e.g., under names of individual Strausses, no data are given, only *see* references to the article on the Strauss family. When two or more articles have the same heading, they are arranged in the sequence: person, place, thing.

Pronunciation is generally indicated only for those parts of proper names which are foreign or unfamiliar. It would have been helpful had more pronunciation aids been provided. The key to pronunciation symbols appears only in the front of the book.

A comparison was made of 400 articles and 140 cross-references in the third and fourth editions. Including the deletion of Hebrew meanings for Biblical entries, approximately 80 percent of the articles in the new edition have been revised in some manner. Some of these revisions are minor cosmetic changes in spelling or word order, while others are major, being evidenced by completely rewritten or greatly expanded articles. About 10 percent of the articles in the third edition have been dropped. Small towns and biographies of personalities of the Western world constitute the major categories of deletions. New articles account for about 13 percent of the fourth edition total. Most new articles are on scientific subjects such as the star *Adhara, Acupuncture,* and *Aardwolf;* third world place-names, such as *Ado, Nigeria,* or the Plain of Adana; or persons recently eminent, such as Hank Aaron and Bella Abzug.

Generally, science articles have received the most revision. Notably, articles dealing with the life sciences have been expanded to include taxonomic descriptions from class through species. Population and other statistical data have been updated, generally to 1970; in any case, the date of each statistic is shown in parentheses. Bibliographies have been updated extensively, but seldom expanded. Root meanings of Latinate terms appear inconsistently. They are not included in new entries, have been deleted from some old entries, and have been retained for others.

Some revisions create problems in locating information. For instance in changing the spellings of Arabic names beginning with "Abu-l ..." in the third edition to "Abu al- ..." in the fourth, no cross-reference was provided from the old spelling. This involves ten personal name entries. Other spelling changes, such as "Aalbory" to "Albory," "Aar" to "Aare," "Aarhus" to "Arhus," "Abdüll Aziz" to "Abd al-Aziz," etc., especially when the new spelling is separated from the old by several entries, did receive cross-references from the old spellings. Further new entries combining more than one entry from the third edition are not always adequately cross-referenced.

A helpful change has been the inclusion of the name of the country for *see* references to variant spellings of place-names, such as the addition of China to the cross-reference from Fort Bayard to Chan-Chaing. The former policy of providing articles on towns with populations of more than 1,000 has been discontinued in favor of a minimum 10,000 population.

The rather extensive table of abbreviations at the entry for *Abbreviation* in the third edition has been dropped. The introductory material of the fourth edition, however, includes a list of abbreviations used in the text. Also, significant abbreviations are themselves entries, such as *Am,* the chemical symbol for the element americium.

Most articles are succinctly written and provide accurate, authoritative data and informed opinion. Some, however, contain ambiguous statements or suffer from imprecise use of language. For instance, the article on *Turkey* states: "European Turkey, which includes Edirne and most of Istanbul, is ..." Since Edirne and Istanbul are the names both of cities and of provinces, the statement may only add to the reader's geographical confusion.

The Committee noted another example of imprecision in the definition of marine biology, which limits the science to the study of plants and animals found in the ocean. This is not correct because marine biology also includes the biology of coastal and estuary life forms. Further, the discussion of zooplankton is limited to protozoa; roe, larva of fish and shellfish, and the copepods are not mentioned. Contrary to the impression left by this article, all plankton are not microorganisms.

Most long articles and many shorter ones conclude with bibliographical references to authorities on the subject. Items are arranged chronologically by publication date. The references are often very abbreviated, referring the reader to "studies by" various authors or "biographies by" various persons, with no indication of the actual titles of the works. For some items, however, the complete title is given. In such cases the publication date and author are always provided for each item. Many of the reference lists have been updated to include more recent titles, editions, or reprints, but few have been expanded since the last edition, and comprehensiveness is not claimed. All books cited appear to be in English. The bibliographies provide a substantial basis for further information if one is interested in becoming better acquainted with a subject treated briefly in *The New Columbia Encyclopedia.*

Cross-references are indicated by *see* references, *see also* references, and by the use of small capitals in text. The latter method, which is mentioned as a footnote on each verso page, has not been consistently followed. For example, the article *Abydos,* an ancient town of Asia Minor, contains no cross-references. Yet eleven items mentioned in the article have separate entries. Two of these are *see* references, but the other nine are substantive articles.

The illustrations are clear, well placed, and quite adequate. There are maps for each state, a locator map for each country or region, and maps for areas of interest such as the Arctic and Antarctica. The illustrations showing devices and processes—capillary, aircraft motions, moldings and column capitals, basilica floorplans, life cycles of animals, and molecular formulae are most successful.

Type for *The New Columbia Encyclopedia* was set by computer. The typeface provides more words per page, yet is far easier to read than that used in the previous edition. The three-column page format is very handsome. The white, nonglare paper also reduces eye strain. The book is thumb indexed and lies flat when opened. The binding is sturdy, and this is essential for such a large, heavy volume.

This extensively revised and updated edition of *The New Columbia Encyclopedia* offers in condensed form authentic and accurate information on a wide range of subjects for the nonspecialist. It is recommended for homes, offices, and all types of libraries. *(Dec. 15, 1976, p.628)*

031 Encyclopedias and dictionaries [CIP] 74-26686

The new illustrated encyclopedia of world history.
Compiled and edited by William L. Langer. 2v. New York, Harry N. Abrams, Inc. [1975]. xxv, 1,368p. 29cm. buckram $65.

The original edition of *Langer's Encyclopedia of World History,* a modernized and revised version of *Ploetz's Epitome* (1883), was published in 1940; successive editions followed in 1948, 1952, and 1968. The first two were reviewed by the Subscription Books Review Committee, which recommended the work especially as a quick reference source.

In 1972 Houghton Mifflin brought out the fifth edition of the *Encyclopedia of World History* at a price of $17.50; that edition is still in print. Now, the Foreword to this new illustrated edition explains that as we are "living in a visually oriented age ... used to seeing history happen ... it seems appropriate to publish an illustrated edition of Professor Langer's classic reference work." The text of this 1975 illustrated edition is identical with the 1972 edition except for the correction of a few minor errors in the Index. The price increase of nearly 200 percent results in part from the incorporation of over 1,900 very fine illustrations which add this title to the impressive catalog of Abrams Artbooks.

While it is true that the volumes embrace the history of the world, emphasis is on the history of Europe; all other continents together receive less space than that given to Europe alone. As with the earlier edition, this is chiefly a handbook of political and military history with only token coverage of cultural events.

Recognized scholars are responsible for the work. William Leonard Langer, the editor and compiler, is Coolidge professor of history (emeritus) at Harvard, a member of the Royal Historical Society, and past president of the American Historical Association. The contributors include scholars who have specialized in such fields as anthropology, European history, Oriental research, the history of science and technology, Ottoman history, and Asian history.

This two-volume set presents the events of world history beginning with prehistoric times and concluding with the space age. The material is grouped in eight broad periods: I. the Prehistoric Period; II. Ancient History; III. the Middle Ages; IV. the Early Modern Period (1500 to 1800); V. the Modern Period (1800 to 1960); VI. the First World War; VII. the Second World War; VIII. the Recent Period, which includes the exploration of space. Within these categories, the material is subdivided by geographic region and then placed into narrower segments in chronological order. For example, Ancient History is arranged:

1. Mesopotamia, to 333 B.C.
2. Egypt, to 332 B.C.
3. Syria-Palestine, to 332 B.C.
4. Anatolia, to 547 B.C.
5. Armenia, to 56 B.C.
6. Iran, to 330 B.C.
7. India, to 72 B.C.
8. China, to 221 B.C.

At the conclusion of each of these sections, a cross-reference leads one to the next segment dealing with the same area, thus enabling the user to trace the entire history of a given country.

The three-column page consists of calendar year in boldface type, month and day when possible, and the corresponding event. Textual explanations then follow with listings ranging from a line or so to a 10- or 15-line paragraph. Each page carries at least one illustration; more often, two or three. This profusion of pictorial material (almost 2,000 illustrations) includes 127 plates in full color, 57 maps, and 104 genealogical tables. For the most part, the illustrations are excellent. The black-and-white photographs (credits given on the final two pages of the Appendix) generally have a proper sharpness of definition and are placed near the text they illustrate. The color reproductions of paintings (sources given beside the picture) are magnificent; they include masterpieces—Bellini's *Doge Leonardo Loredano,* Velasquez' *Maria Anna of Austria,* Howard Pyle's *Battle of Bunker Hill,* Charles Webber's *Fugitive Slaves on the Underground Railroad,* Gilbert Stuart's *George Washington,* and many more.

Unquestionably, this all makes for "absorbing and delightful browsing." The same sentence of the Foreword, however, includes the claim "serious reference work." This latter phrase seems to be an exaggeration, since the absence of notes or bibliography would impede scholarly use.

The Index is detailed and accurate; it appears to include all boldface names and it does give a fair number of cross-references; it does not indicate on which pages illustrations of persons appear. Separate indexes are provided to genealogical tables and maps.

As already indicated, the books are beautifully made. Bound in charcoal cloth with gold lettering on the spine, each volume carries an embossed figure on the cover—volume I, an ancient Egyptian; volume II, a spaceman. The paper is of quality stock, but some of the illustrations are bled to the edge of the page.

Langer's *Encyclopedia of World History* has long been a standard reference work in public, academic, and school libraries. This new illustrated edition, with its quality reproductions, is a successful but expensive publication. Libraries owning the 1972 edition would likely be hesitant to purchase this edition in order to obtain the illustrations, many of which they may have in other sources. On the other hand, libraries may decide that the illustrative enrichment of the text justifies addition of this handsome boxed set to their collections. Recommended.

(Oct. 1, 1976, p.276)

902'.02   History—Outlines, syllabi, etc.   [CIP]   74-31218

The new Oxford atlas.
Prepared by the Cartographic Department of the Oxford University Press. [London], Oxford Univ. Pr. [c1975]. 202p. col. illus. col. maps. 39cm. Linson 4, $19.95.

The New Oxford Atlas is compiled, drawn, and photographed by the Cartographic Department of the Oxford University Press. It is developed from the *Oxford Atlas* of 1951. The atlas is arranged in six sections: physical maps of the oceans; regional maps illustrating relief, climate and geologic formations; the main series of political-physical maps of the world; world thematic maps; thematic maps for the United Kingdom; and the 50,000 entry gazetteer. The Contents lists each map and associated insets, the scale, and the page. There is also a key map index to the main series of maps. Another useful feature is the two-page description of map projections and the list of abbreviations. The atlas utilizes a number of different map projections, among them conical orthomorphic, transverse mercator, and zenithal equidistant. The legend is printed on each map; the bar scale is in miles and kilometers. However, scale equivalent in miles per inch is not provided.

The four single-page maps for the Pacific, Atlantic, and Indian Oceans, and the waters around Antarctica are bled to the edges of the pages. At the scale of 1:50,000,000, they illustrate rifted zones, compression belts, unstable areas, ocean currents, icecaps, etc.

The second section is comprised of seven pages of regional physical maps, also bled to the edge of the page, which include a wealth of information. These use the same altitude layer coloring as the ocean maps but combine it with geologic and climatic data. Through overprinting of letters and numbers, winter and summer climate, temperatures, and duration of wet and dry seasons are presented. Also indicated are elements of geology and structure of the earth, such as sedimentary cover and folded belts. The scale for these maps is approximately 1:25,000,000.

The third major section consists of the main series of 41 maps on 79 pages. All are double-page spreads except the maps of Africa, Southern Africa, and Central South America. The page distribution among major areas is as follows: Eurasia (2), Europe (28), Asia and the USSR (18), Australasia (6), Africa (10), and the Americas (15). Boundaries and major transportation networks are shown, and relief is indicated by a series of layer tints. The scales vary from 1:32,000,000 for the general map of North and South America to 1:1,000,000 for the map of England. The maps are generally medium to small scale and omit many towns, highways, airports, and other man-made features. Also the imbalance in coverage is rather dramatic. For example, 28 of the 79 pages contain 4 maps of Europe, and 5 of these maps are of the United Kingdom. The same number of maps (5) is devoted to the much larger land mass of Canada and the U.S. Australia and New Zealand are covered in 6 pages (3 maps), while the largest country in the world, the USSR, receives 4 pages (only 2 maps) of coverage. Europe, and especially the British Isles are mapped at relatively large scales, generally 1:1,000,000, 1:2,000,000 and 1:4,000,000 while other areas of the world, e.g., North America, are mapped at smaller scales, ranging from 1:5,000,000 to 1:32,000,000.

In the fourth section a series of seven thematic maps portrays world climate, land use and vegetation, population distribution, and growth. In addition the next section has nine thematic maps of the United Kingdom depicting population, land structure, vegetation, geology, mineral deposits, climate, and land use.

The 50,000-entry Gazetteer "is an index of the towns and topographical features shown on the maps." The entries are alphabetized letter by letter and include the following information: name, country, state or province (for selected countries only), map page number, and alphanumeric grid system designator for simplified location on the page. The Gazetteer is arranged five columns per page. According to the Notes on the Use of the Gazetteer, versions of foreign place-names "have been employed which will be most familiar to readers of English language newspapers, etc." Well-known foreign names are entered under both local and Anglicized forms, e.g., both *Wien* and *Vienna.* Rules of transliteration of the U.S. Board on Geographic Names and the British Permanent Committee on Geographical Names have been adopted. The Gazetteer is accurate but does not list all placenames on the maps.

A comparison was made with the fourth edition of the *National Geographic Atlas of the World* (1975, $22.95) which was reviewed by the Committee in the May 15, 1976 *Reference and Subscription Books Reviews. National Geographic* is 50 percent larger in size, contains approximately 50 percent more maps, and 175 percent the number of gazetteer entries. Moreover, *National Geographic* includes considerably larger scale maps. For example, it contains 10 pages of political and physical maps for South America at scales ranging from 1:6,930,000 to 1:12,710,000, whereas the *New Oxford Atlas* has 4 pages of maps for the continent at scales of 1:8,000,000, 1:16,000,000 and 1:32,000,000. *National Geographic* is much more detailed and covers many more towns, natural features, highways, etc. For example, *National Geographic* lists 33 towns located on the Yukon River in Alaska; the *New Oxford Atlas* shows 14. The

National Geographic delineates the extensive Trans-Amazon Highway while *New Oxford* does not. Eighteen pages of ocean maps appear in *National Geographic,* while only 3 pages are provided in *New Oxford*. The information in *National Geographic* also appears more up to date, e.g., the *New Oxford* includes the 1967 Arab-Israeli cease fire lines while the *National Geographic* illustrates the 1974 cease fire lines. However, the *National Geographic* does not contain the 14 thematic maps and does not map geologic formations. Moreover, these maps account for only 20 percent of the maps in *New Oxford,* and the *National Geographic* does include a number of charts and statistical data which duplicate and surpass coverage in *New Oxford.*

Although the *New Oxford Atlas* contains useful climatic/geologic regional maps and world and British thematic maps, the main series of political-physical maps does not provide sufficient detail for an American audience. Comparably priced general world atlases include maps of a larger scale with more balanced representation of the nations of the world. Therefore, *The New Oxford Atlas* is recommended primarily for libraries serving readers who may be interested in Great Britain's geography, geology, demography, vegetation, and land use.

(Oct. 15, 1976, p.343)

†912 Atlases, British [OCLC]

New York art yearbook 1975–1976.
Edited by Judith Tannenbaum. v.1. New York, Noyes Press, 1976. xvi, 288p. 31cm. cloth $24.

New York Art Yearbook 1975–1976 is announced as the first of a series of annual volumes recording art exhibitions in New York City. Coverage is limited to one-person shows at 210 galleries and museums from September 1975 through June 1976. Exhibitions by painters, sculptors, and photographers are included.

The yearbook is unique in that there is no other detailed listing of one-person exhibitions covering an entire New York City season. Although the publisher is apparently new to the subject of art, the editor was a regular contributor to *Arts Magazine* throughout the first half of the 1970s.

The arrangement of the yearbook is simple and clear. The first half of the book is made up of 1,239 brief entries under the names of the artists who exhibited; the second half is devoted to small black-and-white photographic reproductions of representative examples of the artists' works. The galleries and museums housing the exhibitions are listed alphabetically with addresses preceding the biographical section.

In the first half of the yearbook, the entries are presented alphabetically in double-column pages. Entries are under the names by which artists are known, with no cross-reference from the differing real names. As a result, there are no entries under Anna Mary Robertson and Friedrich Stowasser, but there are entries for Grandma Moses and Hundertwasser. Where two artists shared an exhibition, there is only one entry, but there is a reference from the second-named artist to the first-named.

Biographical information is minimal, and there is no indication of how it was obtained beyond an expression of thanks "to the gallery and museum staffs and to the individual artists who provided biographical information, background material, and photographs." In general, the biographical data include birth and death years, colleges and art schools attended, galleries or museums where exhibitions were held, inclusive exhibition dates, and three or four sentences categorizing the artist's work.

Artists who are currently active dominate the exhibitions, and this is reflected in the yearbook's coverage. Only 69 of the 1,239 artists have birth dates earlier than 1901, and of these, only 14 were born before 1876. The earliest artist included is John Singleton Copley (1738–1815).

Pronunciation of artists' names is not indicated. While this omission is not a matter of major concern in a specialized art reference library, one wonders how many generalists will be comfortable pronouncing Jiří Kolář, Aristide Maillol, and Ay-O without a guide.

Black-and-white photographs of works by 1,053 of the artists follow the biographical entries. One representative example of each artist's work is shown. Arranged alphabetically by artist's surname, there are six photographs, each approximately two-and-a-half-inches by three-and-a-half-inches, per page.

The yearbook is sturdily bound and lies flat when opened. Layout is good with easily read typefaces. Each entry is set off from its neighbors, and margins are sufficiently wide to allow rebinding.

The paper used in the biographical section is opaque and nonglare. The black-and-white photographs are printed on heavy glossy stock. The photographs have excellent definition despite the small scale, but the lack of color is disappointing.

New York Art Yearbook 1975–1976 is a specialized reference book which is recommended for libraries whose readers need information on one-person art exhibitions in New York City during one annual season. Large public libraries and institutions supporting art school curricula will find this an essential resource. Although the information on any one artist or exhibition is brief, the yearbook offers further leads; the exhibition dates indicate when the artist's show might have been reviewed, and the gallery name and address supply another source of information. As additional annual volumes are published, the *New York Art Yearbook* will provide a valuable cumulative record of New York City one-person shows.

(June 1, 1977, p.1524)

†708.1747'1 Art—New York (City)—Exhibitions—Yearbooks   76-11654

The ocean world of Jacques Cousteau.
rev. ed. Danbury, Conn., World Pub. Co. in cooperation with Danbury Pr., a division of Grolier Enterprises, Inc., [1975]. 20v. illus. (part col.), maps. tables. diagrs. 28cm. plasticized paper over boards $139.50.

The Ocean World of Jacques Cousteau (hereafter *Ocean World*) is a 20-volume set concerned with the oceans generally and, more specifically, with marine life and exploration. This is a revised edition of *The Ocean World of Jacques Cousteau* produced in 1974. According to the publisher, the 1975 edition resulted from revisions made by Captain Cousteau after thorough reassessment of the original edition.

Jacques Ives Cousteau is, of course, a well-known oceanographer, underwater explorer, and submarine photographer. He is the author of numerous books, including the best-selling *The Silent World* (1953). His documentary films include the award-winning *The Silent World* (1956) and *World Without Sun* (1966). He was partly responsible for the invention of the aqualung, and he participated in making the free-diving bathyscaphe. He promoted the Conshelf project, and he is active in the conservation movement.

The development of *Ocean World* seems very much to have been a team effort involving a number of people in various capacities—project director, managing editor, senior editor, creative director, illustrations editor, science consultant, and the like. Since the project extended over several years, vacancies inevitably occurred so that changes in staff resulted and individual contributors did not necessarily continue in the same positions. After the first six volumes, Peter Ritner was replaced as project director by Steven Schepp, who previously served as managing editor. Ritner is former vice-president and editor-in-chief of World Publishing Company, and Schepp is an author who has written popular materials in the field of science. The production team also included individuals from the Cousteau organization and from the publisher's in-house staff. Credits for the revised volumes are the same as for the original edition.

The *Ocean World* is, according to its publisher, intended for student use through senior high school and for home use by both children and adults. This review will assess the set's appropriateness for this broad spectrum of readers.

The set is comprised of individually titled books, each of which has a basic theme, is subdivided topically, and is discursive in treatment. Volume 1 is typical. Entitled *Oasis in Space,* it has 144 pages including the table of contents and the Index; chapters vary in length from two to eighteen pages; text occupies approximately 35–40 percent of space available with the remainder allocated to photographic plates, charts and diagrams, captions, framed quotations from the text, and the like. The titles of the other volumes are v.2, *The Act of Life;* v.3, *Quest for Food;* v.4, *Window in the Sea;* v.5, *The Art of Motion;* v.6, *Attack and Defense;* v.7, *Invisible Message;* v.8, *Instinct and Intelligence;* v.9, *Pharaohs of the Sea;* v.10, *Mammals in the Sea;* v.11, *Provinces of the Sea;* v.12, *Man Reenters the Sea;* v.13, *A Sea of Legends;* v.14, *The Adventure of Life;* v.15, *Outer and Inner Space;* v.16, *The Whitecaps;* v.17, *Riches of the Sea;* v.18, *Challenges of the Sea;* v.19, *The Sea in Danger;* and v.20, *Guide to the Sea.*

The broad thematic organization of *Ocean World* distinguishes it generally from a more systematic and traditional approach which might have emphasized the academic disciplines such as geography, geology, marine biology, and their appropriate subdivisions. For example, *marine life* or *biology* could have been subdivided by such topics as "ecology," "plant life," "animal life," etc. Further subdivisions could have been taxonomic characteristics, organismic systems, and the like. Cousteau's "horizontal" or thematic arrangement is the more holistic and permits greater attention to interrelationships. Its attendant drawback is a greater dispersion of related material. And since broad themes tend toward indistinct definition, greater reliance must be placed on the thoroughness and precision of the set's indexes. The problem is somewhat exacerbated by the selection of the above named titles for some volumes which make it difficult to know the theme, and indeed the themes of some volumes remain vague even after an examination of the contents. For instance, *Oasis in Space* deals with such various matters as man's dependence on the sea, the origins of life, the essential life drives, the sensual universe of marine animals, the nervous system and how animals "think" and react, behavior and adaptive patterns of some marine animals, and geography of the oceans. It is difficult to see how these relate to the title, or indeed what the title means, and how these topics reflect a common theme. According to the publisher, *Oasis in Space* was intended as a synoptic volume, but the prospective user will not be privy to this information. In any case, considered as a synopsis, the volume has many shortcomings and does not adequately represent the scope of the set.

It should also be noted that occasionally material is included in a volume that seems to have little in common with the theme. For example, in the volume entitled *Instinct and Intelligence,* a section of one chapter deals with the interrelationship between food and sex. No mention is made of instinct or intelligence, and the material might more logically have been placed in the *Act of Life,* which deals with sexual matters, or in the one covering the quest for food.

In general, the first ten volumes treat biological themes, while the last ten concentrate on geography and exploration. No strict separation is made. Volume 13, *A Sea of Legends,* deals with the sea in legend, myth, and art; volume 19, *The Sea in Danger,* looks at pollution and conservation. The volumes concerned with exploration and geography seem generally to be more authoritatively handled than those dealing with biological topics. This may be due to the fact that knowledge in the former areas tends to be strictly cumulative, rather than qualifying, in nature—as is frequently the case in the biological sciences. Inattention to some minute thread within the expanding tapestry of scientific findings can often totally invalidate a statement about the life sciences.

Ocean World also differs from most traditional reference works in its frank espousal of respect for the delicacy of natural relationships and its encouragement of conservational attitudes. The set includes frequent references to Cousteau's own work, as well as the explorations and the historical and contemporary researches of others. Nearly every volume contains references to Cousteau's famous research ship *Calypso.* These personal notes add a dimension of interest commonly lacking in encyclopedic sets.

The material is reasonably accurate, but there are some errors, especially in discussions of biological subjects. Occasionally the errors seem to be the result of oversimplification which can perhaps be defended as inevitable if the material is to be comprehended by children. Were all the exceptions, reservations, and other complexities dealt with, the work would quickly be elevated to a level comprehensible only to specialists. Less defensible are confused presentations or misleading statements, such as the assertion that an average cubic foot of sea water has as many as 20,000 microscopic plants. If by "plants" is meant species of plants, it has not been possible to substantiate this undocumented statement. If individual organisms are meant, this figure conflicts with a subsequent statement that this same volume of water may hold 12 million plant cells or diatoms. But the greatest objection to the assertion is its implication that there is a "typical" volume of sea water and that meaningful statements can be made about it. In fact, the sea is composed of a number of zones—littoral, pelagic, etc.—the populations of which vary greatly. Even in well-defined areas such as the Sargasso Sea, the plants and associated animals tend to cluster so that comparatively lush patches are set off by areas with dilute concentrations of life. And there are other complicating facts such as "rips"—those foamy areas where two ocean currents converge—which tend toward high and diverse populations.

Again, with respect to coverage, there seems to be a bias towards dramatic aspects of marine life. But this is understandable in that unusual behavioral patterns and spectacular creatures are precisely where much interest resides, especially for the younger person or one with more elementary knowledge of marine biology.

The illustrative material which makes up a substantial part of the *Ocean World* is composed largely of photographic plates with occasional maps, charts, and colored drawings. (Volume 13, *A Sea of Legends,* which covers material from the epic of Gilgamesh and the Story of Jason and the Argonauts to the Loch Ness monster and the ballet *Lady from the Sea* is, as might be expected, illustrated primarily, although not exclusively, with drawings and photographs of paintings.) According to the publishers, the set contains more than 2,600 color pictures, 103 black-and-white pictures, and 197 maps, charts, drawings, and tables. In general the illustrative material is well chosen and helpful, although a serious lack in some photographs is scale or size information. A number of illustrations with little reference value, such as a photograph of a city street crowded with vehicular traffic, have been included. These add pictorial substantiation to a chapter on air pollution and frequently enliven and reinforce points made in the text. The charts and diagrams included are generally useful and accurate.

Each volume of the *Ocean World* has an Index, and in the final volume there are a general Index to the set, a Glossary, and a Bibliography.

While all the indexes for individual volumes seem accurate, there is considerable variation in their depth, and all of them leave much to be desired in terms of entry detail. Some typical entries for *Challenges of the Sea,* (v.18), for example, are *Calypso, dolphins, eels, falcon, habitats,* and *mines,* with no further indication of the particular aspect of these entities being dealt with on the pages referenced. Both items indexed for *Calypso* have in fact nothing to do with the ship *per se,* but rather concern incidents that occurred aboard *Calypso,* the one involving the rescue of a circumnavigating sailor in distress and the other an archaeological discovery in the Mediterranean. The only other Index entries provided for the first incident are the names of the small craft and the sailor rescued—neither of particular significance and neither likely to be searched for in the volume. For the second incident, no entries appear in the Index under *archaeology, amphoras* (the vessels recovered), *Greece,* or *Italy* (the vessels were Campanian). The only other reference noted in the Index was an entry for *Sestius, Marcus,* the Roman who owned the sunken ship from which the amphoras were recovered. This inconsistency and shallowness is typical of the indexes to the single volumes. *See* and *see also* references are not used.

The general Index to the work occupies more than 17 pages, set four columns to the page, and contains approximately 2,900 main entries. Animals and plants are entered by common names if such exist; otherwise they are cited by the scientific names. Occasionally a *see also* directs one from normal word order to inverted order. Far more subentries and more precise main entries appear in the general Index than are used in the volume Indexes, but since the organization of the work is loose, much greater detail in indexing would still be desirable. For example, one finds that *bacteria* (which has only three subentries) is covered twelve times within six different volumes. Since none of the volumes appears to treat, say, diseases of marine animals exclusively, how is one to know which, if any, of the citations treat pathogenic organisms? One's patience is tried further by the fact that one of these references is blind. Terms are alphabetized word-by-word with page references to illustrations in boldface. Volume numbers are printed in Roman numerals; page numbers in Arabic. Overall entries are consistently formulated, and citations are accurate. *See* and *see-also* references are used sparingly, and a more useful Index would have resulted if terms had been tied together in a better system of cross-referencing. This is especially true inasmuch as there is no internal referencing in the text of the encyclopedia.

Volume 20 also has a 14-page Glossary and a 4-page Bibliography. As noted above, the language of the text is generally untechnical, and this brief Glossary should be adequate to the needs of the user. The bibliography is divided by subject—general ocean science, evolution, marine archaeology, undersea resources, etc.—and is made up primarily of popular adult materials published in English since 1950 but does have a scattering of technical manuals, textbooks, foreign language books, and earlier publications. The general reading level of books cited would be within the range of good students in the eighth and ninth grades.

The *Ocean World* is printed on coated low-reflectance stock of good opacity in double columns of well-leaded and legible type. The pages are perfect-bound, and the volumes lie flat when opened. The cover boards are covered with plasticized paper, and the spines lack flexibility, having board backstrips which will not withstand protracted use. While type margins are adequate, illustrations extend to the edges, making rebinding a problem.

In summary, *The Ocean World of Jacques Cousteau* is a popularly written encyclopedia of marine life, oceanography, exploration, and conservation with somewhat better treatment of the latter three areas than of marine life. The work's content is adequate for young people and adult slow learners, but its treatment of biological topics tends to make it less suitable for secondary schools and adults capable of addressing more difficult materials. As a reference resource the set has deficiencies in organization and adequacy of access, but since a comparable better work is not available, *The Ocean World of Jacques Cousteau* can be recommended for homes and libraries serving children. *(Jan. 15, 1977, p.742)*

†574.92   Marine biology—Dictionaries || Ocean—Dictionaries   72-87710

The official encyclopedia of baseball.
[By] Hy Turkin and S. C. Thompson. 8th rev. ed., [1976]. New York, Barnes, [c1976]. 715p. 25cm. cloth $14.95 (This ed. now o.p.)

†796.357'021   Baseball—Statistics

See page 6

Official rules of sports and games, 1976–77.
12th ed. Illustrations by H. Radcliffe Wilson and Roger Deer. [London, Kay & Ward Ltd.; distributed in the U.S. by] Sport Shelf, P.O. Box 634, New Rochelle, NY 10802, 1976. illus. 20cm. 862p. cloth $22.50.

This is the twelfth edition of the *Official Rules of Sports and Games.* The first edition was published in 1949; since 1964, the book has been revised every two years, each edition updating its predecessor.

The *Official Rules* is a compilation of rules of various sports and games played primarily in Great Britain. Rules and regulations have been set forth together with the "complete cooperation of the governing associations, unions, and federations of the various sports." Twenty-six of these organizations, all based in England and each representing a different sport, have contributed to the volume.

The book's dust jacket states that "almost every game played today has been included from Archery to Water Polo." This claim is, however, an exaggeration. It is true that the 26 sports included in the volume are major sports in Britain—rugby, cricket, English basketball, volleyball, hockey, bowls, and lacrosse, among others. However, several sports popular in Britain are omitted; examples are gun sports, airborne sports (such as parachuting), and gymnastics. Also, the only aquatic sport included is water polo. Excluded are baseball and softball and the American versions of soccer and football. Readers interested in these and many other sports not represented in the *Official Rules* should consult the colorful and concise *Rules of the Game* (The Diagram Group, Paddington Pr., distributed by Two Continents Publishing Co., 1974).

One of the chapters included in the *Official Rules* is the 44-page one titled "Athletics." The Table of Contents does not indicate that, in accord with British practice, "athletics" includes what Americans refer to as "track-and-field" sports such as cross country, the high jump, shotput, discus throwing, hurdles, and tug-of-war races.

The rules and regulations of each of the 26 sports are covered in separate chapters. With the exception of the chapter on the rules of cricket, each chapter is intended to be a comprehensive and complete statement of the rules of the sport. The chapter on cricket includes all the basic rules of the sport, but because of "reasons of space," some official interpretations of the rules have been excluded.

Although each sport's rules contain different items, the following aspects are covered for all: (1) Standards and measures of playing field (diagrams and drawings often included), (2) Equipment specifications, (3) Dress (drawings included), (4) Scoring (charts included), (5) Rules of playing, along with penalties for misconduct and breaking of rules, (6) Glossary of terms, and (7) General objective of the game.

Metric and/or English units of measurement are cited depending upon the prevailing practice of the sport (e.g., ice hockey uses the metric system; lawn tennis uses both; and bowls employs English units exclusively).

Some of the chapters (rugby fives, real tennis, and bowls) begin with a glossary of terms—something particularly helpful for American readers. Two (rugby union football and basketball) commence with a discussion of the general purpose and object of the game. Many start out with a section on the playing field (e.g., netball, badminton, croquet, water polo); women's lacrosse and men's lacrosse open with a detailed description of the equipment of the sport; and golf begins with a section on "etiquette."

Two major weaknesses of the book are its uneven organization and lack of an index. The rules skip often from specifics to generalities and back to specifics. So many cross-references are made to other sections of the rules which relate to what is being described that the browser is confused. Many of them would be unnecessary if the chapters were organized more uniformly.

The line drawings employed to illustrate rules are small and are generally not very helpful in aiding the reader to understand the text. The full-page diagrams of the playing fields are simple, clear, and accurate but not very attractive.

There is no index, and the Table of Contents does not analyze the information in each chapter; it merely lists the sports for which rules are stated and the pages on which the coverages begin.

This compact book (five by seven and a half inches) opens easily and is sturdily bound. Paper quality is good, and the margins are wide enough to allow for rebinding.

The Official Rules of Sports and Games contains detailed and very precise rules and regulations for games and sports played in Great Britain. It is intended to serve as a reference standard for each sport. Unfortunately, beginners or persons unfamiliar with British sports will find the text hard to follow.

Because of the relatively high price, the British focus of the book, its organizational weaknesses, and the lack of easy access routes to specific information, recommendation is limited to libraries with comprehensive collections on British or international sports. *(July 1, 1977, p.1669)*

†796.018 Sports 51-24610

Outdoor recreation.

[By] Robert G. Schipf. Littleton, Col., Libraries Unlimited, 1976. 278p. 24cm. skivertex $12.50. (Spare Time Guides: Information Sources for Hobbies and Recreation, no. 9)

016.796 Outdoor recreation—Bibliography || Outdoor recreation—U.S.—Bibliography || Outdoor recreation—Canada—Bibliography [CIP] 75-30958

Sports.

[By] Marshall E. Nunn. Littleton, Col., Libraries Unlimited, 1976. 217p. 24cm. skivertex $11.50. (Spare Time Guides: Information Sources for Hobbies and Recreation, no. 10)

016.796 Sports—Bibliography [CIP] 75-33869

Outdoor Recreation by Robert G. Schipf and *Sports* by Marshall E. Nunn are the ninth and tenth annotated bibliographies in the continuing "Spare Time Guide Series" which began in 1973. The books intend to serve as selective buying and reading guides to current, popular, easy-to-locate literature on a wide variety of sports and outdoor activities. Other books in the series cover automobile repair, hunting and fishing, home repair, crafts, stamps and coins, wine, weaving, and railroads. Both Schipf and Nunn are librarians; Schipf is responsible for two other books in this series.

The two volumes under review are arranged by broad subject categories, subarranged alphabetically by author, and entries are numbered consecutively. Additional access is provided by a Table of Contents referring to page number and an Author/Title Index referring to entry number. *Outdoor Recreation* also includes some subject Index entries.

Primary, but not exclusive, emphasis is on U.S. sources. Most inclusions may be presumed to be currently available because the occasional out-of-print item is so indicated. Citations include author, title, publishing information, pagination, special features (e.g., illustrated, bibliography, paperback, price, L.C. card number). The ISBN is included in *Outdoor Recreation* only. Annotations are evaluative and written in an informal style. Cross-referencing in both the body of the bibliographies and the indexes is limited. Following the main list of books are annotated lists of periodicals and associations and a directory of publishers.

Outdoor Recreation covers activities that can be "accomplished alone or with a minimum of companions." Excluded are games and the field generally referred to as athletics, these areas being covered in the companion volume, *Sports*. For activities which may be considered as either recreational or competitive, *Outdoor Recreation* treats the former aspect of this activity, and *Sports* treats the latter. For example, *Away We Go: A Guidebook of Family Trips, One Day Adventures by Car,* and *The Making of Tools* are listed in the recreation volume, while *Match-Winning Tennis, The Olympic Games Handbook,* and *Tuning a Racing Yacht* are in the sports book.

Outdoor Recreation lists 739 books in 10 chapters entitled "Camping and Hiking," "Foods and Cooking," "Identifying and Collecting," "Vehicle Activities," "Winter Activities," "Water Activities," "Aerial Activities," "Country Living," "Animal-Related Activities," and "Miscellaneous." Each chapter is preceded by the author's quite chatty commentary. "Camping and Hiking" receives the most attention; indeed, the distinction between materials included in this chapter and those in the general touring and sight-seeing category is unclear. Also, since there are several titles in this chapter that deal with a variety of miscellaneous outdoor activities, a general category for these entries would have been useful. At the conclusion of the chapter is a listing of "First-Choice Titles" for camping and hiking enthusiasts; none of the other chapters have such listings.

Other chapters in *Outdoor Recreation* are more ambiguous in scope and less thorough in coverage. Gardening sources are included in "Country Living," but so few are listed that the author might have considered excluding them altogether. Similarly, "Animal-Related Activities" is quite limited. There is no material on cats. It might have been more politic if the few dog books had been omitted as well.

Each of the subjects covered in "Miscellaneous" has very few entries. Again, it would seem more appropriate to exclude such activities as photography and physical fitness than to provide only one to three titles. "Foods and Cooking" contains a number of titles that are simply specialty cookbooks without outdoor emphasis. The section on "Automobiles" reveals uncertainty as to whether the automobile should be treated as a sports or a travel vehicle, and it is difficult to determine where the line is drawn between the touring and camping books. Skating is not represented; nor is diving, except as incidental inclusions within general titles.

Although the author admits his difficulty in avoiding subjectivity in the choice of representative titles, the inclusion of *The Foxfire Book,* without mention of *The Whole Earth Catalog,* in "Country Living" is surprising. Also, *Skiing Is a Family Sport* is described as dealing almost exclusively with alpine skiing, a subject area specifically noted in *Outdoor Recreation's* Introduction as being excluded. Furthermore, the author indicates that "almost any other book listed here would be more useful." Other annotations tend to damn titles with faint praise. The Wind Drifters Balloon Club is listed both in the main body of book titles, with a cross-reference to ("see list of organizations") and in the list of organizations. Inclusion of certain periodicals is questionable because their annotations indicate that the titles are not suitable for recreationists, or are no longer being published. In addition, Schipf includes materials he has not even seen.

After the main body of *Outdoor Recreation,* there are 208 periodicals and some 150 organizations in separate listings which are arranged under the same broad subject headings used for the books. Most of these have one-line annotations. The periodical entries are numbered and indexed; the organizations are not.

Sports is a bibliography of 649 books, with 94 periodical titles and nearly 40 sporting organizations included in the supplementary lists. The major U.S. competitive sports, such as baseball, self-defense, and tennis, provide the broad subject framework for the arrangement of the titles. There are also chapters devoted to "General Sports Books" and the "Olympics." Each chapter is composed of two listings: one of reference and the other of general books on the sport. Typical inclusions are materials on how to play the game, biographies of players, histories of the sport, and collections of anecdotes and articles. Even though the emphasis is on recent, in-print items, a small number of "classics" in each field are included. The annotations attempt to give the comparative merits of the various titles.

Unlike its companion volume, *Sports* has no chapter introductions. The annotations are readable and relatively impersonal; the periodical annotations are conspicuously more complete. It appears that all items were examined by the author. Although the periodical listing follows the same outline as the main body of the work, the organizations are arranged alphabetically by name. Access would have been improved had players' names been included in the index; subject indexing is not provided but is unnecessary if one uses the Table of Contents.

Selection criteria appear to have been easier to apply to this volume. Nonetheless, some reference works seem to have been miscast as general titles, and vice versa. Question-and-answer-formatted material sometimes is considered reference, sometimes general. Fairly recent books such as W. Timothy Gallwey's *The Inner Game of Tennis* (New York: Random House, 1974) are included, but the name change of the United States Lawn Tennis Association to the United States Tennis Association is not picked up.

As might be expected, there is overlap between the two guides. Both authors include selections on equestrian, aerial, water, and winter sports, as well as motorcycling and automobile activities; but there is remarkably little repetition of individual titles within those categories. None of the titles dealing with horses, racing, cars, or water activities are repeated. There are three titles on aerial sports listed in both volumes, five out of ten on motorcycles, and five on winter sports.

The volumes are bound in skivertex. They are printed on non-glare paper and have attractive and legible formats. Titles are in heavier type, and running heads of chapter subjects appear at the top of the pages. The margins are adequate for rebinding, and the books lie flat when opened.

The books in the "Spare Time Guide Series" intend to provide librarians, hobbyists, and recreationists with selective, annotated lists of recent materials. *Outdoor Recreation* and *Sports* carry out this intent, despite the sometimes confusing selection criteria applied in *Outdoor Recreation* and the overly-informal annotation style. Both volumes are recommended for purchase by general libraries serving adults and young adults. However, users of *Outdoor Recreation* should bear in mind that the book suffers from imbalance in the coverage of subjects and from ambiguity in the scope.   *(June 15, 1977, p.1596)*

The Oxford companion to German literature.
By Henry and Mary Garland. Oxford, Clarendon Press, 1976. vii, 977p. 24cm. cloth $27.95.

This Oxford Companion adds German to the previously covered English, American, French, Canadian, and classical literatures. Henry Garland is emeritus professor of German at the University of Exeter, England, and is author of *A Concise Survey of German Literature* (1970) and several other works. Mary Garland, his wife, has published works on German authors including *Hebbel's Prose Tragedies* and *Prinz Friedrich von Homburg*.

The volume is organized like the other Oxford Companions: a single alphabet with cross-references; biographies of writers and men of letters; synopses of works; entries on literary movements and styles; entries on figures and events in history, politics, art, and science of importance to literature; entries on intellectual, social, and political background. It is the compilers' "hope that the frequent cross-references will serve to draw attention to the interconnection between literature and all aspects of history." In order to deal satisfactorily with these latter aspects and keep the size of the volume manageable, conspicuous characters in literary works have been omitted. The book covers the period from the earliest record of German literature in the eighth century to the early 1970s. Austria and Switzerland are also included, because the "aim has been to cover in a reasonably representative way every period of the literature of each German-speaking country." Writers like Henrik Ibsen, who spent a major part of their creative life in Germany, and those like Laurence Stern, who influenced indigenous styles, are also included.

Rules for alphabetization and arrangement are given in a prefatory note. Medieval authors are alphabetized by first name; post-sixteenth-century writers are entered under their surnames.

The scope of milieu analysis in entries may be sampled by following up the references under any person or subject. For example, under *Goethe*, one is referred to *Reichskammergericht* and from there to several entries on the Holy Roman Empire (*Reichsstadt, Reichstag, Freie Stadt*), to *Sturm und Drang*, which is in turn tied through *Rousseau*, among others, to the *French Revolution*, the *Napoleonic Wars*, and *Beethoven* (who has one-half column, as do Mozart and Kurt Weill, while Bach has a column). *Napoleonic Wars* (5 columns) itself provides 40 more references, including battles (*Jena, Waterloo*, etc.), rulers (*Friedrich Wilhelm III*, et al.), generals (Clausewitz, et al.), the *Heilige Allianz*, the philosopher *Fichte*, and *Wieland* as well as *Goethe*. From *Rousseau*, one is further referred to *French Revolution*, *Romantik*, J. G. Herder, and Goethe's *Die Leiden des Junger Werthers*. From *Herder* one is led to *Kant* and *Lessing*; from *Romantik* there are q.v.'s to *Fichte*, the brothers Grimm (one and one-half columns), and Beethoven. The entry for *Expressionismus* leads to entries for both art and literature, e.g., *Der Blaue Reiter, Neoromantik, Dekadenz, Nietzsche, Kafka, Werfel*, and is also connected to *Sturm und Drang. Die Reformation* (two columns) has 25 *see* references, including ones to *Martin Luther, Friedrich der Weise, Dürer, Erasmus, Gutenberg*, and *Humanismus. Friedrich II, der Grosse* is linked to *Voltaire* and *Lessing* as well as to *Siebenjähriger Krieg*.

There are many concise (approximately four to six lines) identifications of minor authors, persons of historical significance, cities and places related to history or literature (e.g., "*Kahlenberg*, a hill in Vienna with a famous view"), terms (e.g., "*Fuchs*, a freshman at a German university"), and organizations of historical, political, or literary significance.

Since bio-bibliographical entries constitute the major portion of the volume, a check was made of several standard works to ascertain the comprehensiveness of the *Companion*'s coverage. Two-hundred and sixty-one name entries, including cross-references, appear in the *B* section of the *Companion*. The *B* section of the revised and enlarged *Cassell's Encyclopaedia of World Literature* (New York: Morrow, 1973) lists 77 German-language authors; of these, 19 do not appear in the *Companion*. Seventeen of these omissions are nineteenth- and twentieth-century authors; six are listed as living authors in the 1973 *Cassell's*; four are German-Americans, born in Germany, writing in German (including one who came to Pennsylvania in 1719); eight wrote in Low German. While the *Companion* includes some of the major writers of Low German, e.g., Rudolf Kinau, Klaus Johann Groth, there are no entries for Low German, Plattdeutsch, or Niederdeutsch. All of the 21 German authors in *Columbia Dictionary of Modern European Literature* (New York: Columbia University Press, 1947) appear in the *Companion*. All but one of the 15 German authors born since 1920 listed in the *Penguin Companion to Literature, 2: European* (Penguin Books, 1969) are in the *Companion*. In the section of *Cassell's* article on German literature which discusses post-1945 writers, 27 authors are noted, and only one is not in the *Companion*. The *Companion* lacks only one of the 31 German authors in *Encyclopaedia of World Literature in the Twentieth Century* (New York: Ungar, 1967).

The articles are written in a direct and clear style, blending biographical and bibliographical details with succinct criticism.

The amount of criticism seems keyed to the importance of the author. Goethe is given seven columns discussing his life, milieu, and works, with "q.v." leads to additional discussion of 52 of his works in separate articles under title. A compact one-column critical summation comments on the diversity of his interests—"He is sometimes referred to as the last universal man"—and his works—"They reflect the facets of an extraordinarily rich, multiple, Protean personality, in all its changing moods and varied experiences." While noting that for "a writer of the first rank, Goethe's oeuvre is surprisingly fragmented". . . "Fragmentariness is . . . no defect; it is the essence of his literary genius." Schiller is given three columns, with 23 "q.v." leads to articles under titles of his works and a paragraph of critical summation beginning, "Schiller's character and poetic gifts are dominated by a powerfully developed will, which is embodied in many of his characters, is expressed in the vehemence of his style, and was the supporting element in his modest span of life." Erich Kästner, the author of children's books and recipient of the Hans Andersen prize, whose *Emil und die Detektive* is well known in English translation, receives one column, including three references to separate articles under titles of his works and critical comment within the discussion which also notes that his books were publicly burned during the National Socialist regime. B. Traven is covered in one-third column of brief identification and partial listing of his works. Vicki Baum receives one-half column of brief biography and a partial bibliography. Her writing is characterized as consisting of "light novels which combined dramatic events, erotic complications, a vivid and up-to-date contemporary social background, and a discreet dose of sentiment," and a q.v directs the reader to *Menschen im Hotel, Grand Hotel,* which contains a short plot summary. Additional criticism is usually found under the separate entry for individual works. Pseudonyms are regularly noted and provided with cross-reference.

Title entries, including anonymous works, are well represented. A partial check of anonymous titles within the article on German poetry in the *Princeton Encyclopedia of Poetry and Poetics* (Princeton, N.J.: Princeton Univ. Pr., 1974) revealed that ten works are provided with entries in the *Companion*. Of 50 titles checked, 12 are not in the *Companion,* apparently not being the titles of volumes. In addition to title entries, there are many entries for the much-quoted first lines of poems and hymns, e.g., "Wohlauf! noch getrunken!"

As in the *Oxford Companion to French Literature,* the entries are, with few exceptions, in the language covered in the *Companion.* Cross-references from English to German entries are plentiful. Several are for history entries, e.g., *Austrian Succession, War of the,* see *Osterreichischer Erbfolgekrieg; Thirty Years War,* see *Dreissigjahriger Krieg; Third Reich,* see *Drittes Reich.* These English references are incomplete, evidently used with discretion, for while one finds a reference from *Letter of Majesty* to *Majestätsbriefe,* there is no English reference for *Westfälischer Friede,* although both are referred to in the article *Dreissigjähriger Krieg.* A few general topics are also in English: *Bible, Translations of,* Luther's *Theses, 95,* and *Libraries,* (and a reference from *Bibliotheken,* with a reverse pattern used for *Dictionaries,* see *Wörterbücher*). Titles of works are given only in German with no cross-references from their English equivalents because of the lack of uniform translations. With a few exceptions, such as *Emblem* and *Pastourelle,* literary terms are also in German. Familiarity with German literary terms or referral to an English-German dictionary is necessary, e.g., *Kolportageroman* for chapbook, *Schelmenroman* for picaresque novel.

Representation of literary terms, styles, and movements seems thorough, e.g., *Lied, Moritat* (murder stories in ballad form), *Dadaismus (Dada), Sturm und Drang.* There are many entries for poetics: *Endreim, Rokoko, Nibelungenstrophe, Knittelvers,* and *Alexandriner* but not *Gesellschaftslied,* which is given a full column in *Princeton Encyclopedia of Poetry and Poetics.* However, the *Companion* does have *Gesellschaftsroman.* A comparison of terms and topics in the *B's* in the *Companion* and *Cassell's,* shows parallel entries for *Ballade–Ballad; Baroque; Bible, Translations of; Biedermeier;* and *Blankvers– Blank verse.* For "Bestiary" *Cassell's* provides the heading *Bestiary,* while in the *Companion* one must look under *Physiologus.* Similarly, for *Bucolic (of poetry),* the *Companion* uses *Idylle.*

Several of the entries in the *Companion* are not in *Cassell's: Belletristik, Bildungsroman, Briefroman, Bürgerliches Trauerspiel, Butzenscheibenpoesie.* These, except for "Briefroman" (epistolary novel), do not exist as standard English terms. The last two are untranslatable into simple phrases. Only one entry, *Burlesque,* in *Cassell's* does not appear in the *Companion.*

The volume is in the usual tasteful and functional format of the Oxford Companion series. Since it fills the need for a comprehensive bio-bibliographical and topical dictionary of German literature, *The Oxford Companion to German Literature* is recommended for college, university, and large public libraries and for other libraries needing a reliable reference for German literature. *(Apr. 15, 1977, p.1292)*

†830.03   German literature—Dictionaries

Paper and printing.
†681.767'6   Printing—Juvenile literature || Paper—Juvenile literature   [OCLC] 75-20502

See page 50

Parliaments of the world:
a reference compendium. Edited by the Inter-Parliamentary Union; prepared by Valentine Herman with the collaboration of Françoise Mendel. Berlin, New York, De Gruyter, [c1976]. xii. 985p. 24cm. cloth $73.

Parliaments of the World is a comparative treatment of 56 modern parliaments. Its aim, according to the Introduction, is "to provide all those interested in Parliamentary institutions, particularly persons carrying out research in the field, with both an overall description of those institutions and as much specific data as could be gathered to further the task of comparative analysis." The volume is edited by the Inter-Parliamentary Union, an organization founded in 1889 to promote contacts among these legislative bodies throughout the world. Member countries, most of whose parliaments are described in this volume, cover the full range of geographical location and political philosophy: the USSR, Monaco, the U.S., Sri Lanka, and Poland are among them. The union's International Centre for Parliamentary Documentation, whose function is to collect information on parliaments, was directly responsible for the work. Valentine Herman, who prepared the volume for publication, is a lecturer at the Department of Government of the University of Essex and has coauthored three works on parliamentary government. Françoise Mendel, an assistant who helped Herman, is lecturer in constitutional law at the University of Geneva.

This is not the Inter-Parliamentary Union's first assault on the subject. In 1962 it published a volume entitled *Parliaments,* a second edition of which appeared in 1966. These earlier works are comparative studies dealing with the world's parliaments (55 of them in 1966) in long essays covering such topics as composition, legislative function, relation to the executive, and monetary powers. The present work derives from its predecessors, but the format differs greatly.

Instead of being a collection of essays, it is mainly a grouping of 70 comparative tables which present data on the 56 parliaments and which are alphabetically arranged by country. According to the Introduction, the purpose of the tables is, not only to "enable the reader to ascertain the essential similarities and differences between various parliamentary systems in respect of a given question, but also to find detailed information concerning one or more individual Parliaments." Several pages (two to seven) of explanatory text precede each group of tables.

The volume is divided into six parts. Together they cover all features of the composition, organization, and operation of the parliaments as well as their specific legislative, budgetary, and control functions. Each part, including its tables, covers one broad aspect of parliamentary government. For example, Part 1, "Composition of Parliament," consists of 20 tables which cover many points on how membership in the 56 parliaments is achieved. There are tables on such topics as "Nomination of Candidates," "Filling of Vacancies," "Electoral System," and "The Electorate's Qualifications."

The other five parts of the volume, all similarly organized, are entitled "Organisation and Operation of Parliament," "Legislative Function of Parliament," "Powers of Parliament over Finance," "Control of the Executive by Parliament," and "Other Functions of Parliament." The last part includes tables entitled the "Nomination of Government Officials and Judges" and "Judicial Functions of Parliament."

The tables which comprise the bulk of this reference compendium are typically several pages long and are set lengthwise on the page, with the alphabetical listing of the countries running down the left-hand column. Usually it is possible to compare data on three or four separate points. Table 12 of part 1 provides a good illustration. This ten-page table entitled "Balloting Procedure" lists procedural information on parliaments from Argentina's to Zambia's in four columns entitled "Candidates' Identification on Ballot Paper," "Order of Candidates on Ballot Paper," "Polling Station Authorities," and "How the Votes are Counted." Thus, in scanning the "Order of Candidates on Ballot Paper" column for countries beginning with "C," one quickly discovers that Cameroon, Canada, and Czechoslovakia have alphabetical ordering on their ballots to elect members to their national legislatures, while in Costa Rica the order is determined by political party. The three-and-one-half-page text accompanying Table 12 explains why the specific points were chosen for comparison and makes a few general observations about the variety of balloting procedures used to elect members to the various parliaments of the world.

According to the Introduction, the Inter-Parliamentary Union has made every effort to present accurate material. The information was gathered mostly from questionnaires sent to the various parliaments. In addition, once the draft was prepared, it was submitted to the parliaments for confirmation. All information was to be valid as of September 1, 1974. A check of the data from the various tables against information contained in such standard sources as *Statesman's Yearbook* and *Political Handbook of the World* indicates this volume maintains a high level of accuracy.

Access to the material is provided by a table of contents that lists each of the 70 tables under its appropriate part and also by a subject Index. *See* and *see also* references in the Index are not as ample as they might be; three or four headings sometimes need to be tried before the key to the information is found. However, the Index is accurate.

The binding is strong; the paper is of high quality; and the volume lies flat when opened. The tables are clear and well designed. Entries for each country are ruled off from one another, and the distances between columns of information are sufficiently wide. However, the inner margin is narrow and rebinding may prove difficult.

Parliaments of the World is a well-produced volume which effectively organizes comparative information on 56 parliaments of the world. The material is presented accurately and without bias. The work is recommended for purchase by those libraries whose patrons seek such information.

(July 15, 1977, p.1749)

328'.3 Legislative bodies—Handbooks, manuals, etc. [CIP] 76-17574

Pears cyclopaedia, 1976–1977:
a book of background information and reference for everyday use. Edited by L. Mary Barker and Christopher Cook. 85th ed. London, Pelham Books; dist. in U.S. by Transatlantic Arts, c1976. 1v. (various pagings). illus. maps. 20cm. Econolin (paper composition) $10; to schools and libraries, $8.

Pears Cyclopaedia, a British annual, began publication in 1897 under the direction of Thomas J. Barratt, a partner in Messrs A. & F. Pears, soapmakers. Barratt "believed with equal fervour in Pears soap and Pears Cyclopaedia as weapons in the fight against disease and ignorance"—flyleaf 1956–58 edition. *Pears* is currently published by Pelham Books, a division of the Thomson publishing group, which according to *International Literary Market Place* publishes in the fields of biography, how-to, reference, juveniles, and sports. Lilian Mary Barker has been editor of *Pears* for the past quarter century. Christopher Cook became assistant editor for the 81st edition and is now coeditor. He has been associated with the British Library of Political and Economic Science since 1970 and has recently compiled several reference books, including *British Historical Facts, 1830–1900* and *European Political Facts, 1918–1973.* Alastair N. Worden, a veterinarian and professor of toxicology at the University of Bath, and Sarah E. M. Worden wrote the section on pets. Other contributors are not identified.

Pears attempts to be the "encyclopaedia of the common man" and purports to tackle "the crucial problems facing the world today with a simple yet authoritative approach." Not surprisingly, it sets about this task with a British accent on both the selection and treatment of materials.

The 85th edition is divided into 19 separately paged sections. The number, order, and content of these change from edition to edition. In the 1976–77 volume, *British Law* has been dropped and *Collecting Antiques* and *Pets and Ponies* added. Remaining sections have undergone minor, sometimes insignificant, revision.

Events (section A, 42p.) consists of a chronology of world history, with a heavy emphasis on British and European history and upon contemporary events. The section has been updated through May 1976. *Prominent People* (B, 66p.) includes approximately 2,000 biographies, ranging in length from 2 to 24 lines. About half of the figures are from British history or classical antiquity. *Background to Public Affairs* (C, 48p.) covers current events, grouped according to geographical areas of the world. *Collecting Antiques* (D, 28p.) emphasizes items available in Britain and contains tables of silver and pottery marks. *The World of Music* (E, 26p.) has a 17-page historical narrative devoted completely to the Western tradition and a 6-page glossary of terms. *The World of Science* (F, 74p.) gives a nontechnical, concise overview of modern astronomy, physics, chemistry, biology, anthropology, and ecology. This year's special articles are *How Birds Find Their Way* and *Water Resources. Background to Economic Events* (G, 58p.) concentrates on the British and less-developed economies, with scant mention of the U.S. or, more surprisingly, European economies. *Contemporary Theatre* (I, 54p.) deals exclusively with English-language drama through the 1974 season. *Ideas and Beliefs* (J, 56p.) has articles, occasionally extending to a full column, on religious sects and on concepts and schools of philosophy. *Gazetteer of the World* (K, 188p.) lists some 9,000 places with a line or two of descriptive information. Although called "an index and guide to the maps," which occur in a 36-plate separate color section, the entries are not keyed to the maps. *General Information* (L, 130p.) defines 3,000 terms, from aardvark and abacus to zonda and zoology. *Literary Companion* (M, 60p.) discusses mostly modern British and American novels and poetry. Forty-five novelists receive separate treatment. Six have been dropped from the previous edition, including E. M. Forster and Kurt Vonnegut. *General Compendium* (N, 30p.) contains 23 miscellaneous tables, such as foreign currencies, abbreviations, and wind tables. *Medical Matters* (P, 72p.) defines various diseases and physiological terms. *Psychology* (Q, 30p.) treats modern trends, e.g., behaviorism and learning, but without discussion of such figures as Skinner or Piaget. *Sporting Records* (R, 12p.) covers winners and champions in European, British, and Commonwealth events; the few Olympic champions mentioned are from the 1972 Munich games. *Modern Gardening* (T, 40p.) and *Pets and Ponies* (Z, 31p.) give elementary advice on these subjects. The 25 physical-political maps, indicating heights with standard blue-green-orange-purple-white color gradations, are bound in the center of the volume. The most detail is reserved for maps of Europe. A scale of 1:3,500,000 is used for England, Wales, Scotland, and Ireland; Central Europe is shown at 1:5,000,000, Africa at 1:45,000,000, and South America at 1:50,000,000.

A general Index of only seven pages completes the volume; it is neither systematic nor comprehensive. Each of the topically arranged sections has a separate table of contents and several have their own indexes. There are also occasional cross-references to other sections. Nevertheless, considerable searching is needed for locating some information. No bibliographies are included. The maps and line drawings in the gardening section are the only illustrations.

The margins are very narrow and the binding is weak, but the pages lie almost flat when open. The format is double columns of minute, but clear and legible, type.

No other single-volume British reference work incorporates the same combination of features. *Whitaker's Almanack* covers background and statistical material more extensively. The *Daily Mail Year Book* covers only events of the past year in its chronology section and other matters very briefly.

Pears Cyclopaedia achieves its goal of being a handy, modestly-priced compendium of miscellaneous information but with all the concomitant limitations of a work of this type. One finds sketchy treatments of many topics covered more authoritatively and in greater depth in the larger-scaled and costlier reference tools. Nonetheless, *Pears* provides good browsing material for the curious reader. Although reference librarians may be inclined to look askance, their patrons may well find this collection of miscellaneous facts fascinating. Consequently, *Pears* can be recommended as an optional acquisition item for public libraries and for individuals with a more than casual interest in British affairs. *(July 15, 1977, p.1750)*

†032 Encyclopedias and dictionaries

**Personal name index
to 'the New York times index' 1851–1974.**
v. I "A" of 22v. set [By] Byron A. Falk Jr. and Valerie R. Falk. Succasunna, N.J., Roxbury Data Interface, [1976]. 351p. 26cm. cloth $19.50 + $1.50 mailing; v.II–XXII $63 + $1.50 mailing.

Personal Name Index to 'The New York Times Index' 1851–1974, volume 1, is the first of a projected series of 22 volumes which will index names of people "buried within the New York Times Indexes." The series will cover 3,000,000 names. The Introduction states that this new Index was conceived and designed by a librarian with librarians and researchers in mind. Byron A. Falk Jr. is corporate president of Roxbury Data, and he was project manager for *New York Times Obituary Index* (*Reference and Subscription Books Reviews* July 15, 1970).

The "A" volume contains about 90,000 citations excerpted from almost 2,000 separate listings of the multiple volumes of *The New York Times Indexes* from 1851–1974. The names, segregated by *The New York Times* into Book Reviews, Music, Concerts, Deaths, Disappearances, and other categories, with no cross-references, are consolidated here into a single alphabetical sequence.

Multiple citations to particular names are arranged chronologically. These citations are often accompanied by political or occupational designations. Citations for each name are arranged, with earliest date first, indicating year and page of the *New York Times Index* source volume.

According to the Introduction, *The New York Times'* death listings are included in this series with citations preceded by the letter "d". However, this is not consistently done. For example, there is no "d" citation for R. C. Arbuckle (Fatty).

The book is well designed and has a sturdy binding. The citations are in double columns with wide margins. The print is small but easy to read.

The *Personal Name Index to 'The New York Times Index' 1851–1974* is being produced for researchers, but it could prove useful to anyone who consults *The New York Times Index* for biographical data.

Although this reference tool may ultimately be a valuable timesaving resource, no information as to when subsequent volumes will appear is provided by the publisher. Accordingly, the Committee must withhold recommendation or nonrecommendation until more volumes become available for assessment. *(Mar. 15, 1977, p.1120)*

071.'47' New York Times—Indexes || Biography—Indexes [OCLC] 76-12217

Peterson's annual guides to undergraduate and graduate study.
Editor, Karen C. Hegener. [10th ed., 1976] 6v. plus general index. Princeton, N.J., Peterson's Guides Inc., [c1975]; marketed in the Eastern hemisphere by Bowker Publishing Company, Ltd. paper, illus. 28cm. $70.; to schools, minus 30 percent discount; to libraries, minus 30 percent discount if tax exempt. Individual copies may be ordered: Annual Guide to Undergraduate Study $12., book 1 $10., book 2 $13., book 3 $15., book 4 $10., book 5 $10.

Peterson's Annual Guides were first published in 1966 after Peter Hegener, at that time director of career plans and a member of the admissions committee at Princeton University, recognized the need for a set of reference books, arranged by discipline, which would provide information to help undergraduates choose graduate schools. Hegener is currently publisher of the series. Editions have varied in the number of volumes and their titles.

The six volumes of the 1976 edition are comprised of *Annual Guide to Undergraduate Study* (1,288 pages) and a set of five books providing systematically organized information on graduate school programs in North America. Book 1 (313 pages) is *Graduate Institutions of the U.S. and Canada—An Overview;* book 2 (837 pages) is *Humanities and Social Sciences;* book 3 (1,219 pages) is *Biological and Health Sciences;* book 4 (557 pages) is *Physical Sciences;* and book 5 (478 pages) is *Engineering and Applied Sciences.* A separate 25-page paper Index to the set is in three parts: a list of the chief sections of each book; a list of each field of interest, indicating location in the Guides; and an alphabetical list of institutions with references to their descriptions and abstracts in the various books.

Material in these volumes has been obtained by means of questionnaires sent out annually by the compilers. Data in this edition apply to the 1975–76 school year except for enrollment figures which are from the previous year. Schools which have not replied to the publisher's request for information are listed without descriptions. Throughout the volumes, information is presented in several forms: graphic summaries, directory charts, directory listings, abstracts, and longer institutional descriptions. The last two are written by the schools themselves, following a form provided by the publisher. Any institution may submit them. Small photographs of buildings or student activities plus pictures of the institutions' seals accompany many of the descriptions. Each volume also contains information on the appropriate accrediting process and agencies, additional reference sources covering both publications and associations, and a list of institutional changes in 1975.

The Annual Guide to Undergraduate Study includes over 2,700 two-year and four-year institutions in the U.S. and Canada plus Army and Navy ROTC programs. The first major section is a Directory of General Information. In chart format, this indicates for each school its state, institutional type and control, admissions policy, type of student body, total, undergraduate, and freshman enrollments, faculty size, campus setting, calendar, and accreditation. Next, a Directory of Academic Policies and Enrollment Policies lists institutions alphabetically by state or province. This second chart gives city and zip code, resident and out-of-state tuition fees, room and board costs, degrees awarded, number of major entrance examinations required and recommended, application deadlines, financial data required, special programs and policies, grading systems, and undergraduate enrollment profiles (percentage of women, blacks, commuters, etc.). The Directory of Standardized Test Score Ranges lists all institutions that provided information on the percentages of freshmen receiving ACT composite scores and SAT verbal and math scores in various intervals. A Directory of Majors and Degrees then shows the level of degrees the schools offer in 104 fields, from accounting to zoology. Twelve pages of Abstracts come next—these are 50-word descriptions of colleges that elected to prepare brief statements. Over half this book is made up of the more detailed two-page Full Institutional Descriptions from more than 350 schools which follow immediately after the Abstracts. These include information, in paragraph form, about majors and degrees, library and other facilities, costs and financial aids, admissions requirements with addresses and sometimes telephone numbers of admissions directors, kind of community, etc. Information on ROTC programs has been supplied by their headquarters. Book 1, *Graduate Institutions of the U.S. and Canada—An Overview,* commences with a Graphical Summary that lists in one alphabet over 900 universities and indicates which of 81 broad fields of graduate study each offers, and in which book of this series they are described. Section 2 lists graduate schools giving very brief notes on type of school, setting, degrees offered, enrollment, faculty, tuition and financial aid, deadlines, and address. Institutions in book 1 are those usually characterized as liberal arts or multi-purpose. There are longer descriptions of specific graduate programs. For each of these, information is given on research facilities, financial aid, cost of study and living, student body, community, application procedures, address to which to write, and a list of faculty members.

Books 2 through 5, which identify subject areas available at the graduate level, follow a consistent format. Each commences with a Graphical Summary of fields of interest covered in the book. Universities are alphabetically arranged so that the user can quickly find out which institutions offer which subjects. A Directory section then covers a specific field such as Art/Fine Arts or Civil and Environmental Engineering or Geology. These brief listings include address, faculty size, tuition, number of degrees conferred, etc. Next are the longer descriptive entries, followed by indexes to them and to the directory subjects. Clemson University, for example, has 13 such entries or abstracts in the graduate guides and one in the undergraduate; other institutions have only 1 in the entire set. All told, 187 subject areas are represented in the graduate guides.

The binding of the larger volumes is not especially sturdy, and the paper covers can easily be torn. However, they would probably survive one year's use. All volumes open flat. The print is small and rather hard to read on some of the charts.

In general, the set is easy to use because of its uniform arrangement from volume to volume. Individual volumes can stand alone because all have similar introductory material and indexes, and the directory information is in alphabetical order. The absence of cross-references in the *Undergraduate Guide* lessens accessibility to information on schools such as Malcolm X College, Maui Community College, and Hostos Community College which are listed only under their parent institutions, the City Colleges of Chicago, University of Hawaii, and City University of New York, respectively. It should also be noted that not all colleges and universities are listed, as claimed in the Undergraduate Directory of General Information. Among the missing are Mankato Commercial College in Minnesota, and Vernard College and Maharishi International University in Iowa.

A number of other guides to institutions of higher learning are available. *American Universities and Colleges* (11th ed., 1973) lists over 1,440 which offer a bachelor's or higher degree, but its list of the subject offerings of these schools is limited to 38 fields. Most of the information presented is in the form of narrative descriptions arranged by state and then alphabetically by college. *Lovejoy's College Guide* (1974) contains narrative descriptions of about 3,500 institutions, arranged by state and then alphabetically by name of the school. The list of professional and special programs includes over 500 career fields and tells where the courses are taught. The *College Blue Book* (15th ed., 1975, 3 vols.) contains narrative descriptions of over 3,000 colleges, arranged by state and then by college in the first volume. The second volume presents tabular data on the institutions in 55 columns. The third volume, *Degrees Offered by Colleges and Subjects,* lists 2,000 subjects and then, by state, which institutions offer them and at what degree level. Much of the same material can be found in all of these directories, allowing for the variations in dates. Both the *College Blue Book* and *Lovejoy's College Guide* offer more detailed lists of subjects taught than does Peterson. But the Peterson set is particularly useful because the information on graduate schools is presented separately. Most libraries will need more than one such guide, as well as a collection of college catalogs.

Since these volumes present a vast amount of current information on institutions of higher education in a concise and easily understood format, *Peterson's Annual Guides* are recommended for school, public, and academic libraries serving prospective or current college students, particularly those interested in pursuing graduate study.   *(Nov. 1, 1976, p.418)*

†378.83   Universities and colleges—U.S.   68-1823

Photography.
†771   Photography—Juvenile literature   [OCLC]   75-19997

See page 50

Pirates and buccaneers.
†364.135   Pirates—Juvenile literature ‖ Buccaneers—Juvenile literature   [OCLC]   75-19965

See page 50

The planet we live on:
illustrated encyclopedia of the earth sciences. Cornelius S. Hurlbut, Jr., Editor. New York, Harry N. Abrams, Inc., [1976]. 527p. illus. 29cm. impregnated book cloth $37.50.

The reputation of Harry N. Abrams, Inc., as a publisher of fine art books is well established and respected. In recent years Abrams has produced some reference books per se (e.g., *Encyclopedia of Modern Architecture* and *Medical Encyclopedia for Home Use*) and other works which, though not reference books in form, have reference value. The volume reviewed here is a well selected amalgam of relevant illustration and easy-to-read narrative on the disciplines known collectively as the earth sciences. These include crystallography, economic geology, environmental geology, geochemistry, geomorphology, geophysics, glacial geology, historical geology, hydrology, marine geology, meteorology, mineralogy, oceanography, paleontology, petrology, sedimentology, stratigraphy, space geology, structural geology, tectonics, and volcanology. This encyclopedia has been produced for the general reader and student, not for the specialist in any of the earth sciences.

Editor Cornelius S. Hurlbut, Jr., is very well qualified to supervise the content. His career at Harvard began in 1933, and he currently holds the position of professor of mineralogy emeritus. He has published widely in this field and is coeditor with J. D. and E. S. Dana of the eighteenth edition of Dana's *Manual of Mineralogy*. Working closely with Hurlbut and serving as joint author of the Introduction is William H. Matthews III, regent's professor of geology, Lamar University, Beaumont, Texas, who has written more than 16 books for adults and 12 books for juveniles. There are three other contributing editors, each holding major professional positions in one of the earth science disciplines; five contributing specialists who were also selected for their subject expertise; and a consultant from the American Museum of Natural History. The volume was "planned, prepared and produced" by Chanticleer Press, Inc. Chanticleer's vice-president, Milton Rugoff, is editor-in-chief of this volume. Rugoff also holds outstanding credentials as an author and editor.

For the purpose of analysis, the encyclopedia can be divided into three sections: the front matter, the encyclopedia itself, and the appendixes. In line with the typical lavish use of illustrations, the editors have placed a "Color Portfolio of the Earth Sciences" near the beginning of the volume. The front matter includes, in addition to the table of contents, 32 pages of color plates dealing with such diverse topics as drifting continents, the fossil record, and historical eras. Each illustration in the Portfolio section is accompanied by narrative by Susan Rayfield, who is mentioned on the credits page but for whom no expertise is noted. The publisher describes the "Portfolio" as a series of "pictorial essays;" it is not coordinated with the encyclopedia section of the volume and serves little reference purpose. Superb illustrations of such minerals as apatite, galena, calcite, and selenite are included here but are not cross-referenced from encyclopedia entries for the same minerals. The user can retrieve these pictures and accompanying data only through chance, examination of the table of contents, or page-by-page scanning of the section. Also found in these 48 pages are editorial credits, a list of the 21 subjects—with definitions—which make up the earth sciences, and a three-and-a-half page Introduction which attempts to encapsulate the complex combination of sciences which is the subject of this encyclopedia.

The second and most significant part of the volume is the encyclopedia itself, which covers pages 49 through 488. More than 600 illustrations, limited to black and white and a kind of sepia reproduction, are contained in the main part of the book. Few pages are without illustrations, and most contain two or more. Unfortunately, the text does not refer directly to the illustrations. Moreover, each illustration has its own brief narrative which may or may not be located near it on the page. The user, therefore, must find the number of the illustration and look for the corresponding italicized caption. Both illustrations and their italicized explanations are placed either to the outside left or right of the page, but the layout obviously contributes to aesthetic effect rather than to information retrieval. Most of the graphics are clear and helpful, but the climate zone diagram on p.117 indicates that parts of Greenland have a tropical climate, and the photograph of a manganese nodule on the ocean floor (page 298) is too dark to convey much meaning to the viewer.

The entries themselves seem excellent; they are precise and in language comprehensible to the nonexpert. The publisher claims 1,800 entries, but this number is inflated by counting illustration descriptions as well as the basic A–Z entries. Some entries are as brief as two lines (12 to 15 words), but the majority are much longer (100 to 150 words) and include numerous cross-references. There are a number of still longer articles (e.g., *Apollo Program, Earthquake, Lunar Geology, Waterfall*), each of which has several illustrations and contains several hundred words of description. The editors indicate cross-references by the somewhat unusual method of placing an asterisk before the keyword (e.g., *Emerald*. The variety of *beryl with a deep green color . . .). However, the logic of such signals is not self-evident. When reading an entry to which a cross-reference has been made (e.g., beryl), one is not aware that there is also an entry on emerald, even when it is discussed in a second article. It appears that most of the cross-references are from examples to larger categories or to related topics.

A third section of the volume is an Appendix, which incorporates five components: (1) Metric Conversion Tables; (2) an alphabetical list of the elements, with symbols and atomic numbers; (3) A Table of Mineral Properties; (4) lists of principal features (oceans, seas, mountain peaks, deserts, longest rivers, natural lakes, and waterfalls); and (5) a Guide to Entries by Subject. This last Appendix is a breakdown by the 21 subjects covered in the encyclopedia, with terms related to particular headings colocated under the major heading. However, only main entry terms are listed and each is listed only once—which suggests that any given entry is germane to only one larger category, e.g., *Bauxite* is found under *Economic Geology* but not under *Mineralogy*. Of course, the cross-references found in the actual encyclopedia entries do interrelate the material; therefore this "Guide to Entries" is more indicative of assignment of responsibility to a particular discipline than as an indicator of the interdisciplinary nature of many terms. No page numbers are listed since all terms are main entries which can be found in their alphabetical order.

In order to assess their value, the encyclopedia entries were compared with those in three other tools. The authoritative *McGraw-Hill Encyclopedia of Science and Technology* was used as a control since it is clearly more comprehensive with its multiple volumes. It has the advantage of signed articles; the entries in *The Planet We Live On* are occasionally unsigned. *The Planet We Live On* is easier to read than the *McGraw-Hill Encyclopedia* and, on occasion, has more relevant detail. Some entries found in *The Planet We Live On* can be found in *McGraw-Hill* only after careful use of the Index volume, and even then, the material is not as clearly articulated as in the specific entries of *The Planet We Live On*.

The Committee then compared *The Planet We Live On* with *The New Larousse Encyclopedia of the Earth* (Leon Bertin, rev. ed., New York, Crown: 1972). Its organization precludes effective retrieval of specific facts since it is organized around three synoptic themes: The Present (including discussions of the atmosphere, oceans, glaciers, earth movements, etc.); Earth in the Service of Man (including an emphasis on minerals); and The Past. It is intended to be read consecutively rather than to be consulted for specific information. Its Index includes only a sprinkling of the sample entries drawn from *The Planet We Live On*. The two volumes might complement each other, but *The Planet We Live On* is more useful as a reference source.

The final comparison was made with the in-progress *Encyclopedia of Earth Science Series* (1966–   ) edited by R. W. Fairbridge. The publisher, Van Nostrand, projects a set of specialized volumes, each addressed to a particular phase of the earth sciences, e.g., volume 1 deals with oceanography, volume 2 with the atmospheric sciences, volume 3 with geomorphology, etc. It is not complete, and this fact alone supports the value of *The Planet We Live On*. In actuality, there is little comparison since the single-volume Abrams book does not attempt to provide the level or amount of data found in the Van Nostrand venture. Rather, *The Planet We Live On* fills an obvious gap in the reference literature since it synthesizes a vast amount of information at a level much in demand, i.e., that of the nonexpert.

The Planet We Live On is sturdily bound and printed in Israel on quality stock. Its narrow margins and numerous "cross-page" illustrations make rebinding impracticable.

The inclusion of recent theory and findings within the disciplines encompassed by the earth sciences, such as plate tectonics and lunar geology, give special value to *The Planet We Live On.* Before the appearance of this publication, which was developed for effective fact retrieval in the earth sciences as a whole, no single-volume encyclopedia had been available. These two factors, coupled with the proven expertise of the editors, recommend its acquisition by public, college, and university libraries and high school media centers.

(Apr. 15, 1977, p.1293)

550'.3 Earth sciences—Dictionaries [CIP] 75-29977

Political science bibliographies.

v.II. By Robert B. Harmon. Metuchen, N.J., Scarecrow, 1976. 233p. 22cm. cloth $9.

The Reference and Subscription Books Review Committee did not review v.I in the Scarecrow series of political science bibliographies. This review will, therefore, cover both volumes. Volume I was based on two previous works by Harmon, *A Bibliography of Bibliographies in Political Science* (1964) and *Sources and Problems of Political Science* (1966).

Harmon, acquisitions librarian at San Jose State College, has compiled genealogical, bio-bibliographical, and bibliographical works. These include: *The Cole Family: A Bibliography,* privately printed, 1964; *A Preliminary Checklist of Materials on Harman-Harmon Genealogy,* privately printed, 1964; (with John Ray Harmon) *Descendants of Charles Claymore Bartlett and Annie Katrine Jensen,* Harmonart, 1965; *The Art and Practice of Diplomacy: A Selected and Annotated Guide,* Scarecrow, 1971; *Political Science Bibliographies,* v. 1, Scarecrow, 1973; *Political Science: A Bibliographic Guide to the Literature,* Scarecrow, 1974; *Georgette Heyer: A Preliminary Checklist,* Dibco, 1974; and *The Ghostly Bibliography,* Dibco, 1974.

In the Introduction, the compiler states that "the bibliographies listed in this volume are restricted to separately published works. Books containing bibliographies and bibliographic articles have been excluded." In spite of these restrictions, works of other types, not in the strict sense bibliographies, are included. Among these are catalogs of collections, union catalogs, lists of in-print materials, checklists of government publications, directories of organizations, bibliographies of manuscript collections, and indexes to government publications and periodicals. The titles included in the bibliography appear in the *National Union Catalog* and *Library of Congress Catalog, Subjects: Books.* The Committee surmises that the latter source was the basis for the present compilation.

Inconsistent inclusions and omissions of relevant materials mar *Political Science Bibliographies.* This is true of various forms of materials such as indexes and also of foreign language titles, which are excluded at times for no apparent reason. About two-thirds of the materials sampled by the Committee are in English; French and German titles comprise the bulk of the remainder. However, Serbian, Spanish, Malaysian, Finnish, Portuguese, and Italian titles are also represented.

The citations in the bibliography are arranged under subject headings and are numbered consecutively. There are 913 in the second volume and 790 in the first. Usually entry is by corporate or personal author, but title entries appear occasionally, and in all cases the *National Union Catalog* entry is used. In addition, *NUC* cataloging information is used exclusively with only a few modifications in punctuation. The author states that "wherever possible, brief annotations will be provided, particularly with regard to additional subject areas contained within a bibliography." However, fewer than 10 percent of the sampled materials included annotations, and more than half could as easily have been constructed from the tracings or notes in the Library of Congress copy as from direct consultation of the sources.

For each entry the following information is always included: subject heading, item number, author or entry, title underlined, place of publication, publisher, date of publication, number of pages, and Library of Congress card number.

Most citations are accurate, but editorial errors occur frequently. In item 302, Union of International Associations, *Bibliography of Proceedings of International Meetings,* 1957– Brussels, the subtitle *Bibliographie des comptes rendus des réunions internationales* is omitted. Item 655, Théophile André Dufour, *Recherches Bibliographiques sur les Oeuvres Imprimées de J.-J. Rousseau, Suivies de l'Inventaire des Papiers de Rousseau Conservés à la Bibliothèque de Neuchâtel,* Introd. de Pierre-Paul Plan, New York: B. Franklin, 1971, is a reprint of the 1925 edition, an important fact which cannot be determined from *NUC* but is obvious in the work itself. Item 491, *What's New in Forensic Sciences,* Kenosha, Wis.: Romantini Print. Co., is not identified as the official publication of the American Academy of Forensic Sciences. Item 87, Alex Baskin, *The American Civil Liberties Union Papers: A Guide to the Records, A.C.L.U. Cases 1912–1946,* Stony Brook, N.Y. Archives of Social History, 1971, lacks the Library of Congress card number assigned to it (70-28011). Finally, item 196, Peter Klemensberger, *Die Westmächte und Sardinien Während des Krimkrieges. Der Beitritt des Königreiches Sardinien zur Britischfranzösischen Allianz im Rahmen der Europäischen Politik,* Zurich, Juris-Verlag, 1972, violates Harmon's criteria because it is a monograph with a bibliography on p.277–84.

There is an average of one subject heading for every four citations. According to Harmon these "are as consistent as possible with those used by the Library of Congress." Headings include countries and regions as well as personal names and topics. However, subject cataloging is not subject analysis. The major difference between these and Library of Congress subject headings is that the form subdivision BIBLIOGRAPHIES is not used. Otherwise the majority of headings match Library of Congress. Occasional modifications are made, such as using a general heading where Library of Congress uses a subdivision, e.g., item 422, Louisiana State Bar Association, Library, New Orleans, *Catalogue of Books Contained in the Library of the New Orleans Law Association,* New Orleans, Clark and Hofeline, print, 1881, is under the general heading LAW—US instead of the LC heading LAW—US—BIBLIOGRAPHIES—CATALOGS. At times more familiar headings are substituted for the Library of Congress term, changing INDUSTRIES, LOCATION OF to REGIONAL PLANNING. Of less obvious value is the use of TREATY ON NON-PROLIFERATION OF NUCLEAR WEAPONS in place of ATOMIC WEAPONS AND DISARMAMENT. The use of subject headings assigned in Library of Congress cataloging has resulted in a lack of uniformity for headings. For instance POLITICS has been used as a subdivision in some cases and POLITICS AND GOVERNMENT in others. This inconsistency in subject headings caused by changes by the Library of Congress guarantees a parallel inconsistency within individual volumes and increasingly between volumes in this series. The problem is compounded by the lack of subject indexing and cross-references.

Volume I, with its author and title indexes and subject headings, was intended to provide the user with a "triangular approach to the retrieval of information." Volume II shares this aim. The practical advantage in application of this catchy terminology is not great, and neither volume provides more specific subject approaches to the body of the work other than the headings. In volume II author and title indexes have been merged. In both volumes the indexes are reasonably accurate. Index entries in both volumes refer to item numbers, rather than pages.

Though reliable, the indexing does not provide the multiplicity of subject approaches needed. This omission and the lack of cross-references leave the searcher two choices, neither very good: he/she must either consult the Library of Congress Subject Headings or experiment with the various possible headings in the text under which relevant material might appear. In addition, no item appears under more than one subject heading. This, combined with the omission of indexes or cross-references, obligates the reader to use all relevant headings to make an exhaustive search.

Produced by photo-offset, the format is functional though not aesthetically pleasing. Headings, all in upper case, stand out clearly from citations, which are indented after the individual item numbers. Besides page numbers, there are running subject headings—a feature which helps one locate desired headings quickly. The cloth binding is sufficiently durable, but the machine binding is so tight that a newly acquired volume must be held open to the desired page.

A carefully selected and well-organized list of separately published bibliographies in political science would have been a useful and important addition to the general guides, such as Clifton Brock's *The Literature of Social Science: A Guide for Students, Librarians* (New York: Bowker, 1969) and *Teachers and Universal Reference System: Political Science, Government and Public Policy Series* (Princeton, N.J.: Princeton Research), which with its supplements is a good annual review of the monographic, periodical, and ephemeral literature of the field. However, the two volumes of *Political Science Bibliographies* fail in several respects. The selection of bibliographies is arbitrary, and relevant items have been omitted; more than 90 percent of the titles included lack annotations, and cross-references and subject analysis are inadequate. Not recommended.

(May 15, 1977, p.1447)

016.01632   Bibliography—Bibliography—Political science   [CIP]   72-8849

Pollution.
†614.7   Pollution—Juvenile literature   [OCLC]   75-20517
See page 50

A popular guide to government publications.
Compiled by W. Philip Leidy. 4th ed. New York, Columbia, 1976. xx, 440p. 21cm. cloth $25.

The fourth edition of *A Popular Guide to Government Publications* is a compilation of over 3,000 titles issued between 1967 and 1975 selected from the *Monthly Catalog of U.S. Government Publications*. The first (1953), second (1963), and third (1968) editions listed respectively 2,500 titles published between 1940 and 1950, 2,300 titles issued between 1951 and 1962, and 3,000 titles issued between 1961 and 1966.

William Philip Leidy, the compiler, has had many years of library experience including work in public, engineering, scientific, and business libraries. Now a library consultant, he was most recently a reference librarian in the East Islip (New York) Public Library.

The basis for selection of publications is the same as for earlier editions—interests of the average reader and public libraries. Emphasis, as before, has been placed on titles concerning vocational guidance, health, small business, hobbies, recreation, housing, and other subjects of general interest. Highly technical publications and those too specialized for popular appeal have been excluded. Also excluded, with some exceptions, are legal materials, bibliographies, periodicals, detailed statistical works, and publications soon to become out of date. Only titles in print at the time the guide was compiled are included. Consequently, parts of some of the series listed are omitted.

The guide begins with a short introduction, followed by Acknowledgments, a Table of Contents, and a two-page explanation of how to use the book. This latter section also explains how to obtain government publications. The guide proper lists the publications under 119 alphabetically arranged subject headings. The topics are broad and cover a wide range of headings such as *agriculture, child care, literature, solar heating, United States history, women,* and *youth.* Topics added to this edition such as *pollution, mental health, mental retardation, civil rights,* and *consumer guides,* reflect the expansion of subjects of increased government concern as well as popular interest. Publications are listed alphabetically by title under each heading. Titles are cited as they appear on the title page or as listed in the *Monthly Catalog.* The usual bibliographical information—author (when known), issuing office, date, pagination, notes of illustrations, and stock number—is included. The stock number has been added in this edition to expedite orders from the Government Printing Office. Annotations are provided for titles which are not self-explanatory. Because prices now change so frequently, they are no longer cited. But free publications are appropriately noted. The volume ends with three appendixes and a 22-page Index. Appendix A lists agencies and addresses from which publications may be obtained free or purchased directly. Appendix B lists the addresses of Government Printing Office bookstores, and Appendix C cites libraries which are depositories for U.S. government publications.

The first edition of the guide included some Pan American Union publications which were then represented in the *Monthly Catalog.* These were omitted from the second edition when the *Monthly Catalog* discontinued their listing. They were, nevertheless, reinstated in the third edition, but they are not included in the fourth.

The compiler points out that there are from 200 to 250 titles of general interest in each issue of the *Monthly Catalog.* Thus, it was necessary for him to exercise discriminating judgment in choosing the most appropriate items from among the thousands of available publications. He has succeeded in providing a useful and timely compilation with a clear topical arrangement and accurate indexing. The Introduction, advice for the user, and annotations are in a simple and unpedantic style, obviously written with the layman in mind. For many purposes, the use of the guide will eliminate the need for a tedious search through numerous *Monthy Catalogs* and price lists.

The first editions of the *Guide* were criticized as being oriented toward a rural population. This objection, never entirely justifiable, has now become completely invalid. Although numerous publications of the Department of Agriculture and the Department of the Interior are still included, these are of general interest and do not predominate.

Earlier editions of the *Guide* include the Superintendent of Documents classification number with each entry. It is regrettable that these numbers are omitted from this edition. While classification numbers are no longer needed for ordering purposes, they are necessary to expedite the location of documents in the many libraries which use this classification system. Some titles listed in the guide are likely to be out of print in a short time and available only in libraries.

The compiler has erred in indicating in several instances that congressional publications are sold by committees or by the Senate Documents Office. Congressional publications which are not available free must be purchased from the Government Printing Office.

The only other bibliography similar in scope and arrangement is Linda C. Pohle's *A Guide to Popular Government Publications for Libraries and Home Reference* (Littleton, Colo.: Libraries Unlimited, 1972). This work lists fewer titles than the Leidy guide and is, of course, less up to date.

The earlier editions of *A Popular Guide to Government Publications* are recognized as useful bibliographic sources for the librarian and layman seeking inexpensive, authoritative information on a variety of subjects. The fourth edition continues this tradition. Although its price is double that of the 1968 edition, this latest issue of *A Popular Guide to Government Publications* is recommended for public, school, and college libraries.

(July 1, 1977, p.1670)

015.73   U.S.—Government publications—Bibliography   [CIP]   76-17803

Ports and harbors.
†338.476'272   Harbors—Juvenile literature   [OCLC]   75-19987
See page 50

The Princeton encyclopedia of classical sites.
Edited by Richard Stillwell. Princeton, N.J., Princeton Univ. Pr., 1976. 1019p. 28cm. cloth $125.

The Princeton Encyclopedia of Classical Sites proposes to describe, generally at some length, every site in the classical world where ruins, artifacts, or other tangible evidences of classical culture or industry still exist today, whether *in situ* or displaced, e.g., in museums. The period covered extends from about 750 B.C. to A.D. 565. The geographical area dealt with by the encyclopedia is the classical world in general, extending from northern Scotland south to Morocco and eastward as far as Pakistan. Places or sites are described most often in terms of their archaeological significance with only minor attention bestowed on historical factors. Entries range in length from very short (eight to ten lines) to substantial accounts of a page or more. The entry for Rome is eight pages long (16 columns). The average length of an article is about half a page (1 column).

The Preface states that there are approximately 3,000 entries written by 375 scholars from 16 nations. Each entry is signed, and the front of the book includes an alphabetical list of the 375 authors with their academic or other affiliations. Bibliographies accompany almost every article. They are not annotated. They range in number from 1 entry to about 100 (article on Rome). Their number is in almost direct proportion to the length of the article. An article of about ten lines will have 1; a quarter-column article will have 4 or 5; a full-column article will have a dozen; a still longer article, four or five columns, will have 30 to 40 items. The books cited are in all languages, including Slavic and Greek. The former are romanized, while the latter are sometimes in roman lettering but more often in Greek. The bibliographies are arranged by date (except that two or more items by one author are grouped). Many of the books have 1972, 1973, or 1974 dates. Most of the books were published between 1911 and 1969.

Entries are geographical and not by subject, with the exception of two group entries which will be noted below. Place-names appear in their classical form with cross-references from modern equivalents. A few of these differences are very slight—ROME see ROMA; LONDON see LONDINIUM—hardly justifying a cross-reference. But the majority in their modern dress (Turkish, Spanish, French, English, and so on) bear little resemblance to the antecedent Roman or Greek versions—GUZELHUSAR see TRALLES; ALCALA DE HENARES see COMPLUTUM; PARIS see LUTETIA PARISIORUM; and TROY see ILION.

As noted above, there are two exceptions to the geographical type of entry. One is a group article on ALEXANDRIAN FOUNDATIONS in the Middle East, consisting of brief descriptions of 13 towns established by Alexander in the course of his campaign across Asia. The other group entry is under SHIPWRECKS and is a brief listing of some 30 locations where Roman or Greek ships have been discovered under water or buried in mud at the water's edge. Although these articles are very brief, typically no more than six lines, most of them are accompanied by bibliographical reference to further information. Large regions of the classical world, such as Gaul, Italy, Lusitania, and Numidia have no entries. On the other hand, small islands such as Ithaca, Kerkyra (Corfu), and Rhodes do have separate entries, though there are none for the larger islands of Crete or Sicily.

The scholarship of the articles is exemplary. Some of the contributors of the articles are also authors of books cited in the bibliographies, and these are, in some cases, definitive works on the subject. The editor of the work is Richard Stillwell, emeritus professor of art and archeology at Princeton; director of the American School of Classical Studies, Athens, from 1932–35; and author of several monographs on Corinthian architecture. Stillwell has evidently insisted that contributors adhere to the canons of academic objectivity. Typical of the scholarly restraint found in most of the articles is the entry for TARTESSOS. The author, J. M. Blazquez, a member of the Spanish Institute of Archeology, Madrid, systematically presents the known facts about Tartessos and cites the extant classical writers who mention or refer to it, without commenting on the fact that some of their statements contradict each other. He refrains from speculation as to the possible identification of Tartessos with the mythical Atlantis (incidentally there is no entry for Atlantis anywhere in the volume) and strictly limits himself to a discussion of the site, the literature, and the artifacts. Most of the other articles maintain this aloof stance.

At the end of the volume there are 24 pages of maps indicating the geographical location of all of the sites mentioned in the book with red dots and numbers. Each map is accompanied by an alphabetical list of place-names, with their map coordinates and red-dot numbers. These lists enable readers to locate any place of which they know the name or conversely to identify any site they know only by its geographical location. These maps are the only illustrations in the work, and there is no index.

Absent from the work is any clear criterion for the selection of sites. The closest approximation to a policy is a single sentence in the Preface, stating that the intention is to provide a source of information "on sites that show remains from the Classical period." The editor then goes on to delimit the classical period, both chronologically and geographically, but says nothing further about any criteria for inclusion and gives no explanation of what he means by "show remains."

Since no site selection procedure is specified, one may fault the encyclopedia for seemingly illogical exclusions. In Andalusia, for example, there are entries for Carmo (modern Carmona), Italica (Santiponce), and Astapa (Estepa), among others, but none for Ecija or Ronda, although both these towns have Roman ruins, particularly the latter with its bridge that is still in everyday use. The most surprising omission of all is that of Sevilla, ancient Hispalis, of which there is no mention at all. Hispalis, a former Iberian and Carthaginian town, was captured from the Carthaginians by Julius Caesar in 43 B.C. and built up by him and his successors until it became one of the three principal cites of southern Spain. There are still some Roman monoliths in their original location in the heart of the city of Sevilla, and there are many local tomb stones, sarcophagi, statues, inscriptions, and artifacts in its archeological museum.

One other feature at the end of the book intended to help the user may actually have the reverse effect. Just before the section of maps is a six-page Glossary containing definitions of about 350 technical or difficult terms. A note explains that words used in the text only once are defined at that point and not listed in the Glossary. Neither are terms which are in standard desk dictionaries, unless these definitions are "not readily acceptable." Unfortunately, readers cannot be expected to know in advance whether or not terms they need clarified are adequately defined in desk dictionaries. For example, there is one sentence in the text, speaking of a temple in Selinus, Sicily, which reads in part as follows: "Its plan comprises pronoas, cella, adyton, and opisthodomos in antis. . . . " Three of these five words, *pronoas, cella,* and *opisthodomos,* are in the Glossary, while adyton and antis are omitted. The above-mentioned criterion for inclusion or exclusion in the Glossary may be good in theory but is rather frustrating in practice.

A comparison may be made of the work under review with the earlier (1854) *Dictionary of Greek and Roman Geography* in two volumes by Sir William Smith (London: Murray; Boston: Little, reprinted 1873–78). There are significant differences. Smith's work is a dictionary of all geographical names—countries, regions, rivers, lakes, caves, forests, and so on, as well as cities and towns. The entries are usually short and are intended for the general reader rather than for one with special archaeological interest. Seldom do they describe ruins or artifacts in any detail. In Smith's dictionary, there are many more entries than in the Princeton work. For example, between *DA* and *DAZ,* Smith has 73 entries, against only 13 in the Princeton work, and of these only 7 are in both works. A perusal of any of these seven entries plainly shows the great difference between the two works, even when their coverage overlaps. Smith's article on Damascus, for example, devotes two-thirds of its text to the history of the city, with quotations from Greek, Latin, and Hebrew writings. The Princeton work summarizes the history in 16 lines and devotes three-quarters of a page to a description of the classical remains as they are today and as the city might have been in ancient times. In summary, it may be said that the new Princeton volume performs a quite different function from that of the earlier Smith dictionary, and the latter does not make a good substitute for the former.

The *Princeton Encyclopedia of Classical Sites* is printed on two-column pages on a fairly heavy weight, dull-finish paper with good margins. The book's pages lie flat when it is opened, and the cloth binding appears to be sturdy enough for heavy usage. Greek titles in bibliographies are sometimes in Greek letters and at other times in Roman. Russian and other Cyrillic titles are transliterated into Roman. Greek words are sometimes used in the text, but more frequently the Greek name of an object is spelled out in Roman letters.

The *Princeton Encyclopedia of Classical Sites* fills a definite need for a comprehensive, scholarly, and authoritative encyclopedia of visitable sites of the classical world, with emphasis on their archeological aspects. Each entry also provides a brief historical or other kind of identification statement so that the *Princeton Encyclopedia* also serves as a geographical lexicon, though in this respect it is not as complete as the nineteenth-century work by Sir William Smith. For libraries serving clienteles interested in classical antiquities and for all major research libraries, this work is recommended. *(Feb. 1, 1977, p.854)*

938.003   Classical antiquities || Excavations (Archaeology)   [CIP]
75-30210

Rivers and river life.
†574.526'32   Rivers—Juvenile literature || Stream ecology—Juvenile literature   [OCLC]
75-19983
See page 50

Roads and highways.
†625.7   Roads—Juvenile literature   [OCLC]
75-19986
See page 50

Rocks and mining.
†622.3   Rocks—Juvenile literature || Mines and mineral resources—Juvenile literature   [OCLC]
75-19982
See page 50

Science fiction book review index, 1923–1973.
Ed. by H. W. Hall. Detroit, Gale Research, [1975]. 438p. 29cm. cloth $45.

Science fiction is included in university curricula and is subject to academic analysis and criticism. Such analysis and criticism demands historical perspective and creates a need for a comprehensive index of reviews. H. W. Hall's *Science Fiction Book Review Index* is a response to that need. *Science Fiction Book Review Index* covers reviews of books of science fiction and fantasy which appeared in magazines from 1923 through 1973. Hall is serials librarian at Texas A & M University; he has used that collection to verify the accuracy of the entries.

Only book reviews are indexed; reviews of short stories, movies, and television shows are excluded. The books reviewed are largely science fiction, but this is by virtue of the fact that they were reviewed in a science fiction magazine. *Alice's Adventures in Wonderland* probably does not meet the editor's unstated definition of science fiction, but it is included because it was reviewed in *Luna Monthly*. The magazines cited, beginning with 1970 issues, are also largely concerned with science fiction, but other magazines (e.g., *Newsweek, Kirkus, Saturday Review*) are included as well. Reviews cited in the nonscience fiction magazines are of science fiction books only. "Fanzines" are also represented, commencing with 1970 issues. Hall does not give the etymology of the word, but it seems to refer to magazines produced by amateurs, including fans of science fiction or comic books.

Access to *Science Fiction Book Review Index* is primarily by author of the book reviewed. A 344-page listing of book title entries under author headings comprises the main body of this index. *See* references from pseudonyms to authors' real names are provided. Coauthors and coeditors have no references but are indicated in the data for each book. Where possible, authors' names have been verified from Library of Congress catalogs. Following each author's name is a list of the person's books. Given with each title are the place of publication, publisher, date of publication, and pagination. Library of Congress card numbers also accompany most of the entries. Data are provided for the earliest edition, and hard cover is described unless only paperback is available. A list of review references follows each title. These include a letter code for the magazine, its volume and issue number, page numbers, date, and name of reviewer. A key to the magazine abbreviations code is provided in the preliminary pages of the *Science Fiction Book Review Index*. Books entered under title only are listed separately. Access is also possible via the title index which concludes the *Science Fiction Book Review Index*. Titles are in alphabetical order, each followed by its author.

Hall also includes what is in effect a bibliography of science fiction magazines, 1923–1973. Each entry is by title and includes title changes (with appropriate *see* references), editors, publishers, indexes which covered it, special notes, and a checklist noting missed or skipped issues and numbering errors. The abbreviated title, as it is used in the author list, is also given. Additionally, there is a bibliography of eight indexes to magazines in the genre. These are entered by editor, followed by title, publisher, and place and date of publication. The editors are listed separately, along with the magazines they edited and dates they served in that capacity.

Science Fiction Book Review Index is computer-composed in two columns for the author, title, and magazine directory listings and in four columns for the title index. Use of the directory section is facilitated by the inclusion of a dark vertical line in the center margin. Inner margins are wide; the volume is smythe sewn and lies flat when open. The editor plans to keep it up to date with annual supplements.

This work achieves its expressed intention to serve as an aid to study and research. Examination of the Index and a sample of cited magazines revealed no errors or omissions. *Science Fiction Book Review Index* is comprehensive, carefully edited, and a recommended reference tool for any public or academic library. *(Jan. 15, 1977, p.744)*

016.808883'876   Science fiction—Book reviews—Indexes   [CIP]
74-29085

Signals and messages.
†001.51   Communication—Juvenile literature || Signs and symbols—Juvenile literature   [OCLC]
75-20519
See page 50

Sir Banister Fletcher's a history of architecture.
Revised by J. C. Palmes. 18th ed. New York, Scribner, 1975. xvii, 1390p. illus. 25cm. cloth $24.95.

For most of the 76 years of this century, Sir Banister Flight Fletcher's *A History of Architecture on the Comparative Method* has been a revered source of information and expository illustrations for architecture and art history students. Fletcher (1866–1953) was a professional architect as were his father and brother, and he designed some buildings, but his main interest lay in the history of architecture. In 1896, he published the first edition of his book in collaboration with his father. Although his reputation is based mainly upon his authorship of this work, he was no cloistered scholar. Besides being president of the Royal Institute of British Architects, he was a Common Councillor of the City of London for almost 50 years and was knighted in 1919. He traveled widely and according to R. A. Cordingley, editor of the seventeenth edition of the *History*, he "prided himself on the fact that he had personally visited almost all of the sites and buildings of which he wrote."

The revised and rewritten sixth edition of the *History* (1921) established the pattern for its successors. In it 12 historical styles (mainly European) are defined along with the early styles such as the Egyptian, which contributed to them. The 12 included "Architecture of the British Dominions" and "Architecture of the United States of America." In addition to the 12, there were 5 so-called "non-historical styles" including Indian, Chinese, Japanese, Ancient American, and Saracenic occupying 76 out of 859 pages of the text in the seventh edition. He followed a strict format in presenting each style: section 1, influences including geographical and climatic, social, religious, and historical; section 2, architectural character; section 3, examples (succinct architectural descriptions of distinctive buildings illustrating the style); section 4, comparative analysis of structural variations, e.g., plans, walls, openings, roofs, columns, mouldings, and ornamentation between two neighboring styles such as Greek and Roman, or within styles as in the Italian Renaissance in which details of Florentine, Roman, and Venetian structures were compared. Section 5 was a bibliography.

Brief and direct analyses compressed most of the relevant information into a few sentences, making it easy for students to grasp the essential concepts, design features, and kinship of styles. However, what made the *History* a *Biblia pauperum* for the student was its excellent illustrations. There were many photographs, which were useful, but there were also literally hundreds of small, clear, and highly informative line drawings, sometimes as many as ten to a page and often no bigger than two inches square. One could find a complete analysis of a cathedral including a transverse perspective, floor plan, drawings of the facades, details of internal and external bays, vaults, buttresses, important monuments, decorative elements such as capitals, etc., minute but completely legible in black and white and usually all on one six-inch-by-nine-inch page. Or one could find a page of comparative ornaments of a period, four pages of plans of all the great English cathedrals, a page of types of timber church roofs, or the development and construction of Roman arches, domes, and vaults, and other architectural elements.

After the publication of the seventh edition, the *History* continued through nine more editions, most changes being correction and updating of information with the occasional addition or enlargement of sections. By the sixteenth edition, which was the last Sir Banister edited (1953), the illustrations alone had grown from 100 to over 3,200. The seventeenth edition (1961) was edited by Reginald A. Cordingley, professor of architecture at Manchester University, and had seven contributors. This edition marks the first major enlargement of the book, the additions being mainly in the East Asian and prehistoric areas, and in the updating of the twentieth century past World War II. The book grew to 1,366 pages and the illustrative material was also increased.

With the eighteenth edition, it became evident that format changes must be made because knowledge, particularly of ancient, East Asian, and pre-Columbian sites, had grown so much even since 1961 that the book threatened to become prohibitively unwieldy. The new editor therefore decided to drop the comparative sections and the title now reads, *A History of Architecture*, without the phrase "on the comparative method." Although information from the former comparative sections has often been reworked into the treatments of influences and architectural character, there is no longer a section devoted to comparisons *per se*. Despite the textual modifications, most of the comparative line drawings have been retained. The abridgements and excisions throughout seem logical. As one reads the current edition alongside the earlier ones, the scrupulous care exercised by the editors is apparent.

The new editor is James C. Palmes, formerly librarian (and an honorary Fellow) of the Royal Institute of British Architects. He is supported by 13 contributors most of whom are members of the Institute and several of whom have published in their fields.

The *History* is no longer divided into two parts. The "non-historical" styles have been brought to the front of the book and placed after the Egyptian chapter in a more or less chronological order; Ancient, Near Eastern-India and Pakistan, Japanese. Completely new chapters include those for Sri Lanka, Burma, Cambodia, Tibet, Nepal, Afghanistan, and Pre-Columbian America. The format is the same as that established over the years, except that the comparative section is missing. New chapters have been added for the Renaissance in Russia and in the Scandinavian countries. An interesting chapter on Renaissance and Post Renaissance architecture outside Europe includes colonial architecture in the U.S. and Latin America, South Africa, and India. The final chapter "International Architecture since 1914" has been updated to include the Munich Olympic buildings and the Sydney Opera House (1972-1973), and chapters retained from earlier editions have been revised with the material sometimes reorganized or reworded to make it more logically or more smoothly expressed.

Terminology, particularly archaeological place-names, has been brought up to date. The book still offers a wealth of illustrations. Many new photographs have been added and some of the old ones have been replaced with superior sharp black-and-whites on unglazed paper. In the recently added chapters, photographs predominate. However, most of the earlier line drawings have been retained and about 80 new plans and drawings added. According to the publisher, there are now 3,334 illustrations, 2,039 line drawings, and 1,295 photographs. Each chapter ends with a brief Bibliography and there is a Glossary at the conclusion of the book. The Index provides references to personal and place-names, structures (chapels, palaces, airport buildings, etc.), and subjects which include some cross-references.

The dimensions of the sewn binding are the same. The book is slightly thicker but has lost weight because of the conversion to unglazed paper. The margins remain too narrow to allow for rebinding but the book is flexibly and durably bound. The print is small but clear.

The eighteenth edition of Fletcher's *History of Architecture* is a meticulous, logical, and extensive revision of a classic. It is recommended as a basic reference for academic, public, and school libraries. *(Dec. 1, 1976, p.561)*
720.9   Architecture—History   74-25545

Size.
†620.004'4   Weights and measures—Juvenile literature   [OCLC]   75-19966
See page 50

Skyscrapers.
†690.523   Skyscrapers—Juvenile literature   [OCLC]   75-19971
See page 50

Snakes and lizards.
†598.1   Snakes—Juvenile literature || Lizards—Juvenile literature   [OCLC]   75-19985
See page 50

Soviet Asia:
bibliographies; a compilation of social science and humanities sources on the Iranian, Mongolian, and Turkic nationalities, with an essay on the Soviet Asian controversy. By Edward Allworth. New York, Praeger Publishers, 1975. lxiii, 686p. $35.

Soviet Asia: Bibliographies is a bibliography of bibliographies with an introductory essay on "The Controversial Status of Soviet Asia."

Edward Allworth, the compiler, is professor of Turco-Soviet Studies and director of the Program on Soviet Nationality Problems at Columbia University. Although he is primarily a subject specialist rather than a bibliographer, Allworth's other publications in Soviet Asian studies include several bibliographies of more limited scope. *Soviet Asia: Bibliographies* is one of four books published jointly by the Program on Soviet Nationality Problems at Columbia University and "Praeger Special Studies in International Politics and Government." It is a first edition, with no plans announced for supplements or revisions.

In a tool intended for scholars, Allworth has drawn together citations of about 5,200 bibliographies concerned with topics within the humanities and the social sciences. All entries represent bibliographies which were published in Czarist Russia or the USSR between 1850 and 1970. However, "general bibliographies covering the entire Czarist Empire or USSR have been omitted." The compiler sought to provide inclusive coverage within the stated limits of the bibliography and has made extensive use of the Soviet national bibliographies, annual *Bibliography of Soviet Bibliographies* (*Bibliografiia Sovetskoi Bibliografii*), Soviet bibliographies devoted to particular regions or nationalities, encyclopedias for the purpose of "adding system and filling in the gaps," and several Western sources to correct "the slant, tilt or inefficiencies of Soviet bibliography with its pervasive ideological censorship and massive bureaucracy."

Following a general chapter treating all of Soviet Asia, the book is divided into four principal sections: *Black Sea & West Caspian Littoral, Volga Basin, Central Asia,* and *Siberia & Mongolia.* Each of 38 regions is treated in a separate chapter, which is further subdivided by the following eleven subject categories: *General; Anthropology, Ethnology; Architecture, Art, Music; Economics; Education; Geography; History, Archaeology; Language, Literature; Philosophy, Religion; Political Science, Law;* and *Social Organization.* Bibliographies have not been identified or reported in all subject areas for each region.

Under each subject division, bibliographies in both Russian and indigenous languages are cited alphabetically by personal author or by title for those entries with no author identified. More than 50 percent of the bibliographies cited were published since 1950, and the great majority are 20th-century imprints. A complete entry consists of the following elements: name of the author, editor, or compiler; title of the work and, in cases of journal literature, the title of the journal in which it appears; imprint; pagination; number of copies printed; and a descriptive annotation. Serial titles are frequently abbreviated. Annotations show languages of the text, number of entries, main languages of the entries, time period covered and inclusive publication dates, and exact page numbers. No information about current availability is provided by the annotations. However, asterisks mark those bibliographies which are held by Columbia University Libraries. Only those items owned by Columbia have been examined and verified. "Transliteration follows a modification of the system and tables published in Edward Allworth, *Nationalities of the Soviet East* (1971)."

The coverage offered by Allworth in *Soviet Asia: Bibliographies* is detailed and inclusive. Many items are not readily found elsewhere, and no other single source cites them. No inaccuracies in citations were found.

Use of *Soviet Asia: Bibliographies* is facilitated by a detailed table of contents. Although an alphabetical index by author and title would have greatly enhanced the book's utility as a verification source, this omission is compensated for by the volume's inclusiveness. It is indispensable as a verification tool and guide to existing bibliographies. The volume was produced from camera-ready copy. Pages are clear and readable, and the binding is sturdy.

Soviet Asia: Bibliographies draws together bibliographies which are dispersed throughout many less accessible sources, and no comparable tool exists for the subject matter covered. Its entries are full and the information is clearly organized and presented. This specialized bibliography is recommended for scholarly collections. *(Apr. 15, 1977, p.1295)*

†016.957 Asia—Bibliography || Eastern question (Central Asia)—Bibliography || Russia—Bibliography || Bibliography—Bibliography   73-9061

Spiders.
†595.4 Spiders—Juvenile literature [OCLC]   75-19964

See page 50

Sports.
[By] Marshall E. Nunn. Littleton, Col., Libraries Unlimited, 1976. 217p. 24cm. skivertex $11.50. (Spare Time Guides: Information Sources for Hobbies and Recreation, no. 10)
016.796 Sports—Bibliography [CIP]   75-33869

See page 62

The sports encyclopedia: baseball.
[By] David S. Neft, Roland T. Johnson, Richard M. Cohen, and [Jordan A. Deutsch]. New York, Grosset, [c1976]. 494p. 29cm. cloth $17.95; paper $9.95.
†796.357'64 Baseball—Statistics [OCLC]   73-15137

See page 6

The story of cars.
†629.222 Automobiles—Juvenile literature [OCLC]   75-19993

See page 50

Subject guide to children's books in print:
a subject index to children's books in 8,300 categories. New York and London, R. R. Bowker Co. [c1975]. 459p. 28cm. cloth $20.

Subject Guide to Children's Books in Print is a "cross-referenced alphabetical subject arrangement of the 39,000 children's books" listed in its companion volume *Children's Books in Print, 1975.* Textbooks, toy books, and workbooks are excluded. Both of these bibliographies are annually corrected, expanded, and generally revised by the R. R. Bowker Company's Department of Bibliography in collaboration with its Publication Systems Department.

This sixth edition of *Subject Guide to Children's Books in Print* was produced from records stored on magnetic tape, edited by computer programs, and set in type by computer-edited photocomposition.

In the Foreword, Lillian N. Gerhardt, editor in chief of *School Library Journal,* gives a brief history of the publication, points out the origins of the headings, and indicates the purpose of the publication. Following this is a good two-page explanation on "How to Use Subject Guide to Children's Books in Print."

The 8,300 subject categories were derived mainly from the tenth edition of *Sears List of Subject Headings* and from the Library of Congress subject heading list. Some books have been assigned to a single category; other books have been assigned two or more headings. Thus, the 39,000 titles are reflected in over 50,000 entries.

Within the subject categories, typical entries include author(s), editor(s), translator(s), illustrator(s), title, number of volumes, edition, Library of Congress number, series information, language if other than English, grade range, year of publication, type of binding if other than cloth over boards, price, International Standard Book Number, and publisher. The above information is derived from publishers' catalogs.

Current interests are reflected in the headings, for example, Astrology, Blacks, Bilingual, Monsters, Occult, Outer Space, Rock Music. General and specific terms are used. Occasionally one wishes for more specific terms. For example, there are no headings for Big Foot (there is a heading for Sasquatch) and Loch Ness Monster; however, these are covered under Monsters. There is no entry for pyramid; however, books concerned with pyramids can be found under Egypt—Antiquities.

A Key to Abbreviations precedes the index itself and a Key to Publishers' Abbreviations is found at the end of the volume.

See and *see also* references are used generously. Spot-checking revealed no errors.

The material is arranged in three columns, with the headings in boldface capitals. Most of the print is small but readable. The sturdily bound volume lies flat when opened.

Since many inquiries for children's books begin with a subject request, this tool should be of value to libraries serving children and to bookstore personnel. However, as the Foreword indicates, "*Subject Guide to Children's Books in Print* is designed as an aid, not a replacement, for the children's book specialists who can read any number of thematic overtones, into the fiction and picture books published for children. It is intended as the bibliography from which to start. . . ."

Subject Guide to Children's Books in Print is recommended then as a valuable and convenient subject guide to currently available children's books. *(Sept. 15, 1976, p.200)*

†028.52   Children's literature—Bibliography   [OCLC]   70-101705

A survey of musical instruments.
[By] Sibyl Marcuse. New York, Harper & Row, Publishers, 1975. 863p. illus. 24cm. cloth $20.

Emmanual Winternitz, writing in the introduction to the 1964 Dover edition of Curt Sachs' *Real-Lexikon der Musikinstrumente,* first published in 1913, stated that "Today we are living in a veritable renascence of interest in musical instruments of the past." Further, he paid homage to the *Real-Lexikon* as "an encyclopedic work of unprecedented comprehensiveness and international range, including precise descriptions of instruments from all periods of history on a world-wide basis." A half century later, Sibyl Marcuse, in her previous book, *Musical Instruments: A Comprehensive Dictionary* (Garden City, N.Y.: Doubleday, 1964), cited the *Real-Lexikon* as the "first work to deal exclusively with musical instruments of all peoples and times—[that] . . . marked the beginning of an entirely new era in this science." The purpose of Marcuse's *Musical Instruments* is to provide the English-language reader with a reference work comparable to the Sachs' *Real-Lexikon.*

This new work, *A Survey of Musical Instruments,* reflects Marcuse's accumulated experience as musicologist, historian, and former curator of the musical instruments collection at Yale University. Scrupulously researched, the volume is a major contribution to the field, providing additional scholarship in an area of widening interest.

A Survey of Musical Instruments is divided into four major parts: Idiophones (111 pages), Membranophones (56 pages), Chordophones (368 pages), and Aerophones (278 pages), each of which is a category of instruments within the Sachs Hornsbostel classification scheme. Within each part, the historical development of generically related instruments is followed from their beginnings down to their present status or to their retirement from the musical scene. In addition to the chronological development, there is also a geographical arrangement which is not reflected in the Contents. This chronological and geographical pattern is followed in all four parts of the book.

There are numerous quotations throughout the text. These are taken from items in the ten-page bibliography located near the end of the volume. Parenthesized cross-references in the text refer the user to related subjects. Although this arrangement may seem to indicate a lack of coherence, the volume is well organized and specific items are easily located by using the Contents or the indexes.

Unquestionably, Sibyl Marcuse supplies the reader with an abundance of information about European and non-Western instruments, and one could only wish that there were more concerning the latter. In compiling this comprehensive volume, she has not relied on contemporary sources but has drawn from primary work, i.e., musical texts and treatises, diagrams, and documents. This is reflected throughout the text and in the bibliography.

A Survey of Musical Instruments is not a book to be read through from cover to cover because of the astonishingly vast amount of detailed information and facts it contains. However, as the reader consults it about individual instruments or families of instruments, it seems to work very well. Treatment is understandably uneven because there are practical limitations to how much a single volume can hold.

Although the book runs to more than 350 pages, it contains no footnotes. Their inclusion would have greatly assisted the user. Opening or introductory remarks by the author would have been equally helpful, as such statements could have clarified the author's intention in producing the volume, her method of organization, and also express reservations or limitations the user can expect to encounter.

Another obvious weakness is the paucity of illustrations which in a work of this type would have enhanced its usefulness. The volume contains only 40 illustrations, including the frontispiece, and a brief diagram called General Notes. Although well-captioned, pertinent, and of good quality, these are limited to black-and-white photographs, line drawings, and reproductions of paintings. All illustrations are well positioned in relation to the text.

Although the *Harvard Dictionary of Music* identifies a fifth classification of instruments (electrophones), these are not included in *A Survey of Musical Instruments.* Beginning on page 827, there is a very brief Glossary of 94 terms. Because of the lack of comprehensive coverage of definitions, the layman may wish to consult the *Harvard Dictionary* while using *Marcuse.* Following this, there is a 278-entry bibliography, Works Referred to in This Book. Most of the books are in languages other than English and represent sources quoted in the text. The volume closes with a 20-page Index which is divided into two parts: Index Nominum and Index Rerum. Index citations range in number from one for figures only slightly associated with the history of instruments, such as Michael Arne, Pindar, Voltaire, and Conrad Witz, to 103 for Michael Praetorius.

A Survey of Musical Instruments is a scholarly reference volume which will find immediate welcome in the music sections of public, academic, and research libraries as an excellent supplement to similar works, such as Sach's *History of Musical Instruments* (New York: Norton, 1940) and the largely pictorial *Musical Instruments of the World* (New York: Paddington, 1976), and will have great appeal for the adult music enthusiast. Recommended.   *(Mar. 1, 1977, p.1037)*

781.9'1   Musical instruments || Musical instruments—History   [CIP]   72-9135

Television.
†791.45   Television—Juvenile literature   [OCLC]   75-19996
See page 50

The theater.
†792   Theater—Juvenile literature   [OCLC]   75-20515
See page 50

Time and clocks.
†529.78   Time—Juvenile literature || Clocks and watches—Juvenile literature   [OCLC]
                                                                      75-19977
See page 50

Towns and cities.
†301.36   Cities and towns—Juvenile literature   [OCLC]   75-19989
See page 50

Trains and railroads.
†625.27 Railroads—Juvenile literature || Railroads—Trains—Juvenile literature [OCLC]
75-19973
See page 50

Treasures of Italy.
By Giuliano Dogo. New York, Norton, [1976]. pub. simultaneously in Canada by George J. McLeod, Ltd. 434p. illus. (part col.) plates 25cm. cloth $19.85.

This attractive book is a translation of *Guida Artistica d'Italia* (Milan: Electa Editrice, 1974), the translation being under the auspices of the Italian publisher, with Norton retaining right of approval. Apparently Giuliano Dogo is responsible for the contents of the book; Daphne Newton translated it from the Italian.

Treasures of Italy is an alphabetically arranged dictionary of 1,001 towns and sites in Italy which contain important works of art. Rather than concentrating on the large cities for which individual guide books have often been written, the publisher's aim was to "bring to the visitor's notice the lesser known works which, being hidden away or off the beaten track, are often overlooked." There is no indication of criteria used in selecting places, but their relative importance is indicated by one, two, or three asterisks preceding the entry. Within single paragraphs, which sometimes cover several pages, the reader is given a brief geographical, and sometimes historical, description of the site, followed by listings of monuments, buildings, and museums, with brief accounts of their most important holdings. "We have made no attempt to influence the visitor, leaving the works to speak for themselves," says the Introduction, so that no critical influence is exerted, "but in order to place each item in perspective, the essential dates regarding birth and death, or known limits of the artist's activity are given beside the name."

Treatment of the entries varies from about 100 to 150 words for small places like Eboli or Pitigliano to a page or more for towns as big as Pistoia, Lucca, Pisa, or Assisi. For small places, buildings and collections are listed, and their main features and important artists and architects are brought to the attention of the reader. For larger places, there may be more detailed descriptions of cathedral treasures or museum collections. Archaeological sites are also included.

For the really large cities (e.g., Venice, Florence or Rome), by comparison, the treatment is much briefer. There are, however, several pages devoted to each, with the most important works listed and more illustrations provided (e.g., 26 for Venice and 33 for Rome).

The more than 400 black-and-white and 200 colored photographs are one of the main features of the volume. They are close to the entries they illustrate, usually one or two to a page, and range from two inches square to a full page. The black-and-white illustrations are excellent. The colored plates are usually made up of from two to six small pictures and vary in color fidelity and definition but are generally satisfactory. An Index of artists at the back of the book stars references to pages where illustrations of their works may be found. The titles of works, however, are not indexed. The reader who cannot recall the painter of the "Story of the Cross" at Arezzo will find his name in the paragraph on Arezzo. Alternatively, if the name of the town should elude the reader's memory, he or she can find the coverage in the Name Index under Piero della Francesca. But the reader who knows only the title of the painting is out of luck. Also, if he or she looks only under Francesca, there is no cross-reference to Piero. By the same token, Ca' d'Oro, Palazzo dei Diamanti, and the Visconti Castle may be unfindable unless the reader knows the city or town with which these architectural features are associated. A more complete Index would have given the *Treasures* another level of usefulness.

In addition to the artist Index at the back of the volume, there is a list of places arranged under province. There are some cross-references in the text, usually from English versions of names to Italian—Leghorn to Livorno, for instance.

Comparison of *Treasures* with other art reference tools points up its usefulness. There are 155 entries in the *C* section of *Treasures*. The Committee compared the section with the *C* section in *McGraw-Hill Dictionary of Art* (New York: 1969), *Praeger Encyclopedia of Art* (New York: 1971) and with the *C* section of the Index volume to the *Encyclopedia of World Art* (New York: McGraw-Hill, 1959–68). The *McGraw-Hill Dictionary* has entries for some of the same towns, but usually they are concerned with only one building or monument, and they do not contain a summary of the holdings of the town. *Praeger* has no place entries. There are 70 duplicate entries in the *C*'s of the *Encyclopedia of World Art*, v. XV. Some refer to *Italy* (v. 8) which contains comparable accounts of a total of 341 cities and towns. There are also references to other volumes. The disadvantage of the encyclopedia is that several volumes may have to be consulted to retrieve all relevant information. Fourteen different volumes are cited for Caprarola, for instance. However, all encyclopedia entries include bibliographies, and there are none in the *Treasures*.

Treasures was also compared with a regular guidebook. A check was made of the *C* section in the Index of *Nagel's Encyclopedia-Guide: Italy* (1971). Since this, as a guidebook, is concerned with routing travelers, there is no alphabetical arrangement of places except in the Index.

Treasures' arrangement makes it more responsive to the average reader. *Nagel's* Index includes 368 place-names (against 155 in *Treasures*), but some of these merely refer to places as crossroads or geographical features. *Treasures* lists 62 places not in *Nagel*, and there are 93 listed in both guides. However, of the 93 duplicates listed, *Nagel* omits mention of artistic features for 26 of these places; 30 merely listed artistic features with no descriptions; another 26 are provided with fairly extended accounts but not as complete as those in *Treasures*. Only 11 are equal to, or better, than those in *Treasures*. Most extended accounts in *Nagel* include some discussion of holdings in churches and museums and also of artists. For large cities, the guidebook seems much more complete. Directions as to locations of places and how to get to them are not included in *Treasures*. In format, the *Nagel* is certainly more convenient to carry, being pocket-sized, whereas *Treasures* is hardly a glove-compartment book, measuring, as it does, well over nine by six inches and being printed on heavy glazed paper. It is hardbound in a linen-like cloth, printed in two columns to the page in small but clear print with the entries in bold capitals.

Treasures of Italy is an attractive and useful compilation of important artistic and architectural works located in the cities and smaller towns of Italy. Public libraries with art and travel-minded patrons, academic libraries, and perhaps some large high school libraries will find this guide a worthwhile acquisition. Recommended. *(June 15, 1977, p.1598)*
709.45 Art—Italy—Dictionaries || Architecture—Italy—Dictionaries [OCLC] 76-373988

Trees & shrubs:
a complete guide. [By] Richard Gorer. Newton Abbot, London, North Pomfret, Vt., David & Charles; [1976]. Canada, Douglas David & Charles, Ltd. [1976]. 264p. illus. cloth 26cm. $22.50.

Richard Gorer has also written *Choosing Your Garden Plants* (London: David & Charles, 1972), *Living Tradition in the Garden* (David & Charles, 1974), *Flower Gardens in England* (London: Batsford, 1975), *Multiseason Shrubs and Trees* (New York: International Publications Service, 1971), and *Quick Growing Shrubs* (New York: Heinemann, 1976).

The Introduction states that trees and shrubs included are those "that are generally hardy in the United Kingdom." A further limitation is that all plants described be available in the United Kingdom. The plants must be ones which grow in an insular climate, without protection, with winter temperatures as low as 8°C (18°F) but without prolonged frost, with summer temperatures rarely above 25°C (77°F) with infrequent dry spells, and with an average rainfall evenly spread of 30–40 inches annually. The author excludes plants which grow only in specific parts of the United Kingdom affected by the Gulf Stream. Also excluded are "all plants whose dimensions do not attain a metre [ca. three feet] either vertically or horizontally." Because of space limitations the plants described are "confined to species, with hybrids and cultivars receiving the most perfunctory mention and . . . where the number of hybrids is very large . . . completely disregarded." Using these criteria almost 250 genera and 1,500 species are listed. For most genera there are notes of the number of their species so that it is possible to check the percentage included. For example, chionanthus is said to have only two species, and both are listed. Cistus has about 20 species, and 7 species and 2 hybrids are listed. Clematis has more than 200 species, and 20 species are listed. About 50 species of cotoneaster are recognized, and 32 are listed. There are about 600 species of rhododendron, and 126 are listed. "The most popular garden plant in the world," rosa, has 250 species and thousands of hybrids and cultivars; 54 species are listed.

The catalog is arranged alphabetically by genera and species within genera. Distinctive typefaces used for genera and species and text set off the divisions very clearly, and ample margins and spacing give the double-column page a pleasing appearance and allow the entries to stand out for ease in reading. Almost every page has a line drawing illustrating a distinctive aspect of a species.

The order of data for each entry is uniform: genus (in Latin), botanist connected with its taxonomy, family (in Latin), English name (given only if it is generally used, e.g., *ABIES* Miller Pinaceae Silver fir). Access is only through the genera; there are no references from families or English names. This lack of access through English name makes it difficult for the lay person to use the book. The subentry under species has the same format. The genus annotation tells whether the name derives from a personal name (e.g., Abelia from Dr. Clarke Abel), the region(s) of origin, its general characteristics, tolerances and growing requirements, or propagation. The type of information varies, particularly if such notes are given in the annotations on species. There is often a succinct evaluation, e.g., "They are useful shrubs for their late-flowering propensities and are moderate growers."

The annotation for the species is strictly patterned and uses symbols and abbreviations, given in the Introduction. Plants are identified by type, e.g., "A deciduous shrub to 2m." and "Evergreen tree of up to 50m." Space is economized without making the text unduly difficult for the reader to understand. Technical descriptors are used precisely, and definitions are given in an introductory essay which begins "A tree consists of a central stem or *trunk* from which radiate *branches*" and continues to define leaf—"The leaf consists of the leaf-stalk or *petiole* and the blade or *lamina.*"—flower, fruit, and profile. Technical terms in the essay are italicized. A separate Glossary supplements the essay definitions. A comment is usually made on the species' growth habit. The Introduction defines rates of growth. "Rapid" is 30 centimeters each year, "moderate" 15–30 centimeters each year, "slow" 15 centimeters each year. A concluding note is given on the country of origin, the person who introduced it to the United Kingdom, and the date of introduction.

The volume is very attractively produced; the paper is opaque, margins are generous, and the binding is strong.

The value for U.S. libraries of a volume so specifically designed for British gardeners is questionable. However, gardeners in areas of the U.S. have long used British gardening manuals and adjusted requirements to regional conditions. Also, the annotations for many of the plants in the volume indicate an origin in regions of the U.S. or in parts of the world from which plants have been successfully introduced into this country.

Experienced gardeners reading these annotations on cultivation requirements will know that tolerance of some plants to varying conditions is extensive. It is relatively easy, then, to evaluate the adaptability of many of these species to regions of the U.S. by intelligent use of the author's comments on soil, sun/shade, heat/frost, and other tolerances. Additionally one may use this guide to estimate growth rate, flowering habit, and other characteristics. Landscape gardeners will welcome the information on size of plant, habits, and ornamental aspects. Also of use are the notes for each species on methods of propagation. The book may be used, then, in conjunction with regional guides, such as the third edition of the *Sunset Western Garden Book* (Lane, 1967) or with standard encyclopedias, such as the fourth edition of *Taylor's Encyclopedia of Gardening* (Boston: Houghton Mifflin, 1961) and *Wyman's Gardening Encyclopedia* (New York: Macmillan, 1971), all of which give maps for the U.S. which note appropriate zones when describing plants. For example, for a New Zealand shrub, corokia, two species are listed in Gorer; one of them is listed in the *Sunset Western Garden Book,* along with three other species, as suitable for almost all zones in the western U.S.

Trees & Shrubs is recommended for public libraries and home gardening enthusiasts. *(May 15, 1977, p.1448)*

†635.976   Ornamental trees—Dictionaries || Ornamental shrubs—Dictionaries   [OCLC]
76-4364

Trees and wood.
†674   Lumbering—Juvenile literature || Trees—Juvenile literature   [OCLC]   75-19974

See page 50

United States local histories in the Library of Congress: a bibliography. Edited by Marion J. Kaminkow. 5v. Baltimore, Magna Carta Book Co., 1975, [c1976]. 29cm. buckram $275; v.5: supplement and index $25.

United States Local Histories in the Library of Congress is a condensation in book form of the nearly 90,000 cards in the Library of Congress U.S. local history shelflist (L.C. classes F1–F975 and DU620–DU629). The first four volumes list items received by the Library of Congress until mid-1972. They deal respectively with: Atlantic States, Maine to New York; Atlantic States, New Jersey to Florida; the Deep South, the Southwest, the Middle West, Alaska, and Hawaii; the West, the Northwest, and the Pacific States. The fifth volume is a supplement listing U.S. local history books received by the library between mid-1972 and January 1976. Volume 5 also includes the Index to all five volumes and corrects errors in the first four volumes.

Each volume is divided into sections representing states or geographical areas. Each section is preceded by a selected bibliography and summary of the LC classification schedule for periodicals, museums, general works, collective genealogies, pamphlets, juvenile works, etc., relating to that particular state or area and a listing of countries and cities. This is followed by the actual bibliographical entries in shelflist order. There are approximately 15 entries per page.

According to the editor's note, "the original wording on the Library of Congress catalog cards has not been reproduced in its entirety. The titles of the works have been abbreviated, where possible. Authors' dates, joint authors, detailed descriptions of contents, numbers of copies printed, etc., have been omitted. Brief descriptions of contents and important notes, such as all notes of indexes and bibliographies, have been retained. Where it exists, the Library of Congress catalog card number has been listed at the end of each item to help those who wish to purchase cards. The Library's call number is also listed uniformly on the right-hand side, where the number sequence can be easily followed." While it may have been desirable to include detailed descriptions of contents and other information, this probably would have more than doubled the size and cost of the set. At any rate, one can find most of the information in the *National Union Catalog.*

After each section of entries, there appears a supplementary Index of places. The Index must always be consulted to provide access to any additional entries listed elsewhere. The information from LC cards has been rearranged into a clear and attractive format. The type is easy to read, and main entries have been capitalized to enhance legibility.

In volume 5 a 177-page Index of Personal Names, three columns per page, lists more than 35,000 persons including authors, illustrators, subjects of biographies, writers of introductions and prefaces. Because references are made to volume and page only, it is necessary to read every entry on the specified page to be sure of finding all entries that include a sought-after name. It would be easier for the user if references had been made to the volume and LC classification numbers. However, this is a minor complaint.

The set is durably bound in green buckram, and its pages lie flat when in use. The paper is of dull finish with sufficient margins to permit rebinding.

Because the Library of Congress has the most extensive local history collection in the country, this work is the most complete bibliography on the subject. It should be used in conjunction with *Genealogies in the Library of Congress: a Bibliography* (1972, 2v.), as individual genealogies are not included in this work.

The editor, Marion Kaminkow, has had previous experience compiling this type of bibliography. She has edited such works as *Genealogies in the Library of Congress: a Bibliographical Guide* and *A List of Immigrants from England to America 1718–1759* (with Jack Kaminkow).

United States Local Histories in the Library of Congress is a very valuable addition to libraries supporting extensive programs in U.S. history and to large historical society libraries, where it would be available to the serious researcher of local U.S. history. Because of its inclusion of biographies, city and state directories, and baptism and marriage records, it would also be useful to genealogists. Volume 5, which is available separately, would be of little use without the rest of the set. Recommended. *(June 1, 1977, p.1524)*

016.973 U.S.—History, Local—Bibliography || U.S.—Genealogy—Bibliography—Catalogs || U.S.—Biography—Bibliography—Catalogs || U.S.—Description and travel—Bibliography—Catalogs || U.S. Library of Congress [OCLC] 74-25444

The universe.
†523.1 Astronomy—Juvenile literature [OCLC] 75-19980
See page 50

Vanishing animals.
†591.52 Rare animals—Juvenile literature || Extinct animals—Juvenile literature [OCLC] 75-20510
See page 50

Violets of the United States.
[By] Doretta Klaber. South Brunswick and New York, Barnes, [1976]. 208p. illus. (part col.) 32cm. cloth $40.

Observing that "There are any number of botanical treatises on the violet, written by botanists or by those who first discovered a native violet, but these are technical papers not written for the general public," the late Doretta Klaber produced this book to describe and illustrate wild violets not only for amateur enthusiasts but also for botanical experts. She collected live plants from all over the U.S. and drew them in color, showing their flower and seed stages, root systems, and growth patterns.

Since Doretta Klaber's only claim to expertise was based on knowledge which she developed over years of gardening and studying wild violets, Dr. Norman Russell, a well-known botanist, examined every drawing and confirmed the manuscript's accuracy and clarity.

In addition to the usual introductory sections, *Violets* includes a list of abbreviations of the names of individuals who first assigned botanical names to the various violets described, an extensive acknowledgments section, and a glossary of terms (defined through both words and illustrations): the definitions of descriptive terms in the glossary are based on those by Asa Gray (1810–1888) or *Webster's Third New International Dictionary;* the remaining definitions are translations of violets' Latinate names. The definitions—scaled down for the benefit of the lay reader—convey essentially correct botanical meanings. Included as a further means of clarifying the glossary terms are four pages of black-and-white drawings, each generously labeled, showing plants and their parts, forms of growth, and leaf shapes and toothing.

The major section of the work illustrates and describes 92 species of violets, all but one or two of them recognized species. Each species is illustrated on one or two plates. For convenience in studying and ease of identification, the violets are divided into nine groups. Each plant is characterized by dominant color, by leaf (cut or uncut), and by manner of growth (stemmed or stemless). Each violet is cited by its scientific name (Latin binomial): the name of the genus (i.e., Viola), followed by the epithet or word describing the particular species. After the scientific name is an abbreviation of the name of the person who first assigned the scientific name. Next, the common name or names are listed as is the reference to the colored plate on which the illustration of the plant is found.

Following the heading for each violet or, in some cases, group of closely related violets, is a short narrative description including further information on color, shape, and size; similarities with, and/or differences from, other species; natural environment and incidents of sightings; propagation techniques; growth patterns; and other attributes. This material contains informal comments such as "This delightful plant," "I was enchanted," "a darling seedling that came up in my garden," "I never know what amusing combination of color is going to come up," "given time I might learn to grow them well!!" Nonetheless, because Doretta Klaber's language is not intimidating, the write-ups are very useful in helping amateur enthusiasts to identify and classify wild violets.

Cross-references to other violets (either mentioned in the text or illustrated with colorplates) are sometimes provided. They are helpful in showing various relationships between species. All cross-references checked were correct.

Doretta Klaber faces the usual difficulty assigning common or vernacular names to plants. Since these names, though in common usage, are not standardized, they vary greatly. The Committee checked both the scientific and common names in *Violets* against the American Joint Committee on Horticultural Nomenclature's *Standardized Plant Names,* 2d. ed. The scientific names corresponded exactly, but the common names did vary because of the lack of uniform practice in the field. *Violets* cannot be faulted for such variations.

In some ways, this work is like a roadside guide, especially in its liberal use of drawings. Doretta Klaber also prepared the clear, very detailed, and lovely illustrations for the book. Black-and-white line drawings often appear on the same pages as narratives, but it is the 80 colorplates which are the truly outstanding feature of this work. Each plate is drawn from life, depicts both spring and summer appearance, and shows both flower and seed stages and root systems. Through the illustrations alone, many enthusiasts could easily identify unknown violets. Botanists will find the illustrations a useful addition to the scientific literature.

Concluding this work are several appendixes: a list of nurseries with addresses from which the more unusual violets may be obtained, a listing by region (East and West, Midwest, East, South, and North) of the 92 species distribution in the U.S., and a list of species by hospitable natural environment (sun, shade, and moist places).

There are also a Bibliography and an Index. The Bibliography lists only 13 titles, is not annotated, and includes no titles with imprints later than 1966. Many are agricultural bulletins. While these would be helpful to lay readers, they are very out of date, and libraries are not likely to have them. Five of the books were published prior to 1933.

The Index is in three sections: names of persons, botanical names, and common names. With two exceptions (Norman H. Russell and Edgar T. Wherry), the persons whose names are in the Index are persons who sent Doretta Klaber seeds of, or information about, particular violets. Russell and Wherry are cited in the text as persons who added information about particular violets. Names of botanists who are credited with assigning botanical names are not indexed. The Index sections by botanical and common names each give reference to pages of text as well as to colored plates on which the illustrations appear. A check of the Index revealed that only a small percentage of citations were incorrect.

The book is bound in violet-colored cloth. The print throughout is clear and easy to read, and the quality of paper used for both the text and illustrations is excellent. The margins are adequate if rebinding ever becomes necessary. This book should withstand normal library usage unless its lovely pages fall prey to larceny.

Violets of the United States provides much information about wild violets which would be useful to enthusiasts. Much of the information included is not so readily available elsewhere. *Violets* gives accurate detail without overwhelming the reader with elliptical technical terms and description. Because of the illustrations, this would be an excellent volume for any large botanical collection, even with the errors noted in the Index and the unavoidable inconsistency of common names with those cited in other sources. Purchase is recommended for libraries with such holdings; other institutional and individual buyers should weigh the price against probable value for their patrons.

(June 15, 1977, p.1598)

583'.135   Violets—U.S.—Identification   [CIP]   77-75038

Water resources of the world:
selected statistics. Compiled and edited by Frits van der Leeden. Port Washington, New York, Water Information Center, Inc., [c1975]. xi, 568p. illus. maps. 27cm. cloth, $32.50.

As water problems become more critical, sound planning and management require more and more easily accessible information on water availability and use. According to the Preface, "It is with this in mind that these important water statistics have been selected for handy reference [by] hydrologists, engineers, planners, developers, managers, and other interested persons." Frits van der Leeden, the editor of *Water Resources of the World*, is a consultant on groundwater hydrology and an associate of Geraghty & Miller, Inc., a firm specializing in water resources investigations. "He has served industry and governmental and international agencies ... and has carried out ... studies in many parts of the world." His publications include other Water Information Center titles. This specialty publisher has been responsible for a variety of useful bibliographies and compilations in the field of water and water resources, including *Water Encyclopedia, Water Atlas of the United States* (*Reference and Subscription Books Reviews* Jan. 1, 1975), and *Climates of the States* (*Reference and Subscription Books Reviews* May 1, 1975).

Water Resources of the World is arranged geographically in seven sections: Europe, Africa, Asia, Oceania, North America, South America, and World. Each of the geographical divisions begins with some general statistics relating to the area as a whole, followed by data for individual countries. Each section concludes with a list of references cited in the text. Small territories and islands are entered as, for example, French Pacific Dependencies—New Caledonia, and are easy to find in the Table of Contents or the Index. Altogether, 138 countries and territories are represented. Sections for individual countries vary in length from 1 page for Cuba, Burma, Cambodia, to 8 for Canada, 11 for the USSR, and 30 for the U.S.

Water resources are shown in tables detailing discharge of rivers, rainfall, runoff, groundwater, lakes, and reservoirs. Water use in public water supply systems, withdrawal for power production, and agricultural and industrial purposes are also illustrated. Man's efforts to harness, control, and utilize water are represented in statistics on dams and reservoirs, power plants, municipal water supply systems, sewage disposal plants, and water development projects. (An interesting table appears in the Italian section: Aqueducts of Ancient Rome, with date, name of designer, and carrying capacity.) Not all of this information appears for every country and the types and quantity of data included do not conform to a standard pattern. As a case in point, the editor notes that "On a worldwide basis, information on streamflow proved to be fairly complete, but data on the use of water resources were found to be quite inadequate...."

Dates of sources extend from the mid-1960s to 1974. For instance, all tables in the section on China are excerpted from the 1964 *Water Resources of China* published by Tojin Sha. In contrast, the U.S. sources, mostly of government origin, carry 1970–1974 imprints.

UNESCO and other United Nations publications cited throughout the volume, provide essential reportage on less-developed countries. In several cases, (e.g., Ghana, Afghanistan, Dominican Republic), they serve in place of nationally produced sources. Especially valuable are the references which appear at the end of each chapter. These include papers from national and international conferences and symposia; *Yearbooks* of the International Statistical Institute; publications of the United Nations, UNESCO, FAO, WMO, OAS, and WHO; occasional journal articles, as from the Journal of the American Water Works Association; as well as the works of government agencies.

The summaries of data for the continents as a whole, dealing with power generation, industrial water demand, extensive river systems, help the user to take a regional viewpoint in planning. The final section, World, takes this viewpoint farther by providing not only hydrological and meteorological data, but also population and economic information. It includes material on sewage disposal and water development projects and their costs, along with International, U.S., and European standards for drinking water.

Following the World section appears Explanatory Notes, which might better have been placed within the preliminary pages since they define symbols, abbreviations, and acronyms used in the text. On the verso of the page containing these notes is a handy list of measurement conversion factors. A 30-page Index includes principally geographic names with indented subheadings for subject matter arranged beneath names of countries, continents, and rivers. Subjects are main entries for material in the World section. Spot checking confirms that the Index is accurate, and contains appropriate references to statistical data and the necessary cross-references.

The volume is sturdily bound in blue cloth and the pages lie flat to allow easy use. The type is clear and both words and figures are easily read. There are a few black-and-white maps, mainly of river basins and rainfall distribution, which have generally sharp definition and effectively enhance the text.

Water Resources of the World is an extensive, well-arranged, and easily used collection of data dealing with many aspects of water. As the wide range of sources from which it is drawn are available only in larger collections, it is recommended not only for agencies dealing with water-related problems but for public and academic libraries where there is user interest in hydrological resources.

(Nov. 1, 1976, p.419)

†551.48021   Water supply—Statistics || Stream measurements—Statistics   75-20952

The way to play:
the illustrated encyclopedia of the games of the world. [By] Diagram Group. New York, Paddington Pr., Ltd. [c1975]. 320p. illus. 29cm. cloth $15.95.

The Way to Play describes and illustrates a wide range of indoor games, ancient and modern, American favorites, and those of other nations. Games are grouped under 15 major categories: race board games such as pachisi and plakato; strategic board games (checkers, chess, shogi); tile games (dominoes, Mah Jongg); general card games; target games (marbles, jackstraws, darts); solitaire card games; dice games; table games; three categories of card and table casino and private gambling games; word and picture games (charades, hangman, proverbs); children's party games; and children's card games. Accounts range from 12 to 44 pages, with card games the most heavily represented.

Each unit opens with an imaginative two-page illustration representative of the category. Chess players on a medieval Arab manuscript introduce strategic board games; a layout of lottery tickets precedes games of chance, and a detail of Peter Brueghel the Elder's painting "Children's Games," leads into children's party games. Each major game is briefly placed in time and region. Variants are identified; e.g., pachisi, which requires two-thirds of a double-page spread, shares space with the related games of ashta-kashte and ludo, which fill the remaining one-third. Board layout, equipment, rules or objective of the game, and examples of play are provided. Illustrations of boards, tables, cards, titles, and player position are well executed, and the depictions of people engaged in contest, often in national dress, add to the attractiveness of the volume.

The editors' claimed coverage of more than 2,000 considerably exceeds the 622 entries in the table of contents or estimated 1,000 entries in the Index. Again, the total of 5,000 illustrations, mentioned in promotional material, is exaggerated.

The editors do not claim exhaustive coverage of any category of games, and there are some major omissions. Scarne's *Encyclopedia of Games* (New York: Harper and Row, 1973) covers hundreds of additional card games and variations, game books, and additional game activities for children not described in *The Way to Play*. While some contemporary games such as Monopoly and Scrabble are described, most recent board games such as Perquackey, Acquire, and Probe are omitted. The strength of *The Way to Play* lies in its breadth and variety of coverage, clear instructions, and superior illustrations. The overall quality of printing and binding is high.

The Index is adequate and accurate, while the two-page "How many players?" listing is a useful feature for selecting games for specific or varying number of players.

In summary, *The Way to Play* is an attractive, but selective illustrated description of games. It does not offer exhaustive or authoritative information on complex games or games with many variations, but as an engaging and lucid general survey it can be recommended to public and school libraries.

(Sept. 1, 1976, p.51)

790 Games—Rules || Indoor games—Rules [OCLC] 75-11169

Weather.
†551.6 Weather—Juvenile literature || Meteorology—Juvenile literature [OCLC] 75-19969

See page 50

Webster's collegiate thesaurus.
[Mairé Weir Kay, editor.]. Springfield, Mass., Merriam Co., [c1976]. 1a–32a, 944p. 25cm. cloth, thumb indexed $8.95.

Announced by the publisher as "the first totally new thesaurus in over 120 years," *Webster's Collegiate Thesaurus* is concerned with the general vocabulary of the English language. Drawn primarily from *Webster's Third New International Dictionary*, with its more than 460,000 entries, and making use of the more than 12 million citations in the Merriam-Webster file of English usage, it claims to contain more than 100,000 synonyms, antonyms, idiomatic phrases, and related and contrasted words.

The editor, Mairé Weir Kay, has been assisted by seven editors whom she names in the Preface. No qualifications are stated, and it is assumed that they are all members of the Merriam-Webster staff.

According to the editor, "Each main entry consists of a head word followed by a part of speech label, a sense number when needed, a meaning core (basic definition) with a brief verbal illustration, and a list of synonyms. Lists of related words, idiomatic equivalents, contrasted words, and antonyms follow the synonym list if they are called for." Secondary entries follow much the same pattern except that the meaning core and illustration are replaced by a synonym in small capitals. Under this synonym in its alphabetical place is a meaning core and illustration. A sample indicates that there appear to be about five times as many secondary as main entries. Often secondary entries for some sense meanings are subsumed under a main entry, as for *easy,* where six of its nine senses are indicated by synonyms in small capitals.

The introductory section on the evolution of the thesaurus defines synonym as it is used in the volume. "For purposes of *Webster's Collegiate Thesaurus* a word is construed as a synonym if and only if it or one of its senses shares with another word or sense of a word one or more elementary meanings." These elementary meanings are those stated in the meaning cores given for main entries. A meaning core may be supplemented by a usage note or in a few cases may be replaced by a usage note, as in some interjections, (e.g., *goodbye*). Two verbal illustrations may appear after a meaning core that is broad enough to subsume alternatives, but these have been chosen with discretion and are used sparingly.

Each synonym in a list following a main entry has a boldfaced entry at its own alphabetical place, but related words, contrasted words, or idiomatic equivalents do not, unless the related or contrasted words are included as synonyms in other lists. If a main entry synonym list contains more than ten terms, only nine synonyms have been selected for the secondary entry. Thus it is advisable to check the main entry, not only for the meaning core but for synonyms not found under the secondary entry.

Variant spellings are given in parentheses, which are also used to enclose a particle or particles usually associated with the base word, to indicate usage alternatives in idiomatic expressions, to enclose plural suffixes of words sometimes used in the plural, and to enclose material indicating a typical or, occasionally, a sole object of reference.

Most of the synonym lists are made up of single words, since word equivalents (phrases that function as if they were single words) have been included only when they are so firmly fixed in usage as to be accorded part-of-speech labels in major modern dictionaries. Glosses (phrases that restate the meaning) have been eschewed entirely, and selected idiomatic equivalents are listed separately following the pertinent synonym lists. Fewer word equivalents than idiomatic equivalents appear in the text.

Since the editors have followed such a rigorous policy in identification of synonyms and antonyms, they have supplied separate lists of related words and contrasted words, as noted. These they define as "words which do not quite qualify as synonyms or antonyms under a strict definition of these terms but which are so closely related to or so clearly contrastable with the members of the synonym group that the user of the book has a right to have them brought to his attention under appropriate headings." For example, *deluxe* is given the synonyms *Capuan, luscious, lush, luxuriant, opulent, palatial, plush, sumptuous,* and *upholstered,* with related words being *choice, dainty, delicate, elegant, exquisite, rare,* and *recherché,* and with contrasted words being *coarse, common, ordinary,* and *inelegant.*

A semicolon is sometimes used in the lists of related and contrasted words to separate subgroups of words which differ in their relation to the headword. It is also used to separate antonyms that belong to different classes of opposites. These and other practices intended to produce a high degree of discrimination are clarified in the Introduction following an explanatory chart. Careful reading of this commentary is essential to effective use of the thesaurus.

Double bars prefixing some terms "warn the user that the employment of such a term may involve a problem of diction too complex for presentation in a thesaurus, or a restriction in usage." The user is instructed to consult a dictionary in such cases. Examples are *biggie,* found under *luminary,* and *pip,* found under *dilly.* Asterisks, more sparingly used, indicate vulgar words; for example, *puke* (vomit).

As already noted, this thesaurus is concerned with the general vocabulary, and obsolete, archaic, or extremely rare terms and specialized or technical jargon have been omitted. However, slang has been freely included and listed alphabetically in synonym lists, though not labelled as slang. Some are shown with an asterisk to indicate that they are in vulgar usage. Some of the newer words found in *Webster's 6,000 Words* (Springfield: Webster, 1977) are not in the thesaurus, (e.g., *ego trip, flower children, acid head, groupies, flip out, freak out, sexism,* and *ripoff*). But some words not found among the 155,000 entries in *American Heritage Dictionary* do appear as main or secondary entries, among them *astucious, argute, cathedratic, brocard, amaroidal, atramentous, banausic, gasconade, preux, polly-fox, nipcheese, petit-maître, ipseity, spreaghery, diuturnal,* and *poetling,* to name a few. These are evidently included in an effort to supply words as exactly synonymous as possible, as well as to increase the vocabulary of the user.

The book is stoutly bound in linen print, thumb indexed and printed in small but legible type; its format is suitable for heavy use.

Webster's Collegiate Thesaurus invites comparison with the recently published *Family Word Finder: A New Thesaurus of Synonyms and Antonyms in Dictionary Form.* (Pleasantville, N.Y.: Reader's Digest Association; dist. New York: Norton, 1975. 896p.) Webster's vocabulary contains a number of headwords, chiefly secondary entries, not found in *Family Word Finder,* which gives some entries not found in *Webster's,* though fewer. *Family Word Finder* does not distinguish between synonyms and related words, including among its synonyms some words regarded as related in *Webster's.* Its 10,000 alphabetically arranged main entries each give part or parts of speech, an illustrative sentence or sentences if there are several different shades of meaning or use, a list of synonyms, and a shorter list of antonyms. These are arranged in decreasing order of use insofar as possible, with technical terms, informal, and slang terms given last. Slang is labelled as such. Some of the main entries are accompanied by word origins simply explained, usage notes, notes on spelling and pronunciation of words frequently misspelled or mispronounced, and word histories for related words. A sampling of the vocabularies in the two indicates that *Webster's* includes more unusual words, such as those noted earlier. *Webster's* includes more slang, though it is not so labelled. It is difficult to generalize about the number of senses of a word found in each since, in some cases, *Webster's* gives more senses and in others the *Family Word Finder* has more. In format, *Webster's* lists each part of speech under a bold heading, (e.g., *damned* (adj.) and *damned* (adv.), while *Family Word Finder* lists all parts of speech under one bold heading, also using larger type throughout. Both are stoutly bound: *Webster's* in linen, is printed in small but legible type, and thumb indexed; the other is not thumb indexed.

Though both works have many synonyms in common, there are many headwords in which their choice of synonyms varies. An example which demonstrates *Webster's* use of the more unusual word is *cadence,* with *rhythmus* as a synonym. For *caprice, Webster's* includes *whigmaleerie,* but not *notion* or *quirk,* found in *Family Word Finder,* which gives *garrulity* as a synonym for *circumlocution,* while *Webster's* gives *circumambages, circumbendibus,* and *pleonasm.* All in all, the *Family Word Finder* will probably be easier for the beginner to use, though *Webster's* has a larger vocabulary and discriminates between synonyms and related words. It also includes meaning cores for every main entry.

In summary, the meaning cores and verbal illustrations found at each main entry, the use of double bars when necessary to warn the user to consult a dictionary, the entry of each synonym in its alphabetical place, and the separation of its carefully defined synonyms from related and contrasted words are features which recommend *Webster's Collegiate Thesaurus* for home and library purchase. *(July 1, 1977, p.1671)*

423'.1   English language—Synonyms and antonyms   [CIP]   75-45167

Webster's new students dictionary.

[H. Bosley Woolf, editorial director]. Springfield, Mass., G. & C. Merriam Co., [c1974]. 10a, 1050p. 24cm. illus. tables. pyroxylin on paperboard, without thumb index $6.95. to schools and libraries, text ed. sold by American Book Co., $6.84.

Webster's New Students Dictionary was created as part of a new Merriam-Webster school dictionary series in 1938. The first dictionary entitled *Webster's Students Dictionary for Upper School Levels* was recommended "as a highly satisfactory dictionary for school use from the fifth grade through high school" in *Subscription Books Bulletin,* April 1938. The dictionary was completely redone in 1964 and was retitled *Webster's New Students Dictionary.* Updated revisions were published in 1969 and 1974. All editions except the latest were published solely as textbook editions by American Book Company. The newest revision is the first to be available both in a trade edition from Merriam-Webster and a text version from American Book. *Webster's New Students Dictionary* belongs to a family of dictionaries which includes *Webster's Third New International Dictionary, Webster's New Collegiate Dictionary,* and other dictionaries for schools and families. The publisher states that *Webster's New Students* is "edited for use either as the third dictionary in a three-dictionary progression, being preceded by *Webster's New Elementary Dictionary* and *Webster's Intermediate Dictionary,* or as the second of a two-dictionary progression, being preceded by *Webster's Intermediate Dictionary.*"

G. & C. Merriam Company is a publisher known and respected in the field of dictionaries. In correspondence with the Reference and Subscription Books Review Committee the publisher identifies H. Bosley Woolf as editorial director. The rest of the editorial staff is not identified. Woolf is also editor in chief of the *New Collegiate Dictionary, Webster's Intermediate, Webster's New Ideal Dictionary,* and *Webster's Concise Family Dictionary.*

The publisher informs the Committee that there are 81,000 vocabulary entries. The Committee verifies this is true if all forms of words are included. There are about 50,000 main entries arranged alphabetically letter by letter. This figure of 81,000 may be compared to the 450,000 entries in the unabridged dictionary, the 150,000 in the collegiate, the 57,000 in the 1938 student's dictionary, and to the substantially fewer entries of the intermediate and elementary dictionaries. The entries emphasize standard language but include some slang, dialect, obsolete forms, foreign words, and technical terms; they do not include taboo words or encyclopedic information.

The rationale for the dictionary's selection of entries is stated in the Preface: "The vocabulary entries in *Webster's New Students Dictionary* have been selected chiefly on the basis of their occurrence in textbooks and supplementary reading in all subjects of the school curriculum. The definers have had before them this first hand evidence as well as the millions of examples of usage that underlie *Webster's Third New International Dictionary*. This method of editing ensures the coverage of today's school vocabulary, especially in mathematics, science, and social studies, and at the same time makes certain that the current literary and general vocabulary is not neglected.''

A random sample based on examination of secondary school texts in chemistry, mathematics, and English demonstrated that their vocabulary is, on the whole, to be found in the student's dictionary. There are entries for such words as: *insoluble, precipitate, graph, domain, sagacious,* and *tinctured,* but not for gerbil, scumble, gavial, microcircuit, and spoiler.

The explanatory chart and notes, particularly important to the uninitiated dictionary user, are clearly written and well illustrated, but the Committee wishes that such traditional headings as "Etymology" and "Inflected Forms" had been simplified in order to make them more intelligible to younger students. There is some attempt to identify these linguistic terms in the body of each section, but a more direct approach would have been warranted. Basically, however, the dictionary's practices regarding spelling, capitalization, and pronunciation are clearly indicated.

The dictionary follows standards of American orthography, listing acceptable forms and joining alternative spellings with *also* to indicate equal variants and *or* to indicate secondary variants. An example of this practice is the entry for *through*, "through *also* thru" (and *thru* is an entry that refers the reader to *through*) or the entry for *index* which designates plurality as "indexes *or* indices." Capitalization as well as parts of speech and irregular inflections are indicated. Pronunciation is indicated by phonetics which rely to some extent on diacritical marks. The phonetic alphabet is easy to use and is printed at the bottom of every page as well as in a table at the front of the book. Acceptable variations are noted without indicating preference. American pronunciation, not British, appears to be the standard; for *lieutenant,* | lü-'ten-ent | is included but not | lef-'ten-ent | ; and | 'vīt-e-men | is but not | 'vit-ə-men |.

Etymologies, sometimes omitted in dictionaries on the student level, are included as are definitions which are given historical sequence. They constitute an extremely useful source of information for secondary school students. The argument that historical arrangement is unnecessary and confuses the high school student is specious. A few simple instructions clear up any confusion over the order of definitions, and the historical order often reveals significant patterns of linguistic development that may prove illuminating.

No quotations are used to illustrate definitions, and examples of word employment in typical phrases are less common than in other dictionaries directed to secondary school students. However, word groups set off in angle brackets are often used to clarify distinctions in meaning. The definitions for *life* followed by appended examples: <adult life>, <stirring of life>, <life of the party>, <life tenure>, <life force>, <sex life>, <eyes full of life>, <life of an insurance policy>, and <forest life>.

Synonyms are included where useful (in capitals for cross-reference), and antonyms are not included. Synonym paragraphs are used to solve usage problems as in the case of *imply/infer* or *affect/effect,* and they are used to reveal nuances in meaning e.g., of *wit* and *ghastly*.

A dictionary's visual black-and-white line illustrations can be useful to any student and particularly the young student. However, their presence in this dictionary sometimes seems more capricious than functional. There are illustrations for *frog, goose, salmon, sea horse, lizard*—all rather well known, but none for gecko, Gila monster, gopher, gorgon, hedgehog, hydra, hyena, peccary, llama, salamander, or sea anemone. There are illustrations for simple geometric shapes, e.g., *triangle, rectangle, square, pentagon,* but no illustration for icosahedron. *Scythe, hypodermic syringe,* and *field glasses* are shown, but not fibula, fez, and trestle.

In keeping with their understanding of the dictionary as a word book, the publishers provide little supplementary material. However, sections on abbreviations and signs and symbols are included. Excluded are personal names and place-names. For example, there is no entry for Abraham Lincoln, but there is one for *Lincoln's Birthday,* none for Shakespeare, but one for *Shakespearian,* none for Russia, but one for *Russian*. Some of the supplementary material in the 1964 edition such as the lengthy section "Using Your Dictionary," "The History of Your Dictionary," and "Proper Names" was either dropped or drastically modified.

This dictionary is easy to use, clear, and readable. The pyroxylin-impregnated paper over paperboard binding seems adequate, and the book lies flat when opened, but it has narrow margins. The type is clear. Page makeup is good; the headings are fine, and the illustrations are acceptable.

Webster's New Students Dictionary is a fine, responsibly produced tool and a major revision of its predecessor. Its excellent format, numerous etymologies and vocabulary entries, and employment of usage examples are of great value. It is recommended for high school libraries and students.

(Sept. 15, 1976, p.200)

423   English language—Dictionaries   [OCLC]   74-186330

Webster's sports dictionary.
[Robert D. Copeland, editor]. Springfield, Mass., G. & C. Merriam Co., 1976. 503p. illus. diagrs. 25cm. paper composition non-woven material, $8.95.

In combination, the names Merriam and Webster have become synonymous in this country with the word dictionary. *Webster's Third New International, Webster's New Collegiate, Webster's Biographical,* and *Webster's New Geographical* dictionaries, all published by G. & C. Merriam, are widely used works, and they are highly respected by users in both homes and libraries. *Webster's Sports Dictionary,* claiming to be "the only book of its kind in print," seeks to join other Merriam-Webster dictionaries as a leading title in its field.

According to the Preface, "Webster's Sports Dictionary, like all other Merriam-Webster dictionaries, is based on actual usage as recorded in a mass of examples from numerous printed sources. This dictionary defines terms normally used by participants in various sports and by broadcasters and sportswriters as well as terms used in the playing rules of sports.... The book is intended to serve as a handbook for the casual fan.... For the knowledgeable fan, the book can also serve as a handy reference...."

Robert D. Copeland, the editor, is also associate editor of *Webster's New Collegiate Dictionary*. He and his staff have identified over 7,000 terms from some 100 different sports. The terms come from such team sports as baseball, basketball, football, soccer, and hockey as well as such individual contests as golf and bowling. In addition to competitive sports, terms from such recreational activities as hunting, fishing, scuba diving, and mountain climbing have been included. Trademarks such as Frisbee and Nomex are also defined. Not included are terms from hobby activities, card and board games, and traditional children's games. The expressions included are those "in widespread current use. Only a few terms that are no longer commonly used have been kept for their historical interest." The vocabulary is not limited to American sports; it includes terms from other English-speaking nations, especially words and idioms used in Australia, Great Britain, and Canada. Compound words and phrases appear only when their meaning differs from that of the sum of their component words. For example, 22 such combinations with the word *power* are defined. These include *power alley, power block, power form, power head, power serve, power 20,* and *power I*.

The dictionary is arranged alphabetically (letter by letter). Definitions are clearly written. Various parts of speech spelled alike but unalike in meaning are marked by arabic numerals. The fuller definitions of these homographs are always shown first. Subject labels are provided when usage restricts terms or senses of terms to particular sports. The senses are normally arranged alphabetically by subject label. Unlabeled senses applicable to several sports are routinely listed before labeled senses, and simple cross-references usually follow labeled senses. "Cross-references appear in small capitals and serve three principal functions. The 'see' references direct the reader to a more common variant where the definition is given or to another entry where he will find additional information or a fuller treatment; 'see also' references are used for parallel terms or related terms. The 'compare' references direct the reader to contrasting terms." No pronunciations, syllabication, or hyphenations are indicated.

Verbal illustrations have been used throughout the book to show the entry word in typical context. Enclosed in angle brackets, they have been written specifically for the dictionary or are quotations from major sports sources or personalities. In the examples which follow in this paragraph, the entry words in parentheses have been attributed to the sources which immediately precede them. Commonly cited sports media include the *NCAA News* (*depth*), *North American Soccer News* (*fake*), *Auto Racing* (*field*), *Fishing World* (*fish*), *Sports Record Weekly* (*fistic*), *Motor Trend* (*hot dog*), and *Sports Illustrated* (*kayo*). Among personalities quoted are Whitey Ford (*fat*), Lee Trevino (*gimme*), Eddie Arcaro (*jock*), and O. J. Simpson (*juke*). *Playboy* (*gridiron*), *New Yorker* (*holeable*), *Boy's Life* (*intercept*), and major newspapers are nonsport publications which have contributed examples of current vernacular. In a sample of 228 entries, 8 percent had verbal illustrations. However, only 3.5 percent of the total sample had quotations as verbal illustrations.

The dictionary contains over 200 original drawings and diagrams depicting playing areas, techniques, typical athletic stances, team formations, and game equipment. The drawings, produced by J. A. Collier of the Merriam-Webster staff and Harvey Kidder and Al Fiorentino of Kirchoff/Wohlberg, Inc., are well executed and add to the user's understanding of terms. A large majority (85 percent) of the illustrations are on the same pages as the term they accompany; 10 percent are on facing pages, and 5 percent are on the verso of the page containing the appropriate definition. The 5 percent not immediately contiguous to the text could easily be overlooked by the user since there are no references from definitions to illustrations. The double-page illustration of knots (pages 246–247) is referred to from the definition of each know illustrated with the comment "see illustration at KNOT," but the illustration is neither a *knot*, nor referred to from the general definition of *knot*. This could mislead the reader, especially since the double-page illustration is not given a general heading.

In some cases, cross-references could be improved. For example, *punching bag* is defined as a boxing term meaning "a speed bag or a heavy bag, used to develop strength or coordination in punching." Both *speed bag* and *heavy bag* are defined and illustrated, but there is no reference from the general term *punching bag* to these more specific entries. *Putter* is defined on page 337 and illustrated on page 84 along with other clubs used in golf, but there is no reference to the illustration. Yet there is reference to *club* from the *iron* and *wood* entries. The *wedge* is defined on page 477 with no reference to its illustration on page 84. Fortunately these lapses and inconsistencies are very uncommon in this dictionary. Most cross-references are correct, complete, and helpful. The "compare" references [e.g., *bind* (fencing term)—compare CROISE, ENVELOPMENT; *yawl*—compare KETCH, SCHOONER] are extremely helpful in enlarging the user's comprehension of terms.

There is a three-part appendix: Abbreviations, Referee Signals, and Scorekeeping. Each of some 400 abbreviations of terms, athletic conferences, leagues, and other organizations has been normalized to the one form most likely to be encountered in journalistic writing or sports broadcasting; referee signals are given for football, basketball, and ice hockey; scorekeeping directions and illustrations are provided for baseball and bowling only. There are no references from the text to the appendix.

The Preface states that "As a dictionary, this book gives definitions of terms but does not attempt to provide historical information or statistics, which is more properly the job of an encyclopedia." A few extended entries (e.g., *football, ice hockey, lawn bowling, pari-mutuel betting*), have, however, been included to provide a general understanding of the sports and activities from which the dictionary's vocabulary is drawn.

A comparison was made between entries in *Webster's Third New International Dictionary* and the work under review. Seventy percent of a sample of sports vocabulary was represented in both dictionaries, and direct or easily derivable definitions for all of these words were found in the *New Third International*. However, 30 percent of the words were found exclusively in *Webster's Sports Dictionary*, and retrieval of their specific sports usages was tedious and time consuming. In no case were terms defined in the same wording, and *Webster's Sports Dictionary* generally provided more precise definitions.

Webster's Sports Dictionary is the only reference of its kind in print. Although there are many encyclopedias in the sports field, there is no other work which provides definitions for terms drawn from many sports. *Webster's Sports Dictionary* is recommended for purchase for home, school, public, and academic library use. *(Nov. 1, 1976, p.420)*

796.'03 Sports—Dictionaries [CIP] 75-42076

Who was when?:

a dictionary of contemporaries. [By] Miriam Allen de Ford and Joan S. Jackson. 3d ed. New York, Wilson, 1976. [184p.] 27cm. by 36cm. cloth $30 (U.S. and Canada); $35 (other countries).

The first edition of *Who Was When* covered celebrated individuals who died prior to 1939; the second edition updated the coverage through 1949. The third edition's claimed coverage of 10,000 famous persons from 500 B.C. through 1974 is consistent with the Committee's estimated figure. Approximately half the persons included were born or died since 1800, and more than 2,300 of them were alive during the 20th century. Pythagoras, Pericles, Buddha, and Euripides are among the early entries; Wayne Morse, Georgi Zhukov, Ed Sullivan, and Erich Kästner are among recent representatives.

The late Miriam Allen de Ford, associated with the dictionary since its inception, was a prolific writer. She has at least a dozen books to her credit, including *Love Children: A Book of Illustrious Illegitimates* and *The Theme is Murder*. She also wrote short stories, poems, and articles and was the recipient of poetry prizes plus several Mystery Writers of America awards. For many years Miriam de Ford was associated with the H. W. Wilson Company as a frequent contributor to Wilson biographical reference sources. No information was found regarding coauthor Joan Jackson.

The main section of *Who Was When* is a horizontal presentation of chronological tables with vertical subdivisions of each year according to major broad fields of endeavor. Government and Law, Military and Naval Affairs, Industry, Commerce, Economics, Finance, Invention, Labor, Travel and Exploration, Philosophy and Religion, Science and Medicine, Education and History, Literature, Painting and Sculpture, Music, and a Miscellaneous category are used through 1845. Visual Arts replaces Painting and Sculpture in 1846. In 1849, Aviation is added to the Military and Naval category; Technology is added to Science and Medicine, and Literature becomes Literature and Journalism and is expanded to two columns. At the same time, Travel and

Exploration was dropped, with notable persons in this category appearing thereafter in the Miscellaneous column.

From 500 B.C. until c. A.D. 1200, rulers, philosophers, and religious leaders predominate with scattered concentrations of literary figures. For the first 1,700 years there are 15 military figures, 3 musicians, 13 painters and sculptors, 7 travelers or explorers, and the Roman gladiatorial leader, Spartacus, who appears in the Industry, Commerce, Economics, Finance, Invention and Labor column. These categories plus the miscellaneous section have a total of approximately 50 persons listed up to A.D. 1200.

After A.D. 1200, coverage of both Painting and Sculpture and Travel and Exploration are increased; music entries show a sharp increase after 1500; and by mid-1700 there are entries for each year under most categories. While these emphases in coverage convey a reasonably accurate picture of the social, economic, cultural, scientific, and political emphases of the past, the visual analogy is preserved at the expense of efficient space utilization.

Each entry consists of the name of the famous person followed by an abbreviation indicating birth, death, or flourished dates, or when acceded, deposed, or abdicated.

Entries are accurately placed in the main entry section except for a few erratic double entries, such as Heloise (b. circa 1098, d. 1164) listed as being born in 1079 and 1101; Hilliel, who flourished during the last half of the first century B.C. until the first quarter of the first century A.D. with birth entries for the year 70 and again for 30 A.D.; and a double entry in 1961 for Patrice Lumm and Patrice Lumumba. A comparison of main entries with the alphabetical index entries disclosed no blind reference either from main section to Index or from Index to main entry section. Names in the main entry section are sometimes too abbreviated. Tyrone Power's death is given as 1931, an obvious error if attributed to the younger Power. A check in the Index shows both Tyrone Power, Sr., who died in 1931 and Tyrone Power, Jr., who lived until 1958.

The full name listing in the alphabetical Index section is a valuable and necessary feature. Not only are full names given, but persons with identical names are differentiated by country, occupation, title, or some other descriptive word or phrase. Approximately 500 *see* references from or to pseudonyms, variant names, or foreign forms of spelling are provided. For each Index entry, birth and death dates are provided when known, a date when a person flourished is given when only one date is known, and for monarchs the reigning dates are provided. Thus the dates for Albert, Prince Consort of Victoria, England, are 1819-61, his birth and death dates since he was not the ruler; Victoria (England) is listed as reigning from 1837-1901. This questionable method of entering rulers evidently creates problems for the compilers as well as the user. Index dates for Edward VIII of England are given as 1936-72, while the main section shows him as abdicating in 1936. According to the authors' rules, only 1936 should have been given. Farouk I of Egypt abdicated in 1952, but the book gives no indication of his death date.

Entries all appear to have been chosen selectively. Not all rulers or popes are included, although European rulers and nobility are heavily represented under Government and Law. According to the Preface, unsuccessful revolutionists appear in the column headed Industry, Commerce, etc. While this forewarns readers where they will find Spartacus, it provides no rationale for this peculiar categorization. Again the Preface states that Government and Law lists leaders who actually governed. Listed under this heading we find Sam Adams, Tom Paine, Ben Franklin, Boss Tweed, and many others involved in government, but who were not rulers. Miscellaneous has a varied coverage: persons from the stage and cinema, criminals, sports figures, mistresses, and charlatans are among those included.

Who Was When has an effective page layout with boldface headings and a chronological running head in the upper corner of each page. Contrasting typefaces are used to differentiate between birth and death entries. The volume lies flat when open, and the inner margins are sufficiently wide to permit rebinding. While only 27 centimeters high, the dictionary's 30 centimeter width will extend beyond the edge of standard-size shelving.

Although the third edition of *Who Was When* is a well-selected, chronologically arranged tableau of 10,000 famous deceased persons who are likely to be represented in the typical school curriculum, its reference value is very limited. The student who consults it to determine who might have influenced or interacted with whom may be frustrated. For example, Charles Lindbergh was born in 1902 and died in 1974. *Who Was When* lists well over 2,000 persons who were born and/or died since 1902 and thousands of Lindbergh's contemporaries are still alive today. Also, the policy of listing only deceased persons limits the potential value. Both *Timetables of History* by Bernard Grun (New York: Simon & Schuster, 1975) and *Chronology of World History* by G. S. P. Freeman-Grenville (London: Rex Collins, 1975) offer better opportunities for checking connections between contemporaneous figures than *Who Was When*. However, *Who Was When* is valuable for time line or trend studies relating to broad subject areas. Recommended for high school libraries which should be aware of its limitations.

(July 15, 1977, p.1751)

902'.02   Biography || Chronology, Historical—Tables.   [CIP]   76-2404

Who was who in American history—arts and letters.
Chicago, Marquis Who's Who, Inc. [1975]. 604p. 26cm. cloth, $47.50.

Who Was Who in American History—Arts and Letters is a compilation of material from the five volumes of *Who Was Who in America,* covering the years 1897–1973 and the historical volume for 1607–1896. Included are persons who could be classed as belonging in the professions of the arts or letters—actors, dancers, musicians, artists, sculptors, architects, and authors of all kinds. The result is a roster of about 10,000 biographies of deceased Americans and foreigners who became celebrities in the U.S. Among the latter are Edgar Dégas, Maurice Maeterlinck, Fernandel, Winston Churchill, Sergei Rachmaninoff, Otto Klemperer, and Dag Hammarskjöld. There is an entry for Charles de Saint Memin, born in 1770, who painted the last portrait of George Washington from life. All the biographies have been alphabetized and reprinted exactly as they appeared in the six volumes cited above. In the sample examined by the Committee, approximately 44 percent were authors, writers, critics, journalists, news correspondents, editors, or librettists with the next highest representation (23 percent) being of artists, sculptors, painters, engravers, and other individuals working in the fine and applied arts. Actors, dramatists, playwrights, and performing musicians comprised about 21 percent; composers accounted for 4 percent. The remaining 8 percent included a mixture of more unusual occupations; magician, impresario, monologist, circus executive, goldsmith, and so on. Omitted for unexplained reasons are Alexis de Tocqueville, whose writings are conceded to be classics in the study of American democracy, and William Dunlap (1766–1839), who was described in the Historical Volume as a "theatre mgr., painter, author." Robert Fulton, a notable inventor but not highly regarded as a man of letters, is included. Because of these inconsistencies, the absence of a precise statement of criteria for entrants' eligibility is regrettable.

The book under review is a companion volume to *Who Was Who in American History—The Military* which was released at about the same time, and which has been constructed in the same manner. The Committee will review the military volume shortly.

Even if one is familiar with the volumes of *Who Was Who in*

America, from which these biographies have been excerpted, it is disconcerting to find home addresses cited for persons born as early as the latter part of the eighteenth century. For example, the biographical résumé of De Scott Evans, born in 1847, concludes with the observation that he now "divides his time between New York and Paris, France." Because such information has been transferred without change from the previous separate cumulations, a clearer and more accurate explanation is required than the enigmatic reference to double daggers which reads "Non-current sketches of WHO'S WHO IN AMERICA biographees who were born 95 or more years ago (See Preface for explanation)." There are no double daggers in the volume under review, and no explanation appears in the Preface. Apparently this passage which heads the Table of Abbreviations was lifted from the fifth volume of *Who Was Who in America* without awareness of its irrelevance in its new context.

Entries taken from the recent volume V of *Who Was Who in America* (1969–1973) appear to have been reproduced photographically from that volume. Entries taken from prior volumes have been reset in matching type. In general, the reproduction of original entries has been effectively accomplished. However, one entry, that for Max Reinhardt, has had the last seven lines of the original biography accidentally deleted so that it breaks off in the middle of a sentence. Such incidents are rare and the entire work is easy to use. The three columns per page are set in small but legible type. There are no geographical or topical indexes and, as is the case with other Marquis biography volumes, there are no illustrations.

The work will be most useful in large libraries, both academic and public, that have departmentalized reference services or separate humanities, fine arts, and music divisions because this compact, special biographical cumulation can serve in place of the original six-volume *Who Was Who in America* series. For any library with a heavy demand for biographies in the arts and humanities, *Who Was Who in American History—Arts and Letters* is recommended.   *(Nov. 1, 1976, p.422)*

920.073   U.S.—Biography—Dictionaries   [OCLC]   75-29617

Who's who among black Americans.
1st ed. 1975–1976, v.1. Editor, William C. Matney. Northbrook, Illinois, Who's Who Among Black Americans, Inc., 1976. xxiii 772p. 29cm. sturdite, $45; to schools and libraries, $40.

For a number of years, there has been a need for a comprehensive biographical directory of contemporary prominent black Americans. In an article in the seventh edition of *Who's Who in Colored America* (1950), Jean Blackwell (later Hutson), Curator of the New York Public Library's Schomburg Collection described the biographical directories of Afro-Americans published to that date. Among recent bibliographies *Black Bibliographical Sources: An Annotated Bibliography* (Yale University Library, 1970), *The Negro in the United States: A Selected Bibliography* (Library of Congress, 1970), and the revised edition of the *Harvard Guide to American History* (1974) list no current general biographical directory of black Americans. Volume 1 of the *Ebony Success Library: 1,000 Successful Blacks* (1973) begins to fill the gap but the figure of 1,000 persons is an immediate indication of its limitation. Other books are restricted to occupation, for example, including only ministers or business or political leaders. When one turns to the standard *Who's Who in America* and related directories, one finds the representation of black Americans restricted because of the entry requirement of general high prominence. What has been needed is a directory of persons of achievement today who may or may not be in the public eye but are nevertheless important in their career field or geographical area.

In an attempt to fill this reference need, *Who's Who Among Black Americans* has now been published. The editor, William C. Matney, is a national news correspondent for ABC television and radio. The associate publisher, Ann Wolk Krouse, was vice president of the company which publishes *Who's Who Among High School Students.* A page headed Acknowledgements begins with an introductory paragraph: "Contributing Editors: The following individuals served on an honorary basis and frequently assisted in the development of this publication by reviewing policies, selections and overall objectives." The list of 20 persons that follows includes several nationally known individuals, such as Edward Brooke, Richard G. Hatcher, Jesse L. Jackson, and Vernon E. Jordan.

In a one-page Preface, Matney states that "the inaugural edition . . . comprises the largest total of biographical entries of high achieving Blacks ever published in one volume—approximately 10,000." The directory ". . . reflects the dynamic growth of Black achievement and involvement in all areas of American life over the past several decades." Matney also acknowledges omissions because some institutional and corporate sources declined to provide identification by race or raised the question of invasion of privacy (particularly in federal agencies). He additionally notes that ". . . a few outstanding Black Americans in the nonpublic sector . . . preferred noninclusion . . . to inclusion by race."

"The selection of individuals was based on one characteristic: reference value. Individuals became eligible for listing by virtue of positions achieved through election or appointment to office and by distinguished achievement in meritorious careers." Data were collected mainly by the biographees furnishing biographical data forms. "When individuals failed to furnish their own data, staff compiled the information through independent research."

Matney also states in the Preface that it was ". . . demonstrated merit alone that determined inclusion." Wealth, social position, or an individual's desire to be listed were not sufficient reasons to be included. "In fact, many of the biographees in this edition are engaged in fields marked far more by service than by monetary reward." Three paragraphs of Standards and Criteria note that " . . . primary consideration was given to the extent of an individual's reference interest." The position of responsibility held and the level of significant achievement attained in a career of meritorious activity were the focus for inclusion. "An individual must have accomplished some conspicuous achievement—something that distinguishes him from the vast majority of his contemporaries." It is not clear why some persons are included when they are not of special prominence. For example, in politics, business, medicine, dentistry, and the judiciary, several leaders are not included but less prominent persons are in the book.

A number of leading black professional, social, and political organizations offered special cooperation in compiling the work. Twenty individuals are singled out for special thanks, but their affiliations are not included, and the reason for their listing is not given. Among them are Simeon Booker, journalist, and Stanley E. Scott, former presidential assistant.

The front matter of the directory includes a four-and-one-half-page Glossary of Abbreviations used in the entries. The last page of the introductory material, Sample Biography Keyed to Data, uses the biography of Matney to explain the arrangement of information within each entry. The alphabetical arrangement of the volume is also described.

The directory proper consists of 702 pages of double-column, alphabetically arranged biographical entries. The order in which the information appears is usually: name; occupation; place and date of birth (if given); education; marital status (spouse's name); children (ages); present position/employer; previous positions/employers; memberships, awards, special achievements and military service; and address. Many entries do not include all of this information.

The Committee compared sample entries in *Who's Who*

Among Black Americans with comparable material in *Who's Who in America* (38th ed. 1974–1975), *Who's Who of American Women* (9th ed. 1975–1976), and *Who's Who in American Politics* (5th ed. 1975–1976). Some of the biographees are covered more fully in the general *Who's Whos* than in the work under review. For example, Marian Anderson has more complete information in *Who's Who of American Women* and *Who's Who in America* than in *Who's Who Among Black Americans*. *Who's Who in America* notes how she began her career, and *Who's Who of American Women* indicates that she was one of the first persons named to the National Arts Hall of Fame, that her book, *My Lord, What A Morning*, is an autobiography published in 1956, and that she retired in 1965. *Who's Who Among Black Americans* notes that she is the author of *My Lord* but omits publication data. *Who's Who Among Black Americans* and *Who's Who in America* state she received 23 honorary degrees as compared with 35 in *Who's Who of American Women*.

The late Arna Bontemps is another biographee who receives fuller coverage in *Who's Who in America*. This source provides fuller information on his career than *Who's Who Among Black Americans,* including the years he was at various universities, and lists more of his honors, memberships, and books. However, *Who's Who Among Black Americans* does include a 1931 title, *God Sends Sunday,* which is not in the other list. It is unfortunate that *Who's Who Among Black Americans,* published and publicized as the "1975–1976 edition," did not update its biographical data to include Bontemps' death in June 1973.

On the whole, in the sample entries, the standard directories provide more career information than *Who's Who Among Black Americans*. The remaining entries contain essentially the same information in *Who's Who Among Black Americans* and the other directories. The Committee confirmed considerable unevenness in the currency of biographical data. Honors awarded to Mildred Bailey and Bennetta Washington in 1975 are noted, but the establishment of new home run and stolen base records by Hank Aaron and Lou Brock and Frank Robinson's appointment as first black manager in major league baseball, all occurring in 1974, are omitted. The election of George L. Brown as Colorado's Lieutenant Governor in 1974 is also missed. Titles and dates of publication of James Baldwin's books are listed, but no works of Imamu Amiri Baraka (LeRoi Jones) are mentioned. The amount of information provided for Roy Wilkins is slim compared to that given for less prominent persons. A major strength of the directory is that a wide range of persons is included, such as Huey Newton, Wallace Muhammad, Gladys Knight, Elizabeth Koontz, Margaret Bush Wilson, Roy Innis, and Geoffrey Holder.

At the end of the biographies are a 34-page Cross Index by Geographical Location and a 35-page Cross Index by Career Cluster Groups which offer access routes not usually found in biographical directories. The geographical Index is arranged by state with a further breakdown by city. Persons are listed alphabetically under the city where they reside. Americans living outside the U.S. are listed under the countries where they reside. The career Index is divided into Arts (creative, performing, technical); Behavioral and Medical Sciences (applied, e.g., M.D.s, anthropologists); Business (executives, managers, owners); Educators (administrators, teachers); Government (elected and appointed officials, military); Law (attorneys, judges, law enforcement); Media (broadcast and print journalists, editors, publishers); Organizations (associations, fraternal, unions); and Religion (clergy, theologians).

The geographic Index is generally accurate although the address for Marian Anderson in her entry is c/o Hurok Attractions, New York, N.Y., while the Index lists her under Danbury, Connecticut, where she lives. A second Index error occurs in the entry for Rear Admiral Samuel E. Gravely, Jr., where his office is listed as COMCRUDESGRU Two FPO NY. There is no entry for him in the Index under California or New York (traditional military mailing address states), District of Columbia, or foreign countries.

Another problem in the geographic Index arises in several instances of misspelled place-names. For example, following a large section of persons under *Los Angeles* are individuals listed under Los Angeles Angeles, Los Angelos, Los Angesles, and *Los Angles*. There are also entries in New Jersey under E Orange and East Orange, S Orange and South Orange, and W Orange and West Orange.

Both Indexes and the directory in general suffer from a lack of cross-references. For example, the user has to look under *Cream, Arnold* to find the entry for Jersey Joe Walcott; *Jones, Booker T.,* for the leader of Booker T. and the MGs; *Everett-Karenga, Maulana Ron N.,* for Ron Karenga; *Eikerenkoetter, Rev., Frederick,* for Reverend Ike; and *Alexander, Margaret W.,* for Margaret Walker. In the occupational Index, Arthur Mitchell is listed under *Business* (as Executive Director of the Dance Theatre of Harlem) but not also under *Arts*. Lt. Gen. Benjamin O. Davis, Jr., (ret.) is mentioned under *Business* but his present position listed in the entry is Assistant Secretary in the Department of Transportation for Environment, Safety, and Consumer Affairs. The potential value of the Indexes is not fully achieved.

The book contains a number of misspellings and typographical errors. No illustrations are provided. The book is sturdy, lies flat, is easy to use with running heads at the top of each page, and the print is legible. Inner margins are wide enough to accommodate rebinding if it should be necessary. However, front and back endpapers should be reinforced before the book is put to heavy use.

Who's Who Among Black Americans is a needed but flawed directory of prominent black Americans. It is not comprehensive, because too many writers, educators, city officials, and state legislators are missing. Also the user cannot determine if the persons were overlooked by the publisher or failed to submit material. At the same time, the "reference value" of many entries is doubtful despite the publisher's statement that reference value was the sole basis for inclusion. However, there is no comparable directory and the work is useful because it contains facts about a wide diversity of persons not represented in any other single biographical source. For these reasons, and despite its aforementioned flaws, *Who's Who Among Black Americans* is recommended as an auxiliary reference for secondary school, public, college, and special libraries which already own current editions of *U.S. Who's Who* and have patrons who can use this information. *(Nov. 1, 1976, p.420)*

†920.009′2960   Afro-Americans—Biography—Dictionaries   75-42841

Who's who in American art, 1976.
Edited by Jaques Cattell Pr. 12th ed. New York, R. R. Bowker Co., 1976. xiv, 756p. 29cm. cloth $37.

†705   Artists, American   [OCLC]   36-27014

See page 3

The world book dictionary.
Edited by Clarence L. Barnhart [and] Robert K. Barnhart; prepared in cooperation with Field Enterprises Educational Corporation. William H. Nault, editorial director, Robert O. Zeleny, executive editor, Donald H. Ludgin, special projects editor. 2v. Chicago, Field Enterprises Educational Corporation, [c1976 by Doubleday & Co., Inc.]. 124, 2430p. illus. 29cm. pyroxylin fabric, $59.

The World Book Dictionary, "an integral unit of the Thorndike-Barnhart Dictionary Series," was first published in 1963 under the title *The World Book Encyclopedia Dictionary,* and was commended for school, home, and library use in the September 1, 1963 issue of *The Booklist and Subscription Books Bulletin*.

It has been revised and reissued annually; in 1967 the title was changed to *The World Book Dictionary*. This 1976 edition is a major revision, with the text completely reset.

The dictionary is intended to be used by families and schools. It includes "definitions suited to grade level correlation of information in the dictionary with information in the encyclopedia, and placement of information so that it can be quickly obtained by the user."

In addition to this dictionary, Clarence K. Barnhart, Inc. has had lexicographical responsibility for the Thorndike-Barnhart school dictionaries, the *American College Dictionary*, and the *Barnhart Dictionary of New English Since 1963*. The editor in charge of this edition is Robert K. Barnhart who has been associated with the firm for many years. Policies for the dictionary were reviewed by an International Editorial Advisory Committee, the 46 members of which include renowned scholars Guy Jean Forgue, an authority on H. L. Mencken and American English; Samuel I. Hayakawa; Hans Kurath, a specialist on linguistics and Middle English; Randolph Quirk, eminent expert on English grammar and usage; and M. H. Scargill, director of the lexicographical Center for Canadian English. Also assisting the editorial staff was a large panel of special consultants from a variety of disciplines. The editors of *The World Book Encyclopedia* prepared the special front matter.

The editors state that the 1976 *World Book Dictionary* contains a selected vocabulary of 225,000 words, "the most important and most frequently used words and phrases in the English language" as compared with a vocabulary of 180,000 entries in the first edition. This compares with approximately 150,000 to 160,000 entries in standard desk dictionaries and 450,000 entries in *Webster's Third New International Dictionary*. The source of the vocabulary is a file of quotations gathered by readers who scanned contemporary magazines, newspapers, scholarly journals, and books published in the U.S. and other English-speaking countries. The editors also state that *The World Book Encyclopedia* was utilized as a source for technical and new words not found in previous editions. There are 25,000 new entries, including common and general terms and expressions as well as slang, specialized, and technical and scientific vocabulary; also added are some prefixes, suffixes and combining forms (such as *cosmo-, -drome, nucleo-, politico-*).

Since the dictionary is designed to complement *The World Book Encyclopedia*, geographical and biographical names and other encyclopedic-type information are omitted. Proper names from mythology and legend, foreign words and phrases, abbreviations, acronyms, combination words, and non-American usage are included. Presumably because of the dictionary's intended use for families and schools, obscene vocabulary has been omitted.

Entries are in one alphabet, letter by letter, with subentries for expressions using the key entry word. Words formed by adding suffixes to the main entry word now appear after the main entry word from which they are formed; for example, *breezily* and *breeziness* are included in the entry for *breezy*, whereas in earlier editions they were separate entries. Main entries and subentries are printed in boldface.

The content of entries typically includes syllabication, pronunciation, part of speech label, irregular plurals and inflected forms, definitions, illustrative phrases or sentences, synonyms and etymology. Many entries also contain usage or synonym notes and cite idioms. Syllabication is indicated by thin vertical lines between syllables instead of by the centered dots used in preceding editions. A special system of symbols adapted from the International Phonetic Alphabet is used to show pronunciation; a full key (which includes non-English sounds in words taken from foreign languages) appears in "Using This Dictionary" at the end of the introductory section of the dictionary and also at the beginning of the second volume. Briefer keys appear at the bottom of each right hand page. The key is simple and easily interpreted. Preferred pronunciation is given first; alternative pronunciations are indicated by respelling the affected syllables. Pronunciations given are those which the editors consider to be in current use among educated speakers of English in the United States and in representative areas of Canada.

When a word is used in several parts of speech, all labels are now handily grouped together following the pronunciation; each sense is then treated in a separately labelled paragraph. Inflected forms are shown when they present spelling problems, (for example, *beveled, bevelled* and *programmed, programmed*), while commonly misconstrued Latin and Greek plural nouns (*data, alumni, media, cherubim*), have separate entries.

Definitions are normally listed with the most commonly used meaning first. Each definition is numbered, with closely related senses grouped under a common number and differentiated by letter. Figurative meanings are explicitly labelled as such in this new edition. Definitions are clearly expressed in simple language. Many definitions are followed by helpful illustrative phrases or sentences to show how words are used; some, but not all, of these are quotations. Quotations are from older standard authors (e.g., Shakespeare, Pope, Defoe, Francis Parkman), from modern writers in various fields (Fulton J. Sheen, Winston Churchill, Tom Alexander), contemporary magazines and newspapers (*Science Newsletter, The Wall Street Journal*), and reference works (*Automotive Encyclopedia*). Quotations are not fully cited, nor are they dated, and there is no bibliography of sources used.

Synonyms are relocated in this new edition to follow the particular definitions and illustrative quotations (a practice which makes it easier to relate the two), instead of being grouped at the end of entries as in earlier editions. Etymologies appear in brackets at the end of the entries. An improvement in this edition is the use of explicit cross-references to etymologies in related entries (for example, the etymology under *chaplet* ends with a note *see etym. under chapeau*).

The treatment of idioms has also been changed for the better; where there is a question concerning under which of two words an idiom might be listed (for example, *bear arms*), entries appear under both terms with a cross-reference to the word under which full treatment is given. Idioms appear in one alphabetical list after all the definitions of the main entry word.

Many entries conclude with usage notes (e.g., in *air, but, O.K.*) identified by a boldface arrow, or a synonym note (as in *crop, part, severe*) in which the varying senses of a word or the contexts in which a word is used are more fully explained. A number of informative restrictive labels are used, including *archaic, combining form, dialect,* English-speaking variation (e.g., *Canadian*), foreign language, *informal, obsolete, poetic, prefix* and *suffix,* professional (e.g., *law*), *slang, substandard, trademark, unfriendly usage.* Entries for common prefixes are followed by lists of words containing the prefixes; these are not separately defined (for example, *pre-, un-,* and *non-*).

Attractive new line drawings, prepared in cooperation with *The World Book Encyclopedia* staff, accompany 3,000 words to extend and clarify their definitions. Cross-references and asterisks are used to relate words and illustrations. There are no indications of the sizes of objects illustrated.

A comparison of samples of the vocabularies from the 1976 and the 1972 editions of *The World Book Dictionary* supports the publisher's claim that the new edition has been thoroughly revised. Changes noted include the addition and deletion of entries, added, rewritten, and reordered definitions, new and rewritten illustrative quotations, the relocation of words from main entry to subentry position, and changes in labels, synonyms, spellings, etymologies, and cross-references. Among the new vocabulary found in this sample are *Big Brotherism, epibenthic, light show, male chauvinism, microbus, nonbiodegradable,* and *X rated.* Other new words or senses noted are *busing, digital clock, black hole, fast-food, flaky;* (slang) *bad-mouth, hard core, redline, orthotics, OPEC, color-field, living will, charismatic,* and *turn on;* and used as nouns, *Qiana* and *Watergate.*

The introductory material, printed on colored paper to distinguish it from the dictionary proper, has also been rewritten. Pages 13-124 contain sections now entitled, "Using Your Language," "How to Write Effectively," "Using Different Languages" (i.e., signs and symbols, weights and measures, etc.) and "Using This Dictionary." The vocabulary inventories for grades four through college level remain much the same, but there are some changes in these also.

Type and format have been completely restyled. The new computer-set typeface gives a lighter and more attractive appearance to the page. Each of the three columns on the page ends in a "ragged right" instead of the old flush setting in order to eliminate uneven spacing between words and reduce the amount of hyphenation needed. A table of contents appears in the front of each volume, and there are guide words at the top of each page. The two-volume school and library edition is durably bound in tan, brown, and gold, and it is thumb-indexed.

The World Book Dictionary, designed as a dictionary of the contemporary language for school and family use, is edited by a reputable firm with much experience in the making of dictionaries. It is notable for the presentation of information in a clear and easily comprehended manner. In scope, it falls between the desk and unabridged dictionary. In this 1976 revision, vocabulary and vocabulary treatment have been thoroughly reworked and an improved format has been adopted. The dictionary is recommended for school, home, and library use.

(Nov. 1, 1976, p.422)

423 English language—Dictionaries   [OCLC]

The world chronology series.
v. Dobbs Ferry, N.Y., Oceana Publications, 1972–
24cm. cloth $7.50 per volume.

Argentina:
a chronology and fact book, 1516–1973. Compiled and edited by Russell H. Fitzgibbon. Dobbs Ferry, N.Y., Oceana Publications, 1974. 148p. 24cm. cloth $7.50.
982 Argentine Republic—History—Sources || Argentine Republic—History—Chronology [CIP]   73-20375

Brazil:
a chronology and fact book, 1488–1973. Compiled and edited by Russell H. Fitzgibbon. Dobbs Ferry, N.Y., Oceana Publications, 1974. 150p. 24cm. cloth $7.50.
981 Brazil—History—Sources || Brazil—History—Chronology   [CIP]   73-17058

Canada:
a chronology and fact book, 875–1973. Compiled and edited by Brian H. W. Hill. Dobbs Ferry, N.Y., Oceana Publications, 1974. 153p. 24cm. cloth $7.50.
971 Canada—History—Chronology || Canada—History—Sources   [CIP]   73-7929

England:
a chronology and fact book, 1485–1973. Compiled and edited by Robert I. Vexler. Dobbs Ferry, N.Y., Oceana Publications, 1974. 186p. 24cm. cloth $7.50.
942 Gr. Brit.—History—Chronology || Gr. Brit.—History—Sources   [CIP]   73-17067

Germany:
a chronology and fact book, 1415–1972. Compiled and edited by Robert Vexler. Dobbs Ferry, N.Y., Oceana Publications, 1973. 184p. 24cm. cloth $7.50.
943 Germany—History—Chronology || Germany—History—Sources || Germany—History—Bibliography [CIP]   73-7792

Ireland:
a chronology and fact book, 6000BC–1972. Compiled and edited by William D. Griffin. Dobbs Ferry, N.Y., Oceana Publications, 1973. 154p. 24cm. cloth $7.50.
941.5 Ireland—History—Sources || Ireland—History—Chronology   [CIP]   73-12694

Israel:
a chronology and fact book, 2500BC–1972. Compiled and edited by Barnet Litvinoff. Dobbs Ferry, N.Y., Oceana Publications, 1974. 136p. 24cm. cloth $7.50.
956.94 Palestine—History—Chronology || Israel—History—Chronology || Zionism—History—Sources [CIP]   73-12571

The Netherlands:
a chronology and fact book, 57BC–1971. Compiled and edited by Pamela and J. W. Smit. Dobbs Ferry, N.Y., Oceana Publications, 1973. 152p. 24cm. cloth $7.50.
949.2 Netherlands—History—Chronology || Belgium—History—Chronology   [CIP]   73-5599

These eight volumes are parts of the World Chronology Series published by Oceana Publications Inc. The publisher envisages a series of some 50 to 60 volumes which will be published over a five-year period. Credits are given for the compilers and editors of each volume. Information on their qualifications and background is minimal; in a few instances, university affiliations are indicated.

Each book is devoted to one country's history and is organized according to the following general arrangement: table of contents, foreword of compiler/editor, chronology of events, documents, statistics and charts (in some of the volumes), bibliography (in some of the volumes), and index of names in the chronology. No means of accessing information other than through the tables of contents and name indexes are provided. The Indexes are generally accurate, but are devoid of cross-references.

Each of the volumes under review presents historical facts in calendar order. Year or exact date of each event is given. The editors of the series vary in their presumptions of reader knowledge. Little or considerable background data may be provided. Names, places, and events are referred to most of the time with little or no historical framework provided, and transitions between events are seldom made. The scope of each of the chronologies differs—some are narrowly political, while others cover social and cultural events as well as political ones.

The document section of each of the volumes contains mostly excerpts from primary and secondary historical sources.

Volumes within the series vary enough in their emphasis, approach, and usefulness to merit individual evaluation.

Argentina: A Chronology And Fact Book and *Brazil: A Chronology And Fact Book* are both compiled and edited by Russell H. Fitzgibbon, Professor Emeritus, University of California, Santa Barbara. Each contains a short editor's foreword providing a brief historical context of the events listed. In both volumes, the document sections are larger than the chronology sections.

The chronology of the Brazil book spans the period 1488–1973, and that of the Argentina volume the period 1516–1973; both emphasize political events. A mixture of exact dates and years is provided.

Dates in both chronologies appear to be accurate. A check of specific events in both chronologies against the *Encyclopedia of Latin America* (edited by Helen Delpar) and William Langer's *Encyclopedia of World History* revealed no discrepancies in dates, and no major events in the *Langer* book were omitted from the two chronologies compiled by Fitzgibbon.

The descriptions of the events in both chronologies are generally free from bias and clear.

The document sections are comparatively large. The items deal primarily with political and economic events. Each document is introduced by a short summary of its historical importance. The introductions provide sufficient information for persons unfamiliar with Brazilian and Argentine history to understand why the document was included in the volume.

The document section of the Argentina volume begins with two accounts of the Argentine Indian and ends with a news article on Evita Peron (written by Fitzgibbon) which appeared in the *Los Angeles Times* immediately after her death in 1952. Inclusions, such as this news article, have little significance, and most of the documents in the Argentina volume deal with social, geographic, and economic aspects of Argentine history, as described in letters and histories written in the nineteenth century. The selection of documents is random and arbitrary. For example, the 1824-1826 land law extending the legality of owning large areas of land (referred to in the chronology) is missing, and the 1853 Constitution is only summarized by general subject contents. The Constitution deserves more attention, since it has ruled the country for over 100 years. The volume concludes with an Appendix of statistical, geographical, and demographic information and a chart of Argentine rulers; this is followed by an unannotated Bibliography.

The document section of the Brazil book is much more oriented to political and economic events than that of the Argentina volume. It begins with the 1494 Treaty of Tordesillas and ends with the English translation of the 1967 Brazilian Constitution. The section is not well balanced, being heavily weighted with travelers' accounts. An Appendix of rulers since 1808 and a statistical geographical chart follow the documents. A short unannotated Bibliography follows the Appendix.

Canada: A Chronology and Fact Book is edited by Brian H. W. Hill. The publisher provides no information regarding his credentials.

The foreword does not give a historical summary. It indicates only the editor's conception of the chronology as a "collection of dates from Canadian history considered to be of some historical consequence in the shaping of the modern Canadian nation." The chronology begins with a short section of pre-1600 exploration events (875 is the earliest) and ends with the 1973 launching of a Canadian communications satellite. Specific dates are cited for most of the later happenings. The chronology is primarily limited to incidents in political, economic, and exploration history; cultural and social events are not included. Dates listed in the chronology are accurate. The Name Index is also error-free, but cross-references are omitted.

A listing of Canadian prime ministers and premiers of the various Canadian provinces through 1973 follows the chronology proper.

Documents begin with the Quebec Act of 1784 and end with the 1931 Statute of Westminster which gave autonomy to the Canadian government. All the documents relate to evolution of the Canadian nation. Introductions describing historical significance precede the excerpts from each document. Because of the 1931 closing date, official papers generated by the friction between French and English Canadians are not represented. A short area and population chart follows this portion of the book.

The editor states that the unannotated and topically arranged listing which completes the volume is not "a bibliography of Canadian history but rather represents a random survey of works on different aspects of Canadian history."

England: A Chronology and Fact Book and *Germany: A Chronology And Fact Book* are both edited by Robert I. Vexler who is on the history faculty at Briarcliff College. The forewords of both volumes do not attempt to provide a historical context for the chronologies which follow. Instead, they merely paraphrase the tables of contents.

The volume on England contains a chronology beginning in 1485 with the Tudor Period and ending with the change in Prime Minister Heath's Cabinet in mid-1973. The editor states that "emphasis has been placed on England with factors concerning Scotland and Ireland chosen which bear directly on English developments." Vexler has broken down many of the dates for events listed into months and days; the other editors of this series have not. Also, his chronology of England differs from others in the series by the inclusion of many nonpolitical events, e.g., the publication of Milton's *Paradise Lost* in 1667 and the writing of *Sybil* by Disraeli in 1845. Comparison of accuracy with *Langer* indicates that dates of events are accurately listed and that no major events have been slighted.

In this volume, the Name Index includes royal names in parentheses following each proper name entry. Regrettably, in the Index there are no cross-references from royal names. Pseudonyms are also shortchanged. For example, the entry for George Eliot lists her real name in parentheses (Marian Evans), but there is no entry under Evans.

The document section of the England book contains a short preface indicating that the Magna Carta (which begins the document portion) was included because it "formed a basis for the rights of all Englishmen" and that all succeeding materials were "chosen as a means indicating the subtle methods by which English social, cultural, and political life has [sic] changed." Both domestic policy and foreign developments are covered. Many of the earlier documents are taken from Guy Lee's *Sourcebook of English History. Leading Documents* (New York: Holt, 1900). Each document is preceded by a short descriptive paragraph setting the historical context; readers unfamiliar with English history will find these summaries especially helpful. However, the documents stop at 1958, ending with the Life Peerages Act which gave certain British subjects membership in the House of Lords.

Included is an annotated Bibliography organized by historical period into which previously cited document sources have been integrated. Compared with the bibliographies in the other volumes, this is a more complete and useful listing of titles relating to the subject of the book.

The first date in the chronology of the book on Germany is 1415, but the chronology as a serious entity begins with the Prussian influence (1618) and ends with the 1972 West German traffic treaty with East Germany and transportation pact with Russia. This chronology is more detailed in date specificity than other volumes in the series, and representation includes important political and economic events occasionally interrupted by isolated cultural or scientific milestones, such as the 1876 premiere of Richard Wagner's *Ring of the Nibelungen* and Max Planck's promulgation of the Quantum Theory in 1900. Fifty-five of the hundred pages present twentieth-century events. The editor emphasizes and meticulously documents events leading up to and including the Nazi period. In particular, Hitler's life is followed in great detail from his birth in 1889 to his suicide in 1945. In the post-World War II period, Vexler covers major events in both East and West Germany.

A comparison with Langer's *Encyclopedia of World History* and Morris' and Irwin's *Harper's Encyclopedia of the Modern World* (New York: Harper, 1970) indicates that most dates are accurate. In the section dealing with Nazi Germany, there are some events listed with inadequate explanations. Overall, however, the chronology is as clear and complete as any in this series.

The first document is the Reform Edict of 1807; the concluding one is the Berlin Declaration on German Reunification of July 29, 1957. Each document is prefaced by a short and effective statement describing its historical content and importance. With the exception of some excerpts from Hilter's will, the documents all relate to political and economic/historical events of Germany.

Vexler has also compiled an excellent annotated Bibliography of sources and historical analyses of different periods of German history with separate sections on cultural and military history.

Ireland: A Chronology and Fact Book is compiled and edited by William D. Griffin wh teaches history at St. John's University. The foreword offers little historical context except to mention the interrelationship between England and Ireland in very general terms.

As the foreword states, the chronology "gives proportionately greater emphasis to the modern period of Irish political history." The first entry is "c. 6000 B. C.—First evidence of human habitation in Ireland," but a serious year-by-year account does not begin until the sixteenth century. The final date of the chronology is May-June, 1972 (the Dublin crackdown on the IRA). The chronology is almost exclusively limited to internal political developments. Although the dates of events are consistent with those in Langer's *Encyclopedia of World History,* there are missing references and inadequate explanations. Omitted are references to Bernadette Devlin and her role as spokesperson of the IRA and the split between the provisional and Marxist wings of the IRA. Only a date is cited for the latter event. Also, there are very few references to the political situation of Northern Ireland after the split in 1920 between Eire (Irish Free State) and Northern Ireland.

The documents section begins with Poynings Law in 1494 and ends with an article by 1972 Premier John Lynch of Northern Ireland called "The Anglo-Irish Problem." There are no descriptions of the historical context or significance of the documents. Following this section there is an Appendix consisting of a statistical chart of land area of the counties of both Northern and Southern Ireland, and contemporary and historical population figures (including religious affiliation) for Eire and Northern Ireland. An unannotated Bibliography, organized by time period, follows the statistics.

Israel: A Chronology and Fact Book is compiled and edited by Barnet Litvinoff. This volume is somewhat different from the others, in that the editor has defined his subject not only as "the modern nation-state Israel," but also as "a people whose history has been concentrated in the Holy Land since the beginning of the Biblical era." With no historical setting described in the Foreword, the chronology begins with 2500 B.C.—"Early Bronze Age. First Semitic immigration into Canaan," and ends with the events of 1972. However, the events described up to 1900 hardly even touch the surface of the history of the Jewish people, in or out of the Canaan. Beginning with the twentieth century, the entries in the chronology are all directed to people and events having a bearing on the eventual founding of the state of Israel in 1948. For each year after 1900, at least one event is mentioned; however, months and days of events are not indicated. The accuracy of the events listed is good. Events associated with the state of Israel are listed in short sentences grouped together in short paragraphs under the years the events occurred. The editor avoids controversy by simply inventorying each event rather than commenting on its cause and effect. For example, in 1948, when the state of Israel was set up by UN Mandate and immediately became embroiled in a war with neighboring Arab states, large numbers of Arab Palestinians left their land. Why the Arab Palestinians did this is not revealed; the editor simply states: "Hundreds of thousands of Arabs flee." The index of names in the Chronology is acceptably accurate.

The editor states in his foreword that the document section is exclusively concerned with "the modern movement of Zionism." The first document is the Basle Program, formulated in 1897 by the First Zionist Congress, and the final document is the 1972 UN resolution deploring Israel's occupation of territories resulting from the 1967 war. Most of the material is excerpts from the major documents dealing with the history of Zionism. However, the statement which Chaim Weizmann made before the Palestine Royal Commission in 1936 is reprinted in its entirety. One-paragraph Introductions indicate each document's significance.

Following the documents section is an Appendix including three unclear, incomplete, and superficial maps showing Palestine between 1947 and 1949 and Israel after the 1967 war (the 1973 war is not included). A short statistical section on population and economic growth completes the Appendix. A selected Bibliography with one-sentence annotations ends the volume.

The Netherlands: A Chronology and Fact Book is compiled and edited by Pamela and J. W. Smit. Their Foreword, an excellent two-page overview of the political and religious history of the Netherlands, shows what the Smits call "the idealism and toleration of the founders of the Dutch State" as well as "its ruthless empire building." Although the chronology formally begins with 57 B.C.—"the conquest of the Southern Netherlands by Julius Caesar"—it does not go into detail until 1369, with the unification of the nation under the Burgundian and Hapsburg dynasties. The chronology relates events through 1971, ending with the visit of Queen Juliana to the Republic of Indonesia. A four-page listing of Dutch sovereigns and parliamentary leaders follows the chronology.

Events in the chronology were checked against those noted in Langer's *Encyclopedia of World History* (1972) and the 1972 edition of the *Encyclopaedia Britannica.* None of the dates conflicted, and major historical happenings listed in *Langer* were represented in the Smits' chronology along with a number of lesser events. However, the Smits' list is limited to occurrences of primarily political import. Some events are placed only by year; others have specific dates identified. This variable treatment of dates seems arbitrary. For example, William II's death is noted as having taken place in 1849, while Queen Wilhelmina's birthdate is given as August 31, 1880.

The 76-page document section of the volume begins with the Dutch National Anthem (five of fifteen stanzas are printed), and ends with a speech given by Queen Juliana in 1949 on the occasion of the transfer of Dutch sovereignty over Indonesia to an interim government. Each document is prefaced by two or three sentences which are intended to help the reader understand its historical significance. However, readers unfamiliar with Dutch history will find these brief synopses insufficient orientation. At the conclusion, sources used for the book are identified. Aside from this list, there is no bibliography.

All of the volumes in the World Chronology Series are the typically drab but functional products of offset printing; formats and legibility are adequate. Bindings are sturdy, and pages lie flat with relative ease. The margins are acceptable, although rebinding will be difficult because the document sections of all the volumes have very narrow inner margins.

Since none of the volumes in the World Chronology Series qualify as histories of the nations they cover, their primary use and value resides in their condensed, albeit fragmented and inconsistent, outlines of history and the official and unofficial items they offer to whet the amateur historian's curiosity. No comparable titles exist in print which are in this genre. The world chronologies which are in print, e.g., Butler's *Dictionary of Dates* (1972), Grun's *Timetables of History* (1975), and Langer's *Encyclopedia of World History* (1972), are chronologies only, and they attempt to provide international, rather than special area coverage.

The eight volumes in the World Chronology Series reviewed here are part of an incomplete set and therefore, according to Committee policy, this review concludes with no statement of recommendation. The books vary in focus, comprehensiveness, and organization. The main weaknesses of the volumes are their arbitrariness of coverage, inconsistencies of date notations, the haphazardness of the document sections, and the lack of currency. Therefore, in lieu of obtaining these volumes, librarians are advised to consult other references such as general encyclopedias, *The Statesman Yearbook,* Langer's *Encyclopedia of World History,* Keesing's *Contemporary Archives,* and *Facts on File* to confirm the chronology of events of foreign countries.
(Nov. 15, 1976, p.494)

World directory of environmental organizations.
Ed. by Thaddeus C. Trzyna and Eugene V. Coan, with the assistance of Judith Ruggles, in cooperation with the International Union for Conservation of Nature and Natural Resources. 2d ed. Claremont, CA 91711, Public Affairs Clearing House, P.O. Box 30, 1976. xxx, 258p. 28cm. paper $18.

The Sierra Club has produced a *World Directory of Environmental Organizations* to help meet the current need for information on environment. First issued in 1973, the directory is now in its second edition. Its purpose is "to foster better communication and cooperation among the many organizations throughout the world that are working to defend and improve the human environment" and "to facilitate and encourage study and research on global environment problems by identifying sources of information and expertise."

Founded in 1892, the Sierra Club is a citizens' organization working throughout the world to "maintain the integrity of ecosystems and to restore the quality of the natural environment." The club is a member of the International Union for Conservation of Nature and Natural Resources, a leading world nongovernmental conservation organization founded in 1948. The publisher of the volume, Sequoia Institute, is part of a nonprofit research foundation, Center for California Public Affairs, affiliated with Claremont College. The institute's publishing focuses on environment, natural resources, and regional studies.

Both editors hold doctorates. Thaddeus C. Trzyna is president of the Center for California Public Affairs and is a member of the International Committee of the Sierra Club. His field is political science. Eugene V. Coan is a marine biologist and an assistant to the executive director of the Sierra Club in San Francisco.

The editors define "environmental organizations" as groups concerned with traditional natural resources, conservation, pollution control, cultural heritage preservation, energy policy, urban planning, environmental education, welfare of native peoples, nuclear safety, pest management, solid waste management, population, transportation, and resource recovery.

In setting forth the directory's criteria for inclusion, the Introduction states that it does not give thorough coverage to scientific groups in Western countries because these have less influence on policy than citizens' groups and professional societies. Such groups are included for developing countries where they do influence environmental decisions. Usually most groups whose environmental involvement is based on economic self-interest, such as timber and mining trade associations, are excluded. Only national and regional groups are listed for Australia, Canada, Poland, the U.K., and the U.S. because these countries "have good directories of environmental organizations." However, the Introduction does not cite any of the titles.

The first of the directory's four major parts is a subject list of organizations called a "User's Guide." Thirty-five subject-headings, such as *climate* and *weather modification,* are used. Under each heading organizations are listed with their addresses and citations to pages in the directory where more information is given.

Intergovernmental organizations (United Nations agencies followed by other intergovernmental groups) are listed in the second part. The third part lists bodies of international scope which are not government affiliated, and the fourth part lists national organizations. In this fourth part entries are arranged thus: national directories currently available, government agencies, research or educational groups affiliated with government, and individuals, periodicals, and groups concerned with the environments of external territories.

In parts 2, 3, and 4 the entries follow the same pattern. Each group's name and address are given. English translations of names are given in parentheses in most instances. When there is no headquarters, the address is that of the group's chief official. Other information given may include a description of the group's purposes and activities, founding date, number of members, periodical publications, and membership in the International Union for Conservation of Nature and Natural Resources.

An Organization Index and Acronym Index complete the book.

The second edition claims twice as many entries and more detail than the first edition. This claim is accurate. Defunct organizations have been deleted, and the information has been updated. This was achieved by the incorporation of material sent in by users of the first edition, overseas representatives of the Sierra Club and the Asia Foundation, missions at the United Nations, foreign consulates in San Francisco, and the organizations themselves. The editors also monitored the literature of the field for news and consulted such sources as *Yearbook of International Organizations* and the *Political Handbook of the World.* Users of this edition are also invited to send additions and corrections to the editors, and an address for such correspondence is provided.

The writing is terse, and the page design is easy on the eyes, with two columns of type separated by a dark line.

Names of countries stand out clearly in boldface capitals. The book lies flat for use. The margins are wide enough for rebinding.

The *World Directory of Environmental Organizations* is well designed. It provides a ready source of information on environmental topics. Recommended. *(July 15, 1977, p.1752)*

†639.9025 Conservation of natural resources—Directories ‖ Environmental protection—Directories 75-38124

The world guide to antiquities.
By Seymour Kurtz. New York, Crown Publishers, Inc., 1975. 324p. illus. 29cm. cloth $25.

This copiously illustrated guide attempts a comprehensive survey of the civilizations of antiquity. The volume covers not only the familiar treasures of Greece and Rome, pre-Columbian civilization, the near and Far East, but also less well-known artistic creations such as the prehistoric cave paintings at Altamira in Northern Spain and the Khmer temples at Angkor Wat built between the ninth and sixteenth centuries. Arranged alphabetically from *Abbevillian* (a "long-lasting, early paleolithic period") to *Zuni* ("a Pueblo Indian tribe of the American Southwest"), the approximately 1,550 entries address briefly most aspects of the early cultures of man.

Seymour Kurtz, author of the *Guide,* was coeditor of the third edition of the *Columbia Encyclopedia,* editor and founder of the *Reader's Digest Almanac,* and the *New York Times Encyclopedic Almanac,* and editorial consultant in Europe for Reader's Digest. In addition, Kurtz has been a research associate at the museums of the universities of both Pennsylvania and Kansas, Director of Development for the New School of Social Research, and Chief of Information for the Museum of Primitive Art in New York. Leon Pomerance, vice-president of the Archaeological Institute of America, wrote the short Introduction.

Numerous, full-color illustrations, ranging in size from a quarter to full page, are the most striking feature of the work. There are over 300 pictures all of which are well chosen and usually placed near the entries they highlight. Picture credits cite a long list of internationally important museums, as well as publishing houses and individuals. Reproduction is uniformly excellent with colors that are never garish and, in most cases, seem to do justice to the original.

The text, which consists of entries ranging from a few lines to several pages in length, is generally accurate, clearly written, and free of jargon. The avoidance of technical terms makes the text accessible to a general audience. However, the scholar will be disappointed by the absence of aids to further research; entries lack bibliographies and there is no general listing of works consulted for preparation of the work. Moreover, the *Guide*'s lack of an index will hamper users' searches for specific items of information.

In addition, though the text includes *see* references, the work contains no *see-also* references. For example, there is a general article *Roman Civilization* and also related discussions of the *Palatine, Hadrian's Villa, Pompeii, Capitoline, Diocletian's*

Baths, etc.; a short general article on *Celtic Art,* and an even briefer identification of the *White Horse of Uffington;* a brief mention of Viking ships in *Vikings,* and an article on the *Gokstad Ship Burial* in which the vessel is characterized as "a magnificent example of Viking craftsmanship." Yet no allusions are made in any of these articles to connected coverages. Overlapping or identical topics treated in varying degrees of thoroughness and specificity, along with related illustrations, should have been linked to accommodate the user.

The volume is handsome, solidly bound, and lies flat when opened. Produced in Italy, its pages are printed on high quality, coated paper.

The World Guide to Antiquities should please the popular audience for which it is intended because of its readable descriptions and the high quality of its numerous illustrations. However, the potential value of the work is lessened by its lack of index, bibliographies, and *see-also* references. It is recommended only for those collections where such features are of less importance than browsability and pictorial appeal.

(Nov. 15, 1976, p.496)

930.1   Antiquities—Dictionaries   [CIP]   75-4173

World guide to universities.

2d. ed., part I, Europe. 2v. Edited by Michael Zils. New York and London, Bowker; Munich, Verlag Dokumentation, 1976. 1254p. 21cm. cloth $86 plus shipping and handling charges.

Part I of the *World Guide to Universities* lists the address, telephone number, date of founding, number of students, name of the head of the institution, address of the library, and name of the library director for 638 European universities. Following this information for each university, faculty names are enumerated under subheads of major divisions of the institution. Altogether 95,000 faculty members are represented, about a 50 percent increase over the number appearing in the 1971 first edition. The subject field of each faculty member is almost invariably given. University institutes are generally identified only by name without further identification of address or director. The *World Guide to Universities* lists only full professors for some institutions but does include all ranks for many others. Identification of faculty specialties is generally in English, except for the German, French, and Belgian institutions for which German and French are used. Italian faculty are sometimes reported in English; at other times their listings are in Italian. For Sweden, Swedish appears frequently and alternately with English, and there are other exceptions to the overall pattern of using English for other than the French and German universities and colleges.

There are three indexes. A name (faculty member) Index and an alphabetically arranged Index of subject fields broken down by nation are at the end of volume 2; a table of contents "index" at the front of volume 1 lists the names of institutions alphabetically by nation.

Part II of the *Guide* will cover Africa, the Americas, Asia, and Oceania. It will be available this year at a price to be announced.

The World of Learning, 1975–76 (New York: International Publications Service) provides some of the same information in its "universities" section as the *World Guide to Universities.* The latter is much less pleasing to the eye and not as legible because of its very compact format and small typeface with rather diminutive subheads. Moreover, the *World of Learning* is entirely in English; even in cases where formal titles are occasionally given in the native language, an English translation is provided.

The *World Guide to Universities* does not include museums, galleries, and learned societies found in *The World of Learning.* It does, however, include institutes as noted earlier. While *World Guide to Universities* often restricts itself to full professors, it includes lesser ranks far more often than *The World of Learning,* which rarely picks up faculty below the full professor level. For the University of Genoa, for instance, *The World of Learning* reports that there are 952 teachers and lists by name only about 200 full professors. In comparison, for this institution the *World Guide to Universities* has compiled the names of at least 1,000 junior as well as senior faculty. Nonetheless, although it aims to be comprehensive in scope and up to date, the *World Guide to Universities* lists neither the venerable library school in Copenhagen nor the new school in Aalborg. Both are found in *The World of Learning.* Finally, *The World of Learning* lists institutions only, while a major feature of *World Guide to Universities* is its extensive faculty name index.

The *World Guide to Universities,* part I, is recommended for libraries needing current directory information on European universities and their faculties.   *(May 1, 1977, p.1372)*

†378.002'5   Universities and colleges—Directories

The world of learning, 1976–1977.

27th ed. 2v. London, Europa Publications Limited, 1976; dist. in the U.S. by Gale. 1,992p. 26cm. cloth $73.50.

The World of Learning is a directory of institutions of higher education throughout the world. Volume I begins with 51 pages covering several hundred international educational organizations such as UNESCO, International Union of Geodesy and Geophysics, and the International Committee on Historical Sciences; the remainder of the volume includes entries for institutions in nations ranging from Afghanistan to Qatar. Volume II covers Rhodesia through Zambia and concludes with a 145-page Index of Institutions. Both volumes are arranged alphabetically in English, first by nation, then by class (academic, learned societies, libraries, museums, universities), and finally by name of institution within the nation.

Each country's coverage begins with a listing of major learned societies, indicating for each the address, telephone number, date of founding, officers, purposes and activities, library holdings, number of members, publications, and the names of important fellows or members. Similar data for research institutes, libraries and archives, museums and art galleries, and universities follow. The entries for universities indicate the founding dates, addresses, major administrative officers and deans, number of library volumes, and number of students. For large universities, department rosters of full professors are provided. All in all, more than 24,000 organizations and institutions of higher education, upper echelon staff and faculty, and their fields of research or teaching are covered.

Included are approximately 150,000 persons, with their titles and areas of subject involvement indicated. Unfortunately, there is no index to personal names. By contrast, *The World Guide to Universities* (Europe) does include an index of persons, as well as one for institutions.

As noted earlier, the lists of staff and faculty are limited to administrators and full professors. Furthermore, for most small colleges in the U.S., only senior administrators are listed. Nonetheless, 371 pages are devoted to the U.S. alone. A few serial publications and institutes associated with colleges and universities are listed, but this coverage is inconsistent. Several institutes are listed for Columbia University (New York), for example, while those at the University of Chicago go unreported.

The book's binding is sturdy and flexible, and the book lies flat for easy reading. The use of space and varied typefaces makes *The World of Learning* very easy to use. Despite the lack of an index to persons, this work is recommended for libraries needing an up-to-date international directory in higher education. It will be most useful in academic and large public libraries.

(July 15, 1977, p.1752)

†378.002'5   Education, Higher—Directories || Universities and colleges—Directories

47-30172

Notes and Comments

Along the northern border:
cookery in Idaho, Minnesota, and North Dakota. New York, Arno Pr., 1973. xv, 120, 111, 127p. 22cm. cloth $10.
641.5   Cookery, American—Northwestern States   [CIP]   72-9788
See page 116

America: history and life.
v.11. Part A, Article abstracts and citations, 1974– (issued spring, summer and fall); Part B, Index to book reviews, 1975–   . (issued spring and fall); Part C, American history bibliography (books, articles and dissertations), 1975–   . (issued annually); Part D, Annual index, 1976–   . Eric H. Boehm, editor. Santa Barbara, Cal., American Bibliographical Center–Clio Press, 1974– 28cm. paper, sold on service basis (lowest rate, $155; highest rate, $560).

Individuals may subscribe through the Organization of American Historians. ABC–Clio, publishers of *Historical Abstracts* and ongoing bibliographies in art and political science, have expanded the coverage of *America: History and Life* which for ten years abstracted only the journal literature in the field. To the journal abstracts have been added in volume 11 an author and reviewer index to book reviews in 115 journals; a classified bibliography of books, articles, and dissertations; and an analytical Subject Profile Index. This analysis is based on an examination of parts A-D of volume 11.

Part A, Article Abstracts and Citations, issued spring, summer, and fall, follows with some refinements the arrangement of the earlier volumes begun in 1964. Entries are classified under six broad headings, e.g., North America, Canada, and United States, further divided by period, aspect, or smaller geographic division such as a state or province. The sixth heading, History, the Humanities, and Social Sciences, brings together such topics as archives and libraries, methodology, teaching, and related subjects.

Part A supplies full bibliographic data for each article abstracted, the author's affiliation, and a succinct, informative abstract either signed by a volunteer abstracter, supplied by the journal editor, or prepared by the staff of *America: History and Life.* Staff-prepared abstracts are much briefer than those done by volunteer abstracters, while those supplied by the journals are often longer. Only a few have no abstract, usually articles whose titles adequately indicate contents.

The Subject Profile Index (SP Index) is appended. According to the editors, each index entry consists of an average of 4.5 subject, geographic, and bibliographic descriptors, followed by the chronology of the article, as in *Economic policy, Foreign aid, International trade, Middle East, USA, USSR, 1954–69.* These descriptors are rotated so that the complete profile is cited under each of the terms in alphabetical order, giving a much more analytical approach than the index to *Writings on American History.* This latter title scaled down its coverage in 1974 by eliminating book citations. Currently published by the American Historical Association, the new series, *Writings on American History,* remains an essential key to the contents of journals in this field. For books and doctoral dissertations, *America: History and Life* has effectively assumed the role now vacated by *Writings on American History.* Also included in the 1974 volume of *America: History and Life* are 182 "journal profiles." These are brief scope notes, chiefly for journals of state and local historical societies of the United States, most of them appearing under name of state. They have been considered too specialized in appeal to list each article separately.

No list of journals abstracted appears in Part A, but an examination of contents reveals that, with the exception of the French entries on Canada and more especially Quebec, nearly all of the 6,918 citations in volume 11 are to English-language publications. One finds only an occasional abstract of an article in German, Russian, Spanish, Dutch, Japanese, or some other foreign languages. Title translations are supplied for these. This Part A is particularly useful as a source of abstracts of American and Canadian journal articles.

The same English language emphasis is evident in *Part B, Index to Book Reviews,* which in volume 11 lists 2,404 books published from 1969 to 1974 with citations to reviews appearing in the 1974 issues of 115 scholarly journals published in the United States and Canada. Selected with the assistance of some 225 historians, they include journals of national and regional historical societies and major periodicals in related fields. Only a few, e.g., *American Historical Review,* are indexed in either *Book Review Digest* or *Book Review Index,* thus giving access to a large body of reviews hitherto unindexed. Arrangement is by author, with scrupulous reference to all joint authors and with an appended index to names of reviewers. Books with no authors listed are given at the end. Issued in spring and fall, it includes additional reviews for more than 400 books in the fall issue which were listed in the spring, with citation to the earlier item number. The editors expect to include about 5,500 reviews of 3,000 books annually.

Part C, American History Bibliography (*Books, Articles and Dissertations*) includes all references found in Part A (without the abstracts), Part B (without the citations to reviews), and 1,848 doctoral dissertations selected by the editors after screening 40 pertinent sections of *Dissertation Abstracts International.* Following the same classified order as Part A, it serves as a convenient cumulation of Parts A and B, with the valuable addition of an important source of research in the field, dissertations, which for the most part were completed at Canadian and American graduate schools. It also supplies a broad subject approach to book reviews and dissertations.

Part D, Annual Index follows the same form as the Subject Profile Index in Part A. It supplies in one alphabet a cumulation of the indexes found in the spring, summer, and fall issues of Part A. It also serves as an analytical index to book reviews in Part B and an analytical subject index to dissertations classified under broad subjects in Part C. An Author Index is appended.

Though not as current as *Index Medicus, America: History*

and Life is considerably more prompt in its coverage than the old, pre-1974 series, *Writings on American History*. Also, ABC–Clio has plans for making this important bibliographical service in American history even more current. In the future, most nonabstract article entries will be cited within six months of publication of the original article and abstracts within nine months.

Other features in *America: History and Life* not found in *Writings* are the broader geographical coverage to include Canada, the listing and indexing of dissertations, the index to book reviews, the abstracts of articles, and the Subject Profile Index. It also maintains a computer data base with an on-line computer interrogation service. Tape sales for current and back volumes are planned for 1976.

It is evident that the broader coverage, the improved indexing, and the greater currency make the bibliography much more useful than its predecessor and one which will be essential for the historian and teacher of American history.

(Jan. 15, 1977, p.745)

†016.973   U.S.—History—Bibliography

American and British genealogy and heraldry:
a selected list of books. Compiled by P. William Filby. 2d ed. Chicago, American Library Association, 1975. 467p. 25cm. cloth $25.

The first edition of this book was published in 1970. The author is the director of the Maryland Historical Society and has also been chairman of the Genealogical Committee of the History Section of the Reference Services Division (now Reference and Adult Services Division) of the American Library Association. After 1970, Filby continued to augment his list, interleaving and preparing cards for each new entry he found. The result is that the second edition is more than double the size of the first and contains more than 5,000 entries.

The work is essentially a briefly annotated (or sometimes unannotated) list of 5,125 titles considered valuable in genealogical searches. About 300 serials are included.

The work is well organized, starting with general reference works, bibliographies, and indexes, with representation of standard titles by Norma Ireland, Winifred Gregory, Fremont Rider, and others. Following this is a section devoted to more specialized topics, *Censuses, Place Names, Ethnic Groups, Military and Pension Lists,* and the like. A major portion of the book is devoted to the U.S., divided alphabetically by state. Latin America, Canada, the British Isles, and some parts of the former British Empire, such as India, New Zealand, and South Africa, are dealt with in subsequent pages. The concluding section of the bibliography, about 60 items, treats heraldry, without any regional subdivision. The work ends with a list of Addresses of Publishers and a 100-page Index of authors, some titles, and subjects.

Under each section the genealogical works are listed alphabetically by author, except that in some sections, such as *Religion* or *Ethnic Groups,* there is an initial breakdown by religion or ethnic group and then by author. Entry is by title only when no author can be identified.

Despite the obvious expertise of the compiler, the work is not without flaws. The Introduction states that the publishers are given only for books in print. As a result of this policy one finds in the book hundreds of entries which appear to be complete—author, title, place, and date—but which lack a publisher's name. Since it is well known that many genealogical books are privately published by authors, the first move on the part of a reader wishing to ascertain who published a certain work will be to search the directory in the back of the book under the author's name. Usually it is not there; and since most readers will not have discovered, buried in the middle of a paragraph in the Introduction, the brief explanatory statement that the names of publishers of o.p. books are not listed, they will be both puzzled and frustrated. The value of the listings would have been heightened if full publication data had been provided for each entry, with o.p. designations appended whenever appropriate.

Although some of the annotations in the book are valuable, such as those for Rider's *American Genealogical Index* and for the Newberry Library's *Genealogical Index,* other annotations are unsubstantial, because they merely paraphrase information explicit in the title. For example, for the work entitled *Alaska-Yukon Place Names,* the entire annotation reads "State of Alaska and parts of western Canada." Another item is entered as follows: "Society of Mayflower Descendants. California. *Register.*" The annotation reads "A record of descendants from passengers on the Mayflower."

Besides the Addresses of Publishers already mentioned, there is an Index of one hundred double-columned pages. This indexes, by entry number, all entries that have a personal author, some but not all titles, and subjects. Large subjects or areas, such as *California, Canada, Indians,* are subdivided by form or specific topic, e.g., *Pioneers, Ship Registers.*

The second edition of *American and British Genealogy and Heraldry* will prove to be very useful in genealogical libraries and to all historical and genealogical researchers. Its coverage is extremely wide, and, with the exception of the defects noted above, the work is easy to use. It will also prove useful to libraries that wish to build up their genealogical collections.

(May 1, 1977, p.1372)

016.929'1   U.S.—Genealogy—Bibliography || Heraldry—U.S.—Bibliography || Great Britain—Genealogy—Bibliography || Heraldry—Great Britain—Bibliography.   [CIP]   75-29383

**American architects
from the Civil War to the First World War:**
a guide to information sources. By Lawrence Wodehouse. Detroit, Gale Research Co., 1976. xii, 343p. 23cm. cloth $18.

This volume in the Art and Architecture Information Guide Series is described by the editor as a selected "annotated biographical bibliography" of the most significant American architects from the Civil War to World War I. It is intended as a continuation of Frank J. Roos, Jr.'s *Bibliography of Early American Architecture* (University of Illinois Press, 1968), which covers the period up to 1860. The editor hopes to prepare a sequel which will cover the years from World War I to the present.

Lawrence Wodehouse, professor of architectural history at Pratt Institute, is an architect and city planner as well as an architectural historian. His specialty is nineteenth-century American architecture, with particular emphasis on designers of public buildings. His articles have been published in such journals as *Antiques, Art Journal, Historic Preservation,* and the *Journal of the Society of Architectural Historians.* He contributed 16 entries on architects to the *McGraw-Hill Dictionary of World Biography* (1973).

The first section of the volume is an annotated listing by author of 46 general reference books on American architects and their works. The selection is not confined to publications dealing with the chronological period covered by the bibliography and includes items with imprint dates ranging from 1924 through 1972.

Section II, the major part of the volume, is a "Selected Annotated Biographical Bibliography of American Architects from the Period of the Civil War to the First World War." The 175 architects and partnerships covered are those considered "the most representative architects of each era and those that historians and critics have thought worthy enough to research and comment upon."

Entries are arranged alphabetically by surname, and the main entry for each architect usually includes a brief biographical sketch covering birth and death dates, education and training, employment, partnerships, and citations to obituaries. Also included are listings of the architect's publications and information on the locations of his or her drawings.

This information is followed by annotated entries for selected books and journal articles dealing with the architect (or partnership) and his works. Most of the entries are for biographies or critical evaluations of an architect's achievement. Journal articles on individual buildings are included only if the analysis is signed by the author. Thus, the volume constitutes "an interpretation of architects and their works as seen through the eyes of historians and critics."

A third section of the volume provides a separate list of 46 "Significant Architects About Whom Little Has Been Written." The entries in this section include the biographical information noted above, when available, but contain very few bibliographical references.

The General Index (p.279–330) includes entries for individual architects, major partnerships, authors and titles of books listed in the bibliography sections, and subject areas of particular interest to the study of architecture. Journal articles in the bibliographies are indexed only by author, although this is not mentioned in the explanatory note which precedes the Index. Nor does the note point out that Index references to the general reference works in section 1 are to page numbers whereas references to the other sections of the volume are to entry numbers.

American Architects from the Civil War to the First World War is valuable not only as a guide to the literature on American architects of the period but also for the factual information included in the biographical sketches and annotations. It is serviceable both as a bibliography and a reference source.

(Apr. 15, 1977, p.1295)

016.72'092 Architecture—U.S.—Bibliography || Architecture, Modern—19th century—U.S.—Bibliography || Architecture, Modern—20th century—U.S.—Bibliography || Architects—U.S.—Bibliography [CIP]   73-17525

American book prices current, 1975,
v.81. the auction season September 1974–August 1975. [Edited by Katharine Kyes Leab and Daniel J. Leab]. New York, Bancroft-Parkman, Inc., 1976 [c1976]. xxvii, 1188p. 22cm. casebound $53.50; standing order & prepublication $44.15.

This volume of *ABPC* lists 29,000 entries from more than 180 sales at 14 leading auction houses in London, Paris, Utrecht, Montreal, New York, Philadelphia, Chicago, San Francisco, and Los Angeles. Items which sold for $20 or more are included, but the number of books in non-Western languages which brought less than $100 has been reduced to save space. Incomplete sets of books and runs of periodicals are usually not listed.

As in previous volumes, materials are divided into two types. Part I includes books, broadsides, maps, and charts; Part II (Autographs and Manuscripts) covers original illustrations for printed books, documents, letters, typescripts, corrected proofs, signed photos and signatures, as well as manuscripts.

The editors of *American Book Prices Current* state that "every listing of printed material has been checked as to title, format, date of publication, edition, and limitations." This is an essential set for any library whose users need accurate information on locating, evaluating, and buying and selling old and rare books.   *(Dec. 1, 1976, p.562)*

†018'3 Books—Prices || Autographs—Prices || Manuscripts—Prices

The American clock:
a comprehensive pictorial survey 1723–1900, with a listing of 6153 clockmakers. By William H. Distin and Robert Bishop. New York, Dutton, 1976. 359p. illus. 29cm. cloth $27.50.

The American Clock was written to "serve as a basic reference work for clock collectors at all levels ... it has not been the authors' intent to produce a history of clockmaking in America.... Instead ... collectors will have in this volume a substantial pictorial reference with which to compare the clocks already in their collections or to check the points of a clock to be acquired."

The compiler, William H. Distin, is the administrative assistant to the president of the Henry Ford Museum at Greenfield Village in Dearborn, Michigan, and former curator of the clocks and watches at the museum. He is also a Fellow and former director of the National Association of Watch and Clock Collectors. Robert Bishop, originator and designer of the book, is museum editor in charge of publications at Greenfield Village and the Henry Ford Museum and associate editor of *Antique Monthly*. He has written and coauthored several other books on American antiques.

The Introduction briefly discusses American clock collecting and describes the ways collectors can make use of this book. Ten major sections—nine covering the general types of clocks and one showing clockmaking tools—follow. These sections consist of short introductory passages followed by numbered photographic plates arranged chronologically, 694 in black and white and 84 in color.

The caption of each illustration gives information on the clock's general type, kind of movement, maker, location of maker, approximate date of completion, and height. Several closeups of dials and movements are included. "The majority of the clocks shown ... are published here for the first time. They are fine examples from private or little-known public collections throughout the country."

The ten major sections are followed by a 64-page List of Clockmakers, a Glossary, a Selected Bibliography, and an Index. The list of 6,153 clockmakers provides location and dates of activity for each craftsperson. In some cases, birth and death dates and other identifying information are given. The Bibliography lists 40 titles, 10 published between 1970 and 1975. The Index lists makers whose clocks are illustrated. Clocks, plate numbers, and page numbers are arranged under the maker's name.

The white paper is of adequate quality and is coated on the color pages. The photographic layout is varied, with one to five illustrations of varying sizes per page. Rebinding could be difficult due to narrow inner margins with some illustrations bleeding into the center seam, but the binding seems sturdy.

The American Clock is an attractive and useful volume which will be of value both to individuals and to libraries with patrons interested in antiques.   *(July 15, 1977, p.1753)*

†681.113'03 Clocks and watches—U.S.—Dictionaries || Clock and watch makers—U.S.
76-20201

American drama criticism supplement II.
Compiled by Floyd Eugene Eddleman. Hamden, Conn., The Shoe String Pr., Inc., [1976]. 217p. 23cm. cloth, $9.

The parent volume of *American Drama Criticism* covering the period from the first play produced in America up to 1965 was written by Helen H. Palmer and Anne Jane Dyson and published in 1967 by Shoe String. It included references to book materials and periodical articles, was arranged by playwright, and contained title and playwright indexes. Palmer and Dyson's first supplement in 1970 added critical commentary appearing up to that year. The volume under review follows the format of its predecessors, updates the bibliography to January 1975, and lists more articles about plays in drama group, high school, college, and dinner theater repertories, more plays by women, blacks, and authors better known for other genres; more off-Broadway plays, and a few plays by Canadian and Caribbean playwrights. Two indexes facilitate locating specific information: an Index of Titles and an Index of Authors with birth and death dates noted where available. The Reference and Subscription Books Review Committee is plesed to note that *American Drama Criticism* has broadened its scope, thereby making it more useful to high school, college, and public libraries and their clientele. *(Nov. 1, 1976, p.423)*

†016.792′0973 American drama—History and criticism—Bibliography ‖ Theater—U.S.—Bibliography   [CIP]   67-16009

American literary scholarship: an annual, 1973.
Edited by James Woodress. Durham, North Carolina, Duke Univ. Pr., 1975. 490p. 23cm. cloth $13.50.

†016.81 American literature—Bibliography   65-19450

American literary scholarship: an annual, 1974.
Edited by James Woodress. Durham, North Carolina, Duke Univ. Pr., 1976. 492p. 23cm. cloth $14.75.

016.81 American literature—Bibliography   65-19450

American Literary Scholarship (ALS), written for scholars, students, and general readers, offers a systematic evaluative guide to current published studies of American literature. These bibliographical essays are selective and critical. The scholars who have contributed to the series describe and evaluate published works, identify trends in scholarship, and indicate areas ripe for research. The identified books, periodicals, and dissertations are drawn from 247 journals in the 1974 annual as compared to 164 journals in the initial 1963 edition. In 1973, after a five-year absence, James Woodress resumed editorship of this series. Woodress, professor of English at the University of California at Davis is perhaps best known for his work, *Eight American Authors.* Other noted American literary scholars such as Bernice Slote, Richard Ludwig, Hamlin Hall, and John T. Flanagan have joined him in the preparation of these essays. There have been several changes in these recent volumes: in the 1973 edition there appears a new section, "Foreign Contributions," in which French, Italian, German, Scandinavian, and Japanese critics summarize the year's European and Japanese criticism of American literature; Poe has been moved to a separate chapter, and T. S. Eliot is placed in the chapter on American poetry, 1900–1930s. In the 1974 edition a chapter is devoted to Eliot and Pound; twentieth-century fiction is considered in three rather than two segments; and minor nineteenth-century poets have been transferred to a nineteenth-century general literature chapter.

The volumes in recent years have become more compact, with a change of emphasis from the merely American to the literary. These latest editions continue to be helpful tools in the fine tradition established by Woodress.   *(Jan. 1, 1977, p.684)*

American music 1698–1800:
an annotated bibliography. [Compiled by] Priscilla S. Heard. Waco, Texas, Markham Press Fund, Baylor Univ. Pr., [c1975]. vi, 246p. 24cm. cloth $30; to libraries, $24.

American Music 1698–1800 was prepared as a thesis for the School of Music of Baylor University; whether it has been changed in any way for book publication is not indicated.

The first chapter is devoted to a discussion of Charles Evans and the *American Bibliography,* its various predecessors and descendants, revisions, continuations, strengths, and weaknesses. A second, four-page chapter ("A Survey of American Music Bibliography") is "devoted to a survey of American musical bibliography selected from *American Bibliography* and *Early American Imprints."* Information regarding inclusion policy, format, and arrangement, all of it vital to the effective use of the bibliography, is buried within this chapter.

The bibliography itself is in three sections: (1) entries including musical notation; (2) entries related to music but containing no notation; (3) items which have never been located. The chronological order of the Evans bibliography has been retained, with the later items identified by the American Antiquarian Society inserted chronologically and then alphabetically according to Evans' plan. Each entry carries the Evans number, starred if the document is available in *Early American Imprints,* bibliographic description, and annotation. Annotations range from one brief line to nearly a page, though most of them are four to five lines long.

There is a Table of Abbreviations of sources cited in the annotations and a three-page Bibliography of books consulted.

A 22-page Index of names and titles concludes the work. Since some of the names are not authors but appear in an annotation, the full page must occasionally be scanned to locate the desired entry.

The volume is well bound; the paper is opaque and of good quality, type is clear, and the bibliographic entries are easily seen on the page.

Obviously, this is a very specialized work, and its principal value will be to music libraries and large research-oriented collections. Libraries holding the *Early American Imprints* microprints may wish to add this as a supplementary access tool.
(Mar. 1, 1977, p.1038)

016.7817′73 Music—U.S.—Bibliography ‖ U.S.—Imprints [OCLC]   75-14907MN

American picturebooks
from Noah's ark to the beast within.
By Barbara Bader. New York, Macmillan Pub. Co., Inc., London, Collier Macmillan Publishers, [1976]. 615p. 28cm. cloth $45.

The author states, "The subject of this book is the development of picturebooks. It is not about prize winners or best sellers, although books of both sorts are included. Rather it is based upon an attempt to identify all the picturebooks published; to examine as many as possible; and, in certain instances, to learn of the circumstances of their publication."

Barbara Bader brings to this study a strong background in the publishing field and in the area of critical reviewing. She writes with conviction and insight about authors, illustrators, the content of picture books, the history of their development, and the setting of trends.

Excellently reproduced illustrations from picture books abound—130 of the 700 are in color—and are interspersed throughout the double-column text. The format is pleasing.

There is a wealth of material in this book not available in other publications. However, its lack of consistent organization makes a straightway reading of the book an erratic experience. The table of contents reveals this as it meanders from types of books to individual authors and illustrators to trends without any discernible continuity.

Even though the cutoff date was probably the early part of the 1970s, many important people prior to that time are left out: Anglund, Berenstain, Bonsall, Briggs, Bright, Burningham, Goodall, Hogrogian, Lobel (Arnold), Montresor, Ness, Piatti, Titus, Turkle, and Wildsmith. Because of this, one misses discussion of some significant picture books, such as *A Friend Is Someone Who Likes You, Georgie, The Adventures of Paddy Pork, Anatole,* and *Obadiah the Bold.*

A number of books which are really not picture books are discussed at length. The material on information books, a distinctly different type of literature from picture books, seems out of place. Some of the titles mentioned are for older children than the picture book age group. The Holling books are one example. Also, the coverage of Mother Goose editions is very inadequate, included only quite casually in the pages concerning Rojankovsky. A full chapter on Mother Goose would have been preferable to the inclusion of information books.

The book weighs almost five pounds and is uncomfortable to hold and read for any length of time. Editorial pruning could have made a smaller book, because less detail about many of the books would have sufficed.

The research which went into this book is impressive as evidenced in the Notes and Bibliography which are appended and which will be very helpful to anyone wishing to do further study.

Colleges and large public libraries will find this publication a source for authoritative insight and new information as well as a gold mine of quotation for papers and talks.
(Mar. 1, 1977, p.1038)
741.6'42 Illustrated books, Children's—History and criticism || Illustrators, American || Picture books for children || Children's literature, American—History and criticism   [CIP] 72-93304

American-Southern African relations:
bibliographic essays. Ed. by Mohamed A. El-Khawas [and] Francis A. Kornegay, Jr. Westport, Conn., Greenwood Pr., [c1975]. xvii, 188p. (African Bibliographic Center. Special Bibliographic Series, New Series, no. 1). 22cm. cloth $11.95.
The American Bibliographic Center in Washington, D.C., has been preparing special bibliographic guides on African culture and history for ten years. The bibliography under review is the first in a new special series, the next two books of which will be concerned with Ethiopia and Somalia and will be compiled by nationals of the two countries. The *American-Southern African Relations Bibliographic Essays* is edited by professors of African history at Federal City College, Washington, D.C. They have used the broad experience of the Bibliographic Center's staff in compiling the book. The bibliography is an attempt to satisfy the demand begun in the 1960s for source materials on southern Africa. The bibliography is in the form of six summary essays, each of which is related to a specific facet of southern African-U.S. relations and to which extensive bibliographies of works in English are appended.

Titles of the essays are "American Involvement in Angola and Mozambique" by Mohamed A. El-Khawas, "A Short Bibliographic Essay on U.S. Policy toward Southern Rhodesia (Zimbabwe)" by Sulayman Nyang, "Namibia" by Barbara Rogers, "United States Investments in Southern Africa" by Tami Hultman and Reed Kramer, and "Black America and U.S.-Southern African Relations" and "Conclusion" by Francis A. Kornegay, Jr. All of the contributors have written extensively in periodicals on Africa. Hultman and Kramer are correspondents for the Durham, North Carolina, *Africa News*. The others are regular contributors to the Bibliographic Center's quarterly *Current Bibliography on African Affairs*. Barbara Rogers works with the United Nations FAO/Action for Development Programs for Assistance to Liberation Movements, and Dr. Sulayman Nyang is a Gambian who left the directorship of African Studies and Research at Howard University in 1975 to accept a diplomatic post in Saudi Arabia. The essays vary in length from the 9-page conclusion to the 41-page treatment of "Black America and U.S.-Southern African Relations." Information is given in the form of historical surveys which rely heavily on the literature of the 1950s, 1960s, and 1970s to support the views being espoused. A wide range of sources is cited from books, newspapers, and journals to congressional testimony and mimeographed position papers from oil companies.

The book has been reproduced from photographed copy, which is well designed for ease of use. The inner margins will permit rebinding. As a much-needed assessment of sources of information on U.S. and South African relations, *American-Southern African Relations* will be welcomed by colleges and universities concentrating on black studies and by scholars and researchers in the field of South African politics and relations.
(Sept. 1, 1976, p.51)
016.32773'068 Africa, Southern—Relations (general) with the U.S.—Bibliography || U.S.—Relations (general) with Southern Africa—Bibliography || Africa, Southern—Relations (general) with the U.S.—Addresses, essays, lectures || U.S.—Relations (general) with Southern Africa—Addresses, essays, lectures   [CIP]   75-25331

American women and the labor movement, 1825–1974:
an annotated bibliography. By Martha Jane Soltow and Mary K. Wery. Metuchen, N.J., Scarecrow, [c1976]. viii, 247p. 22cm. cloth $8.
American Women and the Labor Movement is a revised edition of the author's *Women in American Labor History, 1825–1935: An Annotated Bibliography,* published in 1972. Soltow is librarian in the Labor and Industrial Relations Library of Michigan State University, and Wery was a student reference assistant there when she worked on this bibliography.

The earlier book focused on general employment problems of women, but in this volume more emphasis is placed on women as labor-union members. This volume lists 726 numbered items, 268 more than in the previous edition. Books, monographs, journal articles, pamphlets, and U.S. government documents are included, but dissertations and state government documents are not. The material is divided into eight subject categories which are the chapter headings: Employment, Trade Unions, Working Conditions, Strikes, Legislation, Worker Education, Labor Leaders, and Supportive Efforts, such as the National Women's Trade Union League. Some of these categories are further subdivided by topic. Within each division all materials are listed alphabetically by author. Full bibliographic citations are provided. Most of the entries are followed by descriptive annotations ranging in length from a short phrase to three or four paragraphs.

Appendix 1 is a list of 48 women and 21 organizations. Each is accompanied by one or more references to archival collections in the U.S. which contain material about them. There are three indexes. The first is a brief Cross Reference Index, arranged by the chapter headings, with citations to related entries by item number. The second is a rather shallow Subject Index, and the third is an Author Index.

The volume is sturdily bound; the type size is good, margins are wide, and the space between the items is ample.

Because of the concise but informative annotations, this bibliography could be helpful even in libraries owning few of its items. It will be welcomed whenever material is needed on the history of women and of the labor movement in the U.S.
(July 1, 1977, p.1672)
016.3314'0973 Women in trade unions—U.S.—Bibliography || Women—Employment—U.S.—Bibliography   [CIP]   76-40169

Anniversaries and holidays.
By Ruth W. Gregory. 3d. ed. Chicago, American Library Association 1975. xv, 246p. 26cm. cloth $10.50.
Anniversaries and Holidays was originally published by the American Library Association in 1928. A second expanded edition came out in 1944, and now the long-awaited third edition which is a complete updating and enlargement of the previous one is off the press. The intent of the current edition is the same as it was in the in the older editions: "to identify the significant days that are celebrated by the nations of the world or recognized in some way by people with common backgrounds or mutual interests." It is international in scope and has been planned as a resource tool to be used by libraries, teachers, writers, and individuals interested in the history of holidays. The new edition contains 2,736 entries as compared with 1,764 in the second edition. More than 150 countries are represented.

Anniversaries and Holidays retains the tripartite arrangement of the second edition: part one, a chronological calendar of fixed dates; part two, five calendars of movable days (Christian, Islamic, Jewish, and Eastern and Western world calendars); and part three, a six-part Bibliography of books related to anniversaries and holidays (sourcebooks and background material; religious days; international celebrations, ceremonials, and festivals; anniversaries, holidays, and special events days; planning and preparing for anniversaries and holidays; and books about persons related to the calendar). A fairly comprehensive Index of authors and subjects facilitates locating specific information. School and public library reference collections will want to replace their old editions of *Anniversaries and Holidays* with the updated, comprehensive third edition. *(Nov. 15, 1976, p.497)*
394.2'6 Holidays || Anniversaries || Holidays—Bibliography || Anniversaries—Bibliography   [CIP]   75-23163

Annual bibliography of British and Irish history.

Publications of 1975. General editor, G. R. Elton. Atlantic Highlands, N.J. Published for the Royal Historical Society by The Harvester Press, Ltd., Sussex, England, and in the U.S. by Humanities Press, [1976]. ix, 155p. 22cm. cloth $14.75; to schools and libraries, 10 percent discount.

This new annual bibliography covers the history of England, Scotland, Wales, and Ireland. Prepared by the Cambridge historian G. R. Elton with the assistance of 11 experts in the field, it contains about 2,000 scholarly books, articles, and official publications appearing in 1975. It is arranged under 13 sections covering bibliography, archives, reference, and historiography; general works; Roman Britain; England 450–1066; England 1066–1500; England and Wales in the sixteenth and seventeenth centuries; eighteenth-century Britain; nineteenth-century Britain; twentieth-century Great Britain; Medieval Wales; Scotland before the Union; Ireland to c1640; and Ireland since 1640. Each section is divided into topically defined subsections, e.g., politics, religion, intellectual and cultural affairs.

The publications are chiefly British except for sections on Ireland and Scotland, where a number of Irish and a few Scottish titles are found. Only a few were published in 1974 as the aim was to be as up-to-date as possible, though provision has been made for picking up omissions and oversights in subsequent volumes.

The bibliography is distinguished not only for its sound editing but for its bibliographical consistency and generous use of *see-also* references. Pieces in collective works are indexed separately and an item number Index to authors and editors is appended. The separate subject Index, containing both broad and highly specific entries, must be used with the table of contents since "items are entered under categorical headings that correspond to the divisions of the list only if they occur in some section other than that in which one would expect to find such categories listed."

This series will provide a useful annual supplement to the *Bibliography of British History,* published earlier under the direction of the American Historical Association and the Royal Historical Society. It should also have the advantage of being more current than the annual *Writings on British History,* published irregularly. It will be a valuable addition to American academic libraries. *(May 15, 1977, p.1449)*

†016.942   Gt. Brit.—History—Bibliography || Ireland—History—Bibliography   [OCLC]

Annual index to popular music record reviews 1974.

By Andrew D. Armitage and Dean Tudor. Metuchen, N.J., The Scarecrow Pr., Inc., 1976. xix, 597p. 22cm. cloth, $20.

The 1974 edition of this annual index retains the same format as its two predecessors including the 1973 *Index* which was reviewed and commended by the Reference and Subscription Books Review Committee July 15, 1975. In the 1974 *Index,* 14,214 reviews of 5,158 long-playing discs appearing in 61 magazines are represented. Periodicals analyzed for the first time in 1974 are *Black Music, Canadian Composer, Flipside, Listening Post, New Musical Express,* and *Shout.* The 13 sections are arranged by genre, e.g., *rock, mood-pop, folk, jazz, rhythm and blues, popular religious,* and *stage and film.* A discographic essay summarizing the events and listing best recordings of the year, as indicated by the reviews, precedes each section.

The book is well organized for ease of use, includes a Directory of Record Labels, and contains adequate finding devices. The 1974 *Annual Index to Popular Record Reviews* is a handy ready reference for homes and libraries. *(Nov. 1, 1976, p.423)*

†016.789913   Phonorecords—Reviews—Indexes   73-8909

Antebellum black newspapers:

indices to *New York Freedom's Journal,* (1827–1829); *The Rights of All* (1829); *The Weekly Advocate* (1837); and *The Colored American* (1837–1841). Edited by Donald M. Jacobs; assisted by Heath Paley, Susan Parker, and Dana Silverman. Westport, Conn., London, Greenwood Pr., [1976]. 587p. 24cm. cloth $35.

Newspapers have emerged as a reliable reflection of contemporary life, especially valuable when other sources of information are difficult to come by or are nonexistent. Using newspapers to reveal and document facts however, is often time-consuming. This was confirmed by Donald M. Jacobs as he searched for information relating to the subject for his doctoral dissertation. To resolve his frustration he produced separate subject indexes to *Freedom's Journal* (1827–1829), *The Rights of All* (1829), *The Weekly Advocate* (1837), and *The Colored American* (1837–1841). All four of these antebellum black newspapers were published in New York City. Appearing in chronological order, *Freedom's Journey* index is 154 pages long, while *The Rights of All* and *The Weekly Advocate* take up about 40 and 18 pages, respectively. *The Colored American,* published for more than four-and-one-half years, accounts for the most space, about 350 pages.

Topic headings in each index are listed alphabetically with specific items of reportage grouped in chronological order of their appearance in the newspaper. Date, page, and column are indicated. Even advertisements are included. There are numerous cross-references throughout as an aid to location of specific subject matter. The indexes are particularly helpful in expediting location of evidence regarding the numerous organizations which existed during the period covered.

There is little doubt that researchers in black history, especially those seeking documentation of happenings during the years 1827 to 1841, will find this volume useful.

(Dec. 1, 1976, p.562)

016.071'47'1   Afro-American newspapers—New York (City)—Indexes   [CIP]   76-2119

Artillery of the world.

rev. ed. [By] Christopher F. Foss. New York, Scribner, 1976. 202p. illus. 24cm. cloth $7.95.

623.41   Artillery   [OCLC]   76-6642

Helicopters of the world.

[By] Michael J. H. Taylor and John W. R. Taylor. New York, Scribner, [c1976]. 128p. illus. 22cm. cloth $7.95.

629.133'35   Helicopters   [OCLC]   76-318634

Military vehicles of the world.

[By] Christopher F. Foss. New York, Scribner, [1975? 1976?]. 192p. illus. 23cm. cloth $7.95.

†623.74   Vehicles, Military   75-46380

Missiles of the world.

rev. ed. [By] Michael J. H. Taylor and John W. R. Taylor. New York, Scribner, [c1976]. 159p. illus. 23cm. cloth $7.95.

358.17   Guided missiles   [OCLC]   76-9557

Artillery of the World, Helicopters of the World, Military Vehicles of the World, and *Missiles of the World* are companion volumes in the Scribner series which also includes *Armoured Fighting Vehicles of the World, Military Aircraft of the World,* and *Civil Aircraft of the World.* Christopher Foss wrote the artillery (first ed., 1974), military vehicles, and fighting vehicles books; J. H. Taylor and John W. R. Taylor wrote the helicopters and missiles (first ed., 1972) volumes. The series was first published in Great Britain.

Artillery of the World describes towed artillery and fire-control equipment of 18 nations of the world including Communist China, Japan, the Soviet Union, Great Britain, and the U.S. Except for South Africa and India whose extremely brief coverage appears at the end of the lists, countries are arranged alphabetically. Each piece of artillery is described individually, and the volume cites insofar as it is applicable: caliber, weight, width and height, barrel length, elevation, rate of fire, type of feed, ammunition, crew, and towing vehicle. Two hundred of the vehicles are illustrated with black-and-white photographs.

Artillery rockets, Soviet multirocket launchers, U.S. and Soviet self-propelled guns, self-propelled anti-aircraft vehicles, and artillery fire control systems are discussed separately. An 18-item bibliography of current German and English books and journal articles will aid the reader who requires further information. An Index divided into five sections listing equipment, guns, mortars, multiple rocket systems, and vehicles will aid those who know the names and numbers (128mm MRS M-63) of artillery.

Helicopters of the World claims to describe and illustrate "all significant helicopters and rotorcrafts under development, in production and in service throughout the world." Because the author provides neither an explanation of the book's organization nor a table of contents, the only way to discover the book's two-part arrangement is by using it. The larger of the two is an 80-page, alphabetical-by-name-of-helicopter, illustrated discussion of the aircraft. Each craft is identified by country of manufacture. A general description (general purpose, commercial, military, utility, anti-submarine, flying crane, research) is followed by information on power, diameter of rotor, length, empty and gross weight, maximum speed, range, accommodation, and armament. A brief historical description places each craft in perspective with the others.

The second part gives brief illustrated descriptions of 23 autogyros. The Index at the end of the book refers to aircraft by name and cites pages in the book without indicating illustrations.

In *Military Vehicles of the World* Christopher Foss covers a large number of cargo-carrying vehicles used in front-line service by the armies of 23 nations. A brief note on China appears at the end of the alphabetical-by-country arrangement. Military vehicles include trucks, tractors, reconnaissance and recovery vehicles, load and cargo carriers, and jeeps. Specifications for each vehicle are listed: length, width and height, wheelbase, weight, clearance, engine, crew, speed and range, fuel capacity, and tire size. A summary description completes the coverage for each vehicle. The Index at the end identifies machines by name and cites the pages on which they are illustrated and described.

In *Missiles of the World* the user's access to information is aided by the alphabetical arrangement of missiles and an Index. The book claims to cover all Soviet and U.S. intercontinental and submarine-launched ballistic missiles as well as those of Israel, France, Sweden, the United Kingdom, Brazil, Germany, China, Italy, Switzerland, and other nations. Data provided for each missile include a general description, identification of country of origin, name of prime contractor, method of power guidance and control, type of airframe and warhead, length, and range. Development and service are summarized for each missile.

Scribner's quartet of handy little books on artillery, helicopters, military vehicles, and missiles provides current descriptions and illustrations that will be useful to both amateur hobbyists and professionals. High school, public, and military institute libraries will find them inexpensive, worthwhile references.

(July 1, 1977, p.1672)

Asimov's biographical encyclopedia of science and technology:
the lives and the achievements of 1195 great scientists from ancient times to the present chronologically arranged. By Isaac Asimov. New rev. ed. New York, Avon Books, [1976]. 805p. 20cm. paper, $5.95.

Avon Books informs the Committee that the current edition of *Asimov's Biographical Encyclopedia of Science and Technology* is a reprint of the Doubleday book first published in 1972. The book is commendable for its broad coverage of scientists. Public and school libraries will find the paperback edition useful.

(Nov. 1, 1976, p.423)

†509.2 Scientists—Biography

Bibliography of American ethnology.
Marc Cashman, editor; Barry Klein, research editor. 1st ed. Rye, N.Y., Todd Publications, [c1976]. viii, 304p. 26cm. cloth $17.50.

The *Bibliography of American Ethnology* is a partially annotated bibliography of some 4,500 in-print books concerned with American ethnology. The term "American" as used in the book seems restricted to the U.S. The Bibliography is organized into four categories: "General Ethnology" (26 pages with 16 subdivisions), "American Indians" (75 pages with 23 subdivisions for general topics and 68 subdivisions for specific and miscellaneous tribes), "Black Americans" (115 pages with 49 subheadings), and "Other Minorities" (57 pages with 39 subdivisions). There is also an 8-page list of books "received too late for classification." While the book carries no indication of scope, purpose, or audience, the use of an asterisk to indicate books appropriate for readers below the college level and approximate age-level suggestions for such works indicates that the book is intended for use by a wide range of readers. Promotional material from the publisher also advertises the book as comprehensive.

The Reference and Subscription Books Review Committee's examination of the *Bibliography of American Ethnology* leads the Committee to doubt the comprehensiveness of the work and even more importantly to question the balance of treatment, the subject headings chosen as appropriate for classifying the books, and the authority of the editors. There are also various kinds of typographical errors. While the publisher identifies the editor, Marc Cashman, as one who "maintains a graduate degree in education and with experience in free-lance editing" and research editor, Barry Klein as publisher and editor of *Reference Encyclopedia of the American Indian* and the *Reference Encyclopedia of American Psychology and Psychiatry,* it seems that neither Klein nor Cashman has qualifications as an authority in ethnology. This weakness is evident throughout the book. For example, among "Other Minorities," Mexican-Americans and Puerto Ricans are listed but not Cubans, Spanish-Americans, or Latin Americans. The subject headings chosen for black Americans are not consistent, and there are no cross-references to related subjects. There is no reference from *Activism* to *Black Power* or *Nationalism* and none from *Youth* to *Child Welfare* or vice versa. There is a heading for *Antebellum* (presumably pre-Civil War) but none for Civil War, postbellum or the Reconstruction. The listing of in-print autobiographies is meager (only 15, and 5 of these are for Booker T. Washington.) *Raw Pearl,* by Pearl Bailey; *No Name in the Street,* by James Baldwin; and *Yes, I Can* by Sammy Davis, Jr., are among those omitted. *The American Negro Reference Book* (Prentice-Hall, 1966) and also its latest revision, *The Black American Reference Book* (Prentice-Hall, 1976), are both listed, the 1966 book without annotation or reference to the new title. Incidentally, the price, number of pages, and publication year are all cited inaccurately for the new edition. The *Ebony Handbook, Negro Almanac,* and *The World Encyclopedia of Black Peoples* are omitted from the list of reference books on blacks. Lerone Bennett's *Black Power: The Human Side of the Reconstruction, 1867 to 1877* is listed with the books referring to the phrase coined by Stokely Carmichael in 1966. James Haskins' *Witchcraft, Mysticism and Magic in the Black World* is listed under *Culture* rather than *Religion. Malcolm X,* with 10 books listed, is the only individual among the blacks accorded a separate subject heading, while there were others like Martin Luther King, Jr. (with 31 books about him in print in 1975) subsumed under the Biographies heading.

The editors note that "annotations have been provided whenever possible," but there is no explanation of what caused them not to annotate all the books, particularly since they are in print. Some pages have as many as 10 out of 17 books without annotations. When provided, the annotations are generally one- or two-sentence descriptions which do not evaluate the books or attempt to place them in the literature of the subject.

The arrangement of the book under title does not provide easy access to all the information. There are no author or title indexes. This means that the reader is entirely dependent on the editors' subject classifications as being appropriate. Further, there are no cross-references between topics. The running headings in boldface at the top of each page are disconcerting because they list every topic on the page, e.g., Navajo; Nez Perce; Ojibwa, Omaha; American Indians. Except for topics which carry over from previous pages, this is unnecessary because new subjects are prominently centered in boldface, and there is an excessive amount of white space around them.

Admittedly, there is a grave need in the U.S. for a bibliography of books and other materials on ethnic groups like American Indians and blacks, but the *Bibliography of American Ethnology* is not the reliable, authoritative, well-balanced assessment that either scholars or general readers can depend on.

(Sept. 1, 1976, p.52)

016.973'04   Minorities—U.S.—Bibliography || Afro-Americans—Bibliography || Indians of North America—Bibliography   [OCLC]   75-44645

A biographical dictionary of film.
[By] David Thomson. New York, William Morrow and Co., Inc., 1976. ix, 629p. 24cm. cloth and board $16.95.

First published in Great Britain in 1975 as *A Biographical Dictionary of the Cinema,* the title *A Biographical Dictionary of Film* is a misnomer, for the volume concentrates exclusively on directors, producers, actors, and actresses. There are no entries for composers, cinematographers, costume designers, set decorators, and the other important supportive talents one would expect to find in a more comprehensive work. The author, David Thomson, admits that he has prepared "a Personal, Opinionated, and Obsessive Biographical Dictionary of the Cinema" and his partisan perspective permeates each of over 800 entries, which range in length from 250 to 2,000 words. Forewarning his readers, Thomson says that "within nearly every entry there are things that may be startling in a biographical dictionary: the sharp expression of personal taste; jokes; disgressions; insults and eulogies." If he likes an individual, the result can be a glowing paean, as per Robert Mitchum (". . . one of the best actors in the movies") or director Nicholas Ray (". . . one comes away from his work moved by the spectacle of human nature that he has revealed"). On the other hand, a splendid bitchiness pervades the entry for any personality disliked by the author; e.g., Bette Davis (". . . a vulgar, bullying actress, who has made mannerism a virtue by showing us how it expresses the emotion of the self") or Errol Flynn (". . . he was an ineffectual, irritable drunk with brittle bones") or, particularly, director John Ford ("Sheer longevity made Ford a major director. . . . No one has done so much to invalidate the Western as a form"). Because of the author's outrageous presumption, the book is highly entertaining and for the most part its venom is leavened by much astute and honest criticism.

All articles provide subjects' names and places and dates of birth. The entries for directors commence with complete chronological lists of their films; those for actors usually cite films in which they participated in the body of the text with comments, while articles on producers either integrate their films within the text or list them at the end of the entry. Cross-references are used occasionally, (*see* Ginger Rogers) follows the Fred Astaire biography, but not vice versa and some individuals rate brief bibliographies. Animated and underground films are not considered. The predominant audience at which the book is directed is English-speaking, so that original foreign-language film titles have English translations next to them in directors' filmographies. However, when these same films are discussed under an actor/actress, only English translations are used.

The author explains the lack of an index: "Under actors, actresses, and producers, films are given their date and director, so that there is no need to look up anything at the back of the book. Indeed, there is nothing at the back." Some of the inclusions (Debra Paget, Will Rogers, director Mario Bava), are as curious as the exclusions, (e.g., Shirley Booth, Kim Stanley, and epic producer Samuel Bronston), but, on the whole, film buffs and other students of the cinema who are interested in provocative and perceptive film criticism will find the book most stimulating.

(Jan. 1, 1977, p.684)

791.43'092 (B)   Moving-pictures—Biography—Dictionaries   [CIP]   75-20044

Biographical dictionary of the federal judiciary.
Compiled by Harold Chase, Samuel Krislov, Keith O. Boyum, and Jerry N. Clark. Detroit, Gale Research Co., [c1976]. xxvi, 381p. 29cm. cloth $38.

Biographical Dictionary of the Federal Judiciary brings together in one collection data on the professional lives of presidentially appointed federal judges with lifetime tenure. Excluded are federal judges who serve for fixed terms. The following courts are represented: the Supreme Court, 1789–1974; the U.S. Courts of Appeals, 1891–1974; the U.S. Circuit Courts, 1789–1911; the U.S. District Courts, 1789–1974; the U.S. Court of Claims, 1855–1974; the U.S. Court of Customs and Patent Appeals, 1909–74; the U.S. Customs Court, 1926–74; the Commerce Court (now defunct), 1910–13; and the Supreme Court for the District of Columbia (now the U.S. District Court for the District of Columbia), 1863–1936.

The compilers of the dictionary have the following qualifications: Harold Chase and Samuel Krislov are professors of political science at the University of Minnesota, Keith O. Boyum is assistant professor of political science, California State University at Fullerton, and Jerry N. Clark is research director, the Health and Retirement Funds, United Mine Workers of America.

By special arrangement with Marquis Who's Who, Inc., biographies previously published in *Who's Who in America* and *Who Was Who* have been printed in this dictionary. Where Marquis biographies were not available, biographies were developed from state historical society records and other sources. The biographies typically list place and date of birth, parents' names, degrees received, spouses, positions, publications, church membership, political party, home address, and death date.

Keith Boyum and Jerry Clark preface the dictionary with a 14-page interesting study, "Perspectives on Biographical Data on the Federal Judiciary," which discusses the significance of the judges' social and political backgrounds. Throughout the "Perspectives" are tables summarizing the religious and political preferences and occupations of federal judges between 1789 and 1971. The strength of the book lies in the tables and the Appendix.

The main body of the book contains biographies of judges appointed by presidents (from George Washington through Lyndon Johnson), arranged alphabetically by the judges' surnames. An Addendum includes biographies of 229 judges appointed by Richard Nixon. An Appendix alphabetically arranges judges according to appointing presidents Washington through Nixon. The arrangement of judges' names in two lists is awkward. Furthermore, the information given must be used with caution because a number of inconsistencies and inaccuracies have slipped in. On page 32 Henry Luesin was born in 1904; on page 324 he was born a year later in 1905. The first name in Burger's law firm is spelled in two different ways: "Farley" on page 36 and "Faricy" on page 324. Carswell has two different home addresses in the two sections.

The book is well bound and sewn to open flat; the print is clear; the text is in double columns with wide margins. This biographical dictionary is much easier to read than are the Marquis publications.

The clientele for this biographical directory is limited. It is intended for scholars of the judicial process, law, politics, and history, for lawyers, judges, journalists, and students interested in the careers of particular judges. Therefore, the *Biographical Dictionary of the Federal Judiciary* will be useful for law libraries and large academic, research, and public libraries.

(Apr. 15, 1977, p.1296)

347'.73 (B) Judges—U.S. [CIP]   76-18787

The birds of California.
By Arnold Small; with photographs by the author and maps by Robert Sandmeyer & Keith Axelson. New York, Collier Books, a division of Macmillan Pub. Co., [1975, c1974]. xxiv, 310p. 23cm. paper $4.95.

Originally published in hardcover by Winchester Press in 1974 at $12.50, this book has now been reprinted as a trade paperback on heavy paper stock so that the many illustrations retain much of their original effectiveness. However, a majority of the illustrations are bled to the margins so that in many instances the user must press down the pages to view a complete picture.

The author, a college professor, former vice-president of the American Birding Association and president of the Los Angeles Audubon Society, has prepared a manual for both the professional ornithologist and amateur bird-watchers. It supplements the basic text by Joseph Grinnell and Alden H. Miller, *The Distribution of Birds of California,* published in 1944, with more recent and fuller information on habitat and distribution.

About 90 percent of the book, the annotated list of 518 species (chapter 3), and extensive discussion of California's habitats for birds (chapter 4), is enhanced by over 300 black-and-white photographs of birds in their natural environment. Eleven maps show habitats and range throughout the state. The preliminary pages of the book contain a checklist arranged by order, family, and species, with a note on 7 new species added in 1974, bringing California's total to 525. The Index is arranged by common English and scientific name of birds. Page references to illustrations appear in bold-face, and italics refer the reader to specific annotations in chapter 3. Chapter 3, the annotated list, follows the same order as the prefatory checklist, giving seasonal status, habitat, range in California, nesting and breeding habits, and present population and sightings for rarer birds. The latter half of the book, chapter 4, describes the types of habitats: sea and seacoast; fresh-water, brushland, grassland, and savannah; woodlands, deserts, the Great Basin, mountains, forests, and man-made habitats of farms, cities, refuges, etc., including the Salton Sea. The birds to be seen in each area and their characteristics are noted. The text is very readable, meant for the amateur avi enthusiast and also of interest to the general naturalist. It is considered by many "birders" to be the best available field manual for California despite the lack of color illustrations.

(Dec. 15, 1976, p.629)

598.2 Birds—California [OCLC]   73-78829

Birdwatcher's guide to wildlife sanctuaries.
By Jessie Kitching. New York, Arco, 1976. xv, 233p. illus. 21cm. $8.95.

An enthusiastic birdwatcher, hiker, book reviewer, bibliographer, and editor of a newsletter, Jessie Kitching has gathered information on bird sanctuaries in the U.S. and Canada, augmenting her own knowledge with correspondence from refuge managers. Arranged by country and state or province are 296 national, local, and state parks, arboretums, public gardens, and other refuges. Of these, 264 are located in the U.S., 31 in Canada, and 1 in the Virgin Islands. Most of the major and some of the smaller sanctuaries are described.

The directory, which began as a critical survey of bird checklists, gives address, including some telephone numbers; directions for reaching the refuge; number of species sighted; rare, uncommon, or endangered birds; birds commonly seen; facilities and sports on the refuge; precautions to take (e.g., insect repellent); and checklists or other information available from a particular refuge. A very informative introduction includes brief suggestions for "an ideal year in bird refuges" itinerary. A few photographs of some of the spots and a very good detailed index complete this convenient field guide for travelling birdwatchers. It will also be useful in public libraries.

(May 15, 1977, p.1449)

917.3'04 Bird watching—U.S. || Bird watching—Canada || Wildlife refuges—U.S. || Wildlife refuges—Canada [CIP]   76-5388

The black American reference book.
Edited by Mabel M. Smythe. Englewood Cliffs, N.J., Prentice-Hall, [1976]. xxviii, 1026p. tables. charts. diagrs. 25cm. cloth $29.95.

According to its editor, *The Black American Reference Book* represents "in one volume a comprehensive view of the world of Black Americans: history, personality, pressures; social and economic status; political activities; involvement in and contribution to arts and letters; participation and treatment in the popular media, sports, and the armed forces; and other matters related to these categories." In 30 chapters, written by a distinguished group of scholars and writers, the book offers historical and current material on all important facets of the black experience in America.

Like its predecessor, *The American Negro Reference Book* (recommended by *Reference and Subscription Books Reviews* July 1, 1966), *The Black American Reference Book* has been sponsored by the Phelps-Stokes Fund, an agency created in 1911 to stimulate, support, and publish research on the African American. *The American Negro Reference Book* (Englewood Cliffs, N.J.: Prentice-Hall, 1965) contained 25 chapters with an arrangement of contents very similar to that of the work under discussion. In fact, materials in some of the chapters are identical (e.g., Prejudice: A Symposium; Black Influences in the American Theater: Part 1). Topics included in this volume which were not covered in the 1965 edition are "Black Personality in American Society," "Young Black Americans," "Blacks and American Foundations: Two Views," "Black Participation in U.S. Foreign Relations," and "The Popular Media."

The 38 authors of *The Black American Reference Book* are well-qualified and recognized experts in the fields in which they write. Editor Mabel M. Smythe is the vice president of the Phelps-Stokes Fund and an economist, author, and lecturer. She wrote the chapter on "The Role in the Economy" and coauthored with Joseph Douglass the chapter, "The Black Family."

A lengthy explanation with supporting data is given for the use of the term "black" throughout the volume instead of "Black," "Negro," "African-American," "Afro-American," or "colored." Also, an explanation is given for the use of sexually slanted terminology with regard to women contained in the book.

The chapters provide a multidimensional panorama of the black experience in this country. The first chapter, "A Brief History," is by the renowned historian John Hope Franklin. Subsequent chapters deal with blacks' legal status, the black personality, the black population in the United States, the black American worker, the black American in agriculture, the black family, the black woman, young black Americans, educating black Americans, the black professional, blacks and American foundations, Afro-American religion, prejudice, black protest in America, the black role in American politics, black participation in U.S. foreign relations, black Americans and Africa, black influences in the American theater, the black contribution to American letters, Afro-American music, Afro-American art, the popular media, black participation in the armed forces, and the black American in sports.

Fifteen of the chapters contain some form of graphic, either a figure or a table. These will be of value to the reader who is searching for ready-reference sources on specific areas of the black experience in America.

Although the language of *The Black American Reference Book* is consistently clear, the style ranges from popular to scholarly varying with individual authors and the subject content. All of the chapters include either notes or a bibliography, and the 62-page Index is comprehensive and accurate.

The book is attractively bound in cloth. The large, clear print makes for easy reading, and the book lies flat when opened.

The Black American Reference Book achieves its purpose of providing a comprehensive view of the world of black Americans. Though in some chapters it appears prescriptive instead of informative (e.g., "The mission of black newsmen") and though much of the material is duplicative of the 1965 edition, this volume is a useful resource tool. It is a valuable key to current and retrospective information on important phases of the black experience in America. *(July 1, 1977, p.1673)*
301.45'19'6073   Afro-Americans   [CIP]   75-26511

Black American writers past and present:
a bibliographical dictionary. By Teresa Gunnels Rush, Carol Fairbanks Myers and Esther Spring Arata. 2v. Metuchen, N.J., Scarecrow Pr. Inc., 1975. 865p. 22cm. cloth $30.

These two volumes present information on more than 2,000 black writers from the early eighteenth century to the present. *Black American Writers* includes writers of novels, dramas, poetry, short stories, literature for children and young adults, and literary criticism.

The compilers of the volumes, Teressa G. Rush, Carol F. Myers, and Esther S. Arata have been or currently are associated with the Department of English, University of Wisconsin-Eau Claire. Eugene B. Redmond who wrote the Introduction is professor of English and poet-in-residence in ethnic studies, California State University at Sacramento.

The authors of *Black American Writers* state that, "The principles determining the selection of writers have been modified to include (1) those writers of non-fiction whose works are studied in Black Literature courses, and whose works frequently appear in Black Literature anthologies, and (2) those writers from Africa and the West Indies who live and/or publish in the United States, and who also identify with Black American Writers."

Volume I includes writers whose surnames begin with *A-I*, and volume II those whose surnames begin with *J-Z*. A General Bibliography listing the references cited under the individual entries is located in the back of the second volume. Two appended lists, one of black and the other of white critics, historians, and editors, complete the work.

Most of the entries include one or two citations of poems, novels, plays, and other works. The most complete information is given for established or prolific creative figures such as Ralph Ellison, W. E. B. Du Bois, Phillis Wheatley, Imamu Amiri Baraka (Everett Le Roi Jones), Langston Hughes, and Paul Laurence Dunbar. Much less detail is provided for relatively obscure authors such as Carolyn Ogletree, Arthur Boze, William Mahoney, Ann Du Cille, Percy Johnston, and Adam Weber. Very few of the entries in *Black American Writers* include all four kinds of information included in the prefatory Note to Readers: (1) biographical summary, (2) bibliography of writer's works classified by form (e.g., novel, drama, poetry), (3) biographical treatments and criticism of the writer, and (4) interjections (quotations of or about the writer). Altogether, about 600 entries include brief biographical data, and approximately 160 are enhanced by interjections. Photographs are provided for 95 writers.

The inclusion of only the writer's name and a few works in most instances is not surprising when one considers the ambitious scale of the compilers' undertaking. The researcher who consults this source will find it a useful but by no means comprehensive reference tool.

Notwithstanding its lack of comprehensiveness, *Black American Writers* is a worthwhile resource for secondary school, public, and college and university libraries. It will also be welcomed by researchers in black studies. *(Oct. 1, 1976, p.279)*
016.8108'08   American literature—Negro authors—Bibliography   [CIP]   74-28400

Black Americans in aviation.
By Raymond Eugene Peters and Clinton M. Arnold. San Diego, Cal., Neyenesch Printers, Inc., [1975], distributed to the book trade by Aviation Book Co., 555 W. Glenoaks Blvd., Glendale, CA 91202. illus. 85p. 28cm. hardbound $9.95, paper $.95, to schools, 20 percent discount; to libraries, 15 percent discount.

The exploits of black aviators in World War II made the general public aware of their accomplishments. At this time the prejudice that had existed for many years in the flying industry was finally made plainly visible.

Only through perseverance had a sizeable number of blacks become involved with aspects of flying, either as service personnel or as private pilots. Only a few have been able to obtain high level positions in this field even to this day.

The authors of *Black Americans in Aviation* have told the whole sordid story of "the wall" which was seemingly erected early in the century to prevent blacks from entrance into aviation and of the few who hurdled the wall and laid the groundwork for later generations.

The initial section of this book is in four convenient chronological periods: 1903 to 1939; 1939 to 1950; 1950 to 1967; 1967 to 1974. Within this framework, the pioneers of the first period, some of whom learned their flying skills in other countries, are given all too brief coverage. The Civilian Pilot Training Program ushered in the second period which raised the hopes of many of the Air Force Veterans that there would be opportunities for them in the commercial arena. The third period describes the "closed doors," trend and decline of opportunities for blacks in the profession. The fourth period witnesses blacks' movement into key responsible positions as pilots and officers of commercial airlines. Individuals mentioned in this section are merely cited as participants in the struggle to eliminate discrimination and achieve just recognition. Reserved after section II are the biographical sketches of 95 black men and women who have become prominent in the aviation industry. The final section of the book contains listings of members and "Supporters of Negro Airman Activities, in the United States, Caribbean and Canada ... or who are licensed as private or commercial pilots ... or, who own or co-own/manage an airport based activity."

Black Americans in Aviation is profusely illustrated with black-and-white photographs of people and planes. Its Bibliography, however, provides incomplete descriptive data for the sources. In summary, the information in this book provides a convenient starting point for the high school or college student who wishes to investigate various phases of black participation in American aviation. *(Dec. 15, 1976, p.630)*
629.13   Afro-Americans in aeronautics   [OCLC]   76-354788

Black separatism:
a bibliography. [Compiled by Betty Lanier Jenkins & Susan Phillis, under the auspices of Metropolitan Applied Research

Center, Inc.] Westport, Conn., Greenwood Pr., [1976]. xxv, 163p. 22cm. cloth.

In 1969, a group of scholars gathered at Haverford College "to discuss the changing attitudes of the Negro intellectual." From this and following meetings of what became known as the Hastie Group, the idea for this bibliography of black separatism emerged. The aim of the compilers was to provide a selective bibliography of important writings which represent scholarly, journalistic, protest, and polemical points of view.

This valuable bibliography has been published under the auspices of the Metropolitan Applied Research Center (MARC). The "Historical Perspectives" and "The Twenty Years since *Brown*" chapters form the first section. The second section is intended to be functional and is divided into five chapters: "Identity: Individual and Collective;" "Education: Segregation and Desegregation;" "Politics: Coalitions and Alternatives;" "The Economic Order: Black Enterprise, Black Workers and Income;" and "Religion and Race: Church Structures and Redressing Inequities." Within each chapter the entries are listed by author. Books as well as articles and even some papers and correspondence are listed. Unpublished items are available from the MARC library. Following each listing is a brief annotation describing the item.

A convenient Name Index and a Title Index increase the usefulness of the volume.

Following the Preface, which provides the rationale for the book, eight members of the Hastie Group provide comments about the separatist movement of recent times. Kenneth B. Clark is the leadoff observer and sets the subject in perspective. The others are Ralph Ellison, Adelaide Cromwell Gulliver, William B. Hastie, Hyland Lewis, J. Saunders Redding, Bernard C. Watson, and Robert C. Weaver. Each of the comments provides a valuable representation of responses to the purportedly short-lived and minority demands for separation. As is the case with any bibliography, this is a derived work. Only the cited works themselves convey the full flavor and substance of the separatists' argument. *(Sept.15, 1976, p.202)*

016.30145'19   Black nationalism—U.S.—Bibliography   [CIP]   75-23866

Bombers in service:
patrol and transport aircraft since 1960. By Kenneth Munson; illus. by John W. Wood. Rev. ed. New York, Macmillan, [c1975]. 159p. illus. 19cm. paper over board $6.95.
358.4'18'3   Bombers || Transport planes || Airplanes, Military   [CIP]   75-14214

Fighters in service:
attack and training aircraft since 1960. By Kenneth Munson; illus. by John W. Wood. Rev. ed. New York, Macmillan, [c1975]. 175p. illus. 19cm. paper over board $6.95.
358.4'3   Fighter planes   [CIP]   75-12742

Tanks and other armoured fighting vehicles 1942–1945.
By B. T. White; illus. by John W. Wood. New York, Macmillan, [c1975]. 171p. illus. 20cm. paper over board $6.95.
358'.18'09044   Tanks (Military science) || Armored vehicles, Military || World War, 1939–1945   [CIP]   75-28306

Kenneth Munson, a specialist in aircraft who has written several books on the subject, is responsible for the text in the two latest pocketbooks in Macmillan's Color Series: *Bombers in Service* and *Fighters in Service*. John W. Wood, the illustrator, works for the British Interplanetary Service and has illustrated a number of other aircraft books. This collaborative effort has resulted in two handy volumes for the aircraft buff.

Arrangement of the books is similar. Eighty pages of colored illustrations showing split plan view (illustrating upper and lower surface markings) precede specific descriptions of the craft. Accompanying each illustration are performance and structural specifications including the craft's dimensions: number and type of engines, span, length, wing area, maximum take-off weight and cruising speed, service ceiling, and range with maximum payload. Brief chronological summaries of the design, development, production, sales, and service records of individual aircraft complete the book. In the book on bombers, propeller-driven aircraft are illustrated before jet-powered aircraft. Among the craft covered are intercontinental and medium range strategic bombers, short- and medium-range tactical bombers, night interdictors, and low-level strike aircraft. The book on fighters illustrates piston-engined aircraft first and then straight-winged and swept-winged aircraft.

Tanks and Other Armored Fighting Vehicles 1942–45 is part of Macmillan's Mechanized Warfare in Color Series. It is written by the well-known expert on fighting vehicles who also wrote two other volumes in the series: *Tanks and Other Armored Fighting Vehicles 1900–1918* and *Tanks and Other AFVs of the Blitzkrieg Era 1939–1941*. Again the illustrations precede the text with all vehicles from one country appearing together. Three tables at the end of the book show considerable data on the specific vehicles at a glance: "Comparative Data for the Principal Tanks and Other A.V.Fs in This Book," "Full-Tracked Armoured Vehicles," and "Wheeled and Half-Tracked Armoured Vehicles." Public and high school libraries with clientele interested in military hardware will find these three books practical and easy to use. *(Dec. 1, 1976, p.563)*

Books for cooks:
a bibliography of cookery. [By] Marguerite Patten. London & New York, Bowker, 1975. ix, 526. ix, 526p. 24cm. illus. cloth, $19.50 plus shipping and handling.

A selected, annotated list of some 1,700 books, this work was compiled by a writer and speaker well known in Great Britain. Criteria for selection are not stated explicitly. Although choice is weighted in favor of British publications, there is considerable representation of U.S. titles along with a few entries from other countries, either translated or in common Germanic and Romance languages. Braille editions are noted.

The work includes not only titles on the subject of cookery proper, but some books on nutrition, the history of food, and related topics. Most of the items were in print at the time the bibliography went to press, and well over half were published in the 1970s (some in 1976!), though one entry bears the date 1845, and the 1975 edition of *Joy of Cooking* is absent. The arrangement is alphabetical by author, with "Late Entries" in a separate sequence. There are indexes by subject and by title.

Each entry gives the usual bibliographic information, including editions published in various countries (chiefly Great Britain and the United States), together with paging and price. The annotations are disappointing as they lack felicity and often repeat information in titles. Typography, paper, and binding reflect excellent production standards, but the format is extravagantly spacious. This work will find its proper place in larger and specialized cookery collections; it will not (as the promotional material claims) satisfy "the busy housewife."
(Oct. 15, 1976, p.343)

†016.6415   Cookery—Bibliography

Books for inner development:
the yes! guide. Cris Popenoe, compiler. Washington, D. C., Yes! Bookshop, [1976]; distributed by Random House. 383p. 28cm. paper $5.95.

This delightful compilation is not what its title may suggest: it is neither a list of books of general therapeutic interest nor a guide to spiritual reading in any orthodox sense. Rather it is a list of books which are available through a particular Georgetown bookstore (order forms are bound in) and which fall into the general category of what would have perhaps once been called Bohemian: fantasy, folklore, the occult, nutrition, popular anthropology, self-help, and "strange gods"—minus, Popenoe points out, the lunatic fringe (though readers are bound to disagree as to what that comprises). The coverage of Eastern philosophies (pure and applied) seems especially strong. There are 70 sections, from *Alchemy* through *Biorhythms* (not the same as chronobiology), *Cookbooks, Death, Grail and King Arthur, Krishnamurti and Thakar, Natural Childbirth, Occult Novels, Parapsychology,* and *Women,* to *Yoga.* The sections on *Ancient Civilization* and *Buddhism* are subdivided (the latter into general, Tibetan, and Zen). There are separate sections on Edgar Cayce, Wilhelm Reich, *et al.* Some may regret the lack of a section on witchcraft. There is an Author Index but no title index and no subject approach other than through the classified arrangement. Supplements are announced, and a subscription form is included.

Within each section, items are listed mainly by author but with some grouping by subject, e.g., within *Chinese Philosophy,* a section on *Confucius* (from Baum to Yutang), and, under *Bible,* sections on the *Apocrypha* and on *Enoch*—and, under *Cookbooks,* a section on *Bread.* Each item is annotated, many at some length and many very interestingly. Some sections open with helpful essays. Along with many happy surprises, there are occasional jars, e.g., the omission of De la Mare's *The Three Royal Monkeys* and of any titles by Arthur Machen. Macdonald's *The Princess and the Goblin* is included: then why not *The Princess and Curdie, At the Back of the North Wind, Lilith,* and *Phantastes?* But defects are minor, and book selectors and readers' advisors should find this work very useful. A vast treasure chest, it is to be valued for its contents rather than deprecated for its lacks; moreover, it is a work to be read as well as consulted. Finally, it is attractive in appearance and format, despite the fineness of its print. Perhaps it will appeal particularly to library users (presumably numerous and increasing) who are "into" various areas of published materials not adequately treated in conventional storage and retrieval systems and perhaps insufficiently covered by the selection policies of some public and academic libraries. In fact, an hour or two with *Books for Inner Development* may well serve as a mind-opener for selectors whose circles of inquiry and speculation have not expanded beyond what a generation ago was called, a shade complacently, "our heritage." *En fin,* a helpful and, on the whole, balanced guide to "counter-culture" reading. *(May 1, 1977, p.1373)*
†011   Bibliography—Best books   76-16941

Bowker serials bibliography supplement 1976:
to Ulrich's international periodicals directory, 16th edition and irregular serials and annuals, 4th edition. [3d ed.] New York & London, Bowker, [c1976]. xxxiv, 521p. 27cm. paper $22.50.

During the interim biennium when Ulrich's *International Periodicals Directory* and *Irregular Serials and Annuals* are not published, Bowker provides a supplementary updating and revision service which is well worth its purchase price. The current supplement covers more than 7,000 current international serials and features two new sections which update the parent volumes: a list of changes in title and a list of cessations. Also appearing for the first time in the supplement are an ISSN Index to titles in Ulrich's sixteenth edition. The supplement is well designed for ease of use. It is a necessary addition for libraries that require up-to-date information on international serials.
(June 1, 1977, p.1525)
011   Periodicals—Directories   72-2677

The Bradford book of collector's plates 1976:
the official guide to all editions traded on the world's largest exchange. Edited under the direction of Nadja K Bartels and John G. McKinven. New York, McGraw-Hill, [c1976]. unpaged. illus. 29cm. cloth $9.95; to schools and libraries, 20 percent–33.4 percent discount depending on quantity ordered.

The Bradford Book of Collector's Plates claims to be the first illustrated book covering all plates "regularly traded on the world's largest exchange for plate trading" and the only guide identifying all plates listed on the Bradford Exchange.

The 160 unnumbered pages contain, in this order: a Table of Contents; an explanation of the arrangement of the listings in the body of the book; an essay, "The world's most traded art," by the director of the Board of Governors of the Bradford Exchange, J. Roderick MacArthur; the Directory of Plates; a glossary; and several indexes.

The Directory of Plates is arranged by "Bradex number," a series of four figures indicating country of origin, maker, series, and individual plate within the series. In practice, use of this number produces an alphabetical arrangement by country and by maker within each country. Each maker's listing gives information on trademarks, history of the maker, size of plates, composition (porcelain, lead crystal), hanging information ("foot rims pierced for hanging," "back hanger attached"), edition limitation, numbering, and price at the time the plate was first issued. All plates described are illustrated by small (1½ inches by 1½ inches) but very clear black-and-white reproductions.

There is a four-page glossary which, rather surprisingly, includes some marketing terms. Completing the volume are the indexes: Index of Plate Makers and Sponsors; Index of Plate Series by Type and Name; Index of Plate Titles; Index of Plate Artists. "See" references are used as necessary. All references are to Bradex number.

The book, in hard cover, is printed on heavy, nonglare white paper and lies flat when open. The "lowest" Bradex number appears on the upper outside corner of each page, making it very easy to go from index to item.

In this day of "collectibles," a book of this quality, scope, and modest price will probably be wanted by most libraries. It has browsing as well as reference value.   *(June 15, 1977, p.1599)*
738   Plates (Tableware)—Collectors and collecting || Plates (Tableware)—Catalogs   [CIP]
                                                                                    76-16129

British music yearbook:
a survey and directory with statistics and reference articles for 1975. Ed. Arthur Jacobs. London and New York, Bowker, [1975]. xxi, 801p. 21cm. cloth $22.50.

This yearbook, edited by a distinguished critic and historian, is presented as the third issue of *Music Yearbook,* with a title change reflecting "the practical limitation of most of the information provided" (p. xiii) and paving the way for the publication of a parallel title, *International Music Market Place,* which will cover developments other than British. In some areas, e.g., necrology, the present volume continues worldwide coverage. The arrangement is by broad subject area: "Musician of the Year . . ."; "Survey and Statistics"; "Reference" (a variety of essays on legal, vocational, educational, etc., topics); "Directory: Offices and Societies"; "Directory: Professional Performance"; and so on. The pattern, if there is one, is not obvious. A brief Subject Index (p. xv–xvii) is an aid to random access. This work will be admired more for its compact storage of a large quantity of useful data than for the ease with which its content can be retrieved by the uninitiated. *British Music Yearbook* offers a mine of information belied by its modest dimensions.
(Dec. 15, 1976, p.630)
†780.9'42   Music—Yearbooks || Music—Gt. Brit.—Directories

Business information sources.
By Lorna M. Daniells. Berkeley, Univ. of California, [c1976]. xv, 439p. 24cm. cloth $14.95; to schools and libraries, $13.45.

The publication in 1955 of Marian C. Manley's *Business Infor-*

mation: *How to Find and Use It* provided the first guide to printed sources aimed at the businessman who needed information but was not sure where to find it. Based on the author's many years of experience as business librarian at the Newark Public Library, it has been especially useful to staff of public libraries originating or improving service to the business community. This guide had been preceded by Edwin Coman's *Sources of Business Information,* published in 1949. Coman was associated with the Graduate School of Business of Stanford University. Aimed primarily at students, this tool's value to librarians and business organizations too was enhanced by the educational approach and the interesting discussion of reasons for using one source rather than another or for compiling data in a particular manner. A revised edition was published in 1964.

When another revision of *Sources of Business Information* was needed, it was undertaken by Lorna M. Daniells, head of the reference department, Baker Library, Graduate School of Business Administration, Harvard University. *Business Information Sources* has turned out to be an entirely new work, rather than an updated edition, and it is sure to be as indispensable as its predecessors to librarians, students, teachers, and personnel of business organizations of all kinds. An excellent Preface explains this relationship and indicates the scope and limitations of the new volume.

The first part of the book consists of eight chapters describing kinds of business reference sources—bibliographies, indexes, abstracts, directories, statistical and financial sources, data on business and economic trends, including loose-leaf services, periodicals and documents. The introductory material is briefer than in the Coman volumes, but the annotations give full descriptions, often including how-to-use information. Chapters 9 through 20 are subject bibliographies for various fields of business management, starting off with basic textbooks and handbooks and continuing with other sources appropriate for the individual field, including periodicals and lists of associations. Annotations vary in length, but are always clear and to the point. No prices are given. Dates are current through 1975, and the expected availability of new editions announced for 1976 is sometimes given.

Subject categories are more finely broken down than in *Manley* or *Coman*. For example, the Marketing chapter includes these subdivisions: Marketing Systems and Quantitative Methods, Consumer Behavior, Channels of Distribution, Industrial Marketing, Marketing Research, Pricing, Product Development, Public Policy and Marketing, Sales Management, Salesmanship, Consumer Expenditure Studies, Sales Promotion, Advertising, Retailing. This partitioning of the literature reflects changes in approaches to doing business, as well as increased activity. Change also is reflected in extended attention to International Management and Computer and Management Information Systems, but Accounting, Banking, Insurance, and Personnel Management, among others, continue to be important areas. While the emphasis is on recent material in the English language— principally U.S. publications—foreign sources are not overlooked. Chapter 21 is *A Basic Bookshelf,* suitable as the beginning of a company library.

The Index consists of 82 double-column pages (the 1949 edition of *Sources of Business Information* had 36 such pages with perhaps less detailed access to the text). Titles are entered in italics, with authors, publishers and organizations as authors, and subjects also entered. *See* and *See also* references are used, and boldface type indicates the primary page reference when several are given.

The book is sturdily bound, with good margins. Clear print and good paper, with variation in type for captions, entries, and annotations make this volume a pleasure to use. *Business Information Sources* will be valued for its well-planned arrangement and excellent Index as well as its basic content of descriptive bibliographies; it should be useful in libraries of all sizes and in the offices of business, government and nonprofit organizations. *(July 1, 1977, p.1674)*

016.33   Business—Bibliography   [OCLC]   74-30517

Canadian book review annual, 1975.
Edited by Dean and Nancy Tudor and Linda Biesenthal. Toronto, Peter Martin Associates Ltd., dist. in U.S. by Books Canada, Inc., 33 E. Tupper St., Buffalo, NY 14203, 1976. viii, 304p. 26cm. cloth $29.95 (U.S.); $27.30 (Canada); £17.90 (U.K.)

The *Canadian Book Review Annual, 1975* is the first edition of an annual publication which will be of great value to the staff of Canadian school, public, and academic libraries and to non-Canadian librarians who select Canadian books for their readers as well as to anyone interested in Canadian studies. This first venture in providing an evaluative guide to English-language Canadian books covers 682 titles supplied by publishers for consideration in this volume. All titles carry 1975 copyright dates, are reprints of books more than a decade old, or are translations published in 1975. Full bibliographic and order information is provided for each book.

The reviews, written by librarians and other subject specialists, vary considerably in length but average about 250 words. Their quality is uniformly high. The reviewers do not shy away from quoting other reviews or, on occasion, suggesting a better or even cheaper book on the subject. Even though there is considerable variation in literary style from one reviewer to another (all reviews are signed), they are consistent in their treatment of salient points and offer candid critiques. Books are praised or panned, and reasons are always provided for recommendations or reservations.

The reviews are arranged by key subject. Author, Title, and Subject Indexes assist the user in locating specific reviews. A list of contributors' names with brief identifying statements is provided on pages 271–77. Omitted from this list are Dean and Nancy Tudor, editors and contributors to the volume. Readers may be familiar with their reviews of cookbooks; their well-received publication, *Cooking for Entertaining* (New York: Bowker, 1976); and their various compilations of bibliographies and other reference tools.

Future editions of *Canadian Book Review Annual* will probably cover a larger number of titles as more Canadian publishers find that it is in their interest to submit review copies to the *Annual's* editors. *(July 15, 1977, p.1753)*

†028.1   Books—Reviews || Canadian literature—History and criticism

Canadian books for children /
Livres canadiens pour enfants.
Edited by/edité par Irma McDonough. Toronto and Buffalo, Univ. of Toronto Pr., [c1976]. xii, 112p. illus. 25cm. paperback $7.50; to schools and libraries, 10 percent discount; retail, 20 percent discount.

Canadian Books for Children/Livres canadiens pour enfants is based on a checklist of 900 English-language books by Canadian writers and about the country and its people published in Canada and elsewhere which appeared in the August 1974 issue of the quarterly *In Review; Canadian Books for Children*. The present list, expanded to about 1,400 in-print books and magazines, including 159 French-language publications is described as a professional aid for librarians and teachers. It was prepared by seven children's librarians under the direction of Irma McDonough, editor of *In Review*.

Entries are arranged in English and French sections under 24 broad headings such as Picture Books, Folklore, Social Sciences, Science, The Arts, Sports and Recreation, Literature, Fiction, and History. It should be noted that titles listed under Publishers' Series do not appear under the appropriate subject headings.

The works of Lucy Maud Montgomery are an exception; they are listed twice.

Uncritical annotations and an Author-Title Index are provided. The decorations add charm but not substance to the work.

Omission of reading levels for many of the English entries is disappointing especially since adult books are included where the selection among Canadian titles for children is limited. The selection of materials for professional reading is puzzling as it ranges over such disparate titles as *Flowers of Delight* by Leonard De Vries, *Sacred Legends of the Sandy Lake Cree* by James Stevens, Millie Gillen's biography of L. M. Montgomery and *Non-Book Materials; the Organization of Integrated Collections* by Jean Riddle Weihs. This first effort in the preparation of a catalog of Canadian books for children will be welcomed by those who feel that Canadians need to promote the publication of English and French language books in Canada.

As Canadian writing for children and young adults grows and develops, future editions of this work will no doubt reflect the enrichment of the field, and the connection between what is simply Canadian and what is valuable for children will appear less tenuous. *(Jan. 1, 1977, p.684)*

028.52 Children's literature—Canadian—Bibliography [OCLC] 76-3276

Canadian essay and literature index.
v. 2, 1974. Edited by Andrew D. Armitage and Nancy Tudor. Toronto and Buffalo, Univ. of Toronto Pr., 1976. x, 489p. 27cm. cloth $35.

As its title suggests, the *Canadian Essay and Literature Index* is an analytic index of collected essays published in Canada, and as such it is analogous to *Essay and General Literature Index*. However, *CELI* has a much broader scope. In addition to indexing the contents of separately published volumes, it also indexes a large number of periodicals. Moreover, both monographs and serials are indexed for book reviews, poems, plays, and short stories as well as for essays. As a result *CELI* has quickly become an invaluable addition to the bibliographic control of Canadiana.

The 1974 *CELI* follows the same approach taken by the 1973 volume with some major changes being qualitative in nature. Inclusion of anthologies and collections continues to be limited to nontechnical general interest works containing the writings of two or more authors. All titles are English-language, Canadian publications, although a few of the individual articles are neither Canadian nor written in English. For no explained reason, the number of titles has dropped from 91 to 77. As in the previous volume, the periodicals represented in *CELI* have been drawn from the ranks of small literary and general interest magazines not indexed by *Canadian Periodical Index*. A continuing and convenient feature is the list of holdings in 54 major Canadian academic, governmental, and public libraries of periodicals indexed in *CELI*. These are exclusively in English with the exception of two bilingual titles. Their number has risen from 38 to 55, suggesting an increase in the relative importance of serials as opposed to anthologies.

Arrangement of entries continues to be by author, title, and subject. The only exceptions are book reviews, which appear only under the main entries of books being indexed, and poems, which are provided with additional first-line entries wherever this seems advisable. The major innovation in this volume is that the formerly separate sections for poems, plays, and short stories have been integrated into a single section—literature. Essays and book reviews continue as separate categories.

Concerning the future course which *CELI* should or might take, no clear indication is available. The need for additional indexing of English Canadian periodicals may diminish if *Canadian Periodical Index* should succeed in increasing its coverage. The need for the book review section might vanish if the proposed *Canadian Book Review Annual* or *Canadian Book Review Digest* projects should be successfully realized. For the present, *CELI* performs an essential service for Canadian libraries and will be universally appreciated by scholars and others with a strong interest in things Canadian.
(Jan.15, 1977, p.746)

†016.8088 Canadian literature—Bibliography 75-7703

Catalogue of the world's most popular coins.
By Fred Reinfeld and Burton Hobson. 9th ed. New York, Sterling, [c1976]. 480p. illus. 25cm. cloth $14.95; to schools and libraries, $12.69.

Since Fred Reinfeld's death, Burton Hobson has carried on the revision and updating of the Reinfeld catalog, which since 1956 has gained the reputation of being the most comprehensive standard catalog of its kind. The present edition catalogs coins of more than 350 modern countries and the ancient coins of Greece, Rome, and the Mediterranean. More than 5,000 coins are illustrated with black-and-white photographs. They vary in clarity depending on the quality of the originals.

The coins cataloged were minted in a variety of metals; the material used is cited with each coin's description: aluminum, acmonital, billon, brass, bronze, copper, gold, iron, silver, magnesium, nickel, steel, tin, zinc. The prices quoted are for the "coins in the condition in which the particular issue is usually encountered."

The book is well designed in a two-column format. Because it may be subjected to excessive use, it is fortunate that the inner margins will permit rebinding. School and public libraries serving collectors of world coins and coin aficionados in homes will want to acquire the ninth editon of the *Catalogue of the World's Most Popular Coins*. *(May 15, 1977, p.1450)*

737.4'02 Coins [OCLC] 76-1168

The Catholic encyclopedia.
[By] Robert C. Broderick, Virginia Broderick, illustrator. Nashville, New York, Thomas Nelson Inc., [c1976]. 612p. illus. 28cm. cloth $24.95.

The purpose of this single-volume reference work is "to bring forward a broad compilation of new terms and a reassessment of the older, almost archiac descriptive definitions of the past," to include books and notable persons of the Bible, and to provide the reader with "an ecumenical understanding by including terms of a broad spectrum of Christian experience." The book is more a dictionary than an encyclopedia. It is intended for use, not by the scholar of theology, but by the lay minister, student of religion, and the family. As is usual with Catholic publications dealing with doctrinal and moral matters, it bears the *nihil obstat* and *imprimatur* to indicate conformance with ecclesiastical standards.

Robert C. Broderick is a former editor of Bruce Publishing Company, has been a free-lance writer for 30 years, and has written 16 books, among them the *Concise Catholic Dictionary*. Virginia Broderick, his wife, has illustrated many books on Catholic subjects.

With the exception of articles on various non-Catholic denominations and religions, the 4,000 entries, arranged alphabetically word by word, deal with subjects directly related to Catholic beliefs and practices and range in length from 20 words (usually brief definitions of terms) to about 2,500 words for Vatican II. Included in some articles are texts of hymns and prayers, such as *Te Deum,* and a few poems. *See* references are limited in supply for the most part, though a few more might have been added. For example, *Freemasonry* and *Masonry,* *Agnus Dei* and *Lamb of God* have substantially duplicative content, and there are no cross-references. There are no bibliographies, but there is frequent citation to and quotation from pertinent Biblical texts, Vatican II, and documents.

The articles are written in a readable style, and a number of them reflect recent developments. Among the latter are *Mar-*

riage Encounter; Habit, Religious; Parish Council; Fasting; Participation in the Liturgy and Life of the Church; Charismatic Renewal, Catholic; Musical Coordinator; Kiss, Liturgical Use of; Teilhardism; Order of the Mass, New; and Key '73.

The Committee noted a few lapses in editorial control, e.g., the provision of two brief articles with nearly identical content on Dark Night of the Soul, one entered under Dark, the other under Night. Also, it would have been helpful in the entry for Abbreviations (chiefly for Catholic organizations) to indicate those treated as separate entries elsewhere in the text.

Illustrative material consists of 150 attractive black-and-white drawings by Virginia Broderick, accompanying pertinent articles, and 51 photographs, 39 of which are in color. Most of them depict church art and eminent figures, nearly half of them American subjects. Since they do not illustrate specific articles in the text and are separated into four sections, they may be viewed as chiefly decorative. The type is large and clear, the paper opaque, the two-columned text has running heads, and the binding is adequate

In spite of its name, this work is not equivalent to the 16-volume The New Catholic Encyclopedia (New York: McGraw-Hill, 1967–74) and its supplement which contain long, signed, and profusely illustrated articles which treat much more fully and authoritatively the history and contemporary concerns of the Catholic Church. Analytically indexed and with full appended bibliographies for more articles, it is strong in geographical and bibliographical names, most of them not found in The Catholic Encyclopedia.

More comparable and similar in purpose to the work under review is The Maryknoll Catholic Dictionary (New York: Grosset & Dunlap, 1965), compiled and edited by Albert J. Nevins with the assistance of the Maryknollers. Its brief 10,000 entries contain many hymns, terms, and geographical and biographical names not in The Catholic Encyclopedia. On the other hand, the title under review contains a number of new or updated articles as noted above. Small line drawings of vestments and architectural details accompany a few of the Maryknoll dictionary's entries, as well as pronunciation and derivation in many cases, though the encyclopedia sometimes incorporates derivation in the text of an article. On the whole, the treatment of entries in the Maryknoll dictionary is more succinct, with fewer Bible references, no texts of hymns and prayers, or illustrative quotations, all of which are found in the Broderick book. Some of the information given in the appendixes to the Maryknoll dictionary appears in alphabetical order in Broderick but not forms of address, selected biographies of deceased Catholics (dates and occupation only), the American martyrology, or the list of popular saints' names and their meanings. Both include patron saints of places and occupations, with a few in each not found in the other. The Catholic Encyclopedia is alone in giving brief descriptions of 50 Catholic awards, chiefly American; it updates the list of international Catholic organizations; it offers a chronologically arranged roster of popes but does not provide separate articles as does the Maryknoll dictionary; it includes fewer Catholic abbreviations and acronyms, though some are not in Maryknoll.

On the whole, The Catholic Encyclopedia is not as well balanced in its coverage of topics as it should be, and it is quite conservative in its viewpoint. For example, the article on Genocide includes information on abortion as an example of genocide. The entry Narcotics is a cross-reference to Gluttony where the "taking of narcotics . . . without sufficient reason" is described as "venially sinful if taken without a sufficient reason" and "mortally sinful if loss of reason results." Women contains the Pauline Corinthian statement that "women are silent for the burden of proclaiming the word is the function of men"—perhaps in these times an unnecessary inclusion. The article on Psychoanalysis is garbled and disjointed. Finally, there are no articles on Mother Seton and John 23 even though photographs of both personages appear in the encyclopedia.

While The Catholic Encyclopedia does not replace The Maryknoll Catholic Dictionary, it is naturally more useful for recent terms. Its coverage of both old and new terms is broad. It quotes Vatican II documents generously. Its attractive format would make it useful in Catholic homes and school libraries.
(Feb. 15, 1977, p.924)
282'.03 Catholic Church—Dictionaries [CIP]   76-10976

Chambers biographical dictionary.
Edited by J. O. Thorne and T. C. Collocott. 2v. Edinburgh, W. & R. Chambers Ltd., 1974. vi, 1432p. 19cm. paperback $7.95.

The 1961 and 1969 editions of this work were reviewed by the Reference and Subscription Books Review Committee November 1, 1962, and February 1, 1974. The current paperback version is nearly identical to the 1969 edition, although the Introduction states that it "takes account of major events to the end of 1973." An eight-page Supplement containing sixty-seven biographies precedes the main listing of over 15,000 persons. For 6 of the Supplement entrants, only death dates are noted. A 35-page, classified Subject Index refers one from topics such as rain gauges to Palmieri (this instrument's inventor) or from variant forms of names to those used in the dictionary (e.g., from Onze Jan to Hofmeyr).

Minor updating adjustments are common. For Richard Nixon, nine words are added to describe his 1972 reelection; for Nkrumah (the next entry), one line is removed. An entry for George McGovern appears in the Supplement. Sir John Barbirolli's description is updated to include his retirement and death; minor alterations have been made in the entries for Samuel Barber and Jules Barbey D'Aurevilly; and Lyndon Johnson and Harry Truman are given death dates. Dean Acheson's 1969 book Present at the Creation is included, but an earlier title is dropped. Samuel Beckett's 1969 Nobel Prize is noted. These modifications have been made without changing beginning and ending words on the pages involved.

Names in the Supplement run alphabetically from Spiro Agnew to Kurt Waldheim and include such diverse persons as Dietrich Bonhoeffer, Guy Burgess, Sir Francis Chichester, and Pier Pasolini. Some 1974 deaths are noted, such as those of H. E. Bates and Samuel Goldwyn. While the entry on Agnew ends with his resignation, there is no biography of Gerald Ford in the book. Many of the coverages in the Supplement include events and publications of the 1970s.

Volume one of this set includes the names through Jewel. Each volume contains a Key to Pronunciation. As in the 1969 edition, pages are divided into two columns. Last names are in boldface capitals, so each main entry stands out. The print is very small but clear. The volumes do not open flat, inner margins are narrow, and the paper covers seem rather flimsy. The low price, however, will make this edition of Chambers Biographical Dictionary an attractive addition to libraries and personal reference collections.   *(June 15, 1977, p.1600)*
920.02 Biography—Dictionaries [OCLC]

Chambers dictionary of science and technology.
Edited by T. C. Collocott and A. B. Dobson. Totowa, N.J., Littlefield, Adams, [1976, c1974 by W. & R. Chambers Ltd.]. x, 1296p. 20cm. paper $7.95.

Chambers Dictionary of Science and Technology was first published in 1971 and was reviewed in Reference and Subscription Books Reviews December 1, 1972. A revised edition, published in 1974, has now been produced in paperback form as part of a Chambers project to issue some of their reference books in paperback. This paperback edition is in two volumes rather than in the easier-to-use one volume of the hardback edition. The number of pages has been reduced slightly by the omission of the table of igneous and sedimentary rocks that had been appended to the first edition.

The Committee found the first edition contained "up-to-date, brief, but for the most part adequate, definitions of terms used in the whole area of science and technology." The dictionary is especially strong in the latter field. It should be pointed out, however, that since this is a British publication the definitions reflect British usage, as does the spelling. Comparison with the first edition shows that numerous new terms have been added and some definitions have been revised, although some of the scientific definitions not found in the first edition are still missing. The type used is even smaller than that of the first edition but is still readable. The narrow inner margin may make binding difficult.

In spite of its British bias and rather brief definitions, *Chambers Dictionary of Science and Technology* still remains a useful and, in this paperback edition, an inexpensive source for ready reference. *(June 15, 1977, p.1600)*

†503   Science—Dictionaries || Technology—Dictionaries

Checklist of the world's birds;

a complete list of species, with names, authorities, and areas of distribution. [By] Edward S. Gruson, with the assistance of Richard A. Forster. [New York], Quadrangle, The New York Times Book Co., [c1976]. xii, 212p. maps, 24cm. cloth, $10.95.

In the *Checklist of the World's Birds,* Edward S. Gruson, publisher of natural history books and author of *Words for Birds* (New York: Quadrangle/The New York Times Book Company, 1972), and Richard A. Forster of the Massachusetts Audubon Society aspire "to provide as complete a listing of the species of birds of the world as possible, to give the scientific name and an English name common for each of the species, to provide a source to which the reader is referred if more information about the species is wanted, and to give a gross idea of its range." The book is intended for bird listers all over the world.

The book is organized so that both professionals and nonprofessionals can make optimum use of the information. Entry is by scientific name with common name cited in the adjacent column. Species within genera are listed alphabetically, e.g., under Phaethontidae (tropicbirds) three species are cited: Phaethon aethereus (red-billed tropicbird), Phaethon lepturus (white-tailed tropicbird), and Phaethon rubricauda (red-tailed tropicbird). Sources of further information and avifaunal regions are cited by code numbers in columns beside the common name. Some 70 sources are referenced.

The book is well designed for ease of use. A Bibliography of more than 100 books and journal articles includes both scholarly and popular works. Two indexes, one of generic names and one of English names, serve as easy guides to the book's contents. In many ways the Gruson and Forster *Checklist of the World's Birds* will serve as a compact one-volume resource for the layman in place of Peter's 13-volume *Checklist of the World's Birds* (Cambridge: Harvard Univ. Pr., 1931–1970) which has established itself as the authority for professional zoologists. Public, biology, and zoology libraries will find it useful. *(Nov. 1, 1976, p.423)*

598.2'021'6   Birds—Classification || Birds—Nomenclature (Popular)   [OCLC]   72-85239

Children's authors and illustrators:

an index to biographical dictionaries. Edited by Dennis La Beau. Detroit, Gale, 1976. 172p. (Gale Biographical Index Series, no.2.) 24cm. cloth $15.

Children's Authors and Illustrators: An Index to Biographical Dictionaries "has been designed to meet a long-felt need for a convenient, easy-to-use index to biographies of children's authors and illustrators."—Introduction.

The index covers biographical material that appears in 26 separate titles. The introductory note indicates that every effort was made to locate as many biographical dictionaries as possible, with the inclusion also of "significant biographical material in other sources that normally would be overlooked, such as biographical notes in anthologies."

The earliest published volumes listed are *Contemporary Illustrators of Children's Books* by Elinor Whitney and Bertha E. Mahoney [c1930] and *The Junior Book of Authors* by Stanley J. Kunitz and Howard Haycraft [c1934]. Among the latest published volumes are *Children's Literature Review,* v.1 and 2 [c1976] and *Newbery and Caldecott Medal Books, 1966–1975* by Lee Kingman, [c1975]. Among the anthologies listed are *Anthology of Children's Literature* by Edna Johnson and others, and *Story and Verse for Children* by Miriam Blanton Huber.

The publications indexed are devoted entirely to children's authors and illustrators except Gale's continuing series, *Contemporary Authors,* which covers primarily authors who write for adults. Only children's authors listed in *Contemporary Authors* have been cited in the present index.

The Introduction acknowledges that users of *Children's Authors and Illustrators* may know of titles that should have been included; however, it is noted that their absence may be due to unavailability at the time the index was compiled or "to an oversight on our part." Suggestions for future editions are welcomed. The following could be considered as candidates for inclusion: *Books in Search of Children* by Louise Seaman Bechtel, Macmillan [c1969], p.63–138; *Tellers of Tales: British Authors of Children's Books From 1800–1964* by Roger Lancelyn Green, Watts, [c1965]; *The Child's First Books* by Donnarae MacCann, H. W. Wilson, [c1973], p.95–106; *Rascals at Large* by Arthur Prager, Doubleday, [c1971].

The index provides the author's or illustrator's name, the years of birth and death (if provided in the source book). This is followed by a code which directs the reader to the book where biographical information can be found. A spot check revealed no incorrect or blind entries.

The list of codes and corresponding titles appears on the inside of the front and back covers and in the bibliography following the Introduction.

No attempt has been made to standardize spellings, authors' and illustrators' names being transcribed exactly as they appear in the indexed volumes. Persons not entirely familiar with writers' pseudonyms could fail to realize fully the index's potential. For example, Theodore Geisel is also indexed under Theo Le Sieg and Dr. Seuss, and Mollie Hunter is additionally represented as M. Molly Hunter McVeigh McIlwraith and Maureen McIlwraith. Furthermore, dates have not been firmly established.

The entries are arranged two columns to a page. Word-by-word alphabetization is used (e.g., *Old Fag* is followed by *Oldden*). Hyphenated names are considered to be words separated by a space. Initials are filed at the head of the alphabet.

The volume is sturdily bound in dark blue cloth with light blue lettering on the front cover and on the spine. Pages of the book lie open flat. The paper is of good quality, and the typeface and page arrangement are clear.

This index can be a helpful time-saver in a library whether it has few or many of the sources listed because consultation of this tool will reveal whether or not the collection at hand contains biographical material on a given author or illustrator. Where source titles are immediately available they probably can be borrowed from a larger library system.

(July 1, 1977, p.1674)

016.809   Authors—Biography—Indexes || Illustrators—Biography—Indexes || Children's literature—Indexes   [CIP]   76-23534

Children's books
in the Rare Book Division of the Library of Congress:

author/title and chronological catalogs. 2v. Totowa, N.J.,

Rowman and Littlefield, 1975. v.1, 890p.; v.2, 493p. 29cm. cloth $100.

This catalog, listing the 15,000 titles in the Library of Congress Rare Book Division's special collection of children's books plus 1,000 other children's books selected from the Rare Book Division's other collections, represents about 10 percent of the library's total estimated holdings in children's literature. Outside the confines of the library itself and the typewritten pages of some 30-odd Catholic University master's theses, this catalog is the only special listing of any portion of the library's total holdings in this field. Its uniqueness is most apparent in nineteenth- and twentieth-century American children's literature. Ninety percent of this important "collection" (concentrated in PZ5 ff., but also scattered throughout almost every other class in the Library of Congress schedule) is still hidden from public view and accessible only through main entries interfiled among the other millions of titles represented in the library's multivolume printed catalogs. Fortunately, a two-volume printed catalog of this special collection now exists. It is useful and very valuable indeed because it provides access to a sizable sample (no matter how skewed by the necessarily adventitious nature of rare book collecting) of the riches of the library's total holdings in children's literature.

For the eighteenth century and the first decades of the nineteenth century, this catalog has little to offer than can compete with A. S. W. Rosenbach's *Early American Children's Books* (Portland, Maine: Southworth Pr., 1933) and D'Alte Welch's *A Bibliography of American Children's Books Printed Prior to 1821* (Worcester, Mass.: American Antiquarian Society, 1972), and the Rare Book Division has not collected a very significant proportion of twentieth-century children's books. However, the Rare Book Division catalog does indicate quite clearly that there is richness in the library of Congress holdings of mid-nineteenth-century children's books. A count of pages in the chronological volume (v.2), reveals the following rough distribution of period coverages:

Period	Percent of v.2
Prior to 1845	about 20 percent
1845 – 1865	about 20 percent
1865 – 1885	about 20 percent
1885 – 1900	more than 10 percent
1900 – 1950	more than 10 percent
1950 – 1975	less than 10 percent
no date	less than 10 percent

The usefulness of this catalog as a research tool can be demonstrated by examining the year 1865. The Committee compiled a working list of 1865 editions by checking Richard Darling's lists of children's books reviewed in 1865 and 1866, contained in *The Rise of Children's Book Reviewing in America, 1865–1881* (New York: Bowker, 1968), against the *National Union Catalog (NUC)*, Library of Congress Catalogs, and James Kelly's *American Catalogue of Books* (New York: Wiley, 1866–71). In compiling this list, items were discarded if editions earlier than 1865 were found, and any items with 1865 imprints were added as they were discovered under entries for authors gleaned from the Darling citations. The corrected and augmented working list was then checked against the *Rare Book Division* holdings for 1865. Items in both the working list and *Rare Book Division* chronological catalog (v.2) were also checked against author and title entries in the author/title volume of the division catalog to determine if there were earlier editions. The corrected combined list provides an incomplete and tentative, but potentially valuable, preliminary census of first editions of children's books written by Americans and published in the U.S. in 1865. The relative contribution of the new *Rare Book Division* catalog is indicated below in approximate percentages:

Percent of 1865 imprints represented	
Items unique to the working list (Darling, NUC-LC, and Kelly)	40 percent
Items unique to *Rare Book Division* catalog	40 percent
Items common to both lists	20 percent

The *Rare Book Division* catalog is obviously an essential source for anyone seeking comprehensive representation of American children's books published not only in 1865 but during the later years of the nineteenth century. For the two or so decades preceding 1865, it has even more value, for Darling's lists begin with 1865 imprints, thereby making the *Rare Book Division* compilation the most extensive list presently available for checking against NUC-LC and Roorbach's *Bibliotheca Americana, 1820–61* (New York: Roorbach, 1852–61).

Despite the catalog's indisputable worth as a bibliographical resource, it is not an easily used reference tool. In the Introduction the reader is warned against "the many temporary cards prepared within the division by staff with varying training and understanding of cataloging rules" and urged "to check all possibilities of entry in an attempt to determine whether the collection includes a particular title or edition." Regrettably it is not possible to determine from the format how many of these cards are included and how extensively they supplement the *NUC*. These shortcomings, the typographical errors in card copy, and occasional compositional oversights (e.g., an entry in one volume but no corresponding entry in the other) indicate a lack of tight editorial control. Admittedly, if fastidious care had been taken to verify, make corrections, cross check entries, and recatalog wherever necessary, scholars and students who need this catalog would have still been without this key to important Library of Congress holdings. On the other hand, because this work is expensive, the user expects thorough editing or, in the absence of that, a title index (including titles in series) to provide an alternative to the suggested perusal of "all possibilities of entry." In summary, *Children's Books in the Rare Book Division of the Library of Congress* is a unique research tool that whets one's appetite for more. Perhaps scholars can persuade the Library of Congress to print a catalog of its complete holdings in children's literature. Until that time has arrived, these two volumes at least provide an important initial element in the bibliographic structure that must be built before the historical study of nineteenth- and twentieth-century children's literature can become a fruitful discipline. Scholars in this field, graduate students, and some rare book collectors and dealers will find this catalog valuable. Its special nature and cost will make it a feasible purchase only for library school, university, and large public libraries. *(Sept. 1, 1976, p.52)*

028.52 Children's literature—Bibliography—Catalogs || Bibliography—Rare books—Catalogs || U.S. Library of Congress. Rare Book Division [CIP] 75-9605

Choice: a classified cumulation.

2v. of 9v. Edited by Richard K. Gardner and Phyllis Grumm, assisted by Julia Johnson. Totowa, N.J., Rowman and Littlefield, [c1976]. xv, 863, ix, 950p. 29cm. buckram $395 (the set); v. IX (the index) only available separately for $49.50.

Rowman and Littlefield is to be congratulated for seeing the need for a cumulation of the authoritative reviews which were published in *Choice* (ALA's College and Research Libraries division's monthly reviewing journal) during the first ten years of its existence and for devising an easy-to-use format. Credit is also due Richard K. Gardner, who had edited *Choice* through most of its existence, for editing the cumulation in a practical arrangement which will be extremely useful to students, librarians, and others requiring ready access to the reviews.

The cumulation is comprised of exact photographic reprints of the 150- to 175-word reviews as they appeared originally. The only omissions from the cumulation are the longer reviews of reference works which appeared in the editorial sections of *Choice*. The classified arrangement of the social, life, and physical sciences in the reprint was designed in consultation with faculty and students in each subject field; the leading abstracting journal of the disciplines provided an overall classificatory framework. The humanistics and literature sections generally follow the traditional Library of Congress and Dewey Decimal classification schemes. The organization separates the material into eight subject volumes and an Index. General subjects covered are: v.I—reference, library science, humanities, communications, sports, and recreation; v.II—language, literature; v.III—literature, performing arts, philosophy, religion; v.IV—science and technology; v.V—engineering, information science, social and behavioral sciences, business, labor, and economics; v.VI—history; v.VII—history, geography, travel, law, and political science; v.VIII—anthropology, education, psychology, and sociology.

While the user might quarrel with the categories selected for some titles in the first two volumes, e.g., Bayle's *Historical and Critical Dictionary* classified under *Encyclopedias* along with *Encyclopedia Americana, Encyclopedia International, New Book of Knowledge,* and *Hutchison's* and with the placement of Ploski's *Negro Almanac* under *Almanacs* with *Reader's Digest Almanac, The Official Associated Press Almanac,* and other yearbook-type almanacs, thus separating it from works of its own genre like Ebony's *Negro Handbook* and Davis's *The American Negro Reference Book,* titles are usually placed with comparable works. Separate volume indexes might have been helpful to users who do not have the perseverance to check all possible leads. Since no cross-references were observed, the Reference and Subscription Books Review Committee assumes that no title appears under more than one subject.

The Committee hopes that the publisher is able to hold to the announced publishing schedule of producing all nine volumes by June 1977. Public, high school, college and university, and research libraries will find the ten-year cumulation of *Choice* a unique new bibliographic tool which is logically arranged and sturdily bound for many years of service.

(May 15, 1977, p.1450)

†051   Bibliography—Best books || Book reviews—Bibliography

Choosing the right dog:
a buyer's guide to all 121 breeds. [By] John Howe. New York, Harper, [c1976]. vii, 151p. illus. 15 x 21cm. cloth $7.95.

Choosing the Right Dog is a handy well-illustrated book that will aid buyers in selecting the best family dog. Each of the 121 breeds recognized by the American Kennel Club is accorded a one-page description. Information given summarizes the results of a 42-item questionnaire sent to dog breeders and owners. Each breed is described briefly enumerating the countries of origin and development, standard height for male and female, color and type of coat (short, smooth, long-haired), special skills, physical weaknesses to ailments, frequency and type of grooming, and price for a puppy. Other characteristics such as usefulness as a guard or watchdog, compatibility with children, attitude toward strangers and unfamiliar dogs, personality, activeness indoors, barking, difficulty with housebreaking, and temperament are covered briefly. *Choosing the Right Dog* is exceptional for its pinpointing a great deal of consumer information in brief space, and it will be useful in public and high school libraries serving clientele who seek information before purchasing a dog. *(Dec. 1, 1976, p.563)*

636.7'1   Dogs—Buying || Dog breeds [CIP]   75-25041

Choral music in print.
1976 supplement. Ed. by Thomas R. Nardone. Philadelphia, Musicdata, Inc., 1976. $32.

In 1974 the newly published *Choral Music in Print* volumes 1 and 2 was applauded as a unique guide to purchasable choral music scores, comparable in usefulness to *Books in Print.* The two volumes were favorably reviewed in *Reference and Subscription Books Reviews,* Feb. 1, 1975 and July 15, 1975.

This first supplement of *Choral Music in Print* has separate alphabetical actions for sacred and secular music. According to Nardone, the contents consist largely of music from publishers overlooked in 1974 and of works appearing since that time.

In his Preface Nardone notes that one of the criticisms leveled at the first editon was that it omitted many foreign publishers because they failed to respond to requests for information. Over 150 publishers, many of them foreign, have been added in this supplement.

The format and contents of entries adhere to the pattern established in the parent work, with most of the information appearing under the composer's name and cross-referenced from titles unless their composers are anonymous, in which case the information is in the title entry. The *Supplement* retains the handy introductory "Guide to Use" which explains entries. Also provided is a list of abbreviations. The editor says in his Preface that the *Supplement* makes no effort to correct errors made in the first edition." Such corrections are promised in the "completely revised second edition." The *Supplement* does, however, include editions which were "inadvertently omitted" in the earlier edition.

This is a successful update of a most useful tool; so libraries having the first edition will wish to acquire the supplement. Other libraries may find the supplement helpful because of its inclusion of new publications and additional publishers, especially if they have a music collection to keep current and teachers or a musical public to satisfy. *(Nov. 1, 1976, p.424)*

016.784'1   Choral music—Bibliography || Choruses, scores, catalogs

The classic motorcycles.
Edited by Harry Louis and Bob Currie; drawings by Carlo Demand. New York, Dutton, [c1976]. 125p. illus. (part col.) 30cm. cloth $29.95.

In *The Classic Motorcycles* Harry Louis, former editor of *Motorcycle* magazine, describes 32 bikes that have contributed significantly to motorcycle history from 1896 to 1950. Among the motorcycles described and illustrated are sporting bikes like the 1911 Indian, the Moto Guzzi, the A.J.S, and the North Manx; touring bikes like the Harley-Davidson, the Brough Superior, the Ariel Four Square, and the Douglas; and unorthodox bikes like the front wheel drive Negola with its aircraft-type rotary engine, the Nera Car, and the Böhmerland.

Each motorcycle selected for inclusion is described in a one-page presentation which explains the significance of its mechanical specifications and contribution to motorcycling history. Following this are full-view photographs, closeups of selected parts, diagrams, and a capsule description of the characteristics: model name and number, type of engine, capacity of engine in cubic centimeters, bore and stroke in millimeters, compression ratio, kind of carburetor, lubrication, type of ignition, clutch, gear box, frame, brakes, suspension, size of tires, size of gas and oil tanks, and speed in miles per hour. High school and public libraries serving motorcycle buffs will find *The Classic Motorcycles* is a beautifully illustrated and factually informative handbook. *(June 1, 1977, p.1525)*

629.22'75   Motorcycles—History   76-8038

Cloak and dagger bibliography:
an annotated guide to spy fiction, 1937–1975. By Myron J. Smith, Jr. Metuchen, N.J., Scarecrow Pr., Inc., 1976. 236p. 22cm. cloth $9.50.

Compiled by the head librarian of the Huntington (Indiana) Public Library, this annotated guide lists and describes for students and fans of espionage literature and librarians who seek to fill their requests, approximately 1,675 titles. These spy-adventure-intrigue novels written in English between 1937 and mid-1975 are arranged alphabetically by author and then by title.

The Introduction succinctly relates the development of the spy genre, basically a twentieth-century form of fiction inspired by the clandestine activities of operatives during World War II and the Cold War. Many items in the bibliography have brief annotations with descriptions of plots and characters, and special aspects, (e.g., whether books have been made into movies), and citations of variant titles. Symbols indicate whether titles appear exclusively in paperback, are for under-tenth graders, or have an emphasis on humor and/or sex in the story line. Cross-references from pseudonyms to real names are generally correct. The Title Index refers the reader to the serial number ascribed to each title entry. Unfortunately, titles may be buried within annotations. For example, Eric Ambler's *Background to Danger* was first published in England. Although its English title, *Uncommon Danger,* is identified within the annotation, it is listed in the Index only under its American title. Also, works by an author are not always in strict alphabetical sequence in the entry since the annotated works are listed before other titles by the author. This selective annotation policy has been used with authors who employ either the same character(s) or similar plots in many works. The annotations tend to be perfunctory and are not entirely accurate. The one for Carre's *Murder of Quality* is incorrect. Also the designation of 1954–71 as the major era for spy fiction may be open to question.

Two extensive volumes on mystery and detective fiction *Who Done It?* (New York: Bowker, 1969) by Ordean Hagen and *A Catalog of Crime* (New York: Harper & Row, 1974) by Jacques Barzun and Wendell H. A. Taylor already exist and include some of the titles appearing in *Cloak and Dagger.* The Barzun-Taylor work also provides a brief discussion of the spy genre, and all of its titles are annotated. However, both *Who Done It* and *A Catalog* deal with the suspense literature in general and do not hone in on the more specific category of spy fiction. *Cloak and Dagger* draws together works in this specialized genre and is up to date (to 1975). In addition, its designations of age level and format will be appreciated by public and school librarians who wish to expand their holdings of spy fiction.

(Sept. 15, 1976, p.203)

016.823'0872 Spy stories, English—20th century—Bibliography || Spy stories, American—20th century—Bibliography || English fiction—20th century—Stories, plots, etc. [CIP]
75-44319

Collectors' guide to nineteenth-century photographs.
[By] William Welling, New York, Macmillan Pub. Co., Inc.; London, Collier Macmillan Publishers, [c1976]. xvi, 204p. illus. 29cm. cloth $15.95; paper $7.95.

Collectors' Guide to Nineteenth-Century Photographs is a guide to all facets of the subject intended for reference use by private and institutional collectors of nineteenth-century photographs. Arranged for easy use, the book is organized into five chapters which discuss and illustrate the types of photographs (cased, tintypes, stereographs, card photographs, and photographic prints) and five chapters of reference material (photographic literature, miscellany, listings of photographers, archives, and societies). An Appendix lists "Lost Daguerreotype Views of the American West" and "Publishers' Albums, Portfolios, and Books Illustrated with Original Photographs." A Bibliography of 21 basic books on the history and development of photography is appended. The author notes when an out-of-print title is available in reprint. Two indexes, one to the text and one to illustrations, aid in locating specific information.

Private collectors, museums, and special libraries will find *Collectors' Guide to Nineteenth-Century Photographs* notable for its coverage of the subject. *(Sept. 1, 1976, p.53)*

770'.75 Photographs—Collectors and collecting [CIP]
75-22004

Colombo's Canadian references.
[By] John Robert Colombo. Toronto, Oxford, 1976. viii, 576p. 24cm. cloth $14.95.

Colombo's Canadian References should really have been titled *Colombo's Encyclopaedia of Canada* or the *Concise Encyclopaedia of Canada*. It is a substantial compendium of useful and accurate information about Canada by the author of *Colombo's Canadian Quotations* (1974). Included are more than 6,000 brief entries relating to 50 categories: Abbreviations, Agriculture, Architecture, Art, Associations, Aviation, Awards, Broadcasting, Business, Canadianisms, Culture, Education, Entertainment, Eskimos, Events, Fauna, Film, Finance, Flora, Food & Drink, Geography, Government, History, Holidays, Indians, Journalism, Labour, Language, Law, Literature, Manufacturing, Military, Mining, Money, Music, Personalities, Places & Regions, Politics, Publications, Railways, Religion, Resources, Ships, Science, Sites, Society, Sports, Technology, War. Answers are provided to the kinds of questions that come to mind when reading about Canada. What's a *CEGEP?* Where's *Regina?* Why are the Liberals sometimes called *Grits?* Who was *Arthur Meighen?* When was the *Parti Quebecois* founded? There is no other one-volume work to rival it as a source of succinct information on a broad range of topics relating to Canada past and present. The articles are very objective and are written in a consistent and lucid style. References to the sources used are not given, but brief bibliographical citations to the major works of authors, musicians, etc., are provided in the body of the text. Lavish cross-references are indicated by capitalizing names and terms which have their own entries in the book. Thus one is easily led from the article on *The Ecstasy of Rita Joe* to George RYGA, Chief Dan GEORGE, Frances HYLAND, the ROYAL WINNIPEG BALLET, and the NATIONAL ARTS CENTER. Adequate *see* references lead from synonyms, related terms, and acronyms to the appropriate entries. As is usually the case with the Oxford University Press, the book is solidly made and beautifully printed. In particular, the use of a wide variety of carefully coordinated typefaces makes the book extremely easy to consult, although its pages are densely filled. At $14.95, the book is very reasonably priced considering the high quality of its production and quantity and quality of the research which has gone into its preparation. *Colombo's Canadian References* will be indispensable for any Canadian library and doubtless will be purchased for home use by many Canadians. School, public, and academic libraries in the U.S. and elsewhere will find it a useful addition to their reference collections.

(July 15, 1977, p.1753)

971'.003 Canada—Dictionaries and encyclopedias [CIP]

The color treasury of gemstones.
Text by Eduard Gubelin; photographs by Michael Wolgensinger and Eduard Gubelin. Translated by P. B. Lapworth. New York, T. Y. Crowell, 1975, c1969. 138p. illus. 29cm. buckram $9.95.

In the Introduction to *The Color Treasury of Gemstones,* Dr. Gubelin states that, "This book attempts . . . to provide—with a touch of poetry—a comprehensive and easily accessible survey of the gemstone realm." Accessibility is hampered by the lack of an index. What is provided are full-page color photographs of 15 major varieties of gems (diamond, ruby, sapphire, beryl, crysoberyl, emerald, garnet, moonstone, opal, peridot, quartz, spinel, topaz, tourmaline, and zircon) and 9 major varieties of ornamental stones (agate, jade, labradorite, spectrolite, lapis lazuli, malachite, rhodochrosite, rhodonite, and turquoise). The photographs are accompanied by short chapters (one to six pages in length) containing information on the chemical composition, formation, occurrence, recovery, color variations, and properties of each type of gemstone listed. Information on legends, poetry, and quotations concerning various gems and ornamental stones is also included. The author's passing reference to the purported special affinity of women for jewels will seem superfluous to readers holding firm egalitarian opinions.

The major part of the work is devoted to information on individual gemstones. Additional coverage is given to the origins of color in gems, crystal formation, durability, the collecting of rare gemstones, and the carving and engraving of ornamental stones. A seven-page Glossary of Technical Terms completes the book.

Both text and illustrations are printed on heavy white paper with margins large enough to permit rebinding. A full- or half-page color photograph appears on virtually every other page. Particularly effective is the dramatic contrast shown between raw and finished products of the lapidary's art. The photographs have excellent definition and color.

While the lack of an index does diminish the usefulness of this book as a reference tool, the large color photographs and the Glossary of Technical Terms may interest home collectors and school or public libraries in *The Color Treasury of Gemstones.*
(Sept. 1, 1976, p.53)

553'.8   Precious stones—Pictorial works   [CIP]   75-15715

Comparative guide to American colleges.
For students, parents, and counselors. By James Cass and Max Birnbaum. 7th ed. New York, Harper & Row, [c1975]. xxxiii, 749p. 24cm. cloth $15; paperback $6.95.

The first edition of this guide was published in 1964. James Cass is education editor of *Saturday Review,* and Max Birnbaum is professor emeritus of human relations and sociology at Boston University. They are also responsible for the *Counselors' Comparative Guide to American Colleges* and the *Comparative Guide to Two-Year Colleges and Career Programs.*

The Comparative Guide intends "to provide for prospective students and their parents the kind of analytical and comparative data about individual colleges that will offer a sound basis for college selection." It is claimed that every accredited four-year college is included; such specialized institutions as seminaries, service academies, and music and art institutes are omitted. Arrangement is alphabetical by name of the institution or by key word: that is, the College of William and Mary is in the *W's* and the University of Akron is in the *A's.* Cross-references refer the user from such colleges as Medgar Evers to City University of New York. Entries vary in length from a few lines to more than a page; all these pages have two columns.

Most entries provide the following information in paragraph form: address, control (state, independent, or religious), founding date, enrollment (men and women, full- and part-time, graduate and undergraduate), general background statement, admission requirements, percent of applicants admitted, average freshman SAT scores, academic environment including degrees offered, special programs, size of library, percent of faculty with advanced degrees, religious orientation, campus life (regulations, percent leaving campus on weekends, etc.), annual costs and scholarships.

There are three indexes: one groups the institutions by state or territory, another groups them by religious orientation, and a Selectivity Index divides them into the categories of Most Selective, Highly Selective, Very (+) Selective, Very Selective, and Selective, representing the judgment of the authors concerning the scholastic potential of the student body and thus the "academic quality" of the colleges.

Comparison of this edition to the sixth, published in 1973, reveals considerable updating of statistical information and revision of textual material to reflect changes on the campuses. The listing of subject fields and the colleges conferring degrees in each has, however, been dropped; it now forms part of the *Counselors' Comparative Guide. The Comparative Guide to American Colleges* continues to be a helpful "consumer's guide to higher education" and should be in most libraries.
(May 1, 1977, p.1374)

378.73   Universities and colleges—U.S.—Directories   [OCLC]   75-6332

Comparative guide to two-year colleges and career programs.
By James Cass and Max Birnbaum. New York, Harper & Row, [c1976]. xvii, 549p. 24cm. cloth $17.50; paper $6.95.

Unlike the authors' *Comparative Guide to American Colleges,* where all institutions are listed in one alphabet, this volume groups them by state or territory. In the first section more than 1,700 schools are listed, including community colleges, public supported technical schools and institutes, traditional junior colleges, and four-year institutions which offer shorter programs. Information given for each includes address, enrollment, type of control, data of founding, a general statement, admission requirements and average freshman SAT scores, type of degree granted, terminal/career-oriented programs offering good job opportunities, programs preparing students for transfers, costs, and, where residential facilities are found, basic information on the nature of the campus life. Entries average about three to four paragraphs each. Occasional cross-references to variant names are found, and some schools are grouped under districts, systems, or parent universities.

The second major part of this volume is the Index to more than 200 education and training programs below the baccalaureate level. Under each field the schools are listed by state, and, if available, the number of such degrees conferred in 1973-74 is stated. The subjects range from accounting to welding technologies and cover such diverse areas as agribusiness, gunsmithing, interior design, loss prevention security, and physical therapy. Numerous cross-references make this guide easy to use. A list of 80 programs offering above average job opportunities precedes this section.

The book contains a two-and-a-half-page list of the schools with ties to particular religious groups, but it lacks an alphabetical name index. This is probably more of a drawback for a librarian needing quick information on a given school than for someone using it as a guidance and counseling tool. *Comparative Guide to Two-Year Colleges and Career Programs* should be most helpful for libraries serving patrons of high school age or older.
(May 1, 1977, p.1374)

378.1534   Community colleges—U.S.—Directories || Occupational training—U.S.—Directories   [OCLC]   76-5552

The complete book of United States coin collecting.
[By] Norman M. Davis. rev. ed. New York, Macmillan Pub. Co., [c1976]. x, 341p. illus. 22cm. cloth $9.95.

The first edition of this introductory volume was published in 1971. The author's approach is popular in style and is largely based on material found in his syndicated newspaper column, "The Coin Box." Only Davis' personal choices of coins which he considers to be Star-Line (i.e., items recommended as an excellent investment) and coins minted since the first edition have been updated for this revision. Organization, type of information included, and the basic narrative remain mostly unchanged.

The text is divided into six sections: (1) "This Fascinating Hobby," which introduces coin collecting with tips on grading, storing, collecting, clubs, etc.; (2) "From Old Colonials to New Dimes"; (3) "Twenty Cents to Trade Dollars"; (4) "The Romance of Gold"; (5) "Let's Collect These, Too," which covers medals, tokens, commemoratives, private gold, Confederate coins, etc.; and (6) "Mints, Designs, and Other Coin Lore." There are five concluding parts: a Table of Mints, a Complete Star-Line and Marginals List, a Collector's Vocabulary, a Bibliography, and an Index.

Coin collecting has become both a major hobby and a big business in this country. Davis has written a readable, informative guide which the majority of coin collectors can use whether they are beginners or more sophisticated in their approach. Most libraries would wish to add this revised edition to their circulating collections since it does have a well-indexed narrative which covers history, issues, fascinating facts, and numerous suggestions about U.S. coins and how to collect them. At the same time, Mort Reed's *Coins: An Investor's & Collector's Guide* and Joseph Coffin's 4th revision of *The Complete Book of Coin Collecting* might also be considered, if not already purchased, because they are comparable in many respects to the Davis volume noted here. *(Apr. 1, 1977, p.1195)*

†737.4973 Numismatics—Collectors and collecting || Coins   70-117963

The complete guide to salt and fresh water fishing equipment.
By Bill Wisner. New York, E. P. Dutton & Co., Inc., [1976]. 255p. 24cm. cloth $9.95; institutional discount available for orders over 5.

Millions are spent annually on sports fishing equipment. Wisner provides valuable consumer information about the selection and purchase of equipment as well as sources. Though the reader is cautioned to be wary of cheap equipment, the author is quick to advise that the purposes determine the kind and size of the investment. There are many hints about the uses of different lures, lines, and tackle for successful fishing experiences. Comparisons are made between salt and freshwater fishing. Rather than indicating which makes and models are best, the author guardedly suggests that "you can't go wrong" with a particular brand.

Not only does Wisner describe the many varieties and makes of fishing equipment, but he has included information on clothing to wear, a practical glossary of fishing terms and slang, and a list of state fish and game departments. For the avid reader of fishing books, the Bibliography at the end, though far from exhaustive, can be used to build a "broad spectrum" library of 70 titles. The average fishing enthusiast will find most of the information he or she needs about currently available equipment in this compact volume. *(Sept. 15, 1976, p.203)*

688.79 Fishing—Implements and appliances [OCLC]   75-42573

Concise encyclopedia of Jewish music.
[By] Macy Nulman. New York, McGraw-Hill Book Co., [c1975]. xii, 276p. illus. 24cm. cloth $14.95.

Macy Nulman has had a distinguished career as scholar and educator. His *Concise Encyclopedia* "endeavors to make accessible in succinct form detailed information concerning the manifold aspects of Jewish music." Its "500-odd" entries, its Introduction states, "include definitions of Jewish musical terms and vocabulary, the origin and structure of Biblical and post-Biblical instruments, histories and descriptions of Jewish musical organizations and movements, [descriptions of] musical works, and principal published collections." Entries are in alphabetical sequence, and most are brief; explanations are succinct but clear; sources are generously cited. At the end is a brief but instructive five-page chronology. The cross-reference network is clear and far reaching. Illustrations (pictorical and musical) are numerous, well chosen, and well placed. So helpful are Nulman's explanations, so efficient are his cross-references, that his *Concise Encyclopedia*—admirable as a work of reference—might well be used as a textbook. Perhaps Nulman will consider displaying, in a second edition, his cross-reference network as a study outline, with his citations of sources indicating further possibilities for self-education. *(Dec. 15, 1976, p.630)*

781.7'2'924 Music, Jewish—Dictionaries || Music, Jewish—Bio-bibliography [CIP]   74-5053

The concise heritage dictionary.
Boston, Houghton Mifflin, [1976], xii, 820p. illus. maps. ports. 24cm. paper-covered boards $5.95; to schools and libraries, $4.46.

The Concise Heritage Dictionary is based on *The American Heritage Dictionary of the English Language* (Boston: American Heritage Publishing Co., Inc. and Houghton Mifflin Co., 1969) which was evaluated in *Reference and Subscription Books Reviews*, February 1, 1972. Many of the outstanding features of the full-length, 155,000-entry parent publication have been incorporated into the 55,000-entry concise dictionary. Entries emphasize contemporary American English and include names and places, acronyms, abbreviations, phrases, and foreign words and phrases. More than 100 entries contain the usage notes which *The American Heritage Dictionary* developed through its special panel of notable American writers and speakers. Etymologies are given in brief form with many references to an Appendix of Indo-European roots at the back of the book, which is an abridged version of the Appendix in the full-length dictionary. Some 300 illustrations, maps of countries, and charts have been selected, appearing within the text rather than in the outer margins as in the more comprehensive desk edition.

A special feature of the *Concise Heritage Dictionary* is its pleasing format with large, easy-to-read print of excellent clarity and contrast on a durable, opaque white paper stock. The two-column pages contain large headings of beginning and ending words, and a pronunciation key using short, easy words appears across the bottom of each pair of facing pages. Entry words are divided into syllables by dots followed by pronunciation in parentheses. Symbols note the part of speech with verb or plural endings as required. Definitions, numbered when multiple, have often been simplified to brief statements with the current meaning given first. Brackets enclose the etymological note, followed, when required, by additional forms of the word in other parts of speech. For controversial or difficult words, phrases are included which illustrate the use. Usage labels such as "informal," "slang," "non-standard," and "archaic" help to establish the context of many words.

In addition to the small portraits, illustrations, and maps within the columns of text, there are useful full-page charts, a list of books of the Bible, exchange rates for currencies, the geologic time scale, measurement units, proofreader's marks, symbols and signs, and other helpful graphics. These are conveniently consulted because the sturdy binding permits full opening with sufficient center margins. The paper-covered boards, though susceptible to wear at the corners, are satisfactorily sturdy considering the low price.

With its selection of 55,000 words and clear, brief definitions, the *Concise Heritage Dictionary* can serve as an intermediate dictionary for advanced middle school students and secondary school students whose vocabulary requirements cannot be fulfilled by the typical children's dictionary but who are not yet prepared to deal with a desk dictionary in the 100,000-plus entry range. The dictionary is also excellent for general use in the home, school, or office by anyone who likes the brevity and convenience of a concise dictionary or who prefers the clarity of large print. *(Jan. 15, 1977, p./46)*

423 English language—Dictionaries [CIP]   76-4047

Congressional quarterly's guide to Congress.
Edited by Robert A. Diamond and Patricia Ann O'Connor. 2d ed. Washington, Congressional Quarterly, 1976. xxxi, 721p. 293–Ap. illus. 29cm. cloth $49.50.

The first edition of this guide, published in 1971, received general approbation. Although only five years have elapsed, the publisher decided to produce this revised edition because, according to the Introduction, "the rush of important events and the spate of Congressional reforms of the last five years have outdated this admirable work."

The second edition retains the arrangement and style of the first. Those portions of the text itself, especially in the historical section which did not call for extensive revision, have also been preserved intact, although footnotes have been added as an aid to further research. Most of the bibliographies that are scattered throughout the volume have been updated, as have the charts and the biographical section. In addition, the new edition has been visually enhanced by the inclusion of a number of black-and-white photographs.

Some of the major changes between the first and second editions lie in those sections that deal with the powers of Congress and its relation to the Executive. Information on Watergate and its aftermath can be found throughout the volume; the role of Congress in the events themselves is outlined in a section entitled "Watergate and the Executive Privilege." The Appendix includes the complete text of the proposed articles of impeachment against former President Richard M. Nixon which were adopted by the House Judiciary Committee in July 1974. The volume also contains information on the War Powers Act of 1973, the new reform of the electoral system, and the recent changes in House and Senate internal organization and procedures.

The second edition of CQ's *Guide* should prove as valuable a reference tool as did the first. Those public and university libraries that did not buy the first edition would benefit from owning the second; those libraries that have the previous volume may find that the usefulness of the current edition justifies its cost. *(July 1, 1977, p.1675)*

328.73 U.S. Congress   [CIP]   76-41925

Conservation directory, 1976:
a list of organizations, agencies, and officials concerned with natural resource use and management. Ed. by Gloria H. Decker. 21st ed. Washington, D.C., The National Wildlife Federation, [c1976]. xi, 235p. 28cm. paper $3.

The National Wildlife Federation was founded in 1936 to "educate citizens about the need for wise use and proper management of our natural resources." In addition to the *Conservation Directory*, which is published annually, the federation's publications include *National Wildlife*, a bimonthly conservation journal; *Ranger Rick's Nature Magazine*, produced for children 12 times a year; *Conservation News*, a semi-monthly newsletter; and *Conservation Report*, a weekly digest of national conservation legislation.

The *Conservation Directory* has extensive lists of U.S. and Canadian agencies and citizens' groups, colleges and universities offering courses in conservation, Canadian and U.S. fish and game directors and commissioners, conservation and environment offices of foreign governments, and periodicals and directories. Five Indexes in front of the book facilitate locating specific organizations and persons: U.S. Federal Departments, Agencies, Offices; International, National, Interstate Organizations, Commissions; State Territorial Agencies and Citizens' Groups Index; Canadian Federal Government Agencies and National Citizens' Groups; and Canadian Provincial Government Departments and Citizens' Groups Index. A Personal Name Index is at the back. The *Conservation Directory* brings together an extraordinary number of names, addresses, and telephone numbers of organizations and persons involved in conservation. It is updated frequently enough to make it a dependable reference for conservation researchers. *(Sept. 1, 1976, p.53)*

†639.9   Birds, Protection of—U.S. || Game protection—U.S.   [OCLC]   70-10746

Consumer complaint guide 1977.
[By] Joseph Rosenbloom. New York, Macmillan Information, [c1976]. 497p. 22cm. cloth $10.95; paper $4.95.

381'.3 U.S.—Manufacturers—Directories || Consumer protection—U.S.—Directories   [CIP]
                                                                                    76-12834

Consumer protection guide 1977.
[By] Joseph Rosenbloom. New York, Macmillan Information, [1976]. viii, 398p. 22cm. cloth $10.95; paper $4.95.

381'.3 Consumer—protection—U.S. || Complaints (Retail trade)—U.S. || Professions—U.S. || Service industries—U.S.   [CIP]   76-22872

When Joseph Rosenbloom wrote the first edition of the *Consumer Complaint Guide* in 1972, it was welcomed by reference librarians and consumers as a practical handbook of advice and a directory of resources for countering complaints. The 1977 guide expands, updates, and revises its predecessor's coverage. It is arranged in three parts: a brief 38-page section on "The Consumer in the Marketplace;" a helpful 125-page section on "How and to Whom to Complain" which describes 8 resorts for complaints (action services, Better Business Bureaus, industry and trade associations, small claims courts, state and local consumer agencies, voluntary consumer organizations, national and international consumer organizations, and federal agencies); and a 332-page directory of companies, products, and brand names. Coverage in the latter section is quite broad as evidenced by the Committee's sampling of trade and reference books publishers. There is no index; so the book's table of contents and tripartite arrangement must serve as access points for the user.

Rosenbloom wrote the *Consumer Protection Guide* as a complement to the *Consumer Complaint Guide* because the complaint book did not cover the "vital area of complaints involving services of all kinds, both professional and non-professional" in any depth. The *Protection Guide* is essentially a directory of 55 services. Among the 15 professional services that are recipients of complaints are associations representing dentists, medical doctors, nurses, osteopaths, optometrists, podiatrists, funeral directors, and veterinarians. Covered among the other services are travel agents, surveyors, public utilities, pilots, interior designers, and the construction trades. Arrangement is A to Z as indicated in the Contents and then alphabetically by state. Prefacing each subject's directory is an essay describing the service. The essays vary in length commensurate with the services' use by the public. For example, the one for medical doctors is nine-and-a-half pages long and describes training and qualifications, specialties, selection, and complaints about doctors, while the essay for social workers is only one-half page long and discusses only their training and qualifications and procedures for complaint.

Publication of the *Complaint Guide* and the *Protection Guide* in reasonably priced paperback editions brings these practical consumer advisers within the reach of homes and libraries. They supplement and complement John Dorfman's *Consumer Arsenal* (New York: Praeger, 1976) reviewed by the Committee in the April 1, 1977, *Reference and Subscription Books Reviews*.
(June 15, 1977, p.1600)

Consumer sourcebook:
a directory and guide to government organizations; associations, centers and institutes; media services; company and trademark information; and bibliographic material relating to consumer topics, sources of recourse, and advisory information. Paul Wasserman, managing ed.; Jean Morgan, assoc. ed. Detroit, Gale Research, 1974. xiv, 593p. 29cm. cloth $35.

According to the editors of *Consumer Sourcebook*, the purpose of this new directory is to "provide specific names, addresses, and phone numbers of the people and departments designed to handle complaints or redress grievances and to supply information about how and where a product or service can be obtained."

The volume is divided into six sections: "Government Organizations"; "Associations, Centers, Institutes, Etc."; "Media Services"; "Companies and Trade Names"; "Selected Bibliography"; and "Indexes." In the major section of the book, the listing of companies and trade or brand names, entries include the name and address of the organization and individual responsible for assisting consumers. Telephone numbers and names of appropriate departments to contact are provided for less than a fifth of the companies. Some of the omitted information may be found in local telephone directories.

The Committee noted inconsistencies between listings in the *Sourcebook* and entries in other current directories such as the *Encyclopedia of Associations; Thomas' Register of American Manufacturers; Standard and Poor's Register of Corporations, Directors, and Executives; Moody's Book and Finance Manual; Standard and Poor's Corporation Records;* and the *National Zip Code Directory.* Because research and editorial work for the *Sourcebook* was completed early in 1974, some of the entries already need updating. This same criticism applies to listings of some governmental services and radio stations, television stations, and newspapers with consumer assistance programs and departments.

The annotated Bibliography in the *Sourcebook* is its most useful feature. Included in this section are citations for directories, guides, bibliographies, abstracts, and indexes; books and pamphlets; periodicals and newsletters; continuing publications series; and audiovisual materials.

The *Consumer Sourcebook's* three separate indexes (Organization, Personnel, Publication) do not provide assistance for the user looking for organizations in a geographic region, and the Personnel Index is vulnerable to quick obsolescence because of rapid turnover of staffs in corporations and governmental agencies.

The information in the *Consumer Sourcebook* is presented in a two-column-per-page format. Printed on dull-finish paper, the text is highly legible. Unfortunately, the cloth binding does not appear to be strong enough to survive sustained use.

Although the *Consumer Sourcebook* does gather together a vast array of directory information for the curious or complaining consumer, its compilation is flawed by omissions and the inclusion of obsolete data. Also, the editors state no criteria for inclusions. Standard business, government, and telephone directories will generally provide more current and accurate information. *(Sept. 1, 1976, p.53)*

381'.3 Consumer protection—Information services—U.S.—Directories || Consumer education—Information services—U.S.—Directories [CIP] 74-10494

A consumer's arsenal.
[By] John Dorfman. New York, Praeger Publishers, [1976]. viii, 270p. 22cm. cloth $10; paper $3.95.

Jack Dorfman was a former editor at *Consumer Reports.* His latest book, *A Consumer's Arsenal,* is an easy-to-use, conveniently arranged handbook of advice and resources for consumers of all kinds of materials and services. Arrangement of the book is tripartite: "A Tactics Manual for Consumers," "Consumer Protection, State by State," and "Complaint Encyclopedia: Where to Go with What Complaint." The "Tactics Manual" presents a ten-point timetable plan of attack which will fit numerous consumer complaints. The state-by-state discussion of consumer protection is alphabetically arranged by state and lists state consumer protection agencies with their addresses. The complaint encyclopedia directs readers to aid in resolving 50 kinds of complaints generated by diverse sources ranging from advertising and buying clubs to encyclopedias and vocational schools.

The book's table of contents, which lists all topics covered, substitutes as a finding device. Public libraries will find *A Consumer's Arsenal* an excellent directory for consumers who have been short-changed. *(Apr. 1, 1977, p.1195)*

381'.3 Complaints (Retail trade) || Consumer protection [CIP] 75-39956

Contemporary novelists.
James Vinson, editor; D. L. Kirkpatrick, associate editor. 2d. ed. London, St. James; New York, St. Martin's, 1976. xvii, 1636p. 24cm. Holliston sturdite, $35.

Contemporary Novelists was first published in 1972 as one of the volumes in the "Contemporary Writers of the English Language" series. Revisions were planned at approximately three-year intervals for each of the volumes, which in addition to *Contemporary Novelists* (1972, 1976) are *Contemporary Poets* (1971, 1975) and *Contemporary Dramatists* (1973). The first edition of *Contemporary Novelists* is described in the section on biographical dictionaries in *Reference and Subscription Books Reviews 1972–1974* (Chicago: American Library Association, 1975), p.373.

James Vinson, general editor of the series, continues as editor of the second edition of *Contemporary Novelists,* with an associate editor, D. L. Kirkpatrick, new to this volume. The selection of novelists for the biographical entries is based upon the recommendations of 29 advisors. The advisors and contributors are scholars, editors, and writers from the U.S., Britain, and other Commonwealth and English-speaking countries. They are identified in brief biographical notes at the end of the volume, with the essays they have contributed. The selection for the second edition includes some 90 percent of the novelists in the first edition whose literary production has continued into the mid-1970s; and a number of new novelists whose reputations have recently become established. The second edition is larger than the first by 40 biographees and about 200 additional pages. In addition to the entries for the new novelists, there is revised and updated biographical and bibliographical information for the novelists whose entries have been continued into this edition, with publications noted through 1975. The analytical commentary remains the same in most instances.

Each novelist's entry contains a paragraph of biographical facts including nationality, birthplace and date, marriage and children, educational attainments, positions, special activities and achievements, awards and honors, and present address. Following this is a bibliographical section which lists the novelist's publications in chronological order within such forms as novels, short stories or uncollected short stories, plays, verse, and other writings. The works listed are British and American editions of all titles, and first editions of publications of other countries. The editor notes that the uncollected short stories are those published since the author's last collection, plus others the author has mentioned. Some authors have suggested a few bibliographical or critical studies for inclusion and some have indicated where their manuscript collections are held. Extensive checklists and bibliographies of literary criticism do not fall within the scope of this biographical source.

The analytical portion of the entry often contains a statement by the novelist about his or her own feelings and purposes. There is always an excellent analytical and critical commentary by a contributor that highlights the novelist's unique qualities and techniques, themes and concerns, and individual contribution to contemporary literature. The combining of biographical and bibliographical information with discerning analytical commentary by the author and a knowledgeable and appreciative contributor is a distinguishing feature of the volumes in the Contemporary Writers of the English Language series.

Walter Allen's perceptive preface on the state of the novel is repeated from the first edition. He comments on the present "prodigality of talent" and notes the coming into existence of the new literatures of the Caribbean Islands, India, countries of Africa, and other places where English is spoken. However, though *Contemporary Novelists* expresses interest in the novelists of the "new literatures," it does not offer access to their names by national or ethnic group. Other sources must be used if one is unfamiliar with these emergent novelists' individual names.

New to this edition is an appendix of entries for 18 novelists "who have died since the 1950's but whose reputations are essentially contemporary." Among this group are Paul Goodman, Jack Kerouac, Carson McCullers, J. R. R. Tolkien, Richard Wright, and others.

The volume is both sturdy and attractive. The clear print and generous spacing of the various parts of the entry contribute to convenient reference use as well as enjoyable reading.

(Oct. 15, 1976, p.344)

823'.03 English fiction—20th century—Bio-bibliography || American literature—20th century—Bio-bibliography [OCLC] 75-189694

Cookery Americana.
Advisory ed., Louis Szathmary. 15v. New York, Arno Pr., 1973. 22cm. cloth $75.
Along the northern border:
cookery in Idaho, Minnesota, and North Dakota. New York, Arno Pr., 1973. xv, 120, 111, 127p. 22cm. cloth $10.
641.5 Cookery, American—Northwestern States [CIP] 72-9788
Cooking in old Creole days.
[By] Celestine Eustes. New York, Arno Pr., 1973. ix, 90p. illus. 22cm. cloth $5.
641.519763 Cookery, Creole [CIP] 72-9798
Cool, chill, and freeze:
a new approach to cookery. Intro. and suggested recipes by Louis Szathmary. New York, Arno Pr., 1973. xvi, 85, 144p. 22cm. cloth $7.
641.7'9 Salads || Cookery (Cold dishes) || Desserts, Frozen || Refrigerators [CIP] 72-9791
Directions for cookery in its various branches.
[By] Eliza Leslie. New York, Arno Pr., 1973. xv. 511p. 22cm. cloth $12.
641.5 Cookery, American [CIP] 72-9797
Fifty years of prairie cooking.
Intro. and suggested recipes by Louis Szathmary. New York, Arno Pr., 1973. xx, 94, 81, 48, 155p. illus. 22 cm. cloth $10.
641.5 Cookery, American—Middle West [CIP] 72-9794
Handbook of practical cookery.
By Pierre Blot. New York, Arno Pr., 1973. 478p. illus. 23cm. cloth $12.
641.5'973 Cookery, American [OCLC] 72-9789
High living:
recipes from Southern climes. Compiled by L. L. McLaren. New York, Arno Pr., 1973. x, n.p. illus. 19cm. cloth $5.
641.5 Cookery [CIP] 72-9798
Home cookery:
ladies indispensable companion: cookery in Northeastern cities. Intro. and suggested recipes by Louis Szathmary. New York, Arno Pr., 1973. xx, 158, 136p. 22cm. cloth $9.
641.5 Cookery, American—Northeastern States [CIP] 72-9790
The improved housewife.
[By] Mrs. A. L. Webster. New York, Arno Pr., 1973. 214p. illus. 22cm. cloth $7.
641.5 Cookery [CIP] 72-9804
The Kansas home cook-book.
Compiled by Mrs. C. H. Cushing and Mrs. B. Gray. New York, Arno Pr., 1973. xvi, 317p. 22cm. cloth $9.
641.5 Cookery, American—Kansas [CIP] 72-9792
Midwestern home cookery.
Intro. and suggested recipes by Louis Szathmary. New York, Arno Pr., 1973. xxi, 178, 155p. illus. 22cm. cloth $10.
641.5 Cookery, American—Middle West [CIP] 72-9801
Mrs. Porter's new southern cookery book.
[By] Mrs. M. E. Porter. New York, Arno Pr., 1973. xvi, 416p. 22cm. cloth $12.
641.5 Cookery, American—Southern States [CIP] 72-9802

One hundred recipes for the chafing dish.
[By] H. M. Kinsley. New York, Arno Pr., 1973. 182p. illus. 19cm. cloth $5.
641.5'8 Chafing—dish recipes [CIP] 72-9795
Six little cooks.
[By] Elizabeth Stansbury Kirkland. New York, Arno Pr., 1973. xii, 236p. illus. 19cm. cloth $7.
641.5 Cookery, Juvenile literature [CIP] 72-9796
Southwestern cookery:
Indian and Spanish influences. Intro. and suggested recipes by Louis Szathmary. New York, Arno Pr., 1973. xxii, 124, 79, 5, 18, 264p. 22cm. cloth, $12.
641.5 Cookery, American—Southwestern States || Indians of North America—Food [CIP] 72-9803

Cookery Americana is an exact reprint of 27 cookbooks published in 15 volumes. The originals were published between 1845 and 1955. All of the books in the Arno set are in the private collection of Louis I. Szathmary, Chicago restaurateur, chef, food management consultant, and owner of the world famous Chicago restaurant, The Bakery. Szathmary, editor/compiler of *Cookery Americana,* has written an introduction and suggested recipes for each volume in the set. The books illustrate the evolution of U.S. cookbooks over the years, and several of them include material no longer considered within the province of recipe books, e.g., instructions on etiquette, advice on household and family management, and humorous common sense hints on laundry and cleaning.

Since each book is unique in scope and coverage, the Committee will describe each one briefly. *Along the Northern Border* is made up of three separately paged cookbooks, each with its own title page: *Choice Recipes by Moscow Women,* compiled by the Hospitality Committee of the Presbyterian Ladies Aid (Moscow, Idaho), 1931; *Library Ann's Cook Book,* compiled in 1928 by the Minneapolis Public Library; and the fourth edition of the *Y.M.C.A. Cook Book,* printed in 1924. The three cookbooks in this volume present the plain, wholesome dishes and simple but skillful methods of the pioneers along the northern borders of the U.S. The recipes are adapted to local possibilities. Szathmary lists eight tested recipes (two or more from each book) in the Introduction. In *Choice Recipes by Moscow Women,* the Hospitality Committee of the Presbyterian Ladies Aid presents delightful "down-home" dishes. *Library Ann's Cook Book* and the *Y.M.C.A. Cook Book* contain compilations of favorite recipes designed to provide tested family-satisfying meals. The latter includes helpful hints for washing and cleaning clothes, as well as for cooking. Most of the recipes in *Along the Northern Border* should be relatively easy to adjust to today's methods because all three books were written in the early twentieth century.

Creole cooking is the creation of a special amalgam of people —black, Indian, Spanish, French, British, German, and Slavic— inspired by the Louisiana territory's natural resources and its settlers' inherited tastes. The interesting recipes in *Cooking in Old Creole Days* provide the reader with an accurate picture of the Louisiana life style.

Many of the recipes were handed down from generation to generation with slave families. The recipes are indexed under the first word in the recipe: "A Todd Ham" (p.20) is indexed under "A," "To Cook and Serve Tomatoes" (page 38) is indexed under "T," etc. Once the user identifies this irregularity, there is little difficulty in finding recipes in this slender, 84-page book. Tomatoes, one of the main vegetables of Creole cooking, are described in p.38–43. *Cooking in Old Creole Days* is a delight and one of the most pleasing books in the series.

Cool, Chill, and Freeze is made up of two books: Alice Bradley's 1924 *Electric Refrigerator Menus and Recipes,* and *Florida Salads,* which was printed in Boston in 1926. *Electric Refrigerator Menus and Recipes* boasts 27 flavors of frozen desserts. *Florida Salads* is a special cookbook which intends to encourage cooks to make salads an experimental and artistic culinary experience. The recipes in these two cookbooks are designed for the icebox or electric refrigerator. Each book has a detailed Index. The recipes are just as easy to make now as in 1926 and 1928 when the books were published.

Elisa Leslie was one of the first commercially successful cookbook authors in our country's history. From its first publication, her book *Directions for Cookery,* was very much in demand, and the volume was reissued many times—more than 30; *Mansell* states that as many as 60 editions were produced. It is very difficult today to find a copy that does not show the wear and tear of a used cookbook. Elisa Leslie wrote U.S. histories and sociology and education books. Her first cookbook was printed in 1837.

Directions for Cookery, a standard for many years, is one of the more practical cookbooks in the series. Most of the recipes are very explicit, but according to Szathmary they sometimes need reinterpretation to conform with modern American English, e.g., "what we know as roast beef she calls Baked Beef (p.71–72) . . . Who knows today what a 'Middling' is? . . . It is a cut of pork which runs from the shoulder down to the ham."

Among promising territories for reading and culinary exploration are "Sweetmeats including Preserves and Jellies;" "Custards, &c;" (especially Puddings); "Animals Used as Butchers' Meat" (p.497–99). There is a ten-page Index and a one-page "index to Appendix," which has sections called "Containing New Receipts," "Carving," "To Draw Poultry, &c."

Fifty Years of Prairie Cooking has four separate cookbooks within its covers: *A Collection of Choice Recipes,* contributed by the ladies of Des Moines, 1903; *Dorcas Cook Book,* published by the Sioux City, Iowa, Dorcas Society of St. John's Lutheran Church in 1939; *Patriotic Food Show* (the official recipe book with all the demonstrations given during the Patriotic Food Show, St. Louis, Feb. 2–10, 1918); and *Priscilla Cook Book,* compiled by the Overton, Nebraska, Christian Church Priscilla Aid in 1954. These books provide much information on the foods and cooking methods of the pioneers and trailblazers who overcame monotony and hardship to settle the central part of the U.S. The recipes are for robust appetites and include interesting adaptations of customs and cooking methods. They use ingredients and know-how from other sections of the country as well as from other parts of the world. These cookbooks are typically American in their approach; they were compiled by many people in the community, not for their personal financial gain, but rather for a charitable purpose.

Although the recipes from *A Collection of Choice Recipes* and *Patriotic Food Show* would have to be adjusted slightly to satisfy today's cook, *Dorcas Cook Book* (1939) and *Priscilla Cook Book* (1954) are more modern, giving oven temperature and baking time. *A Collection of Choice Recipes* and *Dorcas Cook Book* contain one-page subject indexes. *Patriotic Food Show* and *Priscilla Cook Book* have no indexes or tables of contents, but the books are so short that location of information poses no problem for the user.

Hand-Book of Practical Cookery was written by Pierre Blot, who opened the first cooking academy in New York, shortly after the Civil War. Blot's book combines elegant French recipes with those common to the U.S. in the latter part of the nineteenth century, The *Hand-Book of Practical Cookery* is really a textbook with clear directions, and it is unique for its time. The book begins with a chapter on cooking which defines such terms as boiling, broiling, frying, mixing, and roasting. This is followed by a chapter describing utensils, food, and spices. Each chapter is introduced with a clear definition of the subject followed by a narrative analysis of each recipe which could be equated to today's methods and procedures for cooking. In interpreting these recipes, one must remember that most stoves in 1869 used wood or coal for fuel. Temperature control was at best a guess, whereas today's gas and electric ranges have transformed this aspect of cooking into an exact science. This book concludes with a detailed 13½-page Index.

High Living is one of the smallest of the 15-volume set, but all the recipes have character and are cosmopolitan. The book was created by socialites and artists in San Francisco for the benefit of the Telegraph Hill Neighborhood Association before the San Francisco earthquake of 1906. The book is of particular interest not only because it is one of the very few pre-earthquake California cookbooks, but also because of its elegant, highly sophisticated recipes. It has a Table of Weights and Measures, and a useful subject Index. Although the recipes are easy to follow, judgment must be used in converting to the electric mixer, or blender, e.g., egg nog (p.56). The format is attractive with decorative margins.

The two books in *Home Cookery & Ladies Indispensable Companion* are *Home Cookery,* published in 1853 and *The New Family Book,* printed in 1854. These volumes reflect the significant social changes that the middle of the nineteenth century brought to Boston and New York, the two largest population centers of the Northeast. In Boston, Mrs. Chadwick's *Home Cookery* offered foreign and domestic dishes and *The New Family Book,* published in New York City, included home remedies and etiquette advice in addition to recipes. Both books use considerable amounts of native U.S. food in their recipes and mirror life in Boston and New York at that time.

Home Cookery has a complete Index. *Ladies' Indispensable Companion* has a detailed table of contents but no index. There are miscellaneous recipes for preserving flowers in water, lighting matches in damp weather, curing inflamed eyes, and making cologne.

The Improved Housewife is the first cookbook that reveals an authentic national spirit. It uses many raw materials native to the U.S. The chapter on Marketing Plates discusses the cuts of beef, mutton, pork, veal, and venison. The price per pound is also given: sirloin, 10–12 cents per pound; brisket, 6 cents per pound; clod, 3 cents per pound; chuck, 5 cents per pound; leg of mutton, 8–10 cents per pound; and loin of pork, 6 cents per pound. There is a chapter on Carving that includes the major cuts of meat plus information on fowl, goose, and turkey. "Particulars to be Observed in the Selection of Marketables" also includes turkey, fowls, geese, ducks, shad, herring, lobsters, and crab.

The recipes are numbered. The eight-page table of contents lists recipes under broad general headings. "Miscellaneous Receipts" (p.195–214) includes a diversity of how-to-do-it suggestions such as "To Extract Tar, Paint, Grease, and Stains from Carpets," "To Corn Beef," "To Salt Pork," "To Make Potato Starch," and "To Renew Stale Bread and Cake." All in all, these observations contribute a piquant, nostalgic flavor.

The Kansas Home Cook-Book is one of the first U.S. cookbooks to include advice on style and serving (the appearance of the table, china, and silver) and suggestions as to what foods should be served on what occasions (for family and for company). Thus, American cookery moves beyond bare nutritional necessity to become a formalized art with rules, regulations, and norms.

The Kansas Home Cook-Book, first published in 1874, is interesting because it "gives such a concise yet entertaining glimpse of domestic life, manners, customs, etiquette, and socio-economic conditions of the Midwest in the seventies and eighties." In the section on Useful Hints: To Make Good Black Ink (p.287) and Mrs. E. K. Morgan's remedy to restore old crackers (p.283) are well worth trying. There is also a section on table etiquette and miscellany.

Midwestern Home Cookery is composed of the two cookbooks entitled *Capital City Cook Book* (1906) and *Presbyterian Cook Book* (1875). It includes signed recipes from all over the U.S., suggesting that each contributor invested personal pride in the venture.

The Capital City Cook Book from Madison, Wisconsin, was first published just about a decade later than the *Presbyterian Book*. Although not regional, it is still characteristically a Wisconsin book in that this is the first cookbook with an entire section devoted to cheese.

These books have special appeal, because they contain several recipes for the same items. In the *Presbyterian Cook Book* there are three recipes for brown bread, four for corn bread; and four recipes for biscuits. A detailed subject Table of Contents is provided, but there is no index.

The *Capital City Cook Book* lists seven recipes for corn bread, five for plum pudding, and eight different ways of making sponge cake. A detailed Subject Index is included. *Capital City Cook Book* has a timetable for meats and vegetables (p.150–51).

The New South in the title of *Mrs. Porter's New Southern Cookery Book* connotes a widening of regional horizons and increased hospitality to the influence of Northern manners, habits, and techniques of household management. The recipes are no longer strictly localized being taken from all sections of the U.S., even if their emphasis remains predominantly Southern. Mrs. Porter's cookbook is written for the experienced cook, not for the amateur. The reader finds recipes for arrowroot biscuits, sausage dumplings, widgeon, and teal and canvasback duck.

The 24-page Table of Contents is subdivided under broad subjects. Each general subject has an introductory statement that identifies techniques, procedures, and know-how essential for obtaining the best results for the suggested recipes. *Mrs. Porter's New Southern Cookery Book* was written in Virginia and published in Philadelphia, is easy to read, easy to understand, and easy to follow.

Published by a large silver manufacturing company, *One Hundred Recipes for the Chafing Dish* presents the chafing dish as the key to good food and improved social standing. This volume highlights the shift in emphasis that occurred as interest moved from the kitchen into the dining room—from preparing basic food for the family to serving elegant meals for guests.

One Hundred Recipes for the Chafing Dish includes not only recipes, but also pictures of chafing dishes, identified by manufacturer and model number. The recipes are clearly stated and should be relatively easy to follow. The five-page Index is accurate except for one or two minor discrepancies. For example, the entry for sausage, frankfurter, and cabbage recipe (p.158) is actually frankfurter and cabbage.

Six Little Cooks was one of the first cookbooks written exclusively for children. It was printed in Chicago less than ten years after the great fire. Here one not only learns how to prepare children's dishes of bygone days, but finds out about teaching methods of education and family life during that period of Chicago's history. This book symbolizes the new kinetic America and the concern of Americans for their children's future. In content and purpose it differed significantly from its predecessors. *Six Little Cooks* is primarily nostalgic. Some of the recipes would be difficult to follow using today's kitchen utensils and measurements, e.g., "Apple Pudding" (p.85).

Southwestern Cookery, the final volume in the series, is made up of five Spanish and Indian cookbooks: *Choctaw Indian Dishes,* compiled by Amanda and Peter J. Herdson in Tuskahoma, Oklahoma, in 1955; *Favorite Recipes of Colfax Country Club Women,* compiled by the Colfax County Home Demonstration Clubs of Colfax County, New Mexico, in 1946; *The Garfield Woman's Club Cook Book,* compiled and published by the Garfield, Utah, Woman's Club in 1916; *The Indian Cook Book,* by the Indian Women's club of Tulsa, Oklahoma, in 1933; and the second edition of *The Junior League of Dallas Cook Book,* compiled and edited by members of the Dallas, Texas, chapter of the Association of Junior Leagues of America. While strongly overshadowed and changed by the Anglo-Saxon, German, and French heritages of the settlers, the influence of the American Indians and Spanish conquerors is still visible in the cookery of the Southwest. Thus, strange fragrances and elemental and natural ingredients are just as much a part of the cooking of this region as are the more sophisticated western European recipes. In addition, there are not only Spanish dishes from Spain but also Spanish-American dishes from Mexico and not only recipes of the local Indian tribes, but also those of the Indians transferred to the Southwest by the U.S. government. Certain dishes of that polymorphic cuisine, such as chili, spread throughout the entire North American continent, influenced western Europe, and even affected the diet of the Orient.

Favorite Recipes of Colfax County Club Women and *The Garfield Woman's Club Cook Book* have tables of contents. *The Indian Cook Book* has an Index that is really a subject table of contents. *The Junior League of Dallas Cook Book* is a completely modern cookbook with tables of weights and measures, a timetable for cooking, Table of Contents, and a detailed Subject Index. Since these books are all written in this century, few changes would have to be made in order to bring these recipes into alignment with current practice.

Cookery Americana is sturdily bound in dark red buckram. It has gold lettering with decorative gold patterns on the front covers. The volumes lie flat when opened. Twelve of the volumes are one size (22 centimeters) and the other three are smaller (19 centimeters). Many of the recipes could be easily adapted and followed by the present-day cook, but the set's main value is historical. The major drawback of the books as a set is the lack of a comprehensive index that would provide access to all the material. Since the books may be bought separately, and since some of them have good indexes and guides to the contents, individual volumes in the set may be of value to a limited audience of social historians and epicures.

(Nov. 15, 1976, p.497)

Cooking for entertaining.
[By] Nancy Tudor and Dean Tudor. New York & London, Bowker, 1976. xiv, 256p. 23cm. paper over boards $19.95.

The Tudors, both Canadian librarians with considerable training and experience in cookery and home entertaining, have selected from the plethora of publications on food preparation and service over 800 items—mainly books, pamphlets, and periodicals, with a few filmstrips and motion pictures—which they recommend for a comprehensive collection. Most of the books are published in the U.S. and are in-print; a few classics are either out-of-print or foreign. They have noted the number and level (beginner, intermediate, or advanced) of the recipes in each book, and have starred titles especially useful for a basic library or personal collection. For each entry they provide imprint, paging, price, LC number, and annotation. Lively and absorbing, these entries vary in length from two or three lines to more than a dozen and capture the flavor of each book. They describe content, special features (such as use of good historical material to place the recipes in the context of a particular period or culture), shortcomings (cloying text or lack of index), and sometimes note the qualifications of the author, the publishing history of the book, and its relationship to those of similar genre. For nonprint materials complete trade bibliographic data are given. Chapter headings are: reference and resource materials (included here are a few books on kitchen design, equipment, table settings, etc.); general cookbooks; menu and entertaining cookbooks; specific foods, courses, and special kinds of meals; international cuisine (including American cookery); wine and food; special appliance cookery; party guides; periodicals; and societies, book clubs and further study. In this last category the reader is directed to cooking schools both in America and abroad. A good index facilitates locating material by author, title, and subject. The binding is insubstantial, but the margins are adequate. Although an occasional reader may object to the omission of a favorite book, *Cooking for Entertaining* introduces an impressive array of resources. Notable for its broad coverage, excellent organization, attention to detail, and spirited text, this book will be an appreciated acquisition in most public libraries. *(Dec. 1, 1976, p.563)*

016.6415'68   Cookery—Bibliography || Dinners and dining—Bibliography || Entertaining—Bibliography   [CIP]   76-9841

Cooking in old Creole days.
[By] Celestine Eustes. New York, Arno Pr., 1973. ix, 90p. illus. 22 cm. cloth $5.

641.519763   Cookery, Creole   [CIP]   72-9793

See page 116

The cooks' catalogue:
a critical selection of the best, the necessary and the special in kitchen equipment and utensils. Over 4000 items including 200 extraordinary recipes plus cooking folklore and 1700 illustrations produced with the assistance of the world's leading food authorities. Edited by James Beard, Milton Glaser, Burton Wolf, Barbara Poses Kafka, Helen S. Witty, and Associates of the Good Cooking School. New York, Harper, [1975]. 566p. illus. 29cm. cloth, $15.95.

According to Beard's Introduction, "commercial attachés of 138 countries . . . were asked for information on any manufacturers of equipment associated with food and drink." A half million cataloged items were noted, "and 10,000 . . . ordered for testing."

Over 900 of these pieces of kitchen equipment and utensils described here have been arranged in 11 categories: (1) Measuring and Cleaning Tools; (2) Knives, Sharpeners, and Cutting Boards; (3) Cutting Instruments Other than Knives; (4) Grinders, Crushers, Mashers, Refiners, and Extractors; (5) Multipurpose Machines, Beaters, and Bowls; (6) Stovetop Cooking Utensils; (7) Oven: Casseroles and Pots; (8) Roasting and Broiling Pans, Appliances, and Tools; (9) Baking Pans for Batters; (10) Pastry Baking: Pans and Preparation and Other Tools; (11) Specialty Cookware (for seafood, eggs, ice cream, cooking at the table, health foods, coffee, tea, wine, and others).

Each product is illustrated by a halftone photograph 57 millimeters wide and 36 to 72 millimeters high. Materials dimensions in inches, and price (as of June 1975) are indicated in the caption. Accompanying each pictured item is a lively and lucid 200–300 word summary of its applications and limitations. The name and address of the manufacturer or supplier is easily found through lists at the end of the volume. General historical, factual, and commonsensible information is also offered for each type of equipment. A miscellany of 200 recipes demonstrating utensil usage, drawings of food, and early vintage equipment, and culinary anecdotes is interspersed throughout the *Catalogue*. The expansive informality of the writing may detract from the reference efficiency of the book but will add to its appeal for the unhurried browser. There is a classified, briefly annotated bibliography of some 200 books on food. Complete publication data are provided for the titles. A General Index and a Recipe Index conclude the volume.

Sepia brown drawings and headings add a dollop of old-fashioned design and provide contrast to the predominantly black-and-white layout. Imaginatively varied but functional typography complements and enhances the subject of the book; its binding is substantial, and the pages lie flat for convenient consultation.

The Cooks' Catalogue is a unique and highly useful compilation bound to please any connoisseur of food and drink. Public and academic libraries serving such persons will want to buy this book. *(Oct. 15, 1976, p.344)*

†641.5'028   Kitchen utensils || Cookery   [OCLC]   75-6329

Cool, chill, and freeze:
a new approach to cookery. Intro. and suggested recipes by Louis Szathmary. New York, Arno Pr., 1973. xvi, 85, 144p. 22 cm. cloth $7.

641.7'9   Salads || Cookery (Cold dishes) || Desserts, Frozen || Refrigerators   [CIP]   72-9791

See page 116

Corporate profiles
for executives and investors, 1976–77.
Chicago, New York, San Francisco, Rand McNally, [c1976]. unpaged 27cm. hard cover $19.95; paper $14.95.

Joseph Lloyd Corporation of Winnetka, Illinois, designed *Corporate Profiles for Executives and Investors* for executives, college students, financial analysts, business lawyers, and others who need a guide to some 2,400 publicly held corporations with annual sales exceeding $75 million. Besides sales the other criteria applied for inclusion are that the company be "recognized as a major industrial, financial, manufacturing, insurance, service, or transport corporation." The directory does not claim to give balanced coverage to classes of business or to cover foreign corporations, professional organizations, or credit agencies.

The book is arranged in five sections: Corporations Alphabetically, Corporations Geographically, Corporations by Principal Industrial Activity, Corporations by Standard Industrial Classification, and Executive Force. The first section gives most complete information, and it occupies approximately five-sixths of the book. Here the user can determine the name, address, telephone number, five-year review (1971–75) of sales, net earnings and dividends, current assets and liabilities, debt, interest, stock range, number of shares, number of employees, and names of key operating executives of each business. Running heads and large boldfaced letters of the alphabet in the middle of the page help readers locate information in this section. Since the book is not paged and does not have labeled fingertabs, the last five sections are not easy to locate. Therefore special or business libraries which purchase *Corporate Profiles* will find it expeditious to provide fingertabs or some other devices for marking the sections of the book.   *(May 15, 1977, p.1450)*

338.74058   Corporations—U.S.—Directories || Corporations—U.S.—Finance—Directories   [OCLC]   76-15498

Country experts in the federal government.
By Washington Researchers. Washington, D.C., Washington Researchers, 910 Seventeenth St. NW, 20006, 1976. 19p. 28cm. paper $10.

†353.00025   U.S.—Foreign relations administration—Directories || International relations—Directories || Executive advisory boards—Directories

Industry analysts in the federal government.
By Washington Researchers. Washington, D.C., Washington Researchers, 910 Seventeenth St. NW, 20006, 1976. 25p. 28cm. paper $10.

†353.00025   Administrative agencies—Directories || Independent regulatory commissions—Directories

Washington Researchers prepared *Industry Analysts in the Federal Government* and *Country Experts in the Federal Government* "to assist researchers in identifying facts and sources of information for a given industry" and "to assist researchers to locate valuable information on a variety of countries through utilizing the services of the Federal government country experts." Both booklets are reproduced from typewritten copy and are secured at the bound edge by two staples. Libraries which procure them will thus find it advisable to keep them in binders.

The industry booklet has three sections. The first is an alphabetically arranged Index to the Standard Industrial Classification Codes (SIC) most commonly referred to, e.g., Kites, Elevators, Umbrellas and Parasols, and Zinc, each with its own SIC number. The second is an Index to analysts for the various industries who are at the office of Business Research and Analysis at the U.S. Department of Commerce in Washington, D.C. Descriptors like Food & Kindred Products, Apparel, and Furniture and Fixtures are identified by SIC number. The analysts are named, and their telephone and room numbers are identified. The third section identifies analysts at the Industry Division of the U.S. Bureau of Census.

The booklet on country experts lists experienced individuals who have handled requests for specific information on almost 200 countries worldwide. Services of the experts are free, and they are available by telephone and mail. The specialists are listed by country, federal office in which located, name, telephone and room number. The five federal offices concerned are U.S. Department of Commerce, U.S. Department of State, AID (Agency for Industrial Development), U.S. Department of Agriculture, and the Bureau of Mines.

Washington Researchers, which is not related to any government agency, has announced no plans for updating the booklets. Therefore, both must be used with caution. The company does, however, publish a free quarterly which identifies sources of information for those requiring information on general research, marketing, and economics. *(May 15, 1977, p.1450)*

The country life collector's pocket book.
[By] G. Bernard Hughes; illus. by Therle Hughes. London, New York, Sydney, Toronto, Country Life; distributed in the U.S. by A & W Promotional, 1976. 351p. illus. 16cm. cloth $5.95.

The Country Life Collector's Pocket Book aims "to be an on-the-spot reference in the salesrooms, at exhibitions, in showpiece country house and back-street curio shop—wherever beginner-collectors foregather to share their absorbing hobby." Amateur collectors of antiques in the U.S. will find it of little use because of its emphasis on antiques of Great Britain. However, the consumer advice on what to look for, how to determine dates, and how to detect forgeries and fakes is universal and will be helpful to the collector regardless of locale.

The book is well organized into 20 chapters covering the kinds of antiques (Fans, Pewter and Tin, Portrait Miniatures, Barometers, etc.). Some 800 black-and-white line drawings illustrate the chapters which are unique for imparting a maximum of information in a minimum of words. The 50-page coverage of ceramics is a case in point. About 40 wares are listed and described, and 50 types of marks, including more than 100 initials used in the nineteenth century, are identified. The Index facilitates locating specific information. *(Apr. 1, 1977, p.1195)*
†745.103   Collectors and collecting—Dictionaries || Art—Dictionaries || Furniture—Collectors and collecting   76-022039

Current journals in the sciences.
6th ed. Cambridge, Mass., Harvard Univ. Library; dist. by Harvard, July 1975. 199p. 28cm. paper $9.50.

The latest edition of this list from the science libraries of Harvard University, while not a complete holdings inventory, is nonetheless an impressive and useful compilation. The 7,100 entries are journals in the physical and life sciences, as might be expected, and also engineering, statistics, psychology, and empirically oriented subdisciplines within sociology. Holdings of 22 libraries are represented, the new Godfrey Lowell Cabot Science Library for the first time. Also for the first time, the Francis Countway Library of Medicine is given as an additional location for titles in the list that are held by other Harvard Libraries, although these journals constitute a very small percentage of the Countway holdings which are otherwise excluded.

Entry is under the current title, with reference from the old title if there has been a change, the main entry repeating the earlier title. Holdings are given by date and volume, locations by library symbol, and call numbers are cited if appropriate. Languages are noted for multilingual journals. The Preface explains that the word "journals" is no longer strictly appropriate, as contributing libraries have been encouraged to include other active serials. Examples of these are government report series, annual reviews, and *Houben-Weyl, Methoden der Organischen Chemie*. Although the typeface is entirely block letters, not unusual in this sort of publication, good paper and spacing of the two-column layout assure good legibility. A small map is printed on each page listing libraries with their symbols, telephone numbers, and addresses.

An occasional blind cross-reference or incomplete entry was found by the Committee. Such errors are almost unavoidable in a list compiled from the records of so many separate library units.

Academic and research libraries should find *Current Journals in the Sciences* especially useful because of its inclusion of the foreign language serials in Harvard University's family of distinguished libraries, which includes several botanical collections, the Smithsonian Astrophysical Observatory, and Museum of Comparative Zoology.   *(June 1, 1977, p.1525)*
016.505   Science—Periodicals—Bibliography—Catalogs   [CIP]   74-25034

Diary for the business traveler, 1977.
Edited by Paul B. Finney. New York, Business Week, [1976]; distributed by McGraw Hill. 216p. illus. maps. paper based with pyroxylin finish coating $14.95; to schools and libraries, 20 percent discount.

The expertise and succinct up-to-date coverage of *Business Week* is evident in the *Diary for the Business Traveler*. The book will serve not only as a business calendar but also as an authoritative source of current information for the travel planner who will be in any of the 16 major U.S. cities or the 17 foreign municipalities described. The following information is cited for each city: airports (distance from town, airport hotels, car rentals, best way to get about), hotels (elegant and expensive, moderate and commercial, out-of-the-ordinary, best motel), restaurants (best business breakfast, lunch, dinner; best with private dining rooms, best place to eat alone, best watering hole, where to eat after midnight), getting around (downtown, parking, limousines, taxis, what to avoid), personal information (shops, late-night drug stores, sports clubs, where to get tickets, spare-time activity).

Foreign cities coverage includes country and city briefing data, average monthly temperatures, sources of legal advice, and names of English-speaking doctors. Individuals traveling to the 33 cities covered will find *Diary for the Business Traveler* a compact and valuable source of information. Public libraries will find it useful for travelers of all types.
(May 15, 1977, p.1451)
†910.2   Travel—Guide-books

Dictionary of British antique glass.
[By] Douglas Ash. Levittown, N.Y., Transatlantic Arts, Inc., [c1975]. 210p. 22cm. illus. cloth $12.75.

The alphabetical survey provided by the *Dictionary of British Antique Glass* covers the years from the late sixteenth century to approximately 1840, the period of greatest interest to collectors and students. The author, a Fellow of the Society of Antiquaries and a member of the Glass Circle, has also written *How To Identify English Drinking Glasses and Decanters 1680–1830* as well as books on English and Dutch antique silver and English antique furniture.

The 300 entries in the dictionary cover a wide variety of topics related to the manufacture, design, and uses of glass; e.g., implements used in glassmaking (pontils, pucellas), the shapes and ornaments of stemmed drinking glasses, and glass items designed for special uses, (e.g., coaching glasses, ship's decanters). Also included are entries for many glassmakers of the period as well as for glassmaking centers (e.g., Bristol, Waterford) and individual glasshouses having special historical significance.

While the majority of entries are concise (ranging from one line to several paragraphs), major topics are given more extended treatment. (The longest entry, *decanters*, is approximately 12 pages in length.) The dictionary is written in language "which does not presuppose detailed knowledge of technical terminology on the reader's part."

Numerous cross-references direct the reader to related entries under which additional information can be found. Cross-references are also provided from entry terms not used to those under which the topic is discussed. The absence of an index does, however, necessitate some searching to locate specific points of information covered in the longer articles.

The author has provided 174 line drawings of objects treated in the entries as well as stylistic details and ornamental features of various types of glassware. The dictionary concludes with a Bibliography of 32 works dealing with British glass. (Imprint dates range from 1849 to 1968.)

The *Dictionary of British Antique Glass* makes available in convenient and attractive form a wide range of information, not only about the subject itself, but also about the historical and social factors which influenced the creation and design of glass objects. It will be appreciated by libraries and individuals requiring detailed coverage of the subject. *(May 15, 1977, p.1451)*

748.2'9941 Glassware—Gt. Brit.—Dictionaries || Antiques—Gt. Brit.—Dictionaries [OCLC]
76-356117

A dictionary of British surnames.
By Percy H. Reaney. 2d. ed. with corrections and additions by R. M. Wilson. Boston, Mass., Routledge & Kegan Paul, 1976. lxiv, 398p. 25cm. cloth, $37.75.

The first edition of this work was issued in 1958. It contained about 10,000 entries representing approximately 20,000 family names. This revised edition includes over 700 additional names, a rewritten list of abbreviations bringing the bibliography up to date, and various corrections. The original work was by the late Percy Hide Reaney, a recognized British authority on names. He also wrote *The Origin of English Surnames*, and *The Origin of English Place-Names*, was a member of the Council of the English Place-Name Society, and was active in various local historical societies. Richard Middlewood Wilson, the reviser, who also assisted with the first edition, is Professor Emeritus of English Language at Sheffield University and an authority on Middle English literature. In preparing the second edition Wilson utilized Reaney's files, now in Sheffield University Library, Reaney's personal copy of the first edition which he had emended in anticipation of a new edition, and fresh material of his own.

The entries follow the pattern of the first edition by citing for each name variants, sources, and origin of the surname, with derivatives. This is preceded by a 41-page Introduction by Reaney, reprinted from the first edition, which surveys the origins and development of surnames in general followed by brief comments on those of England, Wales, Scotland, Ireland, and the Isle of Man.

In his Preface to the first edition Reaney acknowledged that "A complete Dictionary of Surnames cannot yet be produced, partly because for many of the large number of surnames surviving material is at present scanty or lacking, partly because of the high cost of such a production. This has meant a strict economy in examples and in exposition and the elimination from the first draft of some 100,000 words and 4,000 names. All surnames included are known to survive. The great majority of those eliminated are local surnames such as Manchester, Wakefield, Essex, etc., which can easily be identified from the gazetteer."

Clearly then there is room for other books on British surnames in the library. Two of the classic titles, Charles W. Bardsley, *A Dictionary of English and Welsh Surnames, with Special American Instances* (Baltimore: Genealogical Pub. Co., 1968) originally printed in 1901, and the same author's *English Surnames: Their Sources and Significance* (first published in 1889 and reprinted in 1969), are worthy of inclusion although later evidence has necessitated correction of some of Bardsley's statements. Two more popular works are Constance M. Matthews, *English Surnames* (New York: Scribner, 1967), in which Mrs. Matthews, a local historian, dealt with some 2,500 names grouped under broad headings arranged in a very readable form, and Basil Cottle, *The Penguin Dictionary of Surnames* (Hammondsworth: Penguin, 1967), which has some 8,000 names from the British Isles, with brief annotations given. For reference collections this present work by Reaney and its companion volume, *The Origin of English Surnames*, 1967, will continue to serve as standard works in this field.
(Oct. 15, 1976, p.344)

†929.4'03 Names, Personal—English [OCLC]

Dictionary of business finance and investment.
By Norman D. Moore. New York, London, Drake Publishers, Inc., [1976]. x, 524p. 23cm. paperback, $9.95.

The *Dictionary of Business Finance and Investment* was first published as a hardcover book in 1975 by Investor's Systems, P.O. Box 1422, Dayton, Ohio 45401. The new paperback edition contains the same 1,500 business and finance terms and definitions that appeared in the original. The book was selling for $14.95 for the library edition when the Reference and Subscription Books Review Committee reviewed it on November 1, 1975. Public and school libraries still interested in purchasing this convenient compendium will want to check the current price of the hardcover edition. Because of this book's ample dimensions, the paperback binding may not be sufficiently sturdy to withstand the wear it will receive.
(Nov. 1, 1976, p.424)

332'.03 Business—Dictionaries || Finance—Dictionaries || Investments—Dictionaries
74-29447

The dictionary of butterflies and moths in color.
By Allan Watson and Paul E. S. Whalley. With an introduction by W. Donald Duckworth, American consultant editor. New York, McGraw-Hill Book Co., 1975. xiv, 296p. illus. 31cm. casebound $39.95.

About 2,000 alphabetically arranged entries for butterflies and moths represent nearly every currently accepted family from every major geographic region. They are entered under scientific name, with popular name following, and with many *see* references for variations and common names. Range, size in centimeters and inches, description, feeding habits, and miscellaneous information are given for each entry.

The well-qualified authors are lepidopterists at the British Museum. Duckworth, the American consultant, is curator of lepidoptera of the National Museum of Natural History in Washington. His Introduction cites the usefulness of the volume not only as a guide to what is known but in determining areas and groups in need of additional study. He also describes the characteristics of lepidoptera and their means of survival, and makes a plea for photographing rather than collecting specimens. Also included are a glossary of 51 terms and a list of 36 recent books considered most useful by the compilers of the text. On the whole, more detailed information on individual species is found here than in the *International Butterfly Book*.

Like the *International Butterfly Book* it is handsomely illustrated, with 144 full-colored plates showing about 1,000 species, many taken at the British Museum, but with a number of life-sized photographs of lepidoptera in their natural habitats. In general, they are arranged from the more primitive families to the more advanced, though the compilers admit that the actual sequence is somewhat arbitrary. Exact citation to each illustration is given in the dictionary section. Comparison with the photographs in the *International Butterfly Book* reveals species in each source not found in the other. However, this volume has fewer crowded pages.

The broad scope, authority of the compilers, and the beauty of the photography commend *The Dictionary of Butterflies and Moths* to serious students. *(Sept. 1, 1976, p.54)*

595.7'81 Lepidoptera—Dictionaries [CIP] 74-30433

Dictionary of geological terms.
Prepared under the direction of the American Geological Institute. [rev. ed.] Garden City, N.Y., Anchor Press/Doubleday, 1976. viii, 445p. 18cm. paper $3.50.

The American Geological Institute first published the *Glossary of Geology and Related Sciences* in 1957. The latest edition entitled *Glossary of Geology* was published in 1972. The *Dictionary of Geological Terms* has been published since 1962 as a paperback abridgment of this authoritative work. In this revised edition, based on the 1972 *Glossary of Geology*, older terms have been deleted or the entries shortened and almost 1,000 new terms have been added to bring the total to 8,500. Now included are definitions for plate tectonics, sea floor spreading, environmental geology, oceanography, and lunar and planetary geology. This expansion has been accomplished in fewer pages than in the first edition by the use of smaller but still readable type.

The entries in this dictionary are arranged alphabetically letter by letter. The terms defined are for the most part those used in North America, although some British and Australian terms are included. The definitions are brief but adequate with an emphasis on current or preferred meaning. For many terms more than one definition is given. In these cases the particular field of geology to which the definition applies is often indicated. Numerous cross-references lead to related or preferred terms.

The *Dictionary of Geological Terms* is an authoritative, relatively up-to-date, inexpensive source of definitions of terms used in the earth sciences. It will have value for students of earth science and hobbyists studying rocks, minerals, and fossils.
(June 15, 1977, p.1601)

550.3 Geology—Dictionaries [OCLC] 73-9004

A dictionary of gestures.
By Betty J. Bäuml and Franz H. Bäuml. Metuchen, N.J., Scarecrow Pr., Inc., 1975. xxxv, 249p. 22cm. cloth $11.

Betty J. Bäuml, professor of Spanish, California State University at Northridge, and Franz H. Bäuml, professor of German, University of California at Los Angeles, have compiled a dictionary of gestures of all times and places. Only verifiable noncodified, nonarbitrary culturally transmitted gestures are included. Sign languages, gestures utilized in narrative dances, and military gestures are excluded. A 20-page Bibliography of foreign and English-language sources precedes the dictionary proper. The general arrangement of the work is alphabetical by part(s) of the body used in executing the gesture, e.g., *ear, eye, hand, lip; ear, finger; ear, finger, mouth; ear, hand; ear, hand, leg; ear, hand, lip*. Under body part, significances are alphabetized, and each gesture is described. For example, under *finger, hand,* gestural equivalents for anger, apotropy, approach, approval, assurance, attention, blessing, bravery, calmness, cheating, cigarette, contempt, copulation, etc., are explained, and definitions are elaborated on when necessary. Sources are cited by author, title, and page. For users who wish to get at information by meaning of the gesture rather than part(s) of the body involved, an Index of Significances is provided. *A Dictionary of Gestures* is a unique classification and description of culturally transmitted gestures which will be useful to those requiring source data on the subject. *(Sept. 1, 1976, p.54)*

152.3'84 Gestures—Dictionaries || Nonverbal communication—Dictionaries [CIP]
75-23144

Dictionary of Ming biography, 1368–1644:
the Ming biographical history project of the Association for Asian Studies. L. Carrington Goodrich, editor; Chaoying Fang, associate editor. New York, Columbia Univ. Pr., 1976. 2v. illus. 27cm. cloth, $85.

Over 100 authorities, half of them mainland Chinese; the rest from other parts of the world, including Taiwan, Sri Lanka, Malaysia, Hong Kong, Korea, India, have written nearly 650 biographies of representative figures, both Chinese and foreign, who contributed to the 276-year period of Chinese history distinguished for its intellectual and cultural pursuits, contact with Europe, and the creation of institutions which have lasted to modern times. This monumental work, begun more than 25 years ago and based largely on original Ming documents, is edited by Dr. Goodrich, author of *A Short History of the Chinese People* and other books on China, and by Chaoying Fang, best known for his work on the authoritative *Eminent Chinese of the Ch'ing Period (1644–1912)*, with the assistance of his wife Lienche Tu Fang.

The signed sketches, with full appended bibliographies, vary in length from about 1,000 to 6,000 words, with a few, such as those on the various emperors of the Ming; Li Chi, the Confucian thinker; and Matteo Ricci, the renowned missionary, running much longer. Covering all classes and professions, from emperors to imperial concubines, scholars, artists, philosophers, missionaries, and monks, the articles are interestingly written with generous inclusion of personal detail. Proper names and book titles are given in Chinese, Japanese, or Korean characters as well as in their romanized form.

In addition to the *see* references included in the body of the articles, there are three Indexes: a complete Index to names, another to book titles, and a most useful subject Index. The latter contains many references to calligraphers, Buddhism, Confucianism, drama, concubinage, eunuchs, envoys, government organization and administration, libraries, medicine, monasteries, museums, punishments, and temples, as well as to a number of place-names.

Four maps and about 30 black-and-white reproductions of paintings of emperors and empresses are the only illustrations included. The type is large, clear, and well leaded. The paper is good and the volumes are stoutly bound.

The authority of the editors and contributors, the importance of the period covered, and the careful editing make this a most useful companion to Hummel's *Eminent Chinese of the Ch'ing Period* and Boorman's *Biographical Dictionary of Republican China.* It helps to fill the need for Chinese biographical sources in the English language. *(Nov. 1, 1976, p.424)*

951'.026 China—History—Ming dynasty, 1368–1644—Biography || China—Biography
[CIP] 75-26938

A dictionary of philosophy.
By A. R. Lacey. London, Routledge & Kegan Paul, 1976. vii, 239p. 22cm. econolin $9.75.

Professor Lacey's *A Dictionary of Philosophy* "aims to give the layman or intending student a pocket encyclopaedia of philosophy, one with a bias towards explaining terminology" (Preface). It contains articles on individual philosophers and schools or movements. The emphasis is clearly on philosophical terms and concepts current in English-language philosophy. The author has also purposely favored epistemology and logic (in a wide sense) both in terms of the number and the length of the entries. The author entries deal with a selection of exclusively

Western philosophers. Treatments are all very brief, listing only these thinkers' most important works and very rarely any secondary literature concerning their thought. The author's intention primarily is to indicate the place which ancient and more recent philosophers occupy in contemporary debates. On the whole, Lacey has been quite successful in performing this task with a fairly complete system of cross-references between author entries. The reader may be guided into the discovery of Aristotle's focal role in modern metaphysics or of Kantian philosophy upon contemporary ethical theory. However, it is a pity that the topical entries are not so thoroughly cross-referenced. Even though the names of many relevant authors occur in the text of an article and in the appended bibliography, more cross-referencing would have been useful. The article *scepticism,* for example, refers generally to the ancient sceptics but does not direct the reader to *Sextus Empiricus,* which is the only article identifying some holders of this doctrine by name. Again, the bibliography in the article *moral sense* mentions Hume but does not refer to Hutcheson or Shaftesbury, whereas the texts of the articles on those two philosophers present them as the principal representatives of the moral sense school. However, this relatively minor shortcoming in no way deprives the topical articles of their main value.

Principal concepts are treated in articles dealing with the various disciplines of philosophy (e.g., *logic, philosophy of history,* and *philosophy of religion*), and cross-references ensure that the reader is introduced to key interrelated subjects. Beyond this, Lacey is content, sensibly enough, to provide succinct sketches of the types of problems that are central to each discipline. In the longer articles a special effort has been made to epitomize significant theories and describe the questions they raise for philosophers of the twentieth century. The author often traces the philosophical problems from the meanings of the terms in ordinary language to their more technical usage in philosophy. All of the longer articles are accompanied by bibliographies. These bibliographies are not systematic, but items are annotated to indicate how they relate to the content of the articles. When necessary, they are also rated in terms of their level of difficulty. Classical discussions of philosophical issues by Aristotle, Hume, Kant, or Mill are regularly mentioned. However, the great majority of the bibliographical references utilize recent (post-1900 or even post-1950) philosophical contributions. In many cases, very recent material is included. Like the text of the articles, these references stress problems and debates in contemporary philosophy. In this sense, Lacey's dictionary can serve as an adequate and up-to-date, though not comprehensive, guide to recent philosophical literature. The shorter articles follow the same general pattern, either with a reduced bibliography or no bibliography at all. Among these shorter entries, the explications which Lacey provides of mathematical or logical theorems, as well as of the various classical logical paradoxes, should be especially helpful to the student and nonspecialist.

In brief, *A Dictionary of Philosophy* is neither a philosophy specialist's handbook nor a historical lexicon of the language of classical philosophy. Its aims are purposely limited to the elucidation of the standard terminology and problems of contemporary English language philosophy. Within these limits, Lacey has created a tool which has no exact equivalent in the English language. His dictionary should prove useful to students interested in the technical developments of contemporary philosophy. In view of the stress which the book puts on current philosophical debates, and because of the fairly large selection of recent periodical material which its bibliographies contain, *A Dictionary of Philosophy* should be especially suitable for libraries which serve students of philosophy or general readers who may require access to a good basic philosophical dictionary. *(July 15, 1977, p.1754)*

A dictionary of the old West, 1850–1900.

By Peter Watts. New York, Knopf, 1977. 399p. 24cm. cloth and board $12.95.

A Dictionary of the Old West is a compilation of more than 2,000 words and phrases in common use in the western states prior to the twentieth century. The definitions vary from one or two lines to two full pages (*badman; barbed wire*), the average being about ten lines. The author, an Englishman, also writes western fiction under various pseudonyms. He has taken his definitions from 192 authorities whom he cites by name and date in the text. In addition he provides a list of 80 "Works Consulted." These lists contain the names of most of the well-known lexicographers of the West—Ramon F. Adams, J. Frank Dobie, Jo Mora, and others—as well as early works such as Bartlett's *Dictionary of Americanisms* (1877) and Gregg's *Commerce of the Prairies* (1844). The book is illustrated with about 185 line drawings, mostly small, and integrated with the text. A list of illustration credits is given at the back of the book. Eleven are by the author himself.

The work is primarily aimed at readers of western fiction, and the words defined are either factual, such as *papoose, saddle-blanket, bridle;* or slang, such as *rookus juice,* for whiskey, or *quirly,* for a cigarette; or westernisms, such as *mustang, lasso, rustler;* or they are Spanish words that have come into the language unchanged, such as *matanza* (a slaughterhouse or area), *partida* (a small group of cattle), or *serape* (a blanket used as a cloak). A few words in common use in the West, but not originating there or used there exclusively, have also been added.

Perhaps 20 percent of the western words are of Spanish origin, either changed a little, as *hackamore* from jáquima, or else unchanged, as in *baile,* a dance; *bajada,* a downhill slope; *hacienda,* a ranch or estate; *vaquero,* a cowboy, and so on.

The origin of all such words is given either as Sp (Spanish), Mex-Sp (Mexican-Spanish), Mex-Sp from Nahuatl, and so on. A few words have been taken from Indian tribes, such as the Navaho word *Belinka* for an Anglo-American, and a few from French, such as *bois de vache,* a euphemism for a buffalo chip, often Anglicized as bushwa or booshwa.

Some of the definitions in the book are a little disappointing. The two-word definition of *bravo* as an adjective meaning "fierce, brave" might not satisfy someone who for the first time comes across the book entitled *The Deaths of the Bravos.* The sole definition of *to bushwack* as meaning "to ambush, to attack in surprise from cover," hardly agrees with Mathews, *Dictionary of Americanisms,* which lists additional meanings "to be a frontiersman," and "to make one's way through unbroken forest." The definition of the word *fofarraw,* given as "fancy or decorated dress," fails to indicate that the dress in question was usually worn not so much by a trapper or mountain man as by his squaw, and that it included not merely dress but also beads and other adornments. The word was originated, says the author, by the mountain men, but even though he cites Mathews as his authority for this, he fails to indicate, as Mathews does, that the mountain men did not make up the word, but derived it from the Spanish word *fanfarrón,* meaning cheap or showy.

Finally, the definition of the expression "to see the elephant" also leaves something to be desired. It is given as meaning "to go to town, perhaps for the first time; to see the world and gain some experience of its sin and glitter." The author connects the word with seeing an elephant for the first time, at a circus, and rather disdainfully cites Bartlett (1877) as saying "doubtless originated from some occurrence at a menagerie." But in the California gold rush the word meant something different. It meant "to have seen everything; to be completely disillusioned," and so it was used by men who had crossed the plains, made their way to the diggings, sweated and labored for months for a few paltry ounces of gold dust, and were often, on their way back to the states, completely used up. They had "seen the elephant." The phrase most probably stems from the circumstance that when a circus arrived in a small town, there would be, during the day of the first evening performance, a parade through the town of all the performers and their animals, with a view to drumming up business for the evening. The elephant, the largest of the circus animals and the most impressive, was always placed last in the parade; hence arose the expression "to have seen the elephant," meaning to have stayed to the end, to have seen everything, to have nothing left for which to wait around. The book under review makes no mention of this California expression and, in general, places more emphasis on words in use among cowboys in the plains states than among the gold miners of California.

In summary, the work is a fine contribution to the lexicography of the Old West, an area never before singled out for complete coverage. The main appeal of the book will be to the reader of western fiction and public libraries that stock the works of Zane Grey, Louis L'Amour, and other western fiction writers would do well to put a copy of this book near their circulating collection. It will surely see a good deal of use.

(July 15, 1977, p.1754)

427'.9   Americanisms || English language—Provincialisms—The West || The West—Social life and customs || English language—19th century   [CIP]   76-13724

Dictionary of tools
used in the woodworking and allied trades, c1700–1970.

By Raphael A. Salaman. New York, Scribner, [c1975] 545p., 27cm. illus. plasticized cloth, $47.50.

This dictionary is intended by its compiler to record and "describe every tool used in the woodworking trades from about 1700 to the present time, and to explain its purpose." Generally coverage has been limited geographically to Great Britain, but tools imported from the U.S. and elsewhere have been included if commonly found in British woodworking shops. Some tools belonging to trades associated with woodworking have been also included, e.g., metal working tools used in the making of associated metal parts or sailmaker's tools because they were frequently found in the tool kits of shipwrights. The years around 1700 were chosen as the starting point because it was about that time that hand tools became increasingly differentiated in response to the demands of a multiplicity of trades. Tools have been dated by means of trade catalogs—used with caution, Salaman notes, for firms often continued to supply tools in limited demand long after they were dropped from catalogs.

Raphael Salaman, who designed and equipped the wheelwright's shop in the Science Museum in London and whose collection of tradesmen's tools is exhibited in the St. Albans City Museum, is an engineer with a lifelong interest in tools and the trades. In addition to the work under review, he is author of the article "Tradesmen's Tools, c1500–1850" in *A History of Technology,* v. IV (Oxford, 1954) and has contributed articles on tools to learned journals. He acknowledges entries by six other contributors on particular trades and tools.

The body of the *Dictionary of Tools* consists of a listing of tools, woodworking and allied trades, and technical terms used in workshops in one alphabetical sequence.

Tools are entered by generic name with subentries for specific tools. Thus *adze* is a main entry followed by such subentries as adze, American; adze; canoe howel; etc. In the event that the generic name is not identifiable from the specific name of the tool, a cross-reference under the specific name directs one to the proper entry, e.g., *old woman's tooth: See Plane, Router.* A main entry for a class of tools commonly includes a definition if needed, alternate terms including historical or dialectal variants, a brief history, a listing of specific types, and other information. In line with his expressed intention to record some of the methods and sayings of the tradesmen who used them and to give some idea of the graceful shapes imparted to the tools by the men who designed and made them, Salaman has also enlivened his book with liberal quotations from documents, histories, trade manuals, and the like, and provides copious illustrations for the various tools listed. The illustrations for the main entries generally include a diagram denominating the component parts of the tool and frequently show historical development: the diagram accompanying the entry *brace* depicts a modern bit stock with labels indicating the head (or nave), quill disc, neck, frame (crank), handle, foot, chuck (Shell or Barber type), and jaws. The radius drawn by the turn of the handle is indicated as the "throw" and the diameter described by the turn of the handle is indicated as the "sweep." Next to the Barber chuck is shown the chuck of a ratchet brace. Six drawings illustrate earlier types of chucks.

Subentries for tools deal with specific models or types or with variations designed for or associated with particular trades. Thus subentries for *brace* include "brace, chairmaker's"; "brace, cooper's"; "brace, corner"; etc. Subentries may be further divided: a corner brace is a general term for a bitstalk design to permit holes to be bored in corners and other awkward or confined spaces. Salaman lists four such braces in alphabetic order, (drill brace, gear frame brace, etc.) plus two brace extension devices, and a *see also* reference to two other tools, a ratchet brace and a hand drill, which permit boring in a confined space. Each type of corner brace is illustrated by a drawing. Generally subentries for tools are illustrated by drawings or engravings taken from trade catalogs and other books. Many were prepared especially for the *Dictionary of Tools.*

Besides the entries for tools, the dictionary also lists articles for the various woodworking and allied trades. Among the trades covered are basket maker, bell hanger, bowl turner, carpenter, joiner, cabinet maker, chairmaker, gunstocker, hoop maker, millstone dresser, sawyer, shipwright, tree feller, and wheelwright—altogether some 55 trades are represented. The articles are not only helpful in understanding the use to which the various tools were put, but provide another dimension to the book registering an important bit of social history in covering many a trade now passed from the scene.

A typical entry for a minor or relatively simple trade includes a definition of the trade and perhaps a brief historical note, an indication of woods or other materials used, and a description of process and the tools used. If appropriate, references are provided to other entries with information on tools used in the trade, or references to other articles for tools used in associated processes.

The articles for the more complex trades are much more extensive and contain a number of subdivisions. The entry for wheelwright can be cited as an example. First, a note indicates that tools used by wainwrights are also included, and a *see also* reference directs the reader to coachbuilder. A brief history of wagon wheels with a separate section on dished wheels is followed by an account of the wheelwright's work including an appreciative comment on the graceful lines of an albeit sturdy wagon as a result of stop-champfering, done originally to lighten the load. A section on materials indicates the chief woods used for the various components of wagons and wheels, and the reasons therefor. Next a description of the workshop, the buildings and yard (much work was done outside), with a comment on layout, which is followed by an account of the process of wheelmaking—making the hub, spokes, and felloes, tiring the wheel, boring the hub for the axle box. Another section lists some 70 special tools associated with the trade—an important feature providing another mode of approach to the entries for tools. In a concluding section the wheelwright's equipment is dealt with in three sections: (1) workshop furniture; (2) spoke tools; and (3) tiring tools. Finally it should be said that the article is copiously illustrated with keyed and labeled diagrams and sketches showing parts of a typical wagon, the components of a wheel (with earlier and later designs of spokes), and workshop furniture and equipment showing its use—all of which are helpful in understanding the trade and its tools.

A third type of entry in the *Dictionary of Tools* deals with terminology, such as *face* (if a tool) or *fan tail* (description of a shape), and other miscellaneous matter: for example, although each trade lists the tools associated with it there are some tools and equipment common to many woodworking trades—these are gathered together and listed under *workshop equipment;* similarly, metal-working tools commonly found in woodworking shops are listed under *metal-working tools.*

All three kinds of entries are tied together as necessary by an excellent system of cross-referencing. English spelling preferences present no problem. When present prevalent English usage differs from American or other dialectal usage, references are provided from the form not used ("Clamp: see *Cramp*") or else the term is explained in a self-contained article. In a close examination of the work with frequent checking, only one blind reference was found.

While one may note the omission of a few items such as the Jorgensen adjustable hand screw and hand clamps commonly found in American workshops, which one would expect to have found their way into English workshops, the coverage of the *Dictionary of Tools* is very comprehensive. The articles are clearly written and vary in length from a single line, in the case of a term being defined, to as many as 15 pages for the longest article on a trade, *wheelwrights.*

Prefatory matter in the book includes a Foreword by Joseph Needham, Master of Gonville and Gaius College, Cambridge, gracefully commending the work; Introduction by the author stating the scope of the dictionary and discussing the question of nomenclature and etymology; a useful "List of Trades Included" with cross-references from trade names not used; a thoughtfully provided and welcome section, "Notes on Using the Dictionary"; a table of "Metric Equivalents"; and Acknowledgements of sources. A concluding Bibliography and References lists journal articles, books and pamphlets, trade catalogs, price lists, directories, etc., and visits or correspondence with specialists during the period 1940–1973.

The book is attractively bound in plasticized navy cloth with gold stamping on spine. Signatures are sewn, pages lie flat when the volume is opened, and the book appears to be sturdily made. The text is attractively printed in legible type with entries in boldface. The first and last entry of each double-page spread are set in italics as guide words at head of page. The text is laid out in double columns on a page of generous width. Margins are adequate for rebinding. Although one might wish the white space at the end of alphabetic sections to be distributed equally to the two columns, the volume represents good book making in both design and execution.

The *Dictionary of Tools* is a comprehensive, well organized, lucid, and literate work which can be recommended generally for secondary school, academic, and public libraries according to their needs and for interested individuals. It is an indispensable item for appropriate special collections.

(Nov. 15, 1976, p.499)

†694.03 Carpentry—Tools || Tools—Dictionaries 75-35054

Directions for cookery in its various branches.
[By] Eliza Leslie. New York, Arno Pr., 1973. xv. 511p. 22cm. cloth $12.

641.5 Cookery, American [CIP] 72-9797

See page 116

Directory of corporate affiliations, 1976:
who owns whom. Skokie, Ill., National Register Pub. Co., 1976. 554, 97p. 28cm. paper $40, includes 5 annual updates; 15 percent discount to libraries for standing orders.

The *Directory of Corporate Affiliations* first appeared in 1976. It is published by the National Register Publishing Company, a subsidiary of Standard Rate and Data Service Inc. Other services of the company directed to business include *The Standard Directory of Advertisers* and *The Standard Directory of Advertising Agencies. The Official Museum Directory,* well known to librarians and commended by the Committee for its accuracy and comprehensiveness, is another of the company's publications put out in cooperation with the American Association of Museums.

In well-designed two-column pages the *Directory of Corporate Affiliations* cites major corporations by name; gives the address including zip code, telephone number, officers, divisions, and subsidiaries; and refers to location of plants by city and state. Access to information is assured by a 97-page listing of all divisions, subsidiaries, and affiliates of parent companies appearing in the main part of the book. Five annual updates included in the purchase price keep the directory up to date by listing new and pending mergers. Some 5,000 such changes are projected for 1976. Offices and business libraries will find the directory a comprehensive guide to the major corporate structures in the U.S. *(Sept. 1, 1976, p.54)*

338 Corporations—U.S.—Directories || Holding companies—U.S.—Directories [OCLC]

Directory of franchising organizations 1976.
[Samuel Small, editor. 17th ed.] New York, Pilot Books, [1976]. 64p. 22cm. paper $2.50.

The *Directory of Franchising Organizations* was first published in 1959. The current edition conveniently lists organizations with franchises available under 38 subject headings like *art galleries, cleaning services, donut shops,* and *motel services. Food-drive-in, carry out restaurants* has the most listings. Each business cited is identified by name and address. The amount of investment required is also cited. Persons seeking information on the availability of small business franchises will find the directory an up-to-date checklist. *(Sept. 1, 1976, p.54)*

†658.87 Franchises (Retail trade)—U.S. [OCLC] 62-39831

Directory of library reprographic services/
a world guide. Compiled and edited by Joseph Z. Nitecki. 6th ed. [Weston, Conn.], published for the Reproduction of Library Materials Section, RTSD-American Library Association by Microform Review Inc., [c1976]. 178p. charts. 23cm. paper $9.95.

Directory of Library Reprographic Services is the sixth edition of a work originally published by the American Library Association as *Directory of Institutional Photocopying Services.* The current name was first used with the fifth edition, published in 1973. The present directory is much increased in size over its predecessor—438 entries as compared with 242. All libraries replying to the letter inviting participation were included in the new edition. The following types of institutions were requested to submit data: (1) all libraries listed in the fifth edition of the directory, (2) libraries in the U.S. (at least two to a state), and (3) libraries outside the U.S. (including all identified national libraries).

The primary value of the book is the identification of the types and costs of services. For convenience of use the book is arranged in four sections. Section one consists of 65 charts of reprographic services. Section two lists complete addresses for placing orders. Section three, "Additional Information on Reprographic Policies and Services," is a microfiche contained in an envelope in the inside back cover. Section four, Supplements, defines 15 terms used in the directory, e.g., *copyflo, photographic prints—silver halide, serials, slides;* summarizes advice in requesting reprographic services, shows a suggested sample library photoduplication order form, lists the five previous editions and compilers of the directory, and cites 15 select-

Directory of newspaper libraries in the U.S. and Canada.

Grace D. Parch, editor. New York, Special Libraries Association, 1976. xii, 319p. 26cm. paper, $9.75.

The Newspaper Division of the Special Libraries Association is responsible for the much needed *Directory of Newspaper Libraries in the U.S. and Canada*. *Cleveland Plain Dealer* librarian Grace D. Parch was chairperson of the directory committee, and has edited the book. Its objective is "to provide convenient, complete, accurate and up-to-date information on newspaper libraries including their collections, services and personnel." The information was obtained from replies received from 66 percent of the 558 newspaper libraries who replied to questionnaires in 1975. The work covers 297 newspaper libraries for 295 U.S. and Canadian newspapers published in English and French.

The book is well arranged for ease of use. Newspapers are listed alphabetically by state or province and by city. Each newspaper's logo serves as caption for the entry, and one or more pages are devoted to each library. Listings include the following information as applicable: newspaper publication frequency, address, telephone number, names of librarian and assistant, circulation as described in the Audit Bureau of Circulations' FAS-FAX Reports—September 30, 1975 and Supplements to ABC Daily Newspaper FAS-FAX Reports—December 10, 1975, indication of group or independent ownership, date of founding of library, number of staff, library hours, resources, kinds of holdings (clippings, photographs, negatives, cuts/veloxes, books, pamphlets, audiovisuals, periodicals, microforms, indexes) special collections, services available to both newspaper personnel and others, and extent of automation.

The directory is well reproduced from typewritten copy. Index references by city aid the user in finding information on specific libraries. They also indicate at a glance how many newspaper libraries a city has. *The Directory of Newspaper Libraries* is commendable for its breadth of coverage and up-to-dateness. Public, college preparatory high school, and college and university libraries will find it fills a long recognized need for a newspaper library directory. *(Nov. 1, 1976, p.424)*

026'.07 Newspaper office libraries—U.S.—Directories || Newspaper office libraries—Canada—Directories [CIP]   76-9751

Directory of registered lobbyists and lobbyist legislation.

2d ed. Chicago, Marquis Academic Media, Marquis Who's Who, Inc., [c1975]. vii, 645p. 29cm. cloth $44.50.

Directory of Registered Lobbyists and Lobbyist Legislation is the second edition of a work previously titled *Directory of Registered Federal and State Lobbyists.* The current volume contains reprints of federal and state regulations concerned with lobbying and lists all federal and state lobbyists who were registered through the spring of 1975. The laws, rules, or ethics codes appear before the listings of lobbyists, with federal laws appearing first and the rest being listed alphabetically by state. Hawaii and Utah are omitted, because registration is not required in those states. The state-by-state listings have all lobbyists and lobbying firms as main entries; these appear in boldface. Information given for each includes the address, telephone number, and organizations they represent. Most of the addresses and telephone numbers are local. Lobbyists who work at the federal level are provided with District of Columbia directory information.

Data were obtained directly from such sources as the journals of the various legislatures, records of the attorney general, secretary of state, clerks, ethics boards, and registration files. These data were supplemented with secondary research to assure uniform listings of information for each listee. The book is well designed, being printed on three-column pages. Access to the contents is facilitated by a Lobbyist Index which cites lobbyists by name and state and an Organization Index which alphabetizes all organizations represented and lists all lobbyists registered on their behalf. Anyone needing accurate and reasonably up-to-date information on lobby legislation and organizations and individuals who lobby will find the *Directory of Registered Lobbyists and Lobbyist Legislation* a reliable tool.

(Sept. 1, 1976, p.54)

†328.73 Lobbyists—U.S.—Directories || Lobbying—Law and legislation—U.S. [OCLC]   75-27033

Directory of special programs for minority group members:

career information services, employment skills banks, financial aid sources. 2d ed. [By] Willis L. Johnson, ed. Garrett Park, Md., Garrett Park Pr., 1975. 400p. 28cm. paperback $9.75 (or $8.50 prepaid).

The *Directory of Special Programs for Minority Group Members* contains a listing of 1,340 organizations and institutions which assist members of minority groups with career information, employment, or financial resources. The editor defines minority group members as persons who describe themselves as black or Afro-Americans; Spanish-speaking, Spanish-surnamed, or of Latin American origin or culture; American Indian; Alaskan native; or Asian-American or Oriental.

This volume, the second edition, is very similar in format to the first edition. However, there are 1,340 organizations listed in this edition, whereas the first edition which was published in 1973 recorded only 920 organizations. Willis L. Johnson, the editor, states that plans have already been made for an expanded third edition.

The format of the directory facilitates convenient access. In the front of the directory, there are (1) an Alphabetical List of Organizations represented in the volume, (2) Program Index of Organizations (e.g., Alaskan Indian Program, etc.), and (3) Sources of Information (other sources are cited at the end of the directory).

The work is divided into four sections. Section 1, General Employment and Educational Assistance Programs, contains information on programs which offer special opportunities for employment, job placement, career information, and financial assistance for either undergraduate or graduate study. Included are over 700 listings of alphabetically arranged organizations. Section 2, Federal Programs, provides a comprehensive list of agencies from which financial and training assistance may be obtained. Section 3, Women's Programs, describes programs which are available to all women regardless of their ethnic identification. Section 4, College and University Awards, presents information about individual academic institutions which offer educational and financial support to minority members.

The entries in the four sections list names, addresses, and descriptions of the support offered by the organizations, agencies, or institutions. The entries in sections 1, 2, and 3 are coded consecutively by numbers ranging from 1–1,158. In Section 4, they are coded by the names of states plus a numerical sequence within the state (e.g., Oregon, OR-1, OR-2). The descriptive annotations are concise but adequate.

Two appendixes (A and B) are located in the *Directory.* Appendix A is devoted to the names and addresses of schools, colleges and universities, and organizations operating Upward

Bound, Talent Search, Special Services, and Special Veterans programs. Appendix B defines terms used in the *Directory*.

Because of its abundance of practical information, this directory will be an invaluable source for guidance and career counselors, placement officers, and minority members wishing to identify occupational, financial, and educational opportunities. Its acquisition is advised for school, public, and academic libraries. Many homes and civic and religious organizations will also find it useful. *(Oct. 1, 1976, p.279)*

370.113 Minorities—Education—U.S.—Directories [OCLC] 75-21928

The economics of minorities:
a guide to information sources. [Edited by] Kenneth L. Gagala. Detroit, Gale, [1976]. x, 212p. Economics Information Guide Series. no. 2. 22cm. cloth $18.

The Economics of Minorities is an annotated bibliography of research on the economic conditions of nonwhite people in the U.S. Included are books, journal articles, and government documents. Nonwhites are described as black Americans, American Indians, Mexican Americans, and Puerto Ricans. The Preface indicates that nonwhites comprise approximately 12 percent of the population and of that 12 percent, 95 percent are blacks. This concentration of the population reflects the composition of research on nonwhites. Within the purview of the phrase "economic conditions," the material includes modern economics and social and political economy. The editor comments: "The researcher who comprehends the effects of social and political forces upon minorities lends realism to his analysis in terms of both methodological design and policy recommendations." This bibliography covers materials from 1965 to the summer of 1974, reflecting that little research on minorities had been done prior to 1965, that scholarly inquiry was stimulated as a result of the urban riots of the mid to late 1960s, and that the quantity of research has declined in the 1970s.

Kenneth Gagala, editor of this volume, has his doctoral degree in economics and has published articles in the *American Economist, Journal of Black Studies, Social Science Record,* and *Journal of Social Studies* among others. He is currently an assistant professor at Cornell University's New York State School of Industrial and Labor Relations and serves as statewide coordinator for Cornell's Labor Studies Program.

The materials are grouped in 12 topical chapters. Their titles indicate the subject matter of the bibliographic entries. The titles are: "Description and Causes of Black Inequality," "The Psychology of Race," "Quality and Economic Returns of Black Education," "Black Movement to and Within Urban Areas," "Blacks in Residential Housing Markets," "Economic Development of the Black Community," "Black Consumers," "Blacks and the Manpower Policies of the Business Community," "Blacks and the Labor Movement," "American Indians," and "Spanish-Americans." Within the 12 chapters, entries are arranged alphabetically by personal or corporate author. Journal articles, books, and documents are interfiled. Citation information is generally complete; however, for a small number of references, obtained by the editor while conducting research for his doctoral dissertation or from journal advertisements, some citations are incomplete. The print is small but clear.

Separate Author, Title, and Subject Indexes serve as aids in using this relatively small volume. The Author Index includes all editors and compilers cited in the text, and the Title Index includes all titles of books, published reports, and theses. In some cases, indexed titles have been shortened. Journals, titles of articles, and chapter titles are not included. The Subject Index contains *see* and *see also* references. There are no cross-references in any other part of the book. In the Subject Index, with the exception of Chicago, Detroit, New York City, and Washington, D.C., individual cities and counties are listed under state name.

Although entries do not provide a comprehensive bibliography, the volume will provide a convenient starting point for persons interested in the development of minority economic conditions. *(June 15, 1977, p.1601)*

330.9'73 Negroes—Economic conditions—Bibliography || Indians of North America—Economic conditions—Bibliography || Spanish Americans in the U.S.—Economic conditions—Bibliography [CIP] 73-17573

Educators guide to free guidance materials:
[a multimedia guide]. Compiled and edited by Mary H. Saterstrom. 15th ed. August 1976. Randolph, Wis., Educators Progress Service, [c1976]. XXI, 395p. 27cm. paper $11.95 plus $.95 for postage and handling.

†370.404 Free materials || Personnel service in education—Bibliographies 62-18761

Educators guide to free health, physical education and recreation materials:
[a multimedia guide]. Compiled and edited by Foley A. Horkheimer. 9th ed., 1976. Randolph, Wis., Educators Progress Service, [c1976]. XIX, 521p. 27cm. paper $11.

†371.7104 Free materials || Physical education and training—Bibliography

Educators guide to free science materials:
[a multimedia guide]. Compiled and edited by Mary H. Saterstrom. 17th ed., August 1976. Randolph, Wis., Educators Progress Service, [c1976]. XXIV, 343, 74p. 27cm. paper $11.25

†372.3 Science—Study and teaching—Bibliography || Free materials

The Reference and Subscription Books Review Committee reviewed four of this publisher's guides dealing with individual media on June 1, 1976. The guides analyzed at that time covered films, filmstrips, tapes, and curriculum materials. The three guides presently under review are relatively newer creations of Educators Progress Service. The guidance book covers 2,061 (1,173 new to this edition) materials in four forms: 795 films; 83 filmstrips and 60 slide sets; 517 tapes, 4 scripts, and 21 audiodiscs; and 391 printed materials. For each medium, four subjects are covered in annotated individual references: career-planning materials, social-personal materials, responsibility, and use of leisure time. Access to the materials is provided by five indexes: Author Index, Subject Index, Source and Availability Index, Australian Availability Index, and Canadian Availability Index.

The health, physical education, and recreation guide lists 2,484 titles of which one-third are new to this edition. Access is provided through five indexes similar to those in the guidance guide.

The *Guide to Free Science Materials* lists more than 1,800 selected free items: 922 films, 40 filmstrips, 36 slides, 1 transparency set, 71 charts, exhibits, magazines, and posters, and 467 other printed materials. Nearly 30 percent of the items are new to this edition. Again, with science materials, the five-part Index helps locate information.

The three Educators Progress Service Guides reviewed here are intended to be used as companions to the publisher's other guides to free materials. They provide the most up-to-date and comprehensive listings of free materials in the subjects covered. They have become invaluable to educators and librarians. *(June 15, 1977, p.1601)*

80 years of best sellers, 1895–1975.
[By] Alice Payne Hackett and James Henry Burke. New York and London, Bowker, 1977. xii, 265p. 24cm. cloth $14.95 plus shipping and handling; 1/3 discount to trade.

This volume gathers the titles which have won the designation "bestseller" and suggests the ways in which American taste and popular literature have evolved since 1895 when the systematic recording of bestsellers began. This edition follows three predecessors which cumulated 50, 60, 70 years respectively. Alice Payne Hackett, former associate editor and current contributing editor of *Publisher's Weekly,* has been compiler of this book of records since its initial appearance in 1945 as *50 Years of Bestsellers.* James Henry Burke has assisted her in collecting data and sales figures for this edition which covers the years 1895–1975.

The material for 1895–1912 comes from *The Bookman,* where the first bestseller lists appeared. The titles for 1912–1975 come from *Publisher's Weekly (PW).* (The term "bestseller" allegedly was first found in print in an old copy of *PW.*)

The opening pages establish a link with the three prior editions by reproducing their forewords. Then a section provides a brief history of bestsellers, followed by sections on "Bestsellers, 1895–1975"; "Bestseller Subjects"; "Bestsellers by Years" (161 pages long and the major portion of the book); "Early Bestsellers"; and "Books and Articles about Bestsellers" (a bibliography arranged by titles with some annotations). The Index interfiles titles and authors in one alphabet.

In "Bestsellers" the combined figures for paperback and hardcover titles form a list of 366 titles—fiction and nonfiction—that have sold more than 2 million copies since 1895. Then there appear separate lists of the 278 hardcover books selling 750,000 copies or more and 276 paperbacks exceeding the 2 million mark. (In *60 Years of Bestsellers,* only 41 paperbacks had sold 2 million or more copies.)

"Bestseller Subjects" reassembles titles which exceeded 1 million sales into 7 popular categories: Children's books; Cookbooks; Crime and Suspense; Do-it-Yourself and Gardening; Poetry; Reference; and Religion. The major section of the book, "Bestsellers by Years," lists top 10 titles, accompanied by thumbnail (one-half to one-and-a-half pages) analyses, or it surveys social and political events, fads, and reading trends for each year. Then three pages of early bestsellers arrange in chronological order American favorites published prior to 1895 such as the *Holy Bible* and *The American Dictionary of the English Language,* by Webster, which have sold more than a million copies. For these works, publication dates are not shown. In summary, this book is an edifying chronological record and chart of Americans' social and cultural interests. It will be a handy tool for anyone curious about popular reading of past years and winners of the sales sweepstakes such as the all-time bestseller in fiction (*The Godfather*). This compact and sturdily bound book should find wide acceptance and use in public, school, and college libraries. *(July 1, 1977, p.1675)*

011 Bestsellers—Bibliography [CIP] 76-49120

The encyclopedia of Africa.
New York & London, Franklin Watts, 1976. 223p. illus. (part col.) maps. tables. diagrs. 31cm. tyvek $14.90.

The Encyclopedia of Africa is a profusely illustrated, thematically arranged overview of the continent of Africa which will be useful to high school students in the U.S. who can cope with the British spellings: "centres," "metre," "fertiliser," "colourful," "enrolment," "defence." The two editorial advisers, J. Knappert, lecturer in Bantu languages, School of Oriental and African Studies, University of London, and J. D. Pearson, professor of bibliography for Asia and Africa, University of London, and the ten members of the Consultant Advisory Board, A. E. Afigbo, M. J. C. Echeru, A. M. A. Imebore, Dr. Millar O. A. Jaja, J. H. Nketia, G. O. Nwankwo, A. F. Ogunsola, G. O. Olusanya, Reuben K. Udo, and Dr. Nnaberenyi Ugonna, bring a wide variety of expertise to the encyclopedia. The articles were written by 34 contributors, but their names or initials do not accompany the material for which they were responsible.

The encyclopedia is conveniently arranged under ten broad themes: "People," "History," "Economy," "Ecology," "Government," "Social Services," "The Arts," "Famous People," "The Land," and "Sport." Broadest coverage is given to the "People" (38 pages), "History" (28 pages), "Ecology" (20 pages), and "Famous People" (16 pages). There is also a 42-page gazetteer which is unusual in that its entries are encyclopedia-length descriptions of the places cited covering the people, economy, history, currency, and government of the nations of Africa. A Bibliography arranged by 25 subjects (religions, economy, wildlife, health and medicine, etc.) will be helpful to those seeking further information. The books cited, however, are not likely to be in the average U.S. high school library, e.g., *Ecology of Tropical and Subtropical Vegetation* (Edinburgh: Oliver and Boyd, 1971) and *Seaports of East Africa* (Nairobi: East African Pub. House).

Features of *The Encyclopedia of Africa* include its easy-to-read political and physical maps, its topical maps of languages, vegetation, temperature, and rainfall, and its charts and graphs of major diseases, major game reserves and national parks, production of minerals, and education enrollment. Sources of statistics are not cited, and the cutoff date for most figures seems to be 1971 or 1972. The Index covers all topics except "The Guide to Peoples and Languages." *(Apr. 1, 1977, p.1196)*

†960.03 Africa—Dictionaries 75-5919

The encyclopedia of air warfare.
[New York, T. Y. Crowell, 1975]. 256p. illus. maps. diagrs. charts. 30cm. buckram over binders board $17.95.

The Encyclopedia of Air Warfare, prepared by Britishers Christopher Chant, Richard Humble, John F. Davis, Donald Macintyre, and Bill Gunston, experienced writers on aviation subjects and pilots, was first published in Great Britain by Hammer House (London) in 1974. The book covers the history of air warfare comprehensively in text and a variety of illustrations. Both front and back endpapers depict aircraft insignia in color for 128 nations. The illustrations are exceptional. There are 320 color profile drawings of the major aircraft with their combat markings; a number of original maps, e.g., "The Zeppelin Raids on Britain," "The Allied Bombing Offensive on Germany," "The Changing Shape of Israel"; numerous detailed charts of specifications and statistics; and about 300 photographs and pictures.

Specific items of information in the text are not as easy to locate as they would have been in a conventionally A to Z arranged encyclopedia, because there are 31 chapters placed more or less in chronological order, with titles which give few clues as to their contents. Examples of such chapter titles are "Flying to Fight," "Portable Armies," "The Elite," and "Death Takes Wings." Furthermore, the Table of Contents listing the chapter titles occupies the lower half of the verso of the title page double spread, while the upper half carries copyright and credit data and the names and credentials of the five authors. Some readers may overlook the Contents and not realize that the encyclopedia is organized around four logical topics: "Pioneers of World War I," "Between the Wars," "World War II," and "The Jet Age." Optimum access to the wealth of material in the book is available only through careful use of the Contents and the Index. For example, someone searching for information on Arab or Israeli aircraft will find neither Israel nor the Arabs listed in the Index. The chapter heading "Wars of Survival—Middle East" gives the clue which leads to text and information beginning on page 230, which contains full-page photographs and descriptions of both Israeli and Arab aircraft used in the Yom Kippur War.

Even with the deficiency of inadequate finding devices, *The Encyclopedia of Air Warfare* is an exceptionally comprehensive and well-illustrated nontechnical reference work on the subject, and as such it will be valuable to students and others interested in air warfare. *(Sept. 1, 1976, p.55)*

358.4183 Airplanes, Military [OCLC] 74-24999

Encyclopedia of American steam traction engines.
By John Norbeck. Glen Ellyn, IL 60137, Crestline Publishing, Box 48, [c1977?]. 320p. (Crestline's Automotive Series). illus. leatherette $19.95; to schools and libraries, $17.95.

This collection of 1,200 black-and-white illustrations (mainly photographs with some ink drawings from early brochures) forms an album with commentary, rather than an encyclopedia, on one source of power used in farming, the steam traction engine. To produce this volume, John Norbeck, who has prepared slide talk shows on steam traction engines and workhorses, conducted an eight-year search and contacted farm agents, clubowners, and antique dealers. He also took many pictures of steam engines and draft animals at various sites. The result is a book containing examples and information on steam traction engines operational today and on types no longer in existence. The book begins with a copiously illustrated discussion of draft horses and their use in agriculture. This section is followed by brief biographies of John Deere and Cyrus McCormick. An annotated chronology describes the development (1845–1907) of the steam traction engine, beginning with the portable (horse- or oxen-drawn) engines. At the beginning of "Manufacturers From A to Z" is an explanation of the parts of a typical steam tractor such as boilers, grates, coil springs, and engine mounts. This is followed by an alphabetical listing of the names and city locations of 87 American and Canadian builders of steam traction engines. The 28 companies that have ceased production are asterisked. The main section of the book (225 pages) consists of drawings and photographs of the builders' machines in alphabetical order—from the 12-horsepower tractor of the Advance Thresher Company to the four-wheel-drive engine of Wood, Taber, & Morse Company. Other steam-powered equipment (threshers, balers, sawmills, stone crushers, and corn shellers) form the final section. A directory of annual shows (U.S. and Canada) and associations as well as a bibliography of books and periodicals of interest to steam traction engine owners should prove helpful to anyone (owners, students, antique dealers) who needs information or has an interest in this subject.

The book's binding is strong, and the pages open flat for easy reading. The illustrations clearly depict the forms of the engine as well as its uses.

Although information is not easily located (there is no index and the table of contents is placed in the center of the book), this album does provide specialized details and illustrations on one area of agricultural history. The *Encyclopedia of American Steam Traction Engines* would be useful in an academic or special library and fun to browse through anywhere. The author invites readers to send him corrections and photographs for a proposed second edition. *(July 15, 1977, p.1755)*

†629.229'2 Traction engines—Pictorial works ‖ Steam engines—Pictorial works ‖ Farm engines—Pictorial works   76-5764

The encyclopedia of comic book heroes.
v.1 Batman, v.2 Wonder Woman. Compiled by Michael L. Fleisher assisted by Janet E. Lincoln. New York, Macmillan, 1976. v.1, xix, 387p. 29cm. illus. cloth $16.95; paper $8.95; v.2, xix, 253p. 29cm. illus. cloth $14.95; paper $7.95.

These are the first two parts of an eight-volume series which will also include Captain Marvel, Plastic Man, and the Spirit (v.3), Green Lantern (v.4), The Flash (v.5), Superman (v.6), Captain America, the Sub-Mariner, and the Human Torch (v.7), and Doctor Fate, the Hawkman, Starman, and the Spectre (v.8). The Batman and Wonder Woman encyclopedias are alphabetical compendia of the character, place-names, and imaginative gadgetry that embody the comic-book lore of this hero and heroine from their first appearance (*Batman:* Detective Comics No. 27, May 1939; *Wonder Woman:* National Comics. All-Star No. 8, Dec. 1941) through 27 adventurous years. The 100-page entry under the hero's name in the Batman encyclopedia forms the nucleus of that volume. It includes a monthly chronicle of his exploits from May 1939 to December 1965 with numerous cross-references which, when followed, lead to every other entry in the volume. The Wonder Woman encyclopedia has the same centripetal and unifying arrangement. In each volume entries conclude with a source indicating comic book series, number and episode title; at times month and year are also provided. Many of the comic book episodes alluded to or described in these two volumes are inaccessible because the issues are long out of print and now in publishers' archives or part of private collections. Consequently, the compiler has taken pains in describing some episodes in detail, "retaining generous portions of the original dialogue and textual narrative."

The compiler states in the Preface that the eight-volume encyclopedia was a seven-year "labor of love" and the first two volumes certainly confirm his singular dedication. However, labors of love often attract only small though devoted coteries. This encyclopedia will be most useful to comic book enthusiasts, sociologists, semiologists, and purveyors of popular culture.
(Apr. 15, 1977, p.1296)

741.5'973 Comic books, strips, etc.—U.S.—Dictionaries [CIP]   76-956

Encyclopedia of German-American genealogical research.
[By] Clifford Neal Smith and Anna Piszczan-Czaja Smith. New York, Bowker, c1976. xiii, 273p. 29cm. cloth, $35, plus shipping and handling.

The Encyclopedia of German-American Genealogical Research was written "to survey the material available to the genealogist seeking to link American lineages with their origins in German-speaking Europe," to "serve as . . . a spur to the fashioning of new research tools," and "to provide American researchers with background material on German customs, sociological stratification, governmental organization, and ethnographic considerations having a bearing upon immigrant ancestors."

Most of the material included in the encyclopedia pertains to central Germany, with an emphasis on southwestern Germany, Baden-Württemberg, Hessen, and Rheinland-Pfalz. It was from these areas that a great number of immigrants came to America. Some information is included on German-speaking people from the countries along the North and Baltic Seas, as well as from Austria, from Switzerland, and from Slavic Europe. Material on the Jews of central Germany is included when extant. The authors feel a special moral obligation to assemble the Jewish-German genealogical data which has survived the Holocaust, and to contribute to the reconstruction of information which was largely destroyed during the Third Reich.

The encyclopedia begins with a brief Preface, followed by a Bibliographic Essay dealing with the published research tools on German-American genealogy. The main body of the work is made up of historical data, statistical studies, records, bibliographies, lists, and charts organized into seven articles. The articles are entitled: "German Ethnic Religious Bodies in America," "Language and Onomastics," "Organization of the Holy Roman Empire German Nation," "Genealogy in Germany," "Jews in Southwestern Germany," "Heraldry," and "German-American Genealogy." A 40-page Index, three columns per page, completes the encyclopedia.

Organization of presentation is consistent and thorough. Each article opens with an outline of topics to be covered. These topics are used as captions within the article and as running heads at the top of each right-hand page. Footnotes are listed at the end of each article. The extensive index contains many "see" and "see also" references.

The articles cover a broad range of material, including a list of the state and county locations of German-speaking congregations in the U.S. in 1906, an explanation of internal dialectical clues in German surnames, essays on the social structure and forms of land tenure in the German states, and a survey of the number of Jewish families living in villages and territories of southwestern Germany in the eighteenth and nineteenth centuries.

Although information concerning the authors of the encyclopedia could not be located, the Preface states that journal articles resulting from their research appear in the "National Genealogical Society Quarterly" and the "Illinois State Genealogical Society Quarterly." *Books in Print* 1975 lists seven monographs written by Clifford N. Smith concerning German- and British-American immigrants (Scottsdale, Ariz., Westland Publ., 1974 and 1975). The authors also plan to publish a volume entitled *American Genealogical Resources in German Archives.*

The encyclopedia is printed clearly on white paper. It has a two-column per page layout with adequate margins and lies flat when opened.

The *Encyclopedia of German-American Genealogical Research* is a thorough, well-organized, understandably written guide to information which has not before been treated in such depth. Its intelligent use of primary sources such a statistical data and records, along with lists, charts, bibliographies, and essays should make this reference source attractive even to persons not of German descent. The work fulfills its purposes of providing background material on the German way of life and surveying the existing genealogical material in both Germany and the U.S. The organization and presentation of data could serve as a model for others considering compilation of genealogical research tools. *(Oct. 15, 1976, p.345)*

973'.04   German Americans—Dictionaries and encyclopedias||German Americans—Genealogy—Dictionaries   [CIP]   75-28205

Encyclopedia of hand-weaving.
By Stanislaw A. Zielinski. New York, Funk & Wagnalls; dist. by T. Y. Crowell, [1976, c1959]. ix, 190p. illus. 23cm. paper $4.95.

This is the first U.S. edition of a title published in Canada by Fitzhenry & Whiteside Ltd, Toronto, and copyrighted by the Ryerson Press in 1959. It is reprinted without change.

Handweaving has become a subject of renewed interest as part of the current renaissance in handicrafts as hobby and home industry. There are many texts on handweaving, some with glossaries, but this is apparently the only encyclopedic work available. As handweaving was practiced in relatively isolated communities in several countries and discontinued as a commercial enterprise in the early nineteenth century as a result of the Industrial Revolution, its vocabulary has remained highly variegated. The terminology was modified and often incorrectly applied in the largely rural areas where the craft persevered.

This book provides complete and exact reference to variant terms (e.g., heddle, U.S., is the same as leash, British), as well as synonyms and alternate spellings. Derivation is noted (e.g., "HEDDLE" (fr. AS [Anglo-Saxon] hofeld, or Scand. Heidle)). There are also separate entries for French, German, and Scandinavian weaving terms, alphabetically listing under each language the term and English equivalent.

Brief articles appear on a variety of topics: *History of Weaving, Weaving, Weaves, Mistakes in Weaving, Dyeing, Navajo Weaving, Colour, Munsell's Theory of Colour, Cotton,* and *Count of Yarn*. A short list of books about weaving appears under the entry heading "Bibliography."

Effective black-and-white illustrations for definitions and articles appear on virtually every page. Weaves showing pattern are usually shown in photographs. Looms, parts of looms, and tools are shown in both photographs and diagrams. Although both types of illustrations are plentiful, there might profitably be even more as some of the definitions of equipment are difficult to visualize. The great majority of the illustrations are of the many drafts and drawdowns (pattern draft and weave plan are alternate terms) expressed both numerically and graphically. ("Draft" is fully defined as are the manners in which it may be represented.) The draft design is given under the name of virtually all weaves and patterns.

This book is sturdily bound, well printed on good stock, and has generous margins.

Its brevity of definitions and articles presupposes some prior knowledge of handweaving. Therefore, users who lack familiarity with the subject may have to consult additionally an encyclopedia, dictionary, or textbook. The *Encyclopedia of Handweaving* should be a worthwhile and inexpensive acquisition for public libraries and persons interested in the weaver's vernacular.   *(July 1, 1977, p.1675)*

741.1'4'03   Hand weaving—Dictionaries   [OCLC]   75-45519

Encyclopedia of information systems and services.
Edited by Anthony T. Kruzas. 2d. international ed. Ann Arbor, Mich., Anthony T. Kruzas Associates, 1974. 1,271p. 29cm. cloth $77.50.

Publication of *Information Systems and Services* has been taken over by Gale Research. They expect to have a second edition off the press later in 1977. A statement on the title page of the second edition describes the work as an international guide to "information storage and retrieval systems, computerized data bases, SDI [selective dissemination of information] services, data base publishers, clearinghouse and information centers, library and information networks, data collection and analysis centers, micrographic systems and services; and consulting, research and coordinating agencies." According to the editor, approximately 1,750 organizations within these categories are described and analyzed.

Anthony Kruzas, editor and publisher of this edition, is a professor of library science at the University of Michigan; he has been on the staff of that institution since 1956. The first edition of this work was published in 1971.

Excluded from the encyclopedia are printed commercial and legal services, "traditional" academic and special libraries, public information offices, computer and micrographics hardware manufacturers and distributors, conventional indexing and abstracting services, and library automation programs confined to such functions as circulation control and acquisitions.

The expansion of entries from the first to the second edition is claimed by the editor to be more than 100 percent. The entries now include 225 foreign organizations from 31 countries.

A Bibliography of 56 items (principally directories, lists, surveys) contains most important sources used to identify potential entries. In addition, approximately 50 newsletters and periodicals were scanned regularly for appropriate data. Most information, however, was obtained directly by telephone, letter, or questionnaires.

The basic descriptive portion of the book has two divisions. The main section is devoted to the major organizations and services. The second part is a supplement consisting of briefer descriptions of organizations not requiring extended coverage, those for which the information supplied was incomplete, and defunct and inactive organizations.

As many of the following 18 items as apply are included in each entry, following a basic outline keyed to general subject headings. The name of the parent organization, significant subunits, and the particular system being described are arranged in alphabetic order. Dates of establishment, related or sponsoring organizations, names of the heads of the unit, total staff in full-time equivalents, a description of the system or service, subject coverage, input or data sources, stored information in all forms, publications, and microform applications and services are then listed. Comparable data on computer applications and services, other services offered, specifications of computer and information processing equipment, user equipment requirements, and use restrictions end the typical entry. When required, remarks and addenda include additional information, name changes, and *see also* references.

A particularly helpful feature of this work is its 13 separate indexes to the basic material. The first, Combined Index to Organizations, Systems and Services, is the most detailed, providing access by subunits and by acronyms.

The Geographic Index arranges U.S. organizations by state and city; foreign organizations are arranged alphabetically by country.

Index 3 lists computerized applications and services. Indexes 4, 5, and 6 are devoted respectively to commercially available data bases, micrographic applications and services, and library and information networks.

Selective dissemination of information (SDI) services, consulting and planning services, research and research projects, data collection and analysis centers, professional associations, abstracting and indexing services, and serial publications are subjects of the remaining Indexes.

The Encyclopedia of Information Systems and Services continues to be a valuable tool for libraries needing material on information systems and their availability as of 1974.

(June 1, 1977, p.1525)

029.025'73 Information services—U.S.—Directories || Information storage and retrieval systems—Directories || Data libraries—U.S.—Directories   [OCLC]   73-3732

Energy fact book 1976.
Arlington, Va., Tetra Tech, Inc., 1911 N. Fort Myer Drive, [c1975]. vi, various paging. 28cm. library ed. $8.95; paper $4.95.

The Reference and Subscription Books Review Committee received both the 1975 and the 1976 *Energy Fact Book* for review at the same time. However, promotional material for the 1976 edition advertises it as the "first issue," and a note attached to the 1975 edition states that "this 1975 Energy Fact Book Review Copy is the same as the 1976 Energy Fact Book except that Part v, 'Who's Who in Energy' has been deleted from the 1976 version."

In his Introduction to the book, U.S. Representative (Washington) Mike McCormack states that the *Energy Fact Book 1976* "is a guide to some of the current and potential alternative sources of energy that can be exploited in planning for a crisis-free energy equilibrium." The information in the *Fact Book* was compiled by U.S. Navy Commander Paul A. Petzrick as part of his duties in directing the U.S. Navy's Energy Research and Development program. Data were taken from eight government agencies, seven publishers and journals, six associations and universities, and five consulting firms. The publisher of the book, Tetra Tech, Inc., is a Pasadena-based consulting firm on energy.

An enormous amount of data presented as well-organized tables, graphs, and figures with sources and references cited is compressed into the small volume. Much of the information is current to December 1974. It is regrettable, therefore, that the book is not designed for better access to the facts. Pages are not numbered consecutively. There are no running heads, and there is no index. The only clue to the contents is a Contents page which cites the four major parts by title and eight Appendixes by topic. A gray three-fourths-inch outer edge is on the outer edge of each part and appendix, but this is not as clearly discernible against the wide-edged page as thumb tabs might have been.

The parts are devoted to an overview of the current energy situation, energy research and development in other countries, energy research and development legislation during the Ninety-third and Ninety-fourth congresses (1974 and 1975), and federal government energy research and development. The Appendixes contain facts on petroleum, natural gas, nuclear power (including a World List of Nuclear Power Plants), coal, coal gasification, coal liquefaction, oil shale, and tar sands.

The *Energy Fact Book 1976* is a valuable compendium of well-documented data on fossil fuels and alternative sources of energy.   *(Sept. 1, 1976, p.55)*

†333.7   Power resources || Energy policy

English language cookbooks, 1600–1973.
Compiled by Lavonne Brady Axford. Detroit, Gale, [1976]. ix, 675p. 29cm. cloth $45.

Axford, a librarian of considerable experience, has divided this massive bibliography into three parts: a title listing, an Author Index, and a Subject Index. In the succinct Introduction, she elucidates the book's organization, the use of cross-references, and treatment of serials.

A listing of approximately 12,000 titles (434p.) is the main body of the work. In it books and periodicals are alphabetized by title (printed in upper case to facilitate use), with complete bibliographic data for each: author, illustrator, edition, place of publication, publisher, date, pagination, illustrations, series, other editions and publishers, and variant titles.

The Author Index collocates all works by or attributed to each author or corporate body and provides short titles sufficient for identification purposes.

The very helpful Subject Index lists some books under several headings. General cookbooks for England, France, and the U.S. are arranged chronologically, while those devoted to the cuisines of states, countries, and nationalities are grouped under appropriate headings and alphabetized. For example, the reader is referred from *North American Indians* to *Native Americans* for a list of books devoted to American Indian cooking. Some headings are general (as *Fruit,* with a cross-reference from *Dates* but not from *Avocados* or *Peaches; Famous People; Restaurants, Recipes of; Restaurants, Eating in,* etc.). Others are specific (as *Chili Con Carne* and *Curries*). The page format is two-column and well spaced, with clear type. Binding is substantial, margins adequate, and the book lies flat when opened. *English Language Cookbooks, 1600–1973,* for which the compiler realistically disclaims comprehensiveness, should be a congenial acquisition for large public, academic, and special libraries which provide resources for historical and sociological research. It will also give pleasure to cookbook collectors and bibliophiles.   *(June 1, 1977, p.1526)*

016.6415   Cookery—Bibliography   [CIP]   76-23533

Enjoy Europe by car.
[By] William J. Dunn. Rev. & enl. ed. New York, Charles Scribner's Sons, [c1976]. xii, 303p. illus. diagrs. charts. 23cm. cloth, $10.95; paper, $5.95.

Enjoy Europe By Car has been revised, updated, and enlarged over the original edition of 1973. This handy reference opens with an Introduction on using the book, planning in advance, and using the appendixes while motoring in Europe. There follow 17 short chapters of consumer advice on such topics as hitchhikers, ferries, mountain driving, fuel and service stations, road maps, and fly-drive tours. Then 22 countries, including the four small nations of Andorra, Liechtenstein, Monaco, and San Marino, are described in detail. The general format is the same for all the countries. Specific information on population, area, currency, gasoline, insurance, customs, auto clubs, and tourist offices in North America precedes the several pages of chatty description and advice. There are one or two full-page, black-and-white scenes for each country. These add little information to the book, and the space could have been used better by road maps. The 11 Appendixes are unique and they will be most useful. They cover such topics as "Automobile Comparison Chart," "Mileage Charts," "Currency Regulations," "International Hotel Code," "Comparative Sizes of Clothing," "Temperature Conversion Chart," and "Useful Phrases for the Motorist." The phrases, covering the repertoire of common car emergencies, are given in 12 languages including the major ones of Western Europe, Yugoslavia, and Greek (shown in Greek letters and with phonetic equivalents in the Roman alphabet). There is an Index to places and a few topics such as car(s), mountain passes, customs, and insurance. The endpapers show 81 road signs in color; these will be most useful to persons unfamiliar with European or international road markings. *Enjoy Europe By Car* is packed with useful information for the traveler unfamiliar with European roads, rules, and countries. Its availability in hard and softcover will make it a handy reference in libraries and homes and to carry on the road in Europe.

(Nov. 1, 1976, p.424)

914'.04 Europe—Description and travel—Guide books || Automobiles—Road guides—Europe
[CIP] 75-43771

The equal rights amendment:

a bibliographic study. Compiled by the Equal Rights Amendment Project, Anita Miller, project director; Hazel Greenberg, editor and compiler. Westport, Conn., Greenwood, [c1976], xxvii, 367p. 24cm. pyroxylin $19.95.

The Equal Rights Amendment Project began in 1974 with a grant from the Rockefeller Foundation to the California Commission on the Status of Women. Its purpose was to "make a national study of the societal impact of conformance of laws to the Equal Rights Amendment, with the goal of promoting public understanding of the issues involved." The project is now independent and publishes a magazine, *The Equal Rights Monitor.*

This bibliography lists historical material on the ERA, argumentative material concerning its impact on society, and writings analyzing its legal effects. Most of the 17-page Introduction is devoted to a concise history of the ERA. The bibliography, consisting of 5,809 numbered items, is divided into five parts: Congressional Publications; Other Government Publications; Books, Articles and Discussions in Books, and Dissertations; Pamphlets, Brochures, Reports, Papers, and Other Documents; and Periodical Material. Author, title, place, publisher, and date are provided for books. Periodical citations give author, title, periodical title, date, and pages; newspapers give page and column as well as date. Most entries are not annotated. There is an Author Index and an Organization Index to the numbered citations; the Organization Index also shows their addresses.

The section on congressional publications lists Senate and House items separately, both in chronological order, beginning with the introduction of the Equal Rights Amendment in 1923. Listed are citations from the *Congressional Record,* hearings, and reports, and it is claimed that "every mention of the ERA in Congress, except for very minor procedural entries," is included. The 5-page section on Other Government Publications includes federal and state items arranged by author. The next 5-page section, Books and Dissertations, is also arranged by author. The 13-page section on pamphlets includes brochures, fliers, and leaflets arranged alphabetically by issuing organization.

The longest section, on periodical material, is further subdivided into five types of publications. Legal periodicals are alphabetized by author or by title where no author is available, as are entries from the academic journals, popular magazines, and special interest newspapers. The cutoff date is January 1976 with a few exceptions in the Addenda. The 1,126 articles in the National Woman's Party magazine *Equal Rights* July 1923–November 1954 are cited in chronological order. Most of the references in the Newsletters grouping are from *Herstory* microfilm; arrangement is by newsletter title and then by date. Articles from nine newspapers which are formally indexed are listed chronologically. A 1914 *New York Times* citation is the earliest item in the volume, and coverage for the *Chicago Tribune, Christian Science Monitor, Los Angeles Times,* and *Wall Street Journal* go through January 1976. Other citations come from *Editorials on File* and from the microfilm collections of *Herstory* and *Women and the Law,* which are not elsewhere indexed.

The binding of this volume is sturdy and the format is pleasing; double-spacing between items makes the citations easy to read. Most libraries will find this bibliography very useful because it brings together information about the ERA which would otherwise have to be sought in a variety of other sources in a convenient form. *(July 15, 1977, p.1755)*

016.342'73 Sex discrimination against women—Law and legislation—U.S.—Bibliography || Women—Legal status, laws, etc.—U.S.—Bibliography || Sex discrimination—Law and legislation—U.S.—Bibliography [CIP] 76-24999

Executive and management development for business and government:

a guide to information sources. [By] Agnes O. Hanson. Detroit, Gale, [c1976]. xiv, 357p. 22cm. cloth $14.50.

Executive and Management Development for Business and Government is a conveniently arranged annotated bibliography of information sources. Information is organized into 14 chapters, each of which covers a specific phase of executive and management development: management education; the company, government, and society; international management and multinational corporations. Subtopics under the general chapter headings aid the user in locating specific sources. For example, chapter 4, "Human Resource Planning, Management, and Accounting," has the following subdivisions: "Human Resource Planning," "Personnel Administration," "Selection Procedures," "Performance Appraisal," "Compensation," "Motivation," "Job Attitudes and Job Satisfaction," "Job Enrichment and Job Restructuring," "Development of Creativity and Innovation," and "Psychology in Management."

Information given in each entry includes author, full title, place, date, and year of publication, and pagination. Annotations are brief and primarily descriptive. Four indexes facilitate locating information, an Author Index, Title Index, Subject Index, and an Index to Proper Names.

Executive and Management Development for Business and Government can be a time-saver for those requiring sources of management and executive information. Business divisions in public libraries and special business libraries will find it most helpful. *(June 1, 1977, p.1526)*

016.6584 Management—Bibliography [CIP] 76-8337

The family guide to Cape Cod:

what to do when you don't want to do what everyone else is doing. [By] Bernice Chesler and Evelyn Kaye; illus. by Joan Drescher. Barre, Mass., Barre Publishing, 1976; distributed by Crown. 310p. illus. maps. charts. 23 and 24cm. cloth and paper over boards, $12.95; to schools and libraries, 20 percent discount; paper, $5.95.

The Family Guide to Cape Cod is intended primarily for use by families travelling on the Cape by car. A preliminary chapter, "Orientation to Cape Cod," gives a wide variety of advisory consumer information ranging from Chamber of Commerce members to mileage charts and material on crafts. Then 16 locations are treated in detail: Barnstable, Bourne, Brewster, Chatham, Dennis, Eastham, Falmouth, Harwich, Hyannis, Mashpee, Orleans, Provincetown, Sandwich, Truro, Wellfleet, and Yarmouth. Another chapter describes trips to Martha's Vineyard, Nantucket, Edaville Railroad, and Plymouth, all of which are not more than one day's drive from the Cape. Each area is illustrated with a hand-drawn map showing salt and fresh water areas, villages, and towns. There is no indication of scale so the user must estimate distances between locations.

Enough information is given on each place to satisfy the average family's requirements: historical briefing, beaches, fishing, libraries, recreational facilities, movies and theaters, and restaurant suggestions. *The Family Guide to Cape Cod* is well designed for ease of use, and it should be helpful for families unfamiliar with Cape Cod. *(Nov. 1, 1976, p.425)*

917.44'92 Cape Cod—Description and travel—Guide books   [CIP]   76-5459

Federal government: Congress.
[New York, Environment Information Center, Inc., 1975–   .] annual, 1st Dec. 1975. 36p. 28cm. paper $10.

Federal Government: Congress is the second update of Environment Information Center's *Energy Directory Update Service,* which is published in two formats, as chapter 01 of the *Update Service* and as a separate annual. The annual is being considered in this note. The first update, *Energy Information Locator,* was reviewed in *Reference and Subscription Books Reviews,* April 15, 1976.

For each of 36 congressional committees (3 joint, 19 House, 14 Senate) similar types of information are provided: committee name, mail address, telephone number, statement of committee jurisdiction in energy matters, key energy-related personnel (name, title, telephone), committee chairperson, energy-related subcommittees (name, chairperson, telephone), energy-related hearings, energy-related legislation. The only reference cited is the Environment Information Center's "organizational data base, which profiles 3,000 federal and state agencies. . . ."

About 200 persons are named, occasionally incorrectly, e.g., Lloyd Bentson should be Bentsen, Edward T. Braswell should be T. Edward Braswell, Ernest J. Carrodo should be Corrado, Richard N. Sharoon should be Sharood. Also, there is no index to retrieve these names.

The list of subcommittees of the Joint Economic Committee fails to include the Subcommittee on Energy, chaired by Edward M. Kennedy. (This subcommittee is cited, however, as sponsor of energy-related hearings.) The name of the subcommittee of the House International Relations Committee, chaired by Donald M. Fraser (Subcommittee on International Organizations), is omitted.

In the absence of a stated cutoff date, certain inconsistencies in the energy-related hearings and legislation are not explained. For example: Hearings of the House Ad Hoc Select Committee on the Outer Continental Shelf as recent as Nov. 19, 1975, are noted, yet the approval on Nov. 4 of HR 4799 as Public Law (PL) 94-124 is not, nor is the approval on Oct. 21, 1975, of HR 8121 (House Appropriations Committee) as PL 94-121.

Examination of a sample of the rather general subject Index, concluding this pamphlet, revealed no errors.

The uneven currency, omissions, and errors noted in *Federal Government: Congress* make this publication of limited value for any library clientele requiring recent and accurate information. *(Oct. 1, 1976, p.279)*

†333.7'025 Power resources—Directories || Energy policy—Directories || U.S. Congress—Directories

A field guide to Pacific states wildflowers:
field marks of species found in Washington, Oregon, California and adjacent areas. Text by Theodore F. Niehaus; illus. by Charles L. Ripper. Boston, Houghton Mifflin, 1976. (Sponsored by the National Audubon Society and National Wildlife Federation.) xxii, 432p. illus. (part col.) 19cm. cloth $10.95.

Number 22 in the Peterson Field Guide Series, *A Field Guide to Pacific States Wildflowers* is in the neatly attractive format familiar to the many users of the series. Listed are 1,492 wildflowers from 77 families, with 1,502 illustrations. These appear in six sections grouped by flower color: white-whitish, yellow, orange, pink-red-purple, violet-blue or blue-purple, brown and green. (Pages are color tipped at top right corner for ease in location.) Each text page is faced with a page of drawings, both in color and black and white. The text gives common and scientific names, family, describes recognition features, size and habitat, and gives range and flowering time. The heading for each text page gives petal number and characteristics, leaf shape, and cross-references. Because this guide is meant to be consulted in the field, the content has been arranged to accommodate quick and convenient identification. There is a detailed introduction explaining identification methods. Picture matching, using color and shape, is based on fieldmarks which give the "exact distinctions between similar species." These are noted in the descriptions and illustrations (with arrow designation) in the color-coded sections, and there are cross-references to differently colored species. The pictorial key is dependent on "visual impressions rather than on technical or phylogenetic features." The key, a botanical design, appears in the margin throughout the text and is a guide to the page where one can use picture matching. The "Family Description and Key" section of the Introduction must be referred to until, through experience in the field, the user's recognition skills have been developed enough to permit direct consultation of the guide. It is noted that there are about 280 plant families in the world and that the groupings in this guide are similar to those in most flower guides.

The ten "Plant Regions of the Pacific States" are described and cover British Columbia to Baja, California, from the Pacific Ocean to the foothills of the Rocky Mountains in Idaho and Utah, and western Arizona. This area includes the greatest variety of ecological habitats and the greatest number of flowering plant species in the U.S. There is a map showing natural features.

The endpapers provide a pictorial glossary. There is an index by both scientific and common names and to the introductory "Family Descriptions and Key." *A Field Guide to Pacific States Wildflowers* should be a useful acquisition for libraries located in the Western U.S. *(Apr. 1, 1977, p.1196)*

†582.13'09 Wild flowers—U.S.—Pacific Northwest || Wild flowers—Handbooks, manuals, etc.

A field guide to the butterflies of the West Indies.
By Norman D. Riley. Boston, Demeter Pr., New York, Quadrangle/The New York Times Book Co., [1975]; distributed to the trade by Harper & Row. 224p. 210cm. cloth $12.50.

Butterflies of the West Indies, with the exception of Trinidad and Tobago, are covered comprehensively for the first time in one field guide. Arranged by family, their description, distribution, and in some cases, caterpillar stages are given along with additional notes. Popular names and citations to colorplates are also included. The 24 plates cover all but 22 of the 293 species described and are the work of two artists, using chiefly specimens from the British Museum of Natural History. Though they lack the brilliance of color photographs, they are mostly drawn in life size and are well suited for identification purposes, showing both the upper and under side of the wings.

A general Introduction with information on morphology, classification, and collecting; brief glossary of 40 terms; handy checklist and distribution table; bibliography of general and faunistic works and articles on taxonomy and zoogeography complete this useful field guide. Its two indexes give English and scientific names of species, with citation to text and illustrations.   *(Sept. 1, 1976, p.55)*

595.7'89 Butterflies—West Indies || Insects—West Indies   [OCLC]   74-25436

A field guide to the mammals:
field marks of all North American species found north of

Mexico. Text and maps by William Henry Burt; illustrations by Richard Philip Grossenheider. 3d ed. Sponsored by The National Audubon Society and National Wildlife Federation. Boston, Houghton Mifflin Co., 1976. (The Peterson Field Guide Series, 5) xxv. 289p. illus. maps. tables. 19cm. cloth $9.95; paper $5.95.

This revision of *A Field Guide to the Mammals* continues the familiar format established for the Peterson Field Guide series and previous editions of this title.

William Henry Burt, emeritus curator of mammals and emeritus professor of zoology, University of Michigan, is the former editor of *Journal of Mammalogy* and of *Special Publications* of the American Society of Mammalogists. He is currently visiting lecturer in biology and associate in the museum at the University of Colorado. The late Richard Philip Grossenheider, who did not live to see this edition completed, was an artist and zoologist and served for a number of years on the staff of the St. Louis Zoological Gardens. This is the second work which Burt and Grossenheider have collaboratively produced, their earlier book being *Mammals of Michigan*.

Coverage and treatment of material for this edition of *A Field Guide to the Mammals* is essentially the same as for the second edition. The number of species described has increased from 378 to 380. As in the previous editions, information on subspecies has been intentionally omitted. Readers interested in subspecies or more extended and detailed information are referred to more technical literature, some of which is listed at the back of the book under "References."

Typical entries include information under six subheadings: "Identification," which indicates salient features for quick recognition; "Similar Species," which notes distinguishing marks useful in differentiating between animals of like appearance; an indication of "Habitat"; "Habits"; "Young," which notes such characteristics as litter size, natal season, gestation period, appearance of young, etc.; and "Economic Status." All measurements in this edition are stated in the metric as well as linear system.

As in the second edition, small maps showing the distribution of 291 species of land mammals are included, but maps for 36 species have been updated for this edition. Range maps are not included for marine species, for species restricted to islands, or mammals limited to a single locality. Each map is generally placed near the page upon which the species is described. References are provided from text to map and vice versa.

The section dealing with cetaceans (whales, dolphins, and porpoises) has been extensively rewritten and amplified, and scientific (Latinate) names have been updated. In addition, many entries in other sections have minor revisions.

The plates for the third edition—the same as for the second edition although printed by a different process—have been gathered into one section in the middle of the book. Previously they had been scattered throughout the guide, thereby frequently interrupting the text without necessarily being directly related to the adjacent content. The mammals exhibited in the plates have arrows pointing to the distinctive recognition features noted in the text. Opposite each plate are listed the common names of the species shown followed by the Latinate name together with very brief descriptions which note regional or seasonal variation. For each species there is an area notation which refers to a quadrisected map of North America north of Mexico. In addition, the page opposite a plate frequently has other illustrative matter: specimen tracks, den entrances, representations of nests, etc.

Additionally, the book includes a section of black-and-white plates showing skulls, keyed to text and range map references on the facing pages. New to this edition are drawings of four marine mammal skulls with the opposing page providing identification and size. As a quick aid in verifying remains of mammals, a table of dental formulae is provided, listing species in accordance with the dentition.

As indicated above, the book contains a section of References for those needing more technical information. This bibliography consists of a brief section labelled "General" materials, followed by a more extensive section headed "States and Provinces," subdivided alphabetically by governmental unit, which lists books, journals, museum bulletins, and federal, state, and provincial documents.

The Index is primarily to animals entered by their common and scientific names. Cross-references relate various common names for the same species and refer from superseded scientific names to those in current use. Illustrations are indicated by page references in boldface type. Range maps and the section of skull illustrations are not indexed but are referenced from the text. The Committee found no blind references in the Index or in text cross-references.

A Field Guide to the Mammals is an attractively printed and sturdily bound handbook on the mammals of the continental U.S. and Canada. It aids quick identification in the field and provides brief essential information in the library.

(Jan. 15, 1977, p.746)

599'.09   Mammals—North America—Identification   [CIP]   75-26885

A field guide to the nests, eggs, and nestlings of British and European birds.

[By] Colin Harrison. [New York], Quadrangle/The New York Times Book Co., distributed to the trade by Harper & Row, [c1975]. 432p. illus. (part col.) diagrs. 20cm. cloth $12.50.

Dr. Colin Harrison is a London-born librarian, teacher, and ornithologist who has written works on bird psychology, plumage patterns, and bone structure. In the *Field Guide* he attempts to supplement the field guides to European birds by "providing additional information on the nesting habits" of 69 kinds of birds, including storks, waterfowl, vultures, cranes, and hawks. The young of each bird are described and pictured with line drawings, and the size and color of the eggs are given.

The book is well arranged to permit easy access to the material. The Contents and Index of English Names and Index of Scientific Names help in locating specific information. Entry is boldfaced under common name (*Kingfishers, Long-tailed Tits, Buttonquail, Swallows and Martins, Cuckoos, Treecreepers*) with the scientific name in italics. For each bird information includes description of nest, breeding season, eggs, incubation, nestling, and nestling period.

The illustrations are outstanding for a book priced at $12.50. One hundred forty-five chicks were painted by Dr. Philip Burton, and Dr. Harrison supervised the photographing of some 700 eggs. Both the egg and the chick illustrations are in color. Zoology libraries will find *A Field Guide to the Nests, Eggs, and Nestlings of British and European Birds* authoritative and instructive.

(Sept. 15, 1976, p.204)

†598.2'94   Birds—Eggs and nests—Identification || Birds—Europe || Birds—Gt. Brit.   [OCLC]   74-25435

50 major film-makers.

Edited by Peter Cowie. South Brunswick and New York, A. S. Barnes and Co., Inc., [1975]. 287p. illus. 29cm. cloth $20.

Culled from the "Five Directors of the Year" sections of the annual editions of *International Film Guide* for the year 1964–1973, *50 Major Film-Makers* contains biographical career essays of directors who "were alive when first featured in the guide" and who produced "important" work during the past decade. Thus, such well-known individuals as John Ford, Jean Renoir, Howard Hawks, Yasujiro Ozu, and William Wyler are conspicuously absent, while Sergey Bondarchuk (who directed only three films in his career at the time of the article, including the dreadful *Waterloo*), Jörn Donner (a Finnish director whose work has had little exposure in the U.S.), Mark Donskoy (USSR), Dusan Makavejev (Yugoslavia), and several others are included who may be unknown to any save the serious film scholar. According to the editor, Peter Cowie, who has written several books on film directors and international film history, some of the directors "were chosen not so much for any individual achievement as for their overall contribution to the cinema."

The entries, arranged alphabetically by director, highlight the "important" films and special techniques of each individual and have been revised and updated when necessary; unannotated filmographies with English-language translations, complete up to December 1974, conclude each director's section. Truly international in scope, the book includes directors from 16 countries. France predominates with ten, followed by the U.S. with eight (including English-born Hitchcock and Turkish Elia Kazan), and Italy with six. Most countries have three representatives: Great Britain (including American-born Joseph Losey), Sweden, USSR, Japan, Czechoslovakia, and Poland, although two of the Polish film-makers, Roman Polanski and Jerzy Skolimowski, have become international in their assignments. The Netherlands has two directors; India, Spain, Finland, Hungary, Yugoslavia, and Argentina each boast one.

50 Major Film-Makers includes 10 articles signed by eight additional authors. Cowie wrote the remaining 40 and has exerted fairly strong editorial control over his guest contributors. Similar information is presented in the same order and style in each of the 50 essays. Black-and-white production and publicity stills are thoughtfully chosen, fairly large and clear; a few grainy individual frame blow-ups are used in cases where stills were not available. At least one photograph in each chapter shows the director in action. A four-and-a-half-page Index to Film Titles concludes the book.

The book will be useful for film buffs, serious film scholars, and libraries serving such patrons. *(Jan. 1, 1977, p.685)*

791.43'023 (B) Moving-picture producers and directors—Biography [CIP] 73-107

Fifty years of prairie cooking.
Intro. and suggested recipes by Louis Szathmary. New York, Arno Pr., 1973. xx, 94, 81, 48, 155p. illus. 22 cm. cloth $10.
641.5 Cookery, American—Middle West [CIP] 72-9794
See page 116

Fighters in service:
attack and training aircraft since 1960. By Kenneth Munson; illus. by John W. Wood. Rev. ed. New York, Macmillan, [c1975]. 175p. illus. 19cm. paper over board $6.95.
358.4'3 Fighter planes [CIP] 75-12742
See page 103

Fischler's hockey encyclopedia.
[By] Stan and Shirley Fischler. New York, T. Y. Crowell Co., [1975]. 628p. illus. 24cm. cloth $15.

This encyclopedia consists of 754 articles covering various aspects of ice hockey: players, officials, fans, equipment, and famous events in the game. The coverage is almost exclusively of the professional hockey scene as represented by the National Hockey League and the World Hockey Association from their beginnings to 1975. The articles are arranged alphabetically with a generous supply of photographs of the players and officials included. About 90 percent of the entries are biographical.

As stated in the Introduction, the editors faced difficult decisions in selecting the entries "We had so many names, so many subjects, that volumes would have been required to find room for everyone. As a result a lot of good men, (and) funny subjects ... made their exit on the cutting room floor." The selection criteria used seem to have been fame, notoriety, and novelty.

It will be a rare hockey buff who will not find something new in this book.

Both editors are well-known hockey writers and experienced observers of the game. Stan Fischler has written over 40 books on hockey and is noted for his acute and often controversial writing. The characteristics of style and viewpoint which the authors employ in their journalism have been carried over to the encyclopedia entries. Their sources are implicit, because bibliographical citations are not provided. A random check against the authoritative *Encyclopedia of Hockey* (New York: Barnes, 1973) verified the accuracy of the entries sampled, and an overall examination of the book revealed no internal errors.

The lively style of this book enables one to read it as if it were a novel (albeit in several sittings), and this perhaps is symptomatic of one of its weaknesses; despite its physical size, its 628 pages do not contain a commensurate amount of hard information. If one wishes to know how many assists Gordie Howe had in 1963, this book will not give the answer; aside from Howe's overall totals (now dated and so no longer accurate), only a partial listing of his year-by-year scoring is given. Even so, this is more detail than is given for most of the other players. Not only is the type large and the layout inefficient but also there is a significant amount of repetition. For example, most player entries given a biographical career synopsis, and facts listed here are often repeated in the text of the entry. As the authors' introduction made clear that space was at a premium, much more effective use should have been made of type and layout.

The alphabetic entry arrangement constitutes another drawback to this book, for it is effective *only if one is already familiar with hockey history.* If one wishes to find out the total goal leader in National Hockey League history, unless one suspects that Gordie Howe is the answer, the only way it can be found in this book is to start at the beginning and read through to the entry under Howe. In short, it is very difficult to use this book for reference purposes unless one is familiar with names of individuals or teams. Conversely, if one is already aware of the names of individuals or teams, there is probably little fresh factual information to be found, although many of the anecdotes may provide amusement.

There are many inconsistencies in the entries included. As stated above, the emphasis is almost exclusively on the NHL and WHA so that the lone entry for the American Hockey League team, the Hershey Bears, is illogical. Cross-references are virtually non-existent. There is no *see also* reference under *Hall of Fame* to the article, *Hockey Hall of Fame.* There is no reference from *Team Canada* to *Russian Hockey,* although its series with the Russians is described in the latter article. Here one also finds an account of the World Hockey Association All-Stars series, but again there is no cross-reference from the *World Hockey Association* article. Similar inconsistencies abound throughout the text; e.g., there is no entry under Michel Briere, but details of his tragic demise are cited in the *Pittsburgh Penguins* article. Since there is no index, these omissions make the reference value of this book meager. As is the case with any hardcover reference work, attempting to keep pace with a volatile sport such as hockey, the passage of each season erodes the currency of its facts. In general, adequate coverage of such sports can only be assured by access to a combination of general histories (i.e., team and sport histories, individual biographies, a single "benchmark" encyclopedia) and current periodicals updated yearly (e.g., NHL and WHA player's guides). The Fischler encyclopedia falls neatly between these two stools.

Most of the objections mentioned above pertain to this work's shortcomings as an encyclopedia. If the book were titled "Fischler's Hockey Gallery," or carried a modest label, it would not be open to these structural criticisms, but could be commended as a beginner's guide to some of the color and lore of professional hockey. It may have value for libraries wishing to supplement their reference collections with an engaging, informal, albeit expensive account of this sport.

(Oct. 1, 1976, p.280)

796.9'62   Hockey   [CIP]   75-12749

5,000 questions answered about maintaining, repairing, and improving your home.
[By] Stanley Schuler. New York, Macmillan Pub. Co.; London, Collier Macmillan Publishers, [c1976]. ix, 416p. 29cm. cloth $15.95; paper $9.95.

The author of ten manuals on gardening, swimming pools, and other aspects of home care has collected a wide range of information and advice in alphabetical order. He takes the reader from air cleaning to wood preserving, including in between, bathrooms, burglarproofing, disinfectants, fire protection, floors, furniture, gutters, heating, septic systems, odor control, pests and wood, 62 subjects in all. He also provides a glossary of more than 500 briefly defined words and phrases not described, or not fully described, elsewhere. A detailed Index (bats, bedbugs, fleas, mildew, etc.) adds to ease of use. There is no preface.

The style of writing is clear and uncomplicated, familiar in tone, with the user addressed as "you." The text for each of the 61 topics is a series of specific questions as the title indicates. The answers range in length from one word (a simple "No" to the question of whether a vapor barrier is required with foil insulation) to about 125 words. The author does not hesitate to indicate when a job should be left to someone more proficient than the average home owner. Readers are advised to take their very dirty and cracked paintings to a professional for cleaning if they are valuable and their andirons with broken legs to a welder. Some answers attempt to dispel misinformation, such as the common assumption that if the humidity in a house is raised, less heat is needed to be comfortable. A number of questions on spots and stains include those made by dogs and children, with homeowners urged to act quickly. Very few drawings and diagrams accompany the text. The repair of electrical appliances, such as typewriters, television sets, tape recorders, and refrigerators is omitted, presumably because these usually require the attention of qualified technicians.

Because of its broad scope, handy arrangement, and good Index, this manual compares favorably with such earlier ones as Bernard Gladstone's *New York Times Complete Manual of Home Repair* (New York: Macmillan, 1966). Clearly printed and stoutly bound, it is well suited for home use and for answering telephone reference questions in a public library.

(Feb. 15, 1977, p.925)

643'.7   Dwellings—Maintenance and repair—Miscellanea || Dwellings—Remodeling—Miscellanea   [CIP]   76-8184

A folk music sourcebook.
By Larry Sandberg and Dick Weissman. New York, Alfred A. Knopf, 1976. x, 260, xivp. illus. hard cover $15; paper $7.95.

Described by its publisher as the "first comprehensive guide to every kind of North American folk music from blues to ragtime, string band to bluegrass, Canadian to Chicano, traditional to contemporary, and to every *aspect* of folk music: the records, the artists, the composers, the styles, the songbooks, the instructional books, the scholarly books, the instruments, the techniques, the centers of activity throughout the country," *A Folk Music Sourcebook* is *not* a sourcebook in the strict sense of the word. It is not a collection of documents serving as primary evidence for the study of folk music. According to CIP data, the work has been identified as a directory, bibliography, and discography. These descriptors provide a partial definition of the *Sourcebook*'s range and depth. It is in four parts: "Listening" (not just discography but characteristics of various traditions); "Learning" (bibliography, including songbooks, reference tools, instructional materials, etc.); "Playing" (advice on performance); and "Hanging Out" (organizations, festivals, etc.). Format varies considerably: there are numerous essays, some by guest contributors, as well as "lists." The end matter includes an extremely useful glossary and an Index. Many items appear in unexpected places, e.g., instructional records in Part III, not Part I. In other words, the content is not organized in an arrangement or sequence immediately discernible to the user. Consultation of the Index is therefore essential to those for whom the work is not a constant companion. Its style, by the way, is more informal than is traditional in reference books, but users must not equate this quality with superficiality or simplism. Quite the contrary; *Folk Music Sourcebook* is not only, as its publishers claim, "comprehensive," but, considering its wide scope, thorough and discriminating. Everywhere is evidence of scholarship and of scrupulous attention to subtleties. All in all, this publication is a treasure house of information and ideas, worthy of becoming the devotee's or specialist's *vade mecum* and likely to be useful in both the reference and the circulating collections of public and academic libraries.

(Feb. 1, 1977, p.856)

016.7817'0973   Folk music—North America—Directories || Folk music—North America—Bibliography || Folk music—North America—Discography   [CIP]   75-34472

Foreign affairs bibliography:
a selected and annotated list of books on international relations, 1962–1972. [By] Janis A. Kreslins. New York & London, R. R. Bowker Co., 1976. xxi, 921p. 26cm. cloth $42.50 plus shipping and handling.

Foreign Affairs Bibliography is a major publication of the Council on Foreign Relations, which was founded in 1921 to promote "a wider and better understanding of international affairs through the free interchange of ideas." The newest bibliography is the fifth to be published under the auspices of the Council. Other volumes in the series covered 1919–1932 (William L. Langer and the late Hamilton Fish Armstrong), 1932–1942 (the late Robert Gale Woolbert), and 1942–1952 and 1952–1962 (the late Henry L. Roberts). The five volumes should be used in conjunction with one another and with *The Foreign Affairs 50-Year Bibliography*.

The 1962–1972 bibliography is a selective annotated list of 11,000 books published from 1962 through 1972. The only exceptions to this cutoff date are translations of works published in 1973 or later, that appeared earlier in another language. Emphasis in coverage is on the period since the outset of World War I. International developments and foreign affairs are given special attention, with the more important books being in the fields of economics, politics, and social development.

As with its predecessors, the current bibliography is organized into three basic parts: "General International Relations," "The World since 1914," and "The World by Regions." Arrangement of entries is alphabetical by author and title under 450 subjects like *secret police, political trials, espionage; military confrontations; integration; peace, disarmament, arms control*. Each annotation describes and analyzes the contents of the book and comments on the authority of the author. Access to works by individual authors is provided by an Author Index. The Index to Title Entries includes only titles not listed under an author's name in the body of the book. College and research libraries and special political science and foreign relations libraries will find that the *Foreign Affairs Bibliography* series is an indispensable guide to significant books on foreign affairs.

(Sept. 1, 1976, p.55)

016.327   International relations—Bibliography   [CIP]   75-29085

The foundation grants index, 1974:
a cumulative listing of foundation grants. Compiled by The

Foundation Center, Lee Noe, grants editor. New York, The Foundation Center, distributed by Columbia University Pr., 1975. xiii, 315p. 29cm. cloth $15.

The Foundation Center was incorporated by the University of the State of New York Board of Regents in 1956 as an independent educational institution whose charge was to gather and disseminate factual information on philanthropic foundations. The center maintains national collections in New York, Washington, and Chicago, and there are 48 regional collections in various locations throughout the U.S. The center publishes *Foundation News* bimonthly. This information is cumulated annually into *The Foundation Grants Index,* the 1974 edition of which is the fifth to be published.

The current volume lists 9,576 grants totalling $701,405,871. Some 260 large national foundations which report directly to the center are the donors. Grants of less than $5,000 are not listed. The *Grants Index* is designed to be used in conjunction with *The Foundation Directory,* which the Committee recommended in the November 15, 1975, issue of *Reference and Subscription Books Reviews* as the standard reference source for basic information on the activities of philanthropic foundations.

The *Grants Index* is arranged in four sections: "Grants" (by state), "Domestic and Foreign Recipients," "Key Words and Phrases," and "Foundation Names." There is no publication comparable to *Foundation Grants Index.* It is an invaluable and dependable source of information on grants that were available in 1974. *(Sept. 15, 1976, p.204)*

001.4'4 Endowments—Directories [OCLC]   72-6018

From radical left to extreme right:

a bibliography of current periodicals of protest, controversy, advocacy, or dissent, with dispassionate content-summaries to guide librarians and other educators. By Theodore Jurgen Spahn and Janet Peterson Spahn. 2d ed., rev & enl. v.3. Metuchen, N.J., Scarecrow, 1976, [c1975]. xiv, 762p. 22cm. cloth $22.50.

From Radical Left to Extreme Right is a unique reference tool "designed to aid in the selection of periodicals in fringe areas not adequately covered in bibliographic guides now available to librarians."

The first edition of this bibliography appeared in 1967 and was followed by a two-volume second edition (1972) covering 272 titles. Six hundred fifty periodicals are described in this third volume of the set. The periodicals are divided into 23 broad subject categories such as feminist, racial and ethnic pride, prisons, conservation and ecology, anticommunist and radical left. Each group is preceded by a brief essay which surveys the section and discusses some of the periodicals that follow. What follows for most (475) of the periodicals is a signed review, averaging one page in length, based on examination of one or more issues of the journal. Each is preceded by the following directory information: the editor's name, business address, frequency of publication, price, beginning date, circulation, format, indexing, availability of back issues, and microfilm.

These reviews often characterize the periodicals and their viewpoints by quoting from the periodical itself or from literature of the sponsoring organization. With surprising frequency, the reviews are written with verve, giving the volume an agreeable flavor. Authors and titles of articles in issues examined are mentioned, and regular features are noted. Most informative is the "Feedback" section printed at the end of the review. Here the publisher who has received a copy of the review may insert a description of overlooked features, take issue with the annotation, or note the demise of the journal. In cases where the reviewer wishes to express a personal opinion, this extra statement is labeled "Reviewer's Judgment."

The unsigned reviews were written by the authors of this volume and include the same directory information provided in signed reviews but are briefer since they usually had no issues to examine. These annotations are most often merely descriptions and statements of purpose provided by publishers or sponsoring organizations.

The authors who, with Robert H. Muller, edited volumes one and two are well qualified to continue the project. Theodore Spahn is an associate professor in the Graduate School of Library Science, Rosary College. He was formerly a bibliographer at the University of Illinois (Chicago Circle) and a lecturer in library science at the University of Michigan. Janet Spahn, a botanical illustrator, formerly served as a reference librarian at Skokie (Illinois) Public Library. Janet Spahn wrote most of the succinct yet comprehensive introductory essays and, with Theodore Spahn, is responsible for the 176 unsigned reviews. The contributors of signed reviews are identified only by name and academic degree. Of the 35 contributors, 29 have library degrees and 6 are unidentified.

There are three indexes: a Geographical Index; a Title Index; and an Index of Editors, Publishers and Opinions.

The Geographical Index supplies the place of publication and is arranged by state and city followed by 26 foreign countries and their cities. Most of the periodicals are in English, and the titles are listed following the name of the city of publication. Unfortunately, the page number where the review appears is not also given here.

The Title Index is cumulative and includes the titles of all periodicals reviewed or mentioned in any of the three volumes of the second edition. (It also includes the titles and addresses of hundreds of periodicals to which the authors have written without receiving a response.) Page references are provided to the review itself and to any other pages where the periodical is mentioned. Numerous cross-references and address and title changes for periodicals cited in the first two volumes are valuable aids.

"Opinions" in the Editors, Publishers, Opinions Index refers to the viewpoints expressed in the sample issues examined by the reviewers. Unexpectedly, this Index also contains in the entries citations to bibliographies of periodicals on such subjects as radical professionals, comics, and dogfighting.

Volume 3 is bound to match volumes 1 and 2, providing a satisfactory format. The typography is legible but lacks polish and is unstimulating.

From Radical Left to Extreme Right is a useful reference work with or without the companion volumes. It presents detailed content-summaries, unavailable elsewhere, of 650 periodicals which provide both primary source material and nonestablishment opinion. Public and academic libraries alike will find *From Radical Left to Extreme Right* an appealing and practical acquisition. *(July 1, 1977, p.1676)*

016.3224'4'0973 U.S.—Politics and government—Periodicals—Bibliography. || Right and left (Political science)—Periodicals—Bibliography. || Radicalism—U.S.—Periodicals—Bibliography [CIP]   79-126558

Getting skilled:

a guide to private trade and technical schools. [By] Tom Hebert and John Coyne. New York, Dutton, [c1976]. xvi, 262p. 22cm. cloth, $12.95; paper $4.95.

Using such sources as the National Association of Trade and Technical Schools, National Home Study Council, American Council on Education, American Personnel and Guidance Association, ERIC Clearing House on Higher Education, College Entrance Examination Board, Brookings Institution, B'nai B'rith Career and Counseling Service, AFL-CIO education department, and Federal Aviation Administration, Washington, D.C., educational consultants Tom Hebert and John Coyne have prepared a handbook of consumer advice on private trade and technical schools that high school students will want to consult. Shying away from the heavy style and traditional arrangement of educational directories, the authors have organized the material into three major sections—(1) six chapters covering case studies, profiles of four types of private trade schools, curriculum, teaching staff, and tuition; (2) six unique appendixes containing a NATTS Directory of Accredited Private Trade and Technical Schools, A Sampler of Nonaccredited Specialty Schools, Nationally Recognized Accrediting Associations for Specialized Occupational Programs, Consumer Advice Offices, Summary of Research Studies, and A Summary of Distinctions between Community College Training Programs and Proprietary Schools; and (3) a Bibliography of 13 types of material including speeches, dissertations and theses, magazine and newspaper articles, market surveys, government documents, and general works.

Location of information is aided by a Table of Contents, an Index, and arrangement of the chapters under well-captioned sections. High school and public libraries will want to acquire *Getting Skilled* as a guide to vocational schools, careers, and colleges for those interested in trade and technical school education. *(Nov. 15, 1976, p.500)*

374.8'73 Vocational education—U.S. || Vocational education—U.S.—Directories || Technical education—U.S. || Technical education—U.S.—Directories [CIP] 75-33053

Glass:
the connoisseur illustrated guides. [By] Ruth Hurst Vose; drawings by C. R. Evans. London, The Connoisseur, [1975]. 222p. illus. (part col.) 22cm. paper over boards $14.95.

Glass, from the "Connoisseur Illustrated Guides" series, "attempts to cover the history of every technique of vessel glass-making in all the main glass-making countries throughout the ages." The author has been a university lecturer and assistant curator at the Pilkington Glass Museum in Lancashire, England, and is presently doing postgraduate research on the archaeology of glassmaking in England.

A brief Introduction describes the chemical composition of glass and summarizes the formation and decoration of glass vessels. Eight chapters discuss glass vessel making from the fifteenth century B.C. to the present. Information is arranged by technique rather than by region or historical period. Techniques described include: core formation, mosaic glass, casting, molding, blowing, and the formation of colored and colorless glass. Decorative techniques include trailing glass threads, layering, filligree, millefiori, enamelling, painting, gilding, cutting, engraving, and acid-etching. Appended to the guide are an Index and Select Bibliography arranged by subject.

The format consists of 2 black-and-white line drawings atop each page, 390 in all, with descriptive paragraphs beneath. This permits knowledgeable collectors to leaf through the book and quickly pick out vessels within their particular fields of interest. Although the drawings are clear and quite detailed, black-and-white photographs would have been more helpful in assisting identification of specific pieces. Eight pages of color photographs, four per page, have been included. Inner margins are quite narrow, especially on pages with photographs. References are given from the text to related color photographs, but not from photograph to text.

Collectors and libraries not owning similar books on the history of glass vessel making may wish to add *Glass: The Connoisseur Illustrated Guides* to their collections.
(Jan. 1, 1977, p.685)

748.2 Glassware—Collectors and collecting [OCLC] 75-512411

A glossary of Faulkner's South.
By Calvin S. Brown. New Haven and London, Yale Univ. Pr., 1976. vii, 241p. 22cm. cloth $12.50.

Readers of Faulkner's works who are unfamiliar with his use of Southern dialect or with the fictional and actual place-names, the local names for flora and fauna, and historical characters will find this alphabetically arranged glossary most enlightening. For each of the more than 4,000 entries is given a page citation to one or more of Faulkner's Southern novels, together with an explanation or an equivalent, e.g., *hull* (Sart.223): *whole.* Only *Pylon* has been omitted because "*Pylon* is in the South but not of it." Also omitted are easily recognizable substandard forms, e.g., *knowned* for *knew,* as well as fictional characters because several listings have already been made and "this glossary is concerned with the factual background of the fiction rather than the fiction as such."

The compiler, a professor of comparative literature at the University of Georgia, grew up in Oxford, Mississippi, and knew William Faulkner and his family intimately. This, plus the acknowledged assistance of Faulkner scholars, lends authority to the work.

An informative introduction and an appendix on Faulkner's geography add to the reference value of the glossary. There is little duplication of the earlier *A Faulkner Glossary* by Harry Runyan, published by Citadel Press in 1964, an alphabetical arrangement of all titles, fictional characters, and places in the published writings, with six appendixes, three of them essentially bibliographies, the others giving a biographical sketch, histories of the principal families of Yoknapatapha County, its geography and documents. Both glossaries are essential to a careful reading of the works of one of the greatest Southern novelists.
(Apr. 1, 1977, p.1196)

†813.5 Faulkner, William Cuthbert—Dictionaries 75-43308

Government publications:
a guide to bibliographic tools. By Vladimir M. Palic. 4th ed. Washington, D.C., Library of Congress, 1975. ix, 441p. 24cm. cloth $6.70.

Palic's *Government Publications* is a greatly expanded revision of the third edition of James B. Child's *Government Document Bibliography in the United States and Elsewhere.* The current bibliography reflects the increase in worldwide government publications by being about eight times larger than its immediate predecessor. The bibliography is conveniently arranged in three sections which treat the United States of America (federal government and states, territories, and local government), International Governmental Organizations (United Nations, League of Nations and other organizations), and Foreign Countries (Western hemisphere, Europe, Africa, Near East, Asia and the Pacific).

Each section has an Introduction which describes and evaluates bibliographic activity in the area. Entries are annotated briefly to indicate the scope and period. Library of Congress call numbers and catalog entries are provided when they are available. A general cutoff date of December 31, 1971 was observed, but a number of later works are included.

Palic's chapter on federal government publications is disappointing because it omits critically important items such as the *Federal Register, Public Papers of the Presidents, American Statistics Index, Statistical Abstract of the U.S., Code of Federal Regulations,* and *U.S. Code.* Also the Supreme Court and the imposing bibliographical apparatus which records decisional law are only peripherally treated.

In contrast, Palic provides exemplary listings of state and territorial publications, historical imprints, and documents relating to foreign governments. The new edition of *Government Publications* will be welcomed by researchers and librarians primarily because of its broad representation of state, territorial, and local government documents, and superior coverage of foreign nations. *(Dec. 1, 1976, p.563)*

016.01573 U.S.—Government publications—Bibliography || Government publications—Bibliography [CIP] 74-34440

The great world encyclopedia.
[Frances M. Clapham, editor]. New York, Two Continents,

[1976]. 278p. illus. charts. diagrs. maps. 31cm. cloth $12.95; to schools, 20 percent discount when 25 or more copies are ordered.

The Great World Encyclopedia is a one-volume edition which originated in London, was printed and bound in Milan, Italy, and is now published in the U.S.

Instead of the usual alphabetical arrangement, this encyclopedia is divided into seven main sections: *"The Universe," "The Arts," "The Living World," "History," "Science and Technology," "Transport and Communications," "The World Around Us."* These broad subjects are further subdivided (e.g., "The Arts" includes *Painting and Drawing, The Minor Arts, Sculpture, Architecture, Literature, Theatre, Music, Dance, Cinema*). Included in these 33 pages devoted to "The Arts" is a definition of the art form, brief history of its development, a page of biographical notes, and illustrations—both colored and black and white. Sometimes a diagram or a chart is included, and in contrast to the white pages, frequent tinted boxes contain a glossary or explanation of terms without pronunciation. About 50 percent of each page is devoted to illustrations ranging from postage-stamp size to some covering more than half the page. Every other page is in full color. The illustrations are photographs, drawings, reproductions—some especially commissioned for this work. For the most part, the illustrations are pleasing and artfully coordinated with the proper text. Adjacent to each illustration is its description. Acknowledgments on the last page indicate the institutional sources of the illustrations (e.g., museums, universities, news agencies, travel bureaus, galleries, governmental offices), but not individual artists' or photographers' contributions. Each of the seven main sections has the same general arrangement as just described. With so many phases of the subject being covered in so few pages and only half of that devoted to text, it is obvious that the coverage of any topic would be brief and that there would be omissions. In the four pages devoted to *Literature,* although there are headings for *Classical Literature, English Literature, European Literature, French, German, Spanish, Portuguese, Italian,* and *Russian Literature,* there is no heading for *American Literature* and no discussion other than the brief mention that Poe, Melville, Twain, and Hawthorne were novelists in America. Eugene O'Neill was the only American author since 1900 listed in the text.

Another area given extremely brief treatment is "The World Around Us." In a four-page discussion of the Americas, there is no subheading, "United States," nor is there any mention that there are 50 states. The usual encyclopedic type of information concerning state flag, seal, products, natural resources, and other pertinent facts is entirely lacking.

The entire explanation of North American politics is: "The politics of North America are dominated by the two powerful democracies of the United States and Canada. Both of these countries have close ties with Europe." There is no explanation anywhere of the term "democracy." There is no mention at all of Mexican politics, and the Canadian provinces are also omitted.

Nowhere in any of the seven divisions is space provided for athletics, sports, hobbies, or recreation. Social issues, such as overpopulation, hunger, abortion, racism, alcoholism, drugs, conservation are all ignored. However, there is a two-page discussion of pollution in the section, *Science and Technology.* Contemporary developments in computers, ultrasonics, and microminiaturization are briefly mentioned in this section. Except for moon exploration, there is very little else of current concern included in the encyclopedia. The entire subject of religion is covered in nine sentences in the section, "The World Around Us."

British spellings and orientation predominate in the spare text. Sentences are grammatically correct and simple enough for the young reader, but subjects do not correlate with the American school curriculum or with the special interests of this country's youth.

Since the encyclopedia is not arranged alphabetically, the reader must depend on the Index to find specific subjects. While there are about 1,600 entries in the five-page, four-column Index, most of the terms are the broad, general words used in headings or subheadings (e.g., "constellations" is in the Index, whereas Hyades and Pleiades, specific constellations mentioned in the text, are omitted in the Index). Frequent errors are noted in paging. *Sirius,* p.90, should be p.8; items discussed on more than one page are frequently listed for only one: *quasar,* p.21 and 91. Page 91 is an error, but a definition is on p.9. Although the explanation at the beginning of the Index states that italic numerals indicate an illustration, very few of the reported 750 illustrations are actually indexed. No help is given to pinpoint on what part of the large, double-column page the reference may be found. Terms in the glossaries scattered throughout the book are not found in the Index, and there is no consistency about what information in boxes is included. *Buses and Lorries,* p.194, is omitted, but *Underground Railways,* also in a box on p.200, is indexed; *Textile Industry,* p.168, is represented, but *Knitting Machines,* in a similar box on the same page, is not. The entire Index is superficially constructed, so use of the encyclopedia as a reference tool is extremely frustrating.

Maps of the six continents and the polar regions are included in the back of the encyclopedia. These are apparently topographical maps, but there is no legend or explanation of any kind to indicate what the different colored areas represent. There are no mileage indications, latitude or longitudinal markings, nor any identification of the source of the maps. The countries are marked off with black boundaries, but states and provinces are not shown. The capitals and a few cities are located, and one or two rivers in each continent are named.

A 13-page gazetteer follows, but because of the dearth of place-names on the maps, it has minimal value as a locational aid. Descriptive notes after each term—rivers, volcanoes, islands, cities, lakes, countries, canals, peninsulas, seas—provide more specific information than that found in the text. If proper maps had been provided, the gazetteer would have been the most useful part of the encyclopedia. According to a note at the head of this section, "Population figures are based on the latest estimates available and for simplicity have been rounded usually to the nearest 1000." While there is no source given for those "latest estimates," the figures do correspond with those used in other statistical works.

The editor named on the title page is Frances M. Clapham. Three names are listed under *Editorial,* and four additional names are printed as contributors and advisers. No credits are given for any of the persons, and data concerning their competence was not verified in any of the standard biographical directories, British or American. No articles are signed, and there are no acknowledgments for literary or artistic contribution.

There is no preface, foreword, or explanation of the encyclopedia's purpose. While not totally inaccurate, the descriptions are so very general, brief, and fragmentary that a good elementary dictionary presents more adequate information. Little attempt has been made to include current topics or to update content. The ineffective arrangement and inaccuracies of the Index make the book's information almost inaccessible.

The format is appealing, paper and print is of good quality, the illustrations are reproduced beautifully, and the price is not unreasonable for this large a volume with so much art work. It might, therefore, serve as a picture book for home browsing. But *The Great World Encyclopedia* does not meet the needs of encyclopedia users because it fails to deliver satisfaction as a reference tool. *(June 15, 1977, p.1602)*

Grosset & Dunlap's all-sports world record book.
[By] David S. Neft, Roland T. Johnson, Richard M. Cohen, and Jordan A. Deutsch. New York, Grosset, [c1976]. 320p. 29cm. cloth $17.95.

The authors of *The All-Sports World Record Book* acknowledge the aid of many organizations and institutions such as the Amateur Athletic Union, The Professional Women Bowlers Association, and the Rodeo Cowboys Association for providing information used in their statistical compilation, although the degree of reliance is not specified. The information for baseball, professional football, and professional basketball has been extracted from the authors' three earlier reference books dealing with these three sports individually. The Preface does not state emphases, limitations, or scope, other than to claim in-depth listings of records, champions, standings, and career leaders for 32 major sports. While there are 32 major groupings, neither the section on Awards nor that for the Olympic Games qualify as sports categories. The number of eligible categories greatly exceeds 32 if one counts various track, field, swimming, diving, and gymnastics events as separate sports or Olympic events such as water polo, canoeing, and many other forms of competition that have been excluded from this volume.

There is representation of international events such as the World Grand Prix of auto races and World Cup Soccer matches in addition to U.S. coverage. Tennis includes Wimbledon and Davis Cup results, while baseball and basketball are treated as exclusively American sports. For some sports, professional competition is statistically highlighted. Baseball, basketball, football, golf, and hockey exemplify this type of treatment. For other sports such as lacrosse, boating, and water skiing, the data are relatively sparse. A comparison of the treatments of boating and basketball should clarify this distinction.

Basketball coverage begins with final season standings for the professional teams beginning with the old National Basketball League of the late 1930s through the NBA (National Basketball Association) and ABA (American Basketball Association) 1974/1975 season. Yearly leaders in such categories as field-goal percentage, free-throw percentage, total points, assists, personal fouls, rebounds, and playing time are given for both the season and the playoffs. Best team performance is listed by year for regular season and playoff games. The top 25 lifetime leaders in field goals, free throws, points, rebounds, games played, shooting percentage, assists, and fouls are listed with boldface type identifying players who are still active. The top 25 single-season individual leaders and top ten team leaders are given for the same categories.

Two pages are devoted to identifying the number of players produced by various colleges and conferences, followed by a table which reflects the change from a sport in which 35.9 points was an average team score to the present 108.8 points per team.

The 25 pages devoted to pro basketball are followed by 6 pages on college basketball. Major tournament champions, runners-up and most valuable tournament player, championship teams of major conferences such as the Missouri Valley Conference, Helms Foundation All American team members since 1925, and all-time scoring records through the 1975–1976 season are provided. AAU Women Champions since 1925 and Men's Championship Teams since 1896 complete the basketball coverage.

In contrast with this rather extensive reportage, the boating section lists Gold Cup winners since 1904 with no indication that this is motorboat racing; yachting's America's Cup results and winners of the Mallory Cup and Adams Cup and first-, second-, and third-place finishers in the Intercollegiate Rowing Association Championship varsity eights for recent years only. The U.S. champions for these various events are given from the late 1800s through 1975. Winning times or speeds are not provided for any category.

Sports are apparently given space in accordance with their importance in the mind of the average American spectator. *Auto Racing, Bowling, Boxing,* and *Horse Racing* focus solely on the professional scene. No rosters are given for U.S. Amateur Boxing Champions since 1888 or the National Collegiate Boxing champions from 1936 through 1960. The more cosmopolitan and comprehensive Menke's *Encyclopedia of Sports* provides these rosters as well as a table of the fight-career records of modern world champions. Menke's compendium also includes steeplechasing and many horse-racing records not found in *All-Sports World Record Book.* On the other hand, the auto-racing listings are much more comprehensive in the latter work.

Badminton, Boating, Fencing, Figure Skating, Gymnastics, Handball, Polo, Speed Skating, Squash Racquets, Table Tennis, Volleyball, Water Skiing, Weightlifting, and *Wrestling* are covered in from one to five pages of information and list U.S. national champions and college champions with world championship rosters for fencing, figure skating, speed skating, and table tennis. *The All-Sports World Record Book* is consistently limited to the American scene. Even in those tables which indicate the winning time, the length of the throw, the amount of weight lifted, or number of points scored, there is no indication of world record performance.

Angling, archery, bicycle racing, bobsledding, cricket, curling, dog racing, field hockey, horseshoe pitching, rifle and pistol shooting, jai alai, roller skating, rugby, softball, and water polo are all represented in Menke's *Encyclopedia of Sports* but excluded from this work. There is also no index to the *All-Sports World Record Book* so that some sports subsumed under the Olympics events are not conveniently accessible. Furthermore, the authors provide no discussions of sports or explanations of events. Although an estimated 100,000 items of information are provided in this single volume, many sports are omitted or receive scant treatment. Libraries and individuals will find very little in *All-Sports World Record Book* that is not currently available in more satisfying form in other comparably priced sources. *(July 1, 1977, p. 1676)*

796.02 Sports—Records [OCLC] 74-18879

Group work in the helping professions:
a bibliography. [By] David G. Zimpfer. Washington, D.C., Association for Specialists in Group Work of the American Personnel and Guidance Association, [1976]. vii, 452p. 22cm. paper, $7.

Group Work in the Helping Professions is the first in a series of materials that the Association for Specialists in Group Work will publish for its members. Dr. David G. Zimpfer, the compiler, has been a member of the education department of the University of Rochester since 1965. He has been involved in personnel guidance and group work for a number of years and has written several publications on the subject. Zimpfer intends his bibliography as "a comprehensive list of books, dissertations, unpublished documents and journal articles on the literature" and "research on group procedures in guidance and counseling in education settings." The cutoff date for entries was June 1975.

The bibliography is organized around two primary listings, a topical listing and an author list. The 12 major topics covered are Groups (Foundations, Philosophy, Purposes, Definitions); Theoretical Formulations in Interpersonal Relationships; Dynamics and Relationships of Group Process, Development of Groups; Types of Group Experience; Applications in Education; Group Outcomes, Productivity, Evaluation; Comparisons of Treatment; New Directions; Professional Issues in Groups; Education of Group Workers; and Transcripts of Group Meetings. Each subject divides its coverage into books and periodicals. The Author Listing refers to pages which cite specific authors.

An Appendix lists 75 periodicals searched systematically by Zimpfer through June 1975. *Group Work in the Helping Profes-*

sions is the most comprehensive bibliography on group work published to date. As such it will be very useful in libraries serving administrators, personnel officers, teachers, parents, and social workers. *(Oct. 15, 1976, p.345)*

016.30118   Social groups—Bibliography || Social group work—Bibliography   [OCLC]
76-363090

Guide to basic information sources in English literature.
By Paul A. Doyle. A Halsted Press Book by Jeffrey Norton Publishers, Inc., New York, John Wiley & Sons, [c1976]. (Information Resources Series). xi, 143p. 20cm. cloth $10.95.

Paul A. Doyle is a professor of English, Nassau Community College, State University of New York, where he has been on the faculty since 1962. He has written a number of books dealing with literary figures.

Both English and American literary materials are included in this selective guide, which attempts to list only the fundamental references and those dealing with the most important writers and trends. Its purpose, according to the Foreword, is "to give the beginner in the library a sense of direction."

Twenty-four categories of material are presented, ranging from standard sources and general survey materials to sections on types of literature, journals, and nonprint information sources. In some chapters the materials are arranged alphabetically, in others chronologically, and in others in the order of their importance. A rough count of the main entries yields a total of somewhere between 400 and 450 titles.

Entries include author, title, number of volumes, place of publication, publisher, and date. Helpful descriptive and critical annotations, some quite lengthy, accompany all of them. Some entries, such as that for Kunitz's *Twentieth Century Authors*, contain references within the annotation to related works: *American Authors 1600–1900*, *British Authors before 1800*, and *British Authors of the Nineteenth Century*. There are occasional cross-references to other entries, but to find all citations to any particular title, the Index must be consulted.

The Index gives chiefly names and titles, although there are some subject entries. Unfortunately, it contains so many errors that the user will often be frustrated. On page 143, for example, which runs from *Twentieth Century Interpretations* through *Zesmer, David M.*, there are 16 incorrect citations, all of them off by only one page. Also, while *Who's Who* and *Who Was Who* are in the Index, *Who's Who in America* and *Who Was Who in America* are not, even though they are described in the text. Hopefully, future editions of the work will contain a corrected Index. *(Mar. 15, 1977, p.1121)*

016.01682   Bibliography—Bibliography—English literature || English literature—History and criticism || Reference books—English literature—Bibliography || Bibliography—Bibliography—American literature || American literature—History and criticism   [OCLC]
75-43260

Guide to Cretan antiquities.
By Costis Davaris. Park Ridge, N.J., Noyes Press, c1976. xiv, 370p. illus. 24cm. cloth $18.

An estimated 400 entries, alphabetically arranged, give brief information on "important cultural, natural, social and technological elements, artistic tendencies, individual works of art, and historical happenings in Crete during several millenia, from the arrival of the first settlers in the island to its liberation in the beginning of this century." The author, presently Director of the Archaeological Museum in Hagios Nikalaos and Ephor for Eastern Crete, has emphasized the great Minoan civilization, with its art, religion, and monuments, while not neglecting Dorian Crete. He has conducted archaeological excavations in Greece for many years.

Small black-and-white art reproductions, drawings, and photographs, some hitherto unpublished, accompany 198 of the articles. Seven maps of important sites and a concordance of illustrations, giving museum inventory numbers and provenance, are appended. An Index to sites gives names in bold letters when a visit is recommended.

Authorities are noted only occasionally in the text of the articles and then only by name. A brief appended Bibliography lists 30 recent English-language titles, chiefly monographs on Minoan art and palaces, and four of R. F. Willetts' important books on Crete. None has the broad coverage of the *Guide to Cretan Antiquities*.

The articles, clearly and succinctly written, range in size from a brief identification of a mythological figure in less than 100 words to about 700 words on the topic of music. Among general subjects, literature receives the least attention. Asterisks which refer the reader to related subjects are augmented by additional *see*-references, e.g., *Occupations of population* see *Industries; Social Structure.* A brief chronology is appended.

The authority of the compiler, broad coverage, convenient arrangement, and well-chosen illustrations commend this handbook to libraries with an interest in the Minoan civilization. *(Dec. 1, 1976, p.564)*

949.98'003   Crete—Antiquities || Crete—History

A guide to critical reviews:
part II: the musical, 1909–1974. By James M. Salem. 2d ed. Metuchen, N.J., Scarecrow, 1976. 611p. 22cm. cloth $20.

This handy guide, part II of a four-part set of titles, revises and expands a 1967 publication which covered the seasons 1920–21 through 1964–65. Part I, *American Drama from O'Neill to Albee*, has already appeared in a second edition, and parts III and IV cover *British and Continental Drama from Ibsen to Pinter* and *The Screenplay from the Jazz Singer to Dr. Strangelove.* In Part II, "The productions listed are, for the most part, Broadway productions, though off-Broadway and off-off Broadway presentations have been included when accurate statistical data could be obtained." There is no master list of sources indexed; but reviews cited are said to have "appeared in general circulation American and Canadian periodicals and in the *New York Times.*" In addition, entries in the collection *New York Theatre Critics' Reviews* (1940–   ) are cited. Arrangement is by title, with cross-references, e.g., "*At Home at the Palace* see *Judy Garland at Home at the Palace.*" For individual items, reviews are cited—as are persons responsible for texts, music, staging, etc., dates of openings, and lengths of runs—but not, regrettably, principal performers. The body of the work is followed by a list of long-run musicals (200+ performances), lists of musicals receiving awards, and indexes to (a) authors, composers, and lyricists; (b) directors, designers, and choreographers; and (c) authors and titles of sources (e.g., the authors and title of the play upon which *O Marry Me* was based).

Libraries will wish to acquire this convenient, up-dated source of citations to easily accessible reviews of musical stage productions. *(May 1, 1977, p.1374)*

016.809'2   Theater—Reviews—Index || Moving-pictures—Reviews—Indexes.   [CIP]
73-3120

Guide to drug information.
By Winifred Sewell. Hamilton, Ill., Drug Intelligence Publications, Inc., [1976]. viii, 218p. 23cm. paper over boards, $12.

Winifred Sewell is an experienced pharmaceutical librarian, bibliographer, and teacher who prepared the *Guide to Drug Information* "to guide the pharmacist or other health professional in his use of the literature throughout a professional career...." The book covers the literature of pharmacy in four conveniently arranged parts. The five chapters in Part I deal with handbooks including annuals and looseleaf and card services. The second part also has five chapters. These deal with primary sources like books, periodicals, patents, government documents, theses, directories, dictionaries, and equipment catalogs.

Part III, the most extensive section, surveys sources outside one's own library. Here one finds exceptionally clear descriptions of the various abstracting services, *Science Citation Index*, reviews, encyclopedic treatises, and other secondary sources. The book concludes with five brief chapters that summarize current and future technology. The fairly comprehensive author, title, subject Index aids the user in locating specific items. The *Guide to Drug Information* gives up-to-date, comprehensive coverage of general and specific sources. It will be especially useful to inexperienced pharmacists searching for information. *(Nov. 1, 1976, p.425)*

†029.96151   Pharmacology—Documentation || Drugs—Bibliography   75-17156

Guide to reference books for school media centers:
1974–75 supplement. [By] Christine L. Wynar. Littleton, Colo., Libraries Unlimited, Inc., 1976. xii, 131p. 24cm. paper composition $8.

This *1974–75 Supplement* updates (through December 1975) the *Guide to Reference Books for School Media Centers* (cloth edition 1973, $17.50; softcover 1975, $10) and continues the objectives, editorial policies, and format of the parent volume. Compiler Christine Wynar, former teacher and school librarian, is on the staff of Libraries Unlimited, Inc., and is also a contributing editor of ALA's *School Media Quarterly*.

In compiling both the *Guide* and the *Supplement* "numerous basic lists and guides were consulted, reviews from major journals were checked and hundreds of books received from publishers were examined." Few titles published prior to 1968 are listed, and these only when they are still recognized as basic or outstanding. Designed specifically as a "basic reference tool . . . for the needs of school librarians, teachers and students, grade K–12," these two titles provide a total of 3,094 numbered and annotated entries.

In both books entries are arranged by author under numerous broad subject headings (59 in the *Guide,* 49 in the *Supplement,* omitting only those where no new titles were identified for inclusion). The first three sections in each are "Media Sources," "Media Selection," and "General Reference." These are followed by the balance of subjects, with subdivisions, arranged in alphabetical order from agriculture to zoology. These headings are readily matched with the major curricular areas in grades K through 12 and also include pets, sports, fashion arts, recreation, and the like. Evidence of the attention given to more recent course offerings is found in the inclusion of such headings as communication media, environmental studies, ethnic minorities, films and filmmaking, and occult sciences.

The first section, "Media Sources," lists bibliographies covering a wide range of media including films, recordings, a variety of microforms, government documents, pamphlets, and free materials. "Media Selection," the second section, includes numerous reviewing tools, bibliographies of print and nonprint materials, and indexes. Included, too, are general selection aids, both basic and selective, conveniently arranged by level—elementary, secondary, junior college, and vocational. The third section, "General Reference," includes bibliographic guides, encyclopedias, almanacs, directories, and biographical reference tools.

The excellent Table of Contents provides easy access to the many subject headings and their subdivisions which are frequently further divided by form, i.e., general works, bibliographies, dictionaries and encyclopedias, handbooks and yearbooks, and directories. An accurate and detailed Index, including authors, titles, and subjects in a single alphabet, refers the user to the numbered entries in the main body of the books.

Each of the numbered entries provides full bibliographic information (author, title, publisher, date, pages, price, and LC card number). Paperback editions are also noted. The annotations, many quite lengthy, describe the scope, coverage, and arrangement of the book and frequently include comments on its strengths and weaknesses. For the more important titles, comparisons with similar books are often made. In addition, numerous related titles are cited as additional references. These titles, followed by an *n,* are also included in the Index. Comment on the level of difficulty is included and, in the *Supplement,* titles recommended particularly for the elementary school are labeled "E." Symbols citing reviews in major journals and listings in standard guides are also provided.

Both the hardbound and paper editions are sturdily bound and should withstand frequent use. Although one may not always agree with the designation "reference" for certain titles and may find others highly specialized, this supplement and the original guide deserve commendation because the compiler is well informed and the annotations are perceptive, two attributes seldom found in selection tools for school media specialists. With the heavy emphasis on selection aids (nearly 100 library science titles including books on library skills, reading guidance, and storytelling), both the *Guide* and *Supplement* belong in library schools as well as in school and public library collections. The broad coverage, the up-to-dateness of the titles included (with a promise of further biennial supplements), the ready access provided by the detailed Table of Contents and Index, and the full annotations offer the media specialist an excellent aid for materials selection.   *(Apr. 15, 1977, p.1296)*

011'.02   Reference books—Bibliography || Instructional materials centers || School libraries [CIP]   73-87523

Guide to special issues and indexes of periodicals.
Editors: Charlotte M. Devers, Doris B. Katz, Mary Margaret Regan. 2d ed. New York, Special Libraries Association, 1976. xix, 289p. 26cm. cloth $14.50.

The new *Guide to Special Issues and Indexes of Periodicals* is a well arranged key to features, supplementary issues, and/or sections which appear annually, semiannually, or quarterly in 1,256 U.S. and Canadian periodicals. The current Guide has 450 more entries than appeared in the first edition which was published in 1962. Also new in this edition are Canadian listings and the subscription address and price of both the parent periodical and the special issues. Examination of the book reveals that a number of reliable methods were used to assure accuracy of data. The periodicals listed represent a broad cross section of journals available. Major industries, professions, and consumer interests are covered.

The *Guide* is designed for quick and easy reference. A comprehensive Index to subjects and associations provides broad access to the information. Wide margins will permit rebinding that will be necessary after heavy use of this much needed updated *Guide to Special Issues and Indexes of Periodicals*. Public, special, and college and university libraries and advertisers, marketing specialists, publishers, and trade and professional associations will find that the *Guide* is well worth the price.
(Nov. 15, 1976, p.500)

016.051   American periodicals—Bibliography || Canadian periodicals—Bibliography   [CIP]   75-25621

A guide to the birds of Panama.
By Robert S. Ridgely; illustrated by John A. Gwynne, Jr. Princeton, N.J., Princeton Univ. Pr., [1976]. xv, 394p. 23cm. cloth $15.

Intended for both amateur and professional bird watchers, this guide describes 883 species. Dr. Alexander Wetmore of the Smithsonian Institution, Dr. Eugene Eisenmann, and the author, all of whom have done extensive field work in Panama, have collaborated on its preparation. Ridgely, with a master's degree in zoology, is engaged in research for a doctorate.

Arranged by family and species, the text follows a uniform pattern, with family accounts including general distribution, approximate size, family characteristics, food preferences, general behavior, style of nest, and the number of species recorded in Panama. Species accounts give description, similar species, status and distribution, habits (including bird call), and range, with an occasional added note. These sections are preceded by brief chapters on climate, migration and local movements, conservation, and plan of the book, with helpful definitions of terms used. Two appendixes list additional species of Southern Middle America and describe a number of localities where birds may be found. The Index gives English and Latin bird names mentioned in the main text but not persons and places. An appended list of about 40 English-language books and articles ranges from the popular Peterson field guides to the incomplete, multivolumed *Birds of North and Middle America* by Robert Ridgway. A foreword carries the endorsement of Dr. Wetmore.

Thirty-two color plates by John A Gwynne are grouped in the center of the book and coordinated with the text by appropriate citations. About 650 of the 883 species are clearly depicted. Fifty line drawings accompany the text descriptions.

The author's extensive field experience and use of existing research represented in a convenient format make this guide desirable for both libraries and bird watchers.

(Feb. 15, 1977, p.925)

598.2'97287 Birds—Panama—Identification [CIP] 75-30205

The Hamlyn junior encyclopedia of nature.
[By] Leonard Moore. London, Hamlyn America; dist. by A & W Promotional Corp., [1976, c1974]. 255p. illus. (part col.) 30cm. econolin $7.95.

The Hamlyn Junior Encyclopedia of Nature is the publication of a well-known English publishing firm based in London, with branch offices in New York, Sydney, and Toronto. They have previously published *The Hamlyn's Younger Children's Encyclopedia* (*Reference and Subscription Books Reviews* March 15, 1977), "a single volume general reference encyclopedia," and *The Hamlyn Junior Science Encyclopedia*, (*Reference and Subscription Books Reviews* May 1, 1977), "devoted to scientific topics of interest to children."

The Junior Encyclopedia of Nature was first published in England in 1974; the volume under review is described as a "second impression," dated 1976. The publishers state that "the author, Leonard Moore, has spent a life-time communicating to young children his enormous enthusiasm for his subject," but no reference is made as to his authority or background for handling the broad subject areas contained in this volume; nor does the author document any of his facts. No information is given on the editor(s), editorial staff, or contributors.

The publisher asserts that the *Encyclopedia of Nature* presents "this world of nature to young readers so that they can grow up to appreciate and understand their natural environment." The sentences throughout are fairly short and uncomplicated. However, elementary-age children in the U.S. may experience some confusion with the occasional British spelling and word usage; with, at this time, the use of the metric system in giving measurements; and with the references to the subjects given in relation to areas of the United Kingdom rather than the U.S.

While the question approach used in some instances may rouse the interest of the younger child, it could turn off older elementary school children who might consider some of the questions patronizing (e.g., "What is a bird?" "What do birds eat?" "What is a fish?"). Further, some children would find it difficult to relate to such questions as "Have you ever lifted a stone or uncovered an ants' nest?" "What could be a better way to spend an afternoon than to walk among the trees and look at the life around?" "Have you noticed that on a beach there is usually a line of seaweed left to dry when the tide is out?" On the other hand, a number of the suggested experiments which could be handled by elementary age students would certainly rouse interest.

In most instances, the author is straightforward in presenting information (e.g., "If you take a walk to a fishmonger's shop, you will see that he sells many kinds of fish for us to eat;" "Seals are better adapted to a life in the water than sea otters, but they come on to land from time to time."). Though basic, descriptive, and often fascinating detail is given on a variety of subjects, the amount of information generally would be of insufficient depth or breadth for satisfactory research beyond the elementary level. Unfamiliar terms (e.g., thorax, anthers, polyps, dreys) are italicized and explained when they first appear in the text.

Perhaps the greatest deterrent against use of the volume as a reference tool is its classified arrangement. The book is organized around three large subject areas: "Air," "Water," "Land." "Air" has subdivisions *The Weather, Birds, Insects,* and *Bats.* "Water" is divided into *Ponds, Amphibians, Fresh-water Fish, Other Fresh-water Inhabitants, The Seashore, Life in the Upper Layers of the Sea.* The third section, "Land," has as its subject divisions *In the Soil, Plants, Mammals,* and *Reptiles.*

The above subject divisions listed in the table of Contents suggest one of the hindrances to the volume's use as a reference source. The subject of *Insects* is dealt with under "Air," and later in relation to life in *ponds* and *in the Soil. Mammals* must be looked for under both "Water" and "Land," while *Bats* appears exclusively within the "Air" section. Duplication of subjects occurs frequently.

A scanning of the Index at the back of the book further demonstrates this duplication. The way in which plants use and give off water is listed under "Air"–*weather,* and plants' relationship to bees is identified in another "Air" article. Under "Water" one finds plants "growing in or near fresh water," "growing on the seashore," and "growing under the sea." Finally, "trees and plants in British woods," "trees and plants in rain forests," "desert plants," "insect eating plants," and a general description of plants and seeds are found under "Land."

Such detailed indexing can, of course, lead to the various subjects for reference, but may be too intricate for the young child. The references from the Index at times lead to very brief information (e.g., one reference to "plants" under "weather" merely states, "this [water vapor] has come from the water of the sea, lakes, rivers, and ponds, and also from animals and plants which lose water vapour as they breathe."). Not only is the reference trivial, it gives false information. Plants do not "breathe" as do animals. Fuller explanation is given of the process two pages later in a description of how plants use water: "as water is used by plants, or moves into the air as water vapour (both from the surface of the soil and from the leaves of plants), it is replaced by more rain." Although breathing is not reintroduced, the explanation is still incomplete.

The Index references at times lead to illustrations which are not labeled. In one instance, reference to a *dragonfly* is to an illustration of such an insect appearing among many others. The textual comment on the page states: "Maybe a large dragonfly will dart towards the nearest pond and butterflies will drift silently through the air." It is possible that many children will be able to identify the pictured butterfly, but few would be able to recognize the dragonfly (unless they turn to a labeled illustration on a later page) or name the numerous other uncaptioned insects in the same illustration. If the illustration is only for decorative purposes, the brief, one-sentence comment hardly warrants an Index reference. Another Index reference to the shrew leads to an unlabeled illustration under the topic "scavengers," while brief information concerning the animal was given many pages earlier in a discussion of "water shrews."

The large, brightly colored, and numerous illustrations add dimension to the text, and most, being well captioned, will give the child a clearer understanding of the subject. In fact as much information is sometimes imparted by the illustration as by the text. However, size relationships are sometimes confusing as in one example where a queen termite appears to be slightly larger than a man standing nearby. On the other hand, the artistic renderings of greatly enlarged details of insect anatomy, cellular structure, fish scales, plankton, and other forms of plant and animal life should extend youngsters' understanding and appreciation of nature.

The absence of references to the U.S., in relation to the subjects handled, may limit its use for children in this country more than the occasional British spelling and word usage. Special mention is made of the study of snowflakes by the eminent Wilson A. Bentley; however, in most cases, references relate subjects to habitats in England, Canada, Australia, India, and Africa even though many of the plants and animals may be found in the U.S. For example, only bird migrations in Europe, Africa, and Canada are mentioned, and attention is given only to the crocodiles and alligators in Africa, India, and America (not the U.S.). Foxes, antelope, and deer are limited to Europe, and reference is made only to desert sands, dunes, and rock formations of the Sahara with no mention of similar natural outgrowths in this country. Only a few references are made to specific locations in the U.S. "Venus fly-trap grows in the boggy parts of Carolina in America"; and an illustration of a gila monster carries the label, "Texas, Arizona, Mexico."

The binding of the volume is econolin, and the corners and spine are overly susceptible to damage. Because illustrations are bled to the inner margins, rebinding would be impracticable.

The Hamlyn Junior Encyclopedia of Nature contains much fascinating general information of interest for children but has limited value for youngsters in the U.S. Because of its awkward arrangement, poor binding, and Commonwealth emphasis, this encyclopedia has only marginal value for American children.

(June 15, 1977, p.1603)

†503   Science—Dictionaries || Children's encyclopedias   76-43609

The Hamlyn junior science encyclopedia.
Edited by Valerie Pitt, John Daintith, and Alan Isaacs. London, Hamlyn/American; dist. by A & W Promotional Book Corp., 1973. 256p. illus. 30cm. cloth $7.95.

The title of the *Hamlyn Junior Science Encyclopedia* is somewhat misleading in that the physical sciences and technology are covered but not the biological sciences. It was written to enable children from 9 to 13 and their parents "to find the answers to hundreds of their questions."

The volume is divided into five nonalphabetical sections: "The Earth and the Universe;" "Measurement, Movement, and Energy;" "Light and Sound;" "Electrons at Work;" and "Discoveries and Inventions." Within each section are 21 to 24 thematically arranged unsigned articles. A five-page Index, four columns per page, completes the book.

Coverage within the 115 articles is brief, each being limited to one double-page spread. Presentation varies from a simple discussion of the various types of pollution to a more complex explanation of how television works. Topics of current interest, such as ecology, fuel, computers, and space travel are included, although the 1973 copyright date means that some information may be out of date. For example, the article on *Length* states that "The Imperial or British system of measurement of length is based on the yard, but in 1975 it will be changed to the metre." The article *Exploring Space* describes U.S. plans for landing an unmanned probe on Mars in the future of 1975. It also states that "flights to Venus have provided little information about the planet" and mentions that the U.S. hopes to launch a large orbiting space station in 1977. In fact, the U.S. launched a skylab as early as 1973; *Mariner* 10 took closeup pictures of the clouds surrounding Venus in 1974, and Viking I landed on Mars in 1976.

Because of the extreme brevity of the articles, the information they provide is sometimes confusing, oversimplified, or incomplete. For instance, the article on the formation of the earth presents only one theory, that of continental drift. In the *Rocks and Minerals* article, no clear distinction is drawn between igneous and metamorphic rocks; it is implied that both types are formed volcanically, whereas metamorphic rocks were originally igneous and sedimentary rocks which were changed by heat or pressure within the earth. Only a single sample of each kind of rock is illustrated. The article on elements and compounds mentions that more than 100 elements exist, but only 20 are listed, and this list is several pages distant from the text.

Color drawings, diagrams, tables, and charts abound. More than 800 illustrations are attractively arranged, two to six per page. They are usually clear and their captions add supplementary information to the articles. Short biographical sketches of scientists and inventors are included, and captioned illustrations suggest simple science activities.

The Table of Contents does not list page numbers for the individual articles. These page numbers are listed on separate Contents pages which head each section. Since the articles are not arranged alphabetically and there are very few *see* references from one article to another, it is necessary to rely on the Index to find all related information. The Index was found to contain few errors but many omissions. Left out are references to ten charts relating to previously presented material and appended to the ends of the main sections. Because they are not directly contiguous to related articles or referred to in the text, they are inaccessible except to a browser.

The publisher's promotional material states that the encyclopedia contains "useful reference lists." No such bibliographies or additional reading lists could be found.

The encyclopedia "was written by a team of scientists," but scientific credentials could be verified for only one editor, Alan Isaacs, who holds a PhD in physical chemistry and has written a book entitled *Introducing Science* (London: Penguin, 1961, New York: Basic Books, 1962). Information on the ten writers and fourteen artists and agents listed on the verso of the title page could not be authenticated in standard biographical directories.

The encyclopedia is clearly printed on white paper. Inner margins are narrow, and some illustrations bleed into the center seam. The layout of text and illustrations is attractive. British spellings ("colour,", "aeroplanes") and terminology ("lorries," and "petrol") are used.

The *Hamlyn Junior Science Encyclopedia* answers many questions in the fields of physical science and technology which might be asked by children from nine to thirteen. However, its brevity of coverage, lack of currency, and errors and omissions in the Index, made more serious because of the nonalphabetical arrangement of the text, make purchase of this book inadvisable for school or public library reference collections.

(May 1, 1977, p.1375)

500   Science—Dictionaries   [OCLC]   74-177514/AC

The Hamlyn younger children's encyclopedia.
Kenneth Bailey. London, Hamlyn, [1972], 1st U.S. ed., 1976, distributed in the U.S. by A & W Promotional Book Corp., 95 Madison Ave., New York 10016. 256p. 30cm. cloth $7.95.

This 256-page volume is divided into 24 sections, beginning with *Our Land and Its People* and concluding with *The Journey into Space.* Since this is a British publication, the first section of 26 pages covers the British Isles—geography, history, government, animals, present status. Subsequent sections deal with flora, fauna, exploration, myths and legends, fine arts, food, medicine, travel, history of man, religion, science and invention, countries of the world, the universe, and the earth.

Brief but generally accurate information is provided. Since the volume's publication in 1972, there have been many developments in the exploration of outer space, and the political geography of Africa has undergone substantial change. Coverage of these areas is conspicuously out of date. Sections range in length from the lead section of 26 pages to 4 pages for *Costumes.* Information is so condensed in *The Hamlyn Younger Children's Encyclopedia* that it probably would not inspire a child to seek more in-depth material.

The book jacket indicates that this volume was specially prepared for children aged eight and over, but the reading level appears most suitable for fifth- to seventh-graders.

British spelling is followed, e.g., aeroplane, colour, flavour, humour, learnt. Areas are given in kilometers and miles.

The volume is profusely illustrated in color, including drawings, paintings, photographs, and maps. There is little or no detail in the maps, but the illustrations are for the most part clear and have eye-appeal.

There is a five-page Index which, though accurate, has minimal reference value because most of its entries lead to a mere phrase or line or two of information.

The volume is bound in bright red cloth. The pages lie flat when opened. Text appears in two columns, broken up with many illustrations and captions per page. The print is clear, and the legends accompanying the pictures are in small but readable type.

Reference value of *The Hamlyn Younger Children's Encyclopedia* is extremely slight, even for younger children, because almanacs, dictionaries, and other children's sets provide more current and thorough coverage of much of its content. Browsability is the volume's chief asset. *(Mar. 15, 1977, p.1121)*

†032 Children's encyclopedias and dictionaries

A handbook for travellers in India, Pakistan, Nepal, Bangladesh and Sri Lanka (Ceylon).
Edited by L. F. Rushbrook Williams. 22d. ed. New York, Barnes & Noble, 1975. xii, 726p. maps. plans. 19cm. cloth, $37.50.

During its 116-year existence this handbook has had a series of distinguished editors. Professor L. F. Rushbrook Williams, a well-known authority on South Asia, is responsible for this and the three previous editions. The introductory information has been extensively revised and now includes sections on the overland route from Europe via Turkey and Iran (which is gaining popularity), package tours, fishing, camping, and trekking. The section on art has been rewritten, and the description of the world famous Khajuraho temples expanded. Because of the growing popularity of Nepal among western tourists it has been substituted for Burma in this edition.

The governments of the five countries represented in this guide have been developing facilities for the traveling public. Airline service and highway travel possibilities are described in some detail. The railway systems, however, still cover far greater areas of the subcontinent; hence the handbook concentrates most on this mode of travel. As a matter of fact, the entire guide is organized by rail routes within each country, 33 in India, 23 in Nepal, 10 in Ceylon, 3 in Pakistan, and 2 in Bangladesh. The sequence of places along each route is identified; tourist attractions are described, and mileages from points of origin are given. Maps and plans of cities are interspersed throughout the handbook.

Towards the end of the book is a directory of places as well as an index of names which make the handbook a kind of gazetteer. Census figures and commentary on irrigation projects and industrial development will interest those who want to know what is going on at present in these countries.

Political events up to August 1975 are summarized for Bangladesh; the cutoff for the other countries is 1972. Kinds of accommodation are characterized, e.g., Circuit Houses, Dak Bungalows, and Railway Retiring Rooms, but specific hotels, lodges, and restaurants are not rated or recommended. However, because of the immense amount of data provided about the culture, landmarks, history, and geography of locales on the Indian subcontinent, this handbook will be invaluable to travel agents, tour organizers, and individuals planning extensive travel in the countries covered. Large public and academic libraries may wish to purchase it for the use of their clienteles.
(Nov. 1, 1976, p.425)

†915.4 Asia—Description and travel

A handbook of African names.
By Ihechukwu Madubuike. Washington, D.C., Three Continents, [c1976]. 233p. illus. 20cm. cloth $9.

Ihechukwu Madubuike, a native of Nigeria, holds degrees in French and philosophy and received his doctorate in French and African literature from the State University of New York at Buffalo in 1973. He has written the *Handbook* for the "black man in diaspora" for whom "the knowledge of African names is invaluable." The *Handbook* will give the reader who is unfamiliar with African names a summary introduction to the names of 17 nations and 20 linguistic groups from Senegal to Guinea and Mali to the Xhosa names of South Africa. For ease of use the book is divided into four parts—a 20-page Introduction; a 151-page, 20-part explication of African names by region and people, including lists of names and their meaning in English; a 23-page alphabetical list of some African names for males and females; and a pronunciation guide which is as consistent as possible with the International Phonetic Guide.

It is unfortunate that the material in *A Handbook of African Names* lacks an index which would facilitate finding specific names for which the origin is unknown. The excitement caused by Alex Haley's *Roots* (New York: Doubleday, 1976) and the impact of its televised version augur well for the success of this handbook, especially among Afro-Americans interested in their multi-faceted heritage. *(May 15, 1977, p.1451)*

929.4'096 Names, Personal—Africa [CIP]   75-25943

A handbook of American literature:
a comprehensive study from colonial times to the present day. [By] Martin S. Day. New York, Crane, Russak & Co., [1976]. xii, 661p. 22cm. paper $9.75.

Originally published in a clothbound edition in 1975 by the University of Queensland Press, Australia, the American printing of the *Handbook* is a paperbound edition with margins too narrow to permit rebinding. This is a reference book designed for foreigners. The author, a professor at the University of Houston, has lectured on American literature in several countries abroad. He excludes writers one would find in other standard handbooks "in favor of American authors and writings that the world outside the U.S.A. now deems important or decidedly interesting." Omitted are formerly prominent authors such as Nathaniel Parker Willis and Bayard Taylor.

The book encompasses fiction, drama, poetry, and nonfiction prose. The subject matter is arranged chronologically. American literature from the seventeenth century to 1914 (Richard Hakluyt and John Smith to Josiah Gibbs and Frederick Jackson Turner) is covered in slightly more than one-third of the book. The remainder is devoted to twentieth-century writers and writing from Eugene O'Neill to Carl Sandburg, John O'Hara, Galbraith, Nevins, Jean Stafford, James Purdy, and Ken Kesey. Critical comments on authors and their contributions to American literature are emphasized, with only scant biographical data and very brief plot summaries. Perhaps the chief value of this reference work

is that it does provide introductory material on writers seldom given in biographical references. It is a book for the beginner, not the advanced student. For larger libraries, the *Handbook* can serve as a supplement to standard literary handbooks.
(Feb. 1, 1977, p.857)

†810.09   American literature—History and criticism

Handbook of practical cookery.
By Pierre Blot. New York, Arno Pr., 1973. 478p. illus. 23cm. cloth $12.

641.5'973   Cookery, American   [OCLC]   72-9789

See page 116

Harper dictionary of contemporary usage.
[By] William and Mary Morris. New York, Harper & Row, [1975]. xxiv, 649p. 24cm. cloth $15.

Of possible value as light reading and, in libraries needing yet another guide to the subtleties of English, of probable value as a reference tool, this work is arranged alphabetically, with generally brief entries and numerous cross-references. Its special feature is the presentation at many points of panels of presumably expert opinion. Under *contact,* for example, the Morrises note that some object to its being used to signify "to get in touch with" and ask the panel, "Would you accept 'Let's *contact* him at once'?" Forty-nine panelists reply. Unfortunately, the trick does not quite come off. The experts—most of them, most of the time—shed little light. The tone is that of a very average talk-show, and the majority of comments are quite banal. The experts emerge as "personalities." The Morrises presumably have a following built up through their many years as syndicated columnists. But there is little to be said for such trivialities as, under *drop-out,* "William Morris, one of the editors of this book, was a *dropout* long before the term was invented, having been forced to take a year's leave of absence from Harvard for economic reasons, returning the next year to earn his degree." However, this is far from being a non-book. There are many pages of useful information clearly presented, and the Morrises give good advice even if some of it may seem a trifle gratuitous.   *(Dec. 15, 1976, p.630)*

428   English language—Usage || English language—Dictionaries   [CIP]   73-4112

Helicopter directory.
By Joseph Mill Brown. New York, Hippocrene Books Inc.; London, Vancouver, David & Charles, Newton Abbot, [c1976]. 128p. illus. 16 x 23cm. paper composition $15.95.

The Helicopter Directory is a compact guide to 116 helicopters currently in service in 9 countries: Argentina (1), France (9), Great Britain (7), Italy (21), Japan (4), Poland (1), U.S. (62), USSR (7), and West Germany (4). Arrangement of the book is by country. One page is devoted to each aircraft. All are illustrated in black-and-white halftones, and there are a few line drawings. A brief description summarizes the capabilities of each vehicle, and brief tabular information on the engine, diameter of rotor, length of fuselage, weight (loaded and empty), cruising speed, rate of climb, hover ceiling IGE and OGE, and range makes for easy comparison of the helicopters. *The Helicopter Directory* will serve as a useful introduction to students and other individuals interested in helicopters. Public and technical high school libraries will find that the book is conveniently organized for ease of use.   *(Nov. 15, 1976, p.501)*

629.133'35   Helicopters—Catalogs   [CIP]   75-44234

Helicopters of the world.
[By] Michael J. H. Taylor and John W. R. Taylor. New York, Scribner, [c1976]. 128p. illus. 22cm. cloth $7.95.

629.133'35   Helicopters   [OCLC]   76-318634

See page 98

High living:
recipes from Southern climes. Compiled by L. L. McLaren. New York, Arno Pr., 1973. x, n.p. illus. 19cm. cloth $5.

641.5   Cookery   [CIP]   72-9798

See page 116

Historical and cultural dictionary of Thailand.
By Harold E. Smith. Metuchen, N.J., Scarecrow, 1976. 213p. 22cm. (Historical and cultural dictionaries of Asia, no. 6). cloth $8.

Scarecrow's "Historical and Cultural Dictionaries of Asia" is edited by Basil C. Hedrick. Saudi Arabia, Nepal, the Philippines, Burma, Afghanistan, Vietnam and India have been treated in the other seven volumes in the series. Harold Smith, author of the Thailand volume, teaches at Northern Illinois University; his subject specialties are Thailand, comparative social organization, and the family. He has written extensively on Thailand. The dictionary contains approximately 1,200 entries concerning "history, Thai Buddhism and other religions, the economy, geography, government patterns, Thai customs and values, communication, artistic production, as well as other subjects."

This dictionary is arranged alphabetically with cross-references to related items. Guide words at the top of each page indicate the first entries on the pages. Entries vary in length from one sentence, such as *Hun Krabok,* to almost two pages for *Rama IV* and *Rama V.* Each of Thailand's 72 provinces is discussed in a separate entry, as are the 72 provincial capitals. "The latter are distinguished from the former by the addition of the word 'city,' since each province and its capital have the same name."

A 55-item Bibliography cites sources to supplement the information contained in the dictionary. This list's usefulness is limited because about half of the titles are published in Bangkok and may not be easily obtainable in the U.S.

About half of the dictionary entries define geographical features (islands, rivers, forests, and mountain ranges) or enumerate population statistics, landmarks, and transportation facilities of the nation's many towns, villages, cities, ports, provinces, and regions. Religious institutions and concepts (e.g., *Buddhism,* and *New-Buddhism, Brahmanism, Protestantism, Cosmology, Karma, Nirvana, Noble Eightfold Path,* and *Wat*), customs and various professional and societal status designations (e.g. *politeness and greeting, cockfighting,* and *Pra Mong, Phu Yai* and *Phu Noi, Nen* and *Sangha*), history (contemporary political figures, kings, dynasties), and culture (music, art, architecture, language) account for most of the remaining definitions.

The dictionary is a ready reference, not intended to give comprehensive coverage. At present there is no other reference which offers the same type of ready reference information on Thailand. The entries are easy to read, and the coverage is adequate for persons seeking basic introductory knowledge about this country, its history and culture.

School and public libraries with patrons interested in Southeast Asian customs and traditions may wish to acquire the *Historical and Cultural Dictionary of Thailand.*
(June 15, 1976, p.1604)

959.3'003   Thailand—Dictionaries and encyclopedias   [CIP]   76-7044

Historical and cultural dictionary of Vietnam.
By Danny J. Whitfield. Metuchen, N.J., Scarecrow Pr., Inc., 1976. (Historical and cultural dictionaries of Asia, no.7). viii, 369p. maps. cloth $13.50.

Scarecrow Press' "Historical and Cultural Dictionaries of Asia" series intends "to provide a source where both the scholar and the casual and interested reader may find factual, somewhat balanced, useful information pertinent to the various nations of Asia." The first books in the series were published in 1972.

Countries covered by the series are Saudi Arabia, Nepal, the Philippines, Burma, Afghanistan, Thailand, and India.

Danny J. Whitfield, author of the Vietnam book, lived in that country for eight years and later was assistant to the director of the Center for Vietnamese Studies at Southern Illinois University, Carbondale. His dictionary contains about 1,300 ready-reference entries on the culture, history, places, people, economics, government, and geography of Vietnam. Most of the entries are longer than the usual dictionary definitions, and many are concise encyclopedia-length treatments. The reader who is unfamiliar with the Vietnamese language should read the prefatory explanation of Vietnamese alphabetization and hyphenation, because the system of alphabetization in the book is an adaptation of the Vietnamese.

Three Appendixes help clarify the contents of the book: an outline of Vietnamese history, prepared by Professor Chingho A. Chen, Chinese University, Hong Kong; a dynastic chronology; and 12 maps which trace the country's history from 111 B.C. to the present. A good Bibliography of works in Vietnamese and English will be useful to those who seek more information. High school, college and university, and public libraries will find the *Historical and Cultural Dictionary of Vietnam* a reliable source of facts on Vietnam. *(Sept. 1, 1976, p.56)*

959.704'003   Vietnam—Dictionaries and encyclopedias   [CIP]   75-38729

Historical dictionary of Honduras.
By Harvey K. Meyer. Metuchen, N.J., Scarecrow, 1976. 399p. (Latin American historical dictionaries, No. 13). illus. maps. 23cm. cloth $15.

The *Historical Dictionary of Honduras* is Meyer's second contribution and number 13 in the series "Latin American Historical Dictionaries" under the general editorial direction of the well-known Latin American scholar A. Curtis Wilgus. The author of the present work "has served in all the professional ranks, in colleges and universities, holding professorships, deanships, and directorships" and is now retired from his last post as professor of education at Florida Atlantic University. Meyer has studied, traveled broadly, and lived in Central America. His other works include *Technical Education in Nicaragua; an Essay Report* (Epsilon Pi Tau, 1958) and *Historical Dictionary of Nicaragua* (Scarecrow, 1972).

In the *Historical Dictionary of Honduras,* the dictionary arrangement has been supplemented by a *q.v.* cross-reference system, which greatly improves this volume over Meyer's earlier *Historical Dictionary of Nicaragua* and makes it easier to find chronologically or topically related items. Multiple entries and *see* references are provided for the many items with variant spelling. However, subject and personal name indexes would greatly improve the work as would some kind of chronological key. The author's unpretentious ink drawings (23 illustrations and 8 maps) enhance the textual descriptions of Honduran geography, culture, and artifacts. The bibliography's usefulness is also limited by the lack of annotations. The impregnated cloth binding is durable but tight enough to prevent the book from remaining open without assistance from the reader. Entries are in upper case and stand out clearly, and running heads assist the reader in finding entries.

There is no other comparable work save the official *El Libro de Honduras* (1957) with its Spanish and English texts, which is out of print, and the *Area Handbook for Honduras* (U.S.G.P.O., 1971), which does not have the breadth of coverage especially in biography. The *Dictionary of Honduras* and the other volumes in the series "serve as convenient source books of historical and contemporary facts and statistics . . . each volume providing in dictionary format a potpourri of pertinent information about key persons, places, events, geography, history and political subdivisions." Meyer has, in addition, established sixfold criteria for selection—"significance, typicality, uniqueness, general interest, structure, eclecticism"—in a volume "planned for travelers as well as scholars." His topics generally fall within one of four loose categories—geography, people, culture, and history. Subject coverage ranges across a wide spectrum to include information concerning local use of terms, flora and fauna, labor, commerce, industry and features of social organization. Meyer covers a range of subjects so broad that many of the items are relatively unimportant. Though including too much is not a serious fault, the entries are usually superficial. For instance, in spite of the disclaimer that the compiler has made no "effort to give complete biographies," the omission of birth and death dates of most biographees is particularly troublesome. However, dates of significant activities of biographees are included. Breadth and variety of subject matter have occasionally led Meyer into minor errors. For instance, the mapache is related to the raccoon, not the weasel. Nevertheless, the variety of materials drawn together in one source makes this volume an attractive purchase. *(June 1, 1977, p.1526)*

972.83'003   Honduras—Dictionaries and encyclopedias   [CIP]   76-4539

A history and bibliography of American magazines, 1810–1820.
By Neal L. Edgar. Metuchen, N.J., Scarecrow Pr., Inc., 1975. v, 379p. 23cm. cloth $15.

Neal L. Edgar, professor and serials librarian, Kent State University Libraries, in *A History and Bibliography of American Magazines, 1810–1820,* successfully fills a bibliographical gap that had existed for the 1810 to 1820 decade. The 269-page bibliography of magazines which comprises the major part of the book is preceded by a 67-page summary of the history of magazines of 1810 to 1820 with commentary on their influence on the culture, literature, and religion of the period. Notes document sources of the data and opinions given in this section.

The most important part of the book is comprised of alphabetically arranged bibliographical descriptions of 223 magazines. As much of the following information as is applicable to each title is given: title, places and dates of publication, editor, printer, type of magazine, frequency, price, size (in inches), length of an average issue, availability, remarks, and footnotes. The remarks are a unique phase of the coverage, and they vary in length with the importance of the magazine and availability of data. A number of magazines of the period focused on religion, e.g., *American Baptist Magazine, Berean, Churchman's Magazine, Evangelical Guardian, Evangelical Record, Evangelical Repository, Gospel Visitant, Herald of Gospel, Kentucky Missionary, Literary and Evangelical Magazine, Literary and Philosophical Repertory, Methodist Review.* Seventeen magazines have the initial word "Christian" in their title.

There are three important Appendixes: an annotated list of 92 exclusions, a Chronological List of Magazines, and a Register of Printers, Publishers, Editors, and Engravers, 1810–1820. The Index at the end of the book provides access only to the names, magazine titles, and subjects mentioned in the Introduction and historical summary, pages 3–74. It is to be used in conjunction with the annotations and Appendixes. *A History and Bibliography of American Magazines, 1810–1820* provides a chronological approach to the 223 periodicals of the period. The information it contains was previously available only through laborious perusal of the alphabetically arranged *Union List of Serials.* Edgar's book will, therefore, be an immensely time-saving reference. *(Sept. 1, 1976, p.56)*

016.051   American periodicals—History || American periodicals—Bibliography   [CIP]   75-11882

Home cookery:
ladies indispensable companion: cookery in Northeastern cities. Intro. and suggested recipes by Louis Szathmary. New York, Arno Pr., 1973. xx, 158, 136p. 22cm. cloth $9.

641.5   Cookery, American—Northeastern States   [CIP]   72-9790

See page 116

How to locate reviews of plays and films:
a bibliography of criticism from the beginnings to the present. By Gordon Samples. Metuchen, N.J., Scarecrow, 1976. x, 114p. 22cm. cloth $6.

Gordon Samples, teacher in the Department of Reference and Instructional Services at San Diego State University, prepared *How to Locate Reviews of Plays and Films* for use by research and reference specialists. For convenience of use, Samples has divided the work into two parts, one devoted to plays and the other to films. Both sections are arranged chronologically, with entries listed logically under specific types of sources. All entries are annotated, with summarizing descriptions intended to direct the user to the reference that best fits his or her needs.

The section devoted to plays has information classified around eight categories: "Chronology of Study Guides," "Review Indexing Services," "Newspaper Indexes," "Dramatic Criticism Checklists," "Collected Reviews of Individual Critics," "Leading Theatre Periodicals," "Leading Reference Guides," and "Play Synopses and Production Controlling Agencies." The films section has eleven classes of information including several French-language sources of information on films.

Since the Index contains only author and title references, the table of contents, which lists the titles of the 19 sections, must serve as the only subject approach to the bibliography.

How to Locate Reviews of Plays and Films is a good introduction to the criticism of plays and films. It should prove useful to students interested in the subject and to librarians involved in guiding readers to basic sources of information.
(May 15, 1977, p.1451)

016.791   Theater—Reviews—Bibliography || Moving-pictures—Reviews—Bibliography
[CIP]   76-3509

The illustrated encyclopedia of rock.
[Compiled by] Nick Logan and Bob Woffinden. New York, Harmony Books; dist. by Crown, [c1977]. 256p. illus. 30cm. cloth $11.95; paper $7.95.

784   Rock music—Dictionaries || Rock music—Bio-bibliography   [OCLC]   76-40219
See page 168

The improved housewife.
[By] Mrs. A. L. Webster. New York, Arno Pr., 1973. 214p. illus. 22cm. cloth $7.

641.5   Cookery   [CIP]   72-9804
See page 116

Incredible.
[By] Kevin McFarland; illus. by Luis Dominguez. New York, Hart Pub. Co., [1976]. 400p. illus. 29cm. cloth $9.95; to schools and libraries, $8.46.

On its book jacket, *Incredible* is subtitled "An Astounding Gallery of Extraordinary People, Unique Structures, Exotic Plants, Unusual Animals, and Unbelievable Events in History." Since the book is awkward to use for specific information, and because it lacks an index, the search for facts is best accomplished by browsing through the contents pages and the text. Searching is further complicated because all curiosities on one subject like animals or people are not described together. Thus, the first narrative is captioned "Garfield Could Write Two Languages at the Same Time." The story at the middle of the book is called "Thomas Stevens Rode Around the World on a High Wheeled Bicycle," and the last entry is "Nelson Crossed the United States on a Unicycle." Some 300 marvels are described, and most of them are illustrated with black-and-white drawings. The style of writing will attract students from junior high school age on up. School libraries can expect *Incredible* to attract reluctant readers. The information given in the book may stimulate such students to read further on the subject. Those who seek documentation of some of the many barely credible statements will be disappointed because sources are not cited and there is no bibliography.
(Nov. 15, 1976, p.501)

†031.02   Children's encyclopedias and dictionaries

Index to black poetry.
[By] Dorothy H. Chapman. Boston, Mass., G. K. Hall, 1974. xxii, 541p. 26cm. cloth, $25.

Approximately 1,000 poets and 5,000 poems, 94 books and pamphlets by individual poets, and 33 anthologies are represented in this index. The author, Dorothy H. Chapman, has held the position of curator of the special collections at Texas Southern University since 1969. Samuel Allen (Paul Vesey), the distinguished lawyer and poet, has contributed the Foreword to the work.

Although a wide chronological period from the eighteenth century to the present is encompassed, the index is limited in coverage. For example, well-known anthologies such as *The Poetry of Black Americans* by Arnold Adoff (1973) and *Modern and Contemporary Afro-American Poetry* by Bernard W. Bell (1972) are omitted. In the Preface, the author states that "the Poetry section of the Heartman Collection of the Texas Southern University Library (Houston, Texas) provided a wealth of sources and works." Dependence upon this collection as a primary source may account for the selectivity of inclusions and imbalance in favor of collected works and pamphlets over anthologies.

The index includes writing for adults and children by American, Caribbean, and African poets with U.S. output receiving the most attention.

The work is divided into three alphabetically arranged sections: (1) a Title and First Line Index, (2) an Author Index, and (3) Subject Index. A Key to Abbreviations for Books Indexed is located at the front of the volume. The structure and headings of *Granger's Index to Poetry* are similar to those of the *Index to Black Poetry*. However, *Granger's* lists titles of volumes and omits pagination, while the work under review abbreviates titles but provides page references, thereby forcing the user to flip back to the key in order to verify complete titles.

The *Index to Black Poetry* is a sturdily bound volume with adequate type size. The book lies flat when opened.

While limited in scope, the *Index to Black Poetry* has unique value for students, scholars, and other readers concerned with the works of black poets. It should be particularly useful in school, public, special, and academic libraries, and in homes where an interest in Afro-American culture exists.
(Oct. 1, 1976, p.280)

811'.008   American poetry—Negro authors—Indexes || Negro poetry—Indexes || Negroes—Poetry—Indexes   [OCLC]   74-8838

Index to book reviews in historical periodicals 1973.
By John W. Brewster and Joseph A. McLeod. Metuchen, N.J., Scarecrow Pr., Inc., 1976, xiii, 443p. 22cm. cloth $15.

Index to book reviews in historical periodicals 1974.
By John W. Brewster and Joseph A. McLeod. Metuchen, N.J., Scarecrow Pr., Inc. 1975. xiii, 514p. 22cm. cloth $17.50.

Index to Book Reviews in Historical Periodicals was prepared initially to cover reviews published in 1974. The work was done by two staff members of North Texas State University library as an effort to meet university student needs for an author/title index to historical book reviews. The first volume, covering 97 English-language scholarly journals and historical society publications mostly from the U.S., was published in 1975. The next volume, published during the spring of 1976, indexes reviews which appeared in 93 periodicals during 1973. A third volume covering 1972 is scheduled for publication in 1976. The two volumes under review index mostly the same titles. However, only the 1973 volume indexes *Agricultural History, American History Illustrated,* the *American Jewish Historical Quarterly,* the *Concordin Historical Institute Quarterly, Inland Seas, Lincoln Herald, Nebraska History, Negro History Bulletin, Nevada Historical Society Quarterly, New Jersey History, Pacific Historian, Pennsylvania Magazine of History and Biography,* and *Social Studies,* while the 1974 cumulation picks up 19 journals not cited in the 1973 volume. Approximately 5,000 books for which reviews have been found are represented in each annual index.

Sufficient information is given for locating every reviewed title, and there are frequent cross-references in the text, which is alphabetical by author. The Index by Title gives only the author's name and does not repeat the complete bibliographic citation. The *Index to Book Reviews in Historical Periodicals* will be useful to students, librarians, historians, and general readers who need a ready-made list of English-language history book reviews published in the years covered by each volume. Because the work is devoted entirely to history, its coverage has greater depth than that of general book review indexes like *Humanities Index (Reference and Subscription Books Reviews, April 15, 1976)* and *Book Review Digest. (Sept. 1, 1976, p.56)*

901'.6 History—Book reviews—Indexes || History—Periodicals—Indexes [OCLC]
75-18992

Index to inspiration:
a thesaurus of subjects for speakers and writers. Compiled by Norma Olin Ireland. Westwood, Mass., Faxon, [1976]. xi, 506p. 24cm. cloth $18.

Norma Ireland has compiled a number of dependable reference books published by Faxon. Included among them are *Index to Fairy Tales, An Index to Monologs and Dialogs, An Index to Women of the World, An Index to Skits and Stunts,* and *An Index to Scientists.* The *Index to Inspiration* is comprised of 4,300 key-word subject headings under which inclusive page- or item-number references to relevant passages in books are arranged by author. All types of subjects are used (e.g., *getting along with others, philosophy, perfection, tobacco, wit's end, zeal*). The subjects are copiously cross-referenced. In preparing the index, Norma Ireland consulted and analyzed 220 books in English, both in and out of print. While most of the books are inspirational or convey a moral, a few are humorous. Among the books analyzed are *Norman Vincent Peale's Treasury of Courage and Confidence,* Helen Keller's *The Open Door,* James Schermerhorn's *1500 Anecdotes and Stories,* and Barbara Walters' *How to Talk with Practically Anybody About Anything.*

Ireland explains the book's arrangement, scope, and use in the Preface. Even though the book lacks an Index, it will be easy to use. The *Index to Inspiration* will provide writers and speakers on nontechnical subjects with clues to inspirational material in a wide variety of books. Public libraries will find it most useful.
(June 15, 1977, p.1604)

†808.882 Quotations, English
75-35464

Index to literary biography.
By Patricia Pate Havlice. 2v. Metuchen, N.J., Scarecrow, 1975. viii, 1,300p. 23cm. cloth $39.50.

Patricia Pate Havlice, a former reference librarian who now writes, is also the author of *Index to Artistic Biography* and *Art in Time.* In *Index to Literary Biography* she indexes 50 literary reference works published between 1931 and 1972, the results being an index to some 68,000 authors of all times. The references indexed are mostly English-language items, but outstanding references in German (4), Spanish (4), and French (5) are also included. Among the works included are Fleischmann's *Encyclopedia of World Literature in the 20th Century,* Kunitz's *Twentieth Century Authors,* Magill's *Cyclopedia of World Authors,* Kunisch's *Kleines Handbuch der deutschen Gegenwartsliteratur,* Bleiberg's *Diccionario de Literatura española,* and *Dictionnaire de littérature contemporaine.*

Entries are arranged alphabetically by author's real name with cross-references to pseudonyms. Dates of birth and death are given, and each author is identified as to nationality and type of writing. Letter codes identified in the preliminary pages are used to refer to the books containing each author's biography. The *Index to Literary Biography* will save time for students and others who need to locate biographies of authors which have been published in English-language references and a limited number of other references in French, German, and Spanish. High school, college, university, and public libraries which serve such students and lay persons not engaged in intensive research will want to acquire the book. *(June 1, 1977, p.1527)*

016.809 Literature—Bio-bibliography—Bibliography || Authors—Indexes [CIP] 74-8315

Industry analysts in the federal government.
By Washington Researchers. Washington, D.C., Washington Researchers, 910 Seventeenth St. NW, 20006, 1976. 25p. 28cm. paper $10.

†353.00025 Administrative agencies—Directories || Independent regulatory commissions—Directories

See page 119

Information sources in power engineering:
a guide to energy resources and technology.
[By] Karen S. Metz. Westport, Conn., London, [Greenwood Pr., 1975]. 114p. 22cm. cloth $11.

Information Sources in Power Engineering is intended to guide engineers and librarians, managers and students, to sources of information concerning power plant engineering for the electric utility industry. Descriptions of sources are divided mainly into two types of chapters, one containing bibliographies and the other lists of organizational and institutional information sources.

Chapters in the first category include "Journals, Newsletters, Translations," "Abstracting and Indexing Services," "Textbooks," "Bibliographies," and "Reference Sources." There is considerable duplication of titles, suggesting faulty organization of data as well as a scarcity of sources specifically applicable to power engineering.

The chapter "Journals, Newsletters, Translations" is an annotated list of 74 publications which offer reports of original research, statistical data, product guides, or patent announcements. Although the main thrust of the book is power engineering, titles concerning energy resources and environmental impact are included because the author believes these topics relate to the production and distribution of energy. The list of titles is balanced in favor of petroleum products with relatively few items dealing with coal, even though this fuel accounts for about 50 percent of the fossil fuels used by the electric utility industry. Finally, trade magazines and newsletters represent a crucial source of current information on the utility industry, and some very important newsletters and magazines are omitted from the list. In the case of newsletters especially, the compiler's decision to omit information concerning price is unfortunate because newsletters are as expensive as they are important. The inclusion of full mailing addresses for these publications would also have enhanced the usefulness of the book.

"Indexing and Abstracting Services" annotates 41 periodicals covering the "engineering, nuclear, and environmental sciences related to electric energy." The chapter consists of a mixture of commonly known and out-of-the-way titles. Coverage of foreign sources is uneven and thus, of dubious value. Finally, there are only a few references directed specifically to power engineering.

The chapter titled "Textbooks" lists, in a topical arrangement without annotation, frequently cites monographs (not textbooks) related to the "generation, production and utilization of electric energy." There are not enough recent imprints, with many entries being at least 20 years old. Because selection was based largely upon frequency of citation, some timeworn and no longer serviceable titles are represented. Also, some important newer and more useful titles are omitted.

"Reference Sources" assembles and annotates directories, statistical sources, and dictionaries, as well as handbooks and other references. Again, few titles are specific to power engineering or they are so dated that their inclusion is questionable. Seventeen bibliographies are cited and annotated in a separate chapter.

A second group of chapters refers the user to agencies which are potential information sources. The chapters "Organizations," "U.S. Government Organizations," and "Information Centers, Services, and Libraries" share the second major weakness of *Information Sources in Power Engineering*. Information given is sometimes either incorrect, incomplete, or misleading. Also, there is unnecessary duplication among these chapters.

Directory information for scientific and technological associations and trade organizations is found in the chapter titled "Organizations." These organizations vary widely in their purposes and in their usefulness as information sources. The author fails to distinguish adequately between research and development organizations, lobbyists, trade and promotional organizations, and planning-coordination groups. Also, entries would be improved by adding names and telephone numbers of offices to be contacted for each type of information.

Federal regulatory agencies, monitoring groups, research agencies, and information services are listed in "U.S. Government Organizations." This chapter contains an occasional incomplete or erroneous identification. For example, a key function of the U.S. Federal Energy Administration is fuel allocation and that duty is not mentioned in the annotation. Also, the U.S. Office of Coal Research is no longer a division of the Department of the Interior but a part of the Fossil Energy Division of the Energy Research and Development Agency. Finally, some pertinent agencies involved in electric power generation are not included—Bureau of Reclamation is an example.

State agencies are not touched upon at all, and discussion of them would have been pertinent in this book.

"Information Centers, Services, and Libraries" describes agencies of government, professional, and trade organizations which offer literature searches in the field of power engineering and related energy topics. This section is also flawed. In some instances, agencies have pertinent data systems which are not mentioned in annotations, and listings for the government laboratories which are part of the U.S. Energy Research and Development Agency are incomplete. Furthermore, the failure to indicate possible charges in this section is misleading because some of the agencies described operate as contract researchers —and they charge substantial fees for their work.

Information Sources in Power Engineering contains an Index which consists mostly of names of agencies and organizations. It includes very few subject entries. Therefore, the guide can best be used by turning directly to the appropriate chapters.

Information Sources in Power Engineering purports to be a guide to information sources concerning power plant engineering for the electric utility industry and to related general energy resources. The volume is unsuccessful as a reference tool because of its insufficient and superficial representation of the literature of power engineering, its inadequate and out-of-date information, and its inefficient organization.

(Apr. 1, 1977, p.1197)

016.6214   Power resources—Bibliography || Power (Mechanics)—Bibliography || Power resources—Information services—Directories || Power (Mechanics)—Information services—Directories   [CIP]   75-32096

Interlibrary Users Association journal holdings in the Washington-Baltimore area, 1977.
[Edited by] Nannette McCarthy Pope. 2d ed. Rockville, Md., Sigma Data Computing Corp., 1977 [xxxx], 660p. 28cm. paper $135.

This union list was established in 1964–65 by the Johns Hopkins University Applied Physics Laboratory Library and in its initial version showed the holdings of only six libraries. By 1976, membership of the Interlibrary Users Association had increased to 65 institutions, and it was decided to prepare a publication for sale to non-members. The 1976 edition, also produced by Sigma Data, covered 7,500 titles; the 1977 edition includes approximately 10,500 journal titles.

An editing committee of volunteers from the association's membership verified all titles, using *New Serial Titles, Union List of Serials,* and *Ulrich's International Periodicals Directory*. Similar titles are differentiated by use of beginning dates, city of origin, or issuing agency. Where necessary, acronyms and initialisms have been spelled out for clarification.

The Foreword explains that latest and successive titles are both used with the option of form designation being left to the discretion of individual libraries. Whenever possible, dates are inserted ahead of superseded titles to show a complete title history; successive titles follow superseded titles. Letters *F* (for former title) and *C* (for current title) are used in giving a title history.

The majority of the 65 member units represented are special and federal government libraries such as the Energy Research and Development Administration and the National Bureau of Standards libraries. Also included are two branches of the University of Maryland library system and two county public libraries (Montgomery and Howard). Most titles in this union list are journals in the fields of science, technology, and social science.

A Directory of Participating Libraries provides the mailing address, telephone numbers, librarian in charge and interlibrary loan specialist, hours of service, interlibrary loan policy, subject strengths, and some general comments.

Since the Washington-Baltimore region is particularly rich in library resources, this tool could prove useful as a supplement to other union lists for libraries heavily dependent upon interlibrary loan for journal articles.   *(July 15, 1977, p.1756)*

†016.050   Periodicals—Bibliography—Union lists || Libraries—Washington-Baltimore Region—Directories || Inter-library loans—Washington-Baltimore Region   76-52599

The international antiques yearbook, 1976.
London, Antiques Yearbooks, [c1976]. distributed in the U.S. by Hearst Books, 250 West 55th St., New York 10019. 918p. illus. part col. 19cm. paper over boards $20.

The title is somewhat of a misnomer as the *Antiques Yearbook* is in essence an annual directory of antique *dealers* in 13 European countries, the U.S., Canada, Israel, South Africa, Australia, and Japan. Dealers are listed alphabetically by town within each country. (For English-speaking countries the arrangement is by town within province or state).

No criteria are given for dealer selection, and directory data for the U.S. are very incomplete. Only one dealer is listed for Hallowell, Maine, a town which has become recognized as the antiques center of the state because of the large number of dealers located there. The inclusion of only 36 dealers for the entire state of Vermont, which is heavily populated with antique shops, is further indication of the spottiness of American representation. The comparatively extensive listings for major European cities lead the Committee to suspect that coverage of that area may be more comprehensive. The editors point out, however, that the listings for Great Britain are limited to dealers especially interested in overseas trade and refer the user to *The British Antiques Yearbook* for a more exhaustive survey of British dealers.

Entries include the dealer's name and address, telephone number, and, in many cases, hours of business. (The last point of information is not included for American dealers, however, although a note identified dealers open only by appointment). Specialties are listed for many but not all entries, tending to be included most frequently for European dealers.

Following the dealer listings for each country are sections including packers and shippers, and auctioneers and salesrooms. The volume concludes with listings of antique dealers' associations, antique and art periodicals, international antiques fairs, and a Specialists Index in which dealers included in the yearbook are grouped by country according to their specialties. The first 40 pages of the book are devoted to color advertisements and dealer advertisements are numerous throughout the volume.

Most dealers and collectors who need the information provided in the Yearbook are likely to purchase their own copies. Few libraries will require the information contained in the dealer listings, and the coverage of antiques dealers' associations and antique and art periodicals is, for the most part available elsewhere. *(Dec. 15, 1976, p.630)*

†745.1'05 Antique dealers—Directories

International bibliography of Jewish affairs 1966–1967:
a select list of books and articles published in the Diaspora. Compiled and edited by Elizabeth E. Eppler. New York, Holmes & Meier Publishers, Inc., [1976]. ix, 401p. 24cm. cloth $22.

Dr. Elizabeth Eppler is the archivist of the World Jewish Congress and librarian and senior research officer at the Institute of Jewish Affairs (London). She has created this selective list to aid research on historical, social, political, and cultural aspects of Jewish life and on relationships between Jews and non-Jews. It is the first in a projected series of retrospective bibliographies which will bring together primary or secondary source information from relevant academic disciplines and areas of public life. Since the *Bibliography* is one of the new projects of the Institute of Jewish Affairs which was transferred to London in 1966, it begins with the period 1966–1967. Biennial volumes are planned for 1968–69, 1970–71, and later years.

The volume is divided into two parts, 1966 and 1967. Within each part, books and articles are arranged alphabetically by author (by title, if the author is anonymous or unidentifiable) within various subject categories. The categories under which information has been gathered include Reference; Biography, Autobiography, and Letters; Society; Science and Scientists; Literature; Yiddish; Hebrew; Jews and Gentiles; Zionism; Israel; Middle East Conflict; The Holocaust; Individual Jewish Community; Legal Problems; Political Problems, Parties, and Movements; Jewish Attitude to Peace; Migration and Refugees; Nationalism; National Minorities; Anti-Semitism; the Arts; and Folklore. Only nonfiction works published outside of Israel and that may be important to researchers are identified. Fiction, drama, and poetry (with some exceptions, such as historical novels or plays on the Holocaust) and works of a purely religious or theological nature have been excluded. Important journals (Jewish and non-Jewish) as well as popular magazines from five continents and both in English and other languages, were consulted to form a bibliography that is truly international. The items deal with history, social and political science and the arts. Both non-Jewish as well as Jewish intellectuals (fron Daniel Moynihan to David Ben Gurion) are represented. The annotations are descriptive rather than evaluative, and where the title indicates the subject, no further commentary is given. Foreign titles in Hebrew, Yiddish, Arabic, Greek, and Russian are translated or transliterated as appropriate. Access is facilitated by name and subject indexes. The cross-references are almost invariably correct. Although the bibliography does not exhaust the range of information on Jewish affairs it gives a focus to this current international topic. It will be interesting to see how succeeding volumes solve the problem of selecting and integrating the prodigious amount of material generated by the Middle East conflict and other recent developments within the much-debated and volatile domain of "Jewish affairs."
(Sept. 15, 1976, p.204)

016.910'039 Jews—Bibliography [CIP]   74-84654

The international butterfly book.
By Paul Smart. New York, T. Y. Crowell, [1975]. 275p. illus. (part col.) 31cm. cloth $19.95.

A fellow of the Royal Entomological Society of London with a life-long enthusiasm for butterflies has written a readable account of their life cycles, environment, mobility, genetics, coloration, and mimicry, with added chapters on famous books and collectors of the past. Also given are instructions for collecting, breeding, and rearing.

The illustrations are outstanding, consisting of over 100 color photographs of living insects in their natural surroundings, plus 61 double-page colorplates showing more than 2,000 specimens, most of them from the collections at the Saruman Museum with which the author is connected. All are life-size photographs.

There is also a systematic list followed by an index which includes all species illustrated or mentioned in the general text. Since the index cites only page locations, the look-up operation can be tedious. This is because many plates contain 30 or more specimens not always arranged in numerical order on the page.

In its contents, this work resembles H. L. Lewis' *Butterflies of the World* (London: Harrap, 1974), which is recognized as one of the more useful recent sources in identification of lepidoptera. Notwithstanding the Index, *The International Butterfly Book* is a very handsome and informative guide.
(Sept. 1, 1976, p.56)

595.7'89 Butterflies || Butterflies—Pictorial works [OCLC]   75-15479

International congress calendar, 1976.
16th ed. [Brussels, Union of International Associations, c1976]. 332p. illus. 30cm. paper $23.

The *International Congress Calendar* is a selective listing of "international congresses, conferences, meetings, symposia sponsored or organized by international organizations or important national bodies in 1976 and subsequent years." No criteria for inclusion are stated in the book, and listings are quite erratic. Book fairs seem not to be cited, and listings for publishing meetings are few. While some association meetings are noted for consecutive years 1976 through 1980, other meetings already scheduled as to time and place for those five years have only the 1976 meeting cited.

The typographical and grammatical errors on the title page lead the Committee to suspect the existence of other lapses in mechanical editing. Useful information located in one of the two major sections may be buried in the book because it is not cross-referenced in the other section or represented in the Indexes. The book's arrangement is satisfactory if the user can trust any section to be comprehensive. One main section is a chronological listing by month and day. The other is a geographical listing by continent, country, and city. There are an Analytical Index, which gives a subject approach to meetings, and two International Associations Title Indexes (the latter for "last minute" entrants). However, the Index terms lack precision. While the Index reference *library, special* 76 Jun 6–10 (Denver) is an unequivocal reference to this year's Special Library Association convention, the Index listing *library, education* 76 Jul 16–24 (Chicago) is surprising as the reference to the 1976 American Library Association. The *International Congress Calendar* must be used with caution and perseverance. For the patient and wary user, it will yield date, place, address of orga-

nizing body, theme, estimated attendance, number of countries represented, and information for many national and international gatherings. *(Sept. 1, 1976, p.56)*
060.58 Congresses and conventions—Directories [OCLC] 60-1648

International film guide 1976.
Ed. by Peter Cowie; associate ed., Derek Elley; television ed., David Wilson. London, The Tantivy Pr.; South Brunswick & New York, A. S. Barnes [1976]. 608p. illus. ports. 17cm. paper $4.95; to schools and libraries, 10 percent discount.

At its low price, users of the *International Film Guide* can tolerate the many advertisements interspersed with the text and the tight binding and inadeqaute inner margins, because the 1976 *Guide* is loaded with facts on films in 50 countries. Features include biographies and filmographies of five directors of the year (Michael Cacoyannis, John Cassavetes, Francis Ford Coppola, Rainer Werner Fassbinder, and Krzysztof Zanussi), a selected list of film festivals occurring in 1976, lists of Academy Awards for 1975 and films that can be used for educational purposes with young people, descriptions of U.S. nontheatrical films, citations for film archives, schools, bookshops, book reviews, and magazines. There is no index, but the Guide to Contents aids in locating general information. Published annually since 1964, the *International Film Guide* will be useful as a source of current information on documentaries, television films, and motion pictures of the year. *(Sept. 1, 1976, p.57)*
791.43058 Moving-pictures—Yearbooks [OCLC] 64-1076

International guide to library, archival, and information science associations.
[By] Josephine Riss Fang and Alice H. Songe. New York, Bowker, 1976. 354p. 24cm. cloth, $15 plus shipping and handling.

The *International Guide to Library, Archival, and Information Science Associations* is a directory of 361 nonprofit associations related to librarianship, documentation, information science, and archives located in 101 countries. The terms "library association" and "library and information science" are defined in the broadest sense. The associations may be either of a general nature or specialized by subject, type of library, and staff, etc. Included are 44 international library associations (organizations which include two or more countries), and 317 national library associations (those open to all qualified members of one country and not covering only certain districts, provinces, or regions). Associations concerned primarily with information policy or indexing techniques and commercially supported organizations are omitted.

The *Guide* was prepared by Josephine Riss Fang, Professor, Simmons School of Library Science, and Alice H. Songe, Reference Librarian, United States National Institute of Education. It is a revision and enlargement of a preliminary edition *The Handbook of National and International Library Associations* (Chicago: American Library Association, 1973). The authors state that it is based upon an extensive literature search, primarily covering the years 1965–1975, and on direct written or personal contact with the organizations themselves.

The following information is noted for each association: name, acronym for and English translation of name, address, executive officers, number of paid and voluntary staff, languages used, major fields of interest, date and place of establishment, organizational aims, structure, finances, membership information (number, types, and requirements of members), association conferences, publications, and activities. Brief bibliographies of articles containing background information on individual associations are appended to most of the entries. There are also a number of special features: a list of acronyms, a list of official journals of library associations mentioned in the text, some aggregate summaries of association activities (e.g., the number and percentage affiliated with the International Federation of Library Associations and number and percentage involved in library legislation), a general bibliography of 121 items dealing with professional library associations published between 1965 and 1975, and an alphabetic list of the 25 countries in which the 44 international library associations are currently located.

The text is arranged in two major sections: International Library, Archival and Information Science Associations and National Library, Archival, and Information Science Associations. There are separate indexes for the chief officers of national and international associations, broad subject areas of concern, official names of library associations, and countries for which information is given.

This directory will be most useful for persons studying trends in comparative librarianship. Academic and larger public libraries may also wish to acquire this new guide.
(Oct. 15, 1976, p.345)
020'.6 Library Associations—Directories || Information science—Societies, etc.—Directories || Archives—Societies, etc.—Directories [CIP] 76-2700

Jane's dictionary of military terms.
Compiled by P.H.C. Hayward. London, Macdonald and Jane's, [c1975]; dist. by Hippocrene Books. 200p. 22cm. cloth $11.95; to schools and libraries, $9.56.
†355.003 Military art and science—Dictionaries

Jane's dictionary of naval terms.
Compiled by Joseph Palmer. London, Macdonald and Jane's, [c1975]; dist. by Hippocrene Books. 342p. 22cm. cloth $11.95; to schools and libraries, $9.56.
†359.003 Naval art and science—Dictionaries

These two dictionaries form part of a trilogy commissioned by the publishers. The third is *Jane's Dictionary of Aerospace Terms,* not included in this review. Both books have been compiled by seemingly well-qualified individuals with some evidence of cooperation. The dictionary of naval terms is considerably larger than its companion, because the latter excludes military words unused since 1900. The disparity in size is further increased because the *Dictionary of Naval Terms* also includes general maritime words and terms of general use in the U.S. Navy, in addition to vocabulary employed by the Royal Navy.

It does seem peculiar that no effort has been made to provide a one-volume dictionary of general military terms to cover all of the armed services in at least the U.S. and United Kingdom, if not all of the English-speaking countries.

Both of these dictionaries, however, do include NATO terms and acknowledge the need for standardization of words and word-meanings growing out of the close cooperation between the British and U.S. services.

The Reference and Subscription Books Review Committee compared the dictionaries with the *Dictionary of United States Army Terms* (AR 310-25) and *Dictionary of Military and Associated Terms* (Joint Chiefs of Staff Publication 1). The conclusion was that a joint dictionary would be useful because of the many overlapping definitions. Even the two Jane's dictionaries include similar definitions. The military dictionary describes *acknowledgement* as "a message from the addressee informing the organization that his communication has been received and understood." The naval dictionary defines the same term as a "report that message has been received and understood." The word *muster,* on the other hand, is not defined in the military dictionary. The user is referred instead to the word "roll," but the definition given in the naval dictionary is the only one that is satisfactory.

Both dictionaries carry appendixes consisting of abbreviations used in the respective branches of service. The military dictionary, however, carries two additional appendixes including "National Distinguishing Letters" of NATO and SEATO participants and "The Order of Procedure of Corps and Regiments of the Regular Army."

Those libraries desiring to have more than strictly British dictionaries on their shelves should consider the aforementioned publications of the U.S. services which seem to be broader in scope. Available as documents from the U.S. Government Printing Office, they tend to be more expansive in their coverage of British and NATO terms and also include those of the SEATO and CENTO countries. Most U.S. libraries are likely to find little use for either *Jane's Dictionary of Military Terms* or *Jane's Dictionary of Naval Terms.* *(June 15, 1977, p.1604)*

The Kansas home cook-book.
Compiled by Mrs. C. H. Cushing and Mrs. B. Gray. New York, Arno Pr., 1973. xvi, 317p. 22cm. cloth $9.
641.5 Cookery, American—Kansas [CIP] 72-9792
See page 116

Keywords:
a vocabulary of culture and society. [By] Raymond Williams. New York, Oxford Univ. Pr., 1976. 286p. 21cm. cloth $10.95; paper $3.50.

In *Keywords* Raymond Williams, professor of drama, Cambridge University, traces the social and literary history of more than 100 words in English. Such words as *alienation, bourgeois, existential, pragmatic,* and *wealth* are traced through the processes of alteration, redefinition, modification, and confusion in essays of from one page for *genetic* to three pages for *evolution.* Arrangement of the book is alphabetical. A Table of Contents lists all the keywords which are discussed. For further reference a selected Bibliography of such works as *The Cambridge Bibliography of English Literature,* the *Oxford English Dictionary,* and the 1934 *Webster's Dictionary* is appended. Writers, scholars, and others concerned with the interaction between the changed meanings of words will find *Keywords* current and informative. *(Sept. 1, 1976, p.57)*
†422 English language—Semantics || English language—Glossaries, vocabularies, etc. [OCLC] 75-39578

Kings, rulers and statesmen.
Compiled and edited by Edward W. Egan, Constance B. Hintz, and L. F. Wise. New York, Sterling, [c1976]. 512p. illus. 24cm. impregnated cloth $20; to schools and libraries, $16.79.

Kings, Rulers and Statesmen, an "enormously expanded" version of a 1967 work, contains chronologies of the rulers of political units from ancient to modern times, including extinct nations and newly born ones. In addition it provides biographical information on many of the entries, and supplemental information is frequently inserted to explain the origins, demise, or a hiatus in the existence of a state. According to the publisher, "this volume which contains the most complete listing of kings, rulers and statesmen ever brought together under one cover, is intended to serve the student and researcher by furnishing a starting point and guide to provide the general reader with information enabling him quickly to find the place of a given historical personage in the chronology of his country."

The new revision was compiled under the editorial direction of Edward W. Egan, L. F. Wise, and Constance B. Hintz; Egan and Wise were also involved with the two earlier editions. Egan has served in the State Department, worked as a free-lance writer, and since 1967 has been a reference book editor for Sterling Publishing Company. He has compiled a number of picture works on France, Italy, Belgium and Luxemburg, Ceylon, Brazil, and Argentina and has written *The Dolphin: Cousin to Man* (New York: Sterling, 1968). No information on his colleagues was found in standard biographical sources. In this latest revision of the handbook, as in its predecessors, acknowledgments include a large number of embassies, consulates, information agencies of foreign countries, museums, and galleries consulted for both information and illustrations.

Kings, Rulers and Statesmen has been increased by more than 20 percent since its first publication. This expansion is due principally to the addition of much new biographical information on previously listed rulers and also to the inclusion of new countries formed during the last eight years. In addition, there is expanded coverage of defunct states which have been absorbed into single modern political entities. The duchy of Anjou listed under France is an example.

The arrangement of the present work remains the same as in previous editions. States appear in alphabetical order followed by the names of rulers arranged chronologically and where appropriate under dynastic name. The name of each state appears in bold italic print and is followed by a note on its origin. "Headings at the top and bottom of pages are designed to alert the reader to the point within the alphabetical order contained within each two-page spread." Typically, the official heads of state are followed by the general section "Statesmen", which frequently contains the premiers or prime ministers who hold the real political power. Because of fluctuations in the focus of real power during the past 300 years, particularly in Europe, this arrangement can be deceptive. Emperors and chancellors, kings and presidents, prime ministers and other titular figures have varied so much in their relative influence on governmental affairs that the "head of state"–"statesman" dichotomy has become meaningless, only a nominal distinction. Readers with slight knowledge of history could easily be misled by the arrangement. Another difficulty with respect to any of the statesmen sections is that the contents are not clearly defined. The section may contain a first minister such as Richelieu of France, a head of treasury such as Hamilton of the U.S. or Colbert of France, or a prime minister such as Nasser of Egypt who also served as president.

The usefulness and appeal of the work have increased because of the inclusion of more biographical information for major personages. Biographical sketches usually run only two or three lines with a very few extending to half a page. Comments on the rulers and other dignitaries range from brief discussions of political significance down to mere anecdotes. Much of this information is available elsewhere. *Webster's Biographical Dictionary* and William L. Langer's *An Encyclopedia of World History* each contain background data on about half of the individuals represented in *Kings, Rulers and Statesmen.* Moreover, representation does not seem even-handed because Western nations receive the most detailed attention. All the kings and rulers of Great Britain, France, and Egypt from ancient times are included, while only dynasty names or partial lists of emperors are cited for pre-1644 China.

As partial compensation for the absence of an index, defunct and subordinate political units "along with the names of dynasties and historical periods are listed in the contents, and some are also cross-referenced in the main alphabetical sequence .... For convenience, the following are also cross-referenced: former names of countries, e.g., *Siam, see Thailand;* geographical terms for areas formerly composed of many small states not well known to the average reader, e.g., Asia Minor, and countries where there is a geographical link but not a clear historical and cultural link, e.g., *Mauretania, see Morocco.*"

Regrettably the Table of Contents does not suffice in place of an index because of its inconsistent provision of entries for dynasties. There is also no easy access to personal names. The searcher who does not know that Temujin was Genghis Khan or that Charles V, the Holy Roman emperor, was also Charles I of Spain, may never find the object of his investigation. The lack of cross-references between members of royal families or from all political subdivisions of states to major headings of states further detracts from the work's usefulness. As a case in point, one is referred to the USSR from Georgia but not to Germany from Baden.

Only a few pictures have been added to the "more than 400 illustrations" of the 1967 edition. The illustrations are often pictures of rulers on stamps and coins or works of art. For modern leaders photographs are usually used. Pictures of landmarks such as the Mosque of Oman also appear. The library binding is durable but tight, requiring that it be "broken in."

In summary, this chronology of world leaders has appeal mainly because of its generous inclusion of dates, intermittently useful annotations, and arresting photographs. Despite its arbitrary arrangement, lack of index, and Western emphasis, high school media centers and public libraries may find *Kings, Rulers and Statesmen* a handy compendium to add to their collections.

(June 1, 1977, p.1527)

†923.1   Kings and rulers   [OCLC]   67-16020

Large type books in print, 1976:
subject index, title index, author index. New York & London, R. R. Bowker Co., c1976. 455, 12p. 28cm. cloth $14.95 plus shipping and handling.

Since Bowker published the first edition of *Large Type Books in Print* in 1970, the number of publishers of such books has increased from 30 to 58, and the number of titles cited has grown from 1,200 to 2,552. This second edition of *Large Type Books* intends "to inform librarians, teachers, and individual readers about the large type materials currently available and where they may be obtained." The book is printed in 18 point type so that persons who cannot read normal size print can use it independently to select titles. The books listed were selected by Bowker staff from 44 catalogs of publishers of large type books. *Large Type Books* aims to list all books produced in 14 point or larger print for persons with varying degrees of visual impairment. The type size of each book is included in its citation.

Large Type Books in Print is made up of three indexes: Subject, Author, and Title. The main index is the Subject Index. It is organized in two categories: General Reading and Textbooks. The general books include books of fiction, general nonfiction, home economics, literature, reference, and religion. Textbooks are listed for business, English language arts, foreign language arts, health and hygiene, home economics, literature, mathematics, music and art, science, social studies, and tests. The Subject Index gives complete bibliographic data for each title: title, series (if any), author, coauthor, translator, illustrator, grade, year of publication, binding, type size, book size, price, ISBN, place of publication, and publisher. The Author and Title Indexes refer to the proper page in the Subject Index where complete information is located. The directory of publishers will be particularly helpful for those who wish to order books. Publishers who print in large type only on demand when books are ordered are cited in the directory with an asterisk to distinguish them, but their titles are not listed in the main body of the book.

Large Type Books in Print is well designed and convenient to use. The new edition will be a tremendous timesaver for those who are limited to books in large type. The Committee hopes that Bowker will revise it frequently. *(Apr. 1, 1977, p.1197)*

†099.016   Bibliography—Editions || Legibility (Printing)—Bibliography   74-102773

Larousse dictionary of wines of the world.
[By] Gérard Debuigne. New York, Larousse & Co., Inc., [1976]. 272p. col. illus. maps. 27cm. linson $14.95.

This is an English translation of the somewhat dated *Larousse des Vins* (1970), which was itself basically a reissue of an earlier work *Dictionnaire des Vins* (1969). The translation is quite clear and also very faithful to the original text. The book is an alphabetically arranged dictionary, with tables at the end giving the Bordeaux Classification, the Climats of Burgundy, VDSQ and AOC wines, and a list of good and great French vintages updated to 1974. There is no index, but the articles contain many *see* references. Entries vary in length from a few lines to several pages and cover wines, vineyards, regions, and the terminology of the wine trade. The emphasis is decidedly French with more than 90 percent of the coverage devoted to French terms and wines. By comparison, Germany is summed up in a handful of entries, usually for large regions. Terms, such as *Qualitätswein* and *Auslese*, and towns and vineyards, such as Piesport and the famous Schloss Vollrads, are not given separate entries. The U.S. has five entries and Canada only one. Even finding an entry may require a knowledge of French—for example, there are entries under *sec* (dry) and *pourriture gris* (grey rot) with no *see* reference from "dry" and "grey rot." Once an entry has been found, the information given is accurate, informative, and reasonably complete. The single outstanding feature of the book, however, is the quality of the illustrations. Every page has at least one full-color illustration and often more. These reproductions of labels, maps, and photographs are not only relevant to the text but also make browsing through the book a genuine pleasure.

The *Larousse Dictionary of Wines of the World* is, despite its shortcomings, a valuable reference work. It belongs on the shelves of most medium and large-size public libraries.

(Apr. 15, 1977, p.1297)

†641.22   Wine and wine-making   75-44852

A library of literary criticism: modern American literature.
v. IV, supplement to the fourth ed. Compiled and edited by Dorothy Nyren, Maurice Kramer, and Elaine Fialka Kramer. New York, Ungar, [1976]. xiii, 605p. 24cm. pyroxylin buckram over binder's board $25; to schools (classrooms), 20 percent discount; to libraries, 15 percent discount.

This volume supplements the fourth edition (1969) of the reference classic whose first edition appeared in 1960. The editors remain the same: Dorothy Nyren, chief of Brooklyn's central public library; academician Maurice Kramer, professor of English at Brooklyn College; and former teacher and editor, Elaine Fialka Kramer. This supplement, using the same format as the parent edition, adds 49 new writers to the 1969 list and updates approximately one-half of its 300 entries.

Many of the standard features found in the parent volumes have been incorporated into the supplement. Between five and ten paragraphs of signed and fully cited criticism accompany each author; these are usually selected from book reviews and may also include commentary extracted from scholarly journals and books. A special effort has been made to use representative British criticism reflecting, according to the editors, "the increasing prestige of and interest in American literature among English critics and readers." A separate bibliography listing the major books and plays of each author and an index to the critics quoted in the main text conclude the work.

This sturdily bound and handsomely produced volume will be a welcome addition to those public and academic libraries owning the core edition. *(Mar. 1, 1977, p.1039)*

810.9'005   American literature—20th century—History and criticism || Criticism—U.S.   [CIP]   76-76599

Literary research guide:
an evaluative, annotated bibliography of important reference books and periodicals on American and English literature, of the most useful sources for research in other national literatures, and of more than 300 reference books in literature-related subject areas. Ed. by Margaret C. Patterson, Detroit, Gale, 1976. xlii, 385p. 22cm. cloth $18.50.

This handy and enterprising little volume purports to provide the kind of bibliography described in its title. The author also includes pointers on where to look first, how to proceed, and what to do to assure a logical sequence in one's search strategy. Limited in both size and scope, this desk reference is characterized by its author as being "a unique starting point for independent literary research."

No information was to be found in conventional reference sources on Margaret C. Patterson other than confirmation of her status as faculty member, Department of English, University of Florida.

The book is intended for use either as a basic guide to key reference works and periodicals relevant to research in English, American, and general foreign-language literatures or as a practical guide for library school students. On a much smaller scale, it has format elements in common with both *Reader's Adviser* and *Winchell*. Although many references commonly used by experienced researchers have been excluded, Patterson has succeeded in creating a compact and reasonably well-arranged inventory of annotated sources. The author intends that her work will also function as a teaching tool. In the introduction, she points out that "readers will grasp quickly the facts about each of the books discussed here. But the long-term, more elusive goal is to encourage the habit of inquiry and the wisdom of perspective." Included in this preliminary section is a four-page outline of strategy to be employed by a literary researcher looking for information on Lord Byron, the English poet.

The main body of the book is comprised of 18 chapters of annotated bibliographies. Chapters *A* through *H* include "General Guides," "National Literatures," "Bibliographies of Bibliographies," "Annual Bibliographies," "Monthly Bibliographies," "Abstracting Services," "Indexing Services," "Genre Search"; chapters *J* to *S* are devoted to English, Irish, Scottish, Welsh, Commonwealth, American, Continental, Comparative, and World Literatures. English and American literatures receive the most entries, over 350 and 125 respectively; Commonwealth and Scottish literatures have the least with only 3 and 6 entries each. Chapters are subdivided whenever multiple topics are described under one heading. Copious cross-references, following after single and grouped entries, expedite access to relevant coverage elsewhere in the volume.

Chapter *T* describes about 350 titles in subject or problem areas of interest to literary researchers. Items are included under the headings Abbreviations and Acronyms, Abel Plan, Addresses, Anonymous Literature and Pseudonyms, Art, . . . Textual Criticism, Translations, and Works in Progress. Some of the citations in this chapter seem arbitrary. Under the heading Dictionaries, one finds only the *Oxford English Dictionary, Barnhart Dictionary of New English since 1963,* and *Webster's New Collegiate Dictionary.* Excluded are the more likely *Webster's New International Dictionary* (2d ed.), *Webster's Third New International Dictionary, Random House,* and *American Heritage* dictionaries. The *New Encyclopaedia Britannica* is the lone item under the heading Encyclopedias. Elsewhere it is suggested that one look in *Current Biography* for persons who have made the headlines since 1940. *The New York Times Biographical Edition* and *Biography News* are not mentioned. However, the three periodicals suggested under Psychology seem particularly apropos. They are *Literature and Psychology, American Imago,* and *Psychoanalytic Review.*

The annotations are inconsistent in quality and size. They are in turn brief and perfunctory, lengthy and rhapsodic, straightforward, or facetious. Some of the information is not current. For example, *Book of the States* and *Municipal Yearbook,* now published in Lexington, Kentucky, and Washington, D.C. respectively, are both listed as being published in Chicago.

All bibliographical entries are sequentially numbered. For example, *The Year's Work in English Studies* is assigned the identification code D63; the last entry in the *P* chapter, "American Writers: A Collection of Literary Biographies," is P890; and the first entry in the next chapter, "The Continental Novel: A Checklist of Criticism in English, 1900–66," is Q900. This system expedites consultation because index references are to the item numbers rather than to less precise page locations. A Short-Title Table of Contents lists the guide's divisions and titles which they include. A commentary on the Dewey Decimal and Library of Congress literature classifications, Glossary of Bibliographical Terms, and analytical Index conclude the book. The guide is durably bound, and its pages lie flat when open. The print is small but legible.

Literary Research Guide is a convenient handbook of value to the postsecondary student doing literary research. Academic and library school libraries may find it a useful supplementary reference. *(Sept. 1, 1976, p.57)*

016.0168   Literature—Bibliography || Reference books—Literature   [CIP]   75-13925

The London stage, 1890–1899:
a calendar of plays ad players. By J. P. Wearing. 2v. Metuchen, N.J., Scarecrow, 1976. 1229p. 23cm. cloth $42.50.

The London Stage, 1890–1899 is a work intended for the specialized user with a strong interest in London theatrical production during the last decade of the nineteenth century. It will be of value to the researcher who needs detailed information from this ten-year period.

The compiler, an assistant professor in the Department of English at the University of Arizona, has constructed a comprehensive calendar of 3,025 London theatrical productions covering the years 1890 through 1899. The work has been announced as the first unit of a series which will provide, year by year, a daily listing of London stage plays and players from 1890 to the present. It is similar in arrangement, content, and purpose to the 11-volume work, *London Stage 1660–1800,* published under various editors by the Southern Illinois University Press between 1960 and 1968.

Working from first-night playbills, Wearing provides not only the varying play titles and actors associated with each play but also supplies the author, genre, number of acts, name of theater, dates and length of run, production staff members, and references to reviews. With occasional exceptions, amateur performances are omitted. Details of adaptation and translation, names of all theaters used for one production, and days when performances were not held are indicated. A key to abbreviations used in the entries is included in the front of the first volume.

Each entry is presented in one paragraph which may run as long as 40 or more lines. The entries are adequately separated from each other, but lengthy entries may require careful reading to locate a desired name. Entries are not justified along the right-hand edge, but the uneven line is not distracting.

Following the ten-year calendar is a 376-page Index. The Index, which makes up more than half of volume II, includes entries for all of the information in the calendar except the names of characters and citations of play reviews. Birth and death dates are occasionally supplied for personal names.

The covers and binding are sturdy, and the paper is opaque, nonglare stock. The narrowness of some of the inner margins is a minor defect because rebinding will probably not be required.

The London Stage, 1890–1899 is a specialized work. It will be little used by readers in the average U.S. library but would be a logical acquisition for any institution seeking to build a comprehensive, scholarly performing arts collection.
(Feb. 15, 1977, p.925)

792'.09421'2   Theater—England—London—Calendars   [CIP]   76-1825

Manuscripts guide to collections at the

University of Illinois at Urbana-Champaign.
[By] Maynard J. Brichford, Robert M. Sutton, [and] Dennis F. Walle. Urbana, Chicago, London, University of Illinois Pr., [1976]. 384p. 29cm. cloth, $9.95.

Maynard J. Brichford, University of Illinois Archivist, Robert M. Sutton, University of Illinois history professor and Illinois Historical Survey Director, and Dennis F. Walle, Illinois Historical Survey librarian, have prepared the first comprehensive inventory of all the manuscript resources of the University of Illinois at Urbana-Champaign. Reprinted from typewritten copy, the book is divided into three separate parts: University Archives, Illinois Historical Survey Library, and Business Archives, History, Library, Rare Book Room.

Part I, University Archives, lists each item in the archives (established in 1963) with a descriptive annotation that also indicates its space displacement in cubic feet. This section includes personal papers of 268 faculty, 46 administrators, 42 students and 33 alumni, and records of 22 non-university organizations.

Part II, Illinois Historical Survey Library, lists the holdings of the library which was established in 1903 as a special reference and research library containing documents and manuscripts on the history of Illinois and the Old Northwest. The collection contains more than 7,500 books in addition to newspapers, pamphlets, brochures, maps, broadsides, term papers, posters, advertisements, and manuscripts. Descriptive annotations are a basic contribution of this part of the book, too.

Part III describes the literary manuscripts in the University library's rare book room, history library, business archives, and Mendel Collection in the natural history museum. Included in this, the shortest section of the book, are 74 rare book collections, 76 business archive collections, 3 history library collections, and 1 natural history museum collection. A comprehensive Index of persons and topics represented in Parts I through III concludes the volume. *Manuscripts Guide to Collections at the University of Illinois at Urbana-Champaign* will be valuable to researchers who have long needed a comprehensive inventory of the University's manuscript collections.

(Nov. 1, 1976, p.425)

016.9773 Illinois. University at Urbana-Champaign—Archives || Illinois—History—Sources—Bibliography || Illinois Historical Survey || Illinois. University at Urbana-Champaign. Library. Rare Book Room   [CIP]   75-38797

Maps to anywhere.
[4th ed.] Hollywood, Cal. 90028, Travel Centers of the World, P.O. Box 1673, [1976?] 190p. 28cm. paper $7.95 prepaid; $8.95 billed.

Maps to Anywhere, first published in 1974, is a sales catalog of primarily maps though it also includes atlases, guidebooks, and other general travel/tourist-related publications. The arrangement is basically alphabetical by name of map or monograph with the titles sometimes readjusted so that the geographical areas become the initial words. A five-column format presents the following information for each item: Travel Centers of the World catalog order number; name of map, atlas, or book (title possibly inverted); publisher code name; wholesale price; and suggested retail price. The last two pages of the catalog list the 110 publishers with one- or two-word assessments of the quality of their products. Represented are major cartographic firms such as Kummerley and Frey, Falk, Nagel, and Michelin.

About 75 percent of the entries are road and topographic maps, 20 percent are miscellaneous travel guides and histories, and the remaining 5 percent are atlases. Of the 3,772 numbered entries, approximately 20 percent are cross-references. Cross-references are used from names of insets to those of full maps; from geographic areas which are covered by maps or books under different titles; and for referral from unused headings, e.g., "Railroad Maps (please see name of country or area desired)." Although most of the entries are for single maps, some include separate listings for parts of series. For example, entry 571 cites 918 sheets of the Canadian 1:250 000 topographic sectional maps. It is estimated that the total representation of individual maps or monographs may exceed 5,000. The entries provide coverage for all areas of the world, from the Bronx to Budapest, and from Libreville to Peking.

The second column, which lists the name of the map, atlas, or book, can vary from the mere designation of town and country to a rather detailed description of the work. Unfortunately bibliographic data are generally inadequate. Omitted are year of publication and edition for books; scale, type, language, projection, and size for maps. Consequently it is often difficult to determine exactly what is being offered for sale. For example, entry 3069 lists only "Sosnowiec, Poland," the name of publisher and prices.

This is an order catalog with the wholesale prices quoted for libraries averaging 30 to 35 percent below suggested retail figures. Although prices are said to remain in effect until February 1, 1977, the compilers warn that they are subject to change without notice.

Examination of the catalog revealed typographical errors, inaccurate numbering of entries, a blind cross-reference, omission of a publisher's code, and minor errors in alphabetization.

The *TCW* catalog is reproduced from typescript and is reprinted on both sides of colored paper. There are occasional photographs and line drawings scattered throughout the volume. The unbound catalog is barely held together by a single staple.

The *TCW* catalog is an order catalog and is not intended as a major reference work. It is not comparable in comprehensiveness or in its provision of bibliographic data to Winch, *International Maps and Atlases in Print* (New York: Bowker, 1974). However, *Maps to Anywhere* is inexpensive and lists a wide variety of maps and travel publications available to libraries at reasonable prices. Despite its limitations, this vendor catalog may be useful for small libraries lacking map acquisitions tools, and it can supplement resources held by larger libraries.

(Jan. 1, 1977, p.686)

†070.579 Maps—Bibliographies || Atlases—Bibliographies

Mathematics dictionary.
[By Robert C. James and Edwin F. Beckenrath and others.] 4th ed. New York, Van Nostrand Reinhold, [c1976]. vii, 509p. illus. 24cm. cloth $17.95; to schools and libraries, 10 percent discount.

Intended for "students, scientists, engineers, and others concerned with the meaning of mathematical terms" and intended to be "reasonably complete in the coverage of topics frequently included in precollege or undergraduate college mathematics courses," this edition of a standard reference work—known since the first edition (1942) as "James and James"—defines nearly 8,000 terms, often with illustrations, formulas, and/or symbols. Seven of the contributors are or were affiliated with well-known California academic institutions: UCLA (five, including Glenn James, deceased, and Beckenrach), Claremont Graduate School (Robert C. James), and California Institute of Technology (Aristotle D. Michal, deceased). The eighth contributor is Homer V. Craig (Texas). Four named translators have provided vocabularies giving English equivalents of mathematical terms in French, German, Russian, and Spanish—the final portion of the book.

Mathematics Dictionary consists of two parts: the first and larger is an alphabetically arranged dictionary; the second is appendix material. In the dictionary, main headings (e.g., DATE) are printed in boldface capitals beginning at the left margin. Subheadings (after date draft, average date, dividend date, etc.) are in boldface type at paragraph indentions. Both types of headings may include other terms in boldfaced terms and *see* references. The major change in this edition is the introduction of more than 300 short biographical statements for important persons from all times. To illustrate this change, one entry in the 1968, third edition, was: "ALEXANDER, James Waddell (1888–). Alexander's subbase theorem. A topological space . . ."; in the 1976 edition the added biographical information is: "ALEXANDER, James Waddell (1881–1971). American algebraic topologist who did research in complex-variable theory, homology and ring theory, fixed points, and the theory of knots." (There is no change in the definition "Alexander's subbase theorem.") A random sampling of biographical entries disclosed death dates as recent as 1973 and 1974. The space devoted to main and subsidiary headings varies greatly, e.g., one-half page for SURFACE, more than two-and-a-half pages for subheadings; one-half page for MATHEMATICS and three subheadings.

The appendix material is in nine sections: (1) denominate numbers (i.e., measures of length, area, volume, money, etc.); (2) mathematical symbols, with eight subdivisions (e.g., arithmetic, algebra, number theory; mathematics of finance; statistics); (3) differential formulas; (4) integral tables (more than 400 integrals); (5) Greek alphabet; (6)–(9) French-English, German-English, Russian-English, Spanish-English indexes, previously mentioned.

Mathematics Dictionary, in its fourth edition, is typographically attractive, sturdy, and lies flat when open, although inner margins are quite narrow. It is suitable for its intended audiences and libraries serving them. *(May 15, 1977, p.1452)*

510.3 Mathematics—Dictionaries—Polyglot || Dictionaries, Polyglot [CIP] 76-233

Mexico especially for women.
[By] Gerie Tully. New York, Abelard-Schuman, [c1976]. xxiii, 421p. 21cm. cloth $9.95; to schools and libraries, $7.16; paper $5.95; to schools and libraries, $4.28.

This guide to Mexico, written specifically for single or unaccompanied women travelers, contains information of value to anyone visiting that country. Its eight sections are Before You Go; Mexico City; Outside Mexico City; The Independence Route (for those interested in colonial history and Old World background); The Coastal Resorts; Baja California; Juarez; and The Land of the Mayas (Villahermosa, Palenque, and the Yucatan Peninsula). Included in Part 1, Before You Go, are descriptions of major fiestas and a calendar of events, government regulations affecting tourists, a list of several hundred common Spanish phrases with English equivalents, and shopping tips. Each of the other parts contains a one- or two-page "welcome" section, except for Mexico City which provides 18 pages describing residential zones, parks, boulevards, and shopping locales. Other sections include advice on hotel accommodations: wining and dining spots (also indicate whether a companion is necessary); sightseeing; sports; and shopping. For major cities, nighttime entertainment and beauty salons (with price ranges for shampoo and set) are included. Deluxe, first-, second-, and third-class hotels are cited throughout. A helpful and accurate Index identifies entry categories within parentheses (hotel, entertainment, pottery, dentist, handicrafts, restaurant).

Without a doubt, *Mexico Especially for Women* offers reliable information and encouragement to the woman traveling alone. However, this compact and lightweight book will be welcomed by anyone anticipating a trip south of the border. *(July 1, 1977, p.1677)*

917.2'04'82 Mexico—Description and travel—1951– —Guide books. || Travelers, Women—Mexico [CIP] 75-44327

Midwestern home cookery.
Intro. and suggested recipes by Louis Szathmary. New York, Arno Pr., 1973. xxi, 178, 155p. illus. 22cm. cloth $10.

641.5 Cookery, American—Middle West [CIP] 72-9801
See page 116

Military aircraft of the world.
[By] John W. R. Taylor and Gordon Swanborough. Rev. ed. New York, Charles Scribner's Sons, [c1975]. 240p. illus. 23cm. cloth $6.95.

When the Reference and Subscription Books Review Committee reviewed *Military Aircraft* in the June 15, 1974, issue of *Reference and Subscription Books Reviews*, the Committee commended the 1973 version of the work as a well-illustrated reference tool. The present edition is updated as of 1975 and follows the organization and arrangement of its predecessors: clear identification of each airplane by name of the craft, specific descriptions of type of engine, span, length, empty and gross weight, speed, range, armament, and a summary history. Since there have been three editions of *Military Aircraft* since the first one published in 1971, only those modelmakers, aviation buffs, and libraries interested in the latest facts and figures on international military aircraft will require the updated version. The two previous editions are still valuable for historical purposes.
(Sept. 15, 1976, p.204)

623.746 Airplanes, Military [OCLC] 75-8340

Military vehicles of the world.
[By] Christopher F. Foss. New York, Scribner, [1975? 1976?]. 192p. illus. 23cm. cloth $7.95.

†623.74 Vehicles, Military 75-46380
See page 98

Missiles of the world.
rev. ed. [By] Michael J. H. Taylor and John W. R. Taylor. New York, Scribner, [c1976]. 159p. illus. 23cm. cloth $7.95.

358.17 Guided missiles [OCLC] 76-9557
See page 98

Modern collector's dolls.
By Patricia R. Smith. Third series. Paducah, Kentucky, Collector Books; distributed by Crown Publishers, New York, 1976. viii, 296p. illus. 28cm. cloth $17.95.

This profusely illustrated guide updates and augments two earlier series by the author, who is also responsible for seven other books on doll collecting. It is arranged chiefly by name of manufacturer, except in a few instances: foreign-made dolls are listed under *Foreign*, then alphabetically by 15 countries; also cloth dolls, though some of these are also under manufacturer.

Most of the dolls are shown in clear, black-and-white photographs usually two-and-one-half-by-four-inches and four to a page. A few also appear in color. Except as indicated they were contributed by the author's husband, Dwight Smith. Accompanying descriptive information includes size, date, and brief details of production, identifying marks, and retail price if bought from a dealer.

Information on individual designers and manufacturers ranges from nothing at all to reprints of Buchwald and Bombeck columns on Barbie dolls under Mattell, the manufacturer. An index to photographs and lists of revised prices for dolls in the first two series are appended. Some typographical errors give evidence of hasty editing but are not too serious since the chief reference value of this guide lies in its photographs and price quotations.
(Apr. 1, 1977, p.1198)

†745.592'203 Dolls—Collectors and collecting

Motion picture market place 1976–1977.
Tom Costner, editor. Boston, Little, Brown and Co., 1976. 458p. 24cm. paper $12.95.

Modeled after Bowker's *Literary Market Place, Motion Picture Market Place 1976–1977* lists the names, addresses, and telephone numbers "of production and equipment services and professional talent" in each state of the U.S., Puerto Rico, and the Virgin Islands under alphabetical headings such as Advertising Agencies, Aerial Services and Aircraft, Agents (Literary). The book has no index although there are cross-references in the listings. Several major headings have subheadings, (e.g., "Camera Cars and Cranes," "Repairs and Modifications," "Sales and Rentals" within "Camera Equipment"). A few of the listings have brief introductory paragraphs, such as "Major Studios," (alphabetized, by the way, in the "M's" rather than the "S's"); others provide brief descriptions for each item, e.g., "Festivals" and "Film Commissions."

The book might be useful for students and professionals who seek information about and contacts in the motion picture industry from the production viewpoint. Because of the lack of an index and the use of film jargon in the subject headings ("Stock Shots," "Screening Rooms"), the book will have most value for persons already conversant with the industry.

(Jan.1, 1977, p.686)

338.4'7   Moving picture industry—U.S.—Directories   [CIP]   76-104

Motion picture performers:
a bibliography of magazine and periodical articles, supplement no. 1, 1970–1974. By Mel Schuster. Metuchen, N.J., Scarecrow Pr., Inc., 1976. x, 783p. 23cm. cloth $27.50.

This volume is a supplement to *Motion Picture Performers: A Bibliography of Magazine and Periodical Articles, 1900–1969* "which examined material on 2,900 performers appearing in selected periodicals from 1900 through 1969." In addition to updating all performers appearing in the basic volume, the author has added material on 2,600 new performers, many of "whose involvement with the motion picture medium is very limited or even nonexistent," (e.g., television stars Carol Burnett, Jackie Gleason, and Irene Ryan). Complete runs of additional periodicals are also included.

Entries are listed alphabetically, with articles listed chronologically beneath each celebrity in standard bibliographic citations. Cross-references are given where the author thought them helpful, as with "Burns and Allen (see also: Allen, Gracie, Burns, George)." Two appendixes—a list of abbreviations, and one of publications documented—conclude the book.

This supplement would be useful to those libraries which already have the basic volume and for individuals interested in articles dealing with performers, including television and radio personalities, who have been prominent in the 1970s.

(Jan.1, 1977, p.686)

016.79143'028   Moving-picture actors and actresses—Biography—Bibliography   [CIP]
70-154300

Mrs. Porter's new southern cookery book.
[By] Mrs. M. E. Porter. New York, Arno Pr., 1973. xvi, 416p. 22cm. cloth $12.

641.5   Cookery, American—Southern States   [CIP]   72-9802

See page 116

Music titles in translation:
a checklist of musical compositions. Compiled by Julian Hogson. London, Clive Bingley: Hamden, Conn., Linnett Books, [1976]. 370p. 23cm. cloth $17.50.

The stated purpose of this volume is "to provide a ready answer to the questions raised by looking for 'Sleepers, wake' in the Breitkopf catalogue or 'Wachet auf' in the Novello catalogue." This is, of course, only one example, but it clearly illustrates the common problem faced by many who use music publishers' catalogs and also library card catalogs.

The volume consists of a list of approximately 14,000 title entries, arranged in a single alphabet, representing some 7,000 Western classical music compositions. Each entry concludes with the name of the composer. No further description of the title is provided, and opus and thematic catalog numbers are not given. For well-known works, the most common alternative language titles are given. In the example above, one can also find "Wachet auf" in English translation as "Wake, awake, for night is flying" and "Now let every tongue adore Thee." Obviously the lack of consistency in translations from other languages into English was a major challenge to the compiler. The multiplicity of English-language alternate titles could confuse the user.

In his Preface, the compiler states, "The initial article, though given first, is disregarded, but subsequent articles count for alphabetisation." Although this practice is fairly consistent for French, German, Italian and Spanish titles, some in Hungarian do not follow this plan. In the Hungarian language the two forms of the article "the" are "a" and "az." Thus, the title "A Magyarokhoz" is improperly placed and should appear in the "M" portion of the alphabet. Likewise, the titles "Az ágyam bírogat," "Az egri menes mind szurke," "Az én szerelmem," and "Az oszi lárma" should not be at the end of the "A" listings but rather, following the stated rule concerning initial articles, in the "A," "E," and "O" alphabetical listings respectively.

Although most of the entries are titles of vocal works (derived in most instances from the first lines of text), the volume contains programmatic orchestral works ("Das Lied von der Erde") and many songs with original titles ("Ah Sylvia"). The intent of the author "was to be as comprehensive as possible with this compilation," and he points out a paucity of Russian and foreign opera titles, "especially in the choruses and arias." He directs the user to the *British Music Yearbook 1975* (Bowker, 1976) for a comprehensive list of available translations of operas.

Among the many common titles missed in this compilation are the favorite arias "Avant de quitter ce lieu" (Gounod's *Faust*) and "Vogelfänger bin ich ja" (Mozart's *Magic Flute*), "Casse-Noisette" (Tchaikovsky's *Nutcracker Suite*), "Le Sacre de Printemps," and "Boeuf sur le Toit." *Betrothel in a Convent*, Prokofiev's opera, is unaccountably represented as *Betrothel in a Priory*. Titles of piano pieces such as Debussy's "Voiles" and "Boite à joujoux" are also left out.

Music Titles in Translation will have to be greatly expanded before it can become a viable reference tool. The Sears and De Charms song indexes alone include more than 20,000 titles, and thorough representation of opera arias could add another 10,000 titles. Many more thousands of titles are associated with works in other musical genres. Much enlargement and refinement of the present checklist will be required before it can serve a useful purpose in either a music or general library.

(Feb. 15, 1977, p.926)

784'.0216   Titles of musical compositions   [CIP]   75-42015

The national directory of grants and aid to individuals in the arts, international:
containing listings of most grants, prizes, and awards for professional work in the U.S. and abroad, and information about universities and schools which offer special aid to students. By Daniel Millsaps and the Editors of the Washington International Arts Letter. 3d ed. Washington, DC, 20003, Washington International Arts Letter, Box 9005, [c1976]. v, 221p. 23cm. paper $13.95.

This is the third edition of a directory which according to its editors lists "most grants, prizes, and awards for professional work in the U.S. and abroad, and information about universities and schools which offer special aid to students." The first edition came out in 1970 and contained slightly more than 1,000 entries in 75 pages; the 1972 edition (155 pages) contained many more entries plus an Index; the third updates the information in the second edition and adds more than 300 new entries. The emphasis is on awards obtainable by individuals as opposed to those available to organizations, usually from private foundations.

Arrangement is alphabetical by sponsor with *see* references from name of specific prizes to the awarding institution or organization. It follows, then, that all awards made by any one institution are listed in the entry for that institution. Each entry gives an address to which an aspiring candidate may write; basic requirements; amount of the grant or award if it is $1,000 or more, although some lesser grants are included "to emphasize the need for their increase"; and restrictions, if any. Deadlines are omitted unless they have remained the same over the years. Each entry is preceded by a symbol indicating the discipline covered by the award and whether the aid is predominantly in the profession or in education for the profession. The key to the symbols precedes the listing.

There is a 34-page Index of awarding institutions listed by discipline. If an institution has grants available in more than one discipline, it will appear in each of the appropriate sections of the index.

The book appears to be sturdy, though in paperback. Inner and outer margins are narrow, with text and symbols placed near the edge of the page so that rebinding might not be practical.

Grants and Aid to Individuals in the Arts has value for student and professional alike and deserves consideration by all libraries.

(July 15, 1977, p.1756)

†001.44 Research grants—Directories || Endowments—Directories || Humanities—Research grants 76-27114

Naval, marine and air force uniforms of World War 2.
[By] Andrew Mollo; illustrated by Malcolm McGregor. New York, Macmillan Pub. Co., Inc., [1976, c1975]. 231p. illus. 20cm. casebound linson $6.95.

Naval, Marine and Air Force Uniforms of World War 2 describes and illustrates in color more than 200 uniforms worn by Allied and Axis war personnel in 27 countries. The book is a companion volume to Mollo and McGregor's *Army Uniforms of World War 2* (London: Blandford Pr. Ltd., 1973). Coverage is selective. All uniforms are not shown, and women's auxiliaries uniforms and the dress of civil and paramilitary groups have been excluded. The uniforms are depicted three to a page. Fifty-one are shown for Great Britain and the Commonwealth, 40 for Germany, 30 for the U.S., 15 for the USSR, 12 for Japan, and 3 for Greece. The illustrations are placed between pages 26 and 109 of the descriptive text. Notes to the plates are brief, and they follow the complete text section. A Bibliography of 36 books, most of which are in English, cites the sources used. There is an alphabetical Index to illustrations by country. Military buffs and nostalgic World War II veterans will find *Naval, Marine and Air Force Uniforms* informative.

(Sept. 15, 1976, p.204)

355.1′4 Uniforms, Military—History || World War, 1939–1945 [CIP] 75-28334

The Negro almanac:
a reference work on the Afro American. Compiled and edited by Harry A. Ploski and Warren Marr. bicentennial ed. New York, The Bellwether Company, 167 E. 67th St., 1976. 1206p. illus. cloth $59.95.

The third or "bicentennial edition" of *The Negro Almanac* continues the stated intent of the first two editions: "to reflect a singular awareness of the expanding dimensions of the black cultural and social experience in the United States." The added objectives of the third edition "have been to update the scholarship of the first two editions and to substantially broaden their scope and coverage." The first (1967) and second (1971) editions were reviewed by the Reference and Subscription Books Review Committee on February 1, 1968 and March 15, 1972, respectively. For the new *Negro Almanac*, the size has been increased to accommodate more words per page, and new sections have been added on "Black Capitalism," "Blacks in Colonial and Revolutionary America," "Black Classical Musicians," and "Prominent Black Americans." The number of tables and charts is increased by 28 and 2, respectively, and the number of illustrations from 441 to 825. There are 600 new illustrations including graphs and charts. The quality of the black-and-white reproductions is good.

Harry A. Ploski, educator and psychologist, continues as compiler and editor. There are some changes in the assignments of other staff members, but their principal responsibilities remain the same. Ernest Kaiser, associate editor of the second edition, has been replaced by Warren Marr II, current editor of *The Crisis,* the official publication of the NAACP. John E. Brown and Roger P. Nelson, special projects editors of the second edition, have been replaced by Richard Rosenthal in the third edition. Michael Duke is new managing editor. Two persons have been added to the staff to provide additional graphics.

The National Urban League is credited with reading "every section of the manuscript" and making "perceptive suggestions." The Frontispiece note calls attention to this volume as "A project of the National Urban League, Inc., made possible through a grant by the Lilly Endowment."

The editors continue to update and increase the number of entries as research uncovers additional information. For example there were 44 entries through 1776 in the 1971 edition under "Chronology," and 65 entries in the 1976 edition. Between the years 1771 and 1799 the number increased from 24 in the 1971 edition to 33 in the current one. The number of "Significant Documents of Afro-American History" advanced from 41 to 44, the number of "Historic Landmarks of Black Americans" from 146 to 162.

Many sections have been redeveloped and largely rewritten. The second edition carried only a brief paragraph which summarized civil rights efforts during the twentieth century. The third edition, however, includes 18 pages of text and pictures citing the civil rights struggle from colonial times to the present day. Other changes include transfer of the Spingarn Medal winners to the Appendix and revision and expansion of topics relating to Civil Rights Organizations. Outstanding and practical features of the new edition are the six-page chart on "National Private Organizations with Civil Rights Programs" and the 20-page chart of "Federal Assistance Programs" which cites government assistance available in such categories as housing, food administration, drug abuse, health care and medical treatment, technical assistance and training, educational grants, voting rights, and public assistance. Addresses are given, contacts are cited, and there is a brief description of each program.

The section on "The Black Woman" has been enlarged from 43 sketches in the second to 64 in the third edition. Newcomers include Margaret W. Alexander, well-known writer and college administrator; Augusta Baker, retired children's library administrator; Mary Treadwell Barry, executive and co-founder of the Pride Corporation; Marian Wright Edelman, prominent attorney of Washington, D.C.; and Dorothy Porter, retired librarian of Howard University's Moorland-Spingarn Collection. Some women who more logically belong in other sections of the *Almanac* have been transferred: Sissiereta Jones, famous opera star of the last century; Constance Baker Motley, New York District Court judge; Sojouner Truth; and Harriet Ross Tubman.

"Black Classical Musicians," one of the four new sections, contains biographical notes on 35 persons. As is done elsewhere in the *Almanac,* presumably less prominent biographees are merely listed with birth and death dates.

The section on "Africa: the Changing Continent" has been changed, revised, and retitled "Africa: the Emerging Nations." The information about each nation has been updated. Angola and the Cape Verde Islands, both of which became independent in 1975, are listed. For each nation, date of independence, population, monetary unit, capital city, principal economic resource, and major language are provided. In some instances the exchange rate for U.S. dollars is quoted. A brief history of the nation up to 1975 concludes the entry.

There is a selected Bibliography section which contains listings that did not appear in the first two editions. Most publications have 1971 to 1975 imprints. The new edition divides the bibliographical listings by subjects: Biography; Culture and Society; Education; Economics; General; History; Juvenile; Literature; Political; Slavery; Africa. Under each heading the items are arranged in alphabetical order. The list was compiled by Ernest Kaiser, bibliographer of the Schomburg Collection of Negro History and Literature, New York Public Library.

The Appendix contains lists of charts, illustrations, Afro-American research resources, and Spingarn medalists. Also included are picture credits.

The Negro Almanac is a useful tool which belongs in any public, school, or academic library because it contains extensive data on blacks' history, accomplishments, and current status in the American milieu that cannot be found in any other one-volume, quick reference source. The two previous editions should be retained because much of their content has been dropped in the third edition. *(Nov. 15, 1976, p.501)*

†973 Afro-Americans—Dictionaries
75-24805

The new guide to study abroad:
summer and full-year programs for high-school students, college and university students, and teachers, 1976–1977. [By] John A. Garraty, Lily von Klemperer, Cyril J. H. Taylor; woodcuts by Gail Garraty. New York, Harper & Row, Publishers, [1976]. xii, 451p. illus. 21cm. cloth, $11.95; paper, $4.95.

John A. Garraty, Professor of History, Columbia University and Walter Adams wrote the first *Guide to Study Abroad* in 1962. In 1969 they changed the title of this useful handbook to *The New Guide to Study Abroad*. For the latest edition of the book Garraty is joined by authors Lily von Klemperer, former director of the Institution for International Education's counseling division, and Cyril J. H. Taylor, President, American Institute for Foreign Study.

The original edition described 146 typical programs of study abroad; the current edition describes more than 500 foreign study programs and includes a special chapter on teaching opportunities abroad and difficult to locate information on study in Asia, Africa, and Eastern Europe.

The book is logically arranged in five parts: Part I "Planning for Study Abroad," Part II "The College and Graduate Student Abroad," Part III "The Postsecondary and Secondary School Student Abroad," Part IV "The Teacher Abroad," and Part V "Foreign Experience Outside the Classroom." Descriptions for most schools include information on sponsorship, academic credits, language requirements, dates of the terms, costs, and source of other information. Work-study and other employment programs are described.

The New Guide to Study Abroad contains practical, up-to-date, and authoritative information on a variety of foreign study programs. High school, college and university, and public libraries will find it a comprehensive reference source.
(Nov. 1, 1976, p.426)

370.19'6   Foreign study∥Universities and colleges—Directories∥American teachers in foreign countries—Employment—Directories   [CIP]
75-23882

News dictionary 1975:
an encyclopedia summary of contemporary history. Judith Trotsky, editor. New York, Facts on File, Inc., [c1976]. 504p. 23cm. cloth $9.50; paper $5.95.

Students and others interested in current history on an annual basis will find *News Dictionary* a well-arranged and cross-referenced guide organized by subject. Information is selected from the large data base at Facts on File, Inc. The subject arrangement may be more convenient for users than the traditional chronological grouping of current events which is usually found in yearbooks and annuals. The latter arrangement separates news by date of occurrence, while *News Dictionary* synthesizes all news on a topic bringing it together (but still citing the date) under one heading. The coverage of *religion* is a case in point. The main subdivisions are Episcopal Church with three numbered paragraphs, Lutheran Church, Roman Catholic Church (five paragraphs), Anglican Church (three paragraphs), Interfaith Developments (three paragraphs), the World Council of Churches, Reform Jewish Torah Commentary . . . (two paragraphs), Black Muslim Developments (three paragraphs), and Church Membership.

The news is summarized in straightforward language. There is no evidence of editorializing bias toward particular points of view. All countries are covered, but as is to be expected in a brief chronicle published in the U.S., emphasis is given to U.S. subjects.

News Dictionary 1975 is the twelfth annual volume in a series. It is distinctive for presenting a cohesive overview of news. It can be used as a starting point leading the researcher into the more exhaustive *New York Times Index*. Public and school libraries will find *News Dictionary* commendable for its ease of use.
(Dec. 1, 1976, p.564)

†905   History—Yearbooks

NIH factbook:
guide to National Institutes of Health programs and activities. 1st ed. Chicago, Marquis Academic Media, 1976. 597p. 29cm. cloth $44.50.

In 1971, Academic Media published the first two volumes in this series, the *NASA Factbook* and *NSF Factbook*. Marquis Academic Media, now a division of Marquis Who's Who, Inc., has published second editions of the aforementioned factbooks and concurrently with them the first edition of the title under review. The first editions of both *NASA* and *NSF Factbook* were compiled by individual editors; the current volumes are apparently staff projects. All volumes published to date in the Factbook series are similar in appearance and arrangement. Each is based on the publications of the agency it describes.

NIH Factbook is divided into seven parts. "Part One: History" reviews important events (1887–1975) leading to the establishment of the 12 research institutes that comprise the NIH. Also included are biographical sketches of the key administrators of the NIH complex. Individual agencies within this group include the National Cancer Institute, the National Heart and Lung Institute, and the National Institute of Child Health and Human Development. "Part Two: Organization" includes an organization chart and information about the mission, history, administration, and program of each institute and division of the National Institutes of Health. "Part Three: Statistics" presents specific facts about total health cost and proportion of research expenditures, R & D funding in the U.S., NIH appropriations, functions of NIH funds, monies available for medical research, research grants awarded by NIH, NIH staff, facilities, and properties. "Part Four: NIH Public Advisory Groups" provides the names, terms of office, and professional affiliations of members of all advisory committees, as well as information about each committee—its authority, structure, functions, and meetings. "Part Five: Research" reviews principal contributions of NIH in various medical areas, such as bio-medical research, cancer, diseases of the eye, cardiovascular research and treatment, viruses and infectious diseases, and child health. "Part Six: Public Health Service grants and awards," the largest section with more than 200 pages, lists all U.S. Public Health Service grants for 1974 and 1973/74 and by state, city, facility, affiliation, principal investigator, and dollar amount of grant. "Part Seven: Indexes" offers two indexes, one for subjects and the other for personnel. Geographical references are included in the Subject Index.

A wealth of information is presented in this volume. Most of it consists of verbatim copies of 1975 editions of several publications of the National Institutes of Health, especially the *NIH Almanac 1975.* Since the 1976 edition of the *NIH Almanac* became available in August 1976, much of the information in *NIH Factbook* is already out of date. The *Factbook's* prime value resides in its bringing together into a single volume directory-type information on NIH personnel and grant recipients. However, this information is available as separate publications from the issuing agencies at a fraction of the cost of the *Factbook.*

Comparison of *NIH Factbook* with the *NIH Almanac 1976* reveals that since the publication of the *Factbook* there have been a number of major changes of institutional personnel, including two new secretaries of health, education, and welfare and a new director and deputy director of National Institutes of Health. In some instances, when changes occurred early enough to incorporate in the *NIH Factbook,* the editors have so indicated with a footnote.

The policy of reprinting a publication with a minimal amount of change can lead to some difficulties: one of the institutes, the National Institute of Neurological and Communicative Disorders and Stroke, underwent several name changes. When the new name appears as a heading in the *Factbook,* the name is changed. But when a name change would have required resetting a page, it has apparently been ignored. The pertinent sections of the 1976 *NIH Almanac* include these changes, and statistics are updated to 1975. In the *NIH Factbook* statistics are mostly for 1974.

The major contribution of the editors was the preparation of the two Indexes. During the process of this review, the Committee found the Indexes to be accurate. In the Subject Index there are *see also* references from superseded to current names of institutes.

The book is printed on good quality opaque paper; the type, although at times quite small, is reasonably legible. Margins are adequate for rebinding. The volume lies flat when opened.

Prospective purchasers will have to weigh the convenience of having the most important data about National Institutes of Health agencies brought together in one volume, complete with personnel and subject indexes, against the advantages of obtaining less costly and more current information directly from the separate agencies of the National Institutes of Health.
(Mar. 15, 1977, p.1121)

†610.6 Public health—U.S. || United States National Institutes of Health—Directories
75-32699

Official Eastern North America map and chart index catalog.
Neenah, Wis. 54956, Box 249, U.S./Canadian Map Service Bureau, Ltd., [c1975]. 186p. 37cm. paper $5.95.
†912.973 Maps—Bibliography || U.S.—Maps || Canada—Maps   75-37001

Official Western North America map and chart index catalog.
Neenah, Wis. 54956, Box 249, U.S./Canadian Map Service Bureau, Ltd., [c1975]. 226p. 37cm. paper $5.95.
†912.973 Maps—Bibliography || U.S.—Maps || Canada—Maps   75-37001

The *Map and Chart Index Catalogs* provide access to more than 200,000 topographic maps and hydrographic charts issued for the most part by U.S. and Canadian governments. The two volumes are similar in arrangement and format, one for Eastern North America and the other for Western North America. The boundary is the Mississippi River due north to Hudson Bay. The U.S./Canadian Map Service Bureau is a private commercial firm which sells the maps and charts listed in these volumes.

Each catalog is divided into ten sections. They are: Map Scales, Equivalents, Symbols; United States Special Interest Maps; United States Topographical Maps—1:250,000 Scale; United States Topographical Maps—1:24,000 to 1:62,500 Scale; United States Raised Relief Maps; Canadian Special Interest Maps; Canadian Topographical Maps—1:250,000 Scale; Canadian Topographical Maps—Up to 1:50,000 Scale; United States Hydrographic Charts and Publications; and Canadian Hydrographic Charts and Publications.

The two volumes reproduce U.S. Geological Survey national and state topographic index maps, National Ocean Survey nautical chart indexes, and indexes for Canadian topographic maps and nautical charts. The individual indexes are available without charge from the government agencies. The Canadian and American map and chart indexes represent nearly the complete contents of the two volumes. The special interest maps (some of which are lists of state, provincial, and lunar maps) and the description of basic map and chart terms occupy only a few pages in each volume. There is a Table of Contents, but no index. Ordering information is clearly presented.

The sales prices are considerably higher than the retail purchase prices cited by government agencies. For example, the U.S. 1:62,500 topographic maps are listed in the catalog at $2, while they can be purchased directly from the U.S. Geological Survey for $1.25. The 1:250,000 Canadian topographic maps, costing $1.50 each if purchased directly from the Canada Map Office, are priced at $3 per map in this catalog.

The U.S. and Canadian topographic and hydrographic indexes are invaluable cartographic aids for the student, researcher, geographer, or backpacker. These *Official Maps and Chart Index Catalogs* are easier to consult than an assortment of index sheets and folded indexes. Libraries will have to decide if the purchase price of these volumes is justified in terms of use and convenience.
(Jan 15, 1977, p.747)

Oil terms:
a dictionary of terms used in oil exploration and development. By Leo Crook. New York, International Publications Service, 1976. 160p. illus. tables. 24cm. cloth, $15.

With the development of the North Sea oil fields, petroleum production has become of interest to an increasing number of people in Great Britain. The equipment used in this industry and especially in the exploration and drilling operations is unique and has developed a vocabulary all its own. Leo Crook, an Englishman with long experience in the field, has compiled this dictionary primarily for newcomers to the industry or those new in their dealings with it.

The book is introduced by a short, ten-page discussion of oil exploration and production. The problems, hazards, and costs of North Sea drilling and production are presented along with comments on land-based operations. The body of the work consists of the definitions with illustrations of some 465 terms, in alphabetical order from *abandon* to *work over job,* with special meaning in the industry. Many of the terms, which may be a single word or a phrase of several words, are defined in only a line or two. The discussion of others—*drill ship, mud, production platform,* and *well*—extends to a page or more. A majority of the terms are connected with oil well drilling and the specialized equipment and geological terms are included. Numerous cross-references help to establish the relationships between the various pieces of equipment discussed.

Most of the equipment and many of the operations defined are also illustrated by black-and-white line drawings. These have been well selected from a variety of acknowledged sources and are valuable in helping the layman, especially, to visualize this equipment. The appendixes consist of several tables pertaining to petroleum production, cost, and use. The most recent of these reflects the situation in 1974. There are a few tables of world-wide statistics but the majority are for the United King-

dom. Although this book was compiled for the British user it would make a useful addition to those libraries where such specialized information is in demand. *(Nov. 1, 1976, p.426)*
†665.5'03   Petroleum—Dictionaries

Old and middle English poetry to 1500:
a guide to information sources. By Walter H. Beale. Detroit, Gale, [c1976]. xxiii, 454p. (volume 7 in the American literature, English literature, and world literatures in English information guide series.) 22cm. cloth $18.

Beale, a university professor who teaches medieval literature rhetoric, and English linguistics, has compiled a useful guide for serious students and teachers of English literature and for librarians attempting to build basic collections.

The bibliography is arranged under two broad divisions, Old English and Middle English poetry. These are further divided into general reference, collections, and background studies, followed by texts and commentary. These two parts are further classified following the lead of such standard bibliographies as the *New Cambridge Bibliography of English Literature.* Treatment is limited to works composed in verse, with an occasional note of works in prose since these are covered in other volumes of the series.

The bibliographic form is consistent throughout, the MLA Style Sheet having served as a general guide. For poems with variant titles and spellings, the *NCBEL* has been used as an authority. For those items not found there, the title and spelling used by the editor of the recommended edition have been followed.

In selection of criticism, studies made within the last 20 years have been emphasized, limited generally to titles in English, but with a number of important foreign titles included. Also, books published very recently by major presses were almost automatically selected. Though no systematic search was made for reprints of every entry, a large number have been included. Only standard editions have been listed, though alternate texts also appear, especially where there are competing texts which complement one another or where the best critical editions are found only in major research libraries.

Annotations are given for almost all entries, ranging from a few stating "Not seen" to those of about 200 words, the latter being critical as well as descriptive commentary. Preferred translations have been noted for virtually every poem in Old English. For Middle English poetry, only a few general collections of translations have been cited, the compiler having taken special care to note the presence or absence of glossaries. Works of literary criticism have been given more emphasis than background or historical studies. In a few cases reviews of books have been noted. Although the compiler does not claim absolute neutrality in all matters, he has attempted "to bring access to the best and the most representative views." In this he acknowledges the help of his colleague, James I. Wimsatt.

Each item is numbered, with 411 items in the Old English and 918 in the Middle English section, though a few additional titles are referred to in the annotations. There are separate indexes for medieval authors and titles index, subjects, and modern editors and commentators. Each item is cited by number and appropriate section. Cross-references in the text refer the user to related items. The Subject Index contains general groupings of Old and Middle English poetry, general themes, major topics of criticism, and non-English medieval authors and titles (e.g., *Augustine*). Contents of collected essays and festschriften are indexed.

This companion to two other bibliographies covering drama and prose literature represents the best recent scholarship in the field, together with the original works. Its logical arrangement, bibliographic consistency, critical annotations, and good format make *Old and Middle English Poetry to 1500* a valuable resource for scholars and academic libraries.
(July 1, 1977, p.1677)
016.829.1   Anglo-Saxon poetry—Bibliography. || English poetry—Middle English, 1100–1500—Bibliography [CIP]
74-11538

One hundred recipes for the chafing dish.
[By] H. M. Kinsley. New York, Arno Pr., 1973. 182p. illus. 19cm. cloth $5.
641.5'8   Chafing—dish recipes   [CIP]   72-9795
See page 116

1,000 great lives.
[By] Plantagenet Somerset Fry. London, New York, Sydney, Toronto, Hamlyn; distributed in the U.S. by A & W Promotional, [1975]. 320p. illus. 25cm. cloth $10.

Plantagenet Somerset Fry is the author of books on antique furniture and history *(They Made History, The Hamlyn Children's History of the World, Rulers of Britain,* and *Answer Book of History).* He wrote *1,000 Great Lives* as a world history for children and young people to use in conjunction with his *Hamlyn Children's History of the World. Great Lives* emphasizes British, Commonwealth, and American notables, but coverage of famous people from other parts of the world is not slighted. Length of each story is commensurate with the importance of the biographee. Included are artists, writers, philosophers, musicians, military persons, scholars, statesmen, and religious leaders.

All persons selected for treatment are deceased, and arrangement is chronological by date of death. The time period covered begins with the 36th century B.C. and ends with 1973. Because of the arrangement and the absence of a list of contents, it is necessary to use the Index when looking for specific information. There are no captions or other devices identifying biographees by century or period.

The design of the book into two columns to a page with name of biographee in boldface and text in easy-to-read type is commendable. Almost every page contains an illustration. Each biographee is identified by birth and death dates and an identifying phrase, "King of the Hebrews," "Italian painter and art historian," "English prison reformer," "Russian statesman." Information is presented in a narrative journalistic style which will appeal to young people. Occasionally Fry's personal opinion is evident as in the treatment of John F. Kennedy: "As a boy he had all that rich boys could have"; or Brahms: "Brahms was not a happy man. He never married, for he was said to be too frightened of women"; or Hitler: "What kind of adjective does one give to a man whose demonic energy took him from a humble role as a painter of picture postcards in a Vienna slum to absolute ruler of the German people, all 80,000,000 of them, and then through hideous war to master of the bulk of Europe?"

1,000 Great Lives is useful as a collective biography of persons famous in a number of fields. Children may enjoy reading the book consecutively or browsing through it. For specific items of information on famous persons (except date of birth and death) students will find the coverage in a good general encyclopedia better.   *(Apr. 1, 1977, p.1198)*
†920.02   Biography

Organ music in print.
Ed., Thomas R. Nardone. Philadelphia, Musicdata, Inc., 1975. x, 262p. library binding $32.

This is the third volume in the Music-in-Print series, which is, for scores, a counterpart to *Books in Print.* Volumes 1 and 2, comprising *Choral Music in Print,* were reviewed in *Reference and Subscription Books Reviews,* Feb. 1, 1975. Most of what was said of this latter guide applies to *Organ Music in Print.* Choice of entry, arrangement, and cross-referencing are similar. Anthologies are analyzed only if components do not exceed six. Users should note an inconsistency in alphabetizing composition titles beginning with articles, e.g., "La cathédrale" under *L* but "English Suite, An" under *E*. There are also many entries for surnames alone. Apparently, faulty and incomplete descriptions in publishers' catalogs have been duplicated without editorial modification. The Guide to Use refers to codes which "make it possible to retrieve, from the data base developed for the 'Music-In-Print' series, specialized listings of music for particular seasons, types, etc." How the retrieval service functions is not specified. Nor are details given concerning the "updating service" mentioned in the Guide to Use. In sum, this is a needed, reasonably comprehensive, and usable tool. Pianists, harpists, flutists, and other instrumentalists would surely welcome companion volumes. *(Feb. 1, 1977, p.857)*

016.7868   Organ music—Bibliography [OCLC]   75-16504

The Oxford children's dictionary in colour.
Compiled by John Weston and Alan Spooner; illustrated by Henry Barnett. Oxford Univ. Pr., 1976. 320p. illus. 20cm. paper-covered boards $6.

"We have included all the words they are likely to meet and want to use for themselves." So state the authors of this dictionary for young readers. It is a small six-by-seven-and-three-fourths-inch volume, bound in glossy illustrated paper boards. There are small colored illustrations throughout which help to define the words which are printed in red type. Variant forms, in parentheses, are in black type. A brief definition follows. Separate meanings are listed under the initial word. In the case of homonyms, the words are numbered and follow one another in the columns.

In comparison to other children's dictionaries currently available on the American market, the *Oxford Children's Dictionary* is far too limited in scope to be considered for library purchase. British spellings and definitions further restrict its usefulness. The lack of any data except spelling and brief definition makes it a dubious purchase even for informal use in the home. *(Jan. 15, 1977, p.747)*

423   English language—Dictionaries, Juvenile [CIP]

Pan Am's USA guide.
[By] Pan American World Airways, Inc. 2d ed. New York, McGraw-Hill, [1976]. 634p. illus. maps. 19cm. $5.95; to schools, 1–4 copies, 20 percent discount, 5 copies and over, 25 percent discount; to libraries, 10 percent discount.

This small, sturdy volume is aimed at the foreign visitor who needs capsule information on each of the 50 states and the U.S. territories of Guam, Puerto Rico, and the Virgin Islands. Following a short introduction, which includes such practical information as currency, public holidays, and normal banking hours, the bulk of the text is arranged in eight regional groupings: Northeast, South, Midwest, Southwest, Mountain States, Pacific Coast, Pacific (Alaska, Guam, Hawaii), and Atlantic (Puerto Rico and the Virgin Islands). Within each region, the member states or territories are individually treated; in addition to pertinent statistics, some history is given for each, the major cities and sights are described, and accommodations, restaurants, and entertainment are listed where appropriate. Price ranges are included. The first edition of the book appeared in 1975 under the title *Pan Am's World, the USA*.

Maureen A. Hickey, representing Pan Am, was editorial supervisor, and the DR Group, Inc., administered and coordinated the project with assistance from the McGraw-Hill World News bureaus. The tone of the guide is very positive: small towns tend to be "scenic"; seafood is usually "succulent"; and many historic buildings are seen as "exquisite." Despite the overwriting, lack of critical commentary, and occasionally passé inclusions, the volume is a useful introduction to the main attractions in each state and could prove helpful in identifying the standard accommodations and restaurants in the larger cities. The index which concludes the work is not as comprehensive as one might wish; it lists major points of interest but omits many of the minor places mentioned in the text. Nevertheless, the volume is factually accurate and nicely designed and could serve as an initial introduction to the U.S. It will be most useful for libraries located outside the U.S. which serve clientele contemplating travel in this country. *(Mar. 1, 1977, p.1039)*

917.3'04   U.S.—Description and travel—1960– —Guide books [CIP]   76-10387

Performing arts research:
a guide to information sources. [By] Marion K. Whalon. Detroit, Gale, [c1976]. xi, 280p. (v.1 in the Performing Arts Information Guide Series) 23cm. cloth $18.

Performing Arts Research is an annotated bibliography of reference resources available to the researcher in the performing arts with the emphasis on theater. Monographs are not included. The closing publication date is 1973, although a few outstanding titles from 1974 are included. Annotations indicate scope, arrangement, special strengths, indexing, and other helpful bits of information about the title under consideration as well as cross-references to related titles, subject headings, or sections.

Following the Preface, "Problems of Research in Theater Arts," the book is divided into seven parts: (I) Guides; (II) Dictionaries, Encyclopedias, and Handbooks; (III) Directories; (IV) Play Indexes and Finding Lists; (V) Sources for Review of Plays and Motion Pictures; (VI) Bibliographies, Indexes, and Abstracts; (VII) Illustrative and Audiovisual Sources. Each part is prefaced by a brief introduction of what the user will find therein. Parts I, II, VI, and VII are subdivided in parallel fashion so that the researcher can go from one section to another for different types of sources in the same field. Since many of the numerous cross-references throughout this bibliography refer to section numbers (e.g., "*The National Union Catalog*. See Part IV-A above" "*Encyclopedia of World Art* . . . For full annotation, see Part II-E"), it would have been very helpful to have had the part numbers added to the section titles which appear as running heads on each page. As it is, the user must go to the Table of Contents to find the page number for the cited part and section, or to the Index under the author's name where he is likely to be confronted with numerous page numbers.

The book concludes with a 29-page Index, with author, title, and subject entries in one alphabet. Titles are distinguished by being set in all capital letters. There are unfortunately omissions from the Index, notably in title listings.

Marion Whalon has an extensive background in public and academic libraries and is currently collection development librarian for Humanities and Fine Arts, University of California at Davis.

This comprehensive bibliography would be a desirable acquisition for academic and public libraries with special theater collections or serving clienteles interested in the field. *(July 15, 1977, p.1756)*

†016.792   Theater—Bibliography

Pictorial souvenirs & commemoratives of North America:
[a guide to ceramic glass and metal souvenir collectables, including world's fair souvenirs]. [By] Frank Stefano, Jr., Ian Henderson, consulting ed. New York, E. P. Dutton & Co., Inc., 1976. xii, 148p. illus. 24cm. cloth and board $10.95; paper $6.95; discounts for five or more copies.

The intent of *Pictorial Souvenirs & Commemoratives of North America* is to "serve as a springboard to bring to light more information about our country's past, as so vividly depicted in one of the most widespread and popular forms of documentary art—the pictorial souvenir." The book emphasizes ceramic souvenirs and in Part I describes and discusses American distributors, the scenes, British, German, American, and Japanese manufacturers, and marks. The text is explicated by black-and-white photographs and by line drawings.

Part II illustrates and discusses commemoratives from world's fairs and expositions. Part III explores non-ceramic commemoratives like picture postcards, ruby-glass, glass paperweights, metal forms, metal relief views, and souvenir spoons. Part IV covers current souvenirs in a brief three pages. A 21-item Selected Bibliography of U.S. imprints is provided for collectors who need to read more about pictorial souvenirs. The Index to text and illustrations will aid the user in locating specific information.

Pictorial Souvenirs & Commemoratives of North America will be useful to collectors as an introduction to souvenir collectibles. *(Apr. 1, 1977, p.1198)*

745.1'0973 Antiques||Souvenirs (Keepsakes)—Collectors and collecting||U.S. in art||Canada in art [CIP] 75-25900

The picture reference file.
General ed., Harold H. Hart. 25v. New York, Hart, [c1976]. 32cm. v.I: A Compendium. kivar 9 $39.50; looseleaf $60. v.II: Humor, wit, & fantasy. kivar 9 $39.50; looseleaf $60; to libraries and schools with standing order, 20 percent discount.

According to the publisher, the first volume of a projected 25 includes within 397 pages 2,228 pictures from 131 sources and serves as a kind of sampler of the range of illustrations to be featured in succeeding volumes: it is appropriately called *A Compendium.* The somewhat randomly selected items range in size from smaller than a square inch to a full page, average about six per page, and consist almost entirely of line drawings. These reproductions are all in the public domain either because they appeared before 1907 or because they derive from works not currently under copyright protection. The 96 categories range from "Aircraft" and "Anger" to "Wild Animals" and "Xmas." A brief caption and an indication of source accompany each illustration unless the subject is self-explanatory. Many of the illustrations appeared originally in magazines of the Victorian period. Sources are listed alphabetically by title at the end of the volume along with imprint data. Exact page citations and issues in which the illustrations originally appeared are not indicated. Omission of this information lessens the *File*'s value, especially for owners of back runs of magazines such as *Leslie's, Scribner's, St. Nicholas,* and *Harper's.* An Index of captions and subjects, including the various categories, completes the work. The illustrations are generally well produced with good margins; the book lies flat for easy copying.

A second volume entitled *Humor, Wit & Fantasy* follows a similar format and includes some 2,100 illustrations from 134 sources arranged in 70 categories. A third volume dealing with animals is next in line for publication. *(July 1, 1977, p.1678)*

704.94 Art—Themes, motives—Sources||Pictures—Sources [OCLC] 75-31405

Plants that *really* bloom indoors.
By George and Virginie Elbert. New York, Simon & Schuster, 1974. 222p. 25cm. paperback, $3.95.

This book is totally devoted to plants which, given proper conditions, will bloom on window sills or under artificial light. The book is divided into two major sections: "Basic Culture for Blooming Plants" and "Blooming Plants Indoors."

Information concerning plant propagation, plant problems, selection of flowering plants, types of lighting, watering, and soil mixes is found in Part I. Each plant is included in 1 or more of the 12 special characteristic lists located at the rear of this chapter. These enable the gardener to select a plant which will grow in particular conditions of light, temperature, etc.

Part II, "Blooming Plants," is an alphabetical guide to 93 flowering plants. Included here is information on their natural habitat, possible display locations, and cultural requirements for healthy growth. The scientific name and several paragraphs describing the growing patterns of each are also provided. Accompanying the description is a black-and-white line drawing of each plant and its bloom. These drawings, identifiable to the gardener familiar with various plants, are too general and may be extremely confusing to the novice attempting to identify visually a plant or plants. The back cover of the book erroneously states that the book is "meticulously illustrated with line drawings and full-color photographs;" the only color photograph evident in this edition is found on the front cover of the book.

The plants are indexed by both their common and scientific names, which is useful in cases where one of the various common names might be known and not the scientific. Where an extremely large plant family exists (begonia, orchid, gloxinia) one must know which family a plant belongs to in order to locate its cultural requirements.

Also included are short sections on where to buy house plants, seeds, supplies, and plant societies and their publications. Other books by the Elberts team have included *Fun with Terrarium Gardening, Fun with Growing Herbs Indoors,* and *Fun with Growing Odd and Curious House Plants.*
(Oct. 15, 1976, p.346)

635.9'65 House plants||Flowers [OCLC] 74-9890

The pocket book of furniture.
Written and illustrated by Therle Hughes. [New York], Country Life, [1975, c1968]. 416p. illus. plasticized cloth $5.95.

The Pocket Book of Furniture is the first American edition of a manual published in England in 1968. Therle Hughes is an English author who has written extensively in the field of English antiques and collecting. His intention in this survey of English furniture is to provide beginners with "a simple outline of the changing periods and their products, to make them familiar with the terms in common use in museums and salesrooms, to indicate the factors governing design and ornament and the techniques applied."

The Pocket Book of Furniture is arranged in 18 sections. Part I is an excellent Introduction giving a succinct overview of the history of English furniture, providing for each period brief information on materials, construction, ornament, other descriptive detail, and suggestions on articles to collect. Part II is an alphabetical glossary of about 200 terms used by collectors relating to materials, construction, ornamentation, design, and the like. Most of the remaining sections (Parts III–XVI) are devoted to discussions of the various categories of furniture—chairs, tables, etc. Dining room furniture, exclusive of tables and chairs, and bedroom furniture, exclusive of beds and chests, are treated as units. Typically, these sections begin with general comments highlighting the development, social context, and variety of the category under examination and then proceed with an alphabetical listing of items in the category, describing the article in its historical setting and its variant details as exemplified by different designers and craftsmen, indicating the woods used, the details of construction, or other pertinent information.

Part XVII is a discussion of some crafts associated with making furniture, such as japanning, inlaying, gilding, turnery, papier mâché. The final section of the text (Part XVIII) is a listing of woods used by furniture makers, not only describing physical appearance which is of marginal value in itself but also frequently indicating use in specific periods, e.g., walnut in Queen Anne period, and satinwood for cross-banding by Sheraton.

The Pocket Book of Furniture is illustrated by more than 1,000 line drawings and it is these that most seriously handicap the book. While they convey the overall lines and proportions of furniture, they are inconveniently placed with reference to the text and niggardly in size, so that necessary details are not exhibited. Some details have separate drawings but not a sufficient number to meet the demands of the text. The problem of inadequate detail is compounded by the fact that several drawings are usually included in one numbered figure and captions frequently make no mention of details referred to in the glossary. Since the text places considerable reliance upon technical terms (unfortunately without internal references to the glossary section) this is a serious drawback.

A brief bibliography of about 65 items lists books under several headings: Histories and Surveys, English Furniture—General, English Furniture—Period Studies, and Reviews of Original Designs.

The book concludes with an Index of seven double-column pages. References to illustrative figures are in boldface. Few cross-references are provided. No blind references were detected, but numerous checks from text to index revealed many lost opportunities to provide better access. The book is internally referenced but the system is not extensive: q.v. references are used apparently for relating material within each one of the eighteen sections comprising the book.

The Pocket Book of Furniture may be compared with Joseph Aronson's *The Encyclopedia of Furniture* (3d rev. ed., New York: Crown, 1965. $9.95). Unlike *The Pocket Book of Furniture,* the encyclopedia is worldwide in scope, although the emphasis is on furniture of Europe and the U.S. The body of Aronson's work is arranged in dictionary form in a single alphabet in oversized format, rather than the compact duo-decimo selected for the *Pocket Book,* and includes entries treating terminology; names of designers and makers; articles on national developments (subdivided by period for major European countries and the U.S.); items of furniture; period styles; woods, decorations and ornaments; hardware; etc. The work is profusely illustrated with photographs and drawings (both generously proportioned and useful)—photographs generally being used to illustrate pieces and drawings to illustrate detail and terminology. Photographs are numbered and referred to from text. Drawings are usually captioned and labelled when necessary and are placed conveniently near the text, which appears less technical and detailed in the *Encyclopedia* than in the *Pocket Book.* While generally unnecessary, an index to provide access to longer articles would be useful in Aronson. *The Encyclopedia of Furniture* also includes a bibliography and a useful "Glossary of Designers and Craftsmen" indicating their nationalities and the period in which they flourished.

The Pocket Book of Furniture has much information and within the limitations noted above may prove to be a useful ancillary reference source in its field for home and public library use. *(May 15, 1977, p.1452)*

†749.242 Furniture—Gt. Brit.—Dictionaries || Furniture—Dictionaries

Policies of publishers:
a handbook for order librarians. By Ung Chon Kim. Metuchen, N.J., Scarecrow Pr., Inc., 1976. 132p. 28cm. paper $7.50.

Policies of Publishers is a convenient source of information on ordering practices and policies of more than 400 U.S. publishing houses. Arranged for ease of use by librarians who order books directly from their publishers, this handbook identifies publishers by name, address, and telephone number and for most companies outlines their policies regarding address for orders, prepayment, discount, return, shipping and billing, back order, and standing order plan. Information given was obtained directly from the publishers. The Index to Publishers is adequately cross-referenced so that the user can readily locate publishers who do not appear in the alphabetical listing. The book is well designed, being photographed in two columns per page from typewritten copy on 8½-by-11-inch paper. The inner margins will permit rebinding. Librarians who order books in all types of libraries will find *Policies of Publishers* a handy single source of information on ordering books. *(Sept. 1, 1976, p.57)*

658.8'12 Publishers and publishing—U.S.—Directories || Acquisitions (Libraries) [CIP]
75-33629

Political handbook of the world, 1976:
governments and intergovernmental organizations as of January 1, 1976. Editor, Arthur S. Banks; associate editors, Rebecca T. Granger, Marilyn Green; intergovernmental organization editor, Muntasir M. Labban. 44th ed. New York, McGraw, 1976. xi, 545p. 29cm. Kivar $19.95; to subscribers $13.95 net.

This forty-fourth edition of the *Political Handbook of the World* is the second edition of the *Political Handbook* assembled and edited at the Center for Comparative Political Research at the State University of New York–Binghamton. The recently redesigned annual presents political and socio-economic data about the nations, territories, and major intergovernmental organizations of the world. While retaining all the positive features of its immediate predecessor (*see* the July 15, 1976, issue of *Reference and Subscription Books Reviews* for an evaluation of the *Political Handbook of the World, 1975*), this new edition incorporates political change and activity occurring during the period from January 1, 1975, to January 1, 1976.

Although format and coverage remain essentially unchanged, this volume is over 10 percent larger than the forty-third edition. Six new independent nations are treated, changes have been made in the official names of several countries, and there is a general updating of listing of cabinet members and heads of state, and social and economic facts and statistics. While statistical data for the 160 countries continue to be summarized in tabular form in an Appendix, area and population figures are now also given with the descriptions of individual nations. The most recent available census figures and estimates of 1976 populations are cited with separate essays; 1973 data from the Cross-National Data Archive at SUNY-Binghamton appear in the Appendix. Each country's monetary exchange rate (generally that which prevailed as of December 31, 1975) has also been added. An important contribution of this reference work continues to be its excellent coverage of national political parties and current political issues for each of the worlds' independent nations.

The Intergovernmental Organizations section, now edited by Muntasir M. Labban, has been revised, lengthened, and includes additional agencies.

The Committee's review of the forty-third edition expressed concern about the absence of a comprehensive index. The Table of Contents has, in this new edition, been supplemented by a detailed index which covers not only the independent countries and intergovernmental organizations, but also includes related and dependent territories.

The clarity of presentation and format remain noteworthy features of this annual. The *Political Handbook of the World,* as an authoritative, current, and comprehensive source for understanding world events, will continue to meet the information needs of a wide range of users. *(Dec. 1, 1976, p.564)*

320 Political science—Handbooks, manuals, etc.
75-4083

Popular song index.
By Patricia Pate Havlice. Metuchen, N.J., Scarecrow Pr., Inc., 1975. vi, 933p. 23cm. cloth $30.

Popular Song Index, compiled by author and former librarian Patricia Pate Havlice, complements Sears' *Song Index* and De Charms and Breed's *Songs in Collections.* Conveniently arranged in three parts, Bibliography of the 301 books indexed,

Index of Titles and First Lines, and Index of Composers and Lyricists, the book provides librarians and interested clientele with a good device for finding words and music to popular tunes, folk songs, hymns, spirituals, songs sung by sailors, and blues. Books published between 1940 and 1972 and containing both words and music were selected for indexing. Cross-references between the indexes are adequate. The text is printed in easy-to-read two-column pages, and adequate inner margins will permit rebinding. The publisher notes that supplements will help keep the material current. *(Oct. 1, 1976, p.280)*

016.784   Songs—Indexes   [CIP] 75-9896

Quotations in history:

a dictionary of historical quotations, c.800 A.D. to the present. [By] Alan and Veronica Palmer, New York, Barnes and Noble, [c1976]. 354p. 23cm. cloth $13.50; 15 percent discount to libraries.

This collection consists of quotations attributed to great historical figures from about 800 A.D. to 1975. The emphasis is on historical rather than literary significance.

The compilers, Alan and Veronica Palmer, have written several books and are known as historians and teachers.

Following the practice of dictionaries of quotations published in England (such as *The Oxford Dictionary of Quotations*), the compilers have arranged approximately 1,600 entries by author or instigator to provide a book "which will verify the form of half-remembered phrases; give the opportunity to enrich spoken or written words from the wisdom of the wise; and provide the delights of author browsing." In contrast to works of predominantly literary quotations, this book is historical in emphasis; from the earliest entry (Alcuin, an adviser to Charlemagne) to the present, it covers approximately 1,200 years. The contributors range from the well known (William Pitt and John F. Kennedy) to the anonymous, from well-established statements to those of dubious authenticity. This collection is marked by lesser-known sayings or statements which were chosen only because they seemed to have historical significance or contemporary relevance.

Also, the compilers include longer passages than is customary in collections of quotations to avoid the distortion that can occur when an abbreviated statement is isolated from its context.

Famous names of political history, travellers, diarists, letter writers, poets, novelists, political theorists, historians are represented. Political songs, slogans, and verses are added to reflect the popular mood as are extracts from nineteenth- and twentieth-century press and chronicles of the Middle Ages. There is a heavy emphasis on European and especially English figures—several pages are devoted to the elder and younger William Pitts, Macaulay, and, more recently, Sir Harold Wilson. Institutions (the Board of Admiralty), documents (Magna Charta), Revolutionary songs, and nursery rhymes as well as anonymous sources ("post war German newspaper") are included. Phrases of dubious authenticity are designated by an asterisk, and an attempt is made to date each entry precisely. With passages from books, the Palmers try to indicate when the quotations were written as well as published.

Two indexes of keywords in context, one of English (more than 100 pages) and one of foreign-language keywords (less than two pages), lead the searcher to the number of the entry. Under each person or institution quoted are *see also* references to other entry numbers where the subject is mentioned.

The Index of keywords reveals an intriguing vocabulary of potential interest to linguists. Dandies, cockades, gaiter button, Nabob, petticoat, phoney, sumpsimus are among the terms represented. The strictly historical or politically relevant descriptors are more commonplace, e.g., nations, machines, law, labour, Smuts, Montesquieu. There is no apparent logic governing the selection of keywords, and they are not particularly helpful.

Despite the claimed exclusion of literary quotations, the entries include well-known writers such as Andrew Marvell and Robert Louis Stevenson, and the historical passages are not necessarily devoid of literary merit (witness the entries for Elizabeth I). In addition, some selections are curious. William Makepeace Thayer, an obscure American writer, is listed with the title of his biography for James Garfield, and Erich Maria Remarque is cited with the title of his most famous work, *All Quiet on the Western Front*. And several entries could be combined, e.g., Hitler's comments on the Sudetenland, both taken from the same speech, are listed separately. The blue cloth binding and the utility grade white paper probably could not sustain heavy use.

Several outstanding dictionaries (Burton Stevenson's *Home Book of Quotations* and Bergen Evans' *Dictionary of Quotations*), which emphasize literary works and also include some of the material gathered in this volume, are available. In addition, historical atlases provide a chronology of events; so it does not appear that this work fills any gaps in historical and reference literature. Given its arrangement by quotation originator and the fact that it is highly selective, this dictionary cannot usually provide what someone said on a topic or what quotations occurred or emerged on specified dates.

Quotations in History does satisfy its authors' expressed definition as a book for browsing, vocabulary enrichment, and quotation verification, gathering in one place phrases of the great and not-so-great of past and recent history. However, its arrangement precludes easy access to quotations, and it is more appropriate for browsing than for reference use.

School and public librarians with tight budgets should proceed cautiously before adding this title to their collections.

(May 15, 1977, p.1453)

†081   Quotations, English 76-1801

Railways of the modern age since 1963.

By O. S. Nock; illus. by Clifford and Wendy Meadway. New York, Macmillan Pub. Co., Inc., [c1975]. 155p. col. illus. 20cm. paper, $6.95.

Railways of the Modern Age Since 1963 is part of the "Railways of the World in Color" series and is the sixth book on railroads that British railway historian Oswald Stevens Nock has written. The little book is packed with information and 80 colored drawings and maps, but it is poorly organized for reference. The colorplates are segregated at the front of the book at an inconvenient distance from the text they illustrate. The text begins on page 89 with topics bearing the same numbers and captions as the color-plates, but one becomes aware of this coordination only after using the book. Seemingly, the plates are not arranged alphabetically or by type of locomotive, because the first ten are labeled "British Railways," "French National Railways," "Turkish State Railways," "Yugoslav State Railways," "Royal State Railway of Thailand," "Iraqui State Railway," "Portuguese Railways," "South African Railways," "Spanish National Railways," and "Danish State Railways."

Within the articles there are helpful cross-references, but there is no text for some specific colorplates. For example, *Diesels in Worldwide Use* discusses plates 3 through 10, but there are no separate articles for the individual plates. The four-page Index is arranged under such broad topics as *carriages, diesel locomotives, electric locomotives, freight cars,* and *steam locomotives.* It does not cite illustrations or provide analytics. The searcher for information on AMTRAK will not find a separate entry under AMTRAK, but rather will find it subsumed under *USA,* which in turn is subsumed under *diesel locomotives* and *electric locomotives.* Most fruitful use of the book, therefore, comes from browsing or from reviewing the illustrations before attempting to locate the text. For the patient searcher, *Railways of the Modern World Since 1963* covers the subject comprehensively with compact descriptions and useful drawings; for others, information seeking will be frustrating.

(Nov. 1, 1976, p.426)

385'.09   Railroads || Locomotives   [CIP]   75-28489

Reference materials on Mexican Americans:
an annotated bibliography. By Richard D. Woods. Metuchen, N.J., Scarecrow Press, 1976. vii, 190p. 22cm. cloth $7.50.

Oriented toward the scholar and the academic library, this annotated bibliography lists 387 Mexican-American items published in the continental U.S. and Mexican works treating the status of this minority in the U.S. It includes monographs and pamphlets, as well as nonprint materials such as films, filmstrips, tapes, and microfiche. Bibliographies appended to books and periodical articles have been omitted.

Richard D. Woods, the compiler, is chairman of the Latin American Studies Department at Trinity University, San Antonio, Texas. He has done considerable work in the field of Chicano Studies and Mexican American bibliography and holds graduate degrees in Spanish, library science, and Ibero-American Studies.

A large number of the entries, arranged alphabetically by author, are bibliographies, checklists, indexes, guides, and directories. A majority of them have been published within the last 15 years, but some older listings also appear. The annotations, which range from 75 to 100 words, are long enough to summarize content effectively. Some of the annotations are critical and point out defects as well as desirable features. For example: "Although this work is quite easy to use, an index with more topics would have aided . . . . Also the introduction does not clarify the relationship . . . . Best for researcher interested in post 1960s. For depth, however, Pino's work would have to complement this."

References are made to church, county, and genealogical records. Thirty-eight U.S. government sources are represented, including such data as statistics of minority group employment (U.S. Civil Service Commission), characteristics of the population (U.S. Bureau of the Census), racial and ethnic enrollment in institutions of higher learning (U.S. Office of Education), how to identify Spanish names (U.S. Dept. of Labor). The selections are not entirely on a scholarly level, as indicated by the final one: "Zelayeta . . . *Elena's Mexican and Spanish Recipes.*"

Use of the book is facilitated by three indexes: author (both personal and corporate), title, and subject. Subject listings are sometimes very broad; 185 references are given under *Bibliography,* 93 under *Education,* and 86 under *Mexico.*

This bibliography on Mexican Americans should be valuable in all academic libraries, as well as in special libraries working in this area. Because some 50 of the items contain bibliographies or other information relevant to the educational development and reading needs of Mexican American children, teachers and library media specialists should also find this work helpful.

(May 15, 1977, p.1453)

016.973'04   Reference books—Mexican Americans || Mexican Americans—Bibliography   [CIP]   76-10663

Research in progress in English and history in Britain, Ireland, Canada, Australia, and New Zealand.
Edited by S. T. Bindoff and James T. Boulton. [rev. ed.] London, St. James Pr.; New York [c1975]. 284p. 24cm. linson 2 $15.

Bindoff and Boulton's first edition of *Research in Progress* was published in 1971, and it was limited to a survey of research being carried on by 1,800 scholars located at British universities. The new edition retains the limitation of its predecessor by excluding research leading to higher academic degrees, but its coverage is more comprehensive because Canada, Australia, and New Zealand have been added and the number of researchers increased to 3,800. Coverage has also been expanded to include research in progress outside institutions of higher learning—museums, archives, societies, and other forms of independent research.

Arrangement of entries is alphabetical by surname of researcher under ten main classifications for English Studies (e.g., Old and Middle English, American Literature, Teaching of English) and two main classes of Historical Studies (World History and British Isles). Within each main class are many subclasses which aid the user in locating research germane to his particular interest. For example, under "English Studies: Language," there are subdivisions for place-names and surnames and for psychosocio-linguistics. Researchers are identified by surname and first and middle initial. The research for each entry is described briefly in one- or two-line phrases, e.g., "Authors and Publishers in the 19th century," "Melville's reputation in England, with a survey of reviews and criticism," "The peasant war in Hungary 1514," "Vagrancy in Georgian England."

The 63-page Index at the end of the book is arranged alphabetically by researcher. Here identifying academic titles like "Dr." and "Prof." are given; the researcher's institutional affiliation is cited; the page reference is given to research cited in the book. A list of Addresses of Universities and Institutions is provided for those who wish to contact researchers. The list gives addresses for colleges and institutes operating under the aegis of large institutions. Accordingly, the University of London has 19 subentries. *Research in Progress in English and History* will be useful to scholars and researchers who need to know what research is underway in these subject fields in Great Britain, Ireland, Canada, Australia, and New Zealand. The Reference and Subscription Books Review Committee hopes that successive editions will increase the geographic coverage of the work.

(May 15, 1977, p.1454)

†907.2   History—Bibliography || English philology—Bibliography   [OCLC]   75-29642

Reverse acronyms, initialisms, & abbreviations dictionary.
Edited by Ellen T. Crowley. 5th ed. Detroit, Gale Research, [c1976]. x, 754p. 29cm. cloth $45.

Reverse Acronyms, Initialisms, & Abbreviations Dictionary is, as it states in the subtitle, a companion volume to Gale Research's *Acronyms, Initialisms & Abbreviations Dictionary.* A review of the fifth edition of *AIAD* appeared in *Reference and Subscription Books Reviews* for Feb. 15, 1977. *RAIAD* takes the 130,000 terms of *AIAD* and rearranges them alphabetically by the meaning of the acronym, initialism, or abbreviation; there are no cross-references. Both volumes are international in scope and contain terms from the fields of aerospace, associations, biochemistry, business and trade, domestic and international affairs, education, electronics, genetics, government, labor, medicine, military, pharmacy, physiology, politics, religion, science, societies, sports, technical drawings and specifications, transportation, and other fields.

The editor of *RAIAD* is Ellen T. Crowley; the assistant editors are Christopher Crocker and Donna Wood. This same team also edits Gale's *Trade Names Dictionary* and *AIAD.*

The terms are arranged in two columns to the page; the type is small but clear. The volume is sturdily bound, opens flat, and has margins generous enough to permit rebinding.

The need for such a volume with its copious representation of terms is questionable. The publishers claim that this volume broadens the scope of *AIAD,* which guides "librarians, businessmen, technical writers, and other researchers through the alphabetical maze." They further claim that *RAIAD* is useful in sorting out inconsistencies, since acronymic terms are not all formed in accordance with any set of rules, and that *RAIAD* helps to avoid cases of mistaken identity. Even if these claims are justified, they would not warrant purchase of *RAIAD* because of characteristics this work has in common with *AIAD*. *RAIAD* fills no perceptible need. *(Mar. 1, 1977, p.1039)*

423.1   Acronyms || English language—Reverse indexes   [OCLC]   76-25734

Rock 100.
[By] David Dalton and Lenny Kaye. New York, Grosset, 1977. 280p. 27cm. cloth $17.95; paper $8.95.

784.092   Rock musicians   [OCLC]   74-27945

The illustrated encyclopedia of rock.
[Compiled by] Nick Logan and Bob Woffinden. New York, Harmony Books; dist. by Crown, [c1977]. 256p. illus. 30cm. cloth $11.95; paper $7.95.

784   Rock music—Dictionaries || Rock music—Bio-bibliography   [OCLC]   76-40219

These titles reflect two approaches to information in a dynamic and difficult-to-define field. *Rock 100* is a collection of biographies of performers whose careers marked clear-cut periods in the history of the genre, or who influenced its development. *The Illustrated Encyclopedia of Rock* has a more conventional reference format and describes European (mainly British) as well as American performers, little-known groups as well as stars.

Rock 100 is a chronology of rock, commencing with its founders and those who developed it as a form of entertainment and concluding with groups and individuals active in 1976. In many respects this volume supplements *Rock On* by Norman Nite (New York: T. Y. Crowell, 1974). Although it lacks the thoroughness and discography of Nite's work, it covers a longer period. The compilers have acknowledged the assistance of popular music historians Joel Whitburn, Charlie Gillette, and Lillian Roxon, who have written extensively on the development of rock. The means by which material was gathered and sources used are not divulged. The terms "rock" and "rock and roll" are treated as equivalents, and artists associated with country, blues, middle-of-the-road, folk, rhythm-and-blues, and soul are included, insofar as they shaped the evolution of rock. Although the title suggests the "top 100" on the weekly charts, essays include information on lesser-known (and often currently obscure) artists as well as the giants (e.g., Elvis). The criterion for selection was "not necessarily how many records these artists sold or even how long they remained in the public eye—but rather the basis of their stature in relation to their audiences, musical contemporaries and probably descendants." The essay format of *Rock 100* somewhat limits its value as a reference tool, a defect mitigated by an Index to names of performers, groups, and albums. The book brings together elusive information in a highly readable form, with many black-and-white photographs. It might prove popular in the circulating collection, but for this purpose it should be purchased in hardcover.

The Illustrated Encyclopedia of Rock was prepared by the editor and the associate editor of the *New Musical Express,* Britain's best-selling rock weekly. Nick Logan had previously produced "The Book of Rock," material originally appearing in 10 weekly pullout supplements to *New Musical Express* in 1973. These were later reproduced as a paperback, *The NME Book of Rock.*

The encyclopedia is a mixture of 650 alphabetically arranged entries, illustrated by 350 full-color prints (including reproductions of album jackets) and 90 black-and-white prints. Artists appear under their surnames, bands under their full titles. If an artist's name is given to a group (Spencer Davis Group, La Belle) that form of entry is generally used. However, a few bands are represented only within entries devoted to their founders (Mothers of Invention under Frank Zappa). The encyclopedia includes all those acts which may be described as mainstream rock music and also some peripheral influences. Entries, arranged four columns to a page, include individual names of performing artists; occasional birth (and death) dates; capsule histories of artists and groups; and discographies. Record companies are listed after the albums, first the American and then the British labels. Sometimes American and British labels are identical. Albums issued through May 1976 are cited in the order in which they were produced, not in the order in which they became available on the market. Cross-references within entries are designated by arrows rather than conventional *see also.* Stars (Allman Brothers Band, Fleetwood Mac) and lesser lights (Poco, Sea Train) are found in the work. In addition, European artists not familiar to most Americans are described.

Information in this sturdily bound reference work is brightly and compactly displayed. The somewhat small print will not dissuade rock fans or anyone in search of facts on rock performers. Although some of the reportage is duplicated elsewhere, inclusion of British and other European performers makes this encyclopedia a plausible supplement to other books on the subject such as Irwin Stambler's *Encyclopedia of Rock, Pop, and Soul* (New York: St. Martin's, 1975).

While several rock histories and popular-music encyclopedias exist, these two books are up to date, may serve as circulating as well as reference tools, and gather in one place supplementary ready-reference information and details that would be hard to find in other sources. For these reasons they should be well received in the reference collections of public and college libraries. *(July 1, 1977, p.1678)*

RSPB guide to British birds.
[By] David Saunders. London, New York, Hamlyn, [c1975] 128p. illus. (part col.) maps. 19cm. cloth $4.50.

The British Royal Society for the Protection of Birds collaborated with the author in producing the *RSPB Guide to British Birds.* The *Guide* is pocket size and easily portable. It describes and illustrates some 200 species of British birds and is well fortified with maps and helpful hints on birdwatching equipment. The book's primary purpose is to aid in identifying and conserving birds; its language is easily comprehensible to young people and adults who are novices at birdwatching. The book divides birds into five groups: ducks, geese, and swans; water birds; seabirds; birds of prey; and land birds. Together the clear descriptions and illustrations of each species give enough detail to enable the user to make accurate identification. The book features a Glossary of 33 terms and a Check List of Birds Recorded in Great Britain and Ireland. School and public libraries and birdwatchers will find the *RSPB Guide* is an economical source of identification information on birds commonly seen in the British Isles.
(June 1, 1977, p.1528)

598.2'941   Birds—Gt. Brit.—Identification   [OCLC]   76-22056

Screen world, 1976, V.27:
[a comprehensive pictorial and statistical record of the 1975 movie season. Compiled by John Willis]. New York, c1976. 256p. illus. 24cm. cloth $12.95.

For more than 25 years, *Screen World* has provided the American public with a good, annual illustrated guide to events in the international world of film. The 1976 guide is notable for its organization, layout, and clear, sharp photographs. A two-page spread showing the 25 top box-office stars of 1975 is followed by the bulk of the directory—a 115-page alphabetically arranged grouping of Domestic Films Released in the United States from January 1 through December 31, 1975. Information given for each includes listing of the cast, film company, producer, director, writer, lyricist, art director, and costumer. The listing of foreign films released in the U.S. is quite comprehensive; it occupies 81 pages. Other features of the 1976 *Screen World* include a list of promising actors for 1975, lists of Academy Award winners for 1975 and 1976, biographies (place and date of birth and school attended) and obituaries of those who died in 1975. The table of contents and an Index of names help to locate specific information. High school, public, and special libraries with a need for an overall directory of moving pictures during a specific year have learned to depend on *Screen World* as an easy-to-use, well-illustrated reference source.

(June 15, 1977, p.1605)

†791.4305   Moving-pictures—Yearbooks   50-3023

Sea fiction guide.
By Myron J. Smith, Jr., and Robert C. Weller. Metuchen, N.J., Scarecrow, 1976. xxix, 256p. 23cm. cloth $10.

Sea fiction is a category of interest to many library users, from casual readers to advanced students of literary formulae. Smith and Weller's guide is an annotated list, arranged by author, of 2,525 works, supplemented by a Pseudonym/Joint Author Index, a Title Index, and a Topical Index. In the list itself, many entries are annotated, most of them briefly, e.g., "An anthology," but some lengthily. Annotations tend to be superficial, e.g., the description of Porter's *Ship of Fools* as "A look at some of the passengers aboard a cruise ship" (an annotation which is, moreover, inaccurate, as officers are looked at along with passengers and the ship in question is not a "cruise ship"). The note on *Moby-Dick* does more but includes the following observation, which may have to some an anti-intellectual ring: ". . . each reader must eventually interpret it according to his own prejudices. . . ." The Subject Index includes an entry for *Mexican War* and even so specialized a cross-reference as "Tea Trade *see* Clipper Ships" but does not constitute a sophisticated guide to themes, character types, and narrative motifs (traditional or innovative as the case may be). Still, *Sea Fiction Guide* may be described as a work likely to prove useful to one category of buffs and to the readers' advisors whose task it is to help them. As a list, it is fairly comprehensive; and perhaps some student of the art of fiction will make it the foundation of a scholarly analysis of the genre.   *(May 15, 1977, p.1454)*

016.823'008   Sea stories—Bibliography || English fiction—Bibliography || American fiction—Bibliography   [CIP]   76-7590

A short guide to the study of Ethiopia:
a general bibliography. Edited by Alula Hidaru and Dessalegn Rahmato. Westport, Conn., Greenwood, 1976. 176p. (Special Bibliographic Series; New Series, No. 2). cloth $12.75.

Compilations of bibliographies dealing with African countries are almost always out of date by the time they appear in print. This guide is even more so because it was prepared four years before publication, prior to the radical changes in Ethiopian politics during and subsequent to Haile Selassie's ouster and demise. This fact is recognized by the inclusion of a bibliographical Introduction by Francis J. Kornegay, Jr., associate editor of the African Bibliographic Center. In his Foreword to the book, Daniel G. Matthews, executive director of the Center, states that Kornegay's Introduction, written in 1976, was developed so that bibliographical resources published after 1972 could be incorporated in the guide.

The value of this contribution to Ethiopian bibliography is based upon the fact that it was "compiled by Ethiopians themselves on what works have been published in Ethiopia or abroad or that they feel really reflect the development of their country."

The compilers caution the user that "this bibliography is not meant to be complete and exhaustive." They felt compelled to prepare such a guide because the only existing bibliographies had consisted of predominantly foreign-language titles or were at least 40 years old.

In an Introductory Note—1972, it is pointed out that "A critical study of a serious nature concerning contemporary Ethiopia is virtually non-existent." They explain that Ethiopian writers may have difficulty getting published if they are "miserly in . . . praise of the society and the power-holders." Also mentioned is the European writer's roseate image of Ethiopia as a "charming and peaceful kingdom where custom and tradition . . . are greatly revered, and where people lead simple but healthy lives." And later, "This romantic image is usually accompanied by a generous dose of high praise for the able leadership, wisdom and farsightedness of the present emperor and his plans for modernization of the country."

The bibliography is in six parts, three of which are subdivided. Part I, "Ethiopian Sources," includes (1) "Old Ethiopian Sources," (2) "Ethiopian Government Publications," and (3) "Ethiopian Periodical Publications." Part II is "Bibliographies on Ethiopia." Part III, "History," is again subdivided as follows: (1) "Highland Ethiopia (Abyssinia)," (2) "Southern Ethiopia," and (3) "Italian-Ethiopian Conflict 1926–1941." Part IV, "Contemporary Ethiopia," contains two subdivisions: (1) "General, Political" and (2) "Socio-Ethnographic." Part V is devoted to "Economy, Natural Resources, Health," and part VI is "Religion, Language, Education."

Bibliographic notes accompany less than 10 percent of the entries. Some of the 2,673 numbered items are not unique because they are repeated in other parts of the bibliography. Because notes are also numbered, the actual number of items is reduced considerably. Most entries are in English, but there are several in Amharic and a few in Italian or French. Some translations into English are included. A stated objective is to satisfy the needs of the general reader rather than the serious scholar. There is a mixture of books, pamphlets, and articles. The greatest value from this compilation will accrue to the library with a sizable collection of serious English and French journals and a good representation of books on Africa published indigenously or in English-speaking countries.

Some of the cited serials likely to be held by American libraries include *The National Geographic; Harper's Monthly; Bulletin, School of Oriental and African Studies; Proceedings of the Royal Geographical Society; Journal of African History; Ethiopian Observer; Harvard African Studies; Journal of the Royal Geographical Society; International Conciliation; Contemporary Review; Blackwood's Magazine; Foreign Affairs; Survey Graphic;* and *Journal of Geography.*

Keeping in mind the limitations cited and the degree of inaccessibility of reliable materials about Africa in general and Ethiopia in particular, *A Short Guide to the Study of Ethiopia* will serve the purpose for which it was intended.

(June 1, 1977, p.1528)

016.916'008   Ethiopia—Bibliography   [OCLC]   76-27128

Significant Americans.
16v. Chicago, Children's Pr., [1976]; [c1973 by United States Historical Society, Inc., Skokie, Ill.; c1975 by Regensteiner Publishing Enterprises, Inc. With excerpts from *People Who Made America*]. illus. ports. 26cm. Permalin cover, $133.25 or $9.25 a v.; to schools and libraries, $99.95 or $6.95 a volume.

Significant American artists and architects.
Janet Tegland, executive editor. Chicago, Children's Pr., [c1975]. 78p. illus ports. 26cm. permalin $9.95; to schools and libraries, $6.95.

709'.22 (B) [920]   Artists—U.S.—Biography—Juvenile literature || Architects—U.S.—Biography—Juvenile literature [Artists || Architects]   [CIP]   75-20688

Significant American authors, poets, and playwrights.
Ida S. Meltzer, executive editor. Chicago, Children's Pr., [c1975]. illus. ports. 26cm. permaline, $9.95; to schools and libraries, $6.95.

810'.9 (B) [920]   Authors, American—Biography—Juvenile literature   [CIP]   75-20689

Significant American blacks.
Donald M. Jacobs, executive editor. Chicago, Children's Pr.,

170 Significant Americans

[c1975]. 78p. illus. ports. 26cm. permalin, $9.25; to schools and libraries, $6.95.
920'.0092 (B) [920] Negroes—Biography—Juvenile literature [Negroes—Biography] [CIP]
75-20676

Significant American colonial leaders.
Morris R. Buske, executive editor. Chicago, Children's Pr., [c1975]. 78p. illus. ports. 26cm. permalin, $9.95; to schools and libraries, $6.95.
973.2'092 (B) [920] U.S.—History—Colonial period, ca. 1600–1775—Biography—Juvenile literature [U.S.—History—Colonial period, ca. 1600–1775—Biography] [CIP]   75-20678

Significant American entertainers.
Janet Tegland, executive editor. Chicago, Children's Pr., [c1975]. 78p. illus. ports. 26cm. permalin, $9.95; to schools and libraries, $6.95.
791'.092 (B) [920] Entertainers—U.S.—Biography—Juvenile literature [Entertainers] [CIP]
75-20677

Significant American government leaders.
Gilbert Miekina, executive editor. Chicago, Children's Pr., [c1975]. 78p. illus. ports. 26cm. permalin, $9.95; to schools and libraries, $6.95.
920'.073 [920] Statesmen—U.S.—Biography—Juvenile literature [Statesmen] [CIP]
75-20685

Significant American historians and educators.
Jack Kent Mandel, executive editor. Chicago, Children's Pr., [c1975]. 78p. illus. ports. 26cm. permalin, $9.95; to schools and libraries $6.95.
973'.07 (B) [920] Historians—U.S.—Biography—Juvenile literature || Educators—U.S.—Biography—Juvenile literature [Historians || Educators] [CIP]   75-20690

Significant American Indians.
Jack Kent Mandel, executive editor. Chicago, Children's Pr., [c1975]. 78p. illus. ports. 26cm. permalin, $9.95; to schools and libraries, $6.95.
920'.0092 [920] Indians of North America—Biography—Juvenile literature [Indians of North America—Biography] [CIP]   75-20683

Significant American inventors.
Alvin W. Quinn, executive editor. Chicago, Children's Pr., [c1975]. 78p. illus. ports. 26cm. permalin, $9.95; to schools and libraries, $6.95.
609'.22 (B) [920] Inventors—U.S.—Biography—Juvenile literature [Inventors] [CIP]
75-20681

Significant American military leaders.
Gilbert Miekina, executive editor. Chicago, Children's Pr., [c1975]. 78p. illus. ports. 26cm. permalin, $9.95; to schools and libraries, $6.95.
355'.092 (B) [920] U.S. Army—Biography—Juvenile literature || U.S. Navy—Biography—Juvenile literature [U.S. Army—Biography || U.S. Navy—Biography || Indians of North America || Military biography] [CIP]   75-20682

Significant American musicians, composers, and singers.
Ida S. Meltzer, Chicago, Children's Pr., [c1975]. 78p. illus. ports. 26cm. permalin, $9.95; to schools and libraries, $6.95.
780'.92 (B) [920] Musicians, American—Biography—Juvenile literature [Musicians] [CIP]
75-20691

Significant American presidents of the United States.
Morris R. Buske, executive editor. Chicago, Children's Pr., [c1975]. 78p. illus. ports. 26cm. permalin, $9.95; to schools and libraries, $6.95.
973'.0992 (B) [920] Presidents—U.S.—Biography—Juvenile literature [Presidents] [CIP]
75-20692

Significant American scientists.
Alvin W. Quinn, executive editor. Chicago, Children's Pr., [c1975]. 78p. illus. ports. 26cm. permalin, $9.95; to schools and libraries $6.95.
509'.2 (B) [920] Scientists—U.S.—Biography—Juvenile literature [Scientists] [CIP]
75-20680

Significant American social reformers and humanitarians.
Gilbert Miekina, executive editor. Chicago, Children's Pr., [c1975]. 78p. illus. ports. 26cm. permalin, $9.25; to schools and libraries, $6.95.
301.24'2 (B) Social Reformers—U.S.—Biography—Juvenile literature [Social reformers] [CIP]
75-21596

Significant American sport champions.
Jack Kent Mandel, executive editor. Chicago, Children's Pr., [c1975]. 78p. illus. ports. 26cm. permalin, $9.95; to schools and libraries, $6.95.
796'.092 (B) [920] Athletes—U.S.—Biography—Juvenile literature [Athletes] [CIP]
75-20684

Significant American women.
Ida S. Meltzer, executive editor. Chicago, Children's Pr., [c1975]. 78p. illus. ports. 26cm. permalin, $9.95; to schools and libraries, $6.95.
920.72'0973 [920] Women—U.S.—Biography—Juvenile literature [Biography] [CIP]
75-20686

Each volume of *Significant Americans* includes brief biographical sketches arranged by subject areas: "Artists and Architects"; "Authors, Poets and Playwrights"; "Blacks"; "Colonial Leaders"; "Entertainers"; "Government Leaders"; "Historians and Educators"; "Indians"; "Inventors"; "Military Leaders"; "Musicians, Composers and Singers"; "Presidents of the United States"; "Scientists"; "Social Reformers and Humanitarians"; "Sport Champions"; and "Women."

Seven executive editors share responsibility for preparation of the set. They are Janet Tegland, instructor of creative writing at Saddleback Community College, Mission Viejo, California and a teacher in the Laguna Beach Unified School System; Ida Meltzer, vice principal of Marine Park Junior High School, Brooklyn, New York; Donald M. Jacobs, Assistant Professor of History at Northeastern University, Boston; Morris R. Buske, Triton College, River Grove, Illinois; Gilbert Miekina, social studies teacher at Southwestern Central High School, Jamestown, New York; Jack Kent Mandel, social studies teacher at John Wilson Jr. High School, Brooklyn, New York; and Alvin W. Quinn, Science Department, Northeastern Illinois University, Chicago, Illinois. Each executive editor is associated with one to three volumes. Five men are listed under "Research and Production," but no indication is given as to their professional qualifications.

Each volume is in four to six chronological sections labeled "Early Period," "Second Period," on up to "Fifth Period," and ending in "Contemporary." Only three volumes depart from this pattern: "Presidents of the United States" (appearing in the order in which they won office), "Sport Champions" (grouped by sport—Baseball, Football, Basketball, Olympics, Chess, and so on), and "Colonial Leaders" (presented in alphabetical order). Therefore, unless the period of history is known in which the individual lived, the Index at the end of each volume must usually be consulted. Lack of a master index and the capricious assignment of biographees to unlikely volumes make the look-up task inconclusive until one has examined two or more books in the set.

There is excessive duplication. Sammy Davis, Jr. appears in "Blacks," "Entertainers," and "Musicians, Composers and Singers" as does Louis Armstrong. Dick Gregory shows up as a "Social Reformer and Humanitarian," "Entertainer," and "Blacks." Marian Anderson is accepted as a "Black" and a "Woman" but not as an "Entertainer." Jackie Robinson is both a "Black" and "Sport Champion," Jim Thorpe is an "Indian" and "Sport Champion," and Babe Zaharias is a "Woman" and "Sport Champion." Comparison of the "Blacks," "Scientists," and "Entertainers" reveals 25 additional instances of overlap and many more duplications occur throughout the set.

Peculiar misplacements abound. Marilyn Monroe is a significant "Woman" as well as an "Entertainer" while Georgia O' Keeffe's womanhood is of insufficient magnitude even though she won entry as an "Artist." Dorothy Day and Margaret Sanger are listed as important "Women" but not as "Social Reformers & Humanitarians." Qualifying for entries in the latter volume are Andrew Carnegie and John D. Rockefeller neither of whom had strong credentials as social reformers. Billie Holiday, Charles Mingus, and Thelonius Monk are cited as "Entertainers" but not as "Musicians." Neither Monk nor Mingus are among the "Blacks." Barney Old Coyote and Martha Graham qualify as "Educators" while George S. Counts and Jane Addams do not merit consideration. Among the "Artists" one finds Worley Wong and Jade Snow Wong, Andrew Tsihnahjinnie, Doris Lee, and Don Kingman. Left out are Josef Albers, Lyonel Feininger, Marsden Hartley, Louise Nevelson, and Ben Shahn. Photographers included in this same volume are Gordon Parks, Edward Steichen, and Alfred Steiglitz. Absent are Ansel Adams, Margaret Bourke-White, and Edward Weston. Classical music composers Pedro Flores, William Fry, Yossele Rosenblat, Gustav Strube, and Clarence White are in the "Musicians, Composers and Singers" volume but Samuel Barber, Norman Dello Joio, Elliott Carter, Carl Ruggles, and Virgil Thomson are excluded.

No evidence is presented to back up statements made about biographees. The description of Mary Baker Eddy's life is inconsistent with the two-volume study by scholar Robert Peel. Andrew Carnegie is pictured only as a great philanthropist and humanitarian. Entirely ignored is the miserly and cruel exploitation of workers employed in his industrial empire. Readers are informed that Bessie Smith bled to death because she was not admitted into a Mississippi hospital but not told that Charles Drew, who developed the means of storing and preserving blood plasma, died because he was denied a white man's blood following an accident. Alice B. Toklas is left out of the sketch of Gertrude Stein. Other errors of omission are frequent.

Information varies in length from a brief paragraph to a three-quarter, two-column page. The format of presentation is inconsistent and confusing. Text within the columns sometimes continues down the full length of the page. At other times the biographies are limited to an upper or lower half of a page with the text continuing across half-columns. Coverage of presidents is relatively extensive, with their life stories absorbing two pages of space. The same information exists in an abundance of other sources, so this volume is wholly superfluous.

The cover illustrations are duplications of those appearing with the sketches and are so poorly executed they add little as an introduction to the subjects. Many of the persons portrayed in these amateurish renditions, particularly those in "Sports" and "Entertainers" bear only a very slight resemblance to their pictures. Other sketches depict live subjects as they looked 20 or more years ago. An attempt is made to differentiate between blacks, Indians, and whites but it fails because the skin tones are grotesquely distorted. Jelly Roll Morton appears to be white, Bert Bacharach is tinted as an American Indian, and Aaron Copland is afflicted with jaundice.

The volumes are sturdily bound in cloth buckram, each cover in a different color. The singer sewing prevents the books from lying open for easy use and the inferior grade of paper will not withstand heavy use.

The editors have not indicated which life stories have been excerpted from *People Who Made America* and which have been created especially for this set. In any case, too few of the individuals in the "Contemporary" category are currently active. The youngest of the baseball 'greats' are Hank Aaron and recently retired Willie Mays. Other dubious entries in this category are Mark Spitz and Don Schollander, no longer actively participating in swimming sports; Johnny Unitas and George Blanda, in the twilight of their careers; a very youthful Kareem Jabbar; and two golf pros, Jack Nicklaus and Arnold Palmer, the latter so tanned that his complexion is indistinguishable from that of the "Indians."

Aside from the noted deficiencies in accuracy, authority, currency, illustrations, and format, the set is pervaded by bias. The editors have tried to compensate for past underrepresentation of minority Americans using their status as a decisive criterion. Such unjust reverse discrimination slights minority accomplishment and helps to perpetuate the evil it seeks to eliminate. The editors should have instead established criteria for what constitutes significance and then striven for equitable representation of all individuals who qualified. As it stands, they have violated Aristotle's maxim that equals should be treated equally and unequals unequally by treating equals unequally and unequals equally.

Even though some of the individuals included in this set are indeed worthy albeit obscure figures, especially among the blacks and native Americans, these persons have generally been granted more accurate, current, complete, and lively coverage in other sources. Most junior level encyclopedias will provide more satisfactory information than that given in the brief sketches in *Significant Americans.* There is no valid reason for any school media center, public library, or family to acquire this set.
(Nov. 1, 1976, p.426)

Six little cooks.
[By] Elizabeth Stansbury Kirkland. New York, Arno Pr., 1973. xii, 236p. illus. 19cm. cloth $7.
641.5 Cookery, Juvenile literature [CIP] 72-9796
See page 116

Sociology of America:
a guide to information sources. Compiled by Charles Mark and Paula K. Mark. Detroit, Gale Research Company, [1976]. 454p. 22cm. cloth $18.

A survey of sociological materials about the U.S., this selective bibliography is a guide to nearly 1,900 recent titles, mostly monographs, dealing with a wide range of subjects. According to the Preface, about 85 percent of the titles are by sociologists. Included are 24 chapters. Four of them are of a general nature, comprising an introduction to resources for the sociology of American life, a list of basic reference works, 129 journals broken down into various subject categories (*Social Psychology, Interdisciplinary Journals, Popular Culture and Mass Media,* and so on), and a list of 126 works dealing with American sociology. The remaining 20 chapters traverse the subdivisions of sociology. *Crime and Delinquency, Education,* and the *Urban Community* account for the most items, 125, 101, and 98 respectively; *Youth,* the *Jewish Community,* and *Women* have the smallest representation with only 40, 46, and 48 entries each. These chapters are sectionalized. For example, within chapter 22, *Crime and Delinquency,* there are small groups of titles (4 to 17) for *Police, Gangs, Organized Crime, Juvenile Courts,* and *Social Policy,* plus eleven other categories. Brief annotations are supplied except where the titles and subtitles are sufficiently explanatory. Besides a topical arrangement there are three indexes: author, title, and subject. The work could help a student find references on a subject, and a librarian could use it as an auxiliary selection tool. It is not indispensable because someone needing books on a given subject could consult the same bibliographical reference tools and scholarly journals as did the compilers of this work. The resultant product would be more current and relevant because of the hectic publication pace and rapid obsolescence of much writing in sociology.
(Apr. 1, 1977, p.1198)

016.3091'73 U.S.—Social conditions—1960- —Bibliography ‖ Sociology—History—U.S.
—Bibliography [CIP] 73-17560

Sources of information in water resources:
an annotated guide to printed materials. [Compiled by] Gerald J. Giefer. [Port Washington, N.Y., Water Information Center, c1976.] xvii, 290p. 24cm. cloth $23.50.

Gerald J. Giefer, librarian, Water Resources Center Archives, University of California, Berkeley, compiled *Sources of Information in Water Resources* as an annotated guide to over 1,100 selected printed references that can be used by students and researchers. In general, the period covered is 1960 to date. Literature of the U.S. is emphasized, and there is no attempt to give balanced coverage to the states or to treat all reference works in existence. Textbooks are outside the scope of the book, and very few journal articles are cited.

Entries have been arranged in a form which is a modification of the water resources categories set up by the Federal Council for Science and Technology Committee in Water Resources Research: General Works; Maps and Atlases; Biology, Agriculture, Chemistry; Conferences and Meetings; Information Transfer; Theses; Water Resources Research Educational Programs; Nature of Water; Water Cycle; Arid Lands; Eutrophication; Geothermal Resources; Groundwater; Meteorology, Climatology, Evaporation and Transpiration; Sedimentation, Soils, Erosion, Subsidence; Water Supply; Foods; Forestry; etc. Within the subject classes, reference books are arranged by forms as applicable: guides and manuals, bibliographies, indexes and abstract journals, encyclopedias, dictionaries, publication lists, handbooks, directories, and data compilations. Full bibliographic data are given, and the annotations are descriptive. A very comprehensive Index of authors, subjects, and titles will aid the user in locating specific information.

Sources of Information in Water Resources will save search time in locating bibliographic material, basic data, and background information on a wide variety of topics related to water resources. *(Oct. 1, 1976, p.280)*

†016.333'91   Water resources development—Bibliography || Water resources development || Water supply—Bibliography   [OCLC]   75-20953

Southwestern cookery:
Indian and Spanish influences. Intro. and suggested recipes by Louis Szathmary. New York, Arno Pr., 1973. xxii, 124, 79, 5, 18, 264p. 22cm. cloth, $12.

641.5   Cookery, American—Southwestern States || Indians of North America—Food   [CIP]
72-9803

See page 116

Sports olympiques album officiel/
Olympic sports official album:
Montreal 1976. By Roger de Groote, translated and adapted from the French by Betty Howell, Toronto, Boston, Little, Brown & Co., 1975. cloth $19.95; to schools and libraries, 20 percent discount.

This beautiful book was printed in Canada by Les Editions Martell, Ltée., and in the U.S. by Little, Brown and Company in association with *Sports Illustrated Magazine*. The U.S. edition with side-by-side columns of French and English text on each page, differs from the Canadian edition in that it has appended to it a thirty-page supplement on buff-colored paper containing a summary of American participation on the International Olympic Committee, a statement about Avery Brundage's advocacy and leadership of the International Olympic movement, a history of U.S. participation in the Summer Olympics from 1896 through the tragedy-dominated Munich games, and a roster of U.S. Olympic champions and medalists.

Approximately 200 photographs and 75 diagrams and schematics are included. Over two-thirds of the photographs are in color, some of them breathtakingly effective stop-motion photographs of straining athletes engaged in competitive events. Also depicted are course and field plans, reproductions of Greek vases decorated with athletic motifs, and ancient and contemporary sites for the games.

The work begins with a 15-page illustrated historical and promotional guide to Montreal, the host city for the 1976 games. Subsequent sections briefly discuss ancient and modern games, symbolism and ceremonial events, prizes, medals, and certificates. This introductory material ends with a table summarizing the number of women and men participants and nations represented at previous games. It was estimated that 9,500 athletes from 132 countries would be present at the Montreal Olympiad.

The main body of the *Album*, 230 pages, is comprised of coverage of sports and events alphabetized according to French spellings. Included are track and field events, rowing, basketball, boxing, canoeing, cycling, fencing, soccer, gymnastics, weightlifting, handball, field hockey, judo, wrestling, swimming, diving, water polo, pentathlon, equestrian sports, shooting, archery, volleyball, and yachting. Statistical tables with rosters of names of all Summer Olympic champions from 1896 to 1972 are provided. For each winner, the dimensions of achievement (distance, weight, score, etc.), country represented, year award was earned, and city hosting the competition are identified. Rules of each sport are summarized with Olympic regulations stressed whenever they differ from U.S. practice.

The text has a promotional ambience which tends to exclude less salubrious aspects of the games' history. Sports which were to be stressed during the 1976 games are also given relatively heavy coverage. (For example, cycling is covered in 16 pages, basketball in less than 4.) A few typographical errors and unfelicitous translations into English were noted by the Committee. Also, given names are omitted in the rosters of winning athletes, and their first initials are not consistently provided.

Print, illustrations, and paper are all of superior quality; the book's pages lie flat when opened, and its binding will stand up well under normal use.

Sports Olympiques Album Officiel/Olympic Sports Official Album: Montreal 1976 is primarily a recollection of past events and not, as its titles implies, a program of the 1976 games. The work lacks an index, providing only a Table of Contents, so that it is unresponsive to readers seeking quick answers to questions pertaining to particular athletes, events, and records. However, it will be appreciated by public and school library patrons because of its attractive layout, superior color photographs, and fascinating array of facts about the 20 last Olympiads.

(Sept. 1, 1976, p.58)

796.4   Olympic games—Revival, 1896–   [OCLC]   75-29964

Stamp collectors' handbook.
By Fred Reinfeld; adapted by Burton Hobson; revised by Beatrice Reinfeld. Garden City, N.Y., Doubleday, [1976]. 160p. illus. 20cm. cloth $5.95.

The introductory third of this brief handbook includes a history of the U.S. postal system, a description of collectors' tools and terms, and a section entitled "Hobby or Investment?" The rest of the volume is a catalog of U.S. stamps from 1847 to 1975, with about two-thirds of the stamps illustrated with black-and-white reproductions adequate for identification. For each is given the quantity printed, when known, identification of portrait or scene, color, whether perforated, and value both unused and used. The catalog is subdivided into regular issues, commemorative issues, air mail stamps, air mail special delivery stamps, special delivery issues, registration stamps, special handling stamps, and parcel post series.

The title is misleading as the handbook deals only with U.S. stamps. The catalog section identifies stamps only by year of issue, not using a numbering system as in the Scott or Minkus catalogs. The one-page Index was obviously edited to fit the last page. It includes some of the terms defined in the introductory chapters and omits many others of equal importance while committing two lines to "postage stamp, catalogue of, 62–159." There is also a reference, "pane, see sheet," but no index entry for "sheet." The handbook would be useful as an introduction to the hobby for children, and the brief history of the U.S. postal system is interesting. However, the book has no value as a reference tool. *(Apr. 1, 1977, p.1199)*

769.56   Postage stamps—Collectors and collecting   [OCLC]   77-111945

State constitutional conventions: 1959–1975;
a bibliography. Compiled by Susan Rice Yarger. Westport, Conn.; London; Greenwood Pr., [c1976]. xxxiii, 50p. 24cm. cloth $10.

Between 1959 and 1975 eighteen states (Arkansas, Connecticut, Florida, Hawaii, Illinois, Louisiana, Maryland, Michigan, Montana, New Hampshire, New Jersey, New Mexico, New York, North Dakota, Pennsylvania, Rhode Island, Tennessee, and Texas) held constitutional conventions. The current Greenwood bibliography is intended as a supplement to E. C. Browne's *State Constitutional Conventions from Independence to the Completion of the Present Union, 1776–1959,* also published by Greenwood. The present book claims to cover "all publications of state constitutional conventions, commissions, and legislative or executive committees, and all special studies prepared for the convention or commission bodies."

The bibliography proper is preceded by a 20-page Introduction written by Professor Richard H. Leach of Duke University and taken in large part from *The Book of the States* section on "State Constitutions and Constitutional Revision." The text of the bibliography is arranged alphabetically by state. Documents are cited chronologically by date of publication. Various documents such as enabling legislation, proceedings, journals, resolutions and rules, public hearings, proposed constitutions, and constitutions as revised and implemented by the electorate are listed. For political science and law libraries *State Constitutional Conventions: 1959–1975,* reproduced from typewritten copy, will serve as a useful bibliography of items produced on this subject during the past 25 years. *(Dec. 1, 1976, p.565)*

016.342'73'024 Constitutional Conventions—U.S.—States—Bibliography || Constitutions, State—U.S.—Bibliography [CIP] 75-40939

The statesman's year-book world gazetteer.
[By] John Paxton. New York, St. Martin's Pr., [c1975]. xiii, 733, 24p. maps. 21cm. cloth $15; to libraries, $12.

The World Gazetteer is designed as a companion to *The Statesman's Year-Book,* which "provides absolutely up-to-date information about every place one is likely to encounter in the course of general reading." In addition to providing basic information on each place cited (location, population by estimate or census, source of income, and facts on history, culture, commerce), the gazetteer provides three added features: a section of definitions of some 900 geographical terms; a selection of comparative statistical tables on crude petroleum production, hydroelectric generating plants, territorial sea limits, telephones in countries having more than 500,000 instruments in 1973, national populations, 23 examples of ocean depth, mountain height, geographical and population figures for large areas of the earth; and 14 colored maps showing some of the places described in the gazetteer. *The Statesman's Year-Book World Gazetteer* is a handy, reasonably priced complement to *The Statesman's Year-Book,* and as such it will be useful in school, public, and college and university libraries.
(Sept. 1, 1976, p.58)

910'.3 Gazetteers [OCLC] 74-16097

Sub-aqua illustrated dictionary.
[By] Leo Zanelli and George Skuse. London, Kaye & Ward; New York, Oxford Univ. Pr., [1976]. 114p. illus. 21cm. cloth $7.95.

This dictionary of underwater diving terms is British in tone and content, but since scuba diving and other subaqueous activities are essentially international in character, the vast majority of terms used—such as "wet suit," "paddleboard," and "quick release belt," as well as more general terms like "lifejacket," "nautical mile," and "sonar"—are in common use by both British and U.S. divers. Occasionally there are minor differences. The British use E.C.G. for an electrocardiogram instead of our familiar EKG, and the spellings of "harbour" and "aluminium" will perhaps be noted as strange by U.S. readers. All entries, except for proper names, begin with lower-case letters.

As is the case in most dictionaries, pages are double-columned. The definitions are usually quite brief, often consisting of only four or five lines and seldom running beyond ten. Exceptions are the entry for the history of diving, which runs to nearly a page (71 lines), oxygen poisoning (36 lines), metal fatigue (30 lines), and hypothemia (23). No etymologies or pronunciations are included. A few British slang terms are to be found, such as "Donald Duck," a phrase describing the unnatural, high-pitched speech of divers while breathing helium; but no strictly American ones were noticed.

The book contains more than 70 black-and-white illustrations, most of them quarter-page size, showing details of present-day, as well as some historical, apparatus for diving, breathing, photographing, measuring, and observing underwater. Very brief, unillustrated biographical sketches of prominent early and contemporary undersea explorers and inventors from Franz Kessler and John Letheridge to Jacques-Yves Cousteau and Emile Gagnan are included. Cross-references are indicated by the symbol°. The entries for many countries (e.g., Costa Rica, Finland, Ireland, Italy, Israel) consist only of the names and addresses of their national association of divers. But there is no entry under the word "clubs," or "associations," or any similar word that might give a complete list of such organizations.

The Preface speaks of the difficulty of deciding what to include and what to exclude. Surprisingly, ordinary words such as "communicate," "contact lens," and "knife" have been included, and "knife" is even illustrated, though the object pictured resembles an ordinary hunting knife and hardly seems to need special definition. On the other hand, "mouth-to-mouth resuscitation" is not defined, nor is "Galeazzi chamber," though there is a biographical entry for Robert Galeazzi after whom this type of decompression chamber was named.

There are a few minor errors and inconsistencies. There is a *see* reference at the end of the article "noble gas" to "radon," but there is no such entry (nor is there an entry for "niton," the former name of "radon"). Among inconsistencies noted are the following: *port* is defined but not "starboard;" *inboard* is defined but not "outboard;" and *gage* is a main entry, while "gauge" is used in combined terms such as *pressure gauge.* Under the entry "conversions" there are a few selected conversion factors, mainly from British measures to metric ones, and the reverse. The factors for converting miles to nautical miles, and the reverse, are given in inexact fractions, while other conversions in the same table, such as litres to pints, use the more precise decimal notation. Incidentally, the word "mile" is not defined, though "nautical mile" and "fathom" do appear as entries, with their values given in meters and feet.

Besides the above brief table of conversion factors, there are other useful tables in the work, such as a table of visibilities, ranging from 50 yards (dense fog—Code 0) to 30 miles (excellent visibility—Code 9); a table of the Beaufort wind scale, as used on both land and sea; regulator air-flow requirements at various depths; and a table of "no-stop times," showing the maximum length of times allowable, under both U.S. Navy and Royal Navy standards, for a diver to remain underwater and still make, from varying depths, a "no-stop" ascent, that is, an ascent from the bottom, at a constant speed of 18 meters per minute, without a decompression stage.

The work concludes with a Bibliography of 286 books dealing with diving, undersea photography, salvage, the ocean floor, and the like, including such classics as Rachel Carson's *The Sea Around Us* and 19 titles by Jacques-Yves Cousteau.

On the whole this small, almost pocket-size, dictionary will prove useful to the ever growing number of scuba divers and other persons interested in exploring the undersea world, both in Great Britain and in the U.S. *(Apr. 15, 1977, p.1297)*

†797.203   Diving—Dictionaries || Skindiving—Dictionaries

Subject guide to humor:
anecdotes, facetiae and satire from 365 periodicals, 1968–74. By Jean Spealman Kujoth. Metuchen, N.J., Scarecrow Press, Inc., 1976. vii, 199p. 23cm. B-grade cloth $8.

Jean Kujoth died while the *Subject Guide to Humor* was being produced by Scarecrow. She was a free-lance bibliographer who had produced eight other Scarecrow books; among them were *Best-Selling Children's Books* (1973) and *Subject Guide to Periodical Indexes and Review Indexes.* For the preparation of the *Subject Guide to Humor,* Kujoth consulted 14 general and subject periodical indexes, e.g., *Biological and Agricultural Index, Index to Legal Periodicals, Social Sciences and Humanities Index,* and *Readers' Guide to Periodical Literature,* searching out 365 periodicals published from 1968 to 1974 which contained humorous, anecdotal, and satiric articles. The result is a list of 1,800 articles and stories that can be used by students and speech writers.

The book is conveniently arranged in four sections: A Classified Section which presents the materials and their sources under 15 general subjects (e.g., religion, social relationships, economics and business, literature, mass media, and publishing), Specific-Subject Index (an analytical index which breaks down the 15 major subjects), an Author Index, and a Title Index. *Subject Guide to Humor* is reasonably priced. It will provide high school and public library patrons with a good guide to humor in journals of the late 1960s and early 1970s.

(May 15, 1977, p.1454)

016.80887   Wit and humor—Indexes   [CIP]   76-4865

A supplement to the Oxford English dictionary.
v.II, H–N. Edited by R. W. Burchfield. Oxford, Clarendon Press, 1976. 1,282p. 31cm. buckram $60.

The *Supplement* when completed will contain vocabulary of "all 'common words' (and senses) in British written English" which came into use during the publication years of the original *O.E.D.* (1884–1928), not already included, together with new vocabulary up to the present day. The earlier *Supplement* of 1933 will be superseded. V.I (*A–G*) of the *Supplement* was reviewed in *Reference and Subscription Books Reviews* May 1, 1973, p.818. Information noted at that time pertaining to the general purpose, methods of preparation, content and arrangement of the entries, and the chronological order of the quotations is also applicable to the present volume. A vocabulary sample of v.I (*A–G*) indicated broad subject coverage of all major academic subjects, with particular emphasis on science and technology. Many diverse sources were used for the new words and for additional uses and meanings of other words.

R. W. Burchfield has continued as editor in v.II (*H–N*). In the Preface, Burchfield recognizes many scholars who assisted with the *Supplement,* some no longer living, others who have been added as consultants for v.II. Unusual numbers of valuable quotations have been collected by several of the individual contributors. The *New York Times, New Yorker,* and regional publications in the U.S., Canada, and Britain have continued to be basic sources. The Hench Collection of quotations from newspapers of several Eastern and Southern cities of the U.S. for the years from 1930 onward has become a new source for this volume, evident in entries for letter *M* and beyond. Contributions from South African English were made by W. R. G. Branford and the staff of the forthcoming *Dictionary of South African English.* A collection of quotations for Australian colloquialisms was made available by G. A. Wilkes of the University of Sydney. Other specialists assisted with words of Japanese and Russian origin.

With the increase of excellent quotation material, v.II (*H–N*) has been greatly expanded in vocabulary and quotations, particularly in its later letters. It contains some 13,000 Main Words divided into 22,000 senses; almost 8,000 defined Combinations within the articles and more than 5,000 undefined Combinations; and 125,000 illustrative quotations. The *Supplement* as originally planned was to be complete in three volumes, but after v.II (*H–N*), an additional two volumes will be required for completion. A bibliography based upon verified book titles of all the works cited in the *Supplement* will be included in the final volume.

In addition to the expansion made possible by new sources of quotations, Burchfield indicates "new areas explored" in vocabulary selection. He cites papers and addresses on a variety of aspects of lexicography which he has recently contributed to learned societies. Some research conclusions, briefly stated in the Preface, are that "offensiveness to a particular group, minority or otherwise, is unacceptable as the sole ground for the exclusion of any word or class of words from the O.E.D." and that the "antiquated historical record" of controversial words ought to be brought up to date "to avoid misunderstanding and consequent hostility." Certain sexual words "once considered too gross and vulgar" have therefore been included. Derogatory ethnic words and expressions have received an exacting treatment, with appropriate designations such as "vulgarly offensive" or "deliberate and contemptuous ethnic abuse." Examples of Burchfield's updating of the "antiquated historical record" are the entries for "Jesuit," "Jew," and "Negro," which have been expanded with recent quotations. The entry for "Negro" notes "the increasing use of the word 'Black'."

V.II (*H–N*) continues the breadth of coverage demonstrated in v.I. This portion of the alphabet contains many entries for the arts and literature as well as the social sciences, sciences, and technology. Entries are comprehensive for such prefixes as *iso, mega, micro, hyper, neuro,* and others. World War II and military vernacular are evident, as are many words and phrases imported into the language from a variety of areas and cultures. The editor notes that particular attention was paid to the vocabulary of the West Indies and Scotland in this volume.

For slang words and expressions, Burchfield acknowledges the Partridge *Dictionary of Slang* as a basic source. V.II (*H–N*) contains entry words, and words and expressions within its longer entries, which are also found in Partridge's *Dictionary of Slang and Unconventional English* (New York: Macmillan Co., 7th ed., 1970) and *A Dictionary of the Underworld* (London: Routledge & Kegan Paul Ltd., 3d ed., 1968). These specialized dictionaries are based upon colloquial speech, and the *Supplement* shares selected vocabulary with them in accord with its scope of " 'common words' (and senses) in British written English." A sample of slang and other words from *The Barnhart Dictionary of New English Since 1963* (New York: Harper & Row, 1973) was found to be in v.II (*H–N*) without exception, perhaps because *The Barnhart Dictionary* cites and shares the definition of "common vocabulary" stated in the original *O.E.D.* A sample of American slang from the Wentworth and Flexner *Dictionary of American Slang* (New York: Thomas Y. Crowell Company, 2d ed. 1975) also correlated to a high degree when the words were cited from written sources. The *Supplement* provides excellent depth in the quotation sources for the selected slang and colloquial words and expressions that fall within its scope but does not take the place of slang and other special dictionaries.

It is difficult to single out individual entries in this volume, which maintains and extends the outstanding lexicography and historical insight of the first volume of the *Supplement.* Among the fascinating-to-read entries in v.II (*H–N*) are "heliport," "high-muck-a-muck," "informatics," "ipsissima verba," "jazz," "jive," "kazoo," "Kilroy," "laugh-in," "lobsterish," "mass medium," "moondoggle," "New Frontier," and "Nixonian." The complete *Supplement* promises to be an essential resource for most public and academic libraries and for anyone who would savor or subtly employ the English language of our time.

(May 15, 1977, p.1455)

423 English language—Dictionaries [British Library CIP]

Tanks and other armoured fighting vehicles 1942–1945.
By B. T. White; illus. by John W. Wood. New York, Macmillan, [c1975]. 171p. illus. 20cm. paper over board $6.95.

358'.18'09044 Tanks (Military science) || Armored vehicles, Military || World War, 1939–1945
[CIP]   75-28306

See page 103

Travel market yearbook, 1975/1976.
Stamford, Conn., Marketing Handbooks, [1975?]. 100p. illus. charts. diagrs. 28cm. paper $20 prepaid.

The 1975/1976 *Travel Market Yearbook* is the eleventh annual, presenting facts and figures that illustrate the interrelationships between travel, travelers' habits, and travel service industries. The hundreds of tables, charts, diagrams, and graphs in the book are derived from reliable sources and will interest the general reader as well as persons in the travel business. Organized into seven chapters ("Travel Market Perspectives," "The U.S. Travel Market: Carriers," "The Travel Service Industries," "The United States Family Car Travel Market," "Travel International," "Travel Advertising and Promotion," and "Traveler Characteristics"), most of the data represent the 1974 calendar year. Examination of the travel service industry chapter reveals the diversity of the illustrative material: "Number of Agencies," "Agency Sales by Purpose of Trip," "Components of Travel Agency Dollar Volume," " 'Very Effective' Ratings of Means to Attract New Customers," and "Agents Rating Types of Information and Other Factors 'Very Important' in Investigation/Selection of Hotel for Client" are titles of well-designed graphs and tables which all appear on one page. Twenty-three additional graphs and tables are provided in the same chapter. There is some explanatory text in each chapter, but most of the space is utilized by displays of statistical data.

Twenty pages of the yearbook contain advertisements, 19 of which are full-page promotional plugs for newspapers and magazines. An Editorial Index cites major topics covered and refers to them by page. However, this Index is not an effective substitute for an analytical index that would give the reader ready access to the wealth of facts contained in the book. For example, such valuable tables as "Visitors to the U.S. from Top Ten Countries" (p.63) and "Growth of the Interstate Highway System 1963 vs. 1974" (p.51) are not referred to in either the Index or the Contents and will go unnoticed unless one browses through the book carefully.

Even with the drawback of inadequate finding devices, the *Travel Market Yearbook* is a good source of information that will be useful to those in the travel or related businesses and to active travelers.   *(Sept. 1, 1976, p.58)*

910.5 Tourist trade—Yearbooks [OCLC]   66-635

Treasures of Britain and treasures of Ireland:
[a traveller's guide to the riches of Britain and Ireland]. Prepared by the Automobile Association. 3d ed. New York, Norton; London, Drive Publications, Ltd., [1976]. 680p. illus. maps. 29cm. cloth $19.75; to schools and libraries, 25 percent discount.

There are several excellent "traveller's guides to Britain," but this is not one of them. On the other hand, it is deserving of a place in any collection of reference material concerned with the archeological, historical, architectural and artistic treasures of Great Britain and Ireland. However, it is publicized as a "traveller's guide," and it should be reviewed as such.

First, the book weighs just a shade under four pounds—hardly the thing to tote about in your knapsack on a weekend walking tour of the southern countries; and it stands over eleven inches high—not too easy to stow in the glove compartment of a small car.

Second, though the work is now in its third edition, it still retains awkward design fixtures which would not endear it to a traveler, especially a non-British one.

Although the guide begins with a 40-page survey of the history of England with particular emphasis on man-made features of cultural significance, its main section is a gazetteer of more than 4,000 place-names in Britain and Ireland (Ireland in a separate alphabet), telling where one may find famous buildings, ruins, houses, castles, colleges, bridges, gardens and giving short or long descriptions according to their importance or interest. About 700 of these items, including many paintings and art objects to be seen inside the various buildings, are reproduced in color photographs. In addition there are about 200 black-and-white illustrations of famous people, places, or things prominent in the history of England, and also drawings of the principal details of British architecture and decoration from Saxon times to the outbreak of World War I. These graphics all add to the aesthetic and reference value of the book.

But the utilization of much of this information is beset with difficulty. First of all, because the book is arranged alphabetically by locality and/or name of structure, guide maps to the more than 4,000 such places are essential. A section of 38 pages of maps is provided, based on Ordnance Survey maps, with a scale of 10 miles to the inch (12½ miles to the inch for Ireland). These are described as "superlative maps" on the dust jacket, but in actual use they appear to be somewhat deficient. First, there are no railroads shown. This is understandable; the book is published for the Automobile Association. But there are no rivers either. Among England's great rivers, only the Severn is identified by name, and the others are shown as extending for only a few kilometers inland from their estuaries. Scanning the maps, one finds an unnamed river flowing from a source just behind London's Lambeth Palace and proceeding eastward, past Greenwich and Tilbury, until it runs out into the sea near Southend, where its estuary is about five miles wide. Omission of such historically important and interesting rivers as the Thames, Avon, Trent, and Clyde is a serious shortcoming in a book billed as a "traveller's guide."

Third, no topography or elevations are shown despite the presence of much hilly terrain in both Britain and Ireland.

Fourth, each map is presented with a two-inch foldout tab, a patented device, so that the western two inches (20 miles) of any map is likewise the eastern 20 miles of the next map. This is a good feature, providing continuity for at least east/west travel. But unless each flap is carefully folded back after each use, the tabs will become frayed.

Next, the maps run across two pages and have such deep gutters that center sections are difficult to read. Also the page numbers are in a peculiar place: in the gutter and at the bottom of the page so that their consultation requires the reader to strain the book slightly.

Lastly, each place in the gazetteer is given a map number and grid reference. The grid coordinates are expressed in capital and small letters instead of in more efficient alpha-numeric combinations.

Treasures of Britain and Treasures of Ireland is being offered for sale in this country, but place-name abbreviations certain to puzzle Americans—Hants., Leics., Glos., Oxon., Salop., and so on—are given without explanation. Furthermore, pronunciations of names of such places as Culzean, or Berwick, or Cholmondeley, or Drogheda are not provided. Only the exceptional

American could be expected to speak these "trippingly on the tongue." Lastly, no precise street or area locations are given, except within London. This may be alright in the country. If you go to visit Melrose, you probably will not need directions to find the Abbey. And if you go to Salisbury, you can hardly miss the Cathedral. But what about Syon House, whose only indication is "Greater London"? Is it in Brentford, Richmond, Twickenham, or Isleworth? And on what precise street or road is the main entrance? The book does not say.

Aside from the above deficiencies which limit the work's usefulness for Americans, the book lacks a preface, and running heads in the gazetteer section, the largest part of the guide, are sometimes confusing because they frequently commingle entry and heading information.

At the back of the book, there is a list of "Famous People: Their Works and Whereabouts" that includes architects, divines, politicians, sculptors, and stained-glass makers, indicating where their works or memorabilia may be seen. Surprisingly, painters are not represented despite the fact that many of their works are illustrated in the guide.

There is also a list of museums in Great Britain, arranged by topics (e.g., Armour, Maritime, and Pottery). Again, collections of paintings are excluded. At the conclusion of the book, there is a glossary entitled "The Language of Experts," divided into ten sections including Architecture, Furniture, Gardens, Silver and Gold, and the Parish Church. This means that if the reader cannot categorize an unknown term, several alphabets must be searched with no certainty of success.

Despite the aforementioned weaknesses of the work, it is an excellent source of information about the cultural treasures of Britain with very fine illustrations of some 700 of the most important of them. Described art objects include those located in out-of-the-way towns and villages as well as those held by prestigious museums. Particularly informative are the brief descriptions of churches, palaces, and other architectural landmarks. The guide belongs in any collection devoted to history of British art and architecture. But as a "traveller's guide" it leaves much to be desired. It is too bulky, too unhandy to use, and it omits too much that a traveler needs to know, such as exact location within a city, correct local pronunciation, proper name of county, names of rivers that will be frequently met with, elevations of land, and much else. *(July 1, 1977, p.1679)*
914.2   Gt. Brit.—Description and travel—Guidebooks || Ireland—Description and travel—Guidebooks   [OCLC]

The treasury of houseplants.
[By] Rob Herwig and Margot Schubert; tr. by Marian Powell. New York, Macmillan Pub. Co., [1976]. 368p. illus. (part col.) diagrs. 22cm. cloth $12.95.

The Treasury of Houseplants is the first American edition of the 1974 Dutch publication, *Het Grote Kamer Planten Boek,* which has also been published in Great Britain as *The Complete Book of Houseplants.* The British publication should not be confused with Charles M. Fitch's 1972 Hawthorn publication with the same title.

The Treasury of Houseplants is a comprehensive guide to the selection, maintenance, and identification of houseplants, covering more than 240 genera and approximately 1,000 individual plants. In addition to full-color close-up photographs of mature plants and, where applicable, their bloom, the book contains detailed black-and-white line drawings depicting methods of propagation, plant repotting, pests, and possible display ideas.

The authors provide detailed information on each plant's name origin, natural habitat, characteristics and approximate number of species, watering, feeding, preferred methods of propagation, and diseases or pests to which it is most susceptible. Concise sections are devoted to terraria (maintenance, planting, and container selection) and, for the advanced or experimenting gardener, cultivation of plants in nutrient solutions.

Three sections have been legibly printed on light green paper: The Practical Care of Houseplants, Survey of Plant Families, and For Quick Reference. These provide background information on how to assure plant survival. Attention is devoted to light and shade conditions in rooms, advantages and disadvantages of various directional exposures, water pH values and their effect on plants, humidity, and the control of pests and disease.

The illustrations are crisp and clear enough to permit easy identification of plants. Most of the illustrations are in colors true to the natural plant. Diagrams are sharp, clear, and easy to follow.

Included in the For Quick Reference section is a cross-reference glossary of 29 technical terms, a classification of plants by light requirements, and the Index. The Index to subjects and common and scientific names of plants facilitates locating specific information.

Other books on houseplants by Herwig include *128 Houseplants You Can Grow, 128 More Houseplants You Can Grow,* and *128 Bulbs You Can Grow.* *(Feb. 1, 1977, p.857)*
635.9'65   House plants   [CIP]   75-34283

TV season 74–75:
programs, stars, creators, award winners, everything on tv in 1974–1975. Compiled and edited by Nina David. Phoenix, Oryx Pr., [c1976]. xxv, 200p. 24cm. cloth $13.95 plus $.95 for shipping and handling.
791.45   Television programs   [OCLC]   76-22622

TV season 75–76:
programs, stars, creators, award winners, everything on tv in 1975–1976. Compiled and edited by Nina David. Phoenix, Oryx Pr., [c1977]. xxxi, 245p. 24cm. cloth $13.95 plus $.95 for shipping and handling.
†791.45   Television programs   76-52260

TV Season is the first reference book to record current facts and statistics on television programs and figures on an annual basis. The 16 preliminary pages in the 74–75 edition contain 5 lists: "Shows Cancelled During 1974–1975 Season," "New Shows 1974–1975" "New Shows Cancelled During 1974–1975 Season," "Summer Shows 1975," and "Emmy Awards." The 1975–76 edition includes the Peabody award winners. The main section of both books is an alphabetically arranged and consecutively numbered listing of 1974–75 and 1975–76 television programs presented by ABC, NBC, CBS, and PBS, as well as currently produced syndicated shows that have national distribution. Time period covered is September 9, 1974 (the first day of the season as designated by the networks), to September 20, 1976.

Information given for each show includes (as applicable): time in minutes, program type (animated film, game show, children's show, documentary, feature film, interview), producer, director, distributor, editor, and production company, writer, music director, and cast. A 15-page, 5-column "Who's Who in TV 1974–1975" and a similar 18-page listing for the 1975–76 volume serve as an Index to names in the main listings. Reference is by show number. The books are sturdily bound and have wide enough margins to permit rebinding. All types of libraries with clientele interested in the history of television and annual programming will find *TV Season* an inexpensive and easy-to-use source of information. *(May 15, 1977, p.1455)*

Ukrainians in North America:
a biographical directory of noteworthy men and women of Ukrainian origin in the United States and Canada. Dmytro M. Shtohryn, editor. Champaign, Ill., Association for the Advancement of Ukrainian Studies, 1975. xxiv, 424p. 25cm. cloth, $27; to shools, $25.

The editor of this biographical directory is D. M. Shtohryn, professor of library administration and head of Slavic cataloging at the University of Illinois Library. Assisted by four other librarians and a professor of economics, he compiled the first Ukrainian "Who's Who" in English. It contains biographical notes on 1,173 U.S. and Canadian residents. Additionally included are sketches of 35 individuals who died during the preparation of the publication, i.e., between 1973 and 1975. Their treatments appear in a separate section at the end of the directory. Information on entrants was obtained through questionnaires and supplemented when necessary by data from secondary biographical sources.

This useful reference book lists many Americans and Canadians of Ukrainian origin who have received recognition for their accomplishments or obtained national and international patents for their inventions.

The selection was based on four main factors: (1) positions and responsibilities held; (2) scientific, scholarly, and professional work; (3) cultural, social, and political activities; and (4) past positions and services. Biographical notes contain the following information: personal data, education, positions, military service, society membership, publications, knowledge of languages besides English, address. The professions and activities of biographees range from spiritual leader (archbishop-metropolitan M. Hermaniuk) to film star (Jack Palance); from artist (William Kurelek) to physician (W. M. Lukash, personal physician to President Ford); from nuclear scientist (G. Kistiakowsky) to educator (L. Dobriansky).

Providing essential information about prominent members of a large Ukrainian segment of the population in the U.S. (over 1,100,000) and in Canada (581,000), the directory will be a valuable addition to a reference collection of any academic and public library. *(Nov. 1, 1976, p.428)*

†301.451 Ukrainians in U.S.—Biography || Ukrainians in Canada—Biography || U.S.—Ukrainians—Biography || Canada—Ukrainians—Biography   [OCLC]
75-31726

U.S. government scientific & technical periodicals.
Compiled by Philip A. Yannarella and Rao Aluri. Metuchen, N.J., Scarecrow Pr., Inc., 1976. viii, 263p. 22cm. cloth $10.

U.S. Government Scientific & Technical Periodicals was compiled by Nebraska librarians Yannarella and Aluri to fill the need for a bibliography or guide "focussing on the federal scientific output, especially of periodicals." The compilers are successful in describing more than 250 scientific and technical periodicals emanating from U.S. government agencies or federal contractors and grantees. Included are primary journals, review serials, indexing and abstracting services, and newsletters covering such subjects as chemistry, physics, engineering, medicine, biology, meteorology, and oceanography. Entries cite the title of journal or series, Superintendent of Documents class number, frequency, issuing agency and address, Depository item number, subscription price, distribution policy and ordering information, summary history of the periodical, and abstract, LC card number, indexing and abstracting services which cover it, and locations holding journal on microfilm.

A second section lists bibliographies and publications issued by U.S. government agencies. Here Superintendent of Documents number, issuing agency, subscription information, earlier titles, and Library of Congress card number are given. College and university libraries and researchers will find *U.S. Government Scientific & Technical Periodicals* useful as a guide to federally sponsored serial publications particularly in the subject fields of oceanography, meteorology, public health, and conservation of natural resources. *(Sept. 15, 1976, p.205)*

016.5'05   Science—Periodicals—Bibliography—Union lists || Technology—Periodicals—Bibliography—Union lists || Catalogs, Union—U.S. || American periodicals—Bibliography—Union lists   [CIP]
75-38740

The vice-presidents and cabinet members: biographies arranged chronologically by administration. 2v. By Robert L. Vexler. Dobbs Ferry, N.Y., Oceana Publications, Inc., 1975. xix, 887p. 26cm. cloth $25 per volume.

According to its editor, Robert L. Vexler, the intention of *Vice-Presidents and Cabinet Members* is "to present the basic information concerning the public and private lives" of the vice-presidents and cabinet officers of the U.S. The sketches, chronologically arranged by administration from 1789 to the end of 1974, present information about each person in a set formula: parentage, education, career prior to appointment or election, principal accomplishments while in office, subsequent career, death, place of burial, and bibliography. The articles, which are generally one to three pages in length, are written in a clear, straightforward manner.

Because biographical sketches of vice-presidents and cabinet officers appear in the *Dictionary of American Biography* and the *National Cyclopedia of American Biography,* libraries having these sources will not need to acquire *Vice-Presidents and Cabinet Members.* This work is reproduced by offset from typewritten copy. Omissions of single letters from words, faulty cross-references, and incorrect dates were noted by the Committee.

There is an extensive Name Index of 46 pages, two columns to a page, in which virtually all the personal names mentioned in the text are included. The work also has an Appendix similar in text and typography to the Executive Officers sections of that useful government document, *Biographical Directory of the American Congress 1774–1971.* The Appendix shows the vice-presidents and cabinet officers for each presidential administration and indicates when they assumed their executive responsibilities. The references in the bibliographies are mostly works of well-known trade book publishers, with recent titles being fairly well represented. Usually a half dozen or so references follow each sketch.

The usefulness of *The Vice-Presidents and Cabinet Members* is limited because information it contains is available in other more carefully edited and authoritative sources.
(Sept. 1, 1976, p.58)

973'.0992   Vice-Presidents—U.S.—Bibliography || Cabinet Officers—U.S.—Bibliography || U.S.—Biography   [CIP]
75-28085

Washington information directory, 1976–77.
[Directory editor: Patricia Ann O'Connor.] [Washington, D.C.], Congressional Quarterly, 1976. xxx, 810p. 23cm. cloth $18.

When the *Washington Information Directory* appeared in 1975, it was described as a pioneering attempt to provide "detailed subject access to information in the Washington metropolitan area, both within and outside the federal bureaucracy" (*Reference and Subscription Books Reviews,* February 15, 1976). Now identified by its editors as an annual, this new edition shows evidence of considerable expansion and revision.

Although the original 16 issue-oriented chapters (e.g., "Employment & Labor," "Law & Justice") remain the same, new subheadings have been added and others changed to reflect a more logical or descriptive organization. Major provisions of the Privacy Act and a list of national religious organizations that maintain offices in Washington have been added to the appendixes. In addition to updating names, addresses, and telephone numbers as necessary, many descriptions of individual agencies have been either rewritten or revised. New organizations appear in many sections, while others have been dropped or moved to more appropriate categories. When an organization is listed under several subjects, its description is not simply repeated, it is revised to reflect aspects of the organization pertinent to each heading. The annotated reference bibliographies have also been augmented, although the annotations continue to lack complete addresses (e.g., zip codes) or publication dates.

Access to individual entries has been greatly improved with the addition of a 30-page Agency and Organization Index, replacing the former two-page Department and Agency Index and the redundant Regional Offices Index. The physical properties of the book have also been enhanced by a cleaner type and a more judicious use of boldface. The entire volume has been reset.

The *Washington Information Directory, 1976–77* continues to provide much valuable information in a unique subject-oriented format. The listings for regional information sources and district offices of members of Congress make it especially useful for referral. *(Mar. 15, 1977, p.1122)*

975.3′0025 Washington, D.C.—Directories || Washington metropolitan area—Directories || U.S.—Executive departments—Directories [CIP]   75-646321

Water publications of state agencies,
first supplement, 1971–1974. a bibliography of publications on water resources and their management published by the states of the United States. Edited by Gerald J. Giefer [and] David K. Todd, with the assistance of Beverly Fish.
Huntington, N.Y., Water Information Center, Inc., [c1976].
xix, 189p. 29cm. cloth $23.

The basic volume of *Water Publications,* published in 1972, listed more than 10,000 titles issued by 335 state agencies to 1970. This supplement with its more than 4,000 titles extends the coverage through 1974 and also lists many pre-1971 titles. A total of 292 agencies is included: those represented in the basic volume, new agencies, and some agencies previously overlooked.

Like the 1972 volume, the supplement was compiled using information supplied by the agencies themselves. (The 1972 Preface explained that in those cases where agencies were unable to comply, such gaps were filled by independent research in the libraries of the University of California, Berkeley; the 1976 Preface is silent on this point.) The earlier Preface also stated that the addition of area, author, and subject indexes was considered but dismissed as impractical because of the substantial increase in size and cost of the volume that would have been required. Indexes are again omitted in the supplement. The editors, Gerald J. Giefer and David K. Todd, are respectively, librarian, Water Resources Center Archives, and professor of civil engineering at the University of California, Berkeley. Beverly Fish's qualifications could not be confirmed.

The basic arrangement is alphabetical by state and thereunder by agency name. Many of the agencies have assigned all or some of their material to named series (e.g., reports, circulars, bulletins) and, if so, that is the pattern followed in this volume.

While the editors have eschewed any claim for completeness, comparison of the titles for 1971 in the Florida section of the supplement with the 1971 titles in the Library of Congress' *Monthly Checklist of State Publications* (v.62–64, 1971–73) and *Florida Public Documents* (1971–73; Tallahassee, 1972–74) suggests comparable coverage, with each source providing some information not in the others. The fact that *Water Publications* has collected only the water-related publications of the states is its raison d'être; it will serve as a useful bibliography for seekers of such specialized material. *(June 1, 1977, p.1529)*

†016.6212 Water supply—U.S.—Bibliography || U.S.—Government publications (State governments)—Bibliography   [OCLC]   72-75672

Webster's secretarial handbook.
Ed. by Anna L. Eckersley-Johnson. Springfield, Mass., Merriam, 1976. 546p. 25cm. cloth $8.95.

The G. & C. Merriam Company, publisher of Merriam-Webster dictionaries, has brought out the first edition of the *Webster's Secretarial Handbook,* covering "every aspect of the modern secretarial function . . . the first [such handbook] oriented extensively to both domestic and multinational businesses."

The publisher claims that this work is the product of the same thorough research and careful editing found in all Merriam-Webster publications and that specialists in business education and private industry were selected to write the 15 chapters in the book. In addition to 2 editors, 12 contributors are listed, but only 1 name could be readily verified in standard biographical sources.

Each self-contained chapter covers one aspect of secretarial work. To illustrate, individual chapters deal with meeting and conference arrangements, dictation and transcription, automated and specialized typewriting, records management systems, basic accounting systems, telecommunication systems, and travel and the multinational character of modern business.

Outstanding features of this handbook are an 83-page chapter on business English, a worldwide holidays chart listing over 300 holidays in more than 100 countries, a discussion of international travel and trade, and 33 pages of business-letter facsimiles. An especially valuable aspect is the coverage given to new fields and new techniques, such as word processing, media typewriting, calculators, electronic data processing, cathode-ray-tube terminals, flow charts, micrographics, and reprographics.

Access to information is facilitated by the physical layout of the book. Each chapter is introduced by its own table of contents. Chapter subsections are signaled by boldface subheadings. Cross-references throughout the text guide readers to related subjects. And finally, a 23-page Index leads the user to specific material.

The book is illustrated with charts, tables, diagrams, and line drawings which depict such business matters as conference seating arrangements, the work station which shows installation of the media typewriter and related supplies and communication devices, basic memorandum formats, sample technical reports, fingering techniques on the calculator keyboard, guide and folder arrangement for an alphabetical filing system, and many other equally practical illustrations.

The Standard Handbook for Secretaries by Lois Irene Hutchinson has long been an authority in matters of business usage and style. It is exceptionally strong in English grammar, spelling, pronunciation, and punctuation; the detailed index is especially good and gives approximately 50 percent more entries than *Webster's Secretarial Handbook.* The two sources complement each other extremely well; the latter supplements the word information given in Hutchinson by the inclusion of valuable information on recent skills and techniques. It should be useful in any library, business office, or home.

(July 15, 1977, p.1757)

651.4 Office practice—Handbooks, manuals, etc. || Secretaries—Handbooks, manuals, etc. [CIP]   76-22498

The weekend education source book.
By Wilbur Cross. New York, Harper's Magazine in association with Harper, [1976]. xv, 296p. 22cm. cloth $12.50.

In the *Weekend Education Source Book,* Wilbur Cross, prolific author of books and journal articles, has produced a unique and utilitarian guide to more than 320 centers in the U.S. which offer short residential courses for adults. Organized into two main sections, one consisting of explanatory and advisory chapters and the other of an educational directory, the book covers religious organizations and church learning centers, colleges and universities, business and professional conferences, government sponsored opportunities, and museum programs. A short bibliography lists books and other publications with information on residential programs for adults. The directory of institutions is arranged alphabetically by state. City and zip code are given for each institution. Coverage includes a brief description of the types of offerings, financial aid available and cost of programs, list of subjects, credits and degrees, living accommodations, and contact for enrollment. More than 4,000 institutions were considered for inclusion, and from these 320 were selected as best meeting the criterion of providing short residential programs for adults. The book is a first step and not a comprehensive compendium of sources for prospective weekend scholars. Its author admits that he had difficulty obtaining information on short residential courses and advises inquiring students to supplement perusal of his data with their own independent research. Indexes to subjects and names and to institutions facilitate locating specific facts. The book does not lie flat when opened; its inner margins are rather narrow for rebinding, and the paper quality is adequate only for the short term of this tool's anticipated usefulness. High school and public library patrons requiring practical guidance on selecting courses for continuing education will find much readily accessible information in *Weekend Education Source Book.* *(Dec. 1, 1976, p.565)*

374.9'73 Adult education—U.S. [CIP] 75-30360

Which wine:
the wine drinker's buying guide. [By] Peter M. F. Sichel and Judy Ley. New York, Harper & Row, 1976. 276p. illus. maps. 24cm. cloth $10.

Which Wine? is a buyer's guide to inexpensive wines which appear on the American market. It is jointly authored by Peter Sichel, whose family has been involved in the wine trade in Europe for many years, and Judy Ley, a consumer who was confused by the "array of labels ever present in a wine shop." The Sichel family is well known for importing moderately priced blended wines of reasonable quality under various labels, the most familiar of which is "Blue Nun." The confused consumer is also a common habitué of the wine shop; so a book to which both contribute should prove useful.

The guide contains some information on wines in general, as well as tips on storage, serving, and tasting. The major part of the book classifies the wines of the world by type. Well represented are the conventional French, North American, German, Italian, Spanish, Portuguese, and Chilean table wines. However, Yugoslavian wines are barely touched upon and Greek, South African, and Australasian wines are entirely omitted. Information given in the discussion of each type is generally accurate and instructive. After the discussion there are a series of taste tests in which individual labels are rated against one another in tabular format. The major headings in these tables are "Best at tasting," "Highly ranked," and "Recommended." The tests show some discretion in that, for certain wine types, none could be placed in the category "Best at tasting." In the tests, wines bearing the Sichel label figure prominently, but, in all fairness, so do those of their competitors. Information included for each individual label, apart from the ranking, is country of origin, producer, price, and, most useful, an availability chart which divides the U.S. into 29 geographical market areas. Lastly, the book contains a chapter which indicates which wines go well with which foods—a subject that is open to broad generalizations as the authors themselves recognize.

Which Wine? is not for the connoisseur, but it will be very useful for the uninformed consumer embarking into the complicated world of wines. It should be included in the collections of medium- and large-size public libraries.

(Apr. 15, 1977, p.1298)

641.2'2 Wine and wine making [CIP] 75-6361

Who's who in golf.
By Len Elliott and Barbara Kelly. New Rochelle, N.Y., Arlington House, 1976. 208p. 24cm. cloth $8.95; to schools and libraries, 25 percent discount.

More than 600 entries are included in this compilation of those "who have made and who are still making significant contributions to golf . . . in Great Britain, Ireland, Canada, South Africa, and South America." Included are all American golfers who have won a senior national championship and all professionals who have won at least one tournament on the Professional Golfers' Association tour or who have made the Ryder cup team. Amateurs who have been selected for a World Cup team or for two or more Walker Cup teams are also represented. Women entrants include professionals who have won at least one Ladies' PGA tour and amateurs who have been chosen for at least one World Cup or two Curtis Cup teams. Nonplayers were selected at the discretion of the editors.

Heads of associations, promoters, golf course architects, teachers, administrators, and golf writers are given brief résumés. Also represented are inventors such as Coburn Haskell, responsible for the rubber-wound golf ball, and Jack Jolly, who originated the liquid core used in today's regulation balls. Entries for major players like Cary Middlecoff, Jack Nicklaus, and Bobby Jones run between ten and fifteen sentences or half a page. Lesser figures receive shorter descriptions. Hugh Philip, a clubmaker born in 1782, and Allan Robertson (1815–1858), an early golfing star and maker of feathery balls, are represented; so are many players born in the 1950s (e.g., Jack Renner, Elizabeth Ann Daniel, and Laura Baugh). The compact but informative summaries include date and place of birth, date of death, height and weight for many of those listed, and a capsule digest of each entrant's career. In addition to details of major tournament victories, there are usually brief personal comments or critiques. Despite an occasional minor editorial lapse, *Who's Who in Golf* is bound to please browsers and succeed as a quick reference tool in public libraries.

(July 15, 1977, p.1757)

796.352'092 [B] Golf—Biography [CIP] 76-21059

Who's who in Greek and Roman mythology.
By David Kravitz. New York: Clarkson N. Potter; dist. by Crown, [1975, 1976]. 246p. 24cm. paper $3.95; cloth $10; to schools and libraries, 20 percent discount.

Few books live up to their publishers' promotion. This one does. As part of the prefatory matter of the book, there is a "Note from the Publisher" which reads, in part: "We believe that this dictionary [sic], with its detailed coverage of an enormous subject, is going to be of immense value to all those who require reference to mythology." The publisher is right.

First published in England in 1975 as *The Dictionary of Greek and Roman Mythology,* the work still retains some British spellings. The American edition is unchanged except for the addition of about 50 line drawings of sundry mythological characters by Lynne S. Mayo. These quarter-and-half-page, rather stark, simplified drawings are more decorative than informative. In some cases they approach the grotesque but are preferable to the prosaic reproductions of classical art that usually grace pages of mythological handbooks.

This double-columned work consists of about 3,600 entries, mostly names of mythological persons, with explanations running from one line to half a page. Besides names of persons, there are entries for such topics as "Seven Wonders of the World," "Seven Hills of Rome," and also entries for beasts, such as peacock, seagull, or snake, which were sacred to, or in some way connected with, one of the divinities. There are also entries useful for crossword puzzle fans, such as *marriage, god of; justice, goddess of, Greek;* and *crops, divinities of* as well as references wherever a topic is associated with several different characters, such as *stag, see Actaeon, Arge, Iphigeneia.*

One of the book's assets is its clarification of mythical characters' complicated familial relationships. This takes the form of ". . . sister of . . ." or ". . . parent of . . . ." When the list of "lovers," as they are termed for either sex, becomes extensive, as in the case of Apollo, Ares, or Jupiter, their partners' names are listed in columnar format, along with the offspring of each union. Synopses of major Greek and Roman legends (e.g., Trojan War, Golden Fleece, Wanderings of Aeneas) and entries for classic poets Homer, Virgil, and Horace provide supplementary information. Strangely, there is no entry for Ovid, the most voluminous of Latin poets.

There is evidence of meticulous editing. Within any one entry, references to another person (such as "sister of . . .") may be verified by looking up that name in its proper place, where the same information will invariably be found. Examination of a score or more of such references failed to reveal any significant omission or contradiction of fact. There is an Appendix containing a calender of festivals celebrated at Rome. In addition, each entry for a festival or divinity so honored concludes with the date(s) of its celebration. The same information is not given for Greek festivals, however. Finally, names which refer to essentially the same divinity, but which differ in the Roman or Greek language, such as Jupiter (Zeus), Minerva (Athena), or Mars (Ares), are entered twice, under each form of the name, with commentary on the Roman or Greek veneration, legends, or tradition. Cross-references are provided between entries because their content varies.

One purpose of this handbook, as stated by its compiler, was to aid persons engaged in figuring out crossword puzzles. The work is indeed useful for this purpose, but it will be welcomed by anyone who needs a quick, handy answer to the frequently asked question, "Who, in mythology, was so-and-so?" It is an appropriate acquisition for the home and public or school library. *(June 15, 1977, p.1605)*

292'.003   Mythologies—Dictionaries   [CIP]   76-29730

Who's who in labor.
New York, Arno Pr., 1976. xxi, 807p. 24cm. cloth $65.

The Preface is signed by Stanley R. Greenfield, managing director, Biographical Directories Division, Arno Press. Felicity Lee, editor of the volume, was assisted by an advisory panel made up of presidents and other officers of nine unions or labor associations, including I. W. Abel, William J. Usery, Jr., and Leonard Woodcock. Entrants in the directory were limited to "persons currently active in the labor movement." Information was obtained by questionnaires mailed to union members and to people associated with labor. Biographees include executive officers, vice-presidents, members of executive boards or councils, heads of staff and trade departments, international and field representatives, officers of district councils or joint boards, certain officers emeriti, and the heads of AFL-CIO state and local central bodies. Persons not associated with unions but represented in the directory include directors and senior executives of federal labor offices, state commissioners of labor, members of the National Panel of Arbitrators of the American Arbitration Association, lawyers and journalists specializing in labor relations, and directors of labor studies centers at various universities and colleges. Data, verified as of November 1975, are given for 3,800 respondents to a questionnaire mailed to 5,000 eligible individuals. The returned questionnaires were edited with the assistance of AFL-CIO Department of Publications and validated by the biographees. Listings include name, union or organization memberships, business address and telephone number, career positions, civic activities, education, clubs, awards and honors, date and place of birth, marital status, spouse's and parents' names and occupations, and home address.

The "Reference Section" at the end of the volume is in seven parts: the history and structure of the AFL-CIO and other federations; directory listing for national union and employee associations; directory of federal and state (by state) government officials serving labor; directory by state of labor studies centers, largely at universities; glossary of labor terms, some with quite lengthy definitions; bibliography of labor periodicals; index by organizations with an alphabetical list of member biographees.

This new "who's who" will be welcomed by public, academic, and special libraries serving persons who are interested in or work with labor organizations. *(Feb. 1, 1977, p.857)*

331'.092 (B)   Trade-unions—U.S.—Officials and employees—Biography || Labor and laboring classes—U.S.—Biography || Trade-Unions—U.S.—Directories   [CIP]   75-7962

Who's who in public relations (international).
Robert L. Barbour, editor in chief; Adrian A. Paradis, editor. 5th ed. 1976. Meriden, N.H., P R Publishing Company, Inc., [c1976]. xiii, 731p. 24cm. paper over boards $45; to schools and libraries, $40 with check.

Who's Who in Public Relations, now in its fifth edition, has been published at irregular intervals since 1959. The present edition contains some 5,000 business biographies of living public relations specialists in 61 countries who were judged by the publishers to be authoritative practitioners "on the basis of background, experience and accomplishment." All data were taken from 20,000 questionnaires filled in by the biographees. Information given for each person includes birth date and place, education, résumé of business career, organization memberships, and honors and achievements.

Most biographees are from the U.S., but 60 other countries are represented in varying degrees of comprehensiveness (Scotland—7, Pakistan—1, Australia—20, Switzerland—49). A geographical index to names facilitates locating specialists in specific regions. *Who's Who in Public Relations* will be useful primarily to those who need to locate out-of-town or overseas public relations personnel. Since many of the biographees are included in general and regional biographical directories which give both personal and business information in greater detail, most seekers of biographical data will have little use for this special directory. *(Sept. 1, 1976, p.59)*

926.591   Public relations—Biography   [OCLC]   62-4348

Who's who in the United Nations and related agencies.
New York, Arno Pr., 1975. xxxiii, 785p. 24cm. cloth, $65.

Nearly a quarter of a century has elapsed since the publication of the last biographical directory of United Nations personnel. This current directory of delegates and senior personnel of the UN and its related agencies thus fills an evident information gap. The categories of persons included were selected by a distinguished advisory panel chaired by Andrew W. Cordier. Biographical information is supplied for more than 3,000 UN administrators, members of governing boards and commissions, senior delegates of member and observer states, UN correspondents, and representatives of nongovernmental organizations.

The biographical data, based on questionnaires sent to each person selected, is current to 1974. A typical entry includes name, position, business address and telephone, languages spoken, career positions, countries of service, education, professional interests, published books and articles, avocational interests, and home address and telephone. The biographical entries are in alphabetical order, with access also provided by a nationality index.

Supplementary features include a very helpful organizational roster of the various organs, specialized agencies, and related organizations in the UN system with the names of level officials; a list of 131 member states as of 1974 with their admission dates; a listing by country of more than 300 UN and related agency installations, with complete addresses and telephone numbers; a list, with addresses and telephone numbers, of the Permanent Missions to the UN in New York and Geneva; rosters of the Presidents of the General Assembly and of the principal officials of the UN and Related Agencies for the years 1946–1974, and a list of depository libraries.

This record of the UN leadership is an important document for current reference, and will be of continuing retrospective value for students of international relations. *Who's Who in the United Nations and Related Agencies* is an essential albeit expensive reference source. It is valuable because much of its information is not available elsewhere. *(Oct. 15, 1976, p.346)*

341.23'092 United Nations—Biography || International Agencies—Biography [CIP]
75-4105

Who's who in twentieth century literature.
[By] Martin Seymour-Smith. New York, Holt, Rinehart and Winston, [c1976]. 414p. 24cm. cloth $12.95.

Who's Who in Twentieth Century Literature is a new work which describes and evaluates the work of about 700 authors. It is written entirely by Martin Seymour-Smith, a British poet and free-lance writer who has published several volumes of poetry and literary criticism.

In his Introduction the author states "My chief wish for this book is that it should act not only as a reference but also as an indication of how many excellent and interesting authors remain unread." Because of space limitations imposed by the publisher, the selection is "necessarily biased toward British and American authors; but major foreign authors are included—and so are some less known writers whom I feel have been undeservedly neglected." The availability of English translations was also a factor in his selection. Despite these restrictions, the author portrays a balanced cross-section of Japanese, Russian, Latin American, European, and African writers. For example, there are commentaries on eight Japanese (Osamu, Kawabata, Yasunari, Tanizaki, Yukio, Ibuse, Toson, and Soseki) and three Nigerian (Achebe, Fagunwa, and Ekwensi) authors. The Introduction does not supply a definition of those who are considered to be twentieth-century writers. Most of those included have done their major work in the twentieth century. A few found here are essentially nineteenth-century figures, for example Henry James, Henry Adams, Mark Twain, Thomas Hardy, Gerard Manley Hopkins, Anatole France, Giovanni Verga, and Arthur Strindberg, but they are treated because of their influence on modern literature, as is pointed out in the entries for them. Also included are representatives of other fields that have affected twentieth-century writing, e.g., Sigmund Freud, Erich Fromm, Carl Jung, Wilhelm Reich, John Dewey, William James, Henri Bergson, Thorstein Veblen, and Hans Arp. Since the selection of authors is admittedly subjective, one should not anticipate equitable representation in this work. In general the authors of the first rank that one expects to find are here. Not all of the minor writers were included because they have been "undeservedly neglected." Some seem to have been included only to demonstrate their dismal quality and undeserving popularity. Seymour-Smith has placed Evgeny Evtushenko, Ayn Rand, Marshall MacLuhan, Robert Creeley, and John Barth in this category. Barth "cannot tell a story, create a character, or hold the unfeigned interest of the most willing reader." As for Creeley, "Most of his poems (*For Love: Poems 1950–1960*, 1962; *Poems 1950–1965*, 1966) are unmemorable, and are in short, imageless lines, broken, unmusical, rigorously pragmatic, faithful to their moment alone."

The entries, all of which have authors as their subject, are arranged alphabetically. Some movements which have been influential are identified, however, under a particular author, e.g., "theatre of the absurd" in the article on Eugène Ionesco. An index provides access to this information on movements as well as to names of authors who have not been given a separate entry but are mentioned in the text. If an author mentioned in the text under another author has a separate entry, his name is followed by "q.v." There are almost no cross-references, even from pseudonyms.

A title beginning with "Who's Who" arouses an expectation of the usual itemization of conventional details of education, career, publications. Nothing could be farther removed from this stereotype than *Who's Who in Twentieth Century Literature*. Although each entry does commence with birth and death dates, pseudonyms where appropriate, and brief identification,

the remainder of the entry is devoted to a concise evaluation of the subject's work as a whole and to characterizations and critical comments on individual works, forthrightly and entertainingly written. Seymour-Smith demonstrates critical acumen and a vast knowledge of modern literature.

He is not afraid to differ from other critics at times or to assess the work of recent writers without benefit of the perspective which time provides. The reader may agree or disagree but will find the opinions provocative and perceptive. Seymour-Smith is favorably disposed towards Dashiell Hammett, Henry Green, Patrick White, Achebe, Erskine Caldwell, and Philip Toynbee. Among authors who displease him are Sinclair Lewis, Iris Murdoch, Lawrence Durrell, J. R. R. Tolkien, and Alexander Solzhenitsyn. The following characteristics are typical: "The notion that Lewis is in any sense important as a writer should be resisted." Iris Murdoch's "novels are a concatenation of current ideas and fads, intelligently understood, but cobbled together without any imaginative faculty." Durrell's *Quartet* "is a feat but it is likely that it will become dated and be seen as a glib mixture of popular Einsteinian physics, Milleresque (q.v.) sex-as-pure-knowledge and cut-price Joyce (q.v.)." Finally, "Solzhenitsyn is a remarkable man; he is by no means a great writer." Some biographical information may be a part of the evaluation, but it is incidental. There are no bibliographies at the end of the entries, but publication dates are given for authors' works mentioned in the text. Occasionally a recommendation of a biography or reference to another critic's view is interjected.

The length of the entries varies from three lines to two or three pages, but the norm is from half-page to a page. According to the Introduction, the length "is not, for many reasons, all obvious, any guide to my own view of its subject's merit."

Seymour-Smith is the author of another reference work which deals with some of the same authors, *Guide to Modern World Literature* (London: Wolfe; New York: Funk & Wagnall, 1973, $13.95). This book, organized by country, treats individual authors within the context of the literary development of the country. In addition to differing in arrangement, coverage, and emphasis from *Guide to Modern World Literature*, *Who's Who in Twentieth Century Literature* includes many authors not in the *Guide*.

The work most nearly comparable to the book under review is *Twentieth Century Writing: A Reader's Guide to Contemporary Literature*, edited by Kenneth Richardson (New York: Transatlantic Arts, 1971, first published in England for Newnes Books, 1969, $15). The work of two editors and 35 contributors, it covers about 1,200 authors, popular as well as serious, with English-language writers predominant and the others limited to those writing in European languages. There are no subject bibliographies. Evaluations are intended to provide an estimate of the author's contemporary standing rather than the contributor's evaluation. *Who's Who in Twentieth Century Literature* has a significant number of authors not included in *Twentieth Century Writing*.

The *Longman Companion to Twentieth Century Literature*, by A. C. Ward (2d ed., London: Longman, 1975, $16.50) is another comparable work. Criteria for selection are similar. For each author there is brief biographical information, a selective listing of works, and a limited characterization or evaluation of writing. Besides the author entries, there are also entries for literary categories, plot summaries, characters, and terms.

Who's Who in Twentieth Century Literature is a useful addition to the shelf of literary guides for modern literature. More individualistic and informally written than the usual reference work, it is also delightful for browsing and should serve students well as a guide and stimulus to reading.

(Sept. 15, 1976, p.205)

809 Literature, Modern—20th century—Bio-bibliography [CIP]
75-21470

A Winterthur guide to American Chippendale furniture:

Middle Atlantic and Southern colonies. [By] Charles F. Hummel. [New York], Crown Publishers, [1976]. 144p. illus. (part col.) 21cm. cloth $6.95; paper $3.95; to schools and libraries, 20 percent discount.

American Chippendale Furniture is one of three guides published in 1976 to celebrate the twenty-fifth anniversary of the opening of the Henry Francis duPont Winterthur Museum. The museum contains a distinguished collection of early American decorative arts, including furniture, ceramics, textiles, folk art, silver, glass, and paintings. The objects, arranged in 125 period rooms, include more than 625 examples of American Chippendale furniture. This guide contains comparative illustrations of 151 pieces, all made between 1755 and 1790 in New York, Philadelphia, and the South. Two-thirds of the pieces illustrated are from Philadelphia, however, with 10 from the South and about 40 from New York.

In a brief historical introduction, Hummel explains that the guide "is arranged to encourage the comparison of forms produced within a given region with those made in other centers." Extensive captions adjacent to the plates point out particular features for comparison and often provide a historical comment. The text presumes a knowledge of terms associated with furniture construction, e.g., splat, crest rail, ear, stile, etc.

Sixteen color plates of excellent quality enhance the volume. The black-and-white illustrations are generally clear, although occasional fuzziness or shadow obscures the detail. A few illustrations bleed into the center margin, making rebinding difficult. A brief list of books and articles for further reading concludes the volume.

Hummel received an M.A. in 1955 in the Winterthur Program in Early American Culture from the University of Delaware. He has been employed at Winterthur since that time and now holds the position of curator. His guide would add depth to any collection of material on antiques or decorative arts in America.
(May 1, 1977, p.1375)

749.2'14   Furniture, Colonial—Middle Atlantic States || Furniture—Middle Atlantic States || Furniture, Colonial—Southern States || Furniture—Southern States || Decoration and ornament—Chippendale style || Henry Francis duPont Winterthur Museum   [CIP]   76-10845

A Winterthur guide to American needlework.

[By] Susan Burrows Swan. New York, Crown, 1976. 144p. 21cm. illus. permacote $6.95, paper $3.95; to schools and libraries, 20 percent discount.

Though small in size (eight-and-one-fourth-inches by five-and-one-half-inches, 144 pages), this book aims to "describe the major needlework methods used in America between 1650 and 1890, give the dates of their popularity, and discuss the stitches used to execute them." The author uses the collections of the Henry Francis du Pont Winterthur Museum to illustrate her text in 101 black-and-white photographs and 16 color plates (not "over 150 illustrations," as the dust jacket claims).

This guide is disappointing on a number of grounds. A major source of vexation is terminology. Swan has elected to use the eighteenth- or nineteenth-century name for the various embroidery stitches. However, there is no glossary to relate these terms to their modern equivalents; nor are stitch diagrams provided. Thus it is frequently difficult to follow the author's discussion of embroidery. The experienced needleworker, by disregarding the misleading text (p.49) and minutely examining the photographs (p.53 and 57), will eventually come to the conclusion that "Queen's Stitch" is what modern embroiderers call Rococo Stitch; the amateur in these matters would be completely lost. The fact that stitch name often precedes verbal description by several pages—"Irish stitch" (i.e., bargello) is introduced on p.37 and finally explained on p.45—adds to confusion. The text is further marred by brevity, some dubious arguments, and by an organization based neither on form (e.g., sampler, bed-hanging) nor on technique (e.g., crewel, drawn thread-work) but on a mixture of the two which produces inconsistencies and overlappings. There is no index to guide the reader. A book based on such a fine collection of historic needlework should have better exploited the possibilities for illustration. The black-and-white photographs are poorly posed and muddy. Although the ambience of earlier American interiors is subtly communicated by the color plates, they also lack crisp definition. Missing are the sharp focus and fine depiction of detail, used in conjunction with larger-scale photography, which make a work such as Safford and Bishop's *America's Quilts and Coverlets* (New York: Dutton, 1972) so instructive.

The 33-item Selected Bibliography of reference and periodical literature is of value, as the latter type of material is often difficult to locate. Otherwise, the book falls short of possessing the qualities of either a good reference tool or of a good discursive work.
(May 15, 1977, p.1456)

746.4'4   Needlework—U.S. || Henry Francis Du Pont Winterthur Museum   [CIP]   76-10602

A Winterthur guide to Chinese export porcelain.

By Arlene M. Palmer. New York, A Winterthur/Rutledge Book; Crown Publishers, Inc., [c1976]. 144p. 21cm. cloth $6.95; paper $3.95; to schools and libraries, 20 percent discount.

This third volume of the Winterthur guide series shows representative examples of the more than 5,000 pieces of Chinese porcelain made for European and American markets, chiefly before 1830, and collected by Henry Francis du Pont. They are now at the Winterthur Museum.

Prepared by the assistant curator of the museum, the book contains 134 illustrations, with 16 pages in full color, of vases, plates, jugs, and other objects, with accompanying size and other descriptive information. Brief introductory chapters on the China trade, manufacture of porcelain, personalized porcelains, and other pertinent information are followed by a selected bibliography of English-language titles.

The richness of the original collection and the qualifications of the compiler make this a very useful introduction to the subject as well as a reflection of 19th-century tastes.
(Apr. 1, 1977, p.1199)

738.2'0951   China trade porcelain || Henry Francis du Pont Winterthur Museum   [CIP]   76-10848

Women in public office:

a biographical directory and statistical analysis. Compiled by [the] Center for the American Woman and Politics, Eagleton Institute of Politics, Rutgers—The State University of New Jersey. New York & London, R. R. Bowker Co., 1976. lii, 455p. 29cm. cloth $19.95.

The Center for the American Woman and Politics was established at Rutgers in 1971, under a Ford Foundation grant, in order to develop knowledge about American women in public life and to increase their participation in it. This directory was developed to meet the need for accurate national data on women in the U.S. holding state and local public offices, both elective and appointive. The only listings on the national level are for women in Congress.

Lists of approximately 13,000 officeholders were obtained, often with some difficulty, from a wide variety of government and nongovernment sources. Two-part questionnaires were then mailed to the women with follow-ups as needed. Fifty percent responded. Among the nonrespondents, 38 percent have only names, positions, and addresses listed, while the remaining 12 percent was compiled from secondary biographical sources. The cutoff date for most of the information is July 10, 1975, with a 21-page addendum for material received by September 1. A few names were also added to take into account the November 1975 election results.

The directory is arranged alphabetically by state with Washington, D.C., appended to the end of the sequence. Within each state, officeholders are arranged alphabetically within these categories: U.S. representatives (there are no senators), state executives and cabinet members, state legislators, county commissioners, township officials, mayors, city council members, judges, and state and local board members and commissioners. Biographical information for the last three groups is omitted.

A complete biographical entry includes the following: name, party designation, date first elected to present position, district number, board and committee assignments, party positions held, previous public offices held, current organizational memberships, education, current occupation, date and place of birth, address and telephone number. Asterisks indicate which material has been drawn from secondary sources. Addendum material follows the same format. The Index lists the surnames and initials of all officeholders and refers to the page on which information is located.

Preceding the directory is a 34-page section entitled Statistical Essay: Profile of Women Holding Public Office. It is based on the second part of the questionnaires filled in by these women. It reports findings on such topics as their family situations, age, political experience, organizational activities, education, residential stability, and committee assignments. Thirty-five tables and a selected bibliography accompany this analysis.

Another table provides a state-by-state summary of the numbers of women in office at each level. The center estimates that women held 5 percent of U.S. public office positions and that 19 volumes the same size as this one would be required to list all the men.

The book is sturdily bound and lies flat when open. Entry names are in capitals, and there are two columns of names on each page.

Who's Who in American Politics 1975–76 (Bowker) includes 18,800 men and women in national and state offices plus mayors and council members of large cities. *Who's Who in Government 1975–76* (Marquis) lists 18,000 names. Many entries in these volumes, or in others in the Marquis *Who's Who* series, do contain more information for each entry, such as names of parents and children, marital status, previous occupations, writings, and honors, if any. However, only a small number of the names in *Women in Public Office* will be found in other biographical directories since they do not attempt to cover local officeholders to any great extent. This new directory will be useful in libraries whose patrons require information about contemporary politics and government. *(Sept. 1, 1976, p.59)*

353.002 Women in politics—U.S.—Directories || Women in public life—U.S.—Directories [OCLC]   75-37487

The word book.
Compiled by Kaethe Ellis. Boston, Houghton Mifflin, [1976]. 384p. 15cm. paper-covered boards $2.95; to schools and libraries, $2.21.

The Word Book is a spelling and word division guide based on *The American Heritage Dictionary of the English Language* (Boston: American Heritage Publishing Co., Inc. and Houghton Mifflin Co., 1969). Some 40,000 selected words are alphabetically arranged in three columns per page and divided into syllables by dots. Stress is indicated through use of boldface and lighter accents. Plural and other endings, irregular inflected forms, and variants are noted as required. Many words with prefixes are included, and a special guide illustrates the rules for forming such compounds. Brief definitions and warning symbols call attention to easily confused pairs, homophones, and other sets of words. The selection emphasizes current American English with many colloquial words and scientific and technical terms. Proper names and nouns are included only when they relate to, or form parts of, other compounds. Obsolete or rare words are not included; nor one-syllable words if they present no spelling or use problems.

Additional helps are a guide to plurals; a "sound map for poor spellers" (to help one look up words when the spelling is unknown); a guide to spelling with basic principles and examples; proofreader's marks; abbreviations; and weights and measures with metric equivalents. The endpapers describe punctuation marks and their uses. This is a sturdily bound, handy little book for students, secretaries, and others who write and type, transcribe, or edit. *(Jan. 15, 1977, p.748)*

428'.1 Spellers || English language—Pronunciation   [OCLC]   76-698

The world atlas of food:
a gourmet's guide to the great regional dishes of the world. [Contributing editor Jane Grigson. London, edited and designed by Mitchel Beazley Publishers Ltd., c1974]. 319p. illus. 30cm. buckram $29.95.

This is a book to read and enjoy. It is more at home on the coffee table than in the kitchen or on the reference shelf. The 26 contributors (including well-known writers such as James Beard, Kenneth Lo, and Elisabeth Lambert Ortiz) together have at least 60 books on food and cooking to their credit, as well as many magazine articles.

The first quarter of the book is devoted to a discussion of ingredients by 37 categories. For each there are references to geographic distribution, ancient and modern methods of processing and preparation, and unusual anecdotes concerning specific foods. Colorful, sometimes flamboyant, illustrations appear on every page.

In the remainder of the book, countries or areas of the world, arranged geographically, are treated individually. For each the text explores the uses of indigenous foods, the development through the centuries of national tastes and customs, and changes brought about through trade and migration. Preferred beverages of each nation are described. An excellent two-color map of each country shows areas associated with particular specialties. Other illustrations in this section are small, black-and-white sketches of various objects connected with food. Many countries, including Russia, Greece, Poland, The Netherlands, Norway, Sweden, and Canada, are covered in two pages each, with one or two representative recipes incorporated into the text. France, China, and the U.S. are allotted a much greater proportion of the text and are treated regionally. Recipes for national specialties appear in conventional form, following the general discussion.

The General Index is spotty and not too dependable. A typical example: "lefser," a Scandinavian bread, does not have its own entry but is listed under Breads. For identification of this sort, Theodora Fitzgibbon's *The Food of the Western World* (New York: Quadrangle, 1976) is, within its scope, a more reliable and complete reference source. Individual countries are covered in much greater detail in the Time-Life series Foods of the World.

The principal reference value of *The World Atlas of Food* is as a one-volume, geographic approach to information about national cuisines. *(July 1, 1977, p.1680)*

641.5'9 Cookery, International || Food   [OCLC]   74-193316

The world encyclopedia of comics.
Edited by Maurice Horn. New York, Chelsea House Publishers, [c1976]. 790p. illus. 31cm. cloth $30; 2v. ed $42.50.

Krazy Kat has come in from the cold. The comics, like the science fiction novel, have fully emerged as a "respectable" concern of scholarship. As a mass medium, these popular art expressions are analyzed not only as a vehicle of sociopolitical comment or criticism but also as an informing influence on popular consciousness and the creative imagination: Italo Calvino's phantasmagorical novel *Cosmicomics* and Thomas Pynchon's convoluted *Gravity's Rainbow* structurally and stylistically reflect comic strip form and fantasy, while Argentinian novelist Julio Cortazar has recently contributed the narrative to *Fantomas contra los vampiros multinacional,* a comic book. The ascendancy of comic book and comic strip art has no doubt occasioned this encyclopedia, the work of 15 contributors under the editorship of Maurice Horn. International in scope, this profusely illustrated work includes, in one alphabetical sequence, descriptions and historical sketches of comics and their characters as well as biographical information on individuals involved in this popular art. A brief history of the comics, a 63-page center section demonstrating the use of color in comics, a glossary of comic terms, the code of the Comics Magazine Association of America, and separate name, title, and media indexes embellish the encyclopedia. An unfortunate oversight is the lack of entries under D.C. (Detective Comics), Marvel Comics, and Classics Illustrated. A historical sketch of at least Classics Illustrated would have been most welcome, since this comic book series seems to have been completely neglected by the contributors. Entries are not consistently provided for both comic artists and the products of their invention. While there are entries for Doonsbury and Gary Trudeau, and Toonerville Folks and Fontaine Fox, there is nothing under Othon Aristides, creator of the popular French character Philémon. There are three indexes which provide access to information: Proper Name Index, Title Index, Illustration Index. A geographical index listing comics alphabetically by country would also have been useful. Since the foreword to this compendium indicates that the publisher intends to "update, revise and enlarge" the work in the future, these slight yet annoying omissions may be rectified in the future. On the whole, *The World Encyclopedia of Comics* is a welcome and impressive initiative within the field of popular culture. *(Mar. 15, 1977, p.1122)*

741.5'03 Comic books, strips, etc.—Dictionaries   [CIP]   75-22322

World of fashion:
people, places resources. By Eleanor Lambert. New York, Bowker, 1976. xi, 361p. 24cm. cloth $18.95.

Eleanor Lambert, author of *World of Fashion,* is a well-known producer of fashion shows, member of the National Council of the Arts, newspaper columnist, and winner of numerous awards and honors for her contributions to the fashion industry. Her guide gathers together facts on the creative people (designers, manufacturers, writers, photographers); manufacturing centers; geographic resources and principal exports; schools; costume collections; and various other aspects of the fashion scene. Arranged by continent and subdivided by region and country, the book covers 67 geographical entities with distinctive styles (for example, Hawaii and Alaska are treated separately and not within the U.S. section). Five African nations (Algeria, Morocco, Sudan, Togo, Republic of South Africa), the major Asian and European countries, Australia and the South Sea islands, the U.S., and seven South American nations are represented. Each country is described in relation to its contribution to modern dress. Then, in a section headed "Fashion and Designers," its established and promising new designers and stage and film costume creators who have had an influence on general clothing styles are listed alphabetically with brief biographical notes and comments on their work. There may also be listings of a country's trade and fashion organizations, honors and awards, institutions offering educational programs in clothing design and merchandising, museums with significant costume collections, and important journals in the field. In addition, names and addresses of directors of organizations, museum curators, and magazine editors are provided. A Hall of Fame chapter completes the main body of the book. Here deceased or retired designers whose influence lingers on are given brief biographical profiles. The roster includes such greats as Adrian, Hattie Carnegie, Christian Dior, Conde Nast, Molyneus, and the recently retired Mainbocher. Listed in the Appendix are winners of the Coty Award for the years 1943 through 1975. A selective Bibliography of about 100 important works on fashion and its history, only two of which are foreign-language publications, and a Name Index conclude this volume. While the biographical notes and descriptions are concise and sometimes cursory, they are consistently current and informative. The guide also offers useful commentary on little known and emerging figures in Africa and Eastern Europe. Its cross-references and Name Index constitute an accurate, basic, but incomplete key to the book's contents. *World of Fashion* should prove helpful and fill public and special libraries' need for a compact source of facts about the people and places in the clothing industry.

(Dec. 1, 1976, p.565)

746.9'2 Fashion   [CIP]   75-43904

World uniforms and battles, 1815–50.
[By] Philip J. Haythornthwaite; illus. by Michael Chappel. New York, Hippocrene, [c1976]. 188p. 20cm. cloth $7.95.

In *World Uniforms and Battles,* Philip Haythornthwaite, an experienced military writer, and Michael Chappell, who has a good reputation as a military artist, collaborate to produce the first book on military uniforms of the period from the Battle of Waterloo to 1850. Both the author and illustrator are British. The book is made up of 65 pages of colorplates, 10 chapters devoted to Europe, 1815–30, 1830–40, 1840–48; European revolutions of 1830–31 and 1848; South America, 1815–50; North America 1815–46; British colonial campaigns, 1815–50; and the U.S.–Mexican War, 1846–47. Also included are five pages of black-and-white plates and lists of primary and secondary sources of information.

The colorplates are clear and decorative; two different uniforms are depicted on each page. Uniforms of European armies are given most coverage: Great Britain, France, Prussia, Spain, Russia, Austria, Baden/Hamburg, Netherlands, Papal States, Holland, Belgium, Poland, Bavaria, Denmark, Sardinia, Piedmont/Milan, and the Roman Republic as compared to those of Argentina, Brazil, the U.S., Mexico, and the Danish West Indies for North and South America. The only British colonial uniforms shown are those for India. Each colorplate is numbered and labeled. The text refers to plates by number and name. The black-and-white plates are numbered but not captioned; and even though they are sharp and clear enough, they seem drab by comparison with the gay colorplates.

The text presents historical summaries of the period covered and then describes the applicable plates in detail. For example, the chapter on European operations 1830–40 covers plates 23–39 and gives detailed descriptions of the uniforms of the royal marines bandmaster, the royal marine artillery officer, the 14th light dragoons sergeant, the 3rd foot guard officer, the royal artillery officer, the 15th foot battalion officer, the 46th foot light company sergeant, trumpeter, 10th Hussars officer, Worcestershire and West Somerset yeomanry officers, officer of the royal rifle corps, private of the rifle brigade, 72nd Highlanders light company and 76th Ross-shire officers buffs battalion company (all British); Prussian N.C.O. 1st and foot guards; Belgian trumpeter and officer; Russian trooper, officer, drum major and N.C.O.; Danish N.C.O. and officer; Papal states trumpeter; Swiss officer; French trooper, private, grenadier, and officer; and Spanish trooper and officer. Historians and model and costume makers will find *World Uniforms and Battles* is a compact, inexpensive source of facts and pictures on battle uniforms of 1815–1850. *(July 15, 1977, p.1757)*

355.1'40934 Uniforms, Military—History || Military history, Modern—19th century   [CIP]
75-45405

Writings on American history:
a subject bibliography of articles, 1973/74.
James J. Dougherty, compiler-editor; Robin Byrnes, assistant editor; Maryann C. Lesso, assistant editor. Washington,

American Historical Association; Millwood, N.Y., Kraus-Thompson Organization, Ltd., 1974– . annual. [v.1: a subject bibliography of articles], 266p. 26cm. buckram, $15.

Beginning with this 1973–74 volume, and continuing in the recently published 1974–75 cumulation, the American Historical Association and the Kraus-Thompson Organization aim to carry on the bibliographic coverage provided by the now defunct *Writings on American History 1902–1961*. While the old *Writings* endeavored to cite all monographic and serial literature of value for the study of U.S. history, with some 11,095 bibliographic entries in the 1960 volume, this new annual limits coverage largely to periodical articles. Even here the treatment is hardly exhaustive. The 1960 cumulation of the old *Writings*, for example, included articles from over 700 periodicals, whereas this 1973–74 volume classifies some 3,800 articles taken in the "Recently Published Articles" (RPA) section of the American Historical Review between June 1973 and June 1974. It should be noted however, that the 1974–75 coverage has been broadened to include articles not cited in RPA. (The RPA section has since been removed from the American Historical review and is offered as a separate journal appearing three times per year.) Over 400 journals and about 350 dissertations are represented in the 1974–75 cumulation.

In addition to the coverage now available for 1973–75, the publishers have recently completed in four volumes, *Writings on American History, 1962–1973; a Subject Bibliography of Articles,* drawn from the RPA for those years. This partially covers the bibliographic gap between the old and new *Writings*.

In addition to utilizing the American Historical Association's system of organizing citations by broad chronological categories and geographical areas, this bibliography lists the articles under some 40 subject headings such as Visual Arts, Woman's History, History of Medicine, and Genealogy. Many of the articles are cross-listed in each of the three categories and a separate author index is provided. Although the bibliography does not have a subject index, nor are the entries annotated, the assigned subject categories, increased to some 60 in the 1974–75 edition, are descriptive and will satisfy most users.

While the compilers admit that "this publication is not the complete answer to the shortcomings of bibliography on American History," it fills a manifest need and belongs on the shelf of any library which endeavors to provide bibliographic coverage of the field of American History. *(Oct. 15, 1976, p.346)*

016.9173 U.S.—History—Periodicals—Indexes [CIP]   74-13435

The year book of world affairs, 1976.
[Editors: George W. Keeton and Georg Schwarzenberger]. Boulder, Colorado, 80301, Westview Pr., 1898 Flatiron Court; published under the auspices of the London Institute of World Affairs, 1976. vi, 347p. 25cm. casebound $27.50; to schools and libraries, 10 percent discount.

The thirtieth survey of this series begins with "Trends and Events," a four-page listing of 70 papers published in previous annuals, grouped under 10 subject headings. These provide the reader with some continuity with the subjects under discussion. The general objective of providing an annual "to make possible analyses in a wider perspective and on the basis of more mature reflection than may be possible in a quarterly or monthly journal" is sustained in this volume.

Adam Curle, professor of peace studies, University of Bradford, leads off with a chapter on "Peace Studies," followed by a group of well-qualified commentators, most of them scholars or persons prominent in public affairs. Twelve of the contributors are based in the United Kingdom; five are associated with universities in Australia, Austria, Canada, and the U.S.; one is head of the Norwegian Permanent Delegation to the United Nations. Economics, nuclear deterence and détente, national and regional concerns are most often covered. The range of subject matter is reflected in the following sample of inclusions in the current annual: Colin Legum, associate editor of *The* (London) *Observer* ("Southern Africa: The Politics of Detente"); A. Nussbaumer, professor of economics, University of Vienna ("Western Market Economies"); R. A. Rieber, assistant professor of political science, University of Utah ("Public Information and Political Leadership in International Organizations"); Margaret Doxey, associate professor and chairman, Department of Politics, Trent University, Ontario ("The Commonwealth Secretariat"); Georg Schwarzenberger, director, London Institute of World Affairs ("The Principles of the United Nations"); Ian Bellany, senior lecturer in politics, University of Lancaster ("The Acquisition of Arms by Poor States"); and Russell Jones, lecturer in Indonesian, School of Oriental and African Studies in the University of London ("Indonesia: Language and Nation Building").

An analytical Index at the end of the volume provides ready access to the subject matter and names included in the 18 articles. *The Year Book of World Affairs, 1976* continues the scholarly tradition of previous publications in the series.
(Mar. 1, 1977, p.1039)

341.053 International relations—Yearbooks || World politics—Yearbooks [OCLC]   47-29156

Author Index

Allworth, Edward. Soviet Asia, 73
Aluri, Rao. U.S. government scientific & technical periodicals, 177
Arata, Esther Spring. Black American writers past and present, 102
Armitage, Andrew D. Annual index to popular music record reviews, 1974, 98
———. Canadian essay and literature index, 106
Arnold, Clinton M. Black Americans in aviation, 102
Ash, Douglas. Dictionary of British antique glass, 120
Asimov, Isaac. Asimov's biographical encyclopedia of science and technology, 99
Avi Yonah, Michael. Illustrated encyclopedia of the classical world, 40
Axford, Lavonne Brady. English language cookbooks, 1600–1973, 131
Bader, Barbara. American picturebooks from Noah's ark to the beast within, 96
Bailey, Kenneth. Hamlyn younger children's encyclopedia, 144
Banks, Arthur S. Political handbook of the world, 1976, 165
Barbour, Robert L. Who's who in public relations (international), 180
Barker, L. Mary. Pears cyclopaedia, 1976–1977, 65
Barnhart, Clarence L. World book dictionary, 86
Barnhart, Robert K. World book dictionary, 86
Bartels, Nadja K. Bradford book of collector's plates 1976, 104
Baüml, Betty J. Dictionary of gestures, 122
Baüml, Franz H. Dictionary of gestures, 122
Beale, Walter H. Old and middle English poetry to 1500, 162
Beard, James. Cooks' catalogue, 119
Beck, Terry-Diane. Foundation center source book, 1975/1976, 33
Beckenrath, Edwin F. Mathematics dictionary, 156
Becker, Robert A. Documentary history of the first federal elections, 1788–1790. v.I., 22
Biesenthal, Linda. Canadian book review annual, 1975, 105
Bindoff, S. T. Research in progress in English and history in Britain, Ireland, Canada, Australia, and New Zealand, 167
Birnbaum, Max. Comparative guide to American colleges, 112

———. Comparative guide to two-year colleges and career programs, 112
Bishop, Robert. American clock, 95
Block, Ann. Children's literature review, 14
Blot, Pierre. Handbook of practical cookery, 116
Boehm, Eric H. America: history and life, 93
Boulton, James T. Research in progress in English and history in Britain, Ireland, Canada, Australia, and New Zealand, 167
Boyum, Keith O. Biographical dictionary of the federal judiciary, 100
Bradley, Van Allen. Book collector's handbook of values 1976–1977, 11
Brewster, John W. Index to book reviews in historical periodicals 1973, 148
———. Index to book reviews in historical periodicals 1974, 148
Brichford, Maynard J. Manuscripts guide to collections at the University of Illinois at Urbana-Champaign, 155
Broderick, Robert C. Catholic encyclopedia, 106
Brown, Calvin S. Glossary of Faulkner's South, 138
Brown, Joseph Mill. Helicopter directory, 146
Burchfield, R. W. Supplement to the Oxford English dictionary, 174
Burke, James Henry. 80 years of best-sellers, 1895–1975, 127
Buske, Morris R. Significant American colonial leaders, 170
———. Significant American presidents of the United States, 170
Carey, Helen B. Gateways to readable books, 35
Cashman, Marc. Bibliography of American ethnology, 99
Cass, James. Comparative guide to American colleges, 112
———. Compartive guide to two-year colleges and career programs, 112
Chapman, Dorothy H. Index to black poetry, 148
Chase, Harold. Biographical dictionary of the federal judiciary, 100
Chesler, Bernice. Family guide to Cape Cod, 132
Clapham, Frances M. Great world encyclopedia, 138
Clark, Jerry N. Biographical dictionary of the federal judiciary, 100
Coan, Eugene V. World directory of environmental organizations, 90

Cohen, Richard M. Grosset & Dunlap's all-sports world record book, 140
———. Sports encyclopedia: baseball, 6
Collocott, T. C. Chambers biographical dictionary, 107
———. Chambers dictionary of science and technology, 107
Colombo, John Robert. Colombo's Canadian references, 111
Cook, Christopher. Pears cyclopaedia, 1976–1977, 65
Copeland, Robert D. Webster's sports dictionary, 82
Costner, Tom. Motion picture market place 1976–1977, 157
Cowie, Peter. 50 major film-makers, 134
———. International film guide 1976, 152
Coyne, John. Getting skilled, 137
Crook, Leo. Oil terms, 161
Cross, Wilbur. Weekend education source book, 178
Crowley, Ellen T. Ancronyms, initialisms, & abbreviations dictionary, 1
———. Reverse acronyms, initialisms, & abbreviations dictionary, 167
Currie, Bob. Classic motorcycles, 110
Cushing, Mrs. C. H. Kansas home cook-book, 116
Daintith, John. Hamlyn junior science encyclopedia, 144
Dale, Edgar. Living word vocabulary, 47
Dalton, David. Rock 100, 168
Daniells, Lorna M. Business information sources, 104
Davaris, Costis. Guide to Cretan antiquities, 141
David, Nina. TV season 74–75, 176
———. TV season 75–76, 176
Davis, Norman M. Complete book of United States coin collecting, 112
Day, Martin S. Handbook of American literature, 145
Debuigne, Gérard. Larousse dictionary of wines of the world, 154
Decker, Gloria H. Conservation directory, 1976, 114
Deer, Roger. Official rules of sports and games, 1976–77, 61
de Ford, Miriam Allen. Who was when?, 83
De Groote, Roger. Sports olympiques album officiel/Olympic sports official album, 172
Deutsch, Jordan A. Grosset & Dunlap's all-sports world record book, 140
———. Sports encyclopedia: baseball, 6

Devers, Charlotte M. Guide to special issues and indexes of periodicals, 142
Diagram Group. Way to play, 80
Diamond, Robert A. Congressional quarterly's guide to Congress, 113
Distin, William H. American clock, 95
Dobson, A. B. Chambers dictionary of science and technology, 107
Dogo, Giuliano. Treasures of Italy, 76
Dorfman, John. Consumer's arsenal, 115
Dougherty, James J. Writings on American history: a subject bibliography of articles, 1973/74, 184
Doyle, Paul A. Guide to basic information sources in English literature, 141
Dunmore-Leiber, Leslie. Book review digest: author/title index, 1905-1974, 11
Dunn, William J. Enjoy Europe by car, 131
Eckersley-Johnson, Anna L. Webster's secretarial handbook, 178
Eddleman, Floyd Eugene. American drama criticism supplement II, 95
Edgar, Neal L. History and bibliography of American magazines, 1810-1820, 147
Egan, Edward W. Kings, rulers and statesmen, 153
Elbert, George. Plants that *really* bloom indoors, 164
Elbert, Virginie. Plants that *really* bloom indoors, 164
El-Khawas, Mohamed A. American-Southern African relations, 97
Elliott, Len. Who's who in golf, 179
Ellis, Kaethe. Word book, 183
Elton, G. R. Annual bibliography of British and Irish history, 98
Eppler, Elizabeth E. International bibliography of Jewish affairs, 1966-1967, 151
Eustes, Celestine. Cooking in old Creole days, 116
Falk, Jr., Byron A. Personal name index to 'the New York times index' 1851-1974, 66
Falk, Valerie R. Personal name index to 'the New York times index' 1851-1974, 66
Fang, Josephine Riss. International guide to library, archival, and information science associations, 152
Fichter, George S. Fresh & salt water fishes of the world, 34
Filby, P. William. American and British genealogy and heraldry, 94
Finney, Paul B. Diary for the business traveler, 120
Fischler, Stan and Shirley. Fischler's hockey encyclopedia, 135
Fitzgibbon, Russell H. Argentina, 88
———. Brazil, 88
Fleisher, Michael L. Encyclopedia of comic book heroes, 129
Foss, Christopher F. Artillery of the world, 98
———. Military vehicles of the world, 98
Foster, David William. Library of literary criticism: Modern Latin American literature, 46
Foster, Virginia Ramos. Library of literary criticism: Modern Latin American literature, 46
Fry, Plantagenet Somerset. 1,000 great lives, 162

Gagala, Kenneth L. Economics of minorities, 127
Gardner, Richard K. Choice: a classified cumulation, 109
Garland, Henry and Mary. Oxford companion to German literature, 63
Garraty, John A. New guide to study abroad, 160
Gersumky, Alexis Teitz. Foundation center source book, 1975/1976, 33
Geifer, Gerald J. Sources of information in water resources, 171
———. Water publications of state agencies, 178
Gifford, Denis. British comic catalogue: 1874-1974, 13
Glaser, Milton. Cook's catalogue, 119
Goodrich, L. Carrington. Dictionary of Ming biography, 1368-1644, 122
Gorer, Richard. Trees & shrubs, 76
Gray, Mrs. B. Kansas home cook-book, 116
Green, Stanley. Encyclopedia of the musical theatre, 28
Greenberg, Hazel. Equal rights amendment, 132
Gregory, Ruth W. Anniversaries and holidays, 97
Griffin, William D. Ireland, 88
Grigson, Jane. World atlas of food, 183
Gross, Charles. Bibliography of English history to 1485, 9
Grumm, Phyllis. Choice: a classified cumulation, 109
Gruson, Edward S. Checklist of the world's birds, 108
Gubelin, Eduard. Color treasury of gemstones, 111
Hackett, Alice Payne. 80 years of bestsellers, 1895-1975, 127
Hall, H. W. Science fiction book review index, 1923-1973, 72
Handel, Beatrice. National directory for the performing arts and civic centers, 55
———. National directory for the performing arts/educational, 55
Hanson, Agnes O. Executive and management development for business and government, 132
Harder, Kelsie B. Illustrated dictionary of place names, United States and Canada, 40
Harmon, Robert G. Political science bibliographies, 69
Harris, William H. New Columbia encyclopedia, 56
Harrison, Colin. Field guide to the nests, eggs, and nestlings of British and European birds, 134
Hart, Harold H. Picture reference file, 164
Hausen, Gitta. International bibliography of the book trade and librarianship, 45
Havlice, Patricia Pate. Index to literary biography, 148
———. Popular song index, 165
Haythornthwaite, Phillip J. World uniforms and battles, 1815-50, 184
Hayward, P. H. C. Jane's dictionary of military terms, 152
Heard, Priscilla S. American music 1698-1800, 96
Hebert, Tom. Getting skilled, 137
Hechlinger, Adelaide. Modern science dictionary, 54

Hegener, Karen C. Peterson's annual guides to undergraduate and graduate study, 66
Herman, Valentine. Parliaments of the world, 64
Herwig, Rob. Treasury of houseplants, 176
Hidaru, Alula. Short guide to the study of Ethiopia, 169
Hill, Brian H. W. Canada, 88
Hintz, Constance B. Kings, rulers and statesmen, 153
Hirzel, Bertha M. Gateways to readable books, 35
Hobson, Burton. Catalogue of the world's most popular coins, 106
Hockheimer, Foley A. Educators guide to free health, physical education and recreation materials, 127
Hogson, Julian. Music titles in translation, 158
Honig, Fred. Baseball encyclopedia, 6
Horn, Maurice. World encyclopedia of comics, 183
Howe, John. Choosing the right dog, 110
Hughes, G. Ernard. The country life collector's pocket book, 120
Hughes, Therle. Pocket book of furniture, 164
Hummel, Charles F. Winterthur guide to American Chippendale furniture, 181
Hurlbut, Jr., Cornelius S. Planet we live on, 67
Ireland, Norma Olin. Index to inspiration, 149
Isaacs, Alan. Hamlyn junior science encyclopedia, 144
Jackson, Joan S. Who was when?, 83
Jacobs, Arthur. British music yearbook, 104
Jacobs, Donald M. Antebellum black newspapers, 98
———. Significant American blacks, 169
James, Robert C. Mathematics dictionary, 156
Jaques, Cattell Pr. American art directory, 1976, 3
———. Who's who in American art, 1976, 3
Jenkins, Betty Lanier. Black separatism, 102
Jensen, Merrill. Documentary history of the first federal elections, 1788-1790. v.I., 22
Johnson, Roland T. Grosset & Dunlap's all-sports world record book, 140
———. Sports encyclopedia: baseball, 6
Johnson, Warren T. Insects that feed on trees and shrubs, 42
Johnson, Willis L. Directory of special programs for minority group members, 126
Kafka, Barbara Poses. Cook's catalogue, 119
Kaminkow, Marion J. United States local histories in the Library of Congress, 77
Katz, Doris B. Guide to special issues and indexes of periodicals, 142
Kay, Ernest. International authors and writers who's who, 43
Kay, Mairé Weir. Webster's collegiate thesaurus, 80
Kaye, Evelyn. Family guide to Cape Cod, 132
Kaye, Lenny. Rock 100, 168

Keeton, George W. Year book of world affairs, 1976, 185
Kelly, Barbara. Who's who in golf, 179
Kerrod, Robin. Concise color encyclopedia of science, 17
Ketz, Louise Bilebof. Dictionary of American history, 19
Kim, Ung Chon. Policies of publishers, 165
Kinsley, H. M. One hundred recipes for the chafing dish, 116
Kirkland, Elizabeth Stansbury. Six little cooks, 116
Kitching, Jessie. Birdwatcher's guide to wildlife sanctuaries, 101
Klaber, Doretta. Violets of the United States, 78
Kornegay, Jr., Francis A. American-Southern African relations, 97
Krafsur, Richard P. American film institute catalog of motion pictures: feature films 1961-1970, 5
Kramer, Elaine Fialka. Library of literary criticism: modern American literature, 154
Kramer, Maurice. Library of literary criticism: modern American literature, 154
Kravitz, David. Who's who in Greek and Roman mythology, 179
Kreslins, Janis A. Foreign affairs bibliography, 136
Krislov, Samuel. Biographical dictionary of the federal judiciary, 100
Kruzas, Anthony T. Encyclopedia of information systems and services, 130
Kujoth, Jean Spealman. Subject guide to humor, 174
Kurtz, Seymour. World guide to antiquities, 91
La Beau, Dennis. Biographical dictionaries master index, 10
———. Children's authors and illustrators, 108
Lacey, A. R. Dictionary of philosophy, 122
Lambert, Eleanor. World of fashion, 184
Langer, William L. New illustrated encyclopedia of world history, 57
Leab, Daniel J. American book prices current, 1975, 95
Leab, Katharine Kyes. American book prices current, 1975, 95
Leidy, W. Philip. Popular guide to government publications, 70
Lengenfelder, Helga. International bibliography of the book trade and librarianship, 45
Leslie, Eliza. Directions for cookery in its various branches, 116
Levey, Judith S. New Columbia encyclopedia, 56
Ley, Judy. Which wine, 179
Litvinoff, Barnet. Israel, 88
Lock, C. B. Muriel. Geography and cartography, a reference handbook, 36
Logan, Nick. Illustrated encyclopedia of rock, 168
Louis, Harry. Classic motorcycles, 110
Lyon, Howard H. Insects that feed on trees and shrubs, 42
Mackay, James. Encyclopedia of small antiques, 27
Madubuike, Ihechukwu. Handbook of African names, 145
Mandel, Jack Kent. Significant American historians and educators, 170
———. Significant American Indians, 170
———. Significant American sport champions, 170
Marcuse, Sibyl. Survey of musical instruments, 75
Mark, Charles. Sociology of America, 171
Mark, Paula K. Sociology of America, 171
Marr, Warren. Negro almanac, 159
Matney, William C. Who's who among black Americans, 85
McDonough, Irma. Canadian books for children/Livres canadiens pour enfants, 105
McFarland, Kevin. Incredible, 148
McKinven, John G. Bradford book of collector's plates 1976, 104
McLaren, L.L. High living: recipes from Southern climes, 116
McLeod, Joseph A. Index to book reviews in historical periodicals, 1973, 148
———. Index to book reviews in historical periodicals 1974, 148
Meltzer, Ida S. Significant American authors, poets, and playwrights, 169
———. Significant American musicians, composers, and singers, 170
———. Significant American women, 170
Menke, Frank G. Encyclopedia of sports, 28
Metz, Karen S. Information sources in power engineering, 149
Meyer, Harvey K. Historical dictionary of Honduras, 147
Miekina, Gilbert. Significant American government leaders, 170
———. Significant American military leaders, 170
———. Significant American social reformers and humanitarians, 170
Migdalski, Edward C. Fresh & salt water fishes of the world, 34
Miller, Anita. Equal rights amendment, 132
Miller, Wayne Charles. Comprehensive bibliography for the study of American minorities, 38
———. Handbook of American minorities, 38
Millsaps, Daniel. National directory of grants and aid to individuals in the arts, international, 158
Mollo, Andrew. Naval, marine and air force uniforms of World War 2, 159
Moore, Leonard. Hamlyn junior encyclopedia of nature, 143
Moore, Norman D. Dictionary of business finance and investment, 121
Morris, Richard B. Encyclopedia of American history, 24
Morris, William and Mary. Harper dictionary of contemporary usage, 146
Munson, Kenneth. Bombers in service, 103
———. Fighters in service, 103
Myers, Carol Fairbanks. Black American writers past and present, 102
Nardone, Thomas R. Choral music in print, 110
———. Organ music in print, 162
Neft, David S. Grosset & Dunlap's all-sports world record book, 140
———. Sports encyclopedia: baseball, 6
Niehaus, Theodore F. Field guide to Pacific states wildflowers, 133
Nitecki, Joseph Z. Directory of library reprographic services, 125
Nock, O. S. Railways of the modern age since 1963, 166
Noe, Lee. Foundation grants index, 1974, 136
Norbeck, John. Encyclopedia of American steam traction engines, 129
Nulman, Macy. Concise encyclopedia of Jewish music, 113
Nunn, Marshall E. Sports, 62
Nyren, Dorothy. Library of literary criticism: modern American literature, 154
O'Connor, Patricia Ann. Congressional quarterly's guide to Congress, 113
———. Washington information directory, 1976-77, 177
O'Donoghue, Michael D. Encyclopedia of minerals and gemstones, 25
O'Rourke, Joseph. Living word vocabulary, 47
Palic, Vladimir M. Government publications, 138
Palmer, Alan and Veronica. Quotations in history, 166
Palmer, Arlene M. Winterthur guide to Chinese export porcelain, 182
Palmer, Joseph. Jane's dictionary of naval terms, 152
Palmes, J. C. Sir Banister Fletcher's a history of architecture, 72
Pan Am's USA guide, 163
Parch, Grace D. Directory of newspaper libraries in the U. S. and Canada, 126
Patten, Marguerite. Books for cooks, 103
Patterson, Margaret C. Literary research guide, 154
Paxton, John. Statesman's year-book world gazetteer, 173
Penzler, Otto. Encyclopedia of mystery and detection, 26
Peters, Raymond Eugene. Black Americans in aviation, 102
Phillis, Susan. Black separatism, 102
Pitt, Valerie. Hamlyn junior science encyclopedia, 144
Ploski, Harry A. Negro Almanac, 159
Pope, Nannette McCarthy. Interlibrary Users Association journal holdings in the Washington-Baltimore area, 1977, 150
Popenoe, Cris. Books for inner development, 103
Porter, Mrs. M. E. Mrs. Porter's new southern cookery book, 116
Quinn, Alvin W. Significant American inventors, 170
———. Significant American scientists, 170
Rahmato, Dessalegn. Short guide to the study of Ethiopia, 169
Ramsey, L. G. G. Complete color encyclopedia of antiques, 15
Reaney, Percy H. Dictionary of British surnames, 121
Regan, Mary Margaret. Guide to special issues and indexes of periodicals, 142
Reinfeld, Fred. Catalogue of the world's most popular coins, 106
———. Stamp collectors' handbook, 172
Ridgely, Robert S. Guide to the birds of Panama, 142
Riley, Carolyn. Children's literature review, 14
Riley, Norman D. Field guide to the butterflies of the West Indies, 133
Roberts, Laurance D. Dictionary of Japanese artists, 20
Rosenbloom, Joseph. Consumer complaint guide 1977, 114

———. Consumer protection guide 1977, 114
Rush, Teresa Gunnels. Black American writers past and present, 102
Rust, Brian. American dance band discography, 1917-1942, 4
Salaman, Raphael A. Dictionary of tools used in the woodworking and allied trades, c1700-1970, 124
Salem, James M. Guide to critical reviews, part II, 141
Samples, Gordon. How to locate reviews of plays and films, 148
Sandburg, Larry. Folk music sourcebook, 136
Saterstrom, Mary H. Educators guide to free guidance materials, 127
———. Educators guide to free science materials, 127
Saunders, David. RSPB guide to British birds, 168
Schapsmeier, Edward L. Encyclopedia of American agricultural history, 23
Schapsmeier, Frederick. Encyclopedia of American history, 23
Schipf, Robert G. Outdoor recreation, 62
Schubert, Margot. Treasury of houseplants, 176
Schuler, Stanley. 5,000 questions answered about maintaining, repairing, and improving your home, 136
Schuster, Mel. Motion picture performers, 158
Schwarzenberger, Georg. Year book of world affairs, 1976, 185
Sewell, Winifred. Guide to drug information, 141
Seymour-Smith, Martin. Who's who in twentieth century literature, 181
Shatzman, Israel. Illustrated encyclopaedia of the classical world, 40
Shaw, John MacKay. Childhood in poetry, 14
Shields, Joyce F. Make it: an index to projects and materials, 53
Shtohyrn, Dmytro M. Ukrainians in North America, 176
Sichel, Peter M. F. Which wine, 179
Sinkankas, John. Gemstones of North America, 35
Sive, Mary Robinson. Environmental legislation, 31
Skuse, George. Sub-aqua illustrated dictionary, 173
Small, Arnold. Birds of California, 101
Small, Samuel. Directory of franchising organizations 1976, 125
Smart, Paul. International butterfly book, 151
Smit, J. W. and Pamela. Netherlands, 88
Smith, Alan. Clocks & watches, 15
Smith, Anna Piszczan-Czaja. Encyclopedia of German-American genealogical research, 129
Smith, Clifford Neal. Encyclopedia of German-American genealogical research, 129
Smith, Harold E. Historical and cultural dictionary of Thailand, 146
Smith, Myron J. Cloak and dagger bibliography, 110
———. Sea fiction guide, 169
Smith, Patricia R. Modern collector's dolls, 157
Smythe, Mabel M. Black American reference book, 101
Snyder, Louis L. Encyclopedia of the Third Reich, 29

Soltow, Martha Jane. American women and the labor movement, 1825-1974, 97
Songe, Alice H. International guide to library, archival, and information science associations, 152
Spahn, Janet Peterson. From radical left to extreme right, 137
Spahn, Theodore Jurgen. From radical left to extreme right, 137
Spencer, Janet. National directory for the performing arts and civic centers, 55
———. National directory for the performing arts/educational, 55
Spooner, Alan. Oxford children's dictionary in colour, 163
Steele, Colin. Major libraries of the world, 53
Stefano, Frank. Pictorial souvenirs & commemoratives of North America, 163
Steinbrunner, Chris. Encyclopedia of mystery and detection, 26
Stillwell, Richard. Princeton encyclopedia of classical sites, 71
Sutton, Robert M. Manuscripts guide to collections at the University of Illinois at Urbana-Champaign, 155
Swan, Susan Burrows. Winterthur guide to American needlework, 182
Swanborough, Gordon. Military aircraft of the world, 157
Szathmary, Louis. Cookery Americana, 116
———. Cool, chill, and freeze, 116
———. Fifty years of prairie cooking, 116
———. Home cookery, 116
———. Midwestern home cookery, 116
———. Southwestern cookery, 116
Tannenbaum, Judith. New York art yearbook 1975-1976, 59
Tarbert, Gary C. Biographical dictionaries master index, 10
———. Children's book review index, 14
Taubert, Sigfred. Book trade of the world. v.II, 12
Taylor, Cyril J. H. New guide to study abroad, 160
Taylor John W. R. Helicopters of the world, 98
———. Military aircraft of the world, 157
———. Missiles of the world, 98
Taylor, Michael J. H. Helicopters of the world, 98
———. Missiles of the world, 98
Tegland, Janet. Significant American artists and architects, 169
———. Significant American entertainers, 170
Thompson, S. C. Official encyclopedia of baseball, 6
Thomson, David. Biographical dictionary of film, 100
Thorne, J. O. Chambers biographical dictionary, 107
Todd, David K. Water publications of state agencies, 178
Trotsky, Judith. News dictionary 1975, 160
Trzyna, Thaddeus C. World directory of environmental organizations, 90
Tudor, Dean. Annual index to popular music record reviews 1974, 98
———. Canadian book review annual, 1975, 105

———. Cooking for entertaining, 118
Tudor, Nancy. Canadian book review annual, 1975, 105
———. Canadian essay and literature index, 106
———. Cooking for entertaining, 118
Tully, Gerie. Mexico especially for women, 157
Turkin, Hy. Official encyclopedia of baseball, 6
Turner, Nolanda. National directory for the performing arts and civic centers, 55
———. National directory for the performing arts/educational, 55
Turner, Pearl. Index to handicrafts, model making, and workshop projects, 41
Uden, Grant. Longman illustrated companion to world history, 48
Underhill, Charles S. Handy key to your "National Geographics," 39
van der Leeden, Frits. Water resources of the world, 79
Van Sickle, Sylvia. Macdonald first library, 50
Vexler, Robert. England, 88
———. Germany, 88
———. Vice-presidents and cabinet members, 177
Vinson, James. Contemporary novelists, 115
von Klemperer, Lily. New guide to study abroad, 160
Vose, Ruth Hurst. Glass, 138
Walle, Dennis F. Manuscripts guide to collections at the University of Illinois at Urbana-Champaign, 155
Wasserman, Paul. Consumer sourcebook, 114
———. Ethnic information sources of the United States, 31
Watson, Allan. Dictionary of butterflies and moths in color, 121
Watts, Peter. Dictionary of the old West, 1850-1900, 123
Wearing, J. P. London stage, 1890-1899, 155
Webster, Mrs. A. L. Improved housewife, 116
Wedgeworth, Robert. ALA yearbook, 2
Weissman, Dick. Folk music sourcebook, 136
Weller, Robert C. Sea fiction guide, 169
Welling, William. Collectors' guide to nineteenth-century photographs, 111
Wery, Mary K. American women and the labor movement, 1825-1974, 97
Weston, John. Oxford children's dictionary in colour, 163
Whalley, Paul E. S. Dictionary of butterflies and moths in color, 121
Whalon, Marion K. Performing arts research, 163
White, B. T. Tanks and other armoured fighting vehicles 1942-1945, 103
Whitfield, Danny J. Historical and cultural dictionary of Vietnam, 146
Williams, L. F. Rushbrook. Handbook for travellers in India, Pakistan, Nepal, Bangladesh and Sri Lanka (Ceylon), 145
Williams, Raymond. Keywords, 153
Willis, John. Screen world, 1976, v.27, 168
Wills, Geoffrey. Concise encyclopedia of antiques, 18
Wilson, H. Radcliff. Official rules of sports and games, 1976-77, 61

Wilson, William K. Directory of research grants 1976–77, 21
Wise, L. F. Kings, rulers and statesmen, 153
Wisner, Bill. Complete guide to salt and fresh water fishing equipment, 113
Withrow, Dorothy E. Gateways to readable books, 35
Witty, Helen S. Cook's catalogue, 119
Wodehouse, Lawrence. American architects from the Civil War to the First World War, 94
Woffinden, Bob. Illustrated encyclopedia of Rock, 168
Wolf, Burton. Cook's catalogue, 119
Woodress, James. American literary scholarship: an annual, 1973, 96
———. American literary scholarship: an annual, 1974, 96
Woods, Richard D. Reference materials on Mexican Americans, 167
Woolf, H. Bosley. Webster's new students dictionary, 81
Wynar, Christine L. Guide to reference books for school media centers: 1974–75 supplement, 142
Yannarella, Philip A. U. S. government scientific & technical periodicals, 177
Yarger, Susan Rice. State constitutional conventions: 1959–1975, 173
Young, William C. Famous actors and actresses on the American stage, 32
Zanelli, Leo. Sub-aqua illustrated dictionary, 173
Zielinski, Stanislaw A. Encyclopedia of hand-weaving, 130
Zils, Michael. World guide to universities, 92
Zimpfer, David G. Group work in the helping professions, 140

Ref.
Z
1035.1
S933
1976/77
JUL 12 1978